Communication for Management

Norman B. Sigband

University of Southern California

Scott Foresman and Company

To My Mother and Father

Library of Congress Catalog Card No. 69-11610
Copyright © 1969 by Scott, Foresman and Company
Glenview, Illinois 60025
Philippines Copyright 1969 by Scott, Foresman and Company
All Rights Reserved
Printed in the United States of America
Regional Offices of Scott, Foresman and Company are
located in Atlanta, Dallas, Glenview, Palo Alto, Oakland, N. J.,
and London, England.

Preface

Every communication, transmitted or received, verbal or nonverbal, internal or external, should be viewed within the broad context of the human communication process. What happens inside and between people as a result of the messages that pass between them is important. If this book were to concentrate—as most texts do—only on the mechanics of written or spoken messages, without examining such contributing factors to interpretation as channel, word use, perception, experience, emotion, and bias, it would be incomplete. We must understand the overall communication process if we are to write successful reports, letters, or memos, give effective speeches, or conduct profitable conferences.

The individual who works in government, business, or industry will find this book useful as a source book and reference guide. The student will find it easy to use, and the teacher will find it adaptable to courses in communication, management, report and business-letter writing, business research, and related areas. It has adequate material and questions for a two-semester or two-quarter course, or selections can be made for a single semester's application. The problems and examples will be found to be practical and factual. Most of them have been drawn from more than twenty years of university classroom experience and time spent working with industry as a consultant.

The design of the text is simple and logical. It is divided into three sections: (1) an overview of the theories and processes of communication, (2) business writing with emphasis on reports, and (3) business letters. These three areas are supplemented by a fourth part, consisting of selected readings relevant to topics in the text, and by a group of appendixes: a brief guide to diction and grammar, a detailed and extensive guide to reference sources, and a treatment of the principles and formats of business letters.

A note on the selected readings: Most instructors are faced with the problem of providing students with supplemental readings to round out text and classroom discussion. References to and library arrangements for specific books, collections of essays, or various magazine articles are thus necessary. I have included carefully selected articles—with appropriate cross references in the text—to give the reader the benefit of convenient and immediate reference to the writings of nationally recognized authorities.

Many of the readings relate to Part I: language, behavior, and the process of communication. This was done purposely for two reasons: to provide an opportunity to note controversial points of view in an area that has many differences of opinion, and also because I felt this was the most important of the three parts of the book.

Because of space considerations, many excellent readings were of necessity omitted, and many of those selected were "cut" to a greater or lesser degree. Of course, I attempted to do no article an injustice when I excised paragraphs and sections. Certainly the theme and key ideas have been retained in all. I hope the student will read these articles not only for the information they contain, but also to serve as springboards for his own thinking, subsequent analysis, and further discussion.

This book is the product of many people. The contribution of the authors of the articles in Part IV is of course substantial, and I am indebted to them. In addition, the comments and work of my students at the University of Southern California and DePaul University have been most valuable. They are the persons who saw, heard, and reacted to much of this material in preliminary form. The ideas and principles of members of the American Business Communication Association, and well as its *Journal*, have had a strong impact on this book. Thanks are also due to Dr. Robert R. Dockson, Dean of the School of Business Administration of the University of Southern California for his encouragement of this endeavor.

And of course, my family deserves my greatest thanks. My wife Joan, has read and reread portions of the manuscript and has made many helpful suggestions. My daughters, Robin, Shelley, and Betsy, encouraged me strongly. These four young women always permitted me, in a discussion of the book, to get a word in edgewise—so long as I kept it in writing.

Norman B. Sigband

Los Angeles
March 1969

Contents

The Problems and Process of Communication in the Business Organization

Listening, the Grapevine, and Employee Publications

Interpersonal Communication

The Written Word in Industry

PART ONE

Communication

CHAPTER ONE

The Process and Problems of Communication

An employee can contribute to his firm not only his skill in accounting, marketing, management, or sales, but something of far greater importance: ideas. It is the man with good ideas who moves ahead rapidly. And it is on the basis of these ideas that companies grow and prosper. Most organizations are quick to reward, by pay and by title, those individuals who present ideas which can be translated into progress and profits. But ideas have value only if they are communicated effectively.

Effective communication is also important for the administrator. For how else does he carry out his management functions except through communication? He must transmit his ideas not only clearly but persuasively. The manager must motivate others to do what he wants them to do, and the effective manager relies on words—words effectively communicated—to motivate those persons around him to do what he wishes.

Most of us assume that we need only speak or write, and we have transmitted what was in our mind to someone else. This is often not true. Transmitting what we know and feel to another individual so that his interpretation of it is what we intended requires careful preparation and diction (word choice), and the other person's desire to receive the idea.

COMMUNICATION IN PRACTICE

We have all had the exasperating experience of suddenly realizing that we did not communicate what we thought we had. This has taken place when speaking or writing to business associates, children, wives or husbands, or friends. As an example, let us eavesdrop on the discussion between an office manager, Robert Gordon, and his immediate subordinate in charge of the tabulating room, Bill Orton.

Good morning, Bill. Come in and sit down. You remember a week ago I asked you to give me a progress report on how well your new equipment is working out; if Pete, that new employee, is working well; and if you were able to straighten out those two key-punch operators who are always bickering. This morning I checked and found that you haven't yet submitted that report, that you fired Pete, and that you still haven't spoken to the two girls. Is this all deliberate on your part, Bill? If it is, you and I had better have an understanding right here and now.

Well, Bob, I didn't know you wanted the report right away. As for Pete, I got the idea you didn't like him, so I let him go when I found him goofing off. And the two girls don't "bicker." You're all wrong about that. Maybe they disagree, but they don't cause any real trouble.

Look, Bill, I gave you specific instructions. If you don't want to follow them, maybe I can find someone who will.

But I do want to follow your suggestions, Bob; that's why I got rid of Pete. And you didn't say *when* you wanted the report. As for the girls, well. . . .

And so the discussion goes. Who was at fault? Both men? Neither one? Or does it make any difference? Office procedure is upset, work routines break down, and a loyal, hard-working employee may be lost.

Actually a careful re-examination of the conversation gives clear evidence of a communication breakdown, misunderstanding, and the harmful effect of feelings and emotions getting out of hand.[1] What did happen in the discussion above? Did Bill deliberately misunderstand? Did Bob communicate clearly? Were the words used with one meaning by one man, but understood differently by the other? And if so, why?

Perhaps we can never determine just exactly what went wrong, but we do know that barriers got in the way of the clear reception of ideas, and caused confusion and errors in interpretation. These breakdowns in communication cost American industry millions of dollars each year in tangible losses; and they are also often responsible for the ill will and antagonism which arise between relatives, friends, and nations.

If we are to improve communication, we must understand the theory and process of communication as well as the barriers, so that we can take action, when necessary, to reduce the number of breakdowns.

---

1. A careful study indicates that in general there is less than 50 per cent understanding between supervisor and subordinate about the nature of the job which the latter is supposed to be doing. Reported in A. S. Hatch, "Improving Boss-Man and Man-Boss Communication," *The Journal of Business Communication,* October 1966.

COMMUNICATION THEORY

MATHEMATICAL THEORY

Communication theory is often divided into the mathematical approach and the behavioral approach. Samuel Morse, who developed a code for use in telegraphic communication, was one of the first to apply a mathematical concept to communication. His code used dots and dashes (symbols) to stand for letters.

In 1948, Claude E. Shannon and Warren Weaver published a book called *A Mathematical Theory of Communication*. This important contribution, largely developed by Dr. Shannon at the Bell Telephone Laboratories, examined the technical problems of transmitting a message from sender to receiver. (He was concerned with the problem of electronic communication and not that of semantics.)

The message begins with an *information source*, the mind of the speaker or writer. He chooses words and organizes them into sentences to encode his message. This message is transmitted as a *signal* (sound or light waves, or marks on a paper). The signal is sent through a *channel*, but it can be garbled by *noise* (distractions, poor handwriting, static). Finally, the communicatee (man or machine) receives the message and decodes it into meaningful symbols. Of Shannon's theory, J. R. Pierce says:

> Suppose we have a message source which produces messages of a given type, such as English text. Suppose we have a noisy communication channel of specified characteristics. How can we represent or encode messages from the message source by means of electrical signals so as to attain the fastest possible transmission over the noisy channel? Indeed, how fast can we transmit a given type of message over a given channel without error? In a rough and general way, this is the problem Shannon set himself and solved.[2]

A further discussion on this topic by Francis Bello appeared in *Fortune Magazine* in 1953. He said:

> In this century man's views, not to say his life, have already been deeply altered by such scientific insights as relativity

2. J. R. Pierce, *Symbols, Signals and Noise: The Nature and Process of Communication* (New York: Harper & Row, 1961), p. 44.

theory and quantum theory. Within the last five years a new theory has appeared that seems to bear some of the same hallmarks of greatness. The new theory, still almost unknown to the general public, goes under either of two names: communication theory or information theory. . . .

The central teachings of the theory are directed at electrical engineers. It gives them, for the first time, a comprehensive understanding of their trade. It tells them how to measure the commodity they are called upon to transmit—the commodity called "information"—and how to measure the efficiency of their machinery for transmitting it. Thus the theory applies directly to telegraph, telephone, radio, television, and radar systems; to electronic computers and to automatic controls for factories as well as for weapons.

It may be no exaggeration to say that man's progress in peace, and security in war, depend more on fruitful applications of information theory than on physical demonstrations, either in bombs or in power plants, that Einstein's famous equation works. . . .

The theory has an unusual joint origin. To M.I.T.'s eminent mathematician, Norbert Wiener, goes the major credit for discovering the new continent and grasping its dimensions; to Claude Shannon of Bell Laboratories goes the credit for mapping the new territory in detail and charting some breath-taking peaks. Wiener's basic contribution was to recognize that communication of information is a problem in statistics, a view he first stated clearly in a secret World War II document that dealt with the problem of shooting down airplanes. He followed this in 1948 with his now famous book *Cybernetics, or Control and Communication in the Animal and the Machine.* The same year Shannon published his great work, *A Mathematical Theory of Communication.* . . .

Information, as used in the theory, is very carefully defined. . . . To Wiener and Shannon, information is contained, to a great or less degree, in any message a communication engineer is asked to transmit. He is not interested in semantics or meaning. . . .[3]

A central principle in this Wiener-Shannon theory is that the encoder takes advantage of the statistical nature of messages. Thus when letters are coded into digits (or "bits"), they can be transmitted quickly and accurately.

3. Francis Bello, "The Information Theory," *Fortune Magazine,* December 1953.

BEHAVIORAL THEORY

Individuals working in the fields of the behavioral sciences and related areas have contributed a great deal in recent years to the field of communications. Outstanding work on theories of human communication has been done by a psychiatrist, Dr. Jurgen Ruesch.[4]

People who are concerned with human communication do not focus on precisely what we say or write, but on how the encoder or decoder perceives and thinks about the message. Dr. Ruesch, for example, feels that an understanding of another's personality is possible only after observation of how that person interacts with himself and others.

Dr. Ruesch's theory of communication includes a recognition of the social situation in which an individual finds himself. He then examines the networks through which communication flows and discusses the transmission and reception of information, the individual's response, and his ability to make changes in his own behavior.

Ruesch recognizes that we all exist in a social situation and that our society has established certain patterns. In the first place, we participate in a *social situation* when people communicate with each other and their behavior is organized around a common task. Each person within that social situation assumes and carries through a *role* which is usually acceptable to him and to those around him at that time.

These *roles* are usually agreed upon by all parties involved. In social situations, *status* is also important, but it is often designated by certain conventions, habits, and patterns in society. The company president has more status than the foreman; the ambassador enjoys higher status in a political situation than his secretary. And in most societies there exist symbols which give us clues to status: job titles, office size and decor, uniforms, clothing, type of car, and so on. Recognition of *roles* and *status* is important, for it influences the *rules* of our verbal and nonverbal communication. The perceptive individual, aware of *roles, status,* and *rules,* constantly makes adjustments in his communication to achieve his goals.

The *rules* of communication vary from society to society. However, if one is to accomplish his goals, he must communicate according to the social situation and the rules. These tell him to whom he may communicate, for how long, in what way, and with what expectation of success. In fact, Eric Berne's best-selling book, *Games People Play* (Grove Press, 1964), is almost totally concerned with communication, and the reactions of individuals to others and to themselves as a result of words.

Nonverbal communication also plays a vital role in transmitting messages. These cues or *instructions,* which derive from facial gestures,

4. See J. Ruesch, "Psychiatry and the Challenge of Communication," *Psychiatry,* XVII (1954).

7

touch, or voice inflections, all help the receiver in understanding the message. The nonverbal message often communicates more forcefully than the verbal one. And it, plus the role and status of the individual, are factors which most of us interpret as carefully as we do the specific words spoken or written.

Dr. Ruesch identifies various communication networks. The *intrapersonal* network is entirely within the individual and involves thinking and feeling. For effective introspection, one must examine his own reception and transmission as objectively as possible. If what he is doing is incorrect, he must recognize it as incorrect before he can change.

There is also the *interpersonal* communication network. This is quite different from the intrapersonal, for it permits expressive action on the part of one or more persons and the conscious and unconscious perception of such action. Perhaps one of the most important factors in this network is the possibility of corrective action through feedback. This feedback is vital if the originator and receiver are to secure some level of effectiveness in the communication process.

In *group* interaction we don't have the potential for equality in sending and receiving messages. Because of this inequality in the flow of information, it is usually more difficult to achieve effective communication with all persons involved. Correction in this situation is somewhat more difficult because of the problems of feedback. However, delayed action (e.g., a question period after a speech) may be used.

A fourth network noted by Dr. Ruesch is *cultural*. Here there is no specific originator or receiver of the message. Certain symbols in our society—cars, clothing, homes, morals, etc.—are part of our cultural network. When one accepts them, ignores them, agrees with them, or rejects them, he often causes conflict within himself. And of course it is almost impossible to correct or change the system because of its powerful and pervasive nature.

Dr. Ruesch is convinced that to understand the human personality, one must understand human communication. In connection with his own psychiatric work, he says ". . . only a master who possesses both knowledge about communication and the skill to alter the patient's communication system through expert feedback and selective response can hope to achieve significant psychotherapeutic results."[5]

THE PROCESS OF COMMUNICATION

The process of communication is a complex function involving all our senses, experiences, and feelings. In the brief discussion which follows,

5. *Ibid.*, p. 17.

no attempt will be made to discuss the process in detail, but an effort will be made to explain what happens when Mr. Able talks or writes to Mr. Baker. Therefore, let's listen to another conversation.

Assume that Able and Baker have been examining and discussing some construction plans for the past three hours. Finally Baker leans back, stretches, and says to Able, "My head is so loaded with figures and statistics that it's going in circles. Besides, the air is hot in here; what do you say we go out for a bite to eat and a cup of coffee."

Baker has had some specific feelings which he has put into words— or encoded. Able, whose mind is still deeply involved with the building plans, listens (completely or partially) and must now receive and under- stand—or decode—Baker's message. But will he decode the message as Baker intended?

Baker is tired, not quite clear about the plans, and hungry. But Able is enthusiastic and wants to get the job done. As a matter of fact, he may be affronted that Baker seems to be implying that he—Able—confused him with his discussion and that is why Baker's head is "going in circles." As for the "hot air" which Baker mentions, Able's interpretation of that— in his mood—is unmistakable.

Yet Baker made a simple, sincere statement whose meaning was obvious to himself. Why, then, did Able suddenly seem angry and ir- ritated with Baker's casual comment?

Able, of course, decoded or interpreted the message on the basis of his feelings, past experiences, thoughts, and perhaps even his desires; he interpreted not only Baker's words but also his gestures, actions, tone of voice, and past relationship. No matter that the interpretation may not be what Baker intended; as far as Able is concerned, it is what Baker intended.

WHAT IS COMMUNICATION?

From our brief discussions, we certainly recognize that communication is not just letters, reports, telegrams, telephone conversations, and in- terviews. It is less obvious: It is the action of people talking, listening, seeing, feeling, and reacting to each other, their experiences, and their environment.

When one person speaks, writes, listens, or gestures to another, there is constant action and reaction between the two. When someone speaks to us, we not only interpret the words we hear; we also listen and give mean- ing to the voice inflection, the face of the person, the thoughts in his eyes, the drumming of his fingers, and the nervous tapping of his toe on the floor. Thus we give meaning to these other stimuli as well as to his words themselves. Added to these are our own internal stimuli: our emotions, feelings, experiences, interests, and a dozen other contributing factors which cause us to perceive actions and words in specific ways.

So communication is much more than talking or writing. We might define *communication* as the transmission and reception of ideas, feelings, and attitudes—verbally and/or nonverbally—which produce a response.

OBJECTIVES OF COMMUNICATION

But we communicate for a purpose, and our basic objectives in communication are generally these:

1. We would like to be understood exactly as we intended.
2. We would like to have the receiver of our message agree and accept that message.
3. We would like to secure a favorable action or response to our message.
4. We would like to maintain favorable relations with those with whom we communicate.

Our definition of *communication* should therefore be revised to read: *Effective* communication is the transmission and reception of ideas, feelings, and attitudes—verbally and/or nonverbally—which produce a *favorable* response.

BARRIERS TO COMMUNICATION

Often the nonverbal external and internal stimuli play an important role in the interpretations we give to words. Sometimes, these stimuli are so strong that we interpret them instead of the words directed to us. When these factors sway our understanding to a degree which does not harmonize at all with the meaning intended by the communicator, they become *barriers* to the clear interpretation of ideas. This, of course, is what happened to our friends, Mr. Able and Mr. Baker. However, if we are more aware of what these barriers are, perhaps we can cope with them better.

Differences in perception of a situation may cause imperfect communication. Our previous experiences largely determine how we will react to specific stimuli. Viewing the same thing, individuals of different ages, cultural backgrounds, and national origins will each perceive something quite different. Each uses his learning, his culture, and his experiences to interpret what he sees. Not only do we see things differently from the way another person sees them, but if two of us hear a statement, we may also interpret (hear or perceive) it differently. (See Rogers and Roethlisberger, "Barriers and Gateways to Communication," Part IV.)

Let us look at Line Foreman Anderson, his supervisor, Assistant Plant Supervisor Benton, and Development Engineer Carleton. They have just come from lunch and are walking back to their shop area. Forty feet ahead of them are seven or eight production workers who work directly under Anderson and in Benton's department. As the three men walk past, the circle of workers suddenly breaks into laughter and back-slapping.

How did the foreman, assistant plant supervisor, and engineer each perceive this? Anderson, who has been having trouble securing cooperation from several of the production-line workers, hears derisive and insulting laughter directed at him. Benton, who prides himself on "running a tight ship with high morale," hears good-natured steam being let off. And Carleton, who works as an engineer with dozens of different shop groups from week to week, didn't even hear the laughter, which came at the precise instant he reached the high point of the story he was telling to Anderson and Benton.

Or let us look at the reaction of three men who watch a large new machine being moved into the shop area. Worker Fenton perceives it as a threat to his job and a replacement for his skills. Production Supervisor Gable views it as an asset which will help him achieve his production levels and thus secure his bonus. And the treasurer perceives it as a further drain on the company's limited resources.

Of course we can't hope to perceive every situation as the other person does, but if we make an honest effort to appreciate his point of view, we will improve the possibility of achieving effective communication.

Lack of interest in the subject matter, on the part of either the speaker or the listener, can be a serious deterrent to the reception of the ideas presented. This lack of interest is basically the result of a difference in perception of the situation. Nevertheless, it is still a lack of interest.

However, interest in the topic under discussion can be aroused in the reader or listener by utilizing an attention-catching opening or a statement so provocative or unexpected that the members of the audience must sit up and take notice. These gimmick devices are, at best, short-term in their overall appeal. Individuals can even be ordered to be interested. "I'll expect that report to be completed and submitted by 4:00 P.M. today. If it isn't, don't bother to come in to work tomorrow!" Certainly a statement like this arouses the interest of the listener in the message; in addition, of course, it arouses his animosity and antagonism, and we have lost one of our objectives of good communication: maintaining favorable relationships.

However, the most effective way to secure the reader's or listener's interest is to motivate him to *want* to pay attention. And the best way to accomplish this is to structure the presentation around the benefits that will accrue to him if he carries through what the speaker or writer suggests. For example, to gain the interest of a group of foremen, a plant manager may point out how production will rise if they follow the suggestions he is making. This increase in production will in turn result in higher compensation or recognition for the foremen. Because most of the foremen are concerned with increased compensation, they probably will be interested in the communication.

The sensitive teacher follows a similar method to arouse student interest in the topic under discussion. He does not initially point out the importance of the subject to mankind, the school, or his department; he indicates how knowledge of the topic will assist the student in understanding the entire field of learning, or making a living, or carrying through a process. The device, therefore, to overcome the barrier of lack of interest is basically an appeal to the self-interest of the individuals to whom the message is directed.

Lack of fundamental knowledge can be a third barrier to the clear communication of ideas. How can you intelligently discuss a problem with those who do not have the background to understand or appreciate the basic concepts of the discussion? Certainly there will be a breakdown in the communication of ideas if a nuclear physicist attempts to explain various high-level principles in his field to individuals who do not have the background to appreciate the material. The same may be true if an engineer attempts to give a technical explanation of a process to a production-line worker. Conversely, it is conceivable that the speaker's or writer's knowledge of his subject is superficial. This also becomes a barrier, for it is always apparent to us when we listen to someone who is, as the saying goes, only one chapter ahead of the class.

Associated with this might be those cases where the communicator's knowledge in a field is so thorough that he makes unconscious assumptions that the other person can't follow. The danger is to assume that the listener has adequate background or fundamental knowledge and then to try to communicate on the basis of this false premise. To overcome this barrier, determine how much knowledge of the subject the recipient of the message possesses before you speak or write to him.

This determination is not always simple. As was indicated earlier, we usually depend on some type of response—verbal or nonverbal—to indicate understanding or lack of understanding. But this response from the recipient of our message may not always be accurate.

The *emotions* of either the sender or the receiver can prove to be another obstacle in the communication of an idea. We have all been in situations where the atmosphere became so emotionally charged that reasonable discussion broke down. When any of us have deep emotional reactions—love, hate, fear, anger—we find it almost impossible to communicate coherently anything but that emotion. The lesson learned here is obvious; calm down before you send or receive ideas. Of course this is easier said than done. It is precisely when our emotions are at a high level that we are most strongly motivated to communicate.

On the other hand, emotions need not be strong and deep to be obstacles; they can be sublimated and repressed and still be deterrents to the clear communication of ideas. And the communicator who is emotionally charged up or enthusiastic often finds that this quality is an asset in helping him communicate.

The *personality* of those involved can be another barrier to communication. We are often so strongly influenced by the personality of the speaker or the writer that we may either accept or reject what he has to say without good reason. Personality is not only confined to an individual, however. It may be a total reaction from an audience; there are many speakers who will attest to the fact that this group or that group reflected a personality that was hostile, friendly, apathetic, disagreeable, sympathetic, or understanding. Of course our recognition of the personalities of others is often tempered by our own, and perhaps when we feel that communication breaks down because of personality, we should first examine our own—difficult as this task is—and attempt to make some changes that will improve understanding.

The *appearance* of the communicator or the instrument he uses to communicate, such as the letter or report, can prove to be another critical factor. A speaker whose coat is awry, whose tie is askew, and whose general appearance is poor is not likely to arouse a favorable response in his listeners. The same is true of a business letter or a report that is typed in heavy block paragraphs, is jammed on the page from side to side and from top to bottom, and has a jagged margin, messy erasures, and few, if any, topic headings. Certainly the unkempt attire of a speaker or the careless and negligent appearance of a written message will prove to be a serious barrier to the communication of ideas. The solution here is simply correction of the fault. If the appearance of the report is poor, the business executive should have no compunction about sending it back to be retyped. The reader may be a thousand miles away from the company, but his knowledge of the firm is influenced by the sheet of paper in his hand; it contributes to his image of the company. Make that image a good one by checking the appearance of the communication.

Prejudice can also seriously impede the transmission of ideas. An unreasonable bias rejects ideas without consideration. Although we sometimes think of prejudice as being confined to race, religion, and color, most of us normally encounter it in a dozen other ways in American industry. It may be a simple but strongly held viewpoint (or perception) on the part of the chief executive or it may be the classic statement of the foreman: "Well, I been here twenty-eight years; we never tried it before, and I'm sure it won't work now."

Of all the barriers to the clear communication of ideas that we can list, bias and prejudice are probably the most difficult to eliminate. The usual answer to these is education, but it is a lengthy and sometimes frustrating job to attempt to educate people out of their deeply held and unreasonable prejudices. Perhaps a better way to overcome deep bias is to show the individual how he will benefit by following a specific course of action. Of course this requires reasoning, and so often deep prejudice is unreasonable to begin with.

Distractions can prove to be another disturbing factor in communication. Clattering typewriters, noisy punch presses, inadequate illumination, hissing ventilation, or uncomfortable temperature conditions may be deterrents to the communication of ideas. It is most difficult for a production-line worker to understand clearly what the foreman wants when they have to shout to one another over the noise of pounding machinery. The same is true in a noisy office situation. But noise is not the only disturbing distraction we encounter. Any upsetting factor which impinges upon any of our senses—visual, auditory, olfactory, or others— may well upset the clear transmission and reception of ideas.

Poor organization of ideas may be a serious barrier to communication. When ideas are clearly and logically presented, it is still not easy to assimilate them, but to compound the situation by presenting thoughts in a confused manner is inexcusable. No contractor lays a brick nor does an engineer position a steel beam without first looking at the blueprint; a surgeon makes no move without examining the laboratory reports and the X-rays; an attorney would never dare file an important case without first drawing up a careful brief; but often we begin to write or speak without first making a "blueprint" of our plan.

Whether the organizational framework of our message is jotted down on the back of an envelope, on a sheet of scratch paper, or carefully typed up as a formal outline, we should not attempt to communicate without knowing precisely where we are going. To do so is to invite disaster. If the listener or reader cannot follow you easily and logically, he will simply shut off his mind and comment to himself, "Oh, that speaker is going in circles; I don't know what he's getting at!" A three-minute oral presentation, a fifteen-line letter, a half-hour speech, or a thirty-page report should all be planned before they are carried through.

There is almost nothing we do, from an evening's recreation to the construction of a twenty-story building, that we do not plan, except our speaking and writing. It should not be that way. We should always plan our communication, whether it is long or short, formal or informal.

Poor listening is perhaps one of the most serious barriers to the communication of ideas. All too often we think of communication as encompassing reading, writing, and speaking. When we consider that approximately 60 per cent of our time is spent listening, it is difficult to understand how or why training in this activity is so frequently overlooked.

Poor listening is often a natural result of the disparity in the time it takes to tell of ideas and the time required to assimilate them. Most of us speak at the rate of about 140 words a minute, but we can assimilate approximately 500 words in the same span of time. It is no wonder, therefore, that the listener's mind begins to wander as he moves further and further ahead of the speaker's ideas.

Often a listener is busy thinking of what he is going to say rather than listening to the speaker. Or perhaps his bias permits him to hear only what he wishes. However, we can train ourselves to assimilate better the ideas directed at us. We can learn to listen actively, to concentrate on what is being said, to listen for the ideas beyond the words, and to appreciate the desires and needs of the speaker.

The supervisor or executive *must* listen carefully. He should know that it is not necessary to agree with a subordinate's statement or request. But it is vital that the manager convey the idea that he understands and appreciates why the employee said what he did say. It is through effective listening that the administrator can control many of the activities under his jurisdiction.[6]

The *complexities of our busy society* present still another barrier. With dozens of communication media bombarding us throughout the day, we have, of necessity, become selective. As contrasted to our grandfather's eight-page newspaper, limited circle of friends, and crystal radio receiver, we live in a veritable torrent of sound and printed words. Sixty- and eighty-page newspapers, weekly news magazines, technical journals in our field, and dozens of reports must be read by each of us, and if we do not get to them, we somehow feel guilty. Furthermore, there are meetings we must attend, friends to visit, the radio to listen to, television shows to look at, and movies to go to. The result is that we become selective; we hear and do not listen; we see and do not assimilate. And this wall of defense serves us to good advantage, for there is too much in our world for us to take it all in; we must choose—or be chosen for.

Because of our busy society, the communicator must recognize that he is constantly competing—competing for the attention of those listening to him speak or those reading his material. He must make his spoken or written message so excellent, so clear, so concise, so interesting, and so compelling that it will rise above all competing communication media, and the listener or reader will *want* to assimilate it.

A final barrier is probably the one which occurs most frequently in

6. See Nichols, "Listening Is a Ten-Part Skill," Part IV.

attempting to communicate ideas. That is *language* itself. Among the problems involved in the use of language for communication are *differences in interpretation of statements*. We have all made what we thought were perfectly clear and simple comments to another only to have that individual misconstrue them completely. Why this takes place is hard to determine; perhaps it is simply due to misunderstanding or an unconscious desire not to carry through the request as it is made. Or perhaps the communicatee gives different meanings to the words from those the communicator intended. Although "fee," "salary," "wages," "payment," "stipend," and "emolument" are listed as synonymous in the dictionary, they each create specific images in our mind. We would never pay a surgeon wages for an operation, nor a ditchdigger weekly fees for his labor. Words have precise meanings, and although the denotations of several may be similar, the connotations, or the meanings we give to words by usage, are often different. As Mark Twain said, "There is as much difference between the right word and the almost-right word as between lightning and the lightning bug."

Then, too, a specific word may evoke different symbols or "pictures" in the minds of people whose backgrounds and experiences are different. What does the word "pig" conjure up in the mind of a steelworker, as compared to a farmer? And what symbol does the word evoke when it is hurled in anger at a person?

Language uses words to convey ideas, facts, and feelings. It is in the interpretation of these words that semantic problems arise, because the meanings for words are not in the words, but in the minds of the people who receive them. (See Hayakawa, "How Words Change Our Lives," Part IV.)

Meanings of concrete words do not vary too much from one person to another. There is little possibility for confusion when we speak of pencil, or paper, or book. But as words become more abstract (democracy, honesty, happiness), they are more likely to be misunderstood. This is also true of words which may carry emotional overtones in a specific society. What "liberal," "radical," "virtue," "morality," and "integrity" mean to the speaker or writer may not agree at all with the listener's or reader's concept of the same word.

Another factor to be considered under language is *inadequate vocabulary*. If our stock of words is poor and forces us to fumble and bumble as we attempt to express our ideas, there will certainly be a breakdown in communication. Although it isn't easy, all of us, with a little concentrated effort, can expand our vocabularies so that we can express our ideas clearly, forcefully, and with facility and not be required to use a second-choice word when the *exact* word would result in a much clearer picture.

We should also make every effort to avoid *errors* in speaking and writing. Whether it is spelling, diction, or pronunciation, an error, when it is made, immediately forces the reader or listener to focus on the mistake. You know how you have been impressed by what might be called minor errors, and how they jump out of the page you are reading or the oral statement to which you are listening. Never minimize or rationalize an error, regardless of how minor; make every effort to make your language choice as correct as possible.

Remember also to choose the *proper level* of language when you communicate with others. To speak or write "above their heads" or down to them condescendingly is to invite misinterpretation, irritation, and confusion. A classic story illustrating this problem is of the plumber who wrote to the Bureau of Standards in Washington, stating that he used hydrochloric acid for cleaning out clogged drains. The Bureau wrote him: "The efficacy of hydrochloric acid is indisputable, but the corrosive residue is incompatible with metallic permanence." The plumber replied that he was glad the Bureau agreed. The Bureau tried again, this time writing, "We cannot assume responsibility for the production of noxious and toxic residue with hydrochloric acid and suggest you use an alternative procedure." The plumber again replied that he was pleased that the Bureau agreed with his findings. Finally the Bureau awoke to the fact that it was not writing at this plumber's level. Thereupon the plumber received a note which said, "Don't use hydrochloric acid. It eats hell out of the pipes."

FEEDBACK

Now, we ask ourselves, if there are so many barriers to the communication of ideas, how do we know when we do get through . . . or, even more important, how do we know when we don't?

After all, most of us just write or speak and then assume that we have communicated what is in our mind to someone else. This may be true; we may have communicated, but chances are also good that we did not.

Perhaps the only way to determine whether or not we have been successful is to secure a response, or *feedback*.

The technical meaning for feedback is somewhat different from the popular conception. In 1948, Norbert Wiener published a book called *Cybernetics* (a branch of science that deals with the theory of such systems as the nerve networks in animals, electronic pathways in computing machines, servo systems for the automatic control of machinery, and other information processing, transmission, and control systems).

One of the primary areas of study in cybernetics is feedback. In this context it applies to the ability of man and some machines to detect an error or deviation from what is desired in an operation, and *feed back* that error to a control mechanism, which then makes the necessary correction. If a satellite destined for the moon moves off course, the deviation is noted and fed back to the controlling mechanism for correction. A thermostat in a home records a temperature too low and feeds back a signal to the furnace which then operates to make a correction. Or an individual's body temperature goes lower than desired; this information is fed back and his physiological control mechanism attempts to bring about the change desired.

Thus a common feature of a control system is that the output produces an effect on the input. In communication engineering this is called feedback, and a control systems engineer refers to this as a "closed loop system."

Of course the similarities of feedback in this technical concept to that in interpersonal communication are immediately apparent. And as a matter of fact, we now have the expression "Have you closed the loop?" This obviously refers to the communicator (encoder) and whether or not he has secured a satisfactory response (feedback) from the communicatee (decoder) and thus satisfactorily closed the loop and thus secured understanding.

The popular meaning for feedback is the verbal or nonverbal response received from the individual to whom a message is directed. It may be a series of words; it may be a raised eyebrow, an angry expression, or a smile; it may be no response at all (which is a response indicating that the message was not heard, not understood, or not accepted). But it is only through the feedback we receive that we can know whether we have communicated our ideas.

If we ask our youngster to open the window and he does it, we know we have communicated successfully. However, if he opens the door, that incorrect response or feedback tells us that communication broke down.

That, of course, is a simple example, but it is valid, for most of the reactions we get during the day are similar. If we speak to an individual and he suddenly raises his eyes or looks puzzled and uncomprehending, we know from that response that we must rephrase and revise our message and present it again. Perhaps then his response will be, "Oh, I see now. But you did confuse me a minute ago when you used all those high-powered words."

The same often happens when we write for our superiors, our subordinates, our colleagues, our teachers, or our students. If they don't understand what we have written, they will ask us for a further interpretation. Their questions (or feedback) tell us how successful we and they have been in exchanging ideas.

But we are often not quite so fortunate in being able to secure an almost immediate response. Sometimes we speak to 50, 150, or 250 persons, or we write a report in Chicago which may be read by 20 different individuals in New York. In such instances, feedback is not offered or is much more difficult to secure.

Then there is the further problem of trying to secure accurate feedback after we have made a presentation. Why do individuals often say "yes" when they are asked, "Do you understand?" "Is it clear?" There are two obvious answers. One is that the communicatee (or decoder) honestly believes that he *does* understand, even though he may not. The second occurs when the recipient of the message is reluctant to disclose that he does *not* understand. He feels (and we must all admit to this) that he will lose face or be embarrassed by this admitted lack of comprehension. And so he says, "Yes, I understand," when in truth he does not.

Every student has experienced this situation when the instructor, after his lecture, says, "Are there any questions?" How often we have been tempted to raise our hand, but as we look around the classroom, no one else has raised *his* hand. We are, therefore, reluctant to raise our own. If the teacher places faith in the feedback he received (which was "no questions"), he can only assume that everyone understood the discussion. He may, however, learn differently when he grades the examination papers (feedback to the teacher) which covered this same topic.

Thus, we all depend on feedback to evaluate the clarity of our communications and to receive and interpret responses to what we say or write. This is as it should be, but we must always remember to weigh the feedback for accuracy and not always trust it completely.

The communicator must keep in mind that he may not have transmitted his message. And he should design as many methods as possible to secure feedback so that he can prove to himself as conclusively as possible that he was successful in transmitting what was in his mind to his listener's or reader's mind.

NONVERBAL COMMUNICATION

It is probably no exaggeration to say that we communicate as many ideas nonverbally (and sometimes informally) as we do verbally. The way we stand, the way we walk, the manner in which we shrug our shoulders, furrow our brows, and shake our heads—all convey ideas to others. But we need not always perform an action for nonverbal communication to take place. We also communicate by the clothes we wear, the car we drive, or the office we occupy. It is true that what is communicated may not be accurate, but ideas *are* communicated.

Ruesch and Kees, in their book *Nonverbal Communication*, divide this area of communication into three parts: sign language, action language, and object language.[7] Sign language is used to communicate basic ideas, such as the wave of a hand which says "hi." Or a "thumbs down" sign which denotes nonacceptance.

Action language results from body movements which convey ideas beyond the immediate purpose of the action. We gain certain insights into an individual's personality by noting how he eats, whether he stands or not when a lady approaches, what position he takes when joining a queue at a box-office, etc.

We also decode object language which, according to Ruesch and Kees, includes the display of material items, either intentionally or unintentionally. These might include jewelry, coats, furniture, cars, and other tangible objects.

CONFLICT BETWEEN VERBAL AND NONVERBAL COMMUNICATION

One of the interesting aspects of communication is the task of decoding two messages transmitted simultaneously. This happens quite often in the verbal—or formal—and nonverbal—or informal—communication situation. We have all been in a situation when an individual has greeted us with "How are you? Good to see you. Come on into my office and chew the fat, you old son of a gun." But the nonverbal communication, consisting of a surreptitious but pained glance at the clock, says something else. Or the guest who says, "Of course we want to see your slides of Europe," as he stifles a yawn and sprawls in the chair. Then there is the employee who tries to sound relaxed and comfortable when he talks to the boss, but his toe tapping the floor like a machine gun tells a different story.

Interestingly enough, whenever the meaning of the nonverbal message conflicts with that of the verbal, the receiver is most likely to find the former more believable.

Does this mean that we should bend every effort to communicate the same message both verbally and nonverbally? It seems to me that if we are transmitting an untruth verbally, it will always conflict with the nonverbal communication. And the alert receiver will almost always be able to determine that a problem exists. Most of us can quickly see the fearful person who truly exists behind the good-humored, back-slapping, joke-telling façade that is displayed. We somehow know quite well how dis-

7. A discussion of a portion of the book by Ruesch and Kees may be found in Randall Harrison, "Non-Verbal Communication: Explorations into Time, Space, Action, and Object," contained in Campbell and Hepler, *Dimensions in Communication* (Belmont, California: Wadsworth, 1965), pp. 162-163.

mally Betty and Joe's marriage is progressing, even though their protestations of undying love for one another are voiced loudly and clearly. The nonverbal message is usually obvious, and if it does not agree with the verbal one, the receiver quickly and almost invariably recognizes the one that is true.

How about Mrs. Housewife who has heard radio commercial after radio commercial extolling the courtesy and cleanliness of the Sun Brite Food Markets. However, she shopped there yesterday and when she asked the "bag boy" to place her groceries in two bags instead of one large one, he looked and acted irritated even though he said "O.K." Furthermore, she found a couple of uncooked kernels of rice lying on the top of the lemon meringue pie she bought. And to top it off, she stepped on a wad of chewing gum in the parking lot and it took her almost fifteen minutes to remove the mess from the bottom of her shoe.

Now, which communication channel will she believe: the formal radio and newspaper announcements which describe the virtues of cleanliness and courtesy to be found in this shining emporium, or the informal communication carried through by the wad of gum, the kernels of rice, and the irritated glance of the "bag boy"?

MEDIA OF NONVERBAL COMMUNICATION

Most of the nonverbal messages that we receive come to us visually. We are quick to see the hurt in one's eyes, the triumphant smile on a face, the twisting, nervous fingers in a lap, and the confidence in one's posture. We also decode the message that is a sudden, frightened tug at our arm when we cross in heavy traffic, or the barely noticeable touching of fingers of two people in love.

Our nose or olfactory sense also plays an important role in nonverbal communication. What a wonderful message we decode when we walk into the cozy comfort of the warm home where a huge Thanksgiving dinner is about to be served. The tantalizing aromas of a roasting turkey, dressing, and pumpkin pie require no words to transmit a message.

SPACE AND TIME COMMUNICATE

Anthropologist Edward Hall, in his excellent and provocative book *The Silent Language*, views culture as communication. He points out that what one sees in a society communicates a great deal about that group's values, goals, and standards. (See Hall, "The Silent Language in Overseas Business," Part IV.)

He presents an especially interesting discussion titled Time Talks and Space Speaks. Does Time really talk and does Space actually speak?

Of course they do, and we've all heard them. The person who arrives late for appointment after appointment seems to be telling us that we aren't very important, or that he is careless, or one of several interpretations based on our perception. And if we note Jack and Bob talking with their heads very close together, we may wonder what secrets or plots are being communicated.

We have formulated rather strict patterns in America for time. A business appointment is usually kept punctually. Although we may keep an individual waiting for five or ten minutes, much longer than that is usually interpreted as an affront.

If Jack is ten minutes late for an appointment with Bob, the latter's interpretation may vary according to the situation. Jack will probably apologize immediately if he is a few minutes late for a business meeting with Bob. However, he may be quite casual about his tardiness if it takes place one afternoon on a week-long fishing trip they are taking together. This is also true of our appreciation of time if we are going to attend a 2:00 P.M. university class or a 2:00 P.M. summer picnic. Most of us feel compelled to be more punctual in the former situation.

Time patterns in our society apply to divisions of the year (which is a time pattern in itself) as well as minutes. Weekdays are usually set aside for work while Saturdays and Sundays are the days on which we occupy ourselves with rest or leisure activities. Or someone will remark, "Now that summer is coming, I'm going to take it easier."

Americans are accustomed to quantifying time. "I will have this done in 30 minutes." "I'll see you at the 3:00 meeting." "Let's establish a six-month deadline for the project." "We'll insert a time penalty clause into the contract. The installation should be completed by December 3; for every day that is required after that, a payment of $100 will be made."

This concern with time is not so precise in other cultures, although the European is fast approaching the North American's interpretation of time. To the Latin American, time is taken more casually, and tardiness does not usually communicate the message it does in the United States. Hall points out that in some cultures, such as the Hopi, time is measured by a series of natural events, not by specific numbers of minutes or days. Time passes according to the ripening of grain, or the completion of the growth of an animal, or the winter rains.

Time certainly communicates. The office worker who is at her desk and begins to work promptly at 8:30 A.M. is surely communicating facts to the office manager which are in sharp contrast to what the young lady is "saying" who casually strolls in, day after day, at 8:40, 8:45 or 9:00 A.M.

How people use space also tells us much. As is the case with time, the utilization of space and what is communicated thereby vary from continent to continent and nation to nation.

We say this is "our property line"; even though no fence exists on it, a neighbor may not encroach upon or over it. "This is the children's section of the yard, and they can mess it up as much as they like so long as they don't spoil my lawn."

In a business situation, an employee occupies a specific space where his desk, chair, and cabinets are arranged. Anyone who occupies, uses, or moves this furniture may encounter antagonism. In the conference room, the position at the head of the table belongs to the president of the company or the chairman of the meeting. If the sales manager occupies that position or decides to use the president's office, desk, and chair, he will surely communicate a message.

Space also speaks in informal situations. The man who usurps your place in the theater ticket line communicates to you. In the home, we have also laid claim to certain areas. There is the "children's play room," "Mother's kitchen," "Dad's workshop," "Grandfather's chair," "the family den," etc.

In personal communication between two people, we often find that the distance varies. Two women who are discussing routine matters of their organization may speak comfortably as they sit two to three feet distant from one another. However, if they are discussing "who would make the best president for their group," or "Betty's recent operation," or "just what is happening between Bob and Dorothy Campbell," the distance may be shortened considerably.

The speaking distance which is maintained in different cultures also varies. In the United States two businessmen may talk about a transaction very comfortably across the desk. However, in most of Europe and in Latin America, the distance is much closer. It is not unusual in Italy to see two men walking down a corridor in an office building, arms around each other's shoulders, talking face to face.

This appreciation of space, when cultures are brought together, sometimes causes problems in oral communication. Hall points out that the North American may well back away from the Latin American, as the latter attempts to convey an idea. This reaction, of one man advancing and one retreating, may cause confusion and antagonism in one or both, which in turn colors the interpretation of the ideas expressed.

Time and space, as examples of nonverbal communication, certainly play an important role in our sending and receiving of ideas.

LISTENING — A VITAL AREA OF COMMUNICATION

Most of us, as noted earlier, spend approximately 60 per cent of our work day listening. Yet we do not always do so very effectively. And because we don't listen well, we frequently encounter communication problems.

As we noted earlier in this chapter, poor listening can prove to be a barrier in the communication of ideas.

It is interesting how frequently and consistently this important aspect of communication is neglected in our educational system. Although most of our youngsters are given extensive training in how to read and write effectively, as well as instruction on how to speak competently, little, if any, time is devoted to listening. On one occasion or another, a teacher may admonish a class with "You'd better listen to this," or "Listen carefully, children," but little is ever said on *how* to listen. Yet it is a vital area for the student and business manager.

We are told that we usually forget from one third to one half of what we hear within eight hours after hearing it! This alone indicates the importance of listening. It is important for the student whose success is dependent on how well he retains ideas and for the manager who must know what is taking place in many areas if he is to make intelligent decisions. The salesman must listen to his customers so that he will know what attributes of his product to sell to this customer as compared to that. The parent must listen to his child so that the latter will learn to express himself and develop the assurance that he may confide in his father or mother. And there are several professional areas which require effective listening as a primary stock in trade: psychiatry, educational and marriage counseling, and business and military personnel interviewing.

In this text, we are especially concerned with the industrial and business situation. And it is about this area that business leader Carl Braun said, "The problem is not one of getting men to talk. The problem is one of getting leaders to listen."

Yes, this is a problem. How do we train people to listen to what they hear?

Let us take the case of Supervisor Morrison. Joe has just approached him to report: "Well, Mr. Morrison, I finally locked up the Carlyle Company order. Boy, was it a mess! But you said it was an emergency job, and I saw to it that it went out today—right on the button. But it *was* miserable. You know, I've been down here every night this week and almost all last weekend. Their specifications are ridiculous, but the order is on its way. And let me tell you, if I never see another job as tough as that, I'll be plenty happy." If Mr. Morrison should now turn to Joe and say, "Great, Joe. Now let's get to work on the Mayberry order," Morrison hasn't listened to Joe at all!

What was Joe *really* saying to Morrison? Of course, we'll never truly know, but we can be sure he was not simply saying that the Carlyle order was difficult. He was probably saying, "How about giving me a pat on the back, Mr. Morrison," or "Why do you give me all the problem jobs?" or "I hate to work nights."

You may say, "But is it Morrison's job, or is it any supervisor's job, to hear what is not said?" The answer is "Yes." The sensitive, concerned, and effective manager will hear what Joe *really* wants to say but is often inhibited from stating directly. These inhibitions may be due to ego, pride, emotions, the position we hold, or our society. But the manager (or anyone) who will make an effort to perceive the situation as the communicator perceives it will listen when he hears.

BARRIERS TO EFFECTIVE LISTENING

One of the basic barriers to effective listening is simply the *inability to concentrate*, which in turn causes facts and ideas to be lost.

This lack of concentration may have several causes. Most of us speak, as noted earlier, at a much slower rate than what the average person can comprehend. This permits the listener to make mental excursions into other areas as he listens to the speaker. For a few seconds he thinks about that faulty car transmission; then he returns to the speaker's topic; then he is off again. This time he wonders about the football game: Will it be worth $5.50 per ticket? And again back to the speaker. But what about vacation? Two weeks in September should be O.K. And back to the speaker. But now the speaker is too far ahead; the listener has missed something vital on one of his excursions. Besides, the topic seems very complex. Oh, well, not concentrating is easier than trying to. Another listener is now just hearing.

One's *emotions* can also cause poor listening. When the speaker makes a statement that disagrees with the listener's concepts, the latter may simply reach up into his brain and turn the communicator off. Or he may concentrate on the statement with which he disagrees as others are stated but not heard.

And the style of clothes the speaker wears (or doesn't wear), the pleasant or disagreeable look on his face, or the posture he assumes may or may not cause the listener to react emotionally and tune him out.

Of course there are many other factors which may affect us emotionally and influence our level of comprehension of what is said: the accent of the speaker, the color of his skin, the mannerisms he employs, and our record of past experiences with him.

WHAT IS INVOLVED IN LISTENING

The good listener makes a definite attempt to listen in three different areas for every statement: facts, feelings, fancy.

Facts

In listening for facts, you should first attempt to determine the theme or the thesis of the presentation. In a speech, this may be stated in the first few minutes. It will probably be noted in different words several times during the talk, and may well serve as a concluding statement.

The basic ideas should then be recognized. What are the four key points in the entire talk? The alert listener will be able to recognize them, even if the speaker doesn't label each specifically. Facts to support the ideas should be assimilated. But of primary importance is to recognize the theme and then the major ideas. Once the ideas are firmly fixed in your mind, they will help you recall specific facts.

If you listen analytically, you can recognize major ideas and separate them from minor ones. Of course this requires your full effort and concentrated attention. But effective listening is hard work and requires your complete concentration.

Taking notes during the talk will also help you retain ideas and facts. And if the talk goes on for any length of time, the good listener will occasionally but hastily review mentally the ideas and facts which have already been cited. But you should never become so absorbed in the task of taking notes that you lose the ideas being transmitted.

Feelings

When you listen for a person's feelings, you must be especially sensitive to listen not only to his verbal but also to his nonverbal communication. In the case of the words he uses, you must give, insofar as you are able, the connotations to the words that he gives. You must also try to understand his ideas, feelings, and biases; you should recognize his point of view, his frame of reference, and remember his salary level, his hopes, and his desires. This can be extremely difficult, but you must try.

You must constantly listen to the other person's nonverbal communication: the gestures of his hands, the tapping of his fingers, the look in his eyes, and the confusion in the lines on his brow.

If his words say, "Well, it really isn't very important to me anyway," but his posture is stiff and tight, his knuckles white, his eyes hopeful, and his forehead glistening with perspiration, you had better hear the nonverbal rather than the verbal message. For if you don't, communication between you will not be effective.

Fancy

How do we separate facts from fancy? When do we know that this statement is based on some evidence, but that one is pure opinion without substantiation?

At times our previous experience with certain persons helps us evaluate the validity of what they say. Also careful listening helps us recognize what facts, if any, have been cited as evidence to justify the suggestions, recommendations, or ideas listed. In the final analysis, this helps us separate facts from opinions which have some basis and merit, and those which are purely fanciful.

BEING A GOOD LISTENER

We all agree that in the busy, highly competitive world we live in, there is little opportunity to listen carefully and sensitively. But if we wish to work, live, and play successfully with others, we must find the time. (See Nichols, Part IV.)

The business manager or executive must *listen;* he must listen in many different ways so that he understands what the communicator says, implies, insinuates, desires, and hopes. The successful manager listens for facts, for feelings, for fancy. Here is a list of suggestions that will help improve communications:

Listen actively for the main theme of the discussion and specific ideas and facts. Concentrate on what the speaker is saying; don't let your mind wander. Make mental notes on each idea and supporting fact. Remain alert; ask questions; note fallacies. Don't attempt to do something unrelated to the discussion while the speaker is talking.

Check your posture. Sit up straight and look directly at the speaker. Don't protest that you listen best when you are relaxed, hands clasped behind your head and feet propped on the desk. This may be true. But your listener may *perceive* from that posture your lack of interest and perhaps discourtesy. The result of his perception will then raise barriers to clear communication.

Listen objectively to his point of view. Try to put aside your preconceived ideas or bias on a topic. You may be correct, but nevertheless try to listen objectively. It is true that you have developed your point of view after years of experience, testing, and examination. But he may have a new approach, a new concept, a new method of doing an old job that is worth putting into operation. Thus you must listen objectively to his idea.

Listen analytically to his presentation. Sometimes we listen to an individual who hasn't organized his ideas too well. He seems to be going in circles; he repeats himself, and he barely mentions a key point. He may spend eight minutes on one point, and two minutes on four other aspects. We must recognize his five points. We, as good listeners, must organize his presentation in our minds as he talks. And we can do this if we listen analytically. We can recognize the theme, then the key ideas, the supporting facts, and the necessary details. To do this requires analytical and active listening.

Our task is much simpler when we listen to the individual who has organized his presentation before speaking. Then we need only follow the major ideas and the supporting facts as he lists them. But many people will address us whose presentations are confused. The responsibility for organizing what they say is now ours.

Listen to his meanings for words. It is almost impossible for us to give the exact connotations to every word that the speaker does. But we can try. If we know something of his background, his values, and his experiences, we can give meanings to words as he intended. Of course we will never succeed completely, especially if the words are abstract (democracy, love, honesty, socialism, morals). However, we can try to give *his* meanings to the words he uses.

When he says, "I think we ought to get on this Carlyle job right away," we must try to interpret "right away" as he does. Does it mean today? in a week? in a month? We have worked with this man for several years, and we know that he is exacting but slow and easy-going. To him, "right away" probably means in a week or two.

What does Mr. Kelly mean when he says, "Tom is a very hard worker." Because you know that Mr. Kelly is an extremely conscientious employee himself and that he rarely gives praise without good reason, your connotation for "very hard worker" will probably be similar to Kelly's.

Circumstances and environment also help us give connotations to words. The words used at a company picnic may have different connotations from the same words used in a similar statement in the conference room.

Listen to and observe the speaker's nonverbal communication. The inflection given to words often determines what meaning should be given to the statement. Our statement above, "Tom is a very hard worker," can carry several different meanings according to which word or words are emphasized, and whether the quotation is made as a question or a statement. The meaning can further change according to the facial expression which accompanies it. A simple declarative statement, "Tom is a very hard worker," carries a derisive connotation if the speaker accompanies it with a broad smile or a curled lip.

We have already talked about nonverbal communication and how important it is to decode it correctly. Of course this applies to the competent listener. He is acutely aware of the important messages that are communicated nonverbally: the knuckles being cracked; the handkerchief being twisted; the confidence in a step; the fear in a posture; the hope on a face. And if these communications do not agree with the words being spoken, he must interpret the one that is accurate.

Listen with empathy, with understanding, and with your heart. It is a communication task which requires your full energy, intelligence, and sensitivity. The results are worth the effort. Open pathways in communication are often the result, rather than the barriers which are all too frequently encountered.

THE RESULTS OF GOOD LISTENING

In the final analysis, effective listening produces many salutary results:

1. When others note that you listen carefully to them, they in turn will usually try to understand you better through more effective listening on their part. Thus, your effective listening often results in making others good listeners.

2. Good listening permits you to secure as much information as the speaker possesses. Your careful listening will usually motivate him to cite as many facts as he is able. When you have as much information as possible, you are in a better position to make accurate decisions.

3. Effective listening usually improves relationships between people. It gives the speaker an opportunity to get ideas, facts, and hostilities off his chest. You will understand him better as you listen; he appreciates your interest in him, and friendships may thus deepen.

4. Disagreements and problems can best be solved when individuals listen carefully to each other. This does not mean that one must agree with the other's point of view; he must merely show that he understands the other person's viewpoint. Everyone wants understanding, and there is no better way of expressing this quality than through sensitive listening.

5. Listening may help the other person see his own problem with greater clarity. Usually when any of us are permitted to talk out a problem, we can more easily determine possible solutions.

6. Listening carefully to another will give you clues on how he thinks, what he feels is important, and why he is saying what he is saying. By understanding him better, you will be able to work better with him. Knowing that Tom is an extrovert, Jim an introvert; that Bob needs frequent praise, that Joe requires very little; all this leads to better understanding of others and thus more harmony.

If we were therefore to summarize what the individual gains who is a good listener, we would surely list *information*, which gives the listener additional knowledge; *understanding* of others and their viewpoints, which assists the listener in working with others; *more effective listening* on the part of others so that the listener's ideas get through; and *cooperation* from others who feel that the listener better understands them.

QUESTIONS FOR STUDY

I. Complete any of the following problems assigned. You may wish to review the chapter and note key points before attempting to solve the problem.

1. Using secondary and/or primary sources, carry through a research project on "Motivation of Employees." Determine what factors are important in motivating individuals and what connection, if any, each factor has with communication.

2. Think of a discussion you held recently with an individual which went awry. Present it as a case analysis. Who was the individual? What was the topic of discussion? Where did it take place? What specific factors caused the breakdown? Why were *those* factors the cause in this particular instance? Add any other factors which you feel are relevant.

3. Check through several secondary sources and record four different definitions of *communication* and their authors. Which one of these do you feel is most accurate and why?

4. Citizens of the United States of America frequently have a different perception of this nation than do the citizens of foreign countries. What are some of the reasons for this difference in perception? How does this difference, or how should this difference, influence our foreign policy?

5. There are a number of barriers to effective communication listed in this chapter. Can just one of these cause a breakdown in communication or are there usually several involved almost simultaneously? Defend your answer.

6. An expression which has recently gained in popularity is "Have you closed the loop?" What connection does this statement have with our discussion of feedback?

7. Under some conditions, communication does not take place successfully even when the stated feedback from the decoder indicates it has. Can you present a situation where this might be true?

8. Many of our statesmen, columnists, and others grandly state that our civil disorders, campus unrest, high crime rate, and violence are

due to "differences in perception." However, recognizing a problem does not solve it. What suggestions do you have for eliminating or alleviating the "Differences in Perception" dilemma which exists in our society?

II. Complete any of the following problems assigned.

1. List and explain informal communication messages which you have received through your senses of sight, touch, and smell in the last week.

2. List and discuss several situations in the classroom and in the typical American office which illustrate the truth of Hall's statement, "Time talks and Space speaks."

3. Is it always possible to "hear" the feelings of the speaker? What factors might prevent this?

4. What specific suggestions can you make to the individual who wishes to improve his listening ability?

5. According to Ralph Nichols and other authorities in the field of listening, what are several of the important factors and habits which contribute to poor listening on the part of the decoder?

6. Carry through the following experiment in serial communication and present your findings to the class.

Secure a picture or an advertisement from a magazine. It should have several items or incidents in it as well as people involved in some activity.

Ask for four volunteers from your class, and request that three leave the room. Ask volunteer number one to remain in the room and show him and the class the picture for two to three minutes. Call volunteer two into the room and tell him to listen to what volunteer one tells the group he (volunteer one) saw, so that volunteer two may tell the group what he (volunteer two) heard.

Ask the class to record very briefly what volunteer one tells them he saw.

When volunteer one finishes telling the group what he saw in the picture, call in volunteer three so that he may listen to volunteer two. Have volunteer two tell the group what he heard volunteer one say. Ask the group to record volunteer two's statements.

Call volunteer four in so that he may listen to volunteer three tell the group what he (volunteer three) heard volunteer two say.

Also ask the group to record volunteer three's comments. Finally, ask volunteer four to tell the group what he heard volunteer three say.

You may wish to distribute a form similar to the following for the group to use:

SERIAL COMMUNICATION			
Observations by Decoder One	Comments by Decoder Two	Comments by Decoder Three	Comments by Decoder Four
1. 2. 3. 4. 5. 6. 7. 8. 9. 10.			
Observations by group members on the communication process:			

At the conclusion of the experiment, indicate what specific principles in serial communication took place. Finally, read the article on serial communication by William V. Haney (Part IV) and compare his observations with yours.

III. Each of the following statements is either a quotation or a paraphrase from a book on language, semantics, or communication theory. Indicate as concisely as possible what you think the authors meant by any of the following quotations:

1. "A second principle of general semantics, non-identity, states that the word is not the thing it represents."

2. "Used correctly they [words] can cause friendliness, humor, and happiness. Used incorrectly, they can cause hatred, loss of faith, hostility, and even death."

3. "To say that we know what a word means in advance of its use is nonsense."

4. "A dictionary is an invaluable guide to interpretation, but we should remember that words do not have a *single* correct meaning."

5. "Meaning is relative to experience."

6. "The most important solution to these problems [communication problems] is to pay attention to feedback. Thus it is important to adapt communication to the receiver's interests. However, this feedback is not always to be trusted."

7. "Seldom does one bother to question the other person whether the terms used in the communication are agreed upon by both parties."

8. "Never mind what words mean. What did the speaker mean?"

9. "Semantics is an exploration rather than a science, which rewards its students with a skill rather than a body of subject matter."

10. "Some companies believe that management can exercise 'stop-go' control over information that employees receive."

11. "A piece of paper money is like a word; it has no value in itself."

12. "Speak, in order that I may see you."

13. "We must never assume that we are fully aware of what we communicate to someone else."

14. "Time talks. It speaks more plainly than words."

15. "Speakers are prisoners of their vocabularies."

16. "Nature has given to men one tongue, but two ears, that we may hear from others twice as much as we speak."

17. "It's what and how you communicate or don't communicate, that makes you what you are to others."

CHAPTER TWO

Communication as a Tool of Management Control

Every member of management must understand that effective communication is an essential tool of good management; and that part of his job is to relay and interpret appropriate information and news, whether good or bad, to his subordinates and superiors. . . .

There is a need to inform employees about matters which affect them or their jobs, to interpret management's position on relevant issues, to persuade employees to take actions best designed to serve the long-range mutual interests of themselves and the corporation.

> Lynn Townsend, President
> Chrysler Corporation[1]

Whether a business, industrial, or government office is large or small, it consists of personnel; in some instances, the number of persons involved is very large; in other cases, small. But whether the people who operate any enterprise are many or few, they must communicate among themselves and with others to get things done. Persons at the executive level of an organization are responsible for making decisions and initiating action. For these individuals to carry out their functions effectively, they must know what is taking place throughout the company.

However, this is much easier said than done. It is very difficult to acquire a truly accurate picture of company activities, especially in organizations where there is a good distance between the man working on

1. Quoted from ICIE *Reporting* (December 1964) in G. Seybold, *Employee Communication: Policy and Tools* (National Industrial Conference Board, 1966), p. 11.

the noisy production line and the division manager seated in his walnut-paneled office (See McMurry, "Clear Communications for Chief Executives," Part IV.) This distance is great not only in terms of physical space, but also in terms of social stratification and professional activities. Because of these distances and what happens to the content of a message as it travels, it is often difficult for the decision maker to know exactly what is taking place on the worker level.

In a small organization, with relatively few steps between the employee and the division manager, the problem of information flow is not great. But in a large corporation, it is frequently difficult for management to know *accurately* the true activities, feelings, and relationships of the people in the factories, shops, and offices.

Information transmitted up or down the line is often distorted unintentionally or by design. The distortions that occur may be the result of honest but inaccurate evaluations of facts and situations, the desire to impress a supervisor, a wish to avoid embarrassment, or an effort to side-step well-deserved blame for a mistake.

The persons concerned with the transmission of information must recognize how vital it is for the decision maker to possess accurate facts and figures if he is to complete his assignment effectively. But people being human beings and not machines, it is often difficult for them to achieve the goal of transmitting clear, complete, and accurate information.

UPWARD COMMUNICATIONS

Employees of all levels, except those in top management, must communicate UP. It is vital that they transmit information clearly, concisely, and accurately, so that this information may be evaluated and analyzed for the purpose of making decisions. The persons in charge may use such data to learn from past mistakes, to exercise better control of current situations, and to plan for future activities.

REPORTS

Among the most important kinds of communication to flow up are reports. These, if carefully controlled in number and content, can be invaluable to the supervisor or executive. He will usually receive them periodically from each of his key subordinates, who should include in their reports important information on the activities of their section, department, or division. The contents of such reports, written by several different department managers, will often overlap: The sales manager will have some comments on advertising; the head of the credit department will make a statement about sales; and the production supervisor may refer to something in the personnel manager's area of responsibility. These comments may very well conflict with each other: The sales director feels that the number of credit accounts should be expanded, but the credit manager feels that "because of present conditions, open-account sales should be drastically curtailed"; the advertising department feels that an additional $10,000 should be expended on TV commercials, but the controller recommends a major cut in advertising expenditures.

Indeed, it is helpful if reports from different sources within a company are in conflict, for the executive receiving these reports must make decisions that are based on as wide knowledge as possible. The action he takes may involve huge sums of money: A production line may be opened or closed, an expensive piece of equipment purchased, a contract signed, or property acquired. The correctness of the executive's decisions depends directly on the quality of the communications he receives from his subordinates; and if the information received is conflicting or overlapping, the executive can then evaluate all aspects of a given situation before making his decision.

If the writing in reports is fuzzy, statements are unclear, references ambiguous, or details inaccurate, the action taken on the basis of the report or reports received may very well turn out to be incorrect and extremely costly. For these reasons the communications that go up must be well done.

Reports may be of two kinds: oral and written. *Oral reports* can be presented in formal fashion before a group, the presentation accompanied by charts, graphs, and other visual aids. Or the oral report can be as simple as a foreman's statement to his supervisor: "We produced 455 units today; we will need a reorder on the cork liners for tomorrow's run."

It is much more difficult to classify *written reports*. One author attempts classification according to purpose (analytical, informative, persuasive). Another writer feels that classification by type (credit, periodic, memo, examination, progress) is more accurate as a deciding factor, while still others prefer field (engineering, marketing, management, medicine) or special (research, public, annual).[2]

But whether written reports are produced periodically or for special assignments, whether they are long or short, or whether they are engineering- or accounting-oriented, they contain statistical and/or narrative information. How they are classified is really of little importance, except to designate or differentiate one from another.

2. See Norman B. Sigband, *Effective Report Writing for Business, Industry, and Government* (New York: Harper & Row, 1960).

Distortion in Reports

As we have already noted, distortions of fact may occur in reports. But how can management secure honesty and accuracy in the reports it receives?

If too much emphasis is placed on the report itself, it may receive more attention and time from the writer than the operation about which he is reporting. There is also the danger that the report will contain information and facts that the writer feels management *wants* to hear, rather than an account of what actually took place. And of course, the report may simply cover up errors, or may present specific events in such a way that the reputation and pride of the report writer and his department or division are maintained.

Perhaps there is no one good way to secure honesty and accuracy in reports except by promoting a cooperative climate where it is obvious that the only goal desired is information, and that penalties are not meted out if errors and failures in a department's operations are reported. Employees should be encouraged to report both achievements and mistakes, and credit should be given for clear presentation of the latter as well as of the former. Certainly the manager is better able to make accurate decisions when he possesses knowledge about situations that did *not* succeed as well as about those that did.

Numbers of Reports

The multiplicity of reports directed to individuals in management positions is sometimes staggering. Some executives have taken speed-reading courses to assist them; others have sharply curtailed the number of reports they will accept; some have hired executive assistants whose job it is to select and mark vital portions of reports; and others have tried to limit the length of reports to "no more than one page."

In many corporations, the number of reports seems to have proliferated without reason. In one company a special report was requested in order to gain an understanding of a potential strike situation. The strike threat passed but no one ever bothered to order the report stopped, and it continues to appear regularly, month after month, although no one now reads it or needs it.

Periodically every company should review its reporting procedure. The lines of reporting should be checked, the individual who does the writing should be evaluated, the honesty and accuracy of the content determined, and the need for the report carefully examined. Unnecessary reports should be quickly eliminated and revisions instituted to secure improvements in other reports.

SUGGESTION SYSTEMS

There are many other possible lines of upward communication. The alert manager utilizes as many of these lines as possible, seizing every opportunity to gain information that will help him make valid and successful decisions.

One of the most popular methods of transmitting information upward is the suggestion box. Since the late 1800's, many firms have encouraged their employees to make suggestions for improving company activities. It was during and after World War II, however, that this method of communicating with management received its greatest impetus. New and faster production methods were constantly sought and the man "on the line" frequently had excellent ideas for improving the efficiency of his own job. His ideas were sought and used, and he was rewarded.

Today, many companies solicit suggestions from all workers, and a monetary reward is usually given when the idea is used. Often the sum offered equals approximately 10 per cent of the first year's savings resulting from the suggestion.

There is value in such systems, for millions of dollars are saved by companies as a result of employee suggestions. And the psychological value an employee receives from his participation in the company's production procedure is immeasurable. However, problems can arise with a suggestion system. Sometimes the suggestion made by a worker makes a supervisor appear inefficient or incompetent because the change was not already instituted by the supervisor. Then there is the delicate task of telling workers that their suggestion has no merit and is not eligible for an award. Still another problem is the amount of money to be awarded.

In some instances the suggestion made might cause the routine of an entire work group to change, or might result in eliminating one member of the group because of a more efficient production procedure. This obviously results in lowered group morale, ill will, and antagonism. The gain made through the suggestion may be lost twice over as a result of worker resentment.

But with all these difficulties, the suggestion system does often lead to improved production and more efficient methods, and it gives management another source of information at the worker level.

PERSONAL CONTACT

Although the impersonal report and the suggestion box are important and useful sources of information for management, executives must keep in mind that they are dealing with people, not with a self-sufficient, emotionless machine. Employees, like executives, appreciate and react favorably to personal interest. If they feel that management is interested in them as people, they will more likely be honest and open and cooperative.

Effective communication depends on dialog; there must be some possibility of response, or feedback. Through face-to-face interaction, management can discover the employee's ideas and goals, the level of rapport which exists, his willingness to share in and work toward the company's objectives, and his feelings about his own place in the corporate scheme.

Face-to-face encounters are as useful for downward communication as for upward, of course. The point is that communication becomes two-way rather than unidirectional.

Interviews

Information is frequently forwarded up to management as a result of interviews held with past, present, and prospective employees. Interviews may be held for placement, to give information, to secure ideas, for orientation of new employees, for evaluation of employees, for a transfer in assignment, for promotion, to discipline employees or hear their complaints, and at the time of an employee's separation from the company. If these discussions are carried through carefully, and the vital information is accurately recorded and used by management, they may be very valuable. Certainly every manager should sit down with each of his subordinates periodically and communicate on a one-to-one basis.[3]

Employee Councils

Employee councils are a valuable means of upward communication. Every department or division in the company elects a representative to serve on the council. All employee representatives meet with management's representatives on a periodic basis—usually once a month. The employee representatives bring the questions and suggestions of their department members to the meeting. Because the employee is not speaking for himself but on behalf of an anonymous member of his work group, he usually will not hesitate to ask questions on the most sensitive issues.

A vital rule of the game requires that management's representatives answer *every* question asked. If an answer is not readily available, then it must be given without fail at the next meeting. Of course, the employee representatives have an equal obligation to answer management's questions if they possibly can. A record of such meetings should be kept by

---

3. An excellent article for reference on the subject is Waldo E. Fisher, "The Interview —A Multi-Purpose Leadership Tool," Part IV.

the council secretary and brief summaries distributed by the representatives to their respective groups.

DOWNWARD COMMUNICATIONS

People work better when they know exactly what their superiors desire of them, what their duties, responsibilities, and privileges are. People need to know what is expected of them—perhaps not in minute detail, but certainly in general terms. For this reason management and supervisors must issue directives and policy and procedural statements to individuals in lower echelons.

How much does an employee "need to know"? The answer rests in the perception of the supervisor and the emotional needs of the employee. Some individuals react strongly and unfavorably when their desires for information go unfulfilled. Others react quite passively.

Then, too, the employee's assignment may result in different levels of "need to know." The punch-press operator who repeats the same operation hour after hour on 12" × 12" squares of copper sheet has a different level of need from the engineer working on long-range corporate planning of computer needs.

One business writer puts it this way:

> Variations in the physical height of people occur within a limited range, and the great majority cluster within certain limits. In the same manner, variations in individual communication needs appear to vary over a certain range, but tend to cluster around a central tendency. Various studies could be brought to bear on this subject, and many more need to be made. If we had all the research information it would be nice to have, I believe we would confirm two tendencies disclosed by presently available research, and abundantly confirmed by observation.
>
> 1) The level of motivation of most people could be greatly increased through knowing more about their jobs, departments, companies, working conditions, and their individual and group relationship to others in their departments, companies, and in other comparable companies.
>
> 2) The average supervisor is far more likely to underestimate, than to overestimate, the extent and depth of employees' interest in the enterprise, and the extent to which additional information, properly used, can motivate a bonus for the enterprise in superior performance. . . .
>
> There is also a close relationship between the amount of

motivational information required, and the overall approach and philosophy of supervision. The company which is satisfied with the over-the-shoulder-watching supervision and places heavy emphasis on the supervisor as an enforcer, requires a different order of communication from the company which expects supervision to emphasize the leader-teacher aspects of the management responsibility.[4]

The announcements, bulletins, and policy statements which tell employees what they need to know must be written clearly and concisely; so clearly, as a matter of fact, that they not only can be understood but cannot possibly be misunderstood.

Employees have a "need to know" in two broad areas. The first is the job itself. Every employee wants to know *what* his task is, *how* it is to be performed, *how* it interrelates with other tasks to achieve the company's goals, *where* and *when* it is to be performed. He wants to know what his duties are and what freedom he has within those limits.

The second area concerns the employee's relationship with his company, his community, and his family. He wants to know *how much* insurance his company carries for him, *why* the company's stock dividends are going down, *what* management thinks about the union's demands, *how* management reacts to equal-employment laws, *where* the new plant will be built, and *what are* the company's goals and objectives.

The first of these two "needs to know" is easily satisfied. Printed job descriptions and on-the-job demonstration and consultation, if done conscientiously, will inform the employee of the nature of his job. In addition, the supervisor should strive to create the kind of atmosphere in which the employees who report to him have no qualms about asking questions or requesting further explanations.

THE LARGER WORLD

Downward communication in the larger area of need to know is not so simple. Perhaps management, when considering issues of basic interest to employees—such as strikes, benefits, lay-offs—have the philosophy that "if we ignore it, maybe it'll go away." But it will not go away. If rumors are flying, the company will suffer. Rumor leads to uncertainty, and uncertainty to fear, and fear to inability to function. For a company to continue to function successfully, there must be mutual trust, loyalty, and interest between management and employees.

4. A. S. Hatch, "Improving Boss-Man and Man-Boss Communication," *The Journal of Business Communication,* October 1966, p. 27.

Virgil B. Day, Vice-President for Management Development of General Electric, had this to say to the annual conference of the International Council of Industrial Editors:

> We have found that informed employees—who know, not only *what* happened, but *why* it happened, and *what it means to them*—can solve problems better and faster.
>
> I am sure that many of you recognize that the goals I have mentioned cannot be sought just at times of crisis . . . during a union negotiation, a poor business year, following a lost order, or when costs threaten a business. You know full well that achieving understanding on basic business goals and problems is not possible with a crash campaign at some crisis period.
>
> In General Electric we decided long ago that we must have *year-around, weekly* and *daily*—even *hourly*—two-way communication with company men and women in order to achieve a mutual understanding of the problems of our business. Our 100 *weekly* and *daily* employee publications continually carry up-to-date news and interpretation on such subjects as these:
>
> ——reports on the sales, profits, employee pay and benefits, and taxes of the previous business period
>
> ——news on orders—*won* and *lost*—and what this means to employment
>
> ——news on financial standing of our insurance program and pension plan, as well as how these benefit plans help employees
>
> ——information on the profit dollars being reinvested in equipment to help make jobs more secure
>
> ——reports on movement of General Electric stock, since half our employees are share owners
>
> ——reports on any disagreements between unions and management—including reports on what is taking place in company-union negotiations, whenever these occur
>
> ——features on what our competition is doing and what this means to employment
>
> ——interviews with typical employees to let them express their views on issues affecting their jobs. . . .
>
> We learned, long ago, that a company and its employees have one major interest in common. This interest is the business and its progress. . . . The Opinion Research Corporation found that "there is a lively worker demand to hear the company's point of view."
>
> In one of our own plants a survey asked: "Do you believe

that management should try to keep you informed of how it feels about union relations matters?"

To this query more than 90% of the union-represented employees answering said "Yes."

A typical comment in these surveys was "Both the company and the union should let people know what's going on."[5]

An examination of General Electric's publications indicates that the policy announced at the executive level is carried through in practice. When I asked about GE's communications to employees, I was told:

> In a few words: General Electric managers communicate extensively on controversial subjects to all levels of employees. Many of the more than 100 unions with which we deal also communicate extensively, so we believe our employees have little difficulty in learning all shades of opinion on such matters as strikes, arbitration, negotiations, automation, profits, goals, expansion, mergers, and legal actions in which the company is involved.[6]

Other major corporations indicated a similar philosophy in letters to me. On the other hand, an executive of a major corporation wrote:

> No matters relating to labor disruption, friction or misunderstandings as strikes, slow-downs, arbitration of grievances, etc. should appear in a house organ. The written word is with us forever. While the situation of today could well change drastically by tomorrow, whatever we write remains for all to see.[7]

This seems to me to be very short-sighted. If we write the truth, there should never be any fear in having it read—whether it is read today or tomorrow. And surely a corporation should not be afraid to express its opinions and policies to its employees—or to its stockholders or its customers or its colleagues.

In contrast to the above opinion is American Airlines' Employee Communication Policy, which states:

5. Virgil B. Day, Vice-President, General Electric Company. An address titled "Communications—A Neglected Key to Competitive Progress" to the Annual Conference of the International Council of Industrial Editors, June 18, 1963.

6. Letter to the author from E. J. Kneeland, Manager, Employee Communication Operation, General Electric Company, December 14, 1966.

7. Letter to the author dated December 8, 1966.

The success of American Airlines, and in turn the success of its employees, is greatly dependent upon the teamwork of personnel at all levels—between staff and line, and between all functions. This teamwork will be in direct ratio to the quality of our communications.

It is therefore the policy of the company that communications will be imaginative, timely, appropriate, and free flowing —that there will be communication downward, upward, and laterally throughout the company.[8]

This policy is then spelled out at management and employee levels. Broadly speaking, the policy is to communicate with *all* employees about *all* company activities, present and projected.

One of the outstanding employee communications programs in the nation is Chrysler's. It is directed by one man, with communications coordinators in the various installations. Chrysler's director of publications works carefully with the coordinators. A recent article describing the Chrysler program said:

[The director of publications] and his assistants also prepare a background information package for the plant communication coordinators. In it are a number of items that will assist each local coordinator . . . and provide him material on which he can build. . . .

Of what does the content in these publications consist? It runs the gamut. It has one thing in common: It is serious-minded, perhaps even occasionally heavy, always substantive stuff—discussions of racial issues, conflicts of interest, competition, patents, union negotiations, absenteeism, local political matters.

Yet not all of it is informational. Features are designed to be interesting in themselves, although the format seldom if ever strays from presenting the "view" within the feature. Features in recent issues have discussed what happens to cars that are scrapped, interviews with wives of employees, stories of second and third shift operations, and so on.[9]

This program thus finds it possible to present and cover topics with strong human interest value and those which are often controversial and sensitive.

8. Quoted by G. Seybold, *Employee Communication: Policy and Tools* (National Industrial Conference Board, 1966), pp. 33-34.

9. "A Report on the Chrysler Program," *Reporting,* July 1965, p. 12.

Areas for Discussion

There seems to be a misunderstanding among some managers about employees' reactions to controversial issues. Some executives mistakenly believe that discussions about profits, union-management controversies, taxes, etc. have no place in company publications; that employees would resent management's treatment of such topics; that employees are not interested in the subjects or in management's point of view. Nonsense!

Every intelligent employee wants to hear both sides. He may actually resent being exposed only to the union viewpoint; he may feel that management is avoiding its responsibilities. Thus management must add to the "Betty is holding hands with N. R. T. from Dept. 21 and wedding bells . . ." type of chitchat, which fills so many pages in today's company publications.

From time to time, management should provide information and opinion on the following topics:

Wage and salary structures: how they are established and revised; how they compare with salary levels in the industry generally.

Benefit programs for employees: the benefits received and the important percentage they add to base pay.

Company products and how they are used by consumers and/or wholesalers; the role of such products in defense efforts, consumer use, or other activities.

Company profits, not as a flat dollar amount, but in relation to sales and job security; profits in terms of investment, replacement of equipment, and company expansion and growth; profits in terms of their value to the community, employees, and others.

Employee-management relationships: Union requests and management's viewpoint should be presented with a careful discussion of each point. Articles covering specific points of controversy and written by labor and management representatives might well appear side by side.

Analysis of strikes or work stops. Discussion of union-management negotiations, arbitration, and rulings.

Whenever possible, representatives of labor should be permitted to present their point of view or rebuttal next to management's in an employee publication.

The company's dependence on customers, dealers, stockholders, suppliers, government agencies, community members, distributors, the general public, and the employees themselves.

The organization of the company, the various products or services it provides, the location of plants, and the number and classification of employees.

The company's short- and long-term goals.

Automation and how it will affect production and personnel.

Reductions in the work force—why they occurred and what the future holds.

Contemplated changes in products, personnel, manufacturing process, etc.

Existing rumors; the basis of the rumor should be explained and the truth told.

Taxes paid by the company and how they contribute to local, state, and federal activities.

Economic trends (inflation, lending, interest rates) and how they affect every wage earner.

Company viewpoints on controversial local and federal issues. Employees should be told frequently how important their views are; they should be encouraged to make those views known to their elected representatives.

The free enterprise system, how it works, and what it does for every citizen.

The role of organized labor and its contribution, under responsible leadership, to national growth and progress.

The opinions and activity of the company in social and cultural areas such as education, civil rights, and social welfare.

The above topics may be classified as sensitive and controversial. That is no reason, however, for their not being discussed fairly, candidly, and honestly in company publications. There are many other subjects, non-controversial but important, that should be given attention. These include:

Employee morale
Attitudes toward jobs
The industry of which the
    company is a part
Promotion policies
Company and employee
    contributions to charity
Company competition
New company products
Company activities in research
    and development
Company's sources of materials
    and its markets

Company quality levels
Company cost reduction programs
The employee's role as a salesman
    for the firm's products,
    services, or image
Absenteeism
Safety programs
Employee's role as a recruiter
Litigation in which the company
    is involved
Possible mergers, sales, or
    diversification

In addition to the two large groups above, the following topics may be treated to the extent consistent with the employee communication policy:

Social news regarding births, marriages, anniversaries, etc.
Recognition of long-service employees and retirees
Awards received by employees and their spouses and children
News of retired employees
Employee classified ad section
Employees and their children in the service
Company celebrations, meetings, and recreation programs
Human interest accounts concerning employees

Union Relations

You can be very sure that the unions represented in your company will recognize the interests of their members. They will discuss in detail the "controversial" subjects listed above; and they will, naturally, discuss them from their own point of view. Management, in fairness to itself and to its employees, should also present its point of view.

Fred Foy and Robert Harper, in an article in *The Harvard Business Review*, said:

> Both sides [management and unions] assemble their arguments. Both sides have their economists and technicians preparing the evidence. Both sides are trying to get their views before key people. But here is the reason that in the important battle for the minds of men, management so far has elected to fight with one arm tied behind it:
>
> 1) Only the unions are vigorously and effectively driving home to their members their arguments and their point of view. Week after week they pour out a flood of carefully planned and well-written articles which—irrespective of geographic area or union identity—advocate more government participation in the economy and reflect a solid front on almost every major policy question. This conclusion is based on a careful study of such union publications as *The CIO News*, *AFL Reporter*, *The American Federationist*, *The Machinist*, *United Rubber Worker*, and *District Fifty News*, circulated to millions of union members.
>
> 2) In contrast, the management publications regularly reaching the same union members fail—with only a few exceptions—to present any point of view about what management feels is good for America. Usually well-written and often beautifully printed, they cover mainly employee social news, company sport activities, and brief news reports about the company. For the most part they are conspicuously silent on such basic subjects as the profit system or on key current issues

before the legislatures. This conclusion is based on an intensive study of some 700 company magazines published for employee consumption.[10]

A Cornell University study cited by Dover found that specific terms and words relating to management-labor activities were used much more frequently in union than in company communications. A sample of publications was carefully selected and studied as to economic content and terms.[11]

Word	NUMBER OF TIMES USED	
	In Union Publications	In Company Publications
arbitration	544	0
negotiation	1297	50
collective bargaining	906	2
strike	1364	0
wage increase	775	18
standard of living	701	38
contract	1359	101
organized labor	679	0

These figures are startling. One can only assume that these so-called sensitive areas are avoided to the same extent in face-to-face discussions.

The Cornell study concluded:

1) Economic concepts in all categories appear much more frequently in union publications than they do in company publications.

2) Union papers deal with very concrete and specific issues, while company papers are more prone to talk in economic generalities. Among the very few terms used more in company papers than in union papers were "production" (371-48); "market" (206-162); "promotion" (68-44); and "free enterprise" (25-0).

3) Union-management relationships are not so frequently treated in company papers as in union publications.[12]

There can be no doubt that management, in too many instances, has concerned itself with the prosaic, the noncontroversial, and the "safe" topics for discussion in company publications.

10. Fred C. Foy and Robert Harper, "Round One: Union vs. Company Publications," *Harvard Business Review,* May-June 1955.

11. C. J. Dover, *Management Communication on Controversial Issues* (Washington, D.C.: Bureau of National Affairs, Inc., 1965), p. 11.

12. Dover, p. 13.

Foy and Harper, in their examination of union publications, found that

—the union leaders' program is carefully planned and consistent. It deals almost exclusively with "breadbasket subjects"; union leaders do not talk in economic abstractions.

—communication with rank-and-file members is aided by excellent publications, which are used to promote social goals. From 45 per cent to 65 per cent of the space in some of these publications is allotted for this type of material.

—repetitious handling of the same subjects is extremely well done and indicates that editors and staff assistants are top-quality journalists.

—many of the union publications follow the same pattern of presentation with little or no deviation in the type of material.

In reviewing company publications, however, they determined that

—management did not counteract union activity on realistic "breadbasket" subjects such as union leaders use as levers to promote national social legislation.

—employee publications frequently take a negative approach to challenging problems—more often resorting to "sniper tactics" against the opponent's case. Management often seemed to be "maintaining its dignity" when the audience it wished to reach understood "toe-to-toe" slugging better.

—controversial subjects were avoided, but at the same time attempts were consistently made to stimulate pride in the virtues of the "American way of life." A steady reading diet of such "flag-waving" stories may prove an insult to the average worker's intelligence, for he too believes in the American way of life. The futility of communicating in this manner has been noted several times in leading business publications.

—management has the same kind of self-interest that union leaders have, but when it has used its private communications media in an attempt to influence national, state, and local domestic legislation, it has done the job so awkwardly that its employees have often been left asking "why" to a lot of questions which should have been squarely faced in public statements.

PRESENTATION

Effective communication must be planned. This is particularly true for the kind of downward communication we are discussing. Inserting an occasional story on stock dividends into the company magazine is essentially useless. Management must present its viewpoints consistently, clearly, honestly, and courteously; and such presentation must be founded on a concrete philosophy of communication, based on the nature and goals of the company.

The Personalized Message

Discussions of various concepts or theories usually become more meaningful when the communicator involves his audience or himself in a situation cited as an example. Figures, percentages, or facts usually stand in isolation until they are related, in some personal way, to us. Although we may not be impressed or shocked by "Twenty-one billion dollars were collected in taxes last year," we certainly pay attention when we read, "Each of you taxpayers contributed a sum in income taxes equal to five times what your father paid in 1937, or enough to buy a brand-new, air-conditioned Pontiac."

The same concept of personalizing communication holds true in communicating with employees in such areas as benefits, safety, loyalty, long-range goals, etc. Compare the following few examples and note how the one that is personalized is more meaningful.

Original: The dollar value in benefits which our employees received last year amounted to the significant sum of $9,500,000.

Revised: Last year each of our employees received in benefits a sum equal to almost two full months of additional salary. This money was used to purchase, at no cost to you, stock in the company, life and health insurance protection for you and your family, enjoyable vacation periods, free university educational benefits, sick leaves, funds for your retirement, and work payment for major holidays.

Original: Corporate sales rose 12 per cent last year, which was the largest increase in any firm in the field of women's apparel. We have reason to be proud of this achievement.

Revised: Our sales increased 12 per cent last year, largely because of the loyalty, hard work, and dedication of our employees. This increase in sales permitted overtime work at premium pay for many of you and an overall average increase in income for each employee of almost $500 last year.

Original: Accidents in our plant last month, directly attributable to negligence and careless handling of equipment, resulted in a total loss of 240 work days. Let's obey *all* safety rules in March.

Revised: We had 32 accidents in our plant last month. These were charged directly to negligence and careless handling of equipment.

Unfortunately three of our fellow workers each lost one or more fingers, one man will be confined to a wheel chair for about three months, and another will be able to see his children through only one eye.

The time and effort we save when we take chances are never worth the price we may pay. Let's make March 100 per cent safe for *every* Allied employee.

In the last example above, a negative situation was personalized. The shock value of this may well serve its purpose, even by offending or upsetting the reader. As for the positive cases (benefits, salaries, profits, new equipment and plant), involving the reader is much more meaningful to him than presenting cold, distant statistics.

A Consistent Policy

If a sensitive situation exists in a company, communication will take place. If the facts are given to the employees, they will discuss those facts; if nothing is said by management, the employees will supply their own "facts." If we accept this axiom—if something exists (or is thought to exist), it will be discussed—then it is in everybody's best interest that the company examine the situation with the employees.

Management must be truthful with the employees. If a topic cannot be openly discussed—because of ongoing negotiations, government request, inadequate data on hand, or any other reason—employees should be so informed. Everyone is much more likely to accept a true statement of that type than some obvious hokum that insults one's intelligence. And nothing will lose employee loyalty and diligence faster than dishonesty or manipulation of information.

It is important that management establish a philosophy of communication, to which it adheres as strictly as possible. A typical corporate statement of communication policy might be:

1) To inform employees of ongoing activities and problems of the company.
2) To tell employees about future company plans, directions, and goals.
3) To explain negative, sensitive, and controversial situations.
4) To communicate to employees as quickly as possible information about important events and situations.
5) To encourage, foster, and build a steady flow of two-way communication.
6) To allocate sufficient funds and company time to implement this philosophy of communication.

DOWNWARD COMMUNICATION MEDIA

Effective, useful, and worthwhile communication may be achieved through several media: magazines, orientation manuals, employee handbooks, annual reports, letters, bulletin boards. If they are produced by habit, these will be just so many bits of paper. If they are used imaginatively and creatively, they can produce results far greater than the time and materials expended on them.

By such creative use of the available media, management will be able:

To inform the employee about company problems, markets, expansion, mergers, personnel, labor relations, sales, profits, new products, diversification plans, finance, etc.

To emphasize the firm's dependence on the efforts, creativity, and loyalty of the employees.

To discuss the employees' responsibilities and status in the firm.

To examine the various benefits which the employees receive and to recognize the dollar value of such benefits as a measure of the firm's interest in the welfare of the employee.

To encourage employees to use company publications as a forum for the expression of ideas.

To examine social issues, government activities, and political affairs.

To present examples of company activities in areas of social welfare, cultural improvement, and educational advancement.

To develop attitudes of loyalty for and interest in company affairs on the part of the employees' families.

To examine in detail, from time to time, specific areas of company activities in an effort to educate in depth each employee about a vital phase of the firm's operations.

Quite obviously, the firm which distributes a weekly newspaper, a sixty-four-page monthly magazine, and periodic bulletins will be able to achieve these objectives more easily than the company that can only afford a thirty-two-page magazine quarterly. However, if the firm is sincere and recognizes the employees' need to know, the integrity of its philosophy of communications will be apparent.

Company Magazines

Because the number of company magazines has grown so dramatically in recent years, it is hazardous even to guess how many are published and distributed today. However, it is safe to assume that almost every firm with more than a few hundred employees issues one periodically. (See Scholz, "How to Make Employee Publications Pay Off," Part IV.) They range all the way from slick, sophisticated magazines printed on first-grade paper stock to eight-page mimeographed affairs hastily stapled together. Most of them are published under the guidance of a company editor whose primary responsibility is the magazine. Many companies use agencies which may be part of an advertising firm, or organizations which specialize in handling company magazines. Companies of this type may be responsible for turning out a number of magazines, each for a different firm.

The house magazine of today seems to fall into one of three types:

1) The most popular is the magazine that runs several feature articles on the industry of which the company is a part, the latest speech of the company president, a story on government affairs; and a fair percentage of the issue is devoted to employee activities, including weddings, retirements, vacations, sports, deaths, awards, educational activities, births, etc.

2) A second type is the "tabloid," which may concentrate on company news, is written in a rather breezy style, and may very well have an employees' classified ad section offering cars, furniture, tools, and miscellaneous for sale.

3) The journal type of company magazine usually carries in each issue several articles of a broad, general nature. There is no news of employees or discussion of the day-to-day activities of the company. An attempt is made to publish only material of a fairly high level. Examples of this type are *The Western Electric Engineer*, Lockheed's *Horizons*, Standard Oil's *The Lamp*, and IBM's *Think*. One issue of the last named, for example, carried articles like "Uncertain Road to the Twenty-first Century" by economist Herman Kahn; "English Spoken: Here, There, and Everywhere" by diplomat William Benton; "How the Body Fights Invaders" by scientist George A. W. Boehm; and "The View from Howrah Bridge" by author James Morris.

As indicated earlier, there is a definite trend in company magazines to come to grips with topics a good deal more substantial than was the case ten years ago. Labor problems, government spending, politics, cost of living, civil rights, and many other areas of common interest are being treated in many publications. It is true that the treatment is cautious, but at least these topics are being discussed.

There is probably no medium that can better carry company information than the thousands of company magazines published today in the United States. They can and should be used for informing employees in important areas and improving good will and understanding between employer and employee.[13]

---

13. For readers interested in this vital area of corporate communications, more information may be secured from The International Council of Industrial Editors. This organization publishes its own magazine *(Reporting)* and holds regional and national meetings.

Company Orientation Manuals

The policies of most companies today are so complex, their fringe benefit programs so detailed, and their rules and regulations so varied that a printed guide is necessary. It is virtually impossible for a new employee to learn all he needs to know about a company in a half-hour discussion with his supervisor.

It is important for both the employer and the employees to have the details available for easy and ready reference. A small company orientation manual, carefully organized and clearly written, should contain the answers to most of the questions every employee has from time to time: What about major medical benefits? And how much does the hospitalization policy cover? How about retirement at 60? or 65? Am I entitled to free safety glasses? How about time off to vote? What about profit sharing? When do I become eligible for four weeks' vacation with pay? Does the company have a stock buying program? How about tuition refunds? What do I do about a grievance? Can I use the credit union?

This is not a booklet of company rules and regulations; it is a clear presentation of corporate policies and employee rights and privileges.

The value of such a manual is obvious. In the first place, it is a time saver for the employee. He doesn't have to check with his supervisor or the personnel department for an answer. He can find it easily for himself and it is stated officially in black and white. Second, everyone receives the same answer to the question. The answer to the inquiry isn't different when it is explained to different employees by different supervisors. Third, and perhaps most important, the employee manual eliminates incorrect answers. Too often a worker checks with other employees or immediate supervisors. If the question is difficult and the people who answer are depending on their memories and twenty-five years' experience with the firm, the information given may well be inaccurate.

A typical organization plan for an orientation manual might include company history and goals, a detailed section on employee benefits, and a careful discussion of corporate policies and practices.

It is a good idea to use a spiral binder or a loose-leaf notebook for the employee manual. Thus, whenever a change takes place in vacation regulations, overtime compensation, cost-of-living adjustment, profit-sharing percentages, etc., it is not necessary to destroy all copies already printed. It is a simple task to reprint the page concerned with new information and substitute it for the outdated page.

The writing level and layout of the orientation manual should be checked very carefully. If a large segment of the work force has a relatively low education level, the writing style should be concise and easy to understand. Sentences should be short and words carefully chosen.

Section dividers and topic headings should be generously used. Pictures, sketches, and completed sample forms should be added where they will do the most good. If Mrs. Groweller, who works on Machine 21, wants to find out about maternity leave, she should be able to find the appropriate paragraph in a few seconds. She should not be forced to struggle through thirty pages on employee benefits before finding it. Topic headings and a good table of contents will help her find the section, and clear, concise writing will help her understand it.

Annual Reports to Employees

Several years ago quite a few of the larger corporations issued annual reports specifically for employees. In most instances they were the same (or nearly the same) as the corporate report to stockholders. To save money, the employee report was often printed in black and white only, on inexpensive paper.

However, problems sometimes arose. Employees wanted to know why their report was different from that of the stockholders, and what was being said to the stockholders that wasn't being said to the employees. In some firms, the annual report to employees was very short and was written and illustrated at an elementary level. This, too, was resented by employees. As a result, few companies today issue a separate report for employees. It is really no more costly to give each employee a copy of the regular corporate report.

In those companies that do not have annual stockholders' reports, the printed annual report to employees certainly serves a useful purpose. It gives the worker an overall view of his company's activities in the preceding year, a listing of corporate goals and objectives, some mention of new processes and developments, listings of income and expenditures, and changes in personnel.

One firm that employs large numbers of recent immigrants with a Latin background has had some success with making its annual report for employees available in either English or Spanish.

Letters to Employees

Management has used letters for years in communicating orders, claims, adjustments, etc. to dealers, customers, and clients. It has used thousands in direct mail sales appeals, and dozens of different form letters to a wide variety of recipients. But it is only recently that business has learned the tremendous value of well-written letters sent to employees.

Perhaps the primary value of the letter is the personal touch it conveys. It is addressed to the employee, delivered to his home, and probably read carefully in an atmosphere that is less hurried and noisy than the shop or office. The content of the letter may well be discussed at the supper table, and thus the family is drawn into company activities and interests. What better way to build company loyalty than to involve the employee's family?

Letters have other advantages as well, not the least of which are their low cost and the speed with which they can be written, reproduced, and mailed.

Topics for Letters. Letters can cover a wide variety of topics very effectively. They can be used to welcome new employees; discuss a safety program; explain new products; announce mergers, expansions, or acquisitions; examine labor problems; discuss company profits; or simply build good will through a sincere expression of appreciation for a job well done.

North American Aviation, Inc., has used letters

> . . . not only to keep employees informed as to a specific labor situation, but also to advise them of other developments within the company. While the weekly publication, *Skywriter,* is designed to carry out this function, it is often desirable to reach employees between publication dates, and letters are then used. Additionally, we have found that letters are desirable when the subject requires lengthy explanation.[14]

Tone. Perhaps there is no aspect of a letter to an employee that contributes more to its acceptance or rejection than its tone. The letter that sounds insincere or ingratiating or pompous or dictatorial is surely doomed to failure. Because letters usually come from the top administrative officers, they are likely to be received by the employee with some skepticism in any case. If they then live up to his somewhat cynical expectations, management would have been better off never to have sent those letters at all.

Here are a couple of letters that seem to do an excellent job in tone, tact, and content:

Dear Mr. Kelly:

Welcome to the Allied Manufacturing Company. We are sincerely happy to have you become a member of the Allied

14. Letter dated December 8, 1966, to the author from Robert H. Scholl, Director, News Bureau, North American Aviation, Inc.

family. You may be sure that each of us will do everything possible to make your stay with us pleasant and enjoyable for many, many years to come.

Since 1949 we have been growing steadily and now have almost 8000 employees working in three different plants in the greater Los Angeles area.

Each of these people contributes a great deal to Allied and we know that you will also. All of us who work for the company recognize that as the company advances, so do we. For this reason we work as a team and try to fill the needs of our customers and take care of ourselves.

Right now we are almost at the "top of the heap" in wage rates in the food processing industry. You and our other employees also participate, without charge to you, in a hospitalization program, major medical coverage, stock option plan, profit-sharing program, and paid vacations. These are only some of the items received on the job; there are others which you will learn about from your supervisor and find discussed in your Allied Information Manual.

But these are only a few of the benefits you will receive as an employee of Allied. There are paid holidays, time off for personal affairs, an excellent company medical system, fine recreation program, and wonderful people to work with. I hope you won't ever hesitate to give the company the benefit of your suggestions. We need your help and advice. Just walk in and talk to your supervisor or to me.

Within the next two weeks, you'll be spending a half day with a Personnel Department representative who will help orient you to all Allied activities. Begin now to think of questions to ask him. And those you have left over, bring to me.

I wish you all good fortune at Allied and I know all your fellow employees join me in saying, "Welcome Aboard!"

Cordially yours,

Frank T. Bailey
President

It is important that the above kind of letter be individually typed and signed. A letter so personal in tone loses its value if it is obviously mimeographed and signed by a secretary or with a rubber stamp. The following letter may, however, be mechanically reproduced, for it is obviously being sent to a large number of people.

Dear

    Just a few hours ago the Board of Directors of your company voted to accept a new program: The Allied Employee Profit-Sharing Plan. I wanted you and your family to know about it just as soon as possible. A letter seemed to be the best way to tell you, and so I'm dashing this off. I'm genuinely excited about this; I hope you will be also.

    What this program means is simply this: Beginning August 1, a specific percentage of the profits of the company go to the employees. As our firm grows, expands, and improves its position, we all benefit. Every single employee now has a real stake in the firm.

    It is entirely possible that an employee will be able to retire from the company ten, fifteen, or twenty years from now and find that he has accumulated a very sizable sum in his Profit-Sharing Account. Such funds will make retirement all the more enjoyable.

    Contributions to your fund come only from company profits; no contribution from you is required. Thus the better job we all do and the higher our profits, the faster our Fund grows.

    You'll be getting a booklet very shortly which explains all the details, and we'll also have some group meetings for discussion.

    I just wanted to bring this marvelous news to you today; I feel, and I'm sure you'll agree, that it is events like this that make Allied a great place to work.

                                   Cordially yours,

                                   Bernard Robinson
                                   President

Pay Envelope Inserts

The message printed on a small card or slip of paper and attached to the employee's pay check is sure to receive attention. A brief announcement, a news bulletin, or a vital piece of company information can be effectively transmitted in this way. There are, however, a few basic rules to keep in mind in order to achieve successful pay envelope inserts.

    The message should be brief and its subject matter of importance. The pay envelope insert should be used only occasionally. If every pay check is accompanied by an insert, and the topics covered are routine, the value of this special little message is soon lost.

Company Bulletin Board

In most companies, bulletin boards are used for motivational announcements (safety, zero defects program, bond drives, etc.) and for announcements of broad general interest such as approaching holidays, scheduled meetings, shift changes, and recognition of outstanding employees. If bulletin boards are strategically located and carefully handled, they can be an extremely valuable device for employee communication.

First of all, they must be well lighted and carefully placed throughout the plant. Effective positions can be found in company cafeterias (within easy reading distance of the waiting line), in locker rooms and employee wash-up areas, next to elevators, in employee lounges, near the time clocks, and next to the vending machines.

The boards must be kept up to date. There is nothing more irritating than reading the same announcement every day for months. Every message should be clean, current, and attractively mounted. Sometimes colored paper can be used as a frame or as background for an important announcement.

Some large firms use two types of bulletin boards. One of these is for the display of routine company information and employee announcements such as meetings of the stamp club, the bowling league tournament, and the retirement party. At times a section is also made available for a "classified" section listing personal items for sale or being sought. The other set of bulletin boards may have glass doors with or without a lock. On this board are displayed official company announcements. This may involve listing new corporate policies, practices, or regulations, as well as official recognition or commendation of outstanding employees.

Another way to handle this is to use one set of boards informally divided with clearly lettered headings: "News and Views" and "Official Company Announcements."

All bulletin boards should be the responsibility of one person who is required to approve the placement of every notice. He should:

1) Place a small printed announcement on all boards that says something like "Notices and announcements may receive a stamped approval for placement from Jack Smith, Dept. 32, Industrial Relations Dept." Every item on the bulletin board thus carries the stamped "Approved for bulletin board display until April 28, 19--."

2) Clear all outdated items from the boards every Monday morning, or at some other logical time.

3) Keep all boards clean, well lighted, uncluttered, and attractive.

Bulletin boards are among the least expensive of all company communication devices and, if properly handled, one of the most effective.

Management and Supervisory Bulletins

Many firms issue a variety of bulletins to their different management and supervisory personnel. In some companies a system has been devised of using different colors of paper for different levels and even different divisions. It is easy to see that this whole system can easily get out of hand. Some employees' jobs require that they see bulletins from several different departments and perhaps from more than one level. The result is that so many announcements cross their desks that soon they read none.

However, these are extreme situations which do not occur too frequently. A carefully controlled system of bulletins can prove to be an excellent way of announcing changes in policy, revisions of procedures, or information that is somewhat confidential.

Many firms feel that policies and procedures should always be communicated to employees by their immediate supervisors rather than through any company-wide announcement. In such cases, bulletins can be very effective in transmitting exactly the same information to all managers and supervisors. It is then their responsibility to communicate such information down. This obviously builds a closer relationship between supervisor and subordinate. It also strengthens the supervisor's authority, as it emphasizes his position as a source of official information.

Here, as in the case of bulletin boards, control is important. Bulletins or management letters should originate only with certain persons who occupy specific positions. They should be written carefully and edited thoroughly. Because they often change or amend company policy, they should be numbered and punched so that a file of them can easily be retained by the originator and the receiver.

It is also a good idea to use a distinctive format with perhaps a colored stripe or headline which seems to say clearly, "Here's some special news; give it your complete attention."

Rack Services

Many firms distribute to employees pamphlets covering a wide variety of topics. These are often stacked in wire racks near employee check-out points or in the company cafeteria. The booklets are free, usually pocket size (about 5" x 7"), and 8 to 12 pages long. The topics are broad and are designed to be of interest to the employee's family as well as himself. Some of the areas covered might be safe driving, voting procedures, the future of air travel, American foreign policy, the work of the United Nations, an explanation of the operations of the stock market, preparing a balanced diet, and other areas of a general nature.

Although some firms write, design, and produce their own pamphlets, most companies purchase theirs from organizations specializing in production of such bulletins. These are well written, cleverly illustrated, and relatively inexpensive. The purchasing company may have its name and insignia printed on the back or front if it wishes, thus adding a little personal touch to the booklet.

Perhaps the factor making this program most attractive to employees is that it is voluntary. If an employee wishes to pick up a booklet or two, they are there; if he prefers not to, he simply doesn't bother. Then, too, there is never any obvious "company sell" in the booklet to arouse his feelings positively or negatively. The booklets are there for his information and reading pleasure if he wants to take them.

Companies that use rack services have found the expenditure worthwhile, for it helps keep employees informed in economic, political, health, cultural, social, and recreational areas while building good will.

EFFECTIVE DOWNWARD COMMUNICATION

Each of the above media can be used successfully in a company of almost any size. Downward communication is vitally important; management must use the media creatively and wisely.

Many employees, especially at the supervisory level, receive so many communications that they ignore some of them. If the communications are read, their contents are often not assimilated. For these reasons, the most effective method must be chosen to make the greatest possible impact on the reader. Before selecting the type of communication desired, management must carefully evaluate the content of the message as well as the intellectual level and specific needs of the person or group to whom it is directed.

LATERAL COMMUNICATIONS

"If someone had just bothered to tell us what was going on, we would have saved two weeks' time."

This comment, or variations of it, is not unusual in industry today. And as organizations grow bigger and more complex, it becomes more than ever necessary for management to maintain control and have knowledge of what is taking place in various divisions, sections, and departments. As individuals become increasingly specialized, they have difficulty communicating with and understanding the ideas of other specialists.

Sometimes we think, in a rather superior way, that there is duplication of work and wasted effort only in the vast government complex. However, in recent years many companies have found that they too are guilty of duplication, redundancy, and inefficiency.

Keeping individuals and departments on the same level of activity informed is primarily the responsibility of management. It is vital that Department A know what projects the related Department B is engaged in, and vice versa. However, it is a waste of time to have *all* departments in the organization apprised of A's activities.

When individuals are not aware of what is taking place in a related department, unnecessary duplication of activity may result in needless expenditure of money; but money is also wasted when reports of activities are circulated to persons not concerned with the projects in question.

Here, then, strict control must be exercised. Management must decide:

1) Who is to be informed of which department's activities;
2) the amount of detail to be contained in such reporting;
3) the medium to be used for such communication.

Management must also understand why department heads are often reluctant to communicate their activities to other department heads. Usually it is not required that the sales department know what is taking place in personnel. At times a myopic department manager may feel, "If no one quite knows all I do and how I do it, I become indispensable." And some are busy empire-building to satisfy their own ego needs. But here again, the successful manager *proves* to all department heads how each benefits from good intracompany communications and thus motivates them to carry the activity through. He can do this by calling his supervisors together periodically and building a climate of total participation and cooperation to achieve the goals that the entire group has selected. Intelligent men appreciate knowing what is being achieved in related departments. And this knowledge can often result in suggestions which lead to more efficient production, greater economies, and better use of manpower.

Communication of information from one department to another can be accomplished by written reports, summaries, digests, or abstracts. Even more can be accomplished by a weekly or biweekly meeting of supervisors who summarize their departments' activities in brief oral presentations. Such meetings should be followed up with short mimeographed or printed minutes of the proceedings circulated to interested personnel.

DEPARTMENT MEETINGS

Meetings of all employees in a unit should be held periodically. This should be a sharing situation, where employees are informed of the unit's goals and objectives and individual or group responsibilities are discussed. Meetings are also valuable for solving problems. The confident and competent manager quickly learns that one of the best ways in which he may untangle a knotty situation is to call his men together and ask them for their advice. Their suggestions are usually sound and practical. And the greatest advantage of getting their suggestions is that they are *theirs*. Thus when the men put their ideas into operation, they have participated in management decision making. Because of this, their acceptance and implementation of the procedure is usually whole-hearted.

In all group meetings the climate is vital. Simply to direct that "each department shall, beginning July 1, hold a weekly meeting of all personnel" will not accomplish our goals. The department head must want to meet with his men; he must want to encourage the expression of ideas; he must want to share his knowledge with them. Simply holding a meeting each Tuesday afternoon, because it is required, soon breeds boredom and antagonism.

Perhaps the best way to convince a department head that he will gain from periodic get-togethers with his subordinates is to show him how well the system works when he and other department heads meet with their superior, and to explain to him the value to *him* of exchanging thoughts, listening sensitively, and discussing ideas with others. He should also be shown how much more effectively his department will work if the employees know what is going on in other departments and how their work adds to the product or service of the company.

Although these meetings should be held periodically, they should not be required. If there is nothing to discuss, no meeting should be held. But a get-together on company time is valuable and should be held monthly, at a minimum, and probably every two weeks at a maximum.

CONFERENCES

One of the most effective methods of exchanging ideas, explaining concepts, and introducing new trends is the well-run conference or meeting. Specialist can talk to specialist, questions regarding terminology can be asked and answered, persons on various management levels can be kept informed, and decision making can take place in a democratic forum. (See Bales, "In Conference," Part IV.)

However, a successful conference is not easy to achieve. Many firms are under the mistaken impression that all that is necessary is to assign fourteen men to the meeting room every Tuesday at 2:00 P.M. and dismiss them at 4:00, and a conference has been held. This is not true. More often than not, what results from such a meeting is confusion, antagonism, and wasted time. The expense involved is also not inconsiderable. Men who attend such meetings usually have high salaries. If fifteen are present in the conference room and each man's "loaded" rate (includes rental, taxes, supporting personnel, etc.) is $10 to $20 per hour, an average conference can cost the firm $200 to $300. This is to say nothing of the cost incurred during the manager's two-hour absence from his desk.

But a conference that is well planned, competently led, and in which those concerned with the problem under consideration participate co-operatively, can prove to be a most effective tool for lateral communication.

According to the American Management Association, a conference is a pooling of ideas and experiences to solve common and individual problems.[15] To be successful, a conference must include at least five factors:

1) There must be a need for the meeting.
2) The "climate" of the conference must be friendly and cooperative.
3) The objectives and plan for the meeting must be clearly established.
4) The participants must be prepared and cooperative.
5) The conference leader must be competent.

Need

Because management personnel are usually busy, it is imperative that there be a need for the conference and definite goals established for the meeting. Nothing is more frustrating for the busy executive than to sit for two hours in a meeting that he feels was unnecessarily called and where nothing is accomplished.

All management personnel should submit topics they would like discussed at a conference. When there is something urgent, or when there are enough topics to make it worthwhile, then a conference can be called.

Climate

Hard feelings, animosities, and antagonism have no place in the con-ference room. But, of course, some individuals will bring such attitudes into the meeting. It is one of the jobs of the leader to try to overcome such reactions.

There should be a desire on the part of the conferees to cooperate and share ideas and knowledge. And, most important, there must be a sincere desire to listen on management's part. Morale drops and further meetings are looked upon as a waste of time by the participants if top management ignores the recommendations made in a conference. Valid decisions reached at a meeting should be carried through by those in responsible positions.

15. American Management Association, "A Guide to Successful Conference Leader-ship," pamphlet.

Objectives

To give a conference direction and form, an agenda must be drawn up, specifying exactly the purpose of the meeting and the goals to be achieved. If the objectives are clearly established beforehand, then the discussion during the meeting will not wander and time will not be wasted.

All participants in the conference should be fully aware of the objectives. A memo similar to the following should achieve this purpose.

CHICAGO LAMP CORPORATION
Inter-Office Memo

To: B. Lapidus, Controller
      G. Lord, Sales Mgr.
      R. Baxter, Office Mgr.
      L. Jameson, Production Mgr.
      P. Portel, Office Mgr.
      S. Young, Personnel Mgr.

      L. Lyons, Research Mgr.
      M. Castle, Traffic Mgr.
      T. Gilroy, Mgr., Div. #1
      A. Barlow, Mgr., Div. #2
      D. Hayworth, Mgr., Div. #3

From: F. Levin, Executive Vice President

Subject: A conference will be held at 1:00 p.m. on June 27, in the company meeting room. Please be present.

Topic for discussion: The advisability of introducing an employee profit sharing program for this company.

Scope of conference: An initial discussion to determine advantages and disadvantages of the plan as well as the basic structure of several types.

Questions for Consideration:

1. The advantages of a profit sharing system to Chicago Lamp Corporation.

2. The disadvantages of a profit sharing system to Chicago Lamp Corporation.

3. A brief explanation of six representative plans widely used in industry (B. Lapidus)

4. The plan in relationship to unions, employee good will, and cost to the company.

Such an announcement, distributed several days before the meeting, has several advantages. It indicates to the conferees the nature of the meeting, so that no one can say, after he sits down, "If I'd known you were going to discuss this, I would have come prepared. I've got all kinds of statistics on this back in my office." The participants will have thought about the subject prior to the meeting.

Secondly, it helps keep the meeting on the topic. If someone brings up a point not completely relevant, the leader can quickly refer to the conference guide as he stops discussion in that unrelated area. It also tells each recipient of the memo who will be present. And it aids the conference leader in his own planning.

Preparation

No matter how well planned a meeting may be, if the participants are not prepared it will be a waste of time. They should study the memo announcing the meeting and then do research on and think about the subject to be discussed. They should also note who else will be present at the meeting and be prepared to work effectively with them. They should come to the meeting to cooperate, discuss, and find solutions for the problems under discussion. Some persons will attend a meeting with a "hidden agenda." These are topics, ideas, or viewpoints they will bring up and communicate. These items may have little or nothing to do with the conference topic but are brought up to impress a superior, criticize a colleague, or fulfill an individual's ego needs. However, the competent conference leader can almost immediately halt discussion on a "hidden agenda" topic by pointing out that it "was not listed on the memo distributed yesterday."

Every member should be motivated to make the conference a success. He can help achieve this goal of success if he prepares—and this he has an obligation to do.

Leadership

The key individual in a conference is a leader. It is no easy task to work with ten to twenty knowledgeable men whose natures differ widely.

There will be some men around the conference table whose personalities are pleasant and easy-going, others who are domineering and tactless. There will be a few who are aggressively good-humored in their talkativeness, and one or two who are moody or obdurate in their reticence. There will be those who are broad-minded and understanding; others whose viewpoints are narrow and biased. In the typical conference group there is usually a wide range of human nature reflected. And the conference leader has the task of bringing order, agreement, and a cooperative spirit from among such groups of diverse personalities—certainly a most difficult task.

The conference leader is not truly a "leader" in our usual meaning of the word. He is more a stimulator, a moderator, a catalyst. He need not be an expert on the topic under discussion, although he should be familiar with it. It is more important for him to be an impartial individual who can skillfully control the conferees. He must have the ability to bring everyone into the discussion, yet see to it that no one monopolizes the meeting. He does not tell the conferees what to think or how to think, but he does motivate them to think.

If he is very competent, his presence in the group will go almost unnoticed as long as the discussion moves along on the topic. But he is quick to pull the meeting back on course when it seems to be slipping away, and to call on the quiet individual whose perceptive ideas are needed.

The excellent booklet, "A Guide to Successful Conference Leadership," should be required reading for every business manager. In it the attributes of a successful leader are listed as these:

He must be a clear, rapid thinker.

He must possess ease of expression.

He must possess analytical ability.

He must be impersonal.

He must not let prejudice influence his leadership.

He must be patient.

He must be tactful in handling people.

He must have poise and self-restraint.

He must possess a sense of humor.

Granted, such a paragon is hard to come by. We who must lead conferences can only try to develop these attributes in ourselves to the greatest degree possible. Indeed, all those who must participate in conferences should try to develop these qualities.

Conference Procedure

The conference should be held in a well-lighted, well-ventilated room. Chairs should be comfortable and ashtrays, note pads, blackboards, easels, or other necessary facilities should be available.

Every meeting should begin promptly at the time called and end at the hour set. No busy manager appreciates waiting twenty minutes while late-comers straggle in, nor does he like returning to his desk an hour past the time scheduled for the conclusion of the conference.

A summarized statement of the meeting should be sent to all participants the day after the meeting. This printed résumé of the points covered and the decisions reached may lessen the possibility of misunderstanding at a later date. And of course certain assignments may be indicated on the summary, to avoid a later "Well, I had no idea you wanted me to do that."

The conference method of discussing problems and reaching decisions may be expensive and time-consuming, but it is democratic and effective. When handled properly it gives the conferees a strong feeling of participation in decision-making activities. It does require extra effort on everyone's part, but I am convinced that the results in personnel development, control, decision making, and management morale make it all worthwhile.

THE GRAPEVINE

There is another medium of communication that exists in every organization of whatever size or structure: the grapevine. It is informal, follows no set patterns of content or direction, moves in various communication networks, and comes from the informal or social organization among employees.

Most managers assume that the information flowing along the grapevine hardly reflects credit on the company, is often inaccurate, and not infrequently causes problems. These assumptions are often correct. But to ignore the grapevine, or hope it will go away, or pretend it does not exist is hardly a solution. The grapevine *does* exist; it *does* carry information; and it *can* be used with benefit. (See Hatch, "Explaining Changes: If You Don't, the Grapevine Will," and Davis, "Management Communication and the Grapevine," Part IV.)

The grapevine, if tapped wisely, can be an excellent source of information. It can tell management what activities certain individuals or groups are engaged in, what their future plans are, and how they feel about company conditions and goals.

Some of the information in the grapevine is accurate and some is not. The wise manager sifts it all and, if he is perceptive and listens carefully, he can often discover situations that have potential for trouble, blow-up, and union difficulties. Once they are recognized, these can be discussed either with individuals or with employee groups, and the situations clarified.

The grapevine also allows individuals to "blow off steam." A subordinate cannot usually talk back to his superior, but he can't simply bottle up his frustrations and antagonisms. If he can tell someone, he will certainly feel better. And for others who have a strong need for recognition, the grapevine serves a useful purpose. This person can be the conveyor of news of "major" importance, news of which no one is yet aware except "top management and I"—news only he was privileged to hear and pass on to others.

The grapevine has many useful functions and does keep the lines of communication open between management and worker. The sensitive manager tries to tune in on the various grapevines existing simultaneously. But he also knows that what these rumors *say* may not be what they *mean*. The frequent rumor that shop supervisor Robinson is going to be transferred to the New Jersey plant may be a desire or a wish of many of his subordinates. Or the strong rumor that this plant is going to close down is merely a way of asking for an answer to why so many of the punch presses and milling machines are being moved out.

In almost every situation, it is unwise to ignore the grapevine. Everything in a company environment will be discussed. If management does not communicate, or does not communicate accurate information about the situation, employees will communicate what best serves their purposes or what they imagine to be the case. But silence will not exist; something will flow and management is wise to let the truth circulate rather than inaccurate and harmful rumors.

One method of working with the grapevine is to identify the "influentials" in the informal organization of the company. These individuals strongly influence the thought and actions of fellow workers. Management should talk through problems with them, asking for their suggestions and making sure they understand contemplated changes or new directions in the firm.

The grapevine can also be handled through an employee council. Here representatives of various departments are encouraged to ask management about the accuracy of any rumors. Many companies also have "question boxes" located around the plant. Employees are encouraged to drop questions in the boxes; a copy of the question and the company's reply are then posted on the bulletin boards.

Another frequently used method is the regular column in the company newspaper or magazine, which lists answers to the grapevine. The questions have either been heard by management or have been sent to the editor by an employee.

Still another method is to have large spikes attached to bulletin boards throughout the plant, with a sign above them: "Spike that Rumor." Employees are encouraged to hang their questions or rumors on the spike. Answers are then supplied on the bulletin boards or in a special column in the plant paper. Sometimes the plant public address system may be used if speed in handling a rumor is important.

Whenever possible it is a good idea simply to state the facts answering the rumor without referring to the rumor. When both the rumor and the facts are cited, it often appears that management is attempting to refute what has been rumored. Employees will typically react, "Well, they can't avoid it any longer; they've got to give us *some* answer now that we've forced them into it."

Regardless of how the rumors on the grapevine are handled, the important step is to handle them. Ignoring the messages will not cause them to disappear. The grapevine is a normal and expected method of communication in the informal organization.

Management must listen to the grapevine with sensitivity and perceptiveness. Careful analysis of what is said can tell management what is really behind a rumor and why it is being circulated. Not only is constructive use of the grapevine possible, but it is a necessary method for securing feedback from employees in any number of areas.

INTERNAL COMMUNICATIONS

Every well-run organization must have a carefully supervised internal communications system. Management is responsible for seeing to it that communications move up, down, and laterally. But they must do more than move. For maximum benefit, these communications, whether written or oral, must be clear, accurate, and concise. If a manager is to manage successfully, if employees are to work together efficiently, if a business is to operate profitably—the company must have an effective communications system.

Such a system must be based on a corporate philosophy of communication which not only encourages two-way communication, but bends every effort to see to it that such lines exist. These lines must carry honest information, in a timely fashion, up, down, and laterally. Where this system exists, the management functions of planning, organizing, directing, coordinating, and controlling are greatly assisted.

QUESTIONS FOR STUDY

I. Complete any of the following problems assigned. You may wish to review the chapter and note key points before attempting to solve the problem.

1. What role do reports play in the decision-making process?

2. What are the specific methods for communicating information up?

3. What factors in our changing society seem to demand that today's employee be better informed about his company's activities than the employee of 50 years ago?

4. Elect four class members to carry through research among five local companies on the firms' philosophy of communication to employees. At the conclusion of the research, have the four students engage in a panel discussion on the differences in the philosophies, how they reflected the companies' attitudes, and whether or not there was any correlation between a company philosophy of communication (or lack of one) and employee attitudes.

5. Design a philosophy of communication for a firm that has 10,000 employees, is 12 years old, manufactures electronic components, and is located in a major urban center.

6. Secure six different company magazines. Analyze their content as to the topics covered and the relative value and interest of such topics to most employees.

7. Some research will show you that many companies have two or three different employee-orientation manuals. One of these may be for hourly personnel, one for salaried, and one perhaps for executive or administrative personnel. Why should several manuals exist (or not exist) within one firm?

8. What must the administrator keep in mind if he wishes to use pay envelope inserts most effectively?

9. Elect several class members to investigate and report to the class on the bulletin board and rack service practices of several firms.

10. Of the three directions of internal communications—up, down, and lateral—which one do you think is generally least efficient? Why?

11. Why do you feel there is frequent criticism of the term "conference leader"? What title(s) might be preferable? Why?

12. Split into groups of 14-17. Choose any one of the topics below, carry through research, issue a request to attend the conference, and then hold such a meeting for 40 minutes.

At the conclusion of the meeting, hold a critique of the leader, participants, conference content, discussion, progress, and related factors.

You may wish to ask the members of your group to simulate specific roles having opposing points of view. Representation from any of the following may be assumed: management and labor; salaried and hourly personnel; professional and nonprofessional plant employees; students and faculty; faculty and school administration; fraternity and independent representatives; etc.

(1) Shall we institute a company profit-sharing program?

(2) Why fraternities should (should not) be abolished.

(3) Why students should (should not) have equal representation with faculty on campus committees.

(4) Should the 10-minute morning and afternoon coffee breaks be abolished and the work day shortened?

(5) Should an employee council be established?

(6) Should employees have a voice in the distribution of company profits?

(7) Should we have two separate cafeterias, one for hourly and one for salaried and administrative personnel?

(8) Should our company attempt to diversify through acquisitions and merger?

(9) Should a "Pass-Fail" grade designation be instituted for all undergraduate classes in place of the present A, B, C, D, F method of evaluating students?

(10) Shall we hire a competent individual to edit the company magazine, or shall we engage an outside firm to carry through the complete assignment?

PART TWO

Reports

CHAPTER THREE

The Report
as a Management Tool

The form of the records that companies keep varies for different areas of activity. They may be a series of charts, a stack of complex data, a collection of blueprints, a computer printout, an envelope of lab results and X-rays—usually accompanied by a written report.

It is this report with which management is primarily concerned. Does it convey—concisely and clearly—what the author wishes to convey? Is it well organized? Does it answer the needs of the reader? Does it contain adequate data to substantiate its conclusions and recommendations? Are its interpretations and evaluations valid? If a report does all this for its readers, it will serve a useful purpose. If it does not, it may impede, confuse, or delay the attainment of the goal.

The record is vital, and we must examine it before we move forward. Whether what it presents is purely informative, or almost entirely persuasive, or primarily comparative, we look into it before making decisions or taking the next step in an organized plan.

THE REPORT AND
THE DECISION-MAKING PROCESS

Managers at all levels are required to make decisions. Sometimes these decisions are simple. They may recommend the hiring of a part-time boy to assist in the office or the shipping of merchandise via rail instead of truck. At other times a decision may involve closing down a series of production lines and throwing 100 people out of work, or acquiring a subsidiary company with sales of five million dollars. These decisions, major or minor, are arrived at after the information concerning the problem has been read and evaluated. If the decision is to be as effective as circumstances permit, then the data presented in the report must be clear, complete, and accurate. All necessary facets of a problem must be presented; all conclusions must be carefully drawn; and all recommendations must be thoroughly substantiated.

The manager, acting in a decision-making capacity, must insist that all reports submitted—written or oral, long or short—be as complete, clear, and accurate as possible. His future, that of his associates, and not infrequently that of the company are dependent on his decision. And his decision is dependent on the report.

DIRECTIONS OF FLOW

A variety of different reports move up to the manager. If he is at top level, he receives them from each of his department heads at periodic intervals. These are frequently in writing, but they may also be oral, as in an interview or a conference. In addition to these formal channels, he also receives data from subordinates through informal communication: while waiting in the lunch line; a casual chat while walking down the corridor; the attitudes reflected by various persons in conversations and at meetings.

Reports also travel down, bringing information to every member of an organization. The data contained in these reports help guide employees and give further direction to continuing activities.

And for each department or division to function most efficiently, reports should travel laterally. Certainly it helps the sales manager if he is aware of the status of production, the problems of personnel, and the plans of marketing. However, it is this lateral communication which operates rather haphazardly in most companies. Many department heads *must* send information up because their superiors require it. The manager *must* send information down if his department is to function efficiently. But he is often too busy to communicate laterally. Furthermore, his interest in other departments is usually minimal, unless something arises unexpectedly which forces him to consult with another department head. For these reasons, lateral communication does not always take place effectively.

WEEDING OUT UNNECESSARY REPORTS

Before the astute manager begins to evaluate the quality of his reports and perhaps introduce some changes in report procedure, he should first determine which reports are necessary. Most of them are vital. Industry, science, and government could not exist if they did not have competent reporting procedures.

But there can also be no doubt that today there are too many reports written by too many people on too many occasions. These documents often serve no purpose except to slow communication and decision making in an organization. Perhaps the reports were initiated by a specific individual to solve a particular problem; the individual and problem may no longer exist, but that report is still prepared, typed, and distributed on the first of each month.

Reports are usually the result of careful thought, extensive research, and hours of writing time. When they are completed on situations which aren't very important and when they are filed without being read, the loss in time, effort, and money is enormous.

If the manager examines the report-writing procedures in his firm, he will often find that some reports are written (and read) almost as a matter of habit. For years Joe, in Employee Relations, has submitted a monthly report on the participation of company personnel in social, athletic, and educational activities sponsored by the firm. It is always filled with statistics, has beautiful color charts, and even photographs now and then. And it is always interesting to some department chiefs to note what percentage of their personnel are participating. But others who receive the same report have no interest in it, and do not read it. Such a report is probably not vital nor needed by most of the people to whom it is directed. If it were compiled quarterly or even semi-annually, and its distribution more carefully controlled, it might serve a valuable purpose.

Then there is the quarterly report on Fire Safety which was begun in 1949. It covers exits, the number of hand fire extinguishers, the condition of all wooden doors, and the status of the manual alarm system. The original report was requested by the city fire department following a disastrous fire in a company forty miles away. Since that date, however, the fire department conducts its own safety inspection of the premises every six months, iron fire doors have been installed throughout the building, the plant has an automatic alarm and sprinkler system, and the compilation of the report makes no sense whatsoever. But it does keep someone busy. And it does result in money needlessly spent.

Every manager, in an effort to increase efficiency and save money, should review his report requirements periodically. In this way some reports can be eliminated, others combined, and new ones initiated. Perhaps one efficient procedure in reviewing which reports are necessary and which are not is to take an inventory every year using a check list like the one illustrated on p. 78.

YEARLY INVENTORY OF COMPANY REPORTS

Type of Report	Purpose	Who Writes It?	Who Reads It? (Distribution)	Vital	Some	Little	None	Action Taken
Monthly Sales Report	To present statistical data and make comments on sales volume, sales trends, and related items	Sales Manager	President, Vice Pres. (East), Vice Pres. (West), Production Mgr., Personnel Mgr., Advertising Mgr., Credit Mgr., Transportation Mgr.	✓✓✓	✓✓✓✓✓			Report Continued
Monthly Personnel Report	To present statistical data and make comments on personnel and personnel activities	Personnel Manager	President, Vice Pres. (East), Vice Pres. (West), Sales Mgr., Production Mgr., Advertising Mgr., Credit Mgr., Transportation Mgr.	✓✓✓	✓✓✓✓	✓		Incorporate into Personnel Manager's Report
Monthly Safety Report	To report number of plant accidents and causes	Plant Manager	President, Vice Pres. (East), Vice Pres. (West), Production Mgr., Sales Mgr., Advertising Mgr., Credit Mgr., Transportation Mgr.	✓	✓	✓✓	✓✓✓✓	Report Continued
Fire Safety Report	To report on plant fire equipment	Head maintenance man	President, Vice Pres. (East), Vice Pres. (West), Production Mgr., Sales Mgr., Advertising Mgr., Credit Mgr., Transportation Mgr.		✓✓		✓✓✓✓✓✓	Eliminate (city inspections held monthly)

Naturally when some reports are eliminated and others incorporated into existing ones, a few people are going to be unhappy. Part of their empire has been destroyed and their importance, they feel, lessened. Because the elimination of reports or changes in their handling are often resisted strongly, the person who has the responsibility for controlling company reports should possess adequate authority.

The manager not only should review the need for every report, but he should also examine the distribution roster. There is no point in having personnel read and file reports if they have little concern with the topic presented.

WHAT TO REPORT

A vital question which frequently arises is "What does management want in reports?" A study was made at Westinghouse in an effort to find some answers to this question. Here is an excerpt from the article describing the study:[1]

> When a manager reads a report, he looks for pertinent facts and competent opinions that will aid him in decision making. He wants to know right away whether he should read the report, route it, or skip it.
>
> To determine this, he wants answers fast to some or all of the following questions:
> What's the report about and who wrote it?
> What does it contribute?
> What are its conclusions and recommendations?
> What are their importance and significance?
> What's the implication to the Company?
> What actions are suggested?
> Short range? Long range? Why?
> By whom? When? How?
> The manager wants this information in brief, concise, and meaningful statements. He wants it at the beginning of the report and all in one piece.
>
> For example, if a summary is to convey information efficiently, it should contain three kinds of facts:
> 1. What the report is about;
> 2. The significance and implications of the work; and
> 3. The action called for.

1. Richard W. Dodge, "What to Report," *Westinghouse Engineer,* July-September 1962, Westinghouse Electric Corporation.

To give an intelligent idea of what the report is about, first of all the problem must be defined, then the objectives of the project set forth. Next, the reasons for doing the work must be given. Following this should come the conclusions. And finally, the recommendations.

Such summaries are informative and useful, and should be placed at the beginning of the report.

The kind of information a manager wants in a report is determined by his management responsibilities, but how he wants this information presented is determined largely by his reading habits. This study indicates that management report reading habits are surprisingly similar. Every manager interviewed said he read the *summary* or abstract; a bare majority said they read the *introduction* and *background* sections as well as the *conclusions* and *recommendations;* only a few managers read the *body* of the report or the *appendix* material. . . .

To the report writer, this can mean but one thing: If a report is to convey useful information efficiently, the structure must fit the manager's reading habits.

This same study indicates that during the entire process of writing the report—from the initial step of problem designation to the writing of the final draft—several conferences should be held. The purpose of these meetings is to make sure that the report writer is proceeding in the direction and at the pace desired by the manager.

The first conference should be held to define the problem and the project. At this point the report writer should learn just what he is to do, what kind of report is desired, and how his work relates to the decisions to be made.

A second conference should be held after the research and investigation have been completed. At this time the report writer can discuss with the manager the findings, their implications, and the evidence discovered. The manager, on the basis of his greater experience and his overall view of company activities, can suggest further investigation or additional areas to be surveyed. He may also suggest what areas should be emphasized in the report, the order of presentation, and methods of presentation.

In the third conference, the "final" outline should be reviewed. If changes in the organizational structure are needed, this is the time to make them, *before* the report is written.

And the fourth meeting should take place after the report is written. At this time the manager may suggest a distribution list and minor changes, but the extent of such change should be limited.

THE DISCIPLINE
OF WRITING A REPORT

Long or short, simple or complex, most reports follow a basic pattern. Perhaps some of the steps are just touched lightly in very short reports or even skipped, but the order is common to every one. The writer should check to determine if he has completed each step on the way to writing his final draft.

Define the problem clearly and accurately
Secure a clear understanding of the purpose of the report
Narrow the topic sufficiently, but not too much
Define the scope of the report exactly
Draw up a tentative outline for the report
Formulate a research plan
Carry through research
    From primary sources
    From secondary sources
Tabulate the quantitative data gathered
Evaluate all material secured
Edit the data
Interpret the data
Complete a detailed outline for the report
Write a rough draft
Insert tables, graphs, visuals
Draw up supplements
Edit the rough draft
Write the final copy

This plan should be completed for every report; actually many of these steps become almost mechanical for the efficient writer. And he may even skip a few if the nature of the report or the situation permits.

Because these steps are basic to report writing, they will be discussed in detail. Several points will be covered below, and the remainder will be examined in the chapters which follow.

DEFINING THE PROBLEM

This is perhaps the most important step in researching and writing a report. It is obvious that if we identify a *symptom* as the *problem*, all the work which follows will in large measure be wasted.

Defining a problem quickly and accurately is an art which requires careful thought, critical evaluation, and mature imagination. It is not unusual for a manager to look hastily at a situation and indicate that AB is the problem, when in fact it is only a contributing factor.

For example, Manager Brickworth notes that production is dropping steadily in Department 41. His immediate reaction to this might be to set up three additional punch presses in that department to increase production. Or to assign 12 more men to increase production. Or to increase the piece rate paid to motivate the workers to higher production. But the drop in production is not due to a shortage of punch presses or men or inadequate pay. None of these is the problem. In this particular instance, production has declined because none of the presses is equipped with safety devices, and as a result an operator suffered a serious hand injury two months ago. All operators now work more slowly and carefully.

Once this is recognized as the problem—and solved—production will increase.

It requires a great deal of skill to separate the symptoms and contributing factors from the problem. The manager should:

1) Always isolate symptoms and causes from the problem.
2) Test to be sure that he has defined the problem *before* he begins to list solutions. Too often, hastily selected solutions are the answers for the symptoms and not for the problem.

In some ways, recognition of the problem by the business manager is analogous to the physician-patient relationship. Tom Peterson's stomach pains, nausea, headache, and general lethargy are symptoms of a much more serious problem—an infected appendix. Treating a symptom may only prolong the illness or even result in the patient's death. The problem must be recognized and solved; all the symptoms then disappear.

But if a mistake is made in this first step of problem identification, those steps which follow may all be faulty.

UNDERSTANDING THE PURPOSE

Not infrequently in business, science, or government a report will be assigned, worked on, written, and submitted—but prove unsatisfactory. The manager may very well read it and then confront the writer with, "But this isn't what I wanted at all! I wanted an *analysis* of the potential sales of this product in our Western Division, and you've given me a *comparison* of its present sales with a competing product!"

Who is at fault? The report writer? The manager who made the assignment? Both men? Neither one?

Actually it makes little difference whose fault it is. But we do know that money has been spent, time wasted, tempers ruffled, and the necessary job not accomplished. Had the *purpose* of the report been clearly established in the mind of the manager, and thoroughly understood by the writer, the controversy probably would not have arisen.

It is this confusion in purpose which so often causes the difficulty. The successful report must start with the manager's knowing exactly what purpose the report is to fulfill. The report writer must then be sure that his understanding of the report's purpose and that of the manager are in basic agreement. If this is not the case, then the research, evaluation, interpretation, writing, and recommendations may all be wasted.

How, then, can the report writer and the manager be sure they both agree on the purpose of the report? Perhaps the best way is through discussion and agreement on a written "Statement of Purpose." Once this has been established, the report writer can move to his next task: limiting his subject.

LIMITING THE TOPIC

Not infrequently in industry the manager will receive or write a report that seems to cover a tremendous topic area. And often, because the coverage is very wide, the depth of the examination is shallow and inadequate. A careful discussion of the *purpose* of the report will often result in a topic's being properly narrowed. If we are sure of what purpose the report is to serve, we can move forward toward narrowing the topic with some accuracy.

The manager who breezily asks for an "information report on the potential for a retail outlet in Centerville" may get a ninety-page document. It may cover eighteen separate areas from "population density" to "local style patterns." And it may have cost $3000 in research, writing, and reproduction time to produce. It is true that the manager *does* want information on Centerville as a retail outlet, but he doesn't want, nor does he need, data in eighteen different areas. Had the topic been limited to "economic and population factors in Centerville," the report writer would not have expended time and effort in undesired areas, such as source of raw materials, market factors, and tax structure, and the manager would have received what he wanted.

Here we can see how vital it is to have a specific idea of the purpose of the report. If it is made clear that the purpose is to determine the income level, buying potential, present population, projected population growth, population age levels, and related factors, then perforce, the topic is limited to "Economic and Population Factors in Centerville." Social, educational, and cultural factors are ruled out as are evaluations of Centerville's industries, transportation facilities, and tax structure. It is possible that information in these areas has already been secured or is not necessary.

Topics can be limited or narrowed by using various devices:

> Time
> Distance; geographical
> Area of activity within society
> (cultural, educational, social, political, etc.)
> Area of industrial activity
> (marketing, production, supervising, research, etc.)

Here is an example of the successive steps in limiting a topic:

> An Analysis of the Automobile
>
> An analysis of the American automobile (geographical)
> An analysis of the sales of the American auto in New York City
> (area of industrial activity and geographical)
> An analysis of the sales of the Mustang in New York City,
> 1969-71 (industrial activity, time, and geographical)
> An analysis of the social implications which motivated consumer
> purchase of the 1969 Mustang in Ann Arbor, Michigan, as
> compared with New York City (all limiting factors)

Of course the report writer should be cautioned: it is possible to narrow a topic to the point where finding information becomes extremely difficult. This can be most frustrating and discouraging.

ESTABLISHING THE SCOPE

Although "limiting the topic" and "establishing the scope" are similar, they are not the same. Each is a separate step in the report writing procedure. It seems to me that "scope" may be freely translated as "depth of investigation."

Let's look at the topic above which was limited or narrowed:

> An analysis of the social implications which motivated con-
> sumer purchase of the 1969 Mustang in Ann Arbor, Michigan,
> as compared with New York City.

It would be possible to carry through a most elaborate series of market studies of consumer motivation. Thousands of dollars could be expended on interviews and questionnaire studies; and social implications in relationship to status, race, and occupation could be examined. But if this were not necessary, it would be silly to extend the *scope* of the study to such a depth.

Here again, it is easy to see how closely related this factor of scope is to the purpose of the report. Certainly the purpose the report is to serve will greatly influence the limitation and the scope of the investigative area. Let us examine another topic, such as the availability of the labor force to support our new plant in Midvale. We could analyze the labor market in the following depth:

I. Availability of Labor
    A. Male   B. Female
            Administrative   Production
            Production   Secretarial
            Skilled   Stenographic
            Professional   Professional
            Technical
            Research

II. Wage Rates
    A. Male   B. Female
            Administrative   Production
            Production   Secretarial
            Skilled   Stenographic
            Professional   Professional
            Technical
            Research

III. Labor-Management History
    A. Certified unions
    B. Strike history
    C. Arbitration results
    D. Potential problems

IV. Housing Availability
    A. Rental
    B. Home purchases
    C. Financing

V. Educational Facilities
    A. Public   B. Private
            Elementary   Elementary
            Secondary   Secondary
            Collegiate   Collegiate

However, if our report does not demand such depth, why should it be carried through? If the scope of our total investigation finds the following plan adequate, it should be our choice:

I. Availability of Labor
   A. Male
      Administrative
      Production
      Skilled
   B. Female
      Production
      Secretarial

II. Wage Rates
   A. Male
      Administrative
      Production
   B. Female
      Production
      Secretarial

III. Labor-Management History
   A. Strike history
   B. Potential problems

IV. Housing Availability
   A. Rental
   B. Home purchases

Now that we have defined the problem, recognized the purpose, narrowed our topic, and established the scope, we have automatically achieved our tentative outline (see Chapter Five). That outline is reflected in the "scope" and requires only some further reflection and editing. Our next step is to determine what kind of research should be carried through and to what depth.

FORMULATING A RESEARCH DESIGN

Here again care must be taken. It is pointless to send out thousands of questionnaires, hold dozens of interviews, examine hundreds of company documents, and evaluate the contents of scores of articles, bulletins, reports, and pamphlets, if such effort is not required. A vital question to ask is, "What research design will best serve our needs, and at the same time conserve our time and funds?"

Should we use a questionnaire or not? Will a research agency do the work better and faster than our personnel, who have plenty to do in their regular assignments? Will 50 interviews really add materially to our results, or should we depend entirely on the results from the 2000 questionnaires? Should we request a literature search from NASA or Department of Defense?

What we are really getting at in the formulation of our research design is this: what research shall we carry through which will give us the data we need for the least expenditure of time, money, and effort? Or, on the other hand, it is possible that specific constraints exist concerning the time and money available. In such an instance, the research plan must be accommodated to the boundaries which exist.

Thus, we may decide, in a particular case, that our research design should include:

I. A search of company records
II. An evaluation of secondary sources
      Magazines
      Journals
      Newspapers
III. A check of government publications
      Technical reports
      Translations
IV. A series of 20 interviews with corporate production managers.

It is quite possible that after we get into the research we will discover that our design must be modified. Perhaps the material in the journals doesn't fill our needs and more emphasis must be placed on interviews; or perhaps the findings presented in the government reports are so definitive, complete, and up-to-date that there is no need to carry through a questionnaire or interview survey. But these questions on the effectiveness of the research design cannot be answered until we begin to use the research materials and evaluate their adequacy.

Let us now move into this next phase: the research situation.

QUESTIONS FOR STUDY

Complete any of the following problems assigned. You may wish to review the chapter and note key points before solving the problem.

1. "Decision making in the business enterprise—large or small—is almost completely dependent on reports. When those reports are not clear, complete, and accurate, the decisions reached are often faulty."

Comment on this quotation. Note the words *clear, complete,* and *accurate.*

2. Individuals who have carried through research in the field of communications have indicated that lateral reporting is usually less complete, accurate, and effective than vertical (either up or down) reporting. Can you explain why this is so?

3. How can effective reporting contribute to management control?

4. The production of a clear, useful report is the job not only of the writer, but also of the manager who requests the report. What responsibilities does he have toward achieving excellence in the final report?

5. Distinguish between "limiting the topic" and "establishing the scope" of a report. Why is each important?

6. Carry through an informal research project on how major reports are written in a specific firm. How is the assignment made? What steps are followed by the report writer after he receives the assignment, and what is done with the final product?

7. Compare your findings from question 6 with those of another student who examined a different firm. What are the similarities and differences and how do these factors affect operations?

8. Secure permission to conduct a report inventory in a firm. Report your findings in a brief memo to the individual who arranged for you to carry through the survey.

9. Explain the difference between "problem" and "purpose" in the writing of a report.

10. "Who will be the reader of the report?" is one of the first questions that must be asked by the report writer. Explain why and indicate the specific areas of the report which will be affected by the differences in the readers.

11. Limit the areas of the following so they are sufficiently narrow to serve as a report topic.

(1) Personnel Requirements in the Aerospace Industry in the 1973-75 Period
(2) The U.S. Balance of Payments and American Foreign Policy
(3) Growth Plans of the Jackson Corporation
(4) Potential for New Firms in the Space Age

(5) Corporate Cost of Fringe Benefits at the Jackson Corporation
(6) Emerging Nations and Their Effect on the GNP of the United States
(7) Population Boom in Latin America
(8) Residential Construction and Population Growth
(9) An Analysis of Employee Attitudes at the Jackson Corporation
(10) Acquisitions and Mergers, 1970-80

12. Limit the areas of the following so they are sufficiently narrow to serve as a report topic.

(1) Student Participation in University Administration
(2) Changes in Curriculum in the American University
(3) The Draft and University Enrollment
(4) Racial Unrest and Its Economic Implications
(5) Recent Trends in the Toy Industry
(6) Foreign Policy and the Viet Nam War
(7) U.S. Economic Policies and the Fluctuations of the British Pound
(8) Atomic Power: the Fuel of the Future
(9) The Computer Programmer
(10) The Computer and Information Storage

CHAPTER FOUR
Research

For decisions to be made accurately on the basis of a report, the content must be as complete as possible. Research is often necessary to uncover data, previous history, and possible future directions. Unfortunately too many report writers do themselves, and their companies, an injustice because they cannot take advantage of the wealth of material which is available to them. And they cannot do so because they are not sufficiently knowledgeable in research techniques to find and use the mountains of knowledge which other persons have prepared for them.

And this is a pity. For the report writer to complete costly research which has been previously accomplished and reported by someone else, or not to find and use valuable data which are available—this is a pity, and unnecessary.

Once the report writer has recognized specifically and precisely what his research problem is, he can begin to move toward its solution. It is then that he is ready to start the research which will help solve that problem. Research becomes vital, for it is true that the dwarf can see farther than the giant, provided he stands on the latter's shoulders. And of course, those are the shoulders of research.

The writer will probably begin by combing secondary sources. What have other researchers on this or related topics recorded in books, magazines, reports, newspapers, and other sources? Once he has determined what others have done, he can pursue areas for which he has, as yet, no answers. He may want to secure information from primary sources: questionnaires, interviews, company records, his own observation, manuscripts, etc.

How deeply he pursues his research will depend on the scope of the examination, the quantity of time and money available for investigation, and the imagination and competence of his research abilities. But it is always a pity to find a researcher who has spent countless hours and days securing information on, for example, "Car Purchasing Habits of Young College Graduates," when a detailed and thorough study of that topic had already been completed, and a government report was available for only 25 cents. What a waste not to build on the work of others.

Not only can research time and effort be saved by using the information sources available, but firms can often produce a superior product by adding to their knowledge. Articles written in German, Russian, and French journals; papers which have appeared in our own professional magazines; and government technical reports and translations—all these may contain information worth thousands of dollars. The effort required to find, read, and use such data is almost nothing as compared to the work of researching the problem itself.

There is no point in the researcher sending out questionnaires or conducting surveys if similar work has been done recently. Therefore the first step is to "look at the record." There is a further advantage in examining the information which has been discovered, interpreted, and recorded. It gives the researcher greater understanding, appreciation, and knowledge about his area. With this, he is better able to define his own investigation and direction. Thus, the first step is to look at the secondary sources, and then move on and attempt to answer very specific questions from research with primary source materials.

SECONDARY SOURCES OF INFORMATION

If the report writer has a relatively broad topic, he may wish to investigate each of the six general sources of secondary information:

1. Books
2. Magazines, journals, and periodicals
3. Newspapers
4. Reports, bulletins, and brochures
5. Government documents
6. Other sources

Through the careful use of indexes, guides, and reference sources, the researcher can rather quickly find the materials on his topic which others have recorded for his use. Our discussion here will be only a brief overview; detailed listings of secondary research sources are to be found in Appendix B.

BOOKS

A mistaken opinion held by many researchers working on a topic of current interest is that anything they might find in books is out of date. It is true that many books do contain outdated information, but books can provide valuable background material unavailable elsewhere. Furthermore, because some publishers can turn a book manuscript into a published work in even a matter of days (e.g., the Warren and Kerner reports), books often contain information which is as up-to-date as any periodical. Don't discount the value of recently published books.

Using the Card Catalog

Most library researchers begin by looking through the card catalog for books on their topic. Title, subject, and cross-reference cards should be checked. Of course the obvious disadvantage of this method is that this particular library may have several books which are completely or partially concerned with the topic, but the researcher may never find the cards identifying the books. Perhaps he skipped the cards, they were misfiled, or a card was never completed and filed because only a chapter or two of a book was devoted to the subject.

Using the Library Stacks

If the report writer can secure admission to the library stacks, he avoids the problem noted above. All he need do is determine what library classification number books on his topic carry, walk over to that section, and there on the shelves in front of him are the books on the topic which this library owns. Naturally he checks with the clerk to determine which ones may have been checked out. However, there is also the possibility that a book may not be catalogued under the same classification which the researcher assumes. This is all the more reason for the investigator to check several different classifications in the stacks.

Using Guides to Books

Both of the above methods have obvious limitations. The researcher only discovers the books which a particular library carries on the subject, not all the books which have been published on the topic. This is when comprehensive guides to published books become very valuable.

MAGAZINES, JOURNALS, AND PERIODICALS

There is probably nothing more exasperating to the researcher than to be told, "I read an article on your topic. It appeared early this year—or maybe late last year; I don't recall the title or the name of the magazine, but it was a *great* article and you should use it. You won't have any trouble finding it; the magazine had a green cover."

Where to begin? Surely not by thumbing through stacks of magazines looking for one with a green cover, but with the excellent indexes to journal articles and the guides to magazine collections which are available.

NEWSPAPERS

The business report writer will frequently find that newspapers are excellent sources for topical information. By using the indexes listed in Appendix B, the researcher can determine significant dates which will guide him in turning to newspapers other than the *Wall Street Journal* and *New York Times*.

REPORTS, BULLETINS, AND BROCHURES

There are thousands of excellent reports, bulletins, and studies issued each year in the United States. They are often published as a public service by universities, foundations, cultural and social institutions, corporations, and professional societies and organizations.

Probably because of the variety of issuing sources, there is no guide which really does an adequate job of indexing all of them. However, the *Vertical File Index* is extremely helpful.

GOVERNMENT DOCUMENTS

Today the United States government publishes more material than any agency in the world. Many of the publications are of an extremely high quality. Technical reports, bulletins, and pamphlets are issued by almost every department, many every week. Here again, the reference guides listed in Appendix B can lead the researcher to quantities of valuable information.

BUSINESS AND CORPORATION DIRECTORIES

Business or trade directories carry a wide variety of information of value in the fields with which they are concerned. Usually they list sources of supply, names and addresses of individual companies, product listings, and product information.

Listed in Appendix B are guides to the several thousand directories which are available. Almost every field, from "Automotive Products" to "Wholesale Jewelers," has a trade directory for national and foreign listings.

Corporation directories are of value to investors, manufacturers, buyers, and others who are interested in securing facts on the financial record and personnel of various companies. Many directories are published annually with supplements appearing throughout the year, so that changes in personnel or operation are brought to the reader's attention as quickly as possible.

MISCELLANEOUS SOURCES OF INFORMATION

In addition to those mentioned above, there are dozens of other sources of information, including annuals and atlases. A tremendous amount of material is issued by institutions, organizations, and associations. Just a few of these are the American Management Association, National Industrial Conference Board, National Research Council, Twentieth Century Fund, Chamber of Commerce of the United States, and the National Association of Manufacturers. The guides, indexes, and directories listed in Appendix B will assist the researcher in finding material in the publications of these agencies.

GUIDES TO REFERENCE SOURCES

The researcher is fortunate today in having a wide variety of reference works which help him find source materials. However, this large number of reference works in itself poses a problem. Fortunately, a solution is available in the form of guides to the reference guides (see Appendix B).

PRIMARY SOURCES OF INFORMATION: SURVEYS

Very often the report writer, after having researched secondary sources, will then find it valuable to investigate primary sources. (Or it may be that he will limit his investigation to primary sources.) These primary sources may be company records, original reports, letters and notes, data secured from interview and questionnaire surveys, and personal observation.

The data secured from primary sources are fresh and new, and the researcher has an opportunity to subject them to his analysis, his evaluation, his interpretation. No other person has added his bias to the information. The data, so to speak, are "raw." The report writer has the responsibility of weighing them together with other facts, then deciding if the firm should sell its product in a new red carton instead of blue, build a plant in Topeka instead of Kansas City, use radio or television commercials, etc.

Today we secure a great deal of information on how people will react to a situation by asking them. Of course, all kinds of subtle methods for phrasing the question are used, but essentially what the researcher is after is the true answer to the question, "If we manufacture a new sports-type car that will seat two people, sell for $2500, and look something like this, will you buy it?" In an article in *Business Week* magazine, it was estimated that U.S. corporations spend over $200 million a year asking such questions in market research.[1]

SELECTING THE SAMPLE

The science of statistical sampling has advanced tremendously in recent years. The researcher who knows precisely what his problem is, who makes up his market, and what degree of reliability he needs, can select a sample and be fairly certain that the answers he receives will prove to be accurate.

Questions are not difficult to ask; it is getting a reliable and truthful answer which compounds our problem. Earlier we discussed feedback in face-to-face discussion and we agreed that it was frequently not accurate. The same problem exists in feedback from primary sources such as questionnaires and interviews. In these cases, however, we try to increase the reliability of the response by assuring (in some cases) our prospective respondent of anonymity. Nevertheless, the problem of truth in feedback still exists. Careful sampling is the first step in increasing the level of accuracy.

What type or how big a sample is selected from the group (or universe) to be studied depends on many factors. In some, a major percentage of the universe may be sampled; in other cases, a small fraction is adequate. In this situation a random sample is the answer, but in another instance it would be wiser to take a stratified, cluster, double, selective, or area sample.

TYPES OF SURVEYS

There are several different methods used to secure information from people. Basically they all depend on posing questions or situations,

1. *Business Week* (April 18, 1964), pp. 90-116.

securing reactions, and then determining how people will act in a practical situation based on their responses to the survey. Among the devices used to secure responses are:

Mail questionnaire
Personal interview
Telephone interview
Unstructured or depth interview
Observation

The first three listed all use a series of questions to secure information. However, each is very different from the other and possesses certain assets and liabilities.

The mail questionnaire has the advantage of relatively low cost per response, and the ability to secure answers from wide geographical points. A sample survey may be completed prior to a mailing of thousands. The cloak of anonymity helps increase responses, and securing answers from hard-to-see people is made much easier with a mail questionnaire. Also, the bias of the telephone or face-to-face interviewer does not enter into the situation.

But there are also disadvantages in the mail survey. To be answered, the survey instrument must be relatively brief; individuals who feel strongly—pro or con—make up the greatest number of respondents. It is also difficult to know if the intended respondent completed the questionnaire or some member of his office staff or family did. Respondents are usually reluctant to give comment (qualitative) answers in a questionnaire because of the effort involved, and we are never quite certain whether those who replied are really representative of our sample.

The personal interview does not solve all our problems; although it has some merit over the mail questionnaire, it also has several liabilities. Perhaps the biggest disadvantage of the personal interview technique is its cost. It is very costly to use competent people as interviewers.

And even with professional interviewers, their bias often enters into the respondent's answer. Securing data through interviewing is time-consuming as compared to a mail survey. And often the respondent doesn't have the time or the wish to stand and chat with an interviewer.

On the other hand, an interviewer can conduct a more lengthy discussion than is usually possible by mail. He can also secure answers to questions in sensitive areas (income, sex, politics, religion), and he can often bring in a reply where a mail survey may fail. Because he can choose his respondents to a certain extent, his survey usually covers a more representative sample.

The telephone interview has several major limitations: questions must be brief and few in number—generally not more than three or four.

Questions requiring any discussion or even careful thought cannot be included, nor can any which are concerned with personal relationships. A youngster may answer, or no one, or a refusal to cooperate may be encountered. On the other hand, telephone interviews are inexpensive, almost anyone can be called regardless of his position or office, and simple information can be secured quickly and easily.

But in all three cases, the mail or telephone questionnaire or the personal interview, a major factor in securing a response is how well the questions are designed. If they are clear and easy to answer, the results will probably be good.

DESIGNING THE QUESTIONNAIRE

It is often said that there is nothing easier to make up than a poor questionnaire, and nothing more difficult than a good one. Here are a few suggestions to keep in mind when formulating a questionnaire:

1. The order of the questions should be logical. There is no point in asking a respondent in question 3 the ages and education level of her children, and then asking her in question 6 if she is married. If the questionnaire does not seem logical and sensible to the respondent, it may be discarded immediately.

2. Easy-to-answer questions should come early in the questionnaire. The respondent who has quickly and easily answered the first eight questions may be very reluctant to discard the questionnaire when he encounters a difficult question on number nine. This suggestion may, however, conflict with the one above, for an easy-to-answer question may not be in logical order, but the researcher can only do what is most advantageous under the circumstances.

3. Questions should be logically interconnected with good transitional phrases and words. This, and the parallel wording of questions, helps the respondent to move easily from one question to the next.

4. Each question should be concerned with one topic only. If the respondent is faced with giving two answers to one question—and only one space is provided—he may discard the form. How, for example, can this question be answered: "Would you like movies on commercial air flights at a slight extra charge?" If the respondent would like movies, but not at an extra charge, how can he answer? And if he would like movies on long flights but not short ones, how does he answer? And if he doesn't want movies at all, whether there is an extra charge or not, how does he so indicate?

5. The questionnaire should be, and should look, easy to answer. Questions should be arranged so that the respondent sees clearly where

he is supposed to indicate his replies. There should be plenty of white space and the numbering should be easy to follow. The word choice should be made carefully so that it is at the respondent's level. And an addressed, stamped envelope should be provided so that a reply can be made easily.

6. Words which might provoke a biased or emotional response should not be used, if possible. Words which might carry an undesirable connotation, or those which might have greatly varying connotations, should be avoided. These are usually abstract terms (happiness, morality, democracy, communism), or those dealing with politics, sex, religion, and race.

7. Questions should be crystal clear; all ambiguity should be eliminated. A question like "What type of soup do you prefer?" can only cause difficulty. One respondent will answer "hot," another "Campbell's," a third "beef noodle," and a fourth "inexpensive." Check every question or present a list of choices, to ensure securing the type of answer desired.

8. Avoid questions which "lead" the respondent to specific answers. Certainly a bias will enter into most respondents' answers if we ask, "Do you prefer General Motors cars?" "Do you usually purchase the best seats when attending a play?" "Do you always drink moderately?" "Do you prefer imported wines?" To avoid biasing, eliminate leading words and give the respondent a list of choices from which to make a selection.

9. Avoid questions which require the respondent to search his memory, or carry through computations. How can we expect an accurate answer to "In what year did you take your first jet trip?" How many people will bother to compute the answer to "How much does your family spend each year on movies?" Both of these questions could cause the questionnaire to be tossed into the wastebasket.

10. Avoid personal questions if possible. Individuals are often irritated when asked to answer questions concerning their political or religious affiliation, sex habits, income, or age. Some success may be achieved by assuring the respondent of anonymity, but if personal questions can be avoided, they should be.

11. Don't ask skip-and-jump questions. Most individuals give up in despair when confronted with "If you answered 'yes' to question 4, skip questions 7 and 8 and go directly to question 9, unless you live in New York, in which case do not answer question 9."

12. Avoid words with "blanket" meanings. Such words are open to a variety of interpretations. The word "often" in the question, "Do you often take your wife out to dinner?" may mean once a month to some husbands and once a week to others.

Following is an example of a well-designed mail questionnaire, reprinted by courtesy of The Western Union Telegraph Company.

SURVEY OF TELEGRAPH CUSTOMERS

1. FROM AN OVER-ALL POINT OF VIEW, HOW SATISFACTORY IS WESTERN UNION MESSAGE TELEGRAPH SERVICE?

☐ *Always Satisfactory*

☐ *Usually Satisfactory*

☐ *Frequently Unsatisfactory*

☐ *Usually Unsatisfactory*

☐ *No Opinion*

2. ON THE BASIS OF YOUR EXPERIENCE WITH MESSAGE TELEGRAPH SERVICE, WOULD YOU SAY THE QUALITY OF THE SERVICE IS PRESENTLY BETTER, ABOUT THE SAME OR WORSE THAN IT HAS BEEN IN THE PAST?

☐ *Better*   ☐ *About the Same*   ☐ *Worse*   ☐ *No Opinion*

3. IS YOUR ORGANIZATION OR COMPANY CURRENTLY SENDING MORE, ABOUT THE SAME NUMBER OR FEWER TELEGRAMS THAN A YEAR AGO?

☐ *More*   ☐ *About the Same Number*   ☐ *Fewer*   ☐ *Don't Know*

(IF FEWER TELEGRAMS) WHAT IS THE MAJOR REASON(S) FOR CURTAILING TELEGRAM USAGE?

_____

_____

_____

WESTERN UNION EFFICIENCY IN ACCEPTING TELEGRAMS

1. BY WHAT METHOD ARE TELEGRAMS **USUALLY** SENT BY YOUR COMPANY?

(Check One Method Only)

☐ *By Telephone*   ☐ *Picked Up by Western Union Messenger*

☐ *By Desk-Fax*   ☐ *By Telex Machine*   ☐ *By Teleprinter Machine*

Other Methods (please explain) _____

2. ARE YOU SATISFIED WITH WESTERN UNION'S PRACTICES IN ACCEPTING TELEGRAMS?

☐ *Always*   ☐ *Usually*   ☐ *Occasionally*   ☐ *Rarely*   ☐ *No opinion*

3. IF THERE IS ANYTHING UNSATISFACTORY ABOUT THE WAY WESTERN UNION ACCEPTS TELEGRAMS, PLEASE TELL US ABOUT IT.

_____

_____

_____

WESTERN UNION EFFICIENCY IN DELIVERING TELEGRAMS

1. AFTER WESTERN UNION ACCEPTS YOUR TELEGRAMS, ARE YOU SATISFIED WITH THE TIME IT TAKES TO DELIVER THEM?

☐ *Always*   ☐ *Usually*   ☐ *Occasionally*   ☐ *Rarely*   ☐ *No Opinion*

2. IF THERE IS ANY ASPECT OF MESSAGE DELIVERY SERVICE WHICH IS NOT SATISFACTORY PLEASE TELL US ABOUT IT.

_____

_____

_____

WESTERN UNION TELEGRAPH SERVICE IN GENERAL

1. WHAT WOULD YOU SAY ARE THE MAJOR SHORTCOMINGS OF MESSAGE TELEGRAPH SERVICE?

   (Please Comment On Any Aspect Of Service Or Your Experience With Western Union.)

   _____
   _____
   _____
   _____

2. WHAT **ONE** PARTICULAR SHORTCOMING LIMITS YOUR USAGE OF TELEGRAMS?

   _____
   _____

3. WHAT WOULD YOU SAY ARE THE **MOST** SATISFACTORY ASPECTS OF MESSAGE TELEGRAPH SERVICE?

   _____
   _____
   _____

4. IF YOU HAVE ANY OTHER SUGGESTIONS ON WHAT MIGHT INDUCE YOU TO INCREASE YOUR USAGE OF MESSAGE TELEGRAPH SERVICE PLEASE TELL US ABOUT IT IN THE SPACE PROVIDED BELOW.

   _____
   _____
   _____
   _____
   _____

(Please feel free to use the back cover.)

If you wish, you may fill out the following:

   *Your Name*_____ *Position*_____

   *Name of organization*_____

And now please return this questionnaire in the stamped, addressed envelope provided. Thank you.

CONDUCTING THE SURVEY

Even with a well-planned questionnaire, a survey will be a failure if it is not conducted properly. Respondents to a survey are doing the researcher a favor, and they should be treated accordingly. The investigator should be courteous—and he must be perceptive, in order to come as close to the "real" responses as possible.

The Depth or Unstructured Interview

Because of the conventions of society and the inhibitions most of us have, we often answer questions as we think they should be answered. If someone asks us if we hate our boss, dislike bridge, or find all television programs a pure delight, we reply as we think society would prefer. But if the replies are not honest, the survey results cannot be valid. It is the feeling of some of the scholars in the field, however, that if you let people talk about a topic freely and easily, their true feelings will become apparent to the skilled interviewer, regardless of the conventions of the society in which they live. This is the theory of depth interviewing: to set up a climate for the respondent so that he will talk freely and frankly about the topic under discussion.

"Tell me how you select a can of coffee when you shop" may produce some very revealing information in the answer.

Personal Observation

A great deal of information can often be secured simply by observing. Researchers will watch how a housewife makes a choice of one breakfast food from among thirty, how she selects a cut of meat, or whether or not she confers with her friend before choosing a cake. Observers also secure data by watching traffic patterns, counting shoppers, noting peoples' restaurant habits, etc.

The Mail Questionnaire

We have already mentioned some of the advantages and disadvantages of mail questionnaires. They are probably used by more researchers, and certainly are better known by the public, than any of the other survey methods. In order to obtain the best results possible, it is important not only that the questionnaire be well done but also that the letter which accompanies it be well written and courteous.

The Cover Letter. In a direct mail survey, the quality of the cover letter will strongly influence whether or not the respondent returns a completed questionnaire. A well-written cover letter may very well motivate him to check every question carefully, and return the questionnaire promptly.[2]

A careful study was conducted which attempted to determine what specific characteristics of the cover letter influenced the percentage of questionnaires returned.[3] Four characteristics were tested:

1) The use of a handwritten salutation and signature to make the letter seem personal.
2) A statement designed to impress the prospective respondent with the importance or social utility of the survey.
3) An explanation of how important the prospective respondent is to the study, and the role he will play in the research by responding.
4) An appeal to the prospective respondents to help the researchers.

Sixteen types of letters were sent out, each a different combination of the four factors listed above. The results indicated that making the cover letter seem personal (1 above) was extremely important in increasing responses. Item 3, explaining the importance of the respondent, also caused the number of returns to increase significantly. The other two factors (2 and 4) seemed to have had very little effect on the rate of response.

The findings here seem to be substantiated in another survey in which a handwritten postscript was added to the cover letter. The postscript, which asked the prospective respondent for help and the early return of the completed questionnaire, increased the response 27 per cent over cover letters without the P.S.[4]

There are many reasons why a questionnaire is not completed and returned, and there is almost no way to design a survey instrument which will ensure a 100 per cent response. At times the questionnaire is received by an individual who has no interest or concern with the topic under discussion; he may be busy; or perhaps his company does not permit him to complete such surveys. These are all understandable reasons for not completing a questionnaire. But why are so many simply discarded? The answer is not too difficult to find in an unsuccessful questionnaire and cover letter: writer-centered, tone too pompous, request too demanding, no explanation of survey purpose, and so on. We do know that

2. See also Norman B. Sigband, "The Cover Letter," *Journal of Marketing,* April 1953.
3. Arnold S. Linsky, "A Factorial Experiment in Inducing Responses to a Mail Questionnaire," *Sociology and Social Research,* IL (January 1965).
4. George Frazier and Kermit Bird, "Increasing the Response of a Mail Questionnaire," *Journal of Marketing,* October 1958.

if the recommendations below are followed, the percentage of responses will be good.

1. Keep the letter brief. Go over the cover letter draft with a blue pencil, striking out every extra word and phrase. The reader is in a hurry and he is busy. State what you want, why you want it, how he will benefit from giving it to you, and *stop*. Under almost no circumstances should the cover letter be longer than one page.

2. Show the respondent the importance of his role in achieving the objective of the survey. We all want to be needed, and we like to know that we are making a contribution to any activity. Tell the respondent *what* the survey hopes to accomplish, and *why* it is important. Couple this with the role of the prospective respondent in the survey, and you will usually have him involved to the extent that he will want to help you.

3. Show the respondent how *he* will benefit from completing the questionnaire—the "you" attitude. Although it may initially seem almost impossible to show the respondent how he will benefit, it usually can be done after some thought. After all, most of your activities are designed to assist someone or something. Just explain the situation honestly. Perhaps you are trying to determine an improved delivery or packaging program. On this basis he will eventually receive a better and more salable product. Or you want his opinion on your use of computers. From this your costs drop and the savings are passed on to him.

4. Inject a personal tone. The research cited earlier seems to prove the value of making the cover letter seem personal. This can be done with a handwritten signature, a handwritten postscript (it may be necessary to simulate these if a large mailing is planned), use of the respondent's name typed to match in the salutation and/or body of the letter, and through the overall tone of the letter itself. Drop all the hackneyed and obsolete phrases, and give the letter a "conversation across the desk" tone.

5. List a due date for returning the questionnaire. Most of us are so busy these days that we have no alternative but to defer completing certain assignments, and yet there are many we want to complete. Somehow, however, the days slip by and we keep putting certain jobs off. If we are specifically asked to do something by August 3, most of us will do it. But we have to be told. And this is what should always be done in the cover letter and again in the questionnaire:

Please return the completed questionnaire no later than August 3.

THE WESTERN UNION TELEGRAPH COMPANY

60 HUDSON STREET

NEW YORK 13, N.Y.

H. C. CRUTCHFIELD
DIRECTOR - MARKETING RESEARCH

May, 1966

Dear Customer:

Some of our customers have wisely observed that although the increasing automation of communications offers many benefits, it can also isolate us from you. With the elimination of human contact, it becomes more and more difficult to keep in close touch with a customer's needs and problems. We agree completely.

For a service organization like Western Union, the preservation of some measure of personal contact is essential. It is this belief which has prompted us to send you the enclosed questionnaire. The expression of your views about various aspects of your message telegraph service will not only better our understanding of your needs and problems, but also enable us to provide the kind of service you would most like to have.

Please take a few moments and let us hear from you. Most of the questions can be answered simply by checking the square opposite the answer which comes closest to your opinion. We hope you will answer all of the questions. When the form is completed, it can be mailed in the stamped, addressed envelope which is provided for your convenience.

Thank you for joining us in this step toward greater understanding. Your cooperation is sincerely appreciated.

Very truly yours,

H. C. Crutchfield

Enc.

Courtesy of The Western Union Telegraph Company

So that we can begin our faster new delivery service to you as quickly as possible, please return the completed questionnaire no later than August 3.

6. Where possible, assure the respondent of confidence or anonymity. If you feel that some questionnaires will be discarded because the respondent does not wish to divulge confidential information, or he fears the embarrassment of being identified, take precautions. Sometimes a simple statement will increase responses by 20 per cent:

Dear Mr. Holt:

In a few days you will receive a letter from me
regarding an important survey we are conducting.
I hope I can count on your cooperation in filling
out the simple questionnaire. Thank you in advance.

Franklin M. Heller

Franklin M. Heller, President
Madison Research Associates

You may be sure that all the information you include will be kept completely confidential.

Of course we don't want you to sign the questionnaire; we are only interested in your answers.

7. Offer survey results if you can. If it isn't too expensive, or doesn't divulge findings you would prefer to keep confidential, offer the respondent a copy of the results. Most individuals who complete a survey are interested in or working in the field with which the study is concerned. If you tell the respondent you will share your new knowledge with him by sending him a copy of your findings, he may very well be motivated to help you by completing the questionnaire. If you wish to assure him of anonymity and also offer him a copy of the results, you can include a postal card, addressed to you, which he may return separately from the questionnaire.

The foregoing are the major factors which help increase responses to questionnaire surveys. There are others, but note in the letter on p. 105, written to accompany the Western Union survey shown previously, how most of the principles listed have been included.

Motivating the Prospective Respondent. Research directors have found that giving the prospective respondent a "reward" will often significantly increase the percentage of completed questionnaires returned. A freshly minted quarter or dime, a coupon which may be traded for a free package of the company's product, a ballpoint pen, or a crisp dollar bill are some of the devices used. Whenever a coin is used, it is wise

MADISON RESEARCH ASSOCIATES
27 EAST 22ND STREET
NEW YORK, NEW YORK 10010, U.S.A.

November 6, 1967

Dear Mr. Holt:

Would you please do me a favor?

A client of ours has asked for our help in determining the familiarity of important men in business and industry with certain companies and their opinions of some others.

You were included in the small, scientifically selected sample to whom the enclosed confidential questionnaire is being mailed. Because our sample contains only a few hundred people, each and every answer is extremely important to the reliability of the results of the survey. So please take a few moments to fill out the short questionnaire and return it in the enclosed stamped envelope.

Our client, and I personally, will be grateful for your help.

Sincerely,

Franklin M. Heller

Franklin M. Heller
President

FMH:mi
Enclosures

P. S. The enclosed coin is simply a token of our appreciation. It may brighten the day of a youngster you know.

to avoid the bald statement "Here's a quarter for your effort." This is to avoid the possible "this is a bribe to get you to help" interpretation.

Sometimes these attachments to the cover letter can save the researcher a significant amount of money. If he sends out 5000 questionnaires and receives 400 which have been completed, the cost per completed questionnaire may be 90¢. If, on the other hand, he mails 2000, each of which has a 25¢ enclosure, and receives a response of 550, his cost may well drop to 70¢ *including* the expense of the coin. Thus these premiums should be considered, but they should always be used with caution. Some prospective respondents will become irritated with what they may consider an unethical device to motivate them to complete and return the questionnaire. And there is also the danger that the respondent who has accepted the coin or coupon may attempt to answer the questionnaire as he thinks the researcher desires, rather than as he honestly feels.

DOCUMENTING THE REPORT

Whenever the researcher cites information which he has secured from another source, he should give credit to that source. Usually that credit is given in a footnote, although it is not unusual to see the source cited in the body of the paper.

When to give credit and when not to has always been a controversial point. If the statistics or information are common knowledge in the field, you should not bother with a footnote. But if the information is the result of some other person's knowledge or research, and is not generally known, reference to that source should be made. If you're not sure whether to give credit, then credit should be given.

But the footnote should also be used for purposes other than a reference to a source. It can be used effectively to:

1. cite information which might be relevant to the report material but not so intimately concerned that it should appear in the body of the report itself.
2. cite statistics or data to support statements made in the body of the report.
3. cite points of view other than those presented in the body of the report.
4. note different points of view among the authorities in the field.
5. offer critical evaluations of major sources used. This might be a comment concerning the excellence of the maps in this journal article, the inaccuracies in that book, etc.

Usually footnotes are found at the bottom of a page and refer to a statement made on that page. However, terminal footnoting has become popular in recent years. This is simply the placement of all footnotes at the end of the chapter, end of a section, or at the end of the report or article. This has an obvious advantage in typing, and also places all the footnotes in one area for easy reference.

As for footnote form, this also is a matter of convention and convenience. Some researchers prefer to cite a minimum amount of information, maintaining that further complete details may always be found—if needed—in a bibliographic entry.

Thus, the form of the footnote and bibliographic entries varies. The basic objectives in documentation are to give proper credit to a source, and to cite enough data so the reader may find that source if he desires. If the footnote or bibliographic entry does this, it is sufficiently complete. However, it is always wise to check with the individual for whom the paper is written. Frequently a standard form is required.

There are a variety of abbreviations used in source documentation to assist the writer. Most of these may be found in manuals covering research papers. However, two which are frequently used are *"ibid."* and *"op. cit."* *Ibid.*, from the Latin meaning "in the same place," indicates that the source is identical to the one preceding. *"Ibid.*, p. 45" means that the source is the same as the one preceding except that the page to which reference is made is now 45.

"Op. cit." refers to a source previously cited but not immediately preceding. It is from the Latin meaning "in the work cited."

SUGGESTED FOOTNOTE FORMS

Alfred G. Smith, *Communication and Culture* (New York: Holt, Rinehart & Winston, 1966), p. 61.

Joseph S. Moag, "Computers, Artificial Languages, and Linguistic Behavior," *The Journal of Business Communication*, IV, 2 (March 1967), 49.

R. R. Aurner and M. P. Wolf, *Effective Communication in Business* (Cincinnati: South-Western Publishing Company, 1967), p. 107.

Norman B. Sigband, *Effective Report Writing for Business, Industry, and Government* (New York: Harper & Row, 1960), p. 510.

U.S. Department of Commerce, *Our Growing Population* (Washington, D.C.: U.S. Government Printing Office, 1961), p. 4.

Ted J. McLaughlin *et al.* [or Ted J. McLaughlin and others], *Communication* (Columbus, Ohio: Charles E. Merrill Books, Inc., 1964), pp. 32-40.

Arthur L. Grey, Jr., and John E. Elliott (eds.), *Economic Issues and Policies: Readings in Introductory Economics,* 2nd ed. (New York: Houghton Mifflin Company, 1965), p. 47.

Los Angeles Times, November 4, 1967, Part II, p. 31.

SUGGESTED BIBLIOGRAPHIC FORMS

Aurner, R. R., and M. P. Wolf. *Effective Communication in Business.* Cincinnati: South-Western Publishing Company, 1967.

Grey, Arthur L., Jr., and John E. Elliott (eds.). *Economic Issues and Policies: Readings in Introductory Economics.* Second edition. New York: Houghton Mifflin Company, 1965.

McLaughlin, T. J., *et al.* [or McLaughlin, T. J., and others]. *Communication.* Columbus, Ohio: Charles E. Merrill Books, Inc., 1964.

Moag, Joseph S. "Computers, Artificial Languages, and Linguistic Behavior," *The Journal of Business Communication,* IV, 2 (March 1967), 47-52.

Sigband, Norman B. *Effective Report Writing for Business, Industry, and Government.* New York: Harper & Row, 1960.

Smith, Alfred G. *Communication and Culture.* New York: Holt, Rinehart & Winston, 1966.

U.S. Department of Commerce. *Our Growing Population.* Washington, D.C.: U.S. Government Printing Office, 1961.

QUESTIONS FOR STUDY

I. Answer the following questions and list the reference source from which you secured the information.

1. What articles appeared on Information Systems in the first two months of last year?

2. What books were published last year on Communications? Limit your list to five titles.

3. How many automobiles were registered in your state last year?

4. Who is the present director of the United States Department of Health, Education, and Welfare?

5. How many students are registered in your state's public university?

6. List those pamphlets which have been published in the last twelve months on the topic of the Poverty Program, Civil Disorders, or Riot Control (choose one topic).

7. What articles did the *Wall Street Journal* have on tariffs in the two months previous to this one?

8. Select a large corporation and then cite the names of the major officers.

II. Answer the following questions and list the reference source from which you secured the information.

1. List pertinent biographical data on the president of your school.

2. What books appeared last year on Unidentified Flying Objects?

3. What articles appeared in the *New York Times* last month on American Foreign Policy (limit to five)?

4. List several books (and their publication dates) which have been concerned with the assassination of John F. Kennedy.

5. How many persons were estimated to be unemployed in your state last year?

6. What libraries in a nearby urban center have files of a major journal in your primary field of interest (list journal title)?

7. How many employees work for the Lockheed Corporation? (Or select some other major corporation for the same question.)

8. What publications were issued last year by the United States Government in your major area of study (limit to five publications)?

III. Answer the following questions briefly.

1. Define the following terms as concisely as possible.
   Sampling   Reliability
   Universe   Random sample

2. Secure a directory in an area of your interest (product manufacture or professional listing) and briefly list its title and the types of information and services it offers.

3. Visit the research division of an advertising agency and determine what types of primary research it uses to secure information on consumer buying habits. Present your findings in a brief report.

4. Visit an opinion research agency and determine what types of primary research it uses to secure information on voters' political preferences. Present your findings in a brief report.

5. What type of questionnaire survey would you use and why to determine:

   (1) Opinions of a specific economic group on a specific TV program?
   (2) Student opinion on the university's administrative organization?
   (3) Air passenger reaction to baggage handling?
   (4) Corporate officers' opinions of Company Profit-Sharing Programs?
   (5) The opinions of management of a specific firm on the effectiveness of that company's internal communication?

6. Secure a questionnaire and then offer your constructive criticism. Divide your criticism into:

   (1) the cover letter;
   (2) the format of the questionnaire;
   (3) the questions, noting *specific* factors in *specific* questions which can be improved or have been handled very well.

7. Find an advertising agency that has used a premium of some type to motivate individuals to respond to a specific questionnaire. Write a brief report on how effective the questionnaire survey proved to be and your analysis of the results. Attempt to secure a sample of the cover letter and questionnaire and attach them to your report.

IV. Offer your constructive criticism of the two cover letters which follow:

1. Dear Mr. _____ :

For some time we have wondered if we could possibly change our delivery schedule to our dealers in the Southern California area from two trips per week to one.

We are aware, of course, that you find a twice-per-week delivery convenient. However, if we can satisfy your needs through a once-per-week call, the savings which we will achieve will be very substantial. These savings can then be passed on to you and our other dealers.

However, we don't wish to influence you one way or another with our comments. Won't you please complete the enclosed questionnaire and return it before January 4 in the stamped envelope enclosed.

2. Dear Mrs. _____ :

There are cake mixes with all the ingredients and some with half the ingredients; there are mixes that require that you only open the box and pour, and abracadabra, the cake is almost done. And there are others which require mixing, stirring, rolling, and folding.

We wonder what your preferences are and we hope you will share your opinions with us. Of course our objective is to bring you Tasty Cake mixes exactly the way you want them.

The enclosed questionnaire will only take a few minutes of your time to complete and . . . oh yes, the certificate will be accepted by your food-store manager in exchange for two free packages of Tasty Cake Mix . . . with our compliments, of course.

V. Complete the assignments which follow:

1. Write a careful criticism of the questionnaire used in the sample formal report in Chapter Nine. The questionnaire is on pages 255-258. Include in your evaluation the appropriateness of the questionnaire for its purpose; the logic and clarity of the questions; and the appearance of the questionnaire.

2. Evaluate the questionnaire on p. 115 using criteria similar to those listed in question 1 above.

3. Evaluate the cover letter and questionnaire which are concerned with rumors (p. 116). Use the criteria noted in question 1 above and in this chapter.

VI. Write the cover letter and questionnaire for each of the following problems:

1. Assume you are the manager of communications of the Gotz Corporation. In the past two months you have noticed a large number of the company's monthly magazines discarded in the employee area. There are also fewer than the usual number being picked up from the racks provided. Send a cover letter and questionnaire to the home of each employee asking him to complete and return the questionnaire. The questionnaire is designed to secure his feelings and viewpoints on the value of the company magazine. Design both the cover letter and questionnaire.

2. Design a brief questionnaire in which you attempt to secure the opinion of part-time graduate students on Saturday classes. If graduate classes were offered on Saturdays, how many students would enroll for them? Would students enroll in such classes in place of present evening classes, or would they be "in addition to"?

3. Send a questionnaire to a selected sample of homeowners in the Bellpark suburban area just outside of Chicago. Attempt to find out if the respondents would be interested in subscribing to a private home protective and patrol service if it were established. The service would cost approximately $50.00 per month. Of course it would be fully licensed by the city. Bellpark homeowners are in the upper-middle and upper economic classes.

4. Your busy travel agency has booked a good many tourist vacation trips to the Far East and Europe in the last five years. You wonder if it would be wise for you to offer a chartered trip this summer to the Near East. Send a questionnaire to a selected sample of your patrons attempting to determine how many would be interested in an inexpensive chartered trip to the Near East, and what month in the summer they would prefer to go.

(The following questionnaire was sent to the graduating students of a large, private midwestern university by an airline.)

1. On the average, how many times each semester did you return home for visits? _____

2. What method of transportation did you usually use?

   _____   _____
   auto   plane

   _____   _____
   bus   rail

3. What is the approximate distance from campus to your home?   _____ miles

4. Which mode of transportation would you have preferred for such trips?

   _____   _____
   auto   plane

   _____   _____
   bus   rail

5. Were it available, what would your reaction be to buying a booklet entitling you to four round trips in a semester for the price of three?

   _____
   very interested

   _____
   somewhat interested

   _____
   not interested

6. Were it available, what would your reaction be to buying a booklet entitling you to six round trips in an academic year for the price of five?

   _____
   very interested

   _____
   somewhat interested

   _____
   not interested

Company Name
Company Address
City and State

Attn.: Mr.

Dear Mr.

One of the most active lines of communication in corporations today is the grapevine, through its medium, the rumor. The problem with this informal communications network is that most often its information is inaccurate and causes uneasiness and feelings of insecurity among employees.

I am an advanced graduate student at the University of Southern California. In partial fulfillment of a course in communications, I have chosen to study the grapevine and rumor, mainly through contacting corporations directly. It is my objective to find out how companies look at this area of communications and their policies for dealing with it.

A lack of similar research material in this area recently has prompted me to contact you. I need your help, and would be very much obliged to you if you could find an opportunity to complete the enclosed questionnaire within the next ten days. A stamped, self-addressed envelope is included for your convenience.

I would like to assure you that this questionnaire is completely anonymous; please do not sign it. All the information you supply will be kept in the strictest confidence and will not be used in connection with your company's name.

I would appreciate your assistance very much.

Yours very truly,

George M. Carrick

A QUESTIONNAIRE CONCERNING CORPORATE GRAPEVINES AND RUMORS
PLEASE COMPLETE AND RETURN BY TUESDAY, DECEMBER 19, 19____

Note: The whole informal communications network in a company is known as the *grapevine*, and *rumor* is the speculative, unwise, or untrue message it carries.

1. Have you ever had a study done within your company to examine the presence and effects of grapevines and their rumors?

    Yes _____ No _____

    If yes, (a) Who did it?

    (b) How was it done?

2. With grapevines, do you attempt to:

    Eliminate them completely? _____
    Integrate their interests with those of your company? _____
    Let them operate at will? _____

3. Are rumors a problem in your company as a barrier to efficient operations?

    Yes _____ No _____

4. Do you have any formal method for uncovering rumors and recording them?

    Yes _____ No _____

    If yes, please explain: _____

    _____

5. Do you instruct or discuss with your supervisory personnel the dynamics of rumor and what should be done to handle it?

    Yes _____ No _____

    If yes, please explain: _____

    _____

6. Do you try to stop

    All rumors? _____
    Just potentially injurious rumors? _____
    None of the rumors? _____

7. What steps does your company take to prevent harmful rumors? Please explain.

    (a) Through top management _____

    _____

    (b) Through staff employees _____

    _____

    (c) Through line employees _____

    _____

8. What subjects do the rumors in your company seem to emphasize? Please rank in apparent descending order of importance from 1 through 9:

    Union relations . . . . _____
    Lay-offs . . . . _____
    Pay scales. . . . . _____
    Processes that are designated "secret"
        or "confidential" . . . . _____
    Feelings about supervisors . . . . _____
    Employee transfers within company . . . . _____
    Fringe benefits . . . . _____
    Working conditions . . . . _____
    Other (please specify) . . . . _____

9. Does your company have a formal procedure for dealing with rumors?

    Yes _____ No _____

10. Please indicate if your company utilizes any of the following techniques for dealing with rumors:

    Yes   No

    (b) Providing those whom you regard as
        key communicators of rumors with the
        true facts about the rumor . . . . ____   ____

    (a) Positive presentation of fact upon fact
        about the content of the rumor to all
        employees . . . . ____   ____

    (c) Confronting the source of the rumor
        early and getting an explanation . . . . . ____   ____

(d) Requesting the help of the union . . . . . ___ ___

(e) Other (please specify) . . . . ___ ___

11. Please indicate if your company attempts to halt rumors from starting by practicing the following:

Yes   No

(a) Guarding against idleness and monotony among employees . . . . ___ ___

(b) Developing faith among employees in the credibility and source of management's communications . . . . . ___ ___

(c) Making rumors a topic for discussion in supervisory training programs . . . . . ___ ___

(d) Keeping all channels of communication open to employees for questions . . . . ___ ___

(e) Encouraging free communication between subordinate and superior about company operations . . . . ___ ___

(f) Providing supervisory personnel with up-to-date information about the company's future plans . . . . ___ ___

(g) Keeping the employee who is to be promoted, demoted, or transferred up-to-date on the latest plans the company has for him in the near future . . . . ___ ___

(h) Other (please specify) . . . . ___ ___

Thank you very much for your time and effort in completing this questionnaire. You may be assured that your answers and any comments you may have added will be kept in the strictest confidence, and in no way used with reference to your company.

VII. Unscramble the following and enter footnotes for each in the order given.

1. Gary A. Steiner, Harcourt, Brace and World, Inc., 1964, New York, Bernard Berelson, p. 205, *Human Behavior.*

2. Yale University Press, *Communication and Persuasion,* Carl I. Hovland, *et. al.,* New Haven, Connecticut, p. 105, 1953.

3. Eugene Walton, p. 47, March—April 1961, "How Efficient Is the Grapevine?" *Personnel,* Volume 38, No. 2.

4. Gary A. Steiner, p. 208, Bernard Berelson, *Human Behavior,* Harcourt, Brace and World, Inc., New York, 1964.

5. *Harvard Business Review,* "Management Communication and the Grapevine," September-October 1953, No. 5, p. 45, Volume 31, Keith Davis.

6. Keith Davis, September-October 1953, Volume 31, No. 5, p. 45, "Management Communication and the Grapevine," *Harvard Business Review.*

7. February 1966, page 103, volume 45, George S. Odiorne, *Personnel Journal,* "How Superstitions in Business Are Created," No. 2.

8. *Business Communications Reader,* J. Harold Janis (ed.), Harper & Row, Publishers, 1958, p. 210, New York.

VIII. Unscramble the following and enter footnotes for each in the order given.

1. Page 49, October 1961, *Journal of Marketing,* Aaron J. Spector, "Basic Dimensions of the Corporate Image."

2. Identical reference to footnote 1 except that page 50 was used.

3. *Printers' Ink,* page 53, Gerald Stahl, "How to Define and Get Identity," March 8, 1963.

4. John W. Riley, Jr., (ed.), New York, 1963, page 150, John Wiley and Sons, Inc., *The Corporation and its Publics: Essays on the Corporate Image.*

5. October 1959, p. 9, *Journal of Marketing*, John F. Bolger, Jr., "How to Evaluate Your Company Image."

6. Identical reference to footnote 4 except that page 180 was used.

7. August 1967, p. 19, *Public Relations Journal*, J. S. Macleod, "The Emphasis Is on Corporate Reputation."

8. Page 64, *Journal of Marketing*, W. T. Tucker, January 1961, "How Much of the Corporate Image Is Stereotype?"

CHAPTER FIVE

Planning, Organizing, and Outlining

Good organization and preparation are the keys to the success of a great many activities in our society. A plan, logically organized and carefully prepared, is vital if a space shot is to function properly, a building is to be erected solidly, a surgical procedure carried through successfully, or a piece of oral or written communication presented effectively. There are few activities, from baking a cake to sending a man into orbit, which take place without a plan or blueprint. But often we write or speak without following a plan, and of course we should not.

How often have you thrown down a magazine, slammed shut a book, snapped off the television set, or tapped someone on the chest with a "Well, what's the point?" How often have you lost interest in an article, a report, or a speech because the communication directed to you seemed to be going in circles? Perhaps you have asked yourself why your attention and interest flagged. The answer might be that the communication was not organized, not planned, not outlined.

THE PRELIMINARY PLAN

An exposition of ideas which proceeds logically and clearly is easy to follow and appreciate. It holds our attention and enables us to look for the facts that concern us. It is for this reason that the intelligent person who wishes to transmit his ideas with clarity and force will design some plan or outline for his communication before he attempts to convey his thoughts to you.

Normally the communicator will formulate two outlines: a tentative one which he will develop as he thinks about his problem and carries through preliminary research, and a final one from which he will write his finished paper. This latter outline will be completed after research, thought, and analysis have indicated necessary changes in the original plan.

FIRST STEPS

Before you can write even a tentative outline, there are several questions you must answer: What is the primary purpose of your letter, report, memo? To whom is it addressed? What are its limitations? What is its scope?

Determining Your Purpose

With almost every communication, we must decide, before we plan the content, "What is the primary purpose of this message?" If we are replying to an inquiry letter, we must recognize that the primary purpose is to answer the inquiry, in either an informative or persuasive way, not offer a sales appeal for the firm's new product, or dun for payment of a past due bill. When we establish the primary purpose of a communication, the organizational pattern for it begins to fall into place.

For example, a letter arrives from a customer asking for our firm's credit terms. Our purpose is simply to *inform* him of our credit terms, and we would organize our reply one way:

1. Acknowledge letter requesting credit terms.
2. Spell out our credit terms in detail.
3. Friendly close.

However, if the customer is asking *for* credit, and we discover that his asset-liability ratio is unsatisfactory, our purpose will be to *persuade* the customer to accept an alternative (e.g., c.o.d. instead of credit), and we would organize our reply differently:

1. Acknowledge letter requesting credit.
2. Explain why it would be of benefit to the customer to improve his asset-liability ratio.
3. Offer c.o.d., explaining its advantages. (The refusal to extend credit is *implicit* in the positive statements made here.)
4. Friendly close.

Dear Mr. Baxter:

Thank you for your letter of August 5 and your request for an open account with our company.

We have checked the data you sent us. Because your store

is relatively new, and your present fixture and construction expenses heavy, we feel it would be to your benefit to improve your asset-liability ratio at this time. As a matter of fact, the Northwest Furniture Association recommends that for safe financial planning, all dealers maintain a 2-to-1 asset-liability ratio.

You can therefore appreciate why we recommend that you permit us to send you your order #214 on a c.o.d. basis. This method assures you of an immediate profit-making 2 per cent discount, a lower inventory level, and no month-end bills.

We are sure you will be delighted with the service and the quality of the merchandise you receive from the Crawford Corporation. We will certainly do everything possible to make your association with us pleasant and profitable.

Please call me collect, Mr. Baxter, and I will start your order on its way to you immediately.

By following this procedure, the correspondent need not say, "Therefore we cannot . . . ," "We find it impossible . . . ," or "We must refuse . . . ." Under ordinary circumstances, if the writer first explains the reason for the refusal, that negative statement need be only implied rather than directly stated.

Identifying Your Reader

Before beginning your plan, you must ask yourself: Who is the prospective reader? At what level shall I write? Should the discussion, charts, graphs, and related materials be presented in a simple or a complex fashion? Is the reader one of the persons involved in financing this building project, a relatively uninterested shareholder who owns three shares of stock, or is he the consulting architect? Will this serve as a release to the newspapers for publicity purposes, or is it to be a detailed report to the board of directors? The level and amount of detail will surely differ for each.

As the reader and level differ, so will the outline. The organizational plan may well change according to the reader. In this case, a chronological approach, which is relatively easy to follow, may be better, while in that one, a cause-and-effect or persuasive plan may be appropriate. More technical detail will be included in one organizational plan, and less in another; or complicated financial facts will be part of one outline but not of another. And there may be other variations reflected in the outline, concerning visual aids, financial data, and length and detail of the narrative. In this way the outline (and therefore the final paper) is designed with the reader in mind.

Defining Scope and Limitations

The next step in building the tentative outline is to choose the major topics to be covered. These are foundation blocks upon which the entire paper will be constructed.

Let us say, for example, that our paper will be concerned with "The Marketing of Our Product in Western Europe." We may choose six major areas for examination:

Market acceptance
Competition
Advertising and sales promotion
Method of distribution
Legal restrictions
Cost of distribution

These six points are probably not arranged in their most logical order, but we do know that they will be the major areas for analysis and investigation in this paper. They become the major headings in our tentative outline.

Now we can begin to divide each one into fairly obvious sub-categories:

Market acceptance
    Housewives
    The teenage market
    Institutional purchasers
    Governmental agencies
Competition
    From similar local products
        Brand A
        Brand B
        Brand C
    From North American products
        Brand AA
        Brand BB
        Brand CC
        Brand DD
    From similar products manufactured abroad
Advertising and sales promotion
    To the consumer
        Newspaper
        Radio
        Television

Direct mail
Point of sales
Miscellaneous
To the distributor
Trade publications
Direct mail
Sales force
Miscellaneous
Etc.

Each of the major points has been subdivided, as indicated above, into subpoints. Those can be further divided. But the important fact to note is the method of developing an organizational plan. Always begin by listing your major topics for discussion and examination. These form the general foundation blocks of the paper. It is only after the major areas have been identified that the writer should move to develop each into subdivisions.

It is a fairly simple matter to list the major points in an analysis. They are usually the specific questions which need to be answered. For example, let us say we are faced with a presentation on "Whether we should undertake to manufacture new product X." The obvious questions which arise are: Do we have the facilities to manufacture it? Is there a market for it? What competition exists? What costs will we incur? What advantages do we stand to gain?

Each of these questions can be easily reworded into a more succinct major topic heading, and then the subpoints under each developed. Let's try another topic for presentation. This time let us assume that we are faced with "The Advisability of Publishing and Distributing a Monthly Employee Magazine." Some of the primary questions to be answered here are: Will such a publication make a significant contribution to employee morale? What will the annual cost of such a venture be? What personnel must we secure to handle the project? What alternatives may accomplish similar ends? What are the experiences in this area of similar industries? Here again, subtopics may now be developed under each major topic.

The writer should not select one major point, develop it into several subordinate points, and these into further subcategories. If he does this, he may well become too involved with a detailed organizational plan for one point, rather than a fairly equal developmental plan for all points in his paper.

Before the investigator proceeds too far in his analysis and the development of his organizational plan, he should check his boundaries and limits. Certainly there is no point in his carrying through research on the first problem above in the area of "Legal restrictions" if it is not necessary. Perhaps the legal restrictions in this instance have been determined and are part of company records already. Or the legal restrictions are known to be minor and are not worth the time and effort to investigate. If an area need not be pursued, for any reason, certainly time and energy should not be expended on it.

The number and content of subtopics must also be limited. There is no need to investigate competition from similar products manufactured throughout the world, or those manufactured in North America, or those manufactured in western Europe, if we will only be concerned with competition from similar products manufactured in France.

The writer who is careful to limit his topic before he becomes too deeply involved in research is wise. Limiting a topic has at least two distinct advantages:

1. An investigation into a narrow area will produce more meaningful results for the serious investigator than a survey of a broad topic. Compare "An analysis of electricity as a fuel for heating purposes" and "An analysis of the specific advantages of electric heat for the new Candle Towers building."

2. Once your limits are defined, your research can be more selective. Areas which are not relevant are not examined; data which are not directly related are discarded; and unnecessary notes are not taken. All attention and effort are focused on the narrow objective.

Limitation of the subject area is vital if the communicator is to get to the heart of his planning and investigation and not dissipate his efforts.

In our research and investigation, we are always limited as to the depth of our inquiry. What are our objectives? How definitive must the study be? What are the needs of the reader? How much time, money, and strength do we have available and expendable on this project? What level of reliability do we need?

Let us say we are writing a report on "The Advisability of Constructing a New Plant in Bennington, Ohio." Our major foundation blocks for investigation are:

Labor
Physical plant
Market
Source of raw materials
Financing
Community attitude
Availability of utilities
Tax structure
Transportation facilities

Our further development of one of these—transportation facilities—results in the following outline:

Transportation facilities
    Shipment of finished products
        Rail
            Santa Fe Railroad
            Southern Pacific Railroad
        Truck
            Commercial trucking firms
            Company trucks
            Leased trucks
        Air
            Commercial air freight
            Chartered air freight
    Comparative analysis
        Cost
            Rail
            Truck
            Air
        Shipment time
            Rail
            Truck
            Air
    Analyses of roads, air terminals,
    water and rail facilities
        Roads
            Freeways, highways, major roads
            Secondary roads
            Access roads (to plant)
        Air terminals (75 mile-radius)
            Passenger
            Freight
        Water facilities
            Ports (import-export)
            Rivers (raw material; bulk products)
        Rail facilities
            Track spurs (on company property)
                Condition
                Ownership
            Terminals
                Railroad companies involved
                Accessibility
            Receiving and shipping points

                    Employee transporation
                        Public
                            Commercial bus routes
                            Rapid transit
                        Private
                            Individual automobiles
                            Car pools
                            Routes to and from residential areas
                        Cost analysis

Now the question is: Shall we carry through an investigation of transportation facilities to the depth indicated above? If there is no need to investigate employee transportation, for example, why should we go into such detail? To do so will waste our time and efforts and disturb the reader who has no need or desire to be informed on the topic to this depth.

REVIEWING THE FIRST STEPS

So we now see that the tentative outline is the result of general thinking and overall analysis of the limits of our investigation and the scope of the topics within the areas selected. Let us review quickly the steps in our organizational development of the subject:

Purpose: Just what is the problem? Is it to compare two systems? Is it to analyze a situation? Is it to cite information for record-keeping purposes? Is it to sell a course of action to a prospect? To explain a technical procedure to a reader? To defend and argue for the acceptance of a procedure?

Reader: Is the reader of the message a technically oriented engineer or a business-minded member of the board of directors? Is he a potential customer or a steady account?

Limitation and Scope: Has the topic been accurately limited on the basis of the reader's needs, desires, and level? Has the depth of the research and of the report, letter, or speech been properly determined?

The tentative outline is developed, of course, as the writer carries through the steps above. At no time should he hesitate to add to or delete from the outline or change its order to a more logical form. The outline is completely flexible and should be treated as a guide to be shaped, changed, and molded as the need arises.

THE FINAL PLAN

As the writer carries through investigation in his primary and secondary sources, he will find that some of the points in his tentative outline are not logical or possible to complete. Conversely, he will discover in his sources that areas which should have been included in his tentative outline were omitted. And so he revises, changes, and polishes his outline until he is satisfied that this point-by-point guide will result in a clear and logically presented paper. This new outline, then, is the final copy that is used as a basis for the preparation of the report or letter. It is often appreciably different from the original outline the writer developed.

In our discussion of the principles of organization, let us answer three questions:

1. What are the values and functions of the outline procedure?
2. What are the mechanics of making up an outline?
3. What are the types of outlines and the methods for their development?

VALUE OF AN OUTLINE

Too often individuals feel that drawing up an outline prior to the presentation of the report or speech is an extra and unnecessary step. "Why," they ask, "should I go through the work? Why not just write the report or prepare the talk?"

There are several very good answers to that question:

1. The writer is assured of the *logical* development of his report, if his outline is logical. It is simple, for example, to move point B under IV to another section of the outline, if an analysis of the organization so indicates. Think how much more difficult it is to move that section after the report has been completed. But when it is done during the outline stage, little effort is involved. And it is much easier to expand or reduce section III in the outline than in the finished report.

The brief example at the top of p. 131 illustrates how easy it is to make changes in the outline to secure a more logical plan.

2. The *proportion* of one part of the outline to the other sections can be easily evaluated. If a section is out of proportion—with either too many or too few data—it is easier to make the correction in the outline than it is in the finished presentation.

Employee Fringe Benefits
I. Insurance Programs
    A. Hospitalization
    B. Major medical
    C. Life
II. Paid Holidays
    A. Seven specific national holidays
    B. Vacation with pay
III. Pension Plan
    A. Company retirement program
    B. Social security
IV. Miscellaneous
    A. Sick leave
    B. Annuity program (employee-sponsored)
    C. Discount purchase of merchandise
    D. Surgical coverage (employee-sponsored)

Employee Training at Allied Telephone
I. Employee Training in the Fairview Plant
    A. Executive training
    B. Engineering training
    C. Shop supervisory training
        1. Leadership classes for superintendents
        2. Foreman training
    D. Office personnel training
        1. Written communications
        2. Office equipment training
II. Employee Training at the Leance Plant
    A. Executive training
    B. Engineering training
        1. Electronic control systems
        2. Engineering cost control
    C. Shop supervisory training
        1. Leadership classes for superintendents
        2. Foreman training
        3. Interpersonal relations
III. Employee training at the Rodman Plant
    A. Executive training
        1. Organizational policy
        2. Effective communication
    B. Engineering training
        1. Electronic control systems

      2. Engineering cost control
      3. Engineering economics
   C. Shop supervisory training
   D. Office personnel training
IV. Employee Training at the Stone Plant
   A. Executive training
   B. Engineering training
      1. Engineering cost analysis
      2. Operations research
      3. Manufacturing processes
        a. Heat treatment of alloys
        b. Casting and molding
        c. Material joining
        d. Metal surface treatment
        e. Material cleaning
      4. Computer use
        a. Analog and digital
        b. Computer codes
        c. Programming principles
   C. Shop supervisory training
V. Employee Training at the Maywell Plant
   A. Executive training
      1. Organizational policy
      2. Effective communication
   B. Engineering training
      1. Engineering statistics
      2. Operations research
   C. Shop supervisory training
   D. Office personnel training

It would appear, in the numbered outline above, that point B under IV has been developed to an extent out of proportion to the other topics. If all the material *is* needed, then perhaps a new major heading should be included; if all the details are not necessary, they should be excised mercilessly. Roman numeral IV will then be in better proportion to the other major headings.

    3. The communicator can use the outline to check on the *completeness* of his own presentation. It is certainly simple to evaluate an outline to determine if all the necessary points have been covered; if they have not, additional items may be inserted easily. But the story is different when one must weld missing paragraphs into a completed paper.

    4. The communicator can evaluate the *order of development* he employed. This is closely related to logic, as discussed above. There

must be some method of logical development to any presentation: chronological, geographical, cause and effect, etc. Here again, it is easier to check the outline and correct inconsistencies than it is to rework the finished paper.

5. An outline *saves time.* This fact is obvious. As the communicator evaluates his outline, he can quickly make additions, deletions, corrections, and revisions. How much more effort is required — and how much more inconvenient it is — to take the same action on a finished paper.

In industry, time and money are frequently equated. Here is Mr. Lowell preparing to answer a letter he has just received from customer Barton. Barton has asked Lowell several specific questions: the availability of the Acme filing cabinets, what colors are in stock, the cost, possible trade-in value of the used cabinets on hand, and details on the construction of the Acme. He further wants to know why the credit of $18.50 that he requested three weeks ago has not been acted on. And, in addition, does Lowell carry the new Handy-Dollar payroll envelopes?

This is a typical business letter to which Mr. Lowell should reply *after* he has made a brief outline of what he will discuss and in what order. But does he make up a little scratch outline? Oh, no. He's much too busy. He seizes the microphone of his dictating unit and replies to customer Barton.

Unfortunately, Lowell forgets to tell Barton the price on the Acme cabinets and he neglects to comment on the $18.50 bill. Yet when Lowell's secretary brings the letter in for signing several hours after it was dictated, the dealer quickly signs it (probably without reading it), and feels that he did a good job.

But, of course, Barton is irritated with the reply he receives and angry with Mr. Lowell. The price of the cabinets was not mentioned, so he assumes they are expensive. As a result, he places his order for $750 worth of filing cabinets with a competitor of Lowell's. In addition, he must send another letter to Lowell and again inquire about the $18.50.

Lowell, because he didn't plan his letter, has lost a sizable and profitable sale and the good will of customer Barton and caused himself the needless expense of writing additional letters. Had Mr. Lowell just taken the time to formulate and check a brief outline such as the following, he would have saved time, money, and a customer:

1. Acknowledge Barton's inquiry letter of December 3
2. Indicate that Acme filing cabinets are available and are on sale
3. Cite details on Acme cabinets
    size
    fireproof, tamperproof

   individual drawer locks
   easy roll drawers
   various colors available
   cost
4. Special price; therefore no trade-ins
5. Explain $18.50 credited on October bill (include photocopy)
6. Cite data and sales appeal on Handy-Dollar payroll envelopes
7. Offer to ship filing cabinets within 24 hours of a collect call
8. Friendly close

Based on this outline, Mr. Lowell will probably dictate a letter much like the following:

Dear Mr. Barton:

  Thank you very much for your letter of December 3 concerning the Acme File Cabinets. Yes, they certainly are available and what's more, they are on sale until December 15.

  This new Acme Cabinet is available in either the four- or five-drawer model. Its all-metal construction is fireproof and the new individual drawer locks by Guardian assure that it is also tamperproof. The roller-bearing drawers make it a delight for the girls and it is available in any one of three decorator colors to match or complement your office decor: gray, blue, and pink.

  Ordinarily priced at $59.50 each, the four-drawer model is being specially offered at $52.50 each or four units for $199.00. The five-drawer model is available at $55.00 each or four for $210.

  Because of the special price, Mr. Barton, used cabinets are not being accepted on the Acme for any trade-in value.

  As for the Handy-Dollar payroll envelopes—yes, we do stock them. In fact, we are the exclusive outlet for them in the Chicago area. The enclosed circular lists all sizes available and the prices. Just check the quantities desired and we'll ship them out.

  You did ask about an $18.50 credit on your order #2161. This credit was made on your October invoice. You'll note it circled in red on the attached photocopy.

  It's been a pleasure giving you this information, Mr. Barton. Just call me collect, and I'll ship the Acme Cabinets out immediately. I know you will be delighted with this quality product which will give you years of satisfactory service.

OUTLINE MECHANICS

How you design your outline is often a matter of personal preference. Some people prefer an elaborate numbering system of Roman numerals and letters all carefully arranged on clean, white stationery; others simply indent subordinate ideas under major headings and find the back of an envelope a convenient place to write. Because most of the mechanics of organizing are personal, and most of us eventually develop our own system, the discussion of mechanics that follows will necessarily be brief.

Designating Major and Minor Points

It is always wise to arrange the items in your outline so that a glance will reveal major areas as opposed to minor ones. It is helpful to think of the most important points as the key ideas and the subordinating ones as items of substantiating evidence.

The most frequently used numbering system is the numeral-letter combination. Roman numerals are used for major points, capital letters for subtopics, and Arabic numerals and lower-case letters for smaller topics. If a further breakdown is necessary, Arabic numerals and letters enclosed in parentheses are used.

I. First Main Heading
   A. First subtopic under main heading
   B. Second subtopic under main heading
      1. First subtopic under B
      2. Second subtopic under B
         a. First subtopic under 2
         b. Second subtopic under 2
            (1) First subtopic under b
            (2) Second subtopic under b
               (a) First subtopic under (2)
               (b) Second subtopic under (2)
II. Second Main Heading

The decimal style is favored by engineers as well as others in science and technology. This system is logical, easy to use, and affords a quick method for referring to specific points.

1. First Main Heading
   1.1 First subtopic under first main heading
   1.2 Second subtopic under first main heading
      1.21 First subtopic under 1.2
      1.22 Second subtopic under 1.2

           1.221 First subtopic under 1.22
           1.222 Second subtopic under 1.22
2. Second Main Heading
    2.1 First subtopic under second main heading
    2.2 Second subtopic under second main heading
        2.21 First subtopic under 2.2
        2.22 Second subtopic under 2.2
3. Third Main Heading
    3.1 First subtopic under third main heading
    3.2 Second subtopic under third main heading
    3.3 Third subtopic under third main heading
        3.31 First subtopic under 3.3
        3.32 Second subtopic under 3.3

There are other methods of outlining, such as simple indentation and the use of specialized symbols. Any system which is accurate, permits easy analysis, and works for you is the one you should use.

Ensuring Parallel Development

In designing the outline, give items of equal importance similar levels of designation under major headings. Thus if "cost of materials" is an immediate subhead to Roman numeral I, it would hardly seem possible that under Roman numeral II "cost of materials" should slip to a sub-subtopic. Points of parallel interest should be listed at similar levels in the outline.

In the brief outline that follows, similar topics are treated under the same level of heading. This assists the reader to follow the organizational plan of development.

Comparison of Employee Communication Media Used at the
Baxter and Condon Companies

 I. Oral Communication at the Baxter Company
    A. Management-supervisor level
        1. Weekly staff meetings
        2. Monthly conferences for each division
    B. Plant-wide assemblies
        1. Meeting held prior to Christmas party
        2. Periodic, to announce major changes or discuss issues affecting all workers
    C. Supervisor-worker level
        1. On-the-job instructions
        2. Twice-yearly merit review
II. Written Communication at the Baxter Company
    A. Company magazine

       1. Content
       2. Frequency of issue
   B. Company orientation booklets
       1. For management and supervisory personnel
       2. For hourly workers
   C. Bulletin board notices
   D. Letters to employees from management
III. Oral Communication at the Condon Company
   A. Management-supervisor level
       1. Weekly staff meetings
       2. Monthly conferences for each division
   B. No plant-wide assemblies have been held
   C. Supervisor-worker level
       1. On-the-job instructions
       2. Yearly merit review
       3. Monthly council meetings
IV. Written Communication at the Condon Company
   A. Company magazine
       1. Content
       2. Frequency of issue
   B. Company orientation booklet
       1. For management and supervisory personnel
       2. For hourly workers
   C. Bulletin board notices
   D. Annual report for employees

Avoiding Overlapping of Ideas

If headings and subheadings are chosen properly, there should be little overlapping of ideas.

If a paper were written from the following outline, there would surely be overlapping in the area of health and health insurance. The result would be a poorly organized, repetitious, and uninteresting analysis. However, if the outline is checked, edited, and revised, the paper that results may have merit.

An Analysis of Employee Fringe Benefits

    I. Insurance Programs
   II. Retirement Programs
  III. Blue Cross Hospitalization Plan
  IV. Employee Discount Purchase Plan
   V. Major Medical Insurance Program
  VI. Time Off with Compensation
 VII. Yearly Health Examination
VIII. Paid Holidays As Indicated in Union Contract

Using a Consistent and Logical Order of Development

Whether your communication is long or short, written or oral, simple or complex, your desire is that it be understood and accepted. This obviously requires that you analyze the content of the message, the nature of the audience, and the purpose you hope to achieve. You go through these steps to secure the most logical order of development for your message. This attribute of logic is vital, for regardless of the excellence of your word choice, the clarity of your sentences, and the appearance of the report, all will fail if the message lacks logic.

The critical businessman may well overlook a misplaced comma or a faulty phrase. But if the presentation lacks logic, the ideas then become suspect, and the reader is reluctant to accept any part of the message, or he may simply "tune himself out." You have certainly read a presentation and then suddenly noted that "this doesn't follow; it's not logical; I can't accept it."

Obviously we cannot hope that all we speak or write will be accepted, but when it is rejected because we *did not present it logically*, then the fault is ours.

Logic in Interpretation. The business communicator must exercise logic in his thinking and in his interpretation of the data which he perceives. He must be cautious so that he does not:

1. Assume that items which are alike in some respects are alike in all respects (Product A and B are similar in price, size, and color. Product A sells well in New York, therefore Product B will also sell well. However, this may not be true, for A and B also differ. A is made of steel, B of plastic; A is packaged in a carton, B is wrapped in paper; A is guaranteed, B is not.)
2. Assume that an item which does not conform to one situation *does* conform to another. (Although most of our respondents indicated they did not prefer a red and blue carton for Wake-up Crunchies, it does not mean they *do* prefer red and white. It may be that some prefer red and yellow or red and brown.)
3. Compare items or situations which are not comparable. (Although we found that advertising Christmas vacation flights to college students was unsuccessful in 1950, can we assume that it will be unsuccessful in 1970? Has the family unit changed? Do flights cost less? Do students have more funds for such purposes? Are "quick" vacations by air more common in 1970?)
4. Permit his bias to enter into his reasoning. (For years we have manufactured our Aristo line in aluminum and it has led all other

brands in sales. Aluminum is the best. How can the Aristo line possibly sell as well if fabricated in plastic?)

These are steps in the logic of thinking the communicator must carry through as he places his own ideas in order. The next step is to analyze his audience, his purpose, and his topic to determine the most logical order of development and presentation.

Analysis and Synthesis. Before we design a plan for presentation, we must be sure we have recognized all or most of the important factors which make up the situation or impinge on it.

Sales of our products on the West Coast have declined very dramatically. Let's *analyze*—or identify the elements—to find out why the decline has taken place: We do not have a West-Coast distribution plant; a large market for patio furniture exists on the West Coast; shipping our outdoor funiture from the Midwest is costly; freight rates for shipping have risen steadily; our West-Coast customers have complained about high shipping costs; surveys show we are not competitive on price with West-Coast manufacturers on similar lines; . . . . Thus, we began with a condition: decreased sales. We then analyzed the situation and attempted to identify the contributing factors.

Or we may be confronted by a number of diverse elements which require *synthesis*, or "putting together," to form a logical whole or pattern: Production has declined very rapidly since the early part of June. Employees have complained about the level of illumination in the production area; a new foreman of the section took over in May; the presses in that department have outdated and slow safety equipment; compensation is on a piece-rate basis; the lead man (assistant foreman) was discharged after he and the new foreman had a severe argument on June 1 . . . . Can these various facts be related or synthesized with each other into some pattern that would result in an overall theme?

Chronological. Here we should select a specific period of time and move forward with our discussion. Perhaps we would want to point out that sales in Area 3 were $80,000 in 1950; five years later they doubled; by 1960 they were over $200,000. In 1965 they reached a quarter of a million dollars and have been steadily rising since. This would all indicate that for the period 1970-75 we should make a much heavier advertising and personnel committment, in the expectation that sales will continue to increase.

Here is a firm that is for sale. On the surface it appears to be a good buy. However, it is important for us to look at its "track record" and note its progress since its formation in 1950. What was its situation in 1950: level of sales, profit figures, number of personnel, product lines, physical plant, development activities, etc.? How did these same areas measure up five years, ten years, and fifteen years later? What trends are indicated as we come to the present? Was there a steady rise over this period of time? Was a plateau reached? Was there a strong decline? If so, in what areas? Details should be added in each of the areas (level of sales, profit figures, number of personnel, product lines, physical plant, development activities) to give unity to the report. However, the order of development of the entire report is chronological, as the message moves forward in five-year blocks from 1950 to the present.

Geographical. In this method we begin at one location and then move to the next. If we are analyzing sales for a corporation that has four district sales offices, and sales headquarters in New York, it would seem logical to begin with a discussion of the activities of the New York office, then go on to an examination of the Chicago office; on to Waterloo, Iowa; to Denver; and finally to Los Angeles. Or we might look at warehousing facilities in Camden, Fort Wayne, and Dallas before analyzing what they should be in the new warehouse going up in San Francisco.

If the report involved an overseas operation, it would seem more logical to treat each European outlet—Paris, Frankfurt, and Brussels—before looking at Addis Ababa, Leopoldville, and Johannesburg.

Spatial. Here the order of development moves from one logical space designation to another. In a plant area, areas might be designated as administrative, manufacturing, packaging, storage, shipping, etc. If we were to examine the illumination levels (or salfety hazards, or decorating schemes, or noise levels) in the entire plant, we would first discuss the aspect in one space (administrative, for example), and then go on to each of the others.

Directional. Here we would simply describe the process or product as it moved in a predetermined direction. For example, the piece part might first be cleaned and sprayed. From there it goes to cutting and polishing. It is then sent to inspection, after which it is sent to production where diodes are attached. Again it is returned to inspection, after which it is sold, and taken from stock. These are the steps followed and the directions in which the item moves.

If we were to follow a state legislative bill from the time it was introduced in the house by a legislator to Committee A to Committee B to the senate to the executive branch to the governor, we would be describing the direction of movement of the bill.

Simple to Complex. This is a valuable method to use when we are faced with explaining a relatively involved situation to a reader who may not have a clear understanding of the fundamentals of the subject. If we begin with simple, easy-to-understand situations and gradually move to more complex areas of the same topic, the reader will be able to follow the explanation presented. If we wish to discuss a new automated production process, we might begin by explaining the fundamentals of a standard production process, then go on the principles of a semiautomated situation, and finally to the complexity of a completely automated arrangement. In writing, we could analyze the simple and parallel parts of a system and then weave them together to show the reader how the complex system is dependent on the several simple parts, and then how it operates in a complex fashion.

Inductive. This is an order of development going from particular or specific to general. Here the writer cites details, specific events, and examples, and finally arrives at a general conclusion. We might for example explain that the quality of the product was high, the price very competitive, the service excellent, and delivery fast: all of which resulted in a year of high sales.

Deductive. Here the method of development is from a general statement to particulars, details, and facts. We might begin by pointing out that a firm's primary activities are dependent on communications. From here we could point out how most external transactions are based on business letters; advertising in newspapers, radio, and TV; reports to government agencies; and proposals to potential customers. Internally, communications take place through such media as news bulletins, company magazines, management memos, interdepartmental correspondence and reports, conferences, meetings, etc.

TYPES OF OUTLINES

The two most frequently used outline forms are topic and sentence. In infrequent cases, a paragraph outline may be used. In addition to a list of items in topic, sentence, or paragraph form, the outline also has a title and a thesis sentence. This thesis sentence should state clearly and concisely the purpose or objective of the message.

Topic Outline

Each entry in a topic outline consists of a few words or a short phrase. This type of outline has several advantages: The writer can jot down ideas quickly and need not bother with structuring each thought into a sentence. With a list of brief topics, the writer has little compunction about adding several, dropping a few, or moving one from one section to another of the outline, and making other revisions as the need arises.

A disadvantage of this type of outline involves the writer's memory. When the two- and three-word headings are examined three weeks after they were written, the writer may have quite forgotten to what the cryptic phrase "Losses—unexpected circumstances" refers. Yet when that entry was made, he knew perfectly well what he wanted to discuss under that point.

A Survey of Fringe Benefits in Industry

I. Insurance Programs
  A. Life insurance programs
    1. Executive level
    2. Other employee level
  B. Hospitalization insurance
    1. Individual
    2. Family plans
  C. Major medical plans
    1. Company-sponsored
    2. Insurance company-sponsored
  D. Surgical plans
    1. Individual
    2. Family plans
II. Vacation and Holiday Plans
  A. Vacation plans
    1. Standard vacation (specific period each year for *all* employees)
    2. Nonstandard vacation
    3. Time
      a. Number of weeks associated with years of company service
      b. Specific periods of time for different levels with no reference to length of service
  B. Paid holidays
    1. In conformity with union contracts
    2. As announced by the specific organization
  C. Extended leave periods (for research, travel, illness, etc.)
    1. With compensation
    2. Without compensation
III. Annuity and Pension Plans
  A. Government-sponsored (social security)
  B. Annuity programs
    1. For executives
      a. Company-employee contributions
      b. Company contributions only
    2. For other employees

   C. Pension plans
     1. Company-sponsored programs
     2. Company-employee-sponsored programs
IV. Profit-Sharing Plans
   A. Broad coverage based on net earnings
   B. Limited employee participation

The topic outline above might serve for a brief survey report on the topic of "Fringe Benefits in Industry." The one which follows could be used as a guide by a businessman dictating a letter to one of his customers.

   Acknowledge Mr. Muldoon's order and letter of July 25
  Indicate order:
     Being processed
     Will be shipped via Illinois Central Railroad
     Scheduled to arrive M's warehouse August 8
     Order complete except #202 chairs; back-ordered
     Billing—usual account procedure
  Answer M's questions:
     Fluorescent desk lamps #105 not available; suggest new model
      #205.
     File cabinets—see p. 32, 1969 catalog
     Typewriter tables, #110, can be shipped immed.
  Close
     Sales appeal on Canon Exec. Desk sets
     Friendly close

Sentence Outline

In a sentence outline, each entry is a complete sentence. This requires that the writer structure his thoughts a little more carefully than with the topic outline. Ideas are stated rather completely and the danger of forgetting what the statement refers to is considerably lessened. A major disadvantage, however, is the predilection the writer often has for converting his sentence outline into his report. This is sometimes done through the simple expedient of connecting the sentences with a few transitional words or phrases. Of course the results are obvious and the skeleton of the outline, which shines through such a letter or report, is so apparent as to make the message hardly worth reading. However, with a little thought the writer can avoid this by remembering that the outline must serve only as a guide to the writing assignment, not as an initial effort to be converted into the final paper.

SUMMARIZING COMMENT
ON PLANNING AND ORGANIZING

The primary theme of this chapter has been: Plan and organize before you communicate.

Whether that plan is formal or informal, whether you use a Roman numeral system, a decimal system, or a simple indentation system makes no difference. The critical factor is to know where you are going, what major and minor points you will cover, and in what order you will present them.

The steps to follow in drawing up an organizational plan are usually similar regardless of the type of communication. Here are the questions the communicator might well ask himself: What are the several key points I must cover? These become the major headings in the outline. What are the details under each major point which need attention? These become the subpoints. And finally, how deeply shall I pursue or examine the topic? Or how many of the subpoints shall I cover?

Your presentation may be a detailed and exhaustive analysis of a complex problem, a relatively routine report which will be the basis for a management decision, an ordinary business letter, a memo, a speech, an oral report, a conference discussion, or any one of dozens of other communications which we are required to make in the course of a business day. But whatever it is, be sure to plan and organize it before you present it. The building which follows a carefully drawn blueprint and the communication which adheres to a logical outline are usually well-constructed products.

Always plan your communication before you present it.

QUESTIONS FOR STUDY

I. Complete any of the following problems assigned. You may wish to review the chapter and note key points before attempting to solve the problem.

1. Although most of us recognize that we should draw up a plan before we make an oral or written presentation, we often do not. Can you explain this apparent lack of logic?

2. List several factors which should be considered before designing a tentative outline.

3. What changes should be made in the following outlines to make them more logical?

(1) *Monthly Sales Report, TRM Corporation*
  I. Total Sales Volume
     A. Sales of Able Line
     B. Sales of Baker Line
     C. Sales of Charlie Line
  II. Sales Personnel
     A. Total number of salesmen
        1. District A
        2. District B
     B. Sales Trainees
  III. Finance
     A. Stock issue
     B. Change in sales personnel compensation policies
  IV. Analysis of sales accounts
     A. Over $50,000 in purchases per year
        1. Number of shipments per year
        2. Average dollar amount per sale
        3. Claim and adjustment record
     B. Over $25,000 in purchases per year
        1. Number of shipments per year
        2. Average dollar amount per sale
     C. Assignment of sales personnel

(2) *An Analysis of Training Activities, Jupiter Corporation*
  I. Basic objectives in corporate training
     A. Management training objectives
     B. Professional training objectives
     C. Skilled training objectives
     D. Training objectives of secretarial personnel and cost
  II. Organization of training department
     A. Administrative
     B. Trainers
     C. Support personnel
     D. Use of outside consultants
     E. Cost of maintaining the department
  III. Programs
     A. Supervisory management courses
     B. Shop courses
     C. Cost reduction courses
     D. Cost of maintaining the programs

IV. Expenditures for training
   A. Direct costs of classes
   B. Indirect and overhead charges

(3) *An Analysis of Recruitment Procedures of Engineering Personnel*
   I. Campus recruitment
      A. Undergraduate engineering students
      B. Undergraduate business students
      C. Undergraduate (misc.) students
   II. Newspaper advertisement recruiting
      A. Mail résumés
      B. Responses from ads in engineering journals
   III. Recruiting through present employees
      A. Bonus methods
      B. Interview procedures for prospective personnel
      C. Disadvantages of recruiting through employees

4. Defend or attack the following statement:
"If the communicator will only take the time necessary to draw up a plan for his written or oral communication, he will, in the long run, save much time and produce a better end product."

5. Select a three- or four-page article in a professional journal and make an outline of it. How logical is it? Do you feel the author would have been wiser if he had organized his article differently? Explain.

6. What is meant by "proportion" in the outline? How is it related to "proportion" in the finished communication?

7. How can an outline be used to check on the "order of development" of a report, letter, or oral presentation?

8. Define and discuss each of the following orders of development:
   (1) Chronological
   (2) Geographical
   (3) Directional

CHAPTER SIX

The Process of Writing

Frequently during the business day, you as a manager are called upon to express your thoughts in writing. Memos, letters, reports, surveys, articles, and a dozen other types of written communications flow from your pen. You, like all of us, hope that each of these presentations will be written with force and clarity. Of course, you don't expect them to be recognized as priceless examples of exposition, but you do appreciate it when the boss or one of your colleagues says, "That report of yours certainly rang the bell."

Unfortunately, this doesn't happen as often as you would like; you find that writing is hard work and what you finally do achieve will very probably not be outstanding examples of business prose. (See Fielden, "What Do You Mean I Can't Write?" Part IV.)

But as businessmen, we must all write, and as long as we must, let's do it as effectively as we possibly can. Writing, like most activities from tennis to surgery, requires specific techniques; these will be discussed in this chapter.

WE COMMUNICATE MORE THAN FACTS

If the businessman wishes to communicate effectively, he must keep the factors of rhetoric, diction, and grammar in mind. But he must remember that in conveying his ideas to others, he is also expressing his feelings. The listener may not interpret the message or the feeling as the speaker intended, but the communicator must be aware that the listener will react in some way.

The feelings which enter into this communication strongly influence the interpretation of the message. For example, picture two young business executives who are also good friends. They play golf together, attend plays and parties together with their wives, and generally enjoy social as well as work relations. On a particular morning, while having coffee, they discuss a new advertising campaign. In the course of the conversation Bob casually comments that Bill's ideas on the presentation are "all wet." Bill, taking no offense, probably replies, "No, I'm not all wet. Here, I'll explain why I'm sure the client will accept. . . ." And so the conversation continues.

But contrast that with the office manager, Frank, who has had several rather heated discussions with the tabulating room director, Marty, about the allocation of floor space. Marty is sure that Frank is unreasonable, unfair, and biased. Thus, when Frank comments that Marty is "all wet," we can easily appreciate why Marty gets angry.

The reactions to "you're all wet" in these two cases are certainly different because the feelings conveyed are different even though the words are the same. But this is true of almost all communications; not only ideas are conveyed, but also feelings.

This, then, is a vital factor for the communicator to keep in mind: Feelings are conveyed along with facts—both in speaking and in writing. It is further necessary to remember that feelings are sometimes conveyed most emphatically when the facts in a statement are ignored.

The interpretation of feelings is based on so many factors: the tone and inflection in the communicator's voice if the message is spoken; the climate of the previous discussion; the context in which the key words are used; the relationship of the people involved in the discussion; and the total life experiences of both.

F. J. Roethlisberger, in his excellent book *Management and Morale*, discusses this important area of communication in detail and refers to it as *sentiments*. He says:

> . . . Words refer not only to things happening outside our skins, but also to our attitudes, feelings, and sentiments toward these objects and events. This means that many statements are expressed which have little or no meaning apart from the personal situation of the person who makes them. . . .
>
> The problem would be simple if when people spoke they labeled what it was they were telling us; if, for example, they would say: "Now I am talking about simple events and uniformities among them in our common experience." "Now I am expressing my sentiments and attitude toward something." "Now I am day-dreaming and satisfying my ego." . . . "Now I am trying to influence your sentiments by using these particular words." . . . We very seldom express our sentiments

as sentiments. One of the most time-consuming pastimes of the human mind is to rationalize sentiments and to disguise sentiments as logic.[1]

What we have said thus far (and going back to the discussion on barriers to communication) is this: The process of sending and receiving information is a complex and difficult task. But difficult or not, this is the way individual men, groups, nations, and peoples carry through their daily activities: They must communicate. And the more effective and accurate this communication is, the better is the relationship that exists in the home, in the office, on the golf course, in the United Nations, and at the summit conferences.

THE JOB OF WRITING

There are many men in industry who find writing a difficult task. Reports do *not* flow from their pens; articles and manuscripts are *not* created easily and quickly; the ideas for speeches do *not* tumble pell-mell on to paper; and even the task of composing and dictating a good business letter is difficult for many of them.

Of course there are a few persons, like Winston Churchill, who are reputed to be very adept at writing. Their pens fly over the blank paper like magic and soon excellent reports and articles are completed. They dictate long, memorable letters, quickly, clearly, and confidently. And they enjoy, and are challenged and exhilarated by, a good, stiff writing assignment.

But for most of us, writing is plain hard work. I would be dishonest if I tried to convince you otherwise; but knowledge of writing techniques and frequent practice will make you a *better* writer. Few of you will ever say, "Writing is easy," but I hope you will say, sometime in your career, "Writing is a challenge and I am confident I can do a creditable job."

It is important that we recognize this difficulty; not because I wish to present a negative aspect of communication, but to prevent a competent individual from becoming discouraged when he encounters difficulty in a writing assignment. No, writing is not easy, but like any task which requires work, effort, and concentration, its satisfactory completion is gratifying and rewarding.

1. F. J. Roethlisberger, *Management and Morale* (Cambridge, Mass.: Harvard University Press, 1959), p. 91.

THE FIRST DRAFT

Most of us do not say precisely and clearly what we mean to say in our first draft. However, we can use a "system" to achieve that final well-written communication. The system is simple. Develop a satisfactory outline. Refer to it as you write a first draft, then revise and rewrite until you are satisfied that your paper says just what you mean it to say in the manner in which you mean to say it.

Getting Ready

Before you actually begin to write, you must be ready to write. You must be in the right frame of mind, have the right atmosphere, and be sure what your purpose is, who your reader is, and what you want to say.

The Writing Environment. Once you have recognized that writing requires time and attention, provide an adequate quantity of both for the job. Don't try to write an important report between meetings scheduled for tomorrow morning; don't attempt to complete that article in the midst of clicking typewriters and chattering discussions; and don't stuff the assignment into your briefcase with the intention of completing it tonight while you watch your favorite TV program.

None of these, or similar methods, will work.

Provide a definite time and place for your writing projects. Of course, few of us are fortunate enough to have as much time as we need, yet we must allocate a reasonable number of minutes for our required writing duties. Surely you will agree that it is foolish to work on a business or research project for days and then try to write a report on the assignment in half an hour. And yet this is often done. A manager who knows that production, financial, credit, and advertising decisions will be made on the basis of the content of his sales report may attempt to dash it off in a spare fifteen minutes after lunch. This is an unwise and often costly attempt to save time.

Topic, Purpose, Reader. What is my precise topic? What is my specific purpose? Who is my reader? Answering these three questions is a basic step in planning and organizing the presentation. Our discussion of these areas in the previous chapter emphasized the importance of recognizing and answering these three questions before the formal task of writing is begun.

We have selected or been assigned a specific topic area. We have checked the topic, limited our boundaries, investigated and determined how deeply we should pursue the problem, and, finally, we have drawn up an outline.

Once we have carried through our research into primary and secondary sources (see Chapter Four), we are ready to begin the task of writing.

Thinking and Reflection. Careful, reflective thinking about all the facets of the communication is a vital step in the writing process. And yet this aspect of communication is rarely mentioned in books on writing. Perhaps it is because the authors feel it should occur continually while the executive draws up his outline, limits his topic, and does his research. And this is true: The manager *should* be thinking about his end presentation.

But what I am talking of here is the devotion of a block of time to reflection on the topic. Just as the researcher devoted time to all his other steps, he should now allocate time to sitting and thinking. This is not random or superficial thinking. Here we are talking about reflective thinking which carefully evaluates each section of the paper. Thought is given to the logic of the design, the psychology of treating this aspect before that one, the tone of the language, the approach to use, the arguments to put forward, the complexity of treatment, the words to be chosen, and how each section fits into the whole communication and how the whole meshes into the writer's overall purpose and the company's objective. Perhaps a primary goal of reflective thinking is to attempt to recognize the reader's frame of reference and determine what arguments, facts, and methods of presentation will motivate and interest him.

To accomplish this takes time and thinking which is truly analytical and reflective. The writer can use his final outline as a guide and carefully proceed from one point to the next, weighing, evaluating, and thinking from beginning to end.

Getting It Said

After the writer has gathered all his material, tabulated and interpreted his data, carefully checked his outline, and is confident that his paper will achieve his stated purpose, he is ready to begin to write.

The writing should be done as rapidly as possible. The purpose at this stage is for the writer to get his ideas on paper. Never mind the somewhat awkward sentence, the word that doesn't quite fit the situation, the obvious repetition, and the wordy paragraph. These will be taken care of in the editing process. The most important assignment now is to get the report, article, or account down on paper.

This stage should go rapidly, for the writer has finished his research and is familiar with his material. His detailed and logical outline is there to serve as a guide, and cards are filled with vital information waiting to be transferred to paper. All that needs to be done now is to write the first draft from the materials at hand and the facts learned.

EDITING AND REVISING

A primary purpose of a piece of exposition is to present data, discussions, descriptions, conclusions, and recommendations as clearly and as accurately as possible. Faulty sentence structure, confusion in ideas, negligence in word choice, or any other carelessness in presentation which impedes the free flow of ideas must be corrected. The time to make these corrections, so that the ideas in the final paper flow smoothly and easily, is in the editing process.

People who have not done a great deal of writing may be somewhat amazed at how much work there is yet to do after the first draft has been completed. That first draft, as a matter of fact, is just the beginning. The serious job of rewriting must now be undertaken.

Sometimes sentences must be reworked completely, paragraphs thoroughly revised, and entire sections reorganized. Many of the famous authors of today attest to the fact that the major portion of their time was not spent in the original composition but in revising and rewriting—again and again—the initial draft. The interesting, easy-to-read, and completely clear piece of management writing is usually the result of writing, revising, editing, correcting, rewriting, revising, and rewriting again, and again, and again. For most of us, the task is arduous and time-consuming. However, the results are always worth the effort.

If at all possible, the communicator should take a "cooling-off" period after he completes his first draft. If he attempts to edit his first draft immediately after writing it, he may well read into the paper what he wishes to read. His awkward sentences, inaccurate words, and errors in grammar, however, will become quite obvious when he can stand back with a few days' distance and review critically.

In writing the first draft, our primary goal was to get the facts down as quickly and creatively as possible. In the editing process, we must proceed more slowly, coldly, and analytically. Material which should be cut or revised should be—drastically and thoroughly.

THE PARTS OF THE WHOLE

When we communicate we attempt to transmit ideas. We select words, order them into sentences, and connect the sentences to build paragraphs. The way we handle these three elements—words, sentences, paragraphs—largely determines how effective we are in getting the understanding we are looking for.

WORDS

It is estimated that we have well over half a million words available to us. Many of these are compound words or those we have borrowed from other languages. Other entirely new words come from advances in the sciences, changes in the world of recreation (television, for example), and the effects of unusual activities such as war.

But in using words we find that some are suited for communicating ideas on the golf course, while others are preferable at the technical conference devoted to the use of transistors in new electronic components. Different levels of words, like different levels of dress, are designed for use in specific situations. You would not wear formal dress to a baseball game or a sport shirt and slacks to an evening wedding. Similarly, you would not ordinarily use slang and jargon in an article for the *Harvard Business Review* or highly complex technical terms in explaining the use of lasers to a Cub Scout group.

Perrin, in his excellent work *Writer's Guide and Index to English*,[2] divides words into two general groups: nonstandard and standard. The former is primarily spoken, characterized by regional colloquialisms, used in conversation but not for business or public affairs. Standard English is of three types: informal, general, and formal. Informal is more often spoken than written; it is used in informal situations and includes shoptalk and slang. General English, both spoken and written, is appropriate in almost any situation. It is commonly used in conversation and writing between friends, usual business letters, newspaper features, magazine articles directed to the general public, and comments on radio and television. Formal English, according to Perrin, is more often written than spoken and is used in literary, scientific, technical, and academic writing and speaking. Perrin emphasizes that these classifications do not involve value judgments.

Correctness

If they are to communicate ideas effectively, words must be used carefully and correctly. There are two categories of words commonly misused: those that sound alike but have different meanings and those that are somewhat similar in sound or have the same root (see Appendix A).

Words that sound alike but are spelled differently and have different meanings (homonyms) are very common in English: where, wear, ware; bear, bare; would, wood; principle, principal; council, counsel; see,

2. Porter G. Perrin, *Writer's Guide and Index to English,* 4th ed. rev. by Karl W. Dykema and Wilma R. Ebbitt (Glenview, Ill.: Scott, Foresman and Company, 1965, 1968).

sea; bow, bough; and many others. Most people know what these words mean; the difficulty comes in spelling them. If in a business letter you write *principle* when you mean *principal*, the recipient will figure out what you mean, but he will have a low opinion of you and the care and attention you gave to him. The rest of your letter must be very good indeed to overcome that impression. But this is primarily a question of spelling, and the problem can be solved by closer attention.

Examples of the second group of misused words also abound: uninterested, disinterested; imply, infer; credible, creditable; unorganized, disorganized; incredible, incredulous. A judge on the bench should be disinterested in the case being tried before him, but surely not uninterested. When I am speaking, I imply something; when you are listening, you infer something.

The writer or speaker who uses *disorganized* when he means *unorganized*, or *healthy* when he means *healthful*, not only lessens the exactness of his statement but confuses the reader or listener, embarrasses himself, and, in the long run, helps corrupt and weaken our language.

The carpenter who uses a screwdriver when he should use a chisel will probably produce a less desirable cabinet; when we use second-rate words (our tools), we will produce ideas which have less impact because they are not expressed as they should be.

Accuracy and Precision

There was once a Russian professor, a wonderful old aristocrat who loved her language. When her students found several English words of varying nuance to translate one Russian word, she would say, "Ah, you see how simple is Russian—we need only one word to mean all those things." When, less often, her students found several Russian words of varying nuance to translate one English word, she would say, "Ah, you see the richness of Russian. We can say things much more exactly."

The student of any foreign language knows that this is true: Some ideas can be expressed with greater precision in some languages than in others. Our language has grown up haphazardly, from many different sources. It is still growing and changing. When a word is needed, it is created, or borrowed from another language; if a word is no longer needed, it is discarded. For these reasons, English is perhaps richer than other languages which are not so fluid.

Because English-speaking ideas, particularly American and particularly in the fields of science and entertainment, are spreading so rapidly throughout the world, their vocabularies are spreading with them. Although the Académie Francaise urges the use of un *autodidacte*, the French people insist on saying un *self-made man*. Throughout France are *self-service* shops. On Moscow streets just before intersections are printed the Cyrillic letters for STOP.

We in turn, particularly in the areas of the arts and cooking, borrow from other languages: French, Italian, German, etc. Sometimes these borrowed words duplicate in actual meaning words already in the language, but with a different flavor, a different feeling.

With the richness and adaptability of our language, there is little excuse for imprecision and inaccuracy. This is as true in business as in any other field.

Words, as names or descriptions, have two distinct traits: denotation and connotation. The denotation of a word is its factual meaning or definition. Its connotation, on the other hand, is the sum of thoughts and emotions it arouses or contains.

A single word may have several denotations. The word *vessel*, for example, may refer to a component in the circulatory system, a container for liquids, or a water-borne vehicle. As a noun, *rest* may mean repose, something used for support, a pause in music, or remainder. Yet there is little chance of confusion among these meanings; the context will make obvious which denotation is intended.

It is the connotations of words that create difficulties in communication. The word *capitalism* denotes the same thing to Americans and Soviets, but the connotations are opposite. Everybody knows what *soldier* "means"; but consider the different emotions the word arouses in a boy proudly fighting in Vietnam and a boy burning his draft card. What different feelings do you have about the words *fat, obese, roly-poly, plump?* All have the same denotation. Manufacturers of a diet food would never say it makes you skinny; they would say it makes you slim or slender. Do you want an after-shave lotion that has a smell, a scent, a parfum, an aroma, or an odor? Yet they all have the same denotation. The picture we wish to paint can be conveyed very accurately with the words we choose for our colors.

Attention to connotation is of primary importance in business communication. We have already seen its significance in advertising; and business letters and reports are a form of advertising—for yourself and your firm. A letter over your name is your image to the recipient; if it creates unpleasant feelings it may be worse than no letter at all.

Remember *who* your reader or listener is, and choose your words with his feelings, his educational and social level, and his needs in mind.

SENTENCES

Writing that is clear, concise, and motivates and persuades others is effective. Effective writing is largely based on well-written sentences, sentences that are cogent and memorable.

In some material we read, the sentences seem to flow into each other smoothly, effortlessly, enjoyably. Other material must be read and reread, for the writing seems choppy, difficult, awkward, and stumbling.

The level of complexity probably has something to do with ease of reading, but more important is style, the way sentences are put together. What factors contribute to effective sentence structure? How does one write sentences that flow rather than stumble? There are, of course, no simple answers, but there are some directions we can follow. First, however, we should be familiar with sentence structure and classification.

Types of Sentences

There are four primary kinds of sentences. The most common is the declarative, which is a positive or negative assertion. Others are the interrogative, which asks a question; the imperative, which expresses a command or a wish; and the exclamatory. These all begin with a capital letter, end with the appropriate punctuation, and usually contain a subject and a verb.

Sentences may be formed in several ways. A simple sentence consists of one independent clause; a compound sentence consists of two or more independent clauses. A complex sentence is composed of one independent and one or more subordinate clauses; and a compound-complex sentence is made up of two or more independent clauses and at least one subordinate clause.

Variety of Sentence Structure

It is important to make writing clear and interesting. One way to do that effectively is to vary sentence structure. Paragraphs composed entirely of compound sentences are monotonous and boring; paragraphs constructed only of simple sentences are choppy, childish, and lacking in grace. However, the judicious use of a simple sentence can give writing force and impact. Complex sentences, because they are made up of independent and dependent clauses, clarify meaning and make for easier reading. Compound-complex sentences, in that they have inherent variety, also give vitality and interest to writing.

For variety within a sentence, use an occasional command, exhortation, exclamation, or question to replace the usual declarative sentence. Or why not modify the usual subject-verb sequence, beginning a sentence with a phrase or subordinate clause to give details as a lead-in to the main idea of the independent clause?

Notice the differences in the examples on p. 157. Compare the abruptness and unnecessary overlapping of the simple sentences, and the monotony of the compound sentences, with the smoothness and variety of the sentences on the far right.

Simple Sentences

Management in any large corporation is dependent on information. This information is secured from many departments within a company. Sales, credit, production, research, advertising, and other departments forward information. This information is sent "up" to management. Often this information is in the form of reports. The information in these reports is usually gathered by each department. It is necessary that the content of these reports be accurate and complete. This is necessary because decisions are made on the basis of the content. Obviously decisions cannot be made if the reports do not contain adequate substantiating data. These data are usually statistical.

Compound Sentences

Management in any large corporation is dependent on information, and this information is received from many departments within the company. Sales, credit, production, research, advertising, and other departments forward information, and this information is then sent up to management. Often this information is in the form of reports, and this information is usually gathered by each department. It is necessary that the content of these reports be accurate and complete and this is necessary because decisions are made on the basis of the content. Obviously decisions cannot be made if the reports do not contain adequate substantiating data and these data are usually statistical.

Variety of Sentence Types

Management in any large corporation is dependent on the information it receives from the sales, credit, production, research, advertising, and other departments. This information, which is sent "up," is usually in the form of reports. The substantiating data (usually statistical) in these reports must be accurate and complete, for decisions are made on the basis of the facts provided.

When sentences are well written, they impress, they persuade, they motivate the reader. Sentence structure that will accomplish these ends must be more than correct grammatically. It must often be dramatic and certainly imaginative.[3]   Here are some good examples:

3. See the Royal Bank of Canada Monthly Letter, "Imagination Helps Communication," Part IV.

Never before has man had such capacity to control his own environment—to end thirst and hunger—to banish illiteracy and massive human misery. We have the power to make this the best generation of mankind . . . or to make it the last. . . .

If we fail to make the most of this moment and this momentum, if we convert our new-found hopes and understanding into new walls and weapons of hostility, if this pause in the cold war leads to its renewal and not to its end, then the shaming indictment of posterity will rightly point its finger at us all.[4]

There is, of course, a danger that the writer may write purely for the purpose of impressing the reader with catchy sentences rather than communicating ideas. This is quickly recognized as an artifice for gaining attention, and such writing soon becomes tiresome.

Revising Sentences

The best way to write, as the old saw goes, is to write. Get your ideas down in black and white; let the sentences flow from your mind to the paper.

After you have written down a complete block of ideas, go back and edit and revise the awkward and wordy sentences. As you become more critical of your own writing and more adept at revising sentences, you will find that your ability will steadily improve.

Lack of Clarity	*Improved*
Burns worked in his Dad's store while attending school, and although he majored in management, I don't think he liked it.	Although Burns majored in management and was a good student while he worked in his Dad's store, I don't think he liked the field.
To fly efficiently, a good pilot should check his plane after every flight.	If a plane is to fly efficiently, it should be checked after every flight.
Many of my friends had managed to ski and I didn't know whether it was possible so I decided to attempt to find out.	Since many of my friends had managed to learn to ski, I decided to try it too.

4. From the speech of President John F. Kennedy to the United Nations, September 20, 1963.

Dangling

Arriving home late, dinner was started immediately.

Improved

Because we arrived home later than usual, we prepared dinner immediately.

Running down the sidewalk near the hospital which was a new modern building built to handle children's cases.

John ran down the sidewalk adjacent to the new children's hospital.

Faulty Sentence Structure

When I first started to play tennis with John, I found that my serve was quite good. Although I had not played for six years.

Improved

When I first started to play tennis with John, I found that my serve was quite good, even though I had not played for six years.

When I write a report, I find that it requires a good deal of concentrated effort and work, this is, as I think of it, necessary when I do any type of writing.

When I write a report, I find that it requires a good deal of concentrated effort and work. This is true, as I think of it, of any type of writing I do.

Perhaps one of the most important reports submitted in any organization is the periodic report. Submitted by each department head for decision-making purposes.

One of the most important reports submitted by department heads in any organization is the periodic report. It is used for decision-making purposes.

Wordy and Archaic
Sentence Structure

The annual report serves, by and large, two very important purposes today and the first of which is the presentation of financial information to stockholders and the second is to build company public relations in the business community at large.

Improved

The annual report serves two primary functions: the presentation of financial data to stockholders and the building of company public relations in the business community.

You will find enclosed, as per your basic request, the report which we have taken the liberty of forwarding to you.

The report that you requested is enclosed.

The few examples on pp. 158-159 demonstrate what can be done when a serious attempt is made to edit and revise. Improvement is not difficult; all that is necessary is a merciless blue pencil and acceptance of nothing less than excellence in sentence structure.

The experienced editor does develop techniques to assist him. One is to evaluate a sentence by reading it aloud and listening. If it sounds awkward to the ear, it should probably be revised. A second device is the method used for rewriting and improving sentences. Many people, when revising an awkward sentence, will scratch out a word here and move a phrase there. The usual result of this minor surgery is that some improvement takes place in the "sick" sentence, but it cannot usually be placed on the "healthy" list. Drastic surgery is often called for. Remove the sentence completely and begin again. The new version will usually say just what you mean.

And a final technique is to use your dictionary and thesaurus; don't be satisfied with the almost-right word. Search your thesaurus until you find the word which conveys *precisely* the thought you had in mind and also gives your sentence the rhythm and tone you desire.

PARAGRAPHS

A paragraph is a group of related sentences which help advance the development of the paper. Each paragraph, though joined to the one before and the one following, develops an individual idea. Thus, carefully constructed paragraphs serve the double purpose of joining and separating. Each paragraph should develop one idea, whether that idea is explicitly stated or not. Each paragraph should add to the reader's knowledge or understanding either of the topic or of the paper itself.

The expository paragraph tells about the topic. It is linked at top and bottom with other paragraphs, but it develops, explains, illustrates, or supports a particular point. It can do this by particularization, by example, by definition of terms, by contrast and comparison, by analysis, by classification, or by narration.

The transitional or emphatic paragraph, on the other hand, assists the reader. A paragraph of transition says, "This is where we have been; that is where we're going—so get ready." The paragraph of emphasis says, "That was an important point we just passed; did you get it?"

When you rewrite your paper, be sure not only that you have chosen the right words and put those words together into clear sentences, but that those sentences are combined into logical, useful paragraphs.

QUALITIES OF WRITING STYLE

Most authorities, in a discussion of writing style, list the three standard qualities of rhetoric: unity, coherence, and emphasis. There are others, however, which certainly deserve more than a passing glance: consideration for the reader, clarity, liveliness, and grace.

It is a writer's style which makes his work uniquely his. This author's work is lively, his is dull, hers is persuasive, and another's is consistently entertaining. These qualities come from the heart of the composition and make up the rather indefinable quality that we label *style*.

Every communication written by a businessman should have an effective style. Of course, few executives will approach the excitement of Hemingway, the humor of Thurber, the insight of Shakespeare, or the precision of Churchill. On the other hand, their writing need not be as dull as an inventory form or as uninspired as a page of stock quotations.

UNITY AND COHERENCE

Every paragraph should develop an idea; a group of paragraphs should move a single topic forward; and the sections of the paper should all contribute to the development of the specific aspect with which the message is concerned.

Irrelevant details and materials which are not directly related to the core idea must be eliminated. Then the paper must be checked to determine if it possesses this quality of "oneness" or unity. Each sentence, each paragraph, each section must march forward toward the objective the writer hopes to achieve. If it does not, strike it out.

Coherence is attained when the ideas are logically interconnected, they smoothly follow one another, and their meaning is clear and easily comprehended. When sentences and paragraphs are connected with transitional words, phrases, and sentences, the whole body of material seems to move interestingly and coherently from one idea to another. In this way, thoughts are not isolated, but they are related to each other and all together they proceed logically toward a specific conclusion.

Transitional words assist in achieving coherence, for they connect sentences to each other. Phrases, clauses, or sentences may also be used as transitional devices between paragraphs. And in a long report or other piece of extended writing, paragraphs help bind the sections within the paper to one another.

Coherence also means clarity and accuracy in writing. This requires attention to word choice, sentence structure, and the many other areas of diction and rhetoric which make any piece of communication informative and valuable to read.

COURTESY AND CONSIDERATION

In any kind of communication, oral or written, business or personal, one of the prime requisites is consideration for the recipient. Courtesy and consideration are easy to achieve, and well worth the effort involved.

In business communication, much more than common courtesy is involved. Discourtesy or thoughtlessness might mean the loss of a good customer or of a large sale. It might mean loss of prestige and status. It will almost surely mean a lessening of respect and approval for you and your company.

Basic to consideration is a knowledge of your reader. If you know who he is, what he wants, and why he wants it, you can even refuse him without offending. Remember to write in terms of "you" rather than "I." A customer is interested in *his* request or complaint, and you must be too.

> It is a literary vice not to seek out the reader's interest. You may tell him what you want in impeccable language and forceful manner, but you fall short of success unless you pay attention to what he wants or can be made to desire. Your ideas must enter, influence and stick in the mind of the recipient.
>
> As a writer, you may protest that some of the failure in communication may be blamed on the receiver, but it is your responsibility as sender to determine in advance, to the best of your ability, all potential causes of failure and to tune your transmission for the best reception.[5]

The second ingredient for a courteous business letter is "Please," "Thank you," "I'm sorry," "I'm delighted." Liberal—but not maudlin—use of these words will give your reader the feeling not only that you are polite but that you *care* about him.

The third ingredient in consideration goes back to knowing your reader. Use words and phrases and ideas that are on his level. If you talk over his head, he will feel unhappy, insecure, and inferior. This is no way to gain confidence. If you talk beneath him, he will be insulted. This, too, will defeat your aims.

Courtesy and consideration, then, are among the easiest things to achieve in communication. Their accomplishment requires from you only sensitivity and a little care.

EMPHASIS

At times we wish to persuade our reader to take specific action as recommended in certain segments of our writing; or perhaps we wish to bring a particular section of the paper into sharper focus. This requires that significant sections be emphasized.

There are a variety of methods that can be used by the business writer

---

5. The Royal Bank of Canada Monthly Letter, Part IV.

to achieve emphasis. There is the simple method of *proportion*, which involves giving more space to a key point than to items of less importance. If the writer spends four pages discussing sales and only half a page on credit, production, and research, it is obvious that he wishes to focus the reader's attention on sales.

Repetition of facts, ideas, or words also helps to emphasize what is desired. At times an idea may be discussed in the paper, presented factually in a table, and commented on again in a further analysis.

The thoughtful positioning or *placement* of ideas within the body of the writing may also be a device to secure emphasis. Statements made in the early portion of the presentation, or at the beginning of a section, often receive special attention.

Attention-catching *words or phrases* may be used to emphasize ideas. This use of dramatic words or alliterative phrases need not be limited to advertising writing; it can be used effectively in expository writing as well.

The use of *mechanical methods* has some value when the writer wishes to emphasize a particular point. Emphasis may be secured by capitalizing words, underscoring phrases, using colored inks, or inserting cartoons, sketches, and photographs. In addition, an idea or thought can be set off by itself with a dramatic amount of white space around it.

But perhaps the most effective way to emphasize a point is through *excellent writing*. One's writing should be so effective, so clear, so persuasive that the reader will remember the ideas because of the quality of the writing and not because of capitalized phrases or underscored ideas.

The writer who uses words with care not only can transmit a picture of his idea to the reader's mind, but he can also arouse a feeling in the reader's heart. To do this requires that the communicator choose his words carefully; that he use similes and metaphors effectively; that he select strong, colorful, active phrases; that he be positive that his sentences present his ideas clearly and accurately; and that he be certain that his entire presentation moves logically and thoughtfully from beginning to end.

Securing emphasis through this method—good writing—is not easy. It requires analysis, time, and constant reference to the dictionary and thesaurus. But it is worth it, for effective writing makes an indelible impression in the reader's mind. A well-written statement may be recalled for years, while an underlined sentence may be forgotten in a few minutes.

LIVELINESS AND GRACE

Liveliness and grace are as important in business writing as in any other kind of writing. Achieving them requires a sensitivity to words and a desire to find the exact words and combinations of words to impart not only facts but feelings. Writing that is a pleasure to read—emphatic phrases, clear and concise statements, ideas which are imaginatively presented—is more likely to achieve its purpose than writing which is dull, awkward, heavy-handed, and pompous.

The writer with *imagination* not only will put himself in the place of his reader but will also look for the word, the analogy, the figure that best expresses what he wants to say. He will avoid clichés and ambiguities, worn-out similes, and irritating redundancies.

Here are some examples of Winston Churchill's liveliness and grace in writing:

> Even though large tracts of Europe and many old and famous states have fallen or may fall into the grip of the Gestapo and all the odious apparatus of Nazi rule, we shall not flag or fail. We shall go on to the end, we shall fight in France, we shall fight on the seas and the oceans, we shall fight with growing confidence and growing strength in the air, we shall defend our island, whatever the cost may be, we shall fight in the hills; we shall never surrender, and even if, which I do not for a moment believe, this island or a large part of it were subjugated and starving, then our empire beyond the seas, armed and guarded by the British fleet, would carry on the struggle, until, in God's good time, the New World, with all its power and might, steps forth to the rescue and liberation of the Old.
>
> Speech to the House of Commons
> on the fall of Dunkirk, June 4, 1940

> Victory lies before us, certain and perhaps near. But years of cruel torment and destruction have wasted the earth, and victory with all its brilliant trappings appears to our strained and experienced eyes as a deliverance rather than as a triumph.
>
> Our hearts go out in thankfulness that we have been saved from annihilation and from enduring the ruin of our country, and that, after all our long, famous history, we shall come through once again with life and honor, surmounting a convulsion that has ravaged the globe.
>
> Speech to the Conservative Party
> Conference March 15, 1945

> I would say to the House, as I have said to those who have joined this government: "I have nothing to offer but blood, toil, tears and sweat."
>
> We have before us an ordeal of the most grievous kind. We have before us many, many long months of struggle and

of suffering. You ask, What is our policy? I will say: It is to wage war, by sea, land and air, with all our might and with all the strength that God can give us; to wage war against a monstrous tyranny, never surpassed in the dark lamentable catalog of human crime. That is our policy.

You ask, What is our aim? I can answer in one word: Victory––victory at all costs, victory in spite of all terror, victory however long and hard the road may be . . . .

First statement to the House of Commons
as prime minister, May 13, 1940

Imagination not only requires that the writer determine the reader's interest and communicate toward that end, but he must also have the imagination to choose words that will strike a chord of response. Notice in the quotation on page 162 that the author says "tune" your transmission, not "adapt" or "design" your transmission. The word *tune* is so much more meaningful and colorful than the others, and it is much more intimately and accurately associated with the terms "transmission" and "reception." Also note the imaginative word choices below:

If you do not wish your letters to be read yawningly, write them wide awake. When a good idea strikes you . . . , ride that idea on the dead run: don't wait to ponder, criticize and correct. You can be critical after your imaginative spell subsides.[6]

Lively and graceful writing will have *variety*; this is as important in prose as it is in music. A good symphony has variety of tone and timing: The tempo is fast and slow; the sound level is high and low; the measures are strong and weak. A monotonous symphony, like a monotonous paper, is boring. In your writing, therefore, use a variety of sentence types; use a short sentence now and then for dramatic impact, an alliterative phrase for rhythm and sound. Choose words that are lively and colorful; try to use new words sometimes; put words into new combinations.

Be aware of alliteration, assonance, and consonance. Read aloud what you have written. Does it *sound* right? Does its sound echo its sense? Does the mood of the language fit the mood of the subject, of the ideas? Write so your reader will *want* to read what you have written.

EDITING SUGGESTIONS

You should review your first draft several times; in each review, give special attention to a specific quality of writing. It is probably most help-

6. The Royal Bank of Canada Letter, Part IV.

ful to begin with unity and relevance. Step back, so to speak, from the paper and determine if every sentence, every paragraph, every section contributes to the theme and purpose. If any portion, whether a word or a paragraph, can be construed as being irrelevant or unnecessary, it should be cut out without compunction.

Then you might check for coherence. Is there good transition between ideas? Do the sentences and paragraphs seem to be logically associated and connected? Do the sections flow into one another easily and smoothly? If the answer to any of these questions is "no," then the transitional devices need improvement.

What about word choice? Does every sentence say precisely what you mean it to? Do the words convey the exact connotation intended? Does this phrase or that clause result in the proper picture in the reader's or listener's mind? No second-rate word or group of words is acceptable here; use your dictionary or thesaurus to find the exact words, the words that will convey the precise idea, tone, and mood. Here is a wonderful opportunity to use lively words, similes, metaphors, and various figures of speech that will give your writing vitality and color.

Then you might go on to check for clarity. If there is any possibility —even a slim one—that a phrase or sentence might be misinterpreted, strike it out and write it again. Don't attempt to change a word here or there; rewrite the entire statement so that it says precisely what you intended.

Emphasis is important and can be achieved by proper placement of key ideas, by inserting topic and subtopic headings, and by the judicious use of detail in discussing the various areas of the report.

Examine carefully all statistical data in your paper. Are the figures confusing? Would the use of charts or graphs make your presentation clearer and easier to read? Tables, charts, diagrams, and other visuals must be used with restraint, but they are an important tool in communication. See Chapter Seven for a detailed discussion of visuals and how they can be used most effectively.

What does a piece of writing look like before and after editing? Below we have a short section of the first draft of a report and the revision after editing.

Original Version

Sales for the month of June were, by and large, higher than they were for a similar period last year, but not appreciably so, at least to the extent where we might now consider sitting on "our laurels" so to speak. As a matter of fact, the increase was only approximately 4.5% over last year's sales which were just average for the industry.

As the reader is probably aware, our three primary lines are children's desks (in three different models), record cabinets (also in three different models), and our two different styles in end tables.

Sales for this period, in all these products, have increased appreciably and we have found it necessary to have a corresponding increase in personnel. As a matter of fact we have increased our sales personnel by two full-time men in each of our five sales districts for a total increase of sales personnel of ten. Thus with a total of 65 full-time sales personnel, we have the largest staff of this type of any company in this field.

But back to the discussion of sales for June of this year. In the area of children's desks, 365 dozen of the model 185 were sold, 413 of the model 186, and 429 of the model 187. This is in contrast to 350, 395, and 405 of the models 185, 186, and 187 respectively in June of last year. Sales of record cabinets also went up quite dramati-

cally but with one exception.

Record cabinet model 201 sold 215 dozen; 202 was 262 dozen; and model 203 sold 185 dozen. These figures also reflect an increase over June of last year with the exception of model 203 which dropped 65 dozen. This is difficult to explain except for the fact that Mr. Barnard of Barnard's Furniture did not like our new styling in 203 and wouldn't order one much less his usual quantity. Of course, he has extremely strong likes and dislikes which we have encountered before. However other dealers declined to order this 203 model also. As for last year's sales on record cabinets, we sold 205 dozen of 201, 251 dozen of 202, and 250 dozen of 203.

On the whole, sales of end tables were increased in June of this year over last year. See appendix one for details.

As for advertising and sales personnel, there are several comments which need discussion so that a better line of integration between sales, personnel, and advertising can be instituted. Cooperation in the past has been somewhat less than desirable.

After Editing

Sales for the month of June were approximately 4.5 per cent higher than the similar period last year. Although this is an improvement, it is not dramatic and we should make every effort to increase this figure in the future.

Sales Volume

The table which follows reflects our sales for this period:

The dramatic decline in sales of cabinet 203 was apparently due to our new and rather unusual design which was not favorably received.

Sales Personnel

To keep up with expanding sales, our personnel in this division was increased a total of 10 (2 per sales district). The sales force now numbers 65 full-time men.

Advertising and Sales Promotion

On June 27, a meeting was held with the heads of the advertising, personnel, and sales departments present. . . .

Model	Sales Volume (in Dozens)	
	June 1969	June 1968
Desks		
185	365	350
186	413	395
187	429	405
Cabinets		
201	215	205
202	262	251
203	185	250
Tables		
101	760	697
102	870	791

The edited version on pp. 167-168 is much easier to read and assimilate than the wordy, unorganized draft on pp. 166-167.

Here are a few examples of edited material. Note how clarity almost always improves when material is made more concise.

Original: The Purchasing Department has a vital, basic, and important responsibility to interview all vendors who make themselves available at Company offices and examine all bids which are submitted by those firms who have been accepted and placed on the approved buyer roster. The Manual for Purchasing Agents, not the 1965 edition but the one published in 1969, contains specific recommendations on completing Request for Quotation forms.

Revised: The Purchasing Department has a responsibility to interview all vendors and examine all bids submitted by those firms listed on the approved buyer roster. The 1969 Manual for Purchasing Agents contains specific recommendations on completing Request for Quotation forms.

Original: Although our sales department is now somewhat short of personnel and understaffed, we are nevertheless bending every conceivable effort to complete our usual top-flight job by calling on each retailer once each month during the 1968-69 period even though this was not the case in the previous period of 1967-68. The sales survey, which was conducted through the utilization of a mail questionnaire, indicated that most of our retailers would prefer to place an order once each month rather than once every few months. In this way they can better control their inventory, always maintain fresh quality merchandise, which is vital with a food product, and learn from the salesman what is new and worthwhile in the marketing of our products.

Revised: Although our sales department is now short of personnel, we are making every effort to call on each retailer once each month during 1968-69. This was not the case in 1967-68. A mail questionnaire survey of our retailers indicated that they prefer to order monthly. In this way they can better control their inventory, always maintain fresh merchandise, and learn from the salesman what is new and worthwhile in the marketing of our products.

Original: The business executive has many duties to carry through in industry today. He is frequently called upon to make decisions involving the expenditure of funds, future corporate plans, and movement of personnel. He also must attend various meetings of a professional nature. In addition to this, he is frequently sought out as a counselor by subordinates. And on some occasions he must serve as the company's representative to community groups. These are only a few of the tasks the modern executive is expected to carry through.

Revised: Today's business executive has many duties to perform. Some of these are:

1. Decision making for the expenditure of funds, for corporate planning, and for the movement of personnel.
2. Attendance at professional meetings.
3. Counseling of subordinates.
4. Serving as the company representative to community groups.

Original: It has been requested of our organization that we offer approval of a 20-year lease arrangement of 200 acres of State property in the Del Monte area (see map enclosure) to the Michaelson Company for proper handling and development of said area. The Michaelson Company would be obliged to immediately prepare plans for a recreation area in the Del Monte area, such plans to be submitted no later than March 1. The lease would further require that a master plan be prepared for the greater Del Monte area of 500 acres (see map enclosure) and that such a master plan for a State Park be presented no later than April 15. The Michaelson Company is further required to begin actual work on the initial Del Monte area and complete all work to the satisfaction of the State Department of Recreation no later than December 1. All agreements between the Department of Recreation and the Michaelson Company are subject to acceptance by the proper state legislative committees.

Revised: The State Legal Division has been requested to evaluate a 20-year lease of 200 acres of State property in the Del Monte area (see map enclosure) to the Michaelson Company. This firm would be required:

169

1. To prepare plans for a recreation area in the Del Monte area to be submitted no later than March 1.
2. To prepare a master plan for the greater Del Monte area of 500 acres (see map enclosure) and submit it no later than April 15.
3. To complete all work on the initial Del Monte area to the satisfaction of the State Department of Recreation no later than December 1.

All agreements between the Department of Recreation and the Michaelson Company are subject to acceptance by the proper state legislative committees.

Robert Gunning[7] offers a series of suggestions which everyone might well keep in mind when writing. His points sound deceptively simple and, like most recommendations, are much easier to make than to achieve. In addition, there is much more to effective composition than the points Gunning makes. Yet his list is a convenient guide against which to check your own writing.

1. Keep sentences short, on the average.

Gunning points out that there is nothing wrong with a clear forty- or fifty-word sentence, as long as balance is achieved with a few that are six, eight, or ten words long. Of course, a short sentence that lacks other qualities of effective communication will have no value.

2. Use the simple rather than the complex.

If we can say, "It was difficult to free the youngster's leg from the drainpipe," why should we say, "Major difficulties of a complex nature were encountered in the process of extricating the lower left limb of the adolescent from . . . ." Write directly, simply, and to the point.

3. Select familiar words.

Use a vocabulary of words that is familiar to your reading group. In one case the best term may be *concomitant strabismus;* in another, it may be *cross-eyed.*

4. Avoid unnecessary words.

Much of the writing done in business today is padded, wordy, and pompous. It is simple to eliminate unnecessary words and thereby improve the writing.

5. Use active, not passive, words.

Passive: Unsatisfactory spraying methods in the paint department have been eliminated through the utilization of new equipment.

Active: New equipment has eliminated unsatisfactory spraying methods in the paint department.

7. *The Technique of Clear Writing* (New York: McGraw-Hill Book Company, 1952). See also Robert Gunning, *New Guide to More Effective Writing in Business and Industry* (Boston: Industrial Education Institute, 1962).

Passive: A sharp drop in production was noted.

Active: Production dropped sharply.

Writing in the active rather than the passive voice results in more alive, more vivid, and more interesting prose.

6. Write as you talk.

In this recommendation, Gunning does not really want you to "write as you talk." If you did, your writing would contain a good deal of repetition, awkward phrases, and most certainly an inexcusable quantity of unnecessary words. What he is suggesting is that our writing reflect the friendly, natural tone we usually use when we talk.

Perhaps it would be more accurate to say that when we write, we should sound as though we are talking.

7. Use terms your reader can picture.

We noted earlier in our discussion that words make pictures in people's minds. When the words are concrete (chair, pen, lamp), the picture in the communicator's mind will probably be similar to that in the receiver's mind.

However, the task of securing the same picture between the sender and the receiver is more difficult when abstract terms are used. Because of this it is better to say "Please pay within three days" than to say "It is highly desirable that payment be forthcoming at your earliest convenience."

Why talk about "unavoidable exigencies which may result from the complexities of morality which infringe on the juvenile's activities" when it is easier to say "Problems of morality frequently confront today's youngsters"?

8. Relate your writing to the reader's experience.

Your writing should present material from the reader's point of view. It isn't enough to explain the company profit-sharing program; it must be explained in relation to the employee and his family, his job, his experiences.

9. Use variety in your writing.

Go from simple to complex sentences, from long to short statements.

10. Write to express and not to impress.

Many of us feel that it is necessary, in our everyday activities, to impress someone with the importance of our job, the outstanding facts in our education, or the world-shaking impact of what we say. Skip such artificiality in writing or speaking. It fools no one. Pomposity is always recognized for what it is.

Throw out the long words, the unusual words, the pompous phrases, and the overlong sentences. They will impress no one, and they do not help express ideas.

These, very briefly, are Mr. Gunning's suggestions for achieving clarity in writing. Several of them are very closely related and appear to overlap. Furthermore, the reader may feel that Gunning reduces effective writing to a too-simple formula. But his suggestions have much to recommend them, and they can be adapted to individual needs.

THE FINAL PRODUCT

Now that the writing and editing of the final draft have been completed, you should check one more aspect of your paper: the overall appearance.

TOPIC HEADINGS

Is each new section properly headed? Will the busy reader be required to read through the sixteen pages on employee fringe benefits to find the section on sick-leave pay or will he be able to find that section quickly because it is preceded by a heading?

You can assist your reader by using topic and subtopic headings. Choose your words for them carefully. Be sure these headings are concise and meaningful.

Every busy executive is delighted when he can skim through a paper and see at a glance the major and minor areas that are discussed. He can quickly note the organizational pattern the writer had in mind and can thus appreciate the method of development and emphasis. With such knowledge, he can then select the specific section or sections that require his detailed study.

The use of headings also assists the writer: He is faced with a constant reminder to deal only with the topic noted. It is difficult to digress when a guide of three or four words heads the section. Thus, topic headings serve as road markers for both reader and writer.

Below are the beginning sections of two reports. Note the advantages of the one which uses topic headings: It is visually more attractive, areas covered are immediately obvious, and the organization of the whole paper is clear.

I.   A report on the activities of the personnel department must include comments in a variety of areas. For example, if we consider training which is under the direction of the Personnel Manager, we must examine shop training, office and clerical, and management training. In the case of shop training, we completed the instruction of eight groups of twenty men each. Each group met for a total of 21 hours of instruction in seven 3-hour sessions.

In the area of office and clerical training, we carried through instruction for eight groups of fifteen persons per group. Four classes were devoted to Office Procedures, and four groups received training in Written Communications. Each class met two hours a week for six weeks.

Management training was carried through on a seminar basis with each of ten groups (twenty men per group) receiving eighteen hours of instruction. Classes met for two-hour sessions once each week for nine weeks. Five groups examined the area of Human Relations, while the other five devoted their time to Management Communications.

The personnel department is also responsible for corporate safety programs and employee health care. In the case of safety, we are concerned with employee accident prevention in two areas. The first is internal or in-plant. In this area, each department (there are 32 designated departments in the company) has one man assigned as the safety officer. He holds this job for one year and receives $50.00 in extra compensation each month. He is expected to attend after-hours safety meetings, give instruction in his department, and do everything possible to protect the health of our employees. We feel this program has been successful, for in our classification of accidents into Categories I, II, and III (see Appendix One for definitions), the number has dropped in the three categories respectively to 28, 46, 150 this year as compared with 48, 72, and 190 last year.

Our external safety program is primarily concerned with our truck drivers, service men, and sales personnel. This program is under the direction of one person in the personnel office. His work has proved successful, as indicated by this year's figures of 18, 24, 38 for Categories I, II, and III as compared to 26, 32, and 48 for last year.

Our employee health care program is divided into three areas: Preventive Medicine, Retired Employees' Health, and New Employee Medical Evaluation. In the case of the first area . . . .

II.   PERSONNEL DEPARTMENT REPORT

The Personnel Department Report which follows covers only three areas: Training, Safety, and Employee Health.

Training

Almost 500 company personnel were involved this year in various training programs:

Shop Training. Eight groups of twenty men each were given instruction in various areas of shop activity. Each group met for three-hour periods once a week for seven weeks.

Office and Clerical Training. Eight groups of fifteen persons each met for two hours once each week for six weeks. Four groups concentrated on Office Procedures, while the other four received instruction in Written Communications.

Management Training. Ten groups of twenty men each met in seminars for two hours once a week for nine weeks. Five groups were concerned with Human Relations, while the other five studied Management Communications.

Safety Programs

The primary purpose of these programs is accident prevention and the development of safety awareness on the part of all employees. For administrative purposes, our safety program is divided into "in-plant" and external. Each of the 32 departments within the company has a designated safety officer who receives additional compensation of $50.00 per month for this added responsibility. His specific assignments include giving safety instruction, attendance at safety meetings, and related duties.

Our external safety program is under the direction of an assistant in the personnel department and covers truck drivers, service men, and sales personnel.

Both programs are proving successful, as the following table indicates:

REPORTABLE ACCIDENTS

Category*	1969	1968
Internal		
I	28	48
II	46	72
III	150	190
External		
I	18	26
II	24	32
III	38	48

*I = minor
II = requiring medical attention
III = requiring home or hospital confinement

Employee Health Care Programs

Although this program was begun five years ago, it has proved extremely popular with our employees. It is presently divided into three areas: Preventive Medicine, Retired Employees' Health, and New Employee Medical Evaluation.

Preventive Medicine

In this particular area . . . .

WHITE SPACE

It is foolish to spend a good deal of time and money on a report or letter and then economize on paper. The generous use of white space in the margins, between sections, above and below tables and charts, and on a title page adds immeasurably to the appeal of your presentation.

The well-balanced page looks inviting; the material is easy to read and easy to assimilate. This is in contrast to the appearance of a "heavy" page that has typing from the very top to the very bottom and only a half-inch margin on either side.

APPENDIXES, CHARTS, SUPPLEMENTS

The technical paper may require various supporting documents. To include this material in the text may upset the continuity of the discussion. This is especially true if such material is somewhat relevant to the topic but not vital. In such cases, the information should be placed in a footnote, if it is brief, or in an appendix. Sometimes a complete set of supporting documents must accompany a study; these can be placed in an appendix.

At times *extensive* tables or charts may serve their purpose better when placed at the end of a paper. Here clever fold-outs, gate folds, and lay-overs[8] can be employed.

Various supplements may also be made part of the whole presentation to aid in understanding. These would include sales promotion materials, statistics, company records, etc.

These are all valuable to include, but if they are not *vital* to the message being presented, they should be attached as additions to the report proper. Nothing should be permitted to interfere with the reader's understanding and assimilation of the core idea of the presentation.

8. A graph reflecting trend lines may be drawn on transparent paper and so inserted that it may be laid over a related graph or chart so that contrasts are made more obvious.

BINDINGS, INTRODUCTORY PAGES, AND REPRODUCTION

Some type of binder is vital for a study, research document, or report. It is usually an important document, and a good binder helps the reader examine it, file it, or forward it to others.

The firm which issues many reports may use a standard binder; other companies can use anything from an inexpensive folder to an attractive plastic spiral affair. Here again, one should not be penny-wise and pound-foolish in his selection of a cover.

Introductory pages, such as the title page, table of contents, or list of illustrations, should be tastefully designed and meaningful in their designations.

How the paper is reproduced depends on the number of copies desired and the size of the budget available. The report writer would now profit from the advice of a printing consultant. Of course, if only a limited number of copies is needed, the report should be typed. The results achieved by a competent secretary, using one of the modern electric typewriters with their contemporary type styles, are invariably excellent.

QUESTIONS FOR STUDY

I. Complete any of the following problems assigned. You may wish to review the chapter and note key points before attempting to solve the problem.

1. "Our words communicate more than the facts in the message." Please interpret this quotation.

2. Can you explain why some of your friends communicate their ideas in both writing and speaking easily and fluently, and others encounter major difficulties in similar tasks?

3. Review S. I. Hayakawa's *Language in Thought and Action* with special reference to his discussion on word denotation and connotation. Summarize his comments briefly and then apply his discussion in the areas of (1) race relations; (2) American foreign policy; (3) the generation gap; and (4) campus unrest.

4. Clip a column from a recent issue of a newspaper. Carefully check the author's remarks and underline key words and phrases which

you feel were purposely selected to arouse some emotional reaction on the part of the reader. You may wish to discuss your interpretation of these.

5. Duplicate the assignment above, but instead of a columnist's contribution, use an advertisement from a magazine or newspaper.

6. Edit the following brief passages to improve coherence, clarity, accuracy, and conciseness:

(1) There are many men who are not at all reluctant to tell their supervisors about their specific responsibilities and their duties.

(2) Sometimes we can, although not in every single instance, control much of our future; we sometimes do not act (or even react) to events so that we may take full advantage of our opportunities.

(3) The Maxwell merchandise which was shipped via a local trucking line whose services we had used on other occasions, consisted of components for our AR 232 Receiver and was designated c.o.d., although previous shipments from Maxwell had always been sent on open account.

(4) We began our operations with three full-time and eight part-time salesmen in just 8000 square feet of space in our Ogden Avenue location. In only three years' time we had grown to a sales staff of 18. That was in 1968. It was in 1965 that we began operations on Ogden Avenue and our next move was to Villa Park where we grew to the sales staff of 18. How we managed with 8000 square feet in 1965 is hard to understand when 40,000 seemed inadequate in 1968 in Villa Park. Also in Villa Park in 1968 we had 20 part-time salesmen.

(5) Initially we had three men serving as officers of the corporation. There was Bob Rheem who acted as head of the group and Tom Bartletti and Max Rubin our treasurer and vice president. Our treasurer had been with the company for several years before he was elected to that position, but the vice president came to us from California Electronics just three months ago. But even though he was a newcomer to the organization, everyone seemed to like him and felt that he always acted in the best interests of the employees and the firm.

Tom Bartletti had worked in the same capacity at two or three other companies so we all seemed to feel he really knew what he was doing and as a matter of fact, he performed his job with a great degree of competency.

Which reminds me that the treasurer we had last year got our tax situation so confused that we are still trying to get a ruling on the depreciation factor on our plant which was originally disallowed.

7. Edit the following sections to improve coherence, clarity, accuracy, and conciseness.

(1) Most of us are dependent on others to get our job completed. And because we are largely dependent on others to accomplish many of the activities that are needed to secure our goals, we must be aware of the sundry and various needs of people. Most authorities in the field list three or four basic needs of individuals. Abraham Maslow lists five needs; Langer presents three; Sigband talks about four.

Certainly we recognize that the most compelling is the physical need which includes the need for warmth, food, shelter, and related items closely associated with physiological functions of the body. Then we have what are sometimes referred to as social needs which include such areas as affection, affiliation, and nurturance. Now in this area we must keep in mind that they exist in two directions: the need to give a feeling of belonging (affiliation), a need to give affection, and a need to take care of others (nurturance). But in addition, we have the need to receive these from others. And, as a matter of fact, if an individual only has the capacity to receive these three social needs, and not give, we sometimes find that such an individual is not as carefully balanced emotionally and intellectually as he should be.

But this is an individual's relationship with another person. What about his relationship with himself which is of course, recognized by his egoistic needs. These are satisfied through accomplishment, responsibility, rewards, recognition, and related factors.

And finally, we must recognize that many persons and individuals (if not almost all) have a need to know. And as a matter of fact, it we don't tell people why the company is doing such and such, or why we bought that new piece of equipment, or whether or not we really are going to buy that small firm in Bayview, that doesn't mean people won't discuss it. And we know that if they don't have an answer for a situation, and we don't tell them, then the grapevine will take over and "explain" the situation. People have a need to know and it will be satisfied one way or another.

Now the interesting thing about all these needs, with the exception of the physical need, is that they can all be fulfilled to a most satisfactory degree the same way: through communications.

A touch on the shoulder, a smile, a wave, a nod of encouragement, a hand symbol for "O.K.," a pat on the back, a cheer, are every bit as vital as communication tools as a letter of congratulations, a name on the door, a picture in the company magazine, and a scroll of achievement.

Communication, therefore, will do much more for you in motivating others than will the threat of penalty or the rewards of money.

(2) An analysis of our production of the Jupiter Relay Systems for use in a variety of military and commercial applications reveals many interesting and important applications. As you may or may not recall, we began the Jupiter line with our Complete Climate unit or the CC 120 and the Bulldog B 220 line for interior assemblies. Each of these came in three capacities ranging from 300 to 400 to 500 watts. These were designated as the 3/w, 4/w, and 5/w units.

An examination of the records going back two years shows a sale of 5000 dozen of the 3/w and 5/w CC 120 units, but only 3200 dozen of the 4/w CC 120 for the same year. Certainly this hardly compared with last year's showing of 8000 and 9000 dozen of the CC 120 in the 3/w, and 5/w units respectively. The 4/w Bulldog (B 220 line) sold as many units last year (10,000) as the CC 120 in the 4/w.

Of course, the B 220 or Bulldog line consistently outsold the CC 120 model. Two years ago the 4/w hit 12,000 dozen in sales, while the 3/w and 5/w sold 15,000 and 14,000 respectively. Last year the Bulldog line dropped in sales probably because Electronics Corporation, one of our biggest customers, lost its government contract. In any event, we sold 11,000 dozen 3/w and 11,500 dozen 5/w.

Actually the sales were not the items of the greatest consideration at Jupiter. Our bigger problem was personnel and we found, probably like other companies, that we suffered from a rather critical shortage of top-flight administrative persons. However, this is not said in a deprecatory manner, but simply indicates that although a clear trend for added administrative personnel may be noted in our statistics, we have taken no specific steps or procedures to implement our Personnel Practices

recommendation committee report of last January which specifically and categorically emphasized to some extent that in 10
to 14 years, 75 percent of the personnel of the Jupiter Company
will retire. As an example of this, it is upsetting to note that
120, 140, 220, 360, and 570 persons retired from Jupiter in the
years 1965 to 1969 in that order. Obviously the figure is now
over 15 percent of our work force which is a serious matter
indeed.

CHAPTER SEVEN

Using Visual Aids

Tables, charts, graphs, drawings, sketches, and pictograms are certainly not new devices for communicating ideas; abundant pictorial representations are found on ancient parchments and on the walls of caves, temples and ancient buildings.

Many of those symbolic messages continue to communicate their ideas clearly and interestingly. However, we are still struggling to make sense of the peculiar lettering some civilizations have left us. Graphic representation tells a story directly; words only do so when the key or code to the lettering is known.

But beyond this, a graph or chart will much more quickly and easily convey an idea or a relationship that carries some complex quantitative aspect than will a series of words. Certainly there is nothing more irritating than trying to understand a complex discussion which cites dozens of different sums of money, tons of production, yearly changes, and percentage differentials. We read through such paragraphs once, twice, and perhaps three times trying to arrange the numbers in some meaningful form. Usually we are unsuccessful, and resort to transferring the statistics from the text to a sheet of paper and then into a rough table. How much better it would have been if the writer had presented such a table in the report itself! The assimilation of statistics is made much easier when they are communicated in carefully designed tables, charts, or graphs. Graphic aids normally permit the statistics to be compared, contrasted, and analyzed with much greater ease than if they had been presented in the narrative discussion.

This chapter contains only a brief overview of visual aids. There have been many different techniques developed in recent years, and the report writer should consult some of the many excellent books and articles concerned with the graphic representation of ideas.

SELECTION

Graphic aids should be used in a report only when they help clarify the data presented. When they are used as "window dressing," or to fill up space, they detract from the basic idea.

WHO IS THE READER?

As in all phases of report writing, the writer must ask himself "Who is the reader?" before choosing the chart or graph. If the report is directed to a group of aerospace engineers, the charts, graphs, and tables can be complex. But if the visual aid is to be included in the corporate annual report to stockholders, a logarithmic chart, for example, would not be appropriate.

The report writer must therefore determine which type of illustration will best communicate the idea to the reader; then he must choose his chart. The writer cannot arbitrarily decide that a line graph, with five different situations represented, is best. It is only best if the reader will find it clear, informative, and easy to understand. If five pictograms should be used in place of a complex line graph for a particular audience, then that is the answer.

This all seems so obvious as to require no comment. But if one simply looks through an annual report or a scientific journal, he will be amazed at how the complexity or simplicity of many of the charts is often not in keeping with the level of the audience.

WHAT TYPE OF GRAPHIC AID SHOULD BE USED?

A second question the report writer must ask himself: What type of chart or table will best tell my story? At times the report writer gets in the habit of using a table for this type of representation, and a bar chart for that, adapting them to almost every situation. He knows them well and can use them effectively, but he runs the risk of not stretching his imagination occasionally to determine if there might not be another, novel and better, way to present the data. If the reader is interested in trends, a series of bars or a line graph might be useful. If, however, he is concerned with specifics and precise data, he would be irritated with bar charts. He wants specific facts and figures, and a table may be the answer.

DESIGNING THE CONTENT

Not only must the report writer determine which type of graphic aid best presents his data, but he must also decide how complex or simple it should be in reference to the data and the reader. One reader will be comfortable with five different information designations on one chart: solid, broken, dotted, dashed, and dot-dash lines. Another reader requires five separate charts. He doesn't have the interest, motivation, or ability to analyze a single complex visual aid. In the two tables shown here, for example, the same information is presented. The first table is difficult to understand, and much more complex than it should be. Table 2, however, is simple in its construction and easy to interpret.

TABLE 1. SALES OF HI DEB SPORTSWEAR (LISTED IN DOZENS)

	June 1969	June 1968	June 1963	Unit Difference 1969 and 1963
Swimsuits				
Bel Air Line	225	200	250	−25
Brentwood Line	250	210	225	+25
Sailing Jackets				
Bel Air Line	350	330	385	−35
Brentwood Line	400	325	380	−20
Summer Blouses				
Bel Air Line	2400	2350	2150	+250
Brentwood Line	1250	1200	1375	−125
Summer Skirts				
Bel Air Line	300	275	285	+15
Brentwood Line	500	475	550	+50
Blazers				
Bel Air Line	950	925	760	+190
Brentwood Line	840	875	800	+40

TABLE 2. SALES OF HI DEB SPORTSWEAR (LISTED IN DOZENS)

	June 1969	June 1968	Percentage Change (approx.) June 1969 with June 1963 (Base Year)
Bel Air Line			
Swimsuits	225	200	−11%
Sailing Jackets	350	330	−10%
Summer Blouses	2400	2350	+11%
Summer Skirts	300	275	+ 5%
Blazers	950	925	+20%
Brentwood Line			
Swimsuits	250	210	+10%
Sailing Jackets	400	325	− 5%
Summer Blouses	1250	1200	−10%
Summer Skirts	500	475	−10%
Blazers	840	875	+ 5%

EXAMPLE CASE OF CHOICE AND DESIGN

Which is the best visual aid to represent the data contained in the following excerpt from a periodic report?

> Twelve of our Star-Economy gasoline stations in the Chicago area were selected to check the effectiveness of the two display stands in generating sales. For purposes of the survey, the stations were designated with numbers from 1 to 12 (see Appendix A for number and address of each station).
>
> The test was conducted from June 5 to June 10 and the total sales for three items were recorded: "Road Safety Flares, package of 4," Unit 201; "All Purpose Med-Kit," Unit 404; and "All Purpose Wrench Kit," Unit 605.
>
> Two different cases were used to display these three items for sale. Six of the cases were our regular 5-foot walnut with chrome trim affairs, while the other six were newly manufactured by the Greeley Company. These were only 2 feet wide, constructed of heavy cardboard, and equipped with a continuously flashing red and yellow electric blinker. Stations 1, 4, 5, 7, 9, and 10 received the 5-foot case, and Stations 2, 3, 6, 8, 11, and 12 the 2-foot case with blinkers.
>
> Total sales of the three items during the six-day test period (Monday through Saturday) were as follows: Stores 1, 2, 3, and 4 sold 350, 820, 870, and 440 respectively. In Stores 5, 6, 7, 8, sales were recorded at 375, 950, 475, and 675 units. Sales of the same units in Store 9 were 550; Store 10, 525; and 11 sold 1150, while Store 12 sold 1050. It would certainly appear that there is a correlation between sales and type of display case. This correlation was also apparent in a similar survey conducted in Detroit early this year.

The examples shown reflect relatively simple material which is easy to assimilate and understand. Obviously the reader finds it easier to compare sales when the stores which have a similar type of case are grouped together, rather than in those charts which present the data in order of store number.

The basic fact to keep in mind is that careful evaluation of the data and the reader should be carried through *before* a visual aid is selected and designed. When properly used, the table, chart, or graph can make a significant contribution in communicating ideas.

SALES OF UNITS 201, 404, AND 605, JUNE 5-10.

Example 1

Station No.	Total Sales
1	350
2	820
3	870
4	440
5	375
6	950
7	475
8	675
9	550
10	525
11	1150
12	1050

Example 2

Station No.	5 ft. Display Case	2 ft. Display Case (Blinker)
1	350	
2		820
3		870
4	440	
5	375	
6		950
7	475	
8		675
9	550	
10	525	
11		1150
12		1050

Example 3

Station No.	5 ft. Display Case	2 ft. Display Case (Blinker)
1	350	
4	440	
5	375	
7	475	
9	550	
10	525	
2		820
3		870
6		950
8		675
11		1150
12		1050

Example 4

Station No.	5 ft. Display Case	Station No.	2 ft. Display Case (Blinker)
1	350	2	820
4	440	3	870
5	375	6	950
7	475	8	675
9	550	11	1150
10	525	12	1050

Example 5

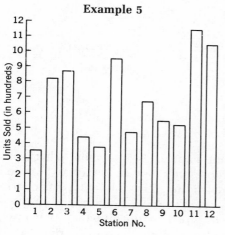

Example 6

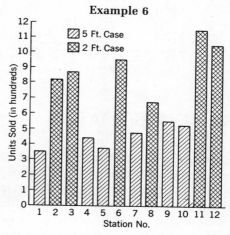

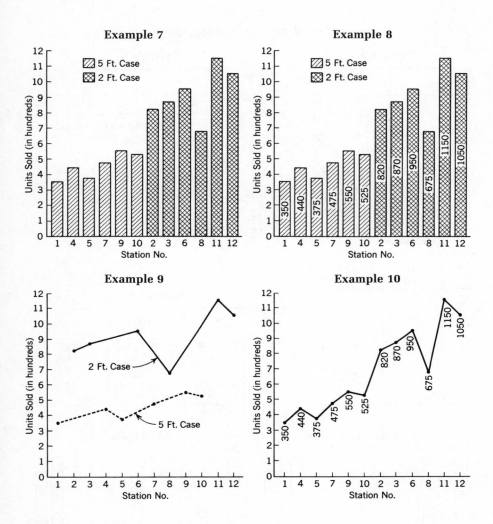

Example 7

Example 8

Example 9

Example 10

MISREPRESENTATION

Sometimes a report writer will present some facts in a table, chart, or graph and omit others. The data he represents may be accurate, but the impression he creates is basically misleading. The following bar chart is an example of selective omission. The casual reader might simply *assume* that several bars have been dropped in the illustration below only to save space, and that sales have been climbing steadily from 1958 to 1967. However, if we examine the section which has been omitted (ostensibly to save space), we find quite a different story. Sales have *not*

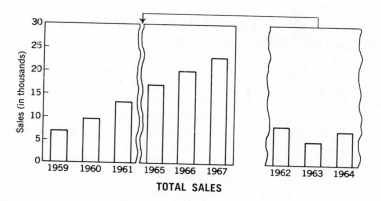

TOTAL SALES

gone up consistently. The chart is therefore accurate but misleading.[1]

Visual distortion is another way to subtly misrepresent statistics. Perhaps the first figure below is not sufficiently impressive. Why not convey it as illustrated in the second figure—or even the third? Note that the base numbers are present on both the horizontal and vertical axes. The tops of the money bags are precisely at 3 and 6 on the vertical axis—but the horizontal dimension has been stretched.

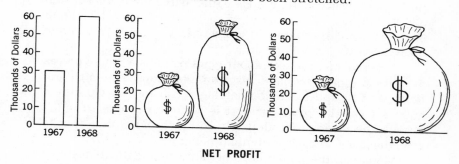

NET PROFIT

Phony statistics are also related in statements which *seem* to convey facts, but, like double talk, really say nothing.[2] The ad which shouts "50% bigger" but neglects to indicate "bigger than what" is an example. Or the "giant 256 sq. in. TV screen"; why "giant"? Certainly 256 sq. in. is 256 sq. in., and adjectives do not increase the size—except to the suggestible mind.

1. There is probably nothing better available on this topic than Darrel Huff's instructive and entertaining book, *How to Lie with Statistics.* Each of us can find in it examples of misleading statistics which we have accepted—or perhaps transmitted.

2. Daniel Seligman, in an amusing and thought-provoking article, "We're Drowning in Phony Statistics" (*Fortune,* November 1961), identifies two varieties of misleading statements: the "meaningless statistic" and the "unknowable statistic."

Newspaper columnist Sydney Harris had the following[3] to say about the half-truths conveyed in misleading words:

A government study of income by occupational groups shows that doctors, as a class, earn about twice as much from the practice of medicine as attorneys do from the practice of law.

But this is only another example of the danger of statistics in a void. For while the great bulk of the doctors' income comes from medicine, a similar percentage of the lawyers' income does not come from law.

Many, if not most lawyers, make as much on the side as they do from their direct law practice. They are involved in many legal deals in forming companies, buying property and "putting paper together." For their services, they are often rewarded with a piece of the action. Most lawyers get rich not from legal fees but from supralegal connections.

Another common fallacy holds that psychiatrists—and especially psychoanalysts—are at the financial top of their profession, because they charge the patient anywhere from $25 to $50 per visit. Actually, these men rank near the bottom of the medical specialties in terms of income, as any accurate breakdown would clearly show.

A psychoanalyst sees about eight patients a day, whereas a well-equipped dermatologist can see more than eight an hour. At $10 a clip, the dermatologist can pull in more than $600 a day. The psychoanalyst is forced to charge so much because he gives proportionately so much more time—not to say attention—to each individual patient.

Moreover, these men have perhaps double the investment in their career than most specialists have. Not only must they go through a longer regimen of study, they must also have several years of their own personal analysis—which is not deductible as an educational or professional expense.

And someone who wants to do child analysis must take an extra two years to be certified for this specialty-within-a-specialty, which may mean he is nearly 40 years old before he begins to earn more than a nominal income. . . .

3. Sydney J. Harris, "What Statistics Don't Show," *Chicago Daily News,* April 19, 1968, page 18. © Publishers-Hall Syndicate 1968. Reprinted by permission.

When we *read* charts, graphs, and illustrations, or interpret statements citing statistics, we should do so critically. Are the ideas conveyed to us accurate and complete? And when we *transmit* ideas through graphic aids or statistics, are we being complete and thorough?

There is probably no statistical reference more commonly used (and misused) than the term *on the average*. It is employed to designate the common characteristics or central tendency of a group.

Because "on the average" is often loosely used to refer to the mean, median, or mode, it is sometimes employed in one context and interpreted in another. For example, in the Dependable Car Sales Company, automobiles were sold in the quantities listed on the dates designated below:

DATE	NO. SOLD	DATE	NO. SOLD
July 1	16	July 11	6
July 2	16	July 12	5
July 5	0	July 13	7
July 6	2	July 14	8
July 7	1	July 15	4
July 8	3		

The *mean* (or arithmetical average) number of cars sold is 6.18. This figure is obtained by totaling the cars sold and dividing by the number of days. The *median* number of cars sold, 5, is the middle number in the array of daily sales arranged from high to low: 1 2 3 4⑤6 7 8 16. The *mode* designates the most frequently recurring number in a group. In this case, 16 occurs twice, the other numbers only once; so 16 is the mode.

Thus "on the average" can be easily misconstrued or misused. The report writer should use it with caution, and the report reader should always question an "on the average" figure. He should determine whether the writer is referring to the mean, median, or mode—and beyond that, he should ask how many cases were included in the sample to secure the figure.

By permission of Johnny Hart and Field Enterprises, Inc.

TABLES

What would your reaction be to the following paragraphs encountered in a production report?

> This month, January 1969, was an especially satisfactory one, for production increased very appreciably.
>
> In our Model 200 line we sold 250 dozen Western in 1968 as compared to 275 dozen in 1969. This was a 10% increase. In the Tally-Ho line we had a +5% jump with 220 dozen in 1969 and only 210 dozen in the previous year. As for the Bronco Line, also in Model 200, there was a 5% decline with 380 dozen sold in 1969 and 400 in 1968.
>
> The story is relatively similar with the model 300. The Collegiate sold 825 dozen in 1969 and 750 dozen in 1968 for a 10% increase. However, both the Fastback and the Touchdown declined. The former took a −5% (from 600 to 570) drop, and the latter suffered a decline of three percentage points when it went from 500 dozen to 485.

Now compare the above with the table below.

FANFARE PRODUCTION, JANUARY 1969 (IN DOZENS)

	January 1969	January 1968	Percentage Change
Model 200			
Western	275	250	+10%
Tally-Ho	220	210	+ 5
Bronco	380	400	− 5
Model 300			
Collegiate	825	750	+10
Fastback	570	600	− 5
Touchdown	485	500	− 3

The foregoing example makes it obvious that a table is far superior to a series of sentences in communicating quantitative ideas. In addition, tables have many other advantages:

1. Materials can be listed concisely.
2. Reference to specific facts can be made quickly.
3. Comparisons between and among statistics can be made easily.
4. The reader can comprehend and assimilate quantitative data listed in tables much more quickly than if the same information were presented within paragraphs in the body of the report.

Authorities in the field of visual aids classify tables in different ways. One group speaks of a *dependent* table, which does not carry a title or subtitle and is explained by the text material which follows or precedes it. The *independent* table, with its title, headnote, and explanatory comments found in the caption and/or footnote, stands by itself. Even if it were viewed without the text material on the page, it would convey a clear and complete idea to the reader.

Tables are also designated as *spot, special purpose,* and *reference.* The *spot* table may be made up of a few figures, set apart from the text in some organized fashion, to make understanding easier.

FACULTY SIZE AT MIDWEST UNIVERSITY

	1967	1966	1965
Professors	110	90	62
Associate Professors	240	230	205
Assistant Professors	320	402	390
Instructors	340	320	290

The *special-purpose* table is somewhat more complex, usually uses column headings and rulings, and often carries a title.

PRODUCTION OF PRINTED CIRCUIT BOARDS (IN THOUSANDS), CIRCUIT SWITCH CORP., MANSFIELD PLANT

Year	Radio			Television		
	#101	#102	#103	#301	#302	#303
1967	150	250	90	580	300	250
1966	120	220	115	510	310	220
1965	110	220	120	420	290	205

The *reference* table usually contains a fairly large quantity of data. The table is ruled, titled, and arranged to facilitate comparisons and evaluations by the reader. It is not unusual to find government reports containing a great deal of information which has been distilled and refined into one or two excellent tables.

Check List for Constructing Tables

✔ Each vertical column should be headed clearly and concisely.

✔ Each reference table should have a number and a title. Subtitles should be used, if necessary, to further clarify or explain the caption.

✔ Comparative data should be placed on a horizontal plane from left to right (the usual direction of the eyes in reading).

✔ Fractions should be noted in decimals.

✔ Standard terms should be used throughout the table (yards, meters, fathoms should all be converted to a standard unit of measure and explained in a footnote).

✔ Tables should always be designed so that reading and understanding are easy. This requires careful ruling, plenty of white space, and clear titling.

CHARTS AND GRAPHS

Charts, graphs, pictograms, and sketches can present information dramatically and skillfully. With a glance at a bar or line chart, the reader can determine the *trend* of an activity. For example, have sales increased? declined? remained stationary?

If the reader is a layman, he may not appreciate the fluctuations of the stock market or the changes in the gross national product if the information is presented in percentages and numbers within the text. But if he sees a tiny money bag next to a giant one, the basic message may be communicated more effectively.

It is true that charts and pictograms do not contain the quantity of specific data a table does, but their purpose is different. They indicate trends, rather than precise data.

PIE OR CIRCLE CHARTS

The "pie" or circle chart is probably one of the most popular visual aids used. It is easy to interpret, does not require extensive art work, and communicates its basic ideas with clarity and simplicity. Although each segment represents a different percentage, the total comes to 100 per cent.

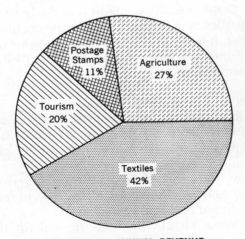

SOURCES OF ANNUAL REVENUE

Because of its popularity, the pie chart has been used extensively in a variety of different ways. Firms use a picture of their product to represent their "pie," and divide it into appropriate segments to represent cost of materials, salaries, depreciation, etc.

192

The report reader should beware of the "pie" which has segments labeled only with verbal designations and no percentage figures. And he should also be skeptical of the pie that has segments numbered consecutively and the legend noted at the bottom of the page. One of the most frequently used illustrations in the game of "lying with statistics" is the pie (or product) chart with out-of-proportion segments. Each segment in the pie chart should be identified (taxes, salaries, advertising), and show the percentage it represents.

BAR CHARTS

As in the case of most illustrations of this nature, the bar chart is constructed so that each point is located in reference to two variables: one a quantity of money, temperature, volume (etc.), usually indicated along the vertical axis; and the other a time, distance, load (etc.) factor, most frequently indicated along the horizontal axis.

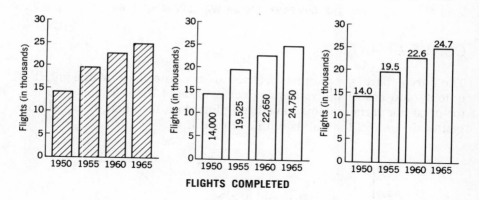

FLIGHTS COMPLETED

Bar charts may be presented either vertically (often called column charts) or horizontally; the length of the bar normally indicates quantity. Ordinarily the variation in bars should only be in length. If a bar is changed in length and width, to designate two variables, confusion in interpretation is likely to result.

Various techniques can be used to make the chart more interesting: bars in a second color, hatching effects, projective drawing, or sketching the company's products in a stylized column form are all helpful.

One of the criticisms leveled at the bar chart is that it does not reflect quantities with precision and accuracy, which is true. When the reader's eye moves from the top or end of the bar to the scale axis, it is impossible for him to determine the exact quantity designation. However, a little imagination can correct that if the sums are placed within the bars or at the top of each bar.

SEGMENTED BAR CHARTS

The segmented bar chart is a simple variation on the pie chart. A single bar represents the total data. However, it is split into segments which are in proportion to the quantities designated. Here also the bar may be horizontal, vertical, or designed to duplicate the company's product.

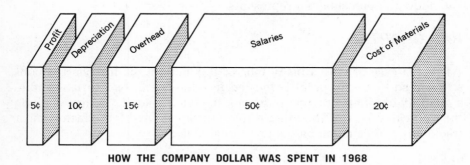

HOW THE COMPANY DOLLAR WAS SPENT IN 1968

CURVE CHARTS

The curve chart is sometimes referred to as a line chart or line graph. It quickly and easily shows trends over periods of time. It is easy to use, for once the various items have been plotted on the chart, it is a simple matter to connect the points with a curved line.

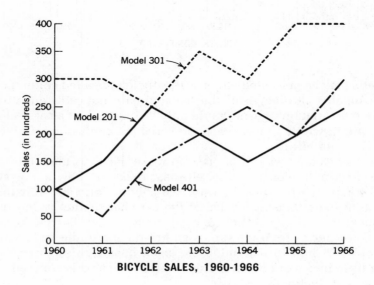

BICYCLE SALES, 1960-1966

A further advantage is the large quantity of information which may be depicted on one chart. It is relatively simple to use multiple curves on one drawing to depict related data. Of course the curves are made up differently (solid, broken, dashed, dotted), for the reader's convenience.

BAND CHARTS AND COMPONENT BAR CHARTS

The band chart is similar to the multiple curve chart except for the shadings. Each shaded section (usually beginning with dark and moving up to lighter colors) represents a quantity.

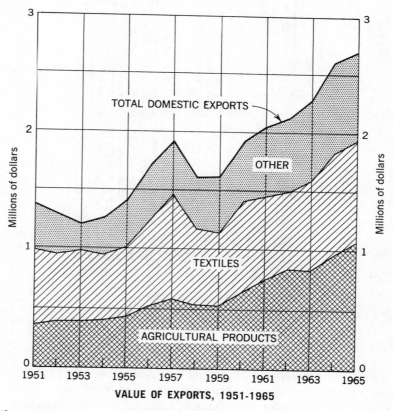

VALUE OF EXPORTS, 1951-1965

The same pattern is followed with the component bar chart. (See top of p. 196).

Both of these charts should be used only to give an impression of general relationships. If the report writer wishes to show exact relationships or precise data, he should use some other visual aid.

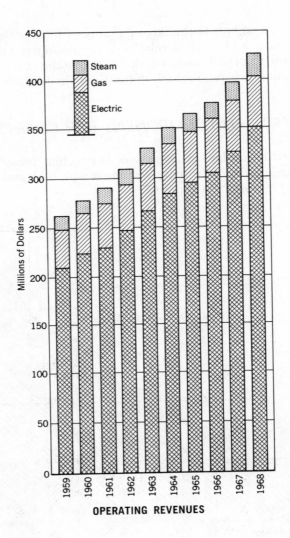

RATIO CHARTS

The usual chart reflects arithmetical changes. The ratio chart is drawn on semilogarithmic paper to illustrate *ratio* or *percentage*.

On an ordinary chart, for example, a change in Army reserve strength from 3000 to 30,000 and Navy reserve strength from 10,000 to 100,000 would be difficult to represent. The major change in the Navy figure might well force the line or bar designations off the chart completely. If these figures were represented on a ratio chart, we would simply be showing the *percentage* of change, which is the same for both Army and Navy.

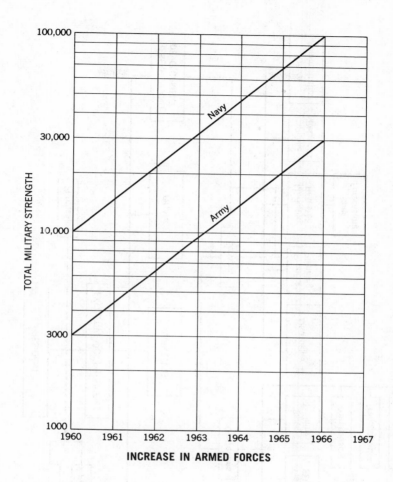

INCREASE IN ARMED FORCES

MISCELLANEOUS GRAPHIC AIDS

ORGANIZATIONAL CHARTS

As the American corporation becomes more and more complex, it is vital for the manager to have a clear understanding of whom he reports to and who reports to him. And every employee usually feels more comfortable when he knows precisely where he stands within the company, exactly who is his boss, and who is his supervisor's boss.

To accomplish these ends, the organizational chart has come into being. The typical vertical chart (shown on p. 198) reads from top to bottom; the horizontal chart is interpreted from left to right. The circle chart shows authority emanating from the center out. A variation similar to the

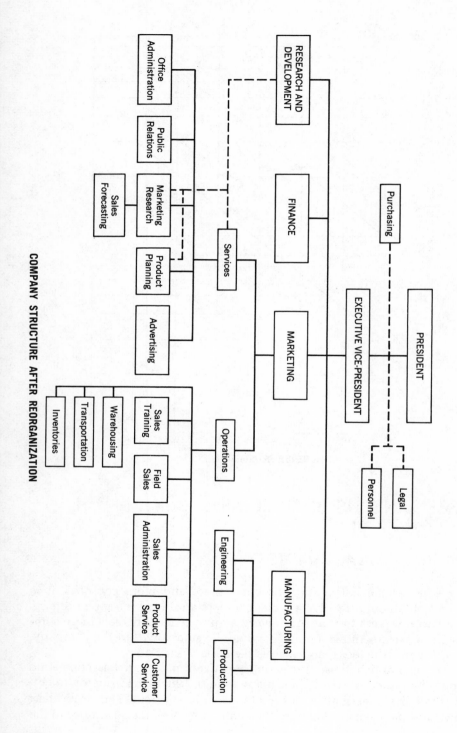

COMPANY STRUCTURE AFTER REORGANIZATION

circle is the beehive chart. (See McMurry, "Clear Communications for Chief Executives," Part IV.) In most organizational charts, solid lines indicate direct relationships and broken lines indicate indirect relationships.

Although authority and the chain of command usually differ between the real situation and what is depicted on paper, the organizational chart does serve an important purpose. Something is needed to give an appreciation of the structure of the company, and nothing does it quite so quickly and easily as an organizational chart.

FLOW CHARTS

Flow charts indicate the direction of movement of a product or a process from the initial stages to completion. Sometimes simplified drawings or symbols are used to represent stages, with arrows to indicate direction. The flow chart, flow sheet, or routing diagram can be extremely helpful to the new employee or anyone who wishes to gain a rapid familiarity with the sequence of activity in a process.

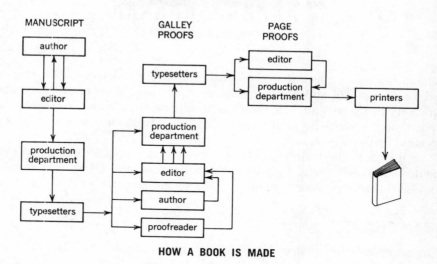

HOW A BOOK IS MADE

PICTOGRAMS OR PICTORIAL CHARTS

The use of drawings has proved especially popular in recent years. For the individual who is hurried, or disinclined to interpret a six-line curve chart, the pictogram is excellent. He can quickly see, for example, that the cost of living has gone up if little market baskets are shown marching up a chart, or that more office buildings were constructed this year than last year if five additional skyscrapers are shown on a pictogram.

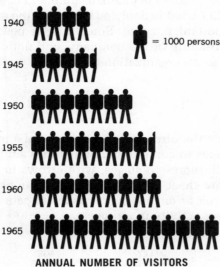

1940

1945

1950

1955

1960

1965

♦ = 1000 persons

ANNUAL NUMBER OF VISITORS

The symbols, such as dollar signs, autos, homes, planes, tires, etc., should all be of uniform appearance and size. Each should represent the same quantity or dimension. The sketches should be simple and so representative that it would be almost impossible for two readers to interpret a symbol differently.

Only a limited amount of uncomplicated information can be presented in a pictogram. For data which have several facets and require thoughtful interpretation, other visual aids are preferable.

MAP CHARTS

For representation that is dependent on geographical or spatial relationships, map charts are excellent. Symbols (trees, oil wells, people, livestock, etc.) can designate quantities, and their position on the map can indicate location.

A map drawn out of proportion to its true land areas can be used to indicate the disparate characteristics of various areas of the nation. For example, a map of the United States depicting manufacturing output has the eastern and midwestern states drawn out of proportion so that they appear much larger than the other states.

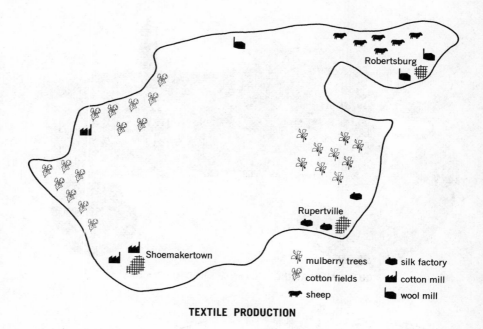

Robertsburg

Rupertville

Shoemakertown

mulberry trees
cotton fields
sheep

silk factory
cotton mill
wool mill

TEXTILE PRODUCTION

CUTAWAY AND EXPLODED DRAWINGS

Cutaway and exploded sketches or photographs are excellent for showing the reader the component parts of a piece of equipment, as well as subsurface areas. They are usually arranged to give the reader a perspective view. A cutaway can often convey a much clearer picture of the intricate interior working parts of a complex mechanical device than could a 5000-word description.

An exploded diagram presents the component parts of a device. Each piece is drawn to show how it fits into, or next to, a contiguous piece. If it is a piece part, for example, each of its segments is exploded. Dotted lines are sometimes used to illustrate how the entire unit is attached to the larger mechanism.

Both the cutaway and the exploded diagram are especially valuable for the technical report. The writer benefits because he can do a much better job of describing a product with one sketch than he can with pages of text. The adept artist can help communicate not only with the care and precision of his drawings, but in his use of imagination. A projective drawing, for example, adds a great deal to a reader's appreciation of depth.

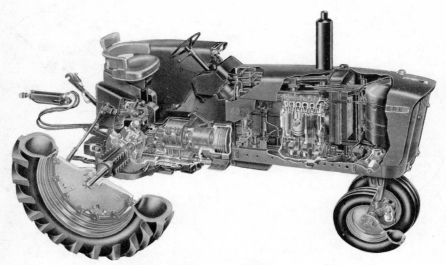

CUTAWAY DRAWING (Courtesy John Deere Company)

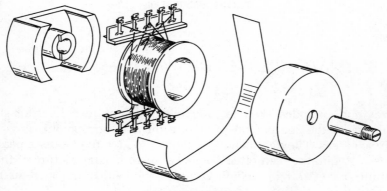

EXPLODED DRAWING

PHOTOGRAPHS

The use of photographs in reports has increased in recent years, and with good reason. They are most persuasive as visual evidence in support of the text. If a report writer wants to indicate that a shield does not bend on impact, he can take a picture at the precise instant of impact. If he wants to prove a cement support cracked, he can take a photo. If an individual wants a view of a piece of property, he need only snap the picture, and then pencil on it the width, depth, frontage, or other pertinent data. The contractor need not draw a diagram of the kitchen he is going to remodel; he snaps the room from several angles, pencils in the dimensions needed, and hours of drafting time are saved.

Another advantage of photographs is the speed with which they can be made. In black and white or color, a Polaroid photo can be snapped and printed in minutes. Photographs are also easier, less time-consuming, and less expensive to prepare than charts and graphs—although they are more expensive to reproduce in printed form.

PLACEMENT OF ILLUSTRATIONS

An illustration should appear in the text if the material it presents is directly related to the topic under discussion, and any explanation, interpretation, or analysis of the statistics in it should appear in the body of the report immediately before or after it. On the other hand, if the tables and charts are meant only to present material which is related to text information or amplifies it—but which is not vital to it—they can be placed in an appendix or supplement.

But the report writer should keep in mind the obvious danger of placing anything important in an appendix. Few readers are inclined to check illustrations not in the body of the text. If the reader can refer to a chart easily and quickly, he will use it. If he is required to flip back and forth between the body of the report and charts in the appendix, he may become irritated and stop referring to the illustrations altogether.

At times a table or chart may be found in a footnote, but it usually seems out of place. The chart almost always appears to be too large for the space available, unless it contains relatively little information. The footnote area at the bottom of a page is not recommended for illustrations.

This chapter has presented only a few of the visual aids which can be used to help convey ideas in report writing. There are many others, such as PERT charts, schematics, block diagrams, etc. But the individual who is convinced that there is some truth to the old cliché about one picture being worth a thousand words will search out the best visual aid for his particular message and his particular reader.

QUESTIONS FOR STUDY

I. Answer the following questions as succinctly as possible.

1. Is it wiser to place a graphic aid in the body of a report, at the end of it, or in an appendix?

2. What factors govern the report writer's choice of a simple or complex graphic aid?

3. If one wished to present the trends in the cost of living since the end of World War II, which type(s) of graphic aid would you recommend and why?

4. What specific attributes do tables possess which make them especially valuable when large quantities of precise data must be presented?

5. Explain the differences among the terms *mean*, *median*, and *modal* averages.

6. Secure an annual report and cut out two graphic aids. Present these two aids with a brief statement of constructive criticism on why the aid does a good or poor job presenting the information it represents. If possible, make specific suggestions for improvement.

II. Present the data in the following problems in any tabular or graphic form which you feel is the most appropriate.

1. In a newspaper advertisement which stresses the theme of *"Everyone flies these days; why don't you?"* depict the increase in the International Airlines fleet from 5 passenger planes 10 years ago as compared to 125 today. The average number of passengers carried today in a one-month period is 120,000 as compared to 3000 for a one-month period 10 years ago.

2. In a campus survey you found that today's college senior divided his dollar into 30¢ for fees and tuition, 32¢ for food and room facilities, 15¢ for recreation, 7¢ for books and supplies, 14¢ for clothes, and 2¢ for miscellaneous. This contrasted with a similar survey made of the class of 1950 when expenditures on the average ran: 6¢ for miscellaneous, 12¢ for recreation, 14¢ for books and supplies, 25¢ for fees and tuition, 25¢ for food and room facilities, and 18¢ for clothes.

3. The Spin-Disk Record Company has divided its sales into three categories: Popular, Classical, and Foreign. An examination of the sales of records to distributors in the United States indicated that in February of 1969, 202,000 Foreign records were sold as compared to 850,000 Pop and 350,000 Classical. In the same month of 1968, 725,000 Pop were sold, 305,000 Classical, and 140,000 Foreign. The figures for February 1969 for Pop, Classical, and Foreign were 8 per cent, 6 per cent, and 8 per cent over the base year sales of 1960.

In Record Club sales, for February 1968, Pop sold 210,000; Classical 65,000; and Foreign numbered 30,000. This was relatively poor as compared to 1969 when sales for Foreign were 51,000; Pop, 290,000; and Classical 105,000. The contrast with the base year (1960) could not be used in this instance simply because no Record Club existed in that year.

4. ABC University is seriously considering the construction of faculty housing near the university campus. At the present time, most faculty live in homes and apartments in the greater metropolitan area of which ABC is a part.

You have just completed a survey of faculty concerning housing and you have found that:

38.5 per cent would be interested in buying a new home near the university.

30.5 per cent would be interested in living in a university-managed apartment building.

10 per cent are undecided.

21 per cent have no desire to move from their present location.

5. In 1969 Argus Oil Corporation had sales of $31,000,000 as contrasted to $12,000,000 in 1963 and $15,000,000 in 1964. In the following year, 1965, sales went to $25,000,000, but dropped to $21,000,000 in 1966. In 1967 and 1968, sales were $26,000,000 and $27,500,000 respectively.

6. Our personnel recruitment efforts have encountered a few problems; however, there has been a steady rise in the number of persons secured in all four quarters last year by our Los Angeles headquarters as contrasted to the Chicago headquarters.

In Los Angeles we were able to secure 45 salaried and 320 hourly personnel in the first quarter, and 62, 60, and 40 salaried in the second, third, and fourth quarters respectively. In the area of hourly workers, we added 360, 390, and 320 in the second, third, and fourth quarters.

However, the Chicago office, with much greater needs, was able to recruit only 40, 45, 45, and 35 salaried personnel in the same calendar year in the quarters from first to fourth. The picture was somewhat different in respect to hourly employees in Chicago. In the first quarter, 450 were added to the payroll and for each of the three quarters following, 610, 650, and 550 were added, respectively.

III. Present the data in the following problems in any tabular or graphic form which you feel is most appropriate.

1. You have just reviewed questionnaires returned by 30 men who received their Bachelor's degree at the same time you did. Ten of those men indicated their income was $12,000; 12 checked $18,000;

3 listed $28,000; and 5 noted theirs as $50,000 or up. What were the mean, median, and modal incomes of the 30 men?

2. Draw an organization chart of the administration and/or instructional staff of the school in which you are enrolled. If you would prefer to use an organization of which you are a member, do so.

3. The number of single-family dwellings constructed in Plainfield, California, in 1969 was 85,000 as compared to 30,000 in 1959; and 25,000 in 1949. In 1949, 170,000 apartment units were constructed as compared to 290,000 in 1959, and 480,000 in 1969.

Present this information to (a) newspaper readers of Plainfield and (b) magazine subscribers of the *California Realtors Monthly*. It should be noted that non-taxable units were not included in any of the data cited above nor were government-owned units.

4. Wage rates for skilled artisans in the construction industry in New York have risen from $4.50 per hour in 1965 to $4.80 in 1966; $5.50 in 1967, $5.90 in 1968, and $6.50 in 1969. This compares with California where the wage rates for the same years went from $4.90 to $5.10 to $5.75 to $6.40 and finally $6.90. In New York, this did not include hospitalization costs (of approximately 30¢ per hour in value) but it did in the California statistics. All other fringe benefits were included in the hourly rates and were essentially the same in both cities.

5. Your evaluation of college records shows that the School of Engineering awarded 850 Bachelor's and 290 Master's degrees in 1969, and 670 Bachelors in 1968 and 550 in 1967. In 1967, 250 Masters were conferred and 210 in 1968. The School of Business Administration awarded 790 Bachelors and 410 Masters of Business Administration in 1966. These figures rose to 910 and 540 in 1967 and jumped in 1968 to 1050 Bachelors and 610 MBA's.

The School of Liberal Arts awarded 1800 Bachelors in 1969 and 650 Masters of Arts. In 1968, the number was 1650 Bachelors and 450 Masters, and in 1967 only 290 Masters and 1750 Bachelors.

All three schools awarded a total of 65 doctorates in 1967; 72 in 1968; and 90 in 1969. Of these figures, four were honorary in each of the three years.

6. Attempt to draw a flow chart tracing the process of registration in your school. You may do this with a specific work process at your place of employment if you prefer.

CHAPTER EIGHT

The Brief Report

As we have noted earlier, most business decisions are based on reports submitted to management. Some of these reports are long, detailed presentations, complete with tables of contents, letters of transmittal, appendixes, summaries, indexes, etc., but most are relatively short, from half a page to several pages in length.

For these reports to be effective, they should reflect certain attributes. They should be accurate and precise in the data they present, clear in style, and logical and orderly in organization. In addition, they should:

1. follow a completely objective point of view unless they are meant to be, and are clearly evident to be, persuasive or sales reports.
2. substantiate all statements made, using either statistical data, quotations, or other forms of evidence.
3. utilize visual representations—charts, graphs, tables, etc.—whenever and wherever they will assist in the presentation of the message.
4. explain any unusual rise, fall, or change in the statistical data presented. If the reader notes that the figures indicate a 40 per cent drop in sales between this month and last, the writer had better explain the reason. If he does not, he will surely hear the irritated voice of the boss shouting for an explanation.
5. present an attractive format. Every report should be easy to read. Use topic and subtopic headings; tables, charts, and graphs; wide margins and plenty of white space.

A well-thought-out and clearly written report frequently brings favorable action—and focuses attention on the writer. One young executive told me of his frustration in suggesting a new product line to several officers in his firm. He said, "I spoke to them about it at meetings, in the corridors, on the golf course, and at lunch. I sent memos and notices, but no one ever acted favorably. One day, I carefully organized a recommendation report. I worked on it, off and on, for a week. I supplied substantiating data, included visual aids, had it neatly typed and bound, and forwarded several copies, asking for a decision at the supervisors' meeting scheduled three weeks in the future. You know something? My recommendations received unanimous approval, and the product has done extremely well—and so have I. It's all the result of the report, which was read, analyzed, and evaluated."

That is what a good report always does: It turns the spotlight on the topic and the writer, and frequently gets action. It is often the basis for decisions to start production lines rolling, halt expenditures on TV advertising, bring about a merger, or any one of dozens of other vital activities.

If one were to visit a hundred American corporations, he would encounter dozens of different formats for reports. Many reports serve the same purpose but are referred to by different names; some have the same name in several companies but different objectives and different formats. It is therefore important to remember that reports may have different designations and formats in different companies but may seek to attain similar objectives.

Let us examine those types which are most frequently used by American companies. Although their purposes may differ, many of the principles of effective reports are found in all.

THE PERIODIC REPORT

The periodic report is perhaps one of the most widely written reports in industry. It is prepared monthly by department managers for their supervisors; weekly by foremen; daily by others; and yearly by corporations for their stockholders. With the exception of the annual report, decisions for future action are almost always made on the basis of periodic reports. Because of this it is absolutely vital that their contents be accurate, clear, complete, and concise. The one who originates the typical weekly or monthly report is usually responsible for the area reported on, and he normally possesses the most knowledge about the topic. For that reason, the reader expects to receive accurate and complete information on the activities for that period, with recommendations (if included) for future action.

Typically the manager who receives a monthly sales report will also receive others covering the same period from production, credit, accounting, research and development, personnel, advertising, and per- haps other departments. For this executive to manage properly, he must be informed, and these reports supply him with the facts and figures on which he bases his decisions. These decisions are not always easy to reach, but they must be made. The executive will often find that there is more disagreement than agreement among the reports. The credit man- ager recommends that all open accounts be limited; the sales director says this is just the time to expand credit. The production manager in- dicates that he finally has six lines running smoothly on open-toe shoe styles for women; but marketing research recommends cutbacks on all open-toe models because of style changes, and a fast move to women's bow tie slippers and slingbacks "or we'll lose a large share of the sum- mer market."

Someone has to make a decision from among the conflicting recom- mendations. And that someone is the executive to whom the reports are directed. Woe unto the writer whose reports are not clearly written or are inadequately substantiated by statistical data. The very future life of the business may well depend on the executive's decisions, and the de- cisions depend on the reports.

Although the format of the periodic report will vary from com- pany to company, certain general elements are fairly standard (see the accompanying examples): the report opening; the various sections of the report, each with an appropriate topic heading; and the signature or the initials of the writer at the end. (If the writer and the reporting manager are the same man, the initials may appear next to the from: typed name in the opening.)

The content of the report almost invariably begins with a summary of activities for the period covered. This is followed by a fairly detailed discussion of the primary topic of the report: sales and sales volume if sent out by the sales manager; production accomplishments and prob- lems if done by the production manager; the numbers of employees, separations, and employee additions if written by the personnel manager.

This primary area is supported by statistical data, facts, and figures. The number and depth of supporting sections will be dependent on the firm's needs and demands. For the monthly sales analysis, some com- panies will limit the report to only the sales activities; other firms will require sections on sales personnel, sales advertising, competition, sales problems encountered, and other related areas. In the case of the person- nel report, one firm may find it desirable and adequate to learn about the present employee level, the number added, dismissed, and separated. Another firm will require a careful presentation of compensation levels, training, safety, union-management relations, and on and on.

The following is an example of a typical periodic report.

HAWTHORNE TOY CORPORATION
Newton, New York

Monthly Sales Report
June, 19____

TO: Robert T. Montgomery, Executive Vice President

FROM: Frank Levin, Sales Manager

DATE: July 1, 19____

Summary

Sales for the month of May have proved to be somewhat heavier than anticipated, and almost 10% above those of May last year.

All items in Group II (metal-mechanical) and Group III (packaged games) have sold as expected. Group IV (plastic items) has moved up to a very satisfactory level. Group V (bicycles) has declined.

Sales of all groups for November delivery are up 15% as compared to the same period last year.

Sales expenses have risen again this month. This has taken place in spite of new efforts to achieve economies.

Sales personnel and advertising expenditures have remained static.

Sales

Although *The Toy Manufacturers Monthly* for April indicated that overall toy sales should be expected to rise approximately 7% in May over last year's figures, our sales reflect about a 10% increase. This may be accounted for by our salesmen's incentive program as well as our introduction of five new items in May.

Group V figures are a cause for concern. Certainly sales in this category should reflect, as they traditionally have, increases in May over April. The reasons for our decline are not clear. However, there may be two important contributing factors:

1. Our higher price to the dealer for our entire bicycle line (as compared to our competitors).
2. Increase in advertising on the part of competitors. Hi-Flyer, for example, has purchased large blocks of TV· time.

SALES VOLUME MAY, 19___ (IN DOZENS)

ITEM	MAY 19___	APRIL 19___	MAY (previous year)
GROUP I (misc.)			
A 100	5750	5700	5200
A 101	6500	6400	5800
B 300	9750	9500	8800
B 303	6700	6500	5900
GROUP II			
M 101	3150	3100	2800
M 102	2500	2500	2200
M 103	2300	2100	2000
M 104	2400	2300	2100
M 105	3500	3400	3250
M 106	3000	2850	2750
GROUP III			
G 405	8500	8450	7800
G 407	7500	7300	6500
G 408	7000	7100	6500
G 409	9500	9350	8200
G 410	3500	3400	3100
GROUP IV			
P 600-5	21,000	20,000	23,000
P 610-5	23,500	24,000	26,000
P 620-5	22,500	22,100	25,000
GROUP V (in single units)			
Whippet			
Girls'	8500	9300	9000
Boys'	12,500	14,000	14,500
Hi-Ride			
Girls'	16,000	16,000	16,500
Boys'	19,000	21,000	20,500
Speedsters			
Girls'	12,500	14,000	13,900
Boys'	16,500	17,500	18,500

Advertising Expenditures

According to Bob Carlton, Advertising Manager, expenditures for magazine and newspaper ads were 5% above May of last year. However, he indicated that we will, for the first time, use TV spot commercials during the summer months. An initial expenditure of $45,000 for TV will be made in two carefully selected areas on the east and west coasts. Sales will be observed carefully and correlations, if any, drawn.

Sales Personnel

The number of personnel, with the exception of trainees, has remained stable.

SALES PERSONNEL

	MAY 19___	APRIL 19___	MAY (previous year)
Salesmen			
Area I	40	38	39
Area II	20	20	22
Area III	25	23	23
Trainees			
Area I	6	3	0
Area II	3	0	0
Area III	3	1	0

Recommendations

It is recommended that an immediate cost analysis be carried through to determine if the wholesale prices on our entire Group V line can be cut 10% so that we may meet competition. Savings on our part could be secured by using plastic instead of rubber handle grips, eliminating the battery-powered road light as standard equipment, and applying two instead of three coats of enamel to the bike frame.

I am again recommending to the Executive Board that all prices in Group III (packaged games) be cut 15% when purchases are made in gross lots. Savings in packaging and shipping costs should account for almost 10% while the remaining 5% will be taken care of through increased sales.

Note in the foregoing report that any situation which is somewhat unusual, as compared to the previous month, is explained. This is evident in the section devoted to Group V sales.

In the periodic report given above, the recommendations appear at the end. Note that, in the paper which follows, two formats (A and B) are presented: one with various recommendations noted from time to time throughout the body of the report; and the same report with all recommendations listed at the end. The method used depends on the complexity of the material, who the reader is, and the company's preferred format.

AMERICAN AUTOMOTIVE ACCESSORIES COMPANY
529 South Madison Avenue
Pasadena, California 91106

MONTHLY SALES REPORT
MARCH, 19____

To: Mr. Douglas Shoemaker, General Manager
From: Harold Palmer, Sales Manager
Date: April 5, 19____

SUMMARY

Sales are up 1.2% from last month and 10.7% from the same period of a year ago. Net profits are up a corresponding amount in spite of added advertising expenditures and increased personnel costs. High unit contribution margins have enabled us to maintain our net return on sales.

While the overall sales picture looks good, the outlook for individual product lines varies from "terrible" to "tremendous." We are passing up opportunities with great growth potential: yet at the same time, we are continuing to carry some product lines which should have been dropped long ago.

Inventories have taken a significant jump (4.6%) from last month, but this is largely attributable to the change in accounting procedure. Our monthly inventory turnover ratio has improved from .70 for March, 1966, to .74 for March, 1967.

SALES VOLUME

Sales volume data are presented below. Items with an asterisk are discussed in the following section.

	March 1967	February 1967	March 1966	% Change 3/66-3/67
Group One				
*Air Conditioners	102,000	100,000	85,000	20.0
*Heaters	23,000	24,000	37,000	(38.0)
	$125,000	$124,000	$122,000	
Group Two				
Chrome Tailpipe Extensions	22,000	22,000	25,000	(12.0)
Headlamp & Door Trim	20,000	20,000	25,000	(20.0)
Mirrors	21,000	20,000	15,000	40.0
*Hood ornaments	4,000	4,000	28,000	(85.7)
Miscellaneous	13,000	14,000	10,000	30.0
	$80,000	$80,000	$103,000	
Group Three				
*Stereo Tape Players	104,000	100,000	50,500	105.9
Radios	83,000	82,000	80,000	3.8
Clocks	15,000	14,000	10,000	50.0
	$202,000	$196,000	$140,500	
Total Dollar Sales	$407,000	$400,000	$365,500	

EXAMPLE A

PRODUCT LINES

I. *Air conditioners.* Sales forecasts continued to be very bright.

> *Recommendations:*
> 1. We should continue our heavy emphasis on this line.
> 2. Truck "camper" market for air conditioners should be investigated.

II. *Heaters.* Sales for auto and truck heaters are showing a downward trend. Analysis of past sales records indicates that this decline has continued for the past five years. Automotive industry statistics on cars sold without heaters as original equipment point out a far greater decline than our own sales drop. As automotive "no heater" sales and our heater sales have always shown a direct positive correlation—*but* with a three-year lag—we appear to be headed for real trouble in this area.

Our salesmen report repeated inquiry about heaters for truck "campers." This appears to be an untapped market.

> *Recommendation:* We should drop standard auto heaters from our sales line. To replace this item, we should consider developing a heater, or heater conversion unit, for truck "campers." Growth potential appears great in this field.

III. *Hood ornaments.* Sales have dropped 86% this year. Last year's sales drop was 5%. The emphasis on auto safety this year may be responsible for this situation. Note that legislation is in process to make hood ornaments illegal.

> *Recommendation:* We should drop this product line as soon as possible.

IV. *Stereo tape players.* Sales increases in this area have been fantastic. *But* we are merely holding our share of the market: This is our big opportunity to push American Automotive Accessories into a period of rapid and profitable expansion. Let's not pass it up.

Evidence continues to support the popularity of the 4-track player over the 8-track player, particularly in the secondary equipment market. We should continue our policy of specialization on the 4-track models.

Recommendations:
1. In spite of sales gains, we should *increase* our efforts on this product line. Increased market penetration is important. Innovation, quality, and availability of product should be of prime concern. Continued heavy advertising to let people know what we have to offer is a must.
2. Strong consideration should be given to stocking a tape library as an addition to our product line.
3. Further consideration should be given to *producing* our own 4-track tapes from marketed stereo "33-1/3's" and 8-track tapes lacking a 4-track line. (Many "garage shop" operators have been finding this a profitable venture.)

ADVERTISING

Our first-quarter increases in advertising expenditures appear to have paid off well in added sales and profits. However, our Accounting Department feels we should cut back advertising "now that we're rolling." I'm strongly opposed to this. Coca-Cola tried cutting back advertising a few years ago— with highly negative results. And what product is better established than "Coke"?

Recommendation: We should not only maintain but expand our advertising program.

PERSONNEL

While our sales have increased 10.7% from one year ago, our sales personnel staff has increased 250.0% for this same period. This situation continues to have me perplexed, but I'm holding off on any staff reduction pending (1) developments in our stereo and air conditioning product line, and (2) the results of our just-completed sales training program.

Recommendation: Sales personnel strength should be maintained another 90 days. The personnel situation will be re-evaluated at that time.

EXAMPLE B

PRODUCT LINES

    I. *Air conditioners.* Sales forecasts continued to be very bright.

    II. *Heaters.* Sales for auto and truck heaters are showing a continued downward trend. Analysis of past sales records indicates that this decline has continued for the past five years. Automotive industry statistics on cars sold without heaters as original equipment point out a far greater decline than our sales drop. As automotive "no heater" sales and our heater sales have always shown a direct positive correlation—*but with a three-year lag*—we appear to be headed for real trouble in this area.

Our salesmen report repeated inquiry about heaters for truck "campers." This appears to be an untapped market.

    III. *Hood ornaments.* Sales have dropped 86% this year. Last year's sales drop was 5%. The emphasis on auto safety this year may be responsible for this situation. Note that legislation is in process to make hood ornaments illegal.

    IV. *Stereo tape players.* Sales increases in this area have been fantastic. *But*—we are merely holding our share of the market! This is our big opportunity to push American Automotive Accessories into a period of rapid and profitable expansion. Let's not pass it up.

    Evidence continues to support the popularity of the 4-track player over the 8-track player, particularly in the secondary equipment market. We should continue our policy of specialization on the 4-track models.

ADVERTISING

Our first-quarter increases in advertising expenditures appear to have paid off well in added sales and profits. However, our Accounting Department feels we should cut back advertising "now that we're rolling." I'm strongly opposed to this. Coca-

Cola tried cutting back advertising a few years ago—with highly negative results. And what product is better established than "Coke"?

PERSONNEL

While our sales have increased 10.7% from one year ago, our sales personnel staff has increased 250.0% for this same period. This situation continues to have me perplexed, but I'm holding off on any staff reduction pending (1) developments in our stereo and air conditioning product line, and (2) the results of our just-completed sales training program.

RECOMMENDATIONS

1. Air conditioners:
   a. We should continue our heavy emphasis on this line.
   b. Truck "camper" market for air conditioners should be investigated.
2. Heaters:
   We should drop standard auto heaters from our sales line. To replace this item, we should consider developing a heater, or heater conversion unit, for truck "campers." Growth potential appears great in this field.
3. Hood ornaments:
   We should drop this product line as soon as possible.
4. Stereo tape players:
   a. In spite of sales gains, we should *increase* our efforts on this product line. Increased market penetration is important. Innovation, quality, and availability of product should be of prime concern. Continued heavy advertising to let people know what we have to offer is a must.
   b. Strong consideration should be given to stocking a tape library as an addition to our product line.
   c. Further consideration should be given to *producing* our own 4-track tapes from marketed stereo "33-1/3's" and 8-track tapes lacking a 4-track line. (Many "garage shop" operators have been finding this a profitable venture.)
5. Advertising:
   We should not only maintain but expand our advertising program.
6. Personnel:
   Sales personnel strength should be maintained another 90 days. The personnel situation will be re-evaluated at that time.

In some companies, a form has been developed for the periodic report which requires the department manager to fill in the blank spaces. This has the obvious advantages of conciseness, the securing of the exact data desired, and a reduction in work for the department head. It also ensures receiving about the same quantity and level of information from the various managers reporting, who may be stationed in different cities throughout the country. Of course, this form may also inhibit discussion and expression of ideas on the part of the writer. However, if management feels that a completed report form serves the purpose, it should be used.

Each firm can develop its own. In this way specific purposes can best be fulfilled. The form illustrated below is used by a relatively small organization in all its divisions (sales, production, personnel, finance, advertising, and administrative).

LEVERET LAMP CORPORATION
Burbank, California

Monthly Sales Report

——— ——
Month   Year

TO:

FROM:

DATE:

Complete *all* blank spaces

Sales Volume

	———	———	———
	Month	Previous Month	Month
	———		———
	Year		Previous Year

Line AM (in dozens)			
AM 100	———	———	———
AM 200	———	———	———
AM 300	———	———	———
AM 400	———	———	———

Line RT (in dozens)
    RT 100   _____   _____   _____
    RT 200   _____   _____   _____
    RT 300   _____   _____   _____

Miscellaneous Items

    _____   _____   _____   _____
    _____   _____   _____   _____
    _____   _____   _____   _____

	Month	Previous Month	Month
	_____ Year		_____ Previous Year

Sales Volume (in dollars)
    Line AM $_____ $_____ $_____
    Line RT   _____   _____   _____
    Misc. Sales   _____   _____   _____

Inventory (in dozens)
    AM 100   _____   _____   _____
    AM 200   _____   _____   _____
    AM 300   _____   _____   _____
    AM 400   _____   _____   _____
    RT 100   _____   _____   _____
    RT 200   _____   _____   _____
    RT 300   _____   _____   _____

Miscellaneous Items

    _____   _____   _____   _____
    _____   _____   _____   _____
    _____   _____   _____   _____
    _____   _____   _____   _____

Comments and Recommendations _____
_____
_____
_____
_____
_____

_____
          Signature

THE PROGRESS REPORT

Business, with all its functions and divisions, is often so big today that a manager may have half a dozen activities going on simultaneously. One unit may have four men carrying on research within the plant, five others engaged in a project for the government 800 miles away, and four attempting to install a new operation in a customer's plastic division. For proper control, the manager must know what progress is being made on each assignment, what problems have been encountered, and when the job will be completed. This control factor is a function of almost every report, but in the progress report it is especially valuable for maintaining close supervision of a continuing activity.

Having knowledge of the progress that is being made permits the manager to coordinate his company's activities and plan for the future.

Progress reports have a further value. The review of progress reports filed on projects in the past assists the manager in planning and working up cost and time estimates for similar operations contemplated for the future. The reports may tell him where problem areas existed, what to avoid, and where to focus attention. Thus they serve as a reference guide.

Every project, whether it is a company audit, the construction of a building, or a scientific research assignment, has a beginning, a work period, and an end. Progress reports conform to this arrangement. There is an initial report, continuing reports, and a terminal statement.

The initial report should cite the background of the project, the need for it, and who sponsors it. In addition, it should review the progress made on the assignment in the period covered by the report. Continuing reports merely recount the activities of the period, and the terminal report presents a final summary and analysis.

Most managers prefer progress reports which give them a brief background to the situation, a detailed summary of the period covered, and a statement of the work to be carried through during the next time block. Problems and obstacles encountered are usually noted, as well as recommendations for solutions.

Like the periodic report, the progress report can also be completed on a form which has been designed for "fill in" purposes. Where a firm has several teams in the field, each working on a somewhat different project, this method can be valuable.

ROBIN CONSUMER RESEARCH AGENCY
Rockefeller Center
New York, New York

Progress Report: 2

Period Covered: October 10, 19____ to October 24, 19____

Date: October 25, 19____

Assignment: Valley Food Centers

Background and Review

During the period October 1 to October 10 the entire Canton Valley was surveyed to determine the best locations for three new food marts. Traffic surveys were taken and population trends analyzed. All details and the proposed sites are noted in the report on this project dated October 11.

Activities for this period

Questionnaire and interview surveys were carried through in the three areas recommended for new stores.

Details on sample size, survey validity, copies of survey instruments, and tabulated results are all available in appendix A for study and analysis.

A recapitulation of the findings indicates the following:

FAMILY INCOME, SIZE, AND LIVING HABITS
Summary of surveys, Oct. 12-19, 19____

	Average income per family	No. of children per family	No. of cars per family
Proposed Site A	$7,500	4.2	.7
Proposed Site B	$9,800	3.2	1.5
Proposed Site C	$18,500	1.5	2

TYPE OF HOUSING

Summary of Surveys, Oct. 12-19, 19___

	Type of Residence	Average No. of Rooms	Average Monthly Rental or Home Value
Proposed Site A	Apt.	4.5	$125.00 per month
Proposed Site B	Apt. or home	5.	$250-275 per month $28,000 to $33,000
Proposed Site C	Home	6.	$35,000 to $58,500

FAMILY EDUCATIONAL LEVEL AND USE OF LEISURE TIME

Summary of Surveys, Oct. 12-19, 19___

	Educ. Grade Completed (head of house)	Read	TV	Movies	Friends	Sports
Proposed Site A	9.5		✔	✔	✔	✔
Proposed Site B	12.5	✔	✔		✔	
Proposed Site C	14.0	✔			✔	✔

PERCENTAGE EXPENDITURES OF FAMILY INCOME

(Listed in per cent of income)

	Residence	Food	Clothing	Medical	Entertainment	Transportation	Misc.
Proposed Site A	20	20	15	15	15	10	5
Proposed Site B	20	25	12	15	12	10	6
Proposed Site C	25	16	18	15	12	10	4

Comments on findings

The survey results are quite consistent with those completed last year in the Jackson area of the state. Some of the findings, as a matter of fact, are startling in their similarity (see Appendix 3, "Comparison of Jackson and Canton Valley Findings").

Steps to be completed

The final area of research to be carried through is the survey of industry, land development and values, and community plans and direction. This will be accomplished in the period October 20 to 30. A final report will be submitted on November 2 together with recommendations.

Clarence Radke

Clarence Radke
Head, Survey Team 3

THE MEMO REPORT

The memo and the memo report can be extremely valuable in transmitting intracompany communications. Completing the memo requires little time or effort, provides a record, and helps to avoid the confusion or misinterpretation which may result when a few words are exchanged in a corridor or over the phone.

More and more today, companies urge their employees to use written memos. The bulletins which circulate to persons in supervisory positions also suggest written memos to subordinates rather than oral directives.

Some managers send out an inordinate number of interoffice memos. They fly from their desks like snowflakes and are directed to superiors, subordinates, and associates. They are often too hastily written and are rarely proofread. Not infrequently they result in confusion, irritation, anger, and embarrassment. When managers feel "Well, it's only a memo—nothing official; I'll put my ideas down and straighten him out," trouble is likely to result.

This illustrates another aspect of the ubiquitous memo which makes it a most potent internal communication tool. In addition to transmitting information, it very often transmits attitudes which build barriers or opens pathways between writer and reader.

Usually multiple copies of memos are distributed, and the tactless directive or message will be read not only by the designated receiver but by all others who receive "information," "carbon," or "file" copies. It is this aspect—that several others read what is addressed to one person—which frequently results in antagonism.

Perhaps one of the most frequent phrases heard in company offices today is "Well, I don't know why he was so sore; I only sent him the memo to keep the record straight." We can understand why "he" was so upset if we keep in mind that carbons of that memo also went to his superiors and fellow supervisors.

Memoranda are important and should be used. However, as much care should be taken with their composition as with any other item of internal or external communication. They should never be looked upon as "only a memo."

For certain specific purposes, memos usually serve better than telephone calls or face-to-face comments.

1. To transmit *exactly* the same information to several people.
2. To put on record the information, policies, or decisions reached at a meeting or conference.
3. To confirm, as a matter of record, a decision or agreement.
4. To transmit information, policies, or directives to an individual.

WRITE IT — ACCEPT NO VERBAL ORDERS

Save Paper - Reply on This Sheet When Possible

	Dept./Orgn.	Bldg./Zone	Plant/Fac.	Division	Date
TO All Department Heads	24	T-21		Hdqrts	Nov. 13, 19___
FROM Sid Hammer, Exec. V.P.					Ext.

SUBJECT Employee nominations for Christmas Award

Please nominate one candidate from your department for

consideration for the Annual President's Christmas Award.

Criteria for outstanding employee performance are noted

in Management Bulletin 101.

All nominations must be in no later than December 10.

Although the format of the memo may vary from company to company, most of them include preprinted designations to be filled in: To, From, Subject, and Date. Every memo should be concise and cover only one topic.

THE LETTER REPORT

For many persons who are accustomed to writing or dictating business letters, completing a brief report in letter form is convenient and easy. However, there are one or two differences between the business letter and the letter report which should be kept in mind.

The tone of the letter report is formal and objective. The writing style is factual; and substantiating data, in the form of tables and charts, are often used. The inside address, salutation, and complimentary close are often dispensed with, although letterhead stationery is used. Topic headings and subheadings are employed liberally. As one would assume, the letter report is almost always sent outside the firm.

LEANCE MANUFACTURING COMPANY
101 Hilton Avenue
Chicago, Illinois

October 21, 19____

TO: Mr. Albert Hill, Manager
Hill, Adams and Hill, Management Consultants

FROM: Robert T. Black, Personnel Director
Leance Manufacturing Company

SUBJECT: Summary of Training Activities, 1960-68.

You indicated that it would be extremely helpful to your firm to learn of the training activities for employees which we carried through from 1960 to 1968. The data which follow are a summary of those activities.

Management Training, 1960-68
Personnel at the management level have been offered three specific courses. These have all been well attended.

Course	Approximate No. Eligible	No. Enrolled	No. of Classes held
Supervision and Human Relations	260	65	3
Decision Making	260	50	3
Effective Written and Oral Communication	260	85	5

Engineering Training, 1960-68

Although a number of courses have been offered to engineering personnel, the response has been very weak. Perhaps the reason for this lies in the engineering work load, which has been extremely heavy due to military and space orders.

Course	Approximate No. Eligible	No. Enrolled	No. of Classes
Cost Control for Engineers	350	45	3
Advances in Electronics	250	25	1
Engineering Reports	350	80	4

Clerical and Office Training, 1960-68

Response by these personnel to the training has been consistently high. However, the company has not offered as many courses as could be filled because of the high turnover of employees in these categories.

Course	Approximate No. Eligible	No. Enrolled	No. of Classes
Office Techniques and Management	425	150	6
Business Letters	300	110	6
Telephone and Filing Techniques	250	50	3

On the basis of your request, shop training has not been included in this report. However, information is available.

Instruction
Instructors for all management-level training plus the
engineering reports classes have been secured from outside
the company. Most of the men used were university
instructors or professional consultants.
All other courses were taught by company personnel.

Administration
All training was carried on under the direct supervision of
the Personnel Department. Mr. Asquith was specifically
charged with the coordination and supervision of
recruitment, assignment, and class direction.

Concluding Comments
This will give you some idea of the training which has been
carried through. If there are any questions I can answer, I
shall be happy to do so. I am eager to work with you on
long-range training plans for our company.

These are some of the short reports which exist, and a sample of the organization and format which are found. There are many others. Credit reports are written by the thousands each week by such firms as Dun and Bradstreet and credit bureaus in urban centers, and also by hundreds of other firms for internal and external use. There are also the reports written in corporations, universities, and government agencies as the result of research. And those which are the result of "An examination of . . ." or "Our investigation into . . ." or "Recommendations for . . . ."

In every instance, these "short form" reports of 1-6 pages should be based on all the principles and steps noted earlier. The writer must recognize what the problem is and who the readers are. He should be positive that he has presented adequate data to substantiate his findings, and that the material is relatively easy to understand and assimilate.

QUESTIONS FOR STUDY

I. Complete any of the following problems assigned. You may wish to review the chapter and note key points before attempting to solve the problem.

1. Survey several large firms in your area and determine what criteria are used for the retention and/or discontinuance of reports. How frequently do the firms carry through such an evaluation?

2. Survey several large firms and attempt to determine the criteria for placing a name on the report distribution list. What methods are used for dropping names on the list?

3. What are several key characteristics of brief reports which make them extremely useful for decision-making purposes?

4. In large companies, monthly periodic reports are usually submitted by department or division managers. Quite often, these will disagree in some fundamental principle. For example, the credit manager may recommend that the company cut back on opening new charge accounts, while the sales manager may recommend that credit be extended or the number of accounts increased. Perhaps the production manager may disagree with the marketing manager's suggestion.

Is such disagreement harmful as far as the decision maker who reads these reports is concerned? Or are there advantages in securing several points of view?

5. Do you feel that it is more helpful to the reader if all the recommendations are presented in one section at the end of the report, or should they be presented individually at relevant points throughout the report? Why do you feel as you do?

6. What are the advantages and disadvantages of a "fill in" report form?

7. How do progress reports serve as control devices in the administrative process?

8. What are the specific advantages of putting very brief ideas into written memo form rather than communicating such ideas orally?

9. What are several of the important attributes of the effective memo report?

10. What differences exist between the letter report and the business letter?

11. Secure a credit report (such as a Dun and Bradstreet report) and comment on the format and areas covered. Note the similarities and differences between it and a standard periodic report.

II. Complete any of the following problems assigned. You may wish to review the chapter and note key points before attempting to solve the problem. You may assume any reasonable facts, data, and information which will make your report more complete.

1. Your firm has managed four apartment buildings for Mr. Robert Arnold for nine years. Two of the buildings include twelve apartments each, one has eight, and the other six apartments. Mr. Arnold passed away two months ago and you have received a request from the executor of Mr. Arnold's estate for information on your management services, and the buildings now part of the estate.

Send a letter report to the executor in which you give him some information on each building, rentals, occupancy rate, management fees, taxes, expenses, and other data which you feel are relevant.

2. Assume that you are the outgoing president of a social organization. You will be graduating and leaving the university next week. The incoming president has requested a brief letter report from you giving him information on his responsibilities in several areas (to members, alumni, and the community in general), meetings, finances, recruitment, and the day-to-day factors involved.

3. Write a letter report which is an analysis of your own time allocation. Do this as accurately as possible noting all areas (scholastic, vocational, recreational, cultural, etc.). If you can make some meaningful recommendations to yourself, do so.

4. You are the manager of the Fairbanks Discount Appliance Center in Parkington. This is one of seven such outlets in the Fairbanks chain. You are permitted to donate in each 12-month period no more than $2000 worth of merchandise to local, certified fund-raising organizations.

Write a letter report to your general manager detailing your store's contributions for the 12-month period just concluded. Note items, their value, the receiving organization, and other relevant data.

5. Send a memo to each of your department heads at the Easley Electronics Company reminding them to announce the annual meet-

ing for employees. At this meeting President Easley will deliver his annual report on the company and answer questions of a broad general nature.

6. You have ten sections, each under a foreman, in your department. These foremen, in turn, supervise a total of about 220 production-line workers. Your entire department has its lunch scheduled from 11:45 A.M. to 12:45 P.M. You have noticed, however, that a large number of these men begin to leave their machines or work tables about 11:30. You have no idea if these men all come from specific sections or if there are several from every section. However, this is costly to the company and your boss has "jumped" on you twice about the early break.

Send a memo to each of your foremen, reminding them that the authorized lunch period is from 11:45 to 12:45. Of course, the time lost when an early break is taken does not help the foremen make their authorized production quotas.

7. At today's meeting of the eight division supervisors it was agreed that (1) there would be no overtime periods in March and April, (2) company tools would no longer be charged out to employees for week-end use, and (3) each employee, beginning on July 1, would have to pay $4.00 toward the cost of a pair of company-issued safety shoes when he ordered such a pair.

Write the memo to the eight supervisors in which you verify and commit to record these rules.

8. Your five foremen supervise a total of 80 men and women who manufacture lamp shades. These are made of a parchment-like heavyweight paper, cottons, silks, and synthetic materials.

A major problem has arisen recently because of the large number of rejects due to dirty and greasy finger- and handprints on the shades. This is extremely costly and unnecessary.

Employees may, if they wish, use cotton gloves which they can draw from supply at no cost. However, most insist that "gloves slow me down." Of course, eating is supposed to be done only in the cafeteria.

Send a memo to your foremen in which you ask for their help in eliminating or alleviating the problem.

9. As the personnel manager of the Top Flite Toy Company, you are required to submit a monthly sales report to the general manager. In this report you comment on the sales of your three major lines of toy airplanes: fighters, bombers, and passenger jets. Each of these

categories has three subgroups. Sales are reported in dozens of units sold. Figures are always compared with sales for the same month last year as well as the previous month. Because of a new Lockheed fighter which has recently proved highly successful in tactical operations, your line of toy fighters has enjoyed a tremendous upswing in sales.

Your sales force has remained relatively stable though you did add four trainees last month.

Although you do not report on sales advertising, you do feel strongly that the budget for buying space in youngsters' magazines, as well as afternoon TV commercial time, should be increased by at least 20 per cent to approximately $90,000 per month.

10. As the personnel director you are required to submit a periodic report each month to the corporate president. You are now writing yours for September (which always shows comparative figures for the previous month as well as the same month last year).

You include production, technical, and skilled artisans under your hourly heading. Salaried categories include clerical, administrative, and professional personnel. You report not only numbers but also salary levels.

Included in your report is training. Last month was quite active and you should list courses and programs as well as approximate cost.

Recruitment is also covered in your report, and for the first time, you will include "Safety," which heretofore was submitted as a separate report by the safety director.

You will probably want to use some graphic aids to assist you in the communication of ideas.

11. You head a team which was assigned the task of conducting a survey of the cities of Bellplaine, Parkview, and Westwood. Your task was to interview individuals designated in a selected stratified sample to determine their reactions to compact foreign cars as compared to American compacts.

This is your first report and you have completed approximately half the survey of the first city, Bellplaine. You find, however, that interviews run an average of 22 minutes (including travel) as compared to the projected 16. This will hold you up. If your team is to stay on schedule, another man will be needed and should be assigned. Your team, under the present situation, will be in Parkview two days later than the original schedule called for. Assume all other necessary facts involved in your survey, and submit a progress report to your research director.

12. Your firm purchased the Sun Brite Lounge Chair Company last year. One of the first tasks was the renovation of the manufacturing facility with special attention to be given to the cafeteria.

This is your second report, six weeks subsequent to the first. In these six weeks, the new loading dock has been put into shape, fluorescent fixtures were wired throughout the factory area, and new furniture purchased for the cafeteria. In addition, complete stainless steel cooking facilities were installed, and ping pong and billiard tables purchased for the lounge area. Changes were also completed in the employee wash-up and locker areas. Labor costs for this work should be reported.

You are running about one week ahead of your schedule.

CHAPTER NINE

The Long Report

From time to time, almost every firm, organization, or institution is required to draw up a detailed report, written after careful investigation and research. Its style is formal and its statements carefully substantiated with facts and figures.

Detailed studies of this type are required so that decisions on major activities may be as accurate as possible. A long report may result from studies involving possible corporate mergers, a detailed analysis of an area for possible development as a shopping center or residential complex. In addition, extensive reports are usually drawn up and studied before production of new items is begun or companies are purchased. And there are dozens of other instances calling for detailed and careful surveys.

Such studies may include trends in population growth, economic analysis, sales potential, cultural contributions, ethnic considerations, national and international affairs, industrial growth in a particular area, and a hundred other contributing factors. Some of these must be examined for one survey, and others for another.

OBJECTIVES

The objectives of a detailed study may be one or more of the following: persuasion, information, comparison, analysis, or argument. The primary purpose of the *persuasive* report is to sell an idea or a product to the reader and his company. It presents all the facts and figures necessary, with an overall tone that is persuasive. A good example might be a long formal report which tries to convince its readers why a new 48-story apartment building to be constructed next year should be heated and air-conditioned by electric power rather than with some other fuel. A report such as this would be directed to several groups of readers: the architects, those who are financing the project, the contractor, and probably the firm which will operate the building or sponsor it. Because these are all intelligent, analytical individuals, there must be adequate statistical data and information to prove every point made. A good deal of very logical reasoning is required, plus an unobtrusive persuasive tone to demonstrate why the building's heating and cooling systems, as well as its kitchen equipment, should be electric rather than gas or oil. Care must be taken to keep this type of report *quietly* persuasive through the logic of its arguments and the strength of its substantiating data. Statements which are overly emphatic or "hard-sell" would surely prove to be negative factors.

The *informational* report is objective and serves only to present data which may be used as a record, or information to serve as the basis for decision making. Perhaps the most frequent fault of this type of report is the presentation of too much information. The scope and limitations of the topic should be carefully defined. The informational report is sometimes referred to as an "investigative" or "research" report.

The *comparative* document is almost always used for the purpose of making a decision. Should we purchase this plant or that one? Should we introduce a new line of brushes or not? Should we open another outlet? Should we stock Product A or competitive Product B? The comparative report is primarily concerned with an evaluation and comparison of two or more products or services.

The *analytical* type of presentation is objective, and attempts to analyze the situation and facts presented. This evaluation and interpretation are not done because the reader cannot do so himself. It may be that the area is somewhat unfamiliar to the reader, or the analysis may have been carried through by the writer simply to save the reader's time.

The *argumentative* report strongly urges a specific course of action and substantiates its recommendations with data and documentation. There is nothing subtle about this "selling job," as contrasted with the persuasive report. It wants the reader to follow a specific course of action and argues for it.

COMPONENTS

The "long report" has, of course, no set number of pages. However, when a report runs to six pages or more, it usually covers a fairly wide area and includes a good deal of information. It is at this point that we begin to think of helping the reader in his assimilation and analysis of the report by including a title page, a table of contents, a summary, and perhaps setting up an appendix for some of the statistical and/or reference data. These devices of organization and format attempt to make the reader's job easier. Some of the specific sections of the long report, in the order in which they would appear, are discussed in the pages which follow. Few reports contain *all* the divisions listed, although most long reports do carry a title page, table of contents, letter of transmittal, summary of the report, and the report proper.

PRELIMINARIES

Title Page

A long report may have both a cover and a title page, although the trend seems to be toward having only one or the other. If both are used, the information is similar, but usually the paper stock of the cover is heavier and affords protection for the report itself.

The title page should carry the report title, for whom the report is written, the author, the group or company issuing the report, and the date.

"Cute" titles should not be used (Pressing Problems: Parker Garment Co.), although there is no reason why a title cannot be informative and interesting. For example, a General Electric report was titled "What They Think of Their Higher Education." And an aircraft company issued one titled "Flying High: A Survey of Supersonic Aircraft."

Letter of Authorization

This letter is not usually found in business reports. However, the first page in government reports often cites the meeting, conference, or legislative action which approved the appropriation of funds for the survey reported on. By clearly setting down the problem, scope, and limitations for research, the letter of authorization can prevent later misunderstanding.

Letter of Acceptance

Although this letter is not written often, it can be used to accept, revise, or change the terms or conditions established in the letter of authorization. It may also be used to cite times, fees, and other contractual obligations if it serves as an agreement between two companies. The letter of acceptance is part of the mechanics leading to the report's assignment and acceptance. It is usually not part of the report, although some government reports display it in an appendix.

Letter of Transmittal

The letter of transmittal almost invariably accompanies the formal report and attempts to "set the stage" for the reader so that he will understand why and for whom the report was prepared. The amount of background detail, the tone, and the choice of language all depend on who the reader is and how much information is given in the report's preface, introduction, or summary. Usually, the letter of transmittal covers the following items:

1. *Authorization* for the research, which can be a direct quotation from the Letter of Authorization.
2. The *purpose* of the project, to tell the reader what the research hoped to achieve.
3. The *limitations* of the report, noting legal restrictions and the boundaries of time and funds which acted as constraints on the researcher. This can be of great help to the writer because it tells the reader what to expect and what not to expect.
4. A listing of certain key *sources*, if they carry special significance which would help substantiate statements made.
5. *Special reference* to a specific finding noted in the report, if the matter is of particular importance and it is desirable to draw the reader's attention to it immediately. At times, recommendations and/or acknowledgments of assistance may be included in the letter of transmittal.

The letter of transmittal can be detailed or brief. Here is an example of each.

Mr. Verne Cates, President
Temple Machine Corporation
115 North Madison Avenue
Los Angeles, California

Dear Mr. Cates:

As requested in your memo of July 19, 19____, I have carried through a study of merchandise returned by our dealers during the previous twelve-month period. The attached report carries my findings and recommendations.

This survey was confined to returned goods which were damaged, unsatisfactory, or unserviceable. The investigation included only our West Coast dealers in Area 4. Some 82 per cent of the returned merchandise came from our Bel Air line.

Please call on me for additional information.

Sincerely yours,

Bernie Robinson

Bernie Robinson

Mr. James P. Failton, Director
Personnel Division
Corwin Manufacturing Company
1501 North Franklin Drive
Mansfield, Ohio

Dear Mr. Failton:

As authorized by your letter of June 27 and based on our proposal of June 16, a survey of personnel in your firm was carried out. The findings are presented in the attached report.

The primary purpose of the survey was to determine personnel attitudes toward working conditions, compensation levels, management, and employee services. All other areas were excluded.

The sources used for data were interviews with a sample of employees, a questionnaire sent to the homes of some of the workers, and reference to other studies of this type in similar firms.

Of particular interest is the very strong feeling about the employee eating facilities. These were severely criticized in almost every instance.

The report contains specific recommendations which we will be happy to discuss further. And of course, we are prepared to explore any other area which may be of interest to you.

Sincerely yours,

Clarence C. Calloway

Clarence C. Calloway
Senior Partner

Table of Contents

The table of contents is prepared after the report has been typed. It lists chapter or section titles and subdivisions. Page numbers are indicated for each. The headings should agree with those in the final outline.

List of Tables or Illustrations

Although not frequently used, an extended formal report may have a list of illustrations and the page numbers on which the tables may be found.

Foreword or Preface

Because the letter of transmittal normally "sets the stage" for the reader, a foreword or preface is not usually found in a report. When one of these is presented, it goes into some detail in pointing out the general scope, purpose, and related factors concerning the survey.

Summary

The summary, sometimes called a *review, brief, abstract, synopsis,* or *digest,* is designed to give the busy reader a concise, bird's-eye view of the entire report.

It should state the problem, the scope of the investigation, the research methods used, the key ideas in the report proper, the conclusions reached, and the course of action recommended. The writing style should be crisp, penetrating, and objective. Topic headings may be used in the summary to assist the reader further.

BODY

The body of most reports can be divided into three major sections: introduction, discussion, and conclusions and recommendations.

Introduction

If the report has a letter of transmittal, a summary section, or other prefatory sections, probably a good part of the introduction has already been presented. In any event, the introduction attempts to give the reader a sufficient background for the report to be meaningful and understandable.

The introduction may include a *history* of the situation and a clear statement of the *problem* to be solved or examined. *Limitations* of the investigation should be noted and the *purpose* of the report should be stated. The *methods of research* used should be explained, and how *validity* or *reliability* of the survey was secured. If specific definitions are important to the clear understanding of the report, they may be presented at this time. The introduction may also tell the reader what the plan of presentation of the report is. If the reader is told that all statistical data may be found in the appendix, that sample questionnaires are in the body, and that this report is based on the initial study dated March 15, 19____, then he will be better able to orient himself and his thinking to the report.

Discussion

The discussion is the vital part of the report and makes up 75 to 85 per cent of the total length. It is in the discussion that the investigator presents his information and his interpretation of it, points out significant facts and relationships among the data, and makes recommendations.

Throughout the discussion, the writer should assist his reader by conciseness and clarity of presentation, use of topic and subtopic headings, and presentation of certain data in easy-to-analyze tables, charts, and graphs.

Conclusions and Recommendations

Conclusions and recommendations are vital in most types of reports. The report writer must be sure that each conclusion or recommendation is thoroughly substantiated by facts, figures, and reliable statements in the body of the report. At no time should the executive who is reading the report ask, "Well, where in the world is the proof for this?" The proof should be in the discussion section of the report.

ADDENDA

After the body of the report are found the appendixes and various supplements, such as copies of questionnaires, interview schedules, diagrams, statistics, maps, and any other information related to the subject of the report that might be of interest to the reader.

SAMPLE
FORMAL REPORT

AN ANALYSIS

of the

COMMUNICATION OF CORPORATE POLICY

within the

PURCHASING DEPARTMENT

of the

JUPITER AUTOMOBILE COMPANY

Report Prepared

by

Arnold Leanse
Executive Assistant to the President

Report Submitted

to

Sydney Hammer, President
Jupiter Automobile Company

Detroit, Michigan
September 25, 19____

TABLE OF CONTENTS

September 25, 19____

Mr. Sydney Hammer, President
Jupiter Automobile Company
Detroit, Michigan

Dear Mr. Hammer:

At the executive board meeting of June 15, there was some discussion concerning the communication of corporate policy to supervisory employees.

You suggested that one department be selected for analysis and a pilot study. Your authorization to me to conduct such a survey was general in nature inasmuch as this initial examination was designed to be experimental and exploratory.

The results of this study of the Purchasing Department seem to indicate that policy is not easily and clearly communicated. They also indicate that a much more thorough and carefully designed survey should be carried out.

It was a pleasure for me to work on this project, and you may be sure that I will be happy to pursue it further, initiate a more thorough investigation, and/or answer any questions you or the board members may have.

Respectfully yours,

Arnold Leanse

Arnold Leanse
Executive Assistant

ii

PREFACE

"Recent research suggests that those who rely principally on memos, letters, manuals and other printed material to communicate statements of policy not only fall short of achieving the desired results but actually contribute to new problems of misunderstanding."[1] This statement, if true, strikes hard and unmercifully at the practices of a large number of corporations which, because of their size, have come to depend on the written word as their chief means of effecting corporate policy.

Although business management spends millions annually improving its already sophisticated dialogue with computers, it appears that it has not overcome the more fundamental problem of man-to-man communication. Different firms have attempted different methods: meetings, bulletins, memos, magazines, discussions, announcements, and a dozen other media of communication. Some firms have used all these methods, a few companies have used several, and there are firms which have used none. Research is still required to determine what results in success. In the pages which follow, a description of the communication process of one department is outlined. An analysis is attempted and recommendations for improvement are offered.

1. David Bushnell and William Wood, "Are You Getting Across to Employees?" *Nation's Business*, LIII (July 1965), 75.

INTRODUCTION

BACKGROUND OF STUDY

This report was undertaken to examine the nature of the media and techniques used to transmit management policy and, to a limited extent, to evaluate their effectiveness, within the Purchasing Department.

SCOPE OF REPORT

This report is limited to a discussion of the most common means by which management policy is communicated within the Purchasing Department. No attempt is made to assess qualitative features. All other areas of communication in which the department is engaged (external letters, reports, bulletins, etc.) were excluded from the study.

The survey questionnaire, used to secure primary source material, was circulated to a sample group of 75 persons in the department. It is felt that data are thus accumulated from a large enough sampling to be statistically significant for purposes of this report, and give some indication of the general situation.

METHOD OF GATHERING DATA

The questionnaire shown in Appendix A was developed by the writer to secure the required data for this report. It was designed to be informal and easily completed by providing check-off blocks where possible. Twenty-five purchasing supervisors and fifty assistant purchasing supervisors were selected to complete the questionnaire. To fairly reflect overall company practice, an equal number of prospective respondents was selected from each of the firm's five operating divisions. To obtain a degree of objectivity, the respondents were requested not to sign their questionnaire. Because the number of participants was relatively small, every effort was made to secure responses from all those selected. This was accomplished by sending a second mailing to each prospective respondent asking him to complete the questionnaire if he had not already done so. (See Appendix B.)

In addition to the questionnaire, discussions were held with the Vice President in charge of the Purchasing Department and other corporate staff members concerning various aspects of corporate policy implementation.

-1-

Secondary source information was obtained from the Business Library of the Detroit Public Library plus the company library facilities.

SUMMARY

There appears to exist an uneasy but common assumption that policy, once transmitted (through various media described in this report), is understood and followed by its recipients. According to Robert N. McMurry, a noted consultant in the field of personnel, industrial relations, and market research, "The overestimation of the effectiveness of the communication media employed is one of the greatest sources of managerial error in dealing with customers, personnel, and the public."[2] This study has attempted to disprove or substantiate this opinion in reference to the Jupiter Automobile Company.

Data obtained by the questionnaire survey method indicate that corporate policy is disseminated to employees by division policy manuals, functional policy manuals, meetings, and memos. Most of the literature reviewed by the writer in connection with this report indicates that the face-to-face method of communicating policy is preferred where it can be accomplished with some degree of facility. This was substantiated in one study in which the presidents of 51 companies were asked to select the two most preferred methods of communicating "very important policy."[3]

They responded as follows:

		Votes
1.	Call a meeting of management personnel and explain orally	44
2.	Hold personal interview with key personnel	27
3.	Announce policy in a management bulletin	16
4.	Explain the policy in an interoffice memo	14
5.	Explain the policy on the telephone or intercom	1

2. Robert N. McMurry, "Clear Communications for Chief Executives," *Harvard Business Review*, XLIII, No. 2 (March-April 1965) 132.
3. Henry H. Albers, *Organized Executive Action*, New York: John Wiley & Sons, Inc., 1962, p. 328.

-2-

COMMUNICATIONS

GENERAL

Prior to examining the communication of policy as it relates to the Purchasing Department and its functions, it may be helpful to stop a moment and define the term "communications." In its simplest form, it may be said to be ". . . the transfer of information between two or more persons."[4]

A more meaningful concept is developed by considering what Charles E. Redfield calls "administrative communications." This concept narrows the scope of communications to those processes that are institutionally determined by an organization for use primarily within its own framework. It consists of the following five italicized elements: A *communicator* who *transmits messages* to a *communicatee* to influence the behavior of the communicatee, as seen in his *response.*[5] Of particular interest and concern is the fifth element, "response." In the paragraphs that follow, an attempt will be made to determine if this element is actually present in the flow of policy information within the Purchasing Department. *Is* there a response, and is it the response desired by the corporate management?

COMPANY STRUCTURE

The corporation within which the Purchasing Department operates is a large multi-division automotive firm employing some eighty to ninety thousand employees. Each of the operating divisions is managed on a semi-autonomous basis with its own executive staff and division policy-making authority. These divisions look to the corporate headquarters for overall corporate administrative and functional policy.

Purchasing Department Functions

The term "Purchasing Department" is used in this report to designate the organization within the corporation responsible for the activities of purchasing, subcontracting, material

---

4. Albers, *op. cit.,* pp. 351-352.
5. Charles E. Redfield, *Communication in Management*, Chicago: University of Chicago Press, 1958, p. 7.

—3—

control, and surplus sales. Approximately 1200 of the corporation's employees are engaged in purchasing activities. First- and second-line supervisors to whom the survey questionnaires were sent were selected because this is the critical area which must be examined to learn whether policy is reaching the lowest levels of the Purchasing Department.

POLICY DISSEMINATION

The normal method for disseminating corporate policy to headquarters and division personnel is by means of company directives. As stated in the preface of the Company Directives Manual:

> "Company Directives are the formal means for establishing and communicating to General Offices and division management company-wide policies and operating requirements. Company Directives will be implemented by division Presidents in their division operating manuals. Division implementation may include necessary additional instructions, but will not distort the original intent or exceed any stated limitations."

Understandably, such policies must leave as much room as possible for interpretation to permit effective implementation by the users. To secure understanding of and compliance with company directives, each operating division publishes a division operating manual which integrates corporate and division policies. Each major functional group within the company—Manufacturing, Engineering, Personnel, Financial, and Purchasing—also publishes a policy manual which is prepared and controlled at the corporation's general offices.

Obviously there are means of conveying policy other than by the formal written statements discussed above. Letters from executives, oral directives, and conference decisions are but a few. Normally, however, these methods for expressing policy statements are used for expediency, and are usually supplemented later by formal policy directives.

POLICY ACCESS

The above discussion of policy sources leads to the questions of who is on the policy receiving end and what are they doing with it? To get a better understanding of this problem, the questionnaire described in preceding

—4—

paragraphs was designed to determine what policy direction was being received by supervision. The supervisors were asked to specify which of the company's policy manuals they had access to and their frequency of use. Following is a summary of their replies:

TABLE I

COMPANY POLICY STATEMENTS, ACCESS AND FREQUENCY OF USE BY SUPERVISORS

HAVE ACCESS TO:		Yes	No
Corporate Directives		25%	75%
Division Operating Manual		90%	10%
Purchasing Department Manual		100%	0%

FREQUENCY OF USE:	Frequently	Occasionally	Never
Corporate Directives	10%	60%	30%
Division Operating Manual	60%	30%	10%
Purchasing Department Manual	100%	0%	0%

The supervisors were also asked to indicate other policy sources which were available to them. Their responses included the following:

1. Letters from division management
2. Letters from corporate purchasing management
3. Security manual
4. Organization manual
5. Purchasing Division bulletins
6. Department personnel manual
7. Program management instructions
8. Desk instructions
9. Armed Service Procurement Regulations
10. Standards Manual
11. Material Stock catalog

Communicating Policy Downward

In order to find out what the supervisors were doing with the policy directives they received from higher management, they were asked to indicate the means by which they communicated policy to their subordinates. Table II

—5—

summarizes their responses to this question. The
supervisors indicated the various media which they used.

TABLE II

SUPERVISORS' MEANS OF COMMUNICATING POLICY TO SUBORDINATES

	% of Total Responses
Subordinates' Direct Access to:	
Company Directives	30
Division Operating Manuals	90
Purchasing Department Manuals	100
Other Functional Department Manuals	80
Regularly Scheduled Meetings at:	
Division Level	10
Department Level	40
Section Level	60
Occasional Meetings at:	
Division Level	10
Department Level	40
Section Level	90
Periodic Letters Concerning Policy from:	
Division Level	50
Department Level	80
Section Level	70
Occasional Letters on Policy from:	
Division Level	20
Department Level	30
Section Level	30

FEEDBACK

To complete the communication cycle, including the element
of response discussed in earlier paragraphs, the
questionnaire asked supervisors about feedback. The
questionnaire posed the question in two categories: (1) How
does the subordinate get something off his chest? and
(2) How does the supervisor do likewise? Tables III and IV
below reflect the related responses. Here, too, the individuals
used several different media to communicate.

−6−

TABLE III

HOW SUBORDINATES COMMUNICATE UPWARD TO THEIR SUPERVISORS

	% of Total Replies
Personal conversation with supervisor	100
Personal conversation with supervisor's superior	50
Personal conversation with fellow employees	70
Participation in section and department meetings	100
Voluntary correspondence to supervisor	60
Required periodic work status reports	90
Correspondence with other functional departments	50
Employee Progress Interview	100
Suggestion Program	60

TABLE IV

HOW SUPERVISORS COMMUNICATE UPWARD

	% of Total Replies
1. Personal conversation with boss	100
2. Personal conversation with boss's supervisor	30
3. Staff meeting participation	80
4. Written letters to boss or higher	40
5. Required periodic work status reports	100

ANALYSIS OF DATA

Table I reveals that only a small percentage (25%) of the supervisors have access to company directives issued from the corporate level. Those who do have access to company directives use them only occasionally. The supervisor's principal source of policy support is through the division operating manuals and the Purchasing Department Manual. The "other sources" of policy which the supervisors named were, in all but three cases, used only occasionally. Although one respondent reported that he never referred to either company directives or his division's operating manual, it is doubtful that he could function effectively without referring to his division operating manual at least occasionally.

Table II indicates that those policy sources that are available to the supervisor, as reflected in Table I, are also accessible to the supervisor's subordinates. It is interesting to note that a large percentage (80%) of supervisors reported that their subordinates have access to other functional department manuals. However, in reporting other sources of policy to

−7−

which *they* had access, only 30% of the respondents referred to other department functional manuals. This may have been due to faulty structure of the questionnaire.

Forty per cent of the respondents reported that department meetings are held regularly. The questionnaire indicates that section meetings are held on a regular basis by 60% of the supervisors. Occasional section meetings were reported by 90% of the supervisors. This indicates either that occasional meetings are held in addition to the regular meeting or that the question was not clearly stated and was misunderstood.

A rather significant number of supervisors reported that periodic memos emanating from all levels of the company were being transmitted to their subordinates. The structure of the questionnaire did not permit amplification as to how this was being done. It is also not clear whether such memos are being transmitted directly to employees or whether the supervisor is instrumental in circulating the memos among those reporting to him.

Tables III and IV, which indicate the ways in which the supervisor and his subordinates communicate upward, present no surprises. The conventional vehicles of personal conversation with one's superior and participation in staff meetings are the most popular means of feedback. The employee progress review was also looked upon as an important means of upward communication. Although some responses indicated that a subordinate sometimes writes to, or discusses problems with, his supervisor's boss, most of the respondents did not feel this practice was being followed. Periodic work status reports seem to be the "way of life" for both supervisors and their subordinates.

Surprisingly, two important and costly sources of management policy were overlooked by the responding supervisors: the weekly company newspaper and the training programs. The company frequently issues advance policy information on such matters as new employee benefits, plant rules, etc., in the company newspaper. Training programs are often designed to provide instruction pertaining to company policies.

—8—

Seventy per cent of the supervisors recognized personal conversation with fellow employees as a common means of communication. To this investigator, this type of communication appears closely related to "grapevine" communication, which certainly transmits policy information in one fashion or another.

CONCLUSIONS

Due to the limitations mentioned in the section "Scope of Report," the information gathered and reviewed does not provide sufficient detail to determine, with any degree of reliability, the effectiveness of policy flow within the Purchasing Division. However, I feel that, by and large, first-level supervisors are using all means at their disposal to convey company policy to their subordinates. How to determine the extent to which the policy has actually been understood, believed, assimilated, and accepted is a closely related subject that will be explored in a subsequent report to determine policy flow.

RECOMMENDATIONS

1. Further in-depth studies of the best means of transmitting company and functional policy within the Purchasing Division should be conducted. Such studies should include thorough analyses and recommendations for eventual adoption of the most effective means presently employed by operating divisions of the company and by other firms in related industries.

–9–

2. Develop a uniform Purchasing Division management information system that will highlight the problem areas and reduce emphasis and reporting requirements in less crucial areas. A discussion of this type of approach is included in the November 1965 issue of the *Systems and Procedures Journal.*[6]

3. Provide training to all purchasing supervisors in written and face-to-face communications.

4. Establish norms for conducting group meetings to assure effective policy interpretation and participation by attendees.

5. Establish review and audit function to assure understanding and effective implementation.

6. Review policy directives to ensure that they provide adequate flexibility for operating personnel to implement them efficiently.

7. Consider recommendations of supervisors for improving communications.

6. William R. Robins, "Getting Better Results from Management Information Systems," *Management Review*, LV, 2 (February 1966), 51-54; condensed from *Systems and Procedures Journal* (November-December 1965).

APPENDIX A

Dear Purchasing Department Supervisor:

Communicating ideas, policies, and directives is never easy. And it becomes especially difficult in an organization as large as ours.

My special task is to determine how well company policy is communicated to you, and how you then transmit it down the line. With the information I receive, I can make suggestions to top management which, hopefully, will make your job easier. I can also incorporate your ideas into our Division Manual.

Please don't bother signing the questionnaire. The names of those responding will not be included in the report nor revealed to others.

One last favor: I am working on a tight deadline and I would greatly appreciate your returning the questionnaire, in the pre-addressed envelope enclosed, no later than September 5, 1966.

Thank you very much.

Sincerely yours,

Arnold Leanse

Arnold Leanse
Executive Assistant

−11−

APPENDIX A

QUESTIONNAIRE
(75 mailed, 60 responded)

I. *Policy Access*

	Yes	No
A. Do you have access to Company Directives issued by the Corporate Office?	15 *	45
B. Do you have access to your division's Operating Manual?	54	6
C. Do you have access to the Purchasing Department Manual?	60	0

D. How often do you refer to the following:

	Frequently	Occasionally	Never
Company Directives	6	36	18
Division Operating Manual	36	18	6
Purchasing Department Manual	60	0	0

E. What other policy sources do you have access to and how often do you refer to them?

_____	☐	☐	☐
_____	☐	☐	☐
_____	☐	☐	☐

II. *Policy Downflow*

A. In which of the following ways are the people reporting to you made aware of operating policy? (Check applicable boxes.)
1. Direct access to policy manuals
   a. Company Directives — 18
   b. Division Operating Manual — 54

*Numbers indicate those responding. These numbers have been converted to percentage figures in the body of the report.

–12–

    c. Purchasing Department Manual   60

    d. Other functional department manuals   48

2. Regularly scheduled meetings

  At what level?   Division 6 Dept. 24 Section 36

3. Occasional meetings as required

  At what level?   Division 6 Dept. 24 Section 54

4. Periodic departmental letters which extract information from policy sources

  Issued at what level?

         Division 30 Dept. 48 Section 42

5. Only occasional department letters

  Issued at what level?

         Division 12 Dept. 18 Section 18

6. Other sources (specify)

_____

_____

_____

III. *Feedback*

  A. Here are some ways people reporting to you may get something off their chest. Please check those that you feel are being used.

    1. Personal conversation with you as supervisor   60

    2. Personal conversation with your superior   30

    3. Personal conversation with fellow employees   42

    4. Participation in section and department meetings   60

    5. Voluntary correspondence to you   36

    6. Required periodic work status reports   54

    7. Correspondence with other functional departments   30

    8. Employee Progress Interview   60

    9. Suggestion Program   36

    10. Other means (specify)

_____

_____

_____

  B. By the same token, how do you get something off your chest?

    1. Personal conversation with your boss   60

    2. Personal conversation with your boss's superior   18

    3. Staff meeting participation   48

    4. Letters to your boss or to a higher level   24

5. Required periodic work status reports 60
6. Other means (please specify)

_____
_____
_____

IV. *Recommendations (Supervisor's Recommendations for Communications Improvement)*
Briefly, what are some suggestions you might have to improve the flow of communication with respect to:

A. Periodic Work Status Reports
   1. Include more narrative—less statistics
   2. Stress brevity and wider distribution among affected groups
   3. Establish and use a consistent format
   4. Require such reports only when essential

B. Staff Meetings
   1. Discuss only items of interest to the group as a whole
   2. Allow more time for question-and-answer period, encourage participation
   3. Stress brevity with defined agenda, publish minutes, assign action items
   4. Limit size of groups

C. Division Operating Manuals
   1. Emphasize broad policy—less detail, to provide greater flexibility for implementation
   2. Provide index
   3. Decongest procedures and eliminate "gray" areas

D. Purchasing Department Manual
   1. Emphasize broad policy—less detail
   2. Establish formal plan for review to assure compliance
   3. Decongest directives and procedures, and eliminate "gray" areas
   4. Too big. Should be actionalized in separate binders
   5. Implementing instructions by divisions should be improved
   6. Occasionally too restrictive—should provide greater latitude for implementation

V. *Remarks*

—14—

APPENDIX B

Dear Purchasing Department Supervisor:

About two weeks ago I sent you a questionnaire concerning the communication of corporate policy.

If you completed and returned it, thanks a million. If you were too busy at the time, or away on vacation, here is another blank questionnaire. Please fill it out today and send it back; my deadline date of September 5 is fast approaching.

As soon as all the questionnaires are in, we can revise our divisional manual in an effort to make your job somewhat easier.

Thank you very much for your cooperation.

Arnold Leanse

Arnold Leanse
Executive Assistant

–15–

BIBLIOGRAPHY

BOOKS

Albers, Henry H. *Organized Executive Action.* New York: John Wiley & Sons, Inc., 1962.

Redfield, Charles E. *Communication in Management.* Chicago: University of Chicago Press, 1958.

Sigband, Norman B. *Effective Report Writing for Business, Industry, and Government.* New York: Harper & Row, 1960.

PERIODICALS

Bushnell, David S., and Wood, William R. "Are You Getting Across to Your Employees?" *Nation's Business,* LIII, 7 (July 1965), 74-77.

McMurry, Robert N. "Clear Communications for Chief Executives," *Harvard Business Review,* XLIII, No. 2 (March-April 1965), 131-147.

Robins, William R. "Getting Better Results from Management Information Systems," *Management Review,* LV, 2 (February 1966), 51-54.

THE CORPORATE ANNUAL REPORT

Perhaps the best-known example of a long report is the once-a-year summary of company activities issued by thousands of corporations.

During the last half of the nineteenth century, it was most unusual for firms to issue annual reports. In fact, one railroad replied to a request for a financial statement with "We make no reports and publish no statements."[1]

But in 1900 the New York Stock Exchange requested all its listed members to publish financial information. And because more and more stockholders wanted such information, the practice grew. By the second quarter of the twentieth century, the trickle grew into a stream, and by the 1960's it became a torrent. In 1966, it was estimated that some 140 million copies of annual reports were issued by American firms.[2]

There were several factors which contributed to this major change in the number of annual reports published. Since 1934, the Securities and Exchange Commission has required that annual reports be issued to all shareholders of those corporations which are listed on the stock exchange. Many states have similar requirements. The New York Stock Exchange also requires a financial report to shareholders.

Then in 1964 the federal government broadened its "full disclosure" law by insisting that larger unlisted firms also disclose substantially the same financial information that has been obtained from listed firms under the 1934 Securities Exchange Act. The 1964 directive also requires that financial statements in corporate annual reports "be prepared and presented on substantially the same basis as the financial statements in officially filed reports" with the SEC.[3]

Various professional groups, educators, and businessmen have also encouraged corporations to issue more thorough, more meaningful, and more readable statements.[4] Among such organizations are the American Institute of Certified Public Accountants and the Financial Analysts Federation.

Financial World Magazine, through its annual survey, has also contributed a great deal to the improvement of annual reports. This is a yearly program in which some 5000 companies submit their reports for consideration as deserving of gold, silver, and bronze "Oscar" awards.

1. "The Corporate Reporting Explosion in Print: Annual Reports." Speech delivered by Howard L. Sherman, Director of the *Financial World Magazine* Annual Report Survey, Hotel Commodore, New York, January 19. 1966.
2. *Ibid.*
3. *Ibid.*
4. See Norman B. Sigband, "Writing the Annual Report," *Advanced Management* (January 1952).

Recognition is given to those corporate reports which are outstanding in content, completeness, readability, and attractiveness.

Today's shareholder wants to know how "his" company is being managed. His desire for a clear, concise, and complete picture have, together with management's awareness of its public responsibility, contributed to better and more complete reports.

As a result of all this, the corporate annual report is no longer a drab, superficial statement of company activities. Today it is usually a well-written document, divided into narrative and financial sections, enhanced by attractive colors, excellent visual aids, and appealing format.

A *Fortune Magazine* article[5] had this to say about the corporate annual report:

> The exercise [of writing and producing the annual report] in a large corporation can monopolize the attention of top management and turn the staff upside down. Public-relations men, concerned with the rounded image, find themselves arrayed against the lawyers, cautious by nature, and conservative-minded executives who are afraid of being burned by telling too much. The financial people grouse when their beloved statements are overshadowed by corporate messages and four-color photographs. Divisional vice presidents argue for equal space (if the year's record has been a good one) or better billing. Such feuding can escalate to a very high level; the chief executive, or someone very close to him, may have to step in at a critical moment to act as arbiter, and calm the roiled waters.
>
> Usually all the time is well spent. The annual report is of unique importance to a corporation; it is, in fact, the one chance that a company has each year formally to tell its share owners and the world at large what it has done, is doing, and plans to do. Besides being management's proud report of performance (or in some cases its *mea culpa*), the report reflects a corporation's character, creates its public image, and makes available information of interest to share owners and security analysts. What it says may have a direct bearing on the price of its securities; how it says it reflects the character of management and may well attract or repel potential customers.

PURPOSES OF THE ANNUAL REPORT

The primary purpose of the annual report is to present an informative summary of company activities to stockholders, each of whom owns a

5. Samuel W. Bryant, "How's the Annual Report Coming?" *Fortune Magazine* (January 1964), p. 105.

share of the company and is interested in learning about the progress which the firm has made during the previous year, its financial structure, its profits, its union-management relations, its expansion of facilities, its new product development, its relationship with government agencies, its long-range objectives, etc.

But the annual report has still another purpose today. It attempts to build good will among its shareholders, and sell its products, stock, and company image to others. This is one reason why corporations distribute many more reports than they have stockholders. American Telephone and Telegraph, with 2.7 million stockholders, printed 3.6 million reports in 1966. Continental Oil had 43,000 stockholders but published 93,000 copies of its 1966 report.[6]

The additional copies go to employees, educators, suppliers, government agencies, libraries, securities analysts, brokerage firms, banks, foundations, financial institutions, insurance firms, university endowment officers, financial editors of newspapers and magazines, legislators, and many others.

With this wide readership, the annual report writer is confronted with a major problem in composition. How does he adjust his style, word choice, financial data, complexity of charts, and overall content to the variety of reader levels and interests?

To accomplish a good job, the writer must weigh every word, examine every sentence, check every graph, and evaluate every page to make sure that *all* his readers will find the report interesting and valuable.

One author made this observation in a national publication about the purpose of the annual report:

"Good or bad, the annual report has become the single most important document a company publishes. A readable report can help a company's long-range profitability in a variety of ways. Besides its primary mission of helping stockholders place a proper evaluation on the company's stocks, it can help sell products and services, recruit superior personnel, improve employee relations, win the support of community leaders and government representatives."[7]

CONTENT AND MAKE-UP OF THE ANNUAL REPORT

The content of the annual report can usually be divided into three major sections: the introductory section (letter of transmittal and table of con-

6. Howard L. Sherman, *op. cit.*
7. William H. Dinsmore, "Dear Stockholder: Everything Looks Rosy." *Harpers,* XXIII (March 1965), p. 138.

tents), the narrative portion, and the financial information.

The president or chairman's letter to the stockholder (letter of transmittal) is usually a crisply worded summary of the highlights of the year's activities. It gives the reader a bird's-eye view of the entire report and serves a purpose similar to that of the letter of transmittal in the typical formal report.

This letter should be friendly, and written from the stockholder's point of view. A stiff, formal, "boardroom" tone will build few friends among the stockholders who live on farms and in towns and cities throughout the country. This letter *is* the corporation to many; it is vital that it build good will.

The narrative portion of the report may contain comments on the company in relation to the following:

1. *Products and services.* The stockholder is interested in learning about the specific products the company handles and what services it makes available to its customers. A word should be offered on new items contemplated, the reactions of customers, future markets, advertising and marketing programs, and other areas which are related to the firm's products.

2. *Plants and equipment.* The stockholder is also interested in learning about and seeing pictures of the various plant locations; what new buildings are being constructed; and what additional equipment has been ordered.

3. *Employees.* The report should discuss how many employees the firm has, what benefits are extended to them, payroll information, programs available, educational activities, employees in community affairs, employee health and safety records, etc.

4. *Labor relations.* A clear and frank discussion of company relations with unions should be presented. If the firm has had labor problems, strikes, or disagreements during the year, they should be discussed objectively. The stockholder has learned something about the firm's problems from newspaper articles; he deserves a clear and honest explanation of this sensitive area.

5. *Stockholders.* How many stockholders are there? How and where are they distributed? What are their interests?

6. *Government.* What percentage of the firm's production goes to the government? What are the future trends likely to be? What interest do federal agencies have in the company? Have investigations been completed? Are they contemplated?

7. *Community.* Some comment should be made on the firm's relations with and contributions to the community. Have employees held public office? What recognition or complaints have been directed to the company?

8. *Research and development.* Where is the firm going? Does it con-

template expanding its product line? Is it going to diversify? Will it merge with other firms?

The foregoing are only some of the areas to discuss in the annual report. There are many others. Some firms will want to treat some topics in depth; others may prefer to treat similar areas superficially.

The financial information in the annual report is vital to most readers. The data should be complete, objectively presented, and noted in a style that is easily understood by the average stockholder.

All necessary statistics should be presented in a comprehensive balance sheet which lists all necessary areas and permits comparison with previous years' records. As for the financial narrative, the American Management Association feels that it is almost as important as the conventional figures. It can serve to amplify the statistics, to explain certain conditions, to qualify various items, and all in all, to throw additional light on the firm's financial picture.[8]

Howard Sherman, Director of *Financial World*'s annual report survey, indicated that every report should contain or include:

A minimum of twelve pages, including the cover.

Highlights, for a quick summarization of the year's results in comparison with the prior year's performance. Inclusion of percentage change figures enhances the value of this section.

An informative, easy-to-read message from the chairman and/ or president.

A comprehensive narrative review of the twelve-month period just concluded. Operating and financial matters to be covered include, for example, prospects for each of the company's divisions, research and development, nature and cost of acquisitions, marketing and advertising details, sales breakdowns, and future financing plans.

Comprehensive balance sheet and profit-and-loss statement, with comparative figures for two years, and adequate footnotes.

Statement of earnings and dividends on a per share basis, for both the current and the previous year, at a minimum.

Statistical data for a sufficient number of items, preferably for ten years.

8. *Preparation of Company Annual Reports,* American Management Association, Inc., Research Report Number 10, New York.

Source and disposition of funds statements.

Certification by independent public auditors.

A high degree of technical excellence in design and typographic art so as to help the reader absorb the hard information in the quickest possible time.[9]

Presenting figures for the last five or ten years is now commonplace; longer periods are not unusual. This is vital for the serious reader who wishes to follow financial trends in the firm.

To all these criteria against which an annual report should be measured, I would add, again, the quality of clear, concise, and readable writing.

The guidelines set down by the American Management Association for good reporting are excellent: The report must be complete; it must be interesting; and it must possess clarity of expression.

PRODUCTION AND DISTRIBUTION

Collecting information from various divisions or subsidiaries of a large corporation, securing excellent photographs, and amassing accurate statistical data is a major task in itself. But then to take all this and present it clearly and concisely in a limited number of pages—to the satisfaction of the company's officers and stockholders—is a real feat.

That is why most firms make one competent person responsible for the production of the annual report. If he is wise, he prepares a timetable which is rigidly followed: narrative explanation of the following areas is due on this date; financial data on that date; selection of photographs and drawings of graphs completed by this time; and presses roll on this date. If it is not done this way, information will trickle in, changes will be made constantly, and confusion will result.

A careful plan for the distribution of the annual reports should also be followed. Of course every stockholder receives a copy, but many other persons and groups should be considered, for, as noted earlier, the annual report can be a potent good-will builder. Among those who might well receive a copy are:

Company employees	Community leaders
Company suppliers	Newspaper and magazine
Financial analysts	editors

9. Howard L. Sherman, "Twenty-five Years of Annual Report Progress," *Financial World Magazine* (June 30, 1965), p. 69.

Educators	Brokerage firms
Government agencies	Legislators
Bank officers	Radio and TV
University and foundation	commentators
investment officers	Libraries
Customers	Clergymen
Investment club officers	Officers of service groups

With stock ownership in America becoming commonplace rather than unusual, a company which does not produce an excellent report does itself a disservice. Many firms have found that there is some correlation between an outstanding report and stock sales and corporate image.

QUESTIONS FOR STUDY

I. Complete any of the following problems assigned. You may wish to review the chapter and note key points before attempting to solve the problem.

1. List and briefly discuss several different types of reports having different objectives.

2. Secure a persuasive and/or a comparative report. Submit it together with an evaluation noting the specific areas within the report that justify your classification.

3. Assume that you have completed a survey of the training activities of the Fairbanks Steel Corporation. You used company records going back ten years, information secured from interviews with employees, employee questionnaire surveys, and secondary sources which reported training activities of other firms. Prepare the letter of transmittal which will convey your formal report to the president of Fairbanks.

4. Assume that your instructor has requested a detailed report from you on formal and informal communication networks in an organization. You have secured your data by direct observation within the organization, structured and unstructured interviews with the personnel involved, and secondary sources. Prepare the letter of transmittal which will accompany your report.

5. Complete title pages for the reports noted in problems 3 and 4 above. Assume that both reports were completed during this month in New York.

6. Prepare a title page for a formal report concerning stock market fluctuations and apparent economic causes. The report was prepared last month by the Economics Department of your college for distribution at an Economics and Monetary Seminar that your School of Business sponsored.

7. Prepare a title page for a report which contains an analysis of the relation between educational attainment and annual income. The report was completed by the Department of Education of your state for distribution to PTA's and other groups interested in helping to reduce the number of high school drop-outs.

II. Assume that you are in charge of the four-man investigation team assigned to carry through an analysis of the Department of Weights and Measures of Lyons, Illinois. Using the data in the problem below, present a formal report to the City of Lyons, Illinois. On the basis of your findings, conclusions, and recommendations, the City Council may vote to take specific action concerning the organization, purposes, and operations of the Department of Weights and Measures.

You may add or delete any reasonable quantity of information.

DEPARTMENT OF WEIGHTS AND MEASURES

This unit was established by City Ordinance in 1942 and had as its primary purpose:

The inspection of all scales, weights and measures together with the business firms using such devices. Periodic checks, on a careful sampling basis, were to be carried through to ensure that retail measuring devices (store scales, measures, and balances) ensured the consumer of full weight in all food and non-food products. Packaged items were to be checked to ensure that printed weights and costs conformed to actual weight.

Wholesale purveyors were also to be checked (foods, coal, oil, etc.).

Miscellaneous scales (taximeters, parking lot clocks, etc.) were also to be evaluated.

Violations were subject to city legal action as set down in Lyons City Statute 21-234.

Unit Personnel Organization

At the present time the department numbers 260 personnel as compared to 180 in 1960, 160 in 1955, 110 in 1950, and 40 in 1942.

The department has one director and four assistant supervisors:

consumer foods, consumer non-foods, wholesale, and miscellaneous. They are designated Units I, II, III, and IV, respectively. Unit I has 110 inspectors, Unit II has 40, Unit III has 60, Unit IV has 20, and there is a clerical office and lab staff of 25.

Problem Areas

Although complaining citizens' letters to the Division and the Mayor have always come in, the number has increased tremendously since early 1965. Most of these accuse food store operators, both chain and independent, of short-weighting merchandise. The letter writers charge that meat and produce prepackaged items carry overcharges of 10¢ to 50¢; this is due to false listing of weights on the printed labels.

Gas station operators are also accused of having "fast" counters on pumps which charge for more gasoline than is actually delivered.

Complaints at the wholesale level and about parking lot clocks and taximeters are almost nonexistent.

Findings Within the Department

The supervisors in charge of Units I, II, III, and IV have held their positions 24, 20, 4, and 6 years respectively.

Inspectors of Units I and II are assigned to different sections of the city and as near to their own homes as possible. Some inspectors have been checking the same business establishments for many years. Unit III and IV inspectors are required to cover different areas of the city in accordance with their supervisors' directives.

All inspectors are required to complete a performance report twice each week at Headquarters. Days are staggered so that all personnel are not in the office at any one time.

Unit I has three Chief Inspectors; Unit II has one; Unit III has four; and Unit IV has one.

Your interviews within the department uncover a great deal of animosity of Unit III and IV members for I and II personnel. Three or four men in Units III and IV commented bitterly on the fact that their Chief Inspectors are "rough, require 20 calls per day, and bounce anyone even suspected of taking a nickel." This is in contrast, they imply, to the men in I and II "who drive their Cadillacs to the same place, hold second full-time jobs, and fly to Hawaii every few months to spend their 'earnings.'"

Although these comments came from only a few men, the others in III and IV exhibited no great loyalty or respect for personnel in I and II.

Interviews with the supervisors led you to believe that Units I and II were "easily run," with few rules and almost no "checking on the checkers" being carried through. Units III and IV personnel were obviously closely supervised.

Your review of performance reports on file clearly indicated sloppy reporting in Units I and II, incomplete findings, lack of clarity, omission of signature and facts, and dozens of reports which would prove value-less in court action. In Units III and IV, each report was complete and signed by the inspector and his chief.

Outside the Department

Your analysis of consumer food stores revealed that several did short-weigh on meat, grocery, and produce packaged items. These purchases were, of course, made anonymously. Other personnel in the audit team disclosed that several of these same outlets had been inspected but never found in violation.

Interestingly enough, most such violations were found in very low income, transient neighborhoods with a high percentage of Negro and Latin American residents. The same findings were determined with gasoline stations.

Interviews with store managers indicated their determination to be extremely honest, but of course, "sometimes moisture dries out and a package may lose ½ ounce or so."

Interviews with several neighborhood group officers and church officials in low income areas determined that they had run their own surveys and found that

(1) specific independents and chains made a practice of short weight, and

(2) it was common knowledge that such stores paid off city inspectors.

Of course, this was all hearsay and no documentation nor substantiation were available.

For some reason the store managers in upper income sections (Westwood, Bel Air, Prairie Palisades) reported extremely few visits by inspectors. Some indicated that they had never seen an inspector. Curiously enough, as many inspectors were assigned (at least on the books) to these areas as to other sections of the city.

Laboratory Procedures

The laboratory procedures seem almost completely haphazard. Packages of food and non-food items are stacked everywhere; inspectors' labels on the items are often incomplete or nonexistent; the method of checking weights and prices is not set down; refrigerators overflow with foodstuffs; and many items approved seem to go home with inspectors rather than to public institutions as required. The lab personnel do not seem very competent.

The lab supervisor is an elderly gentleman who was transferred in from the police department after an accident which incapacitated him. "Yes, he knows his system isn't very good, but one day he's going to get some smart book man from college over, who will set up a system—maybe even new-fangled like IBM."

Expenditure of Funds

Money for the department's purchase of all over-the-counter items comes from a fund administered by the department supervisor. It is given out on signatures. The form lists only unit number, items purchased, date and signature. It does not list store, station, or place where purchase was made.

Inspector expenditures have gone up dramatically in the last 5 years:

1968	$26,540
1967	21,500
1966	16,300
1965	14,800
1964	14,200

Legal Procedures

Interviews with the city attorney and his subordinates were held. All comments in reference to the Department of Weights and Measures were negative. Cases could almost never be tried (especially at the retail level) because of extremely poor records left by inspectors or lack of clear-cut evidence. When cases were brought before the courts, inspectors frequently did not appear, their records were not available, or they were reluctant to testify.

III. Write a formal report on any one of the topics listed below or one which your instructor assigns. If you choose your own topic, you should submit the title and a brief outline for your instructor's approval.

Your instructor will designate which (or all) of the following sections should be included in your report. The approximate length may be designated.

Cover	Body of Report
Title Page	Introduction
Letter of Transmittal	Discussion
Table of Contents	Conclusion
List of Figures	Recommendations
Preface	Appendix
Acknowledgment	Bibliography
Summary	Index

1. The Grapevine in Industrial Communications
2. Informal Lines of Communication in Industry
3. Industrial Training in Listening

4. Industrial Training in Communication
5. Industry's Attitudes Toward the Importance of Communication as a Management Skill
6. Industry's Suggestions on Collegiate Education in Communication
7. The Mathematical Theory of Communication
8. The Shannon-Weaver Communication Theory
9. Jurgen Reusch's Contributions to the Field of Communication
10. The Position of the Industrial Director of Communication
11. Research in Communication Breakdowns in Industry
12. How a Selected Group of Firms Have Attempted to Improve Vertical Communication
13. Development and Use of the Employee Orientation Manual
14. Trends in the Corporate Annual Report
15. Labor Unions' Communications to Members
16. An Analysis of the Union's and Management's Printed Communication Media to Workers
17. The Accountant as a Communicator
18. Printed Versus Interpersonal Communications to Employees
19. What Does the Corporate "Director of Communications" Do?
20. Communications and Company Morale
21. Employee Comprehension of Company Communications
22. Do Company Communications Motivate or Antagonize the Worker?
23. What Does the Employee Hear When Management Speaks?
24. Information Retrieval
25. Attitude Change as a Result of Communication (among consumers; among the public in response to political situations; among students involved in campus activities)
26. An Explanation of the "Semantic Differential"
27. The Information Explosion and the Computer
28. Decision Making and Communication
29. Listening as a Management Tool
30. Can a Corporate Image be "Structured"?

IV. Complete either of the following examination reports assigned. You may wish to review the chapter and note key points before solving the problem. You may assume any reasonable facts, data, and information which will make your report more complete.

You will probably want to add visual aids to assist your reader.

1. Your firm, Westwood Furniture Corporation, has begun a program of acquisitions in an attempt to diversify and thus gain strength in areas that are extremely active. The Board of Directors has committed itself to the acquisition of firms serving the aerospace industry. By so doing, they feel that administration and control will be easier and more efficient.

On March 1, you and three other men were each asked to "check out" a company that was under consideration. Each person is to evaluate the firm and submit a recommendation report to the Board of Directors prior to April 10. Their quarterly meeting is scheduled for the 15th, at which time decisions will be made.

You were assigned to gather data on the Kellogg Fastener Corporation. You were in and out of the firm throughout March and you were able to watch operations, review records, and interview personnel. You have all kinds of information—most in helter-skelter form—and you're now ready to write your report.

Kellogg manufactures several basic types of fasteners (rivets) for aircraft use. These are made of aluminum alloys, lightweight steel, and a few selected types are titanium. The company is run by Mr. Albert Kellogg and his two vice-presidents (and sons), Joe Kellogg in charge of sales, and Mike in charge of production.

The company has three primary product lines: the SR22 (hi-strength steel rivets); the AR32 (aluminum); and the TR92 (titanium). Each line has three basic models and production is measured in pounds. Models A, B, and C of AR32 have increased in production. Kellogg sold 6000 pounds of Model A in 1967 as compared to 5200 pounds in 1966. Models B and C were both up from 6000 pounds in 1966 to 8400 in the following year. In the case of the steel rivets, Models A and C rose from 9200 and 9600 pounds respectively in 1966 to 12,000 and 12,500 in 1967. However, Model B of SR22 dropped from 8500 pounds in 1966 to 6100 in 1967. This may be due to the head which seems to snap off under slightly greater than usual pressure.

Perhaps the greatest potential lies with the titanium line (TR92), for each of the new supersonic planes, "air busses," and tactical aircraft uses from 400,000 to 3,000,000 titanium rivets. Of course there is much competition in the area even though demand for titanium fasteners has skyrocketed throughout the aircraft industry. Kellogg has hardly kept pace with 15,000 pounds of TR92 Model A in 1967 as compared to 13,000 in 1966. Models B and C, however, each rose from 18,000 pounds in 1966 to 24,000 in 1967.

One of the factors that impressed you was the sales force. In 1949, when the company was founded in Hawthorne, California (where the plant is still located), Mr. Kellogg had 4 salesmen calling on the aircraft plants. Today the sales force numbers 15 under Joe Kellogg. When you asked Joe if he had tried to sell the Kellogg line to other industries (boating, shipping, truck manufacturer), he said that they keep thinking about it, "and one of these days I'm going to get a flyer out and really get involved. Surely they use our products and there's no reason why they shouldn't buy ours."

The plant itself is about 38 years old and was used to build piston

272

plane motors before Kellogg bought it. The water lines need replacing as does the illumination. The loading docks are very awkward and the cafeteria and so-called employee areas are in terrible condition. You estimate it would cost about $125,000 to put the 160,000-square-foot plant in decent shape. The offices are almost in the production area, and the parking facilities for the 380 employees consist of an unpaved lot next to the plant.

The employee picture is not too good. There has been a relatively high turnover among the production workers. These are primarily of Latin American background. Since 1964 there have been 3 strikes (Local 405 of the Aerospace Union) and each strike has resulted in higher wages. Approximately 35 to 45 workers leave and are replaced each month. Many complain about the poor eating facilities, the strict supervisors, and the lack of fringe benefits.

The fastener industry on the whole is excellent. More and more fasteners are used on all types of vehicles including aircraft. Methods for their application have been improved tremendously. High-speed rivet guns and mechanical inserters permit one person to fasten two sheets of aluminum 16 feet long in 8 minutes using 96 fasteners.

Lines of authority and channels of communication at Kellogg are completely confused. The Kelloggs have no compunction about giving orders on the line and completely ignoring the foremen or lead men. Production workers often go right to supervisors or officers and skip their immediate superiors. Housekeeping in the plant is rather poor and pilferage seems high though no specific figures on the latter are available.

The profit picture at Kellogg is excellent. In the years 1962 to 1967, the net profit has risen from $84,000 to $96,000 in 1963. In 1964, it was $140,000; in 1965, $165,000, and in 1966, $128,000. However, in 1967, it jumped to $175,000. The price that is desired for the operation is $1,900,000 plus a 5-year contract for each Kellogg to remain in his present position at his present salary. The president now draws $55,000 per year and the heads of production and sales, $40,000 each per year. The $1,900,000 includes the site, plant, and all equipment and fixtures. Even though you're no expert in this area, you feel that figure is not at all unreasonable.

2. You have just completed a survey of the training facilities of the Jet Air Corporation on the request of the president. He felt that training within the company was fragmented, took place under different supervisors, was wasteful because it was duplicative, and was too costly.

He has asked you to prepare a report on all training within the company, the cost during each of the last two years, the number of people involved, your evaluation of the effectiveness of the various programs, and your recommendations.

You have found that there are 5 trade courses being offered for hourly personnel; 4 courses (in three different plant locations) for office personnel; and 8 different courses for management personnel.

In addition, the company runs 8 three-day seminars for engineering personnel each year.

Each year three executives are sent to the University of Southern California's Management Policy Institute, and special sessions are conducted periodically on computer use and technology.

Outside consultants and Jet Air personnel are used as instructors.

Assume all course titles, costs, test results, and data secured as a result of talking to supervisors regarding the effectiveness of the courses.

You may wish to do some research in secondary sources so that you will have adequate data to write an excellent report.

V. Complete any of the following problems assigned.

1. Although the annual report is addressed to the company's stockholders, there are many other types of readers. Name at least five additional groups that read the annual report carefully, and indicate what their primary objective is in examining corporate reports.

2. Secure two annual reports from one company; one should be current and one should have been issued at least five years earlier. Compare the following areas and note similarities and differences in the two reports.

> The president or chairman's letter of transmittal
> Labor relations
> Employees
> Government relations

3. Write a short essay on the steps, procedures, and administrative factors involved in producing an annual report. This will require primary research within a company as well as the use of secondary sources.

If two or more individuals each choose a different corporation, interesting comparisons can be drawn in oral reports or a panel discussion presented by those involved.

4. Many individuals contend that the large sums of money spent on producing elaborate and costly reports are wasteful. All the necessary information, the argument continues, could be mimeographed and the funds which would then be saved could be paid to stockholders as dividends. Do you feel that major expenditures made on costly, colorful reports are wise or wasteful? Why?

5. Survey fifteen to twenty owners of common stock who receive annual reports. Design a questionnaire in which you attempt to determine what segments of the reports are read most intensively, why this is so, what action is taken (if any) as a result of the reading, how the stockholder feels toward the company, whether the reader finds it simple or difficult to understand the report, how meaningful he finds the visual aids, whether the report increases good will toward the company or not, and related questions.

When you have completed your survey, present the results in either a written or an oral report.

6. Carry through research on the *Financial World Magazine* annual report contest. Secure several annual reports which were selected for prizes this year and last, and present an analysis of their contents based on the criteria for selection established by the magazine.

CHAPTER TEN

The Job Résumé

INTRODUCTION

Most of the people you know are delighted with their positions and find each working day an enjoyable adventure. But there are many other individuals in our society who are not particularly happy with their jobs, and there are even those who thoroughly dislike their assignments. In addition to these groups there is still another, made up of persons who really have no strong feelings one way or another about their daily labors, but who are not challenged nor working at their full potential. Often they are earning far less than they should.

Surely the situations above are no exaggeration. A formidable segment of the members of our society, when asked "How do you like your job?" will reply rather resignedly, "Oh, it's O.K.; nothing special of course, but it's a job. And I guess a job's a job."

And you may reply, "But if it isn't what you want, what you enjoy, why not get a new one?"

The reaction to this may be an embarrassed silence or a "Holy smokes, you just don't quit a job and go out and find a new one, you know!"

Well, of course not. None of us is inclined to "just quit," but there is much to be said for leaving a position when it proves less than satisfactory.

Too many people in our society remain in jobs for too many years—unhappy and dissatisfied, giving themselves and their families ulcers, bad tempers, and neuroses. The competent and hard-working person who is unhappy with his position or is insufficiently challenged should have absolutely no compunction about attempting to secure a new job. And one of the most effective ways to find that new position is through the letter of application.

Peter Drucker, a leading management writer, has this to say on the subject:

> To know when to quit is therefore one of the most important things—particularly for the beginner. For on the whole young people have a tendency to hang on to the first job long beyond the time when they should have quit for their own good.
>
> One should quit when self-analysis shows that the job is the wrong job—that, say, it does not give the security and routine one requires, that it is a small-company rather than a big-organization job, that it is at the bottom rather than near the top, a specialist's rather than a generalist's job, etc. One should quit if the job demands behavior one considers morally indefensible, or if the whole atmosphere of the place is morally corrupting—if, for instance, only yes men and flatterers are tolerated.
>
> One should quit if the job does not offer the training one needs . . . .
>
> But the most common reason why one should quit is the absence of promotional opportunities in the organization. That is a compelling reason.[1]

These are favorable times for securing new associations. The manpower needs of industry continue to increase, and the demands for competent professional personnel are high. For the individual who feels that he can "do better," this is the time to explore the job market.

Such exploration will always result in a profitable conclusion. Either the person will find a better job, or he will learn that his present assignment is about as good as he can secure in the present job market. If the latter situation is determined, he may well accept his job, his level, and his salary and thus overcome his feeling that he should be "doing better."

COMMUNICATION AND
THE EMPLOYER-EMPLOYEE RELATIONSHIP

It is extremely important that effective communication take place between the job seeker and the company representative who interviews him. Whether this communication is written or oral, it should be thorough and accurate. Neither the employee nor the employer wishes to

1. Peter F. Drucker, "How to Be an Employee," reprinted in *Psychology Today*, 1, 10 (March 1968), 74.

become involved in an association that is less than satisfactory. Time is lost, training is wasted, and egos are bruised.

Therefore, an honest flow of two-way communication is necessary. The employee may thus learn whether his personality, talent, interests, and goals conform to the firm's patterns. And the company, in turn, may determine if the prospect can make a meaningful contribution to the organization's growth.

SOURCES FOR SECURING NEW JOBS

Although there are a variety of different sources for the job seeker, just four will be reviewed here.

For the college student, recent college graduate, or graduate student, there is probably no agency as effective (and as inexpensive) as his school placement bureau.

The placement officers are experienced in various phases of personnel testing, counseling, and evaluation; they are usually acquainted with most corporate personnel directors in their areas; and they and their staffs are dedicated to serving the needs of the student.

Hundreds of companies have their recruiters make regular calls on universities to interview prospective employees. All of this is done through the college placement services, and at no cost to the student or the college.

Employment agencies and executive placement services are also responsible for finding jobs for thousands of persons each year. These are commercial ventures with fees paid to the employment agency either by the individual who has secured a new position or by the firm that has hired him.

Most executive placement services are doing a fine job in placing management-level personnel. And many employment agencies are also performing valuable services. However, the job hunter should always be sure that he and the agency have a clear understanding on what the fees will be and precisely what obligations and responsibilities each party has. And it goes without saying that the applicant should sign employment agency agreements only after he has carefully read the terms of the contract.

The job seeker might do well to investigate a third possible source for employment. That is his professional association's job placement services. Accounting, advertising, office management, operations research, engineering, and almost every other professional and semi-professional group have placement services for their members. These should be carefully investigated.

But one of the most effective ways of all to secure a new position is through letters of application or résumés.

Most new college graduates will secure their full-time positions through the campus recruiters from large companies or the part-time position they held will become full-time.

However, it is quite possible that the position which seemed so right two or three years ago is now recognized to be a "dead end," lacking in challenge, or not satisfying. This, then, is the time to send out eight or ten letters and take the interviews offered as a result of the mailings.

The letter of application is certainly not restricted in its use to those persons who are looking for a first job, but it can be used by those who have a position but wish to improve themselves.

STEPS PRECEDING
THE WRITING OF THE LETTER

Like any important assignment, the writing of the letter of application should be preceded by careful planning and analysis.

SELF-ANALYSIS

First we must ask some questions about ourselves: What do I have to offer the prospective employer? What professional attributes do I possess? What are my specific capabilities? How expert am I in areas 1, 2, and 3? Do I enjoy working with others or not? How fluent am I in French? Can I handle the ABC computer? Do I like to assume responsibilities? What is my level of initiative? Do I work well with others? How well do I supervise others or take orders from others?

Peter Drucker says the prospective employee should ask himself these questions concerning the job he takes:

1) Do you belong in a job calling primarily for faithfulness in the performance of routine work and promising security? Or do you belong in a job that offers a challenge to imagination and ingenuity—with the attendant penalty for failure?

2) Do you belong in a large organization or in a small organization? Do you work better through channels or through direct contact? Do you enjoy more being a small cog in a big and powerful machine or a big wheel in a small machine?

3) Should you start at the bottom and try to work your way

up, or should you try to start near the top? On the lowest rung of the promotional ladder, with its solid and safe footing but also with a very long climb ahead? Or on the aerial trapeze of "a management trainee," or some other staff position close to management?

4) Finally, are you going to be more effective and happy as a specialist, or as a "generalist," that is, in an administrative job?[2]

These are just a few questions we might well ask ourselves *before* we begin to hunt for the job. The more we learn about the job in an interview, and the more we know about our own desires and capabilities, the more easily we can determine whether or not this type of position would be one we would work in most efficiently and enjoyably.

RESEARCHING THE JOB AND THE JOB MARKET

Perhaps the first item to be checked is the specific job. If our abilities permit us to apply in two or more areas, which specific type of job has the best potential in the years ahead? Should I concentrate on computers, or inventory control, or cost accounting, or auditing, or personnel management if I have the ability and knowledge in each of these areas? Of course the opportunities which become available within the company in the years ahead will also determine the job one goes into. But we can help shape our future by making specific choices early in our career.

The second area to check is the job market itself. Examine the classified ad section of local as well as out-of-town newspapers; read the "job opportunities" section of your professional journals; examine the list of "jobs available" at your college placement office; take interviews with company recruiters who visit your school; read the job opportunity bulletins sent out by the government agencies and corporations; secure suggestions from your college professors, friends, and associates; check such books as the *The College Placement Annual*. And finally, and sometimes most effectively, send out letters of application to top-level firms, and take the interviews which result.

What about the companies in which employment is available? This is a third area to research. What are the firms' futures? What are their objectives? Do they or will they participate in space-age technology?

2. Peter Drucker, *op. cit.*

What are their earning records? Their plans for expansions? Diversification? What do the records reflect as to financial and personnel growth? What facts can be gained from their annual reports? What do knowledgeable people think about this firm? Does the company have a reputation for retaining its personnel for long periods or are there frequent changes and turnover among their employees?

Because our future success is intimately associated with that of the company which employs us, we should make every effort to take a position with a firm whose future is bright and dependable.

TYPES AND FORMS OF LETTERS OF APPLICATION

Basically there are two types of letters of application: the *solicited* letter, in which a firm, government agency, or institution solicits your assistance through an advertisment, an announcement, or a letter; and the *unsolicited* letter, in which you send an inquiry to one or more firms, asking about job openings and requesting an interview.

If you reply to an announcement, you know an opening exists, but you will encounter competition. An interesting and inviting ad which prompted you to write will probably also bring letters from 50 to 100 other applicants. You don't face this level of competition when you mail an unsolicited letter. But, on the other hand, the company may have no immediate opening for you. This should not be a major deterrent, however. Large industrial corporations usually have dozens of persons working in management, finance, engineering, accounting, and marketing areas. If an opening does not exist today, there will surely be one next month, and many corporations are quite willing to hire you today for the opening which is certain to appear in the near future.

The formats for solicited or unsolicited letters are:

One-part: Brief presentation of all necessary facts in a letter.

Two-part: Introductory and summarizing cover letter accompanied by a separate data or résumé sheet.

Job brochure: A booklet containing half a dozen or so pages which outlines in detail education, experience, membership in organizations, honors, awards, copies of letters of reference, and samples of work. This is usually used by an executive with a good deal of experience.

Let us now look at the attributes and make-up of *all* types of job-seeking letters and then come back to examples of the complete message presented in various forms.

LETTER ORGANIZATION

The application letter, like the sales letter, attempts to sell. In the case of the latter, it attempts to sell a product or service, but in the application letter, the writer tries to sell himself.

Like the sales message, the application letter can be divided into a section which attempts to arouse the reader's interest in the job seeker, then describes the background which makes the applicant eligible for the job, continues with proof for the statements made by citing degrees, places of former employment and references, and concludes with a request for an interview (or the sale itself).

AROUSING INTEREST

The prospective employer is not usually impressed with cute or clever openings, nor is he intrigued with the stereotyped "this is in reply to your ad" beginning.

> On June 5 I shall receive my degree from Central College and then will be ready to take a professional position with your firm.

> This is in reply to your ad which appeared in the June 27 issue of the *Daily Times*.

> After many years of study and application, I have reached my goal and am now available to consider the position you have available.

Besides being completely uninspired, the openings above are oriented around the writer. Those openings which follow are concisely worded, give the reader a quick look at the applicant's qualifications, and indicate how the company can benefit from the job seeker's abilities. The employer's attention is arrested when the applicant crisply indicates his major attributes and how they will help the company. This is the time for the writer to use the "you" attitude sincerely and effectively.

> Your recent advertisement for a college graduate with a degree in marketing and some part-time business experience seems to fit my qualifications.

> A college degree in accounting, a CPA certificate, and three

years' experience working directly under a corporate controller should certainly qualify me for the position you described in yesterday's *Sunday Sun*.

Ability to type, take dictation, speak intelligently to customers, clients, or patients, come up with an original idea occasionally, and be pleasant and good-humored are surely the attributes you'd like in the "Gal Friday" for whom you advertised. I have these qualities plus a good many others. Here are some details.

The three openings above do have some merit; they are rather fresh and original and indicate how the applicant's abilities will help the firm. For some jobs, such as advertising and copy writing, it might be advisable to inject a real "attention-getting" statement, an intriguing sentence, or a startling and clever paragraph.

The opening statement also affords a good opportunity to let your reader enjoy a capsule account of your primary selling points: experience, education, special abilities, etc.

DESCRIBING YOUR ABILITIES

In the one-part letter of application, clear and specific statements on your education, experience, leadership abilities, and awards should be made. In the two-part letter, these accomplishments are alluded to rather generally in the cover letter and specifically listed in the data sheet.

The description should be written to "match" the job's requirements or the ad's demands. If experience is emphasized in the job description and you possess it, this should be treated in some detail. If education is vital or leadership qualities important, then they should be emphasized. The sample letters displayed later in this chapter illustrate several different methods of handling these situations.

PROVING YOUR STATEMENTS

In the description section of the application letter, your references, degrees, and former employers (all proof of your abilities) may be indicated specifically in the one-part letter, but only referred to in the cover letter of a two-part application. Here again, the specifics are listed in the résumé or data sheet.

In listing degrees it is wise to indicate specific areas of study. When noting previous employment, a brief description of duties and responsibilities should appear so that the prospective employer has some idea of what you can do. And the same is true of any activities which illustrate leadership qualities: offices held, meetings conducted, articles written, conferences attended, etc.

SECURING THE INTERVIEW— THE REQUEST FOR ACTION

In both the cover letter for the résumé and the one-part letter of application, the final statements are usually concerned with making arrangements for the job interview. This should *not* be a simple "If you are interested, please call me" or "If you have any questions, I shall be pleased to answer them."

Your request for an interview should be emphatic and positive, and should clearly state that you want the interview so that you can tell the prospective employer about your attributes in greater detail than the letter permits. Perhaps an implied statement can be made that indicates that what has been said in the letter is only "part of the story" (as it can only be) and that the interview is desired to expand, add, and clarify details.

> May I have an interview so that we can discuss in greater detail my education, experience, and other qualifications for the position. I can be reached . . . .

> I would appreciate an opportunity to meet with you so that I can explain more completely how my experience, education, ability to work hard and take responsiblity, all qualify me for the job. Please call or write . . . .

> When can we get together? The sooner the better so that I can give you a more complete picture of how a degree in accounting, six years of responsible work as assistant to the controller, and a desire to work very hard where opportunity is unlimited can be put to use by the Cantrel Corporation.

THE COMPLETE LETTER OF APPLICATION

Here are several examples of one- and two-part letters of application. Note that some are more detailed than others, some include references, others do not. In general, they use a factual and persuasive approach.

18127 Oak Street
Fargo, North Dakota
July 20, 19____

Box 221 AM
Sunday Star
Denver, Colorado

Dear Sir:

Your ad requests a recent college graduate who has had some experience in insurance work. My degree in management, two years with a large life insurance firm, and a sincere desire to work hard should qualify me for the position.

In June of this year I received my college degree from Illinois State University. I majored in management with a special interest in personnel. I also took as much work as my program would permit in finance and accounting.

Three years ago I held a summer job in National Insurance Company's personnel division. I continued working there during the school year (on a part-time basis, of course), and full time during the summer periods. Although my initial duties were clerical, I was soon interviewing, testing, and carrying through duties in connection with securing salaried office personnel.

Since receiving my degree I have continued working for National. However, the opportunities with this firm are somewhat restricted and I would like to associate myself with a company that offers potential for growth and advancement in management positions.

During my collegiate career I received recognition for leadership in social and academic endeavors.

Between 19____ and 19____ I completed my service obligation. I am thus not subject to the draft.

I shall be pleased to meet with you, explain my background in more detail, and list work and academic references. I can meet with you at your convenience; just telephone (701) AX 2-1000, extension 201, or write to the address above.

Sincerely,

John Holmes

John Holmes

3760 Marquette Avenue
Hartford, Connecticut
December 10, 19____

Box 1726
Kansas City Star
Kansas City, Kansas

Gentlemen:

Thorough college training in marketing and finance,
ambition, and a desire to work hard are the qualities an
efficient man will need to fill your position of assistant
advertising manager. I am sure that after you evaluate my
qualifications you will find that I am that man.

Education

In February I will receive my Bachelor of Science in
Commerce degree from Hartford University. My major field
of study included the following courses: principles of
marketing, problems in marketing, advertising, retailing,
sales management, market research, marketing seminar, and
foreign marketing. Besides courses in marketing, my
university training included study in such related fields as
finance, management, accounting, business communications,
economics, business law, and statistics.

Experience

While my experience in marketing and particularly
advertising is limited to college work, an example of my
ambition and ability to learn quickly is demonstrated by the
job I have had for the past three years. During that time I
worked for Sears, Roebuck and Co. During my employment

-2-

I was promoted from a stock man to supervisor in charge of stock men. This process usually takes five years.

Personal

I am twenty-one years of age and in excellent health. I enjoy football, baseball, basketball, and bowling. I am also an active member of the Marketing Society, Society for the Advancement of Management, and the Finance Society.

References

I have personally contacted the persons listed below and they have consented to offer a thorough report on my capabilities and my character.

Mr. Vernon Cates
Division Manager
Sears, Roebuck and Co.
Corporate Headquarters
Hartford, Connecticut

Dr. Philip Pendleton
Department of Advertising
Hartford University
Hartford, Connecticut

Dr. Robert E. Cantel, Chairman
Department of Marketing
Hartford University
Hartford, Connecticut

Mr. William B. Myers
2809 South Patterson Avenue
Chicago, Illinois 60634

I have given you all the information I believe is pertinent, but only through an interview can I tell you my entire story. Please call me at (203) 738-1212 to arrange an interview at your convenience.

Very truly yours,

Martin T. Mackay

Martin T. Mackay

4812 North Adams Street
Boston, Massachusetts
May 20, 19____

Box MAR 721
Boston Daily News
Boston, Massachusetts

Gentlemen:

Next month I shall graduate from Boston College armed with
a Bachelor of Science Degree in Commerce, lots of ambition,
and a willingness to work hard. A position as an executive
secretary with the top qualifications you desire is just what
I have been looking for. Please consider my training and
background for the opening in your firm.

EDUCATION—

I have attended Boston College for four years majoring in
Business Education. I have a basic knowledge of business in
the areas of marketing, finance, management, business law
and economics. My liberal arts background has been
excellent, with special emphasis on English, including
courses in business communication and report writing.

SECRETARIAL SKILLS—

Dictation and accurate transcription are second nature to
me. I take shorthand at better than 120 words per minute

-2-

and can type accurately at the rate of 70 words per minute. While at Boston College, I took a course in office machines, in which we learned the basic skills on the comptometer, adding machines, and the automatic calculator.

WORK EXPERIENCE—

The cost of a college education is, as you know, quite expensive. I have always worked part time to help pay expenses and at the same time, I have maintained above-average grades. This has taught me responsibility as well as the ability to organize my time.

I am employed on a part-time basis by Shippey and Shippey, a legal firm, located at One North LaSalle Street, Boston. My duties include heavy dictation, complete charge of the filing system, and other secretarial duties.

From January 19____ until November 19____, I was employed by New England Insurance Company as a stenographer in their Correspondence Department. This job consisted primarily of dictation, transcription, and switchboard "relief."

May I come in for an interview to discuss my qualifications with you in greater detail? I can be reached at Walnut 1-0771.

Very truly yours,

Jane Allen

(Miss) Jane Allen

2107 North Kansas Street
Milwaukee, Wisconsin
December 3, 19____

Box 221 BAM
Milwaukee Gazette
Gazette Building
Milwaukee, Wisconsin

Dear Sir:

This morning's *Milwaukee Gazette* carried your advertisement for a "recent graduate accountant" with "a desire to work in a broad area of private accounting." With my educational background, practical experience, and ability to work rapidly and efficiently, I am sure that I could be a valuable asset to your company.

Education

On February 7, 19____, I shall receive my Bachelor of Science Degree from the University of Wisconsin's College of Commerce, where I have majored in accounting and minored in management. I have successfully completed all the basic courses in accounting plus two in auditing, two in taxes, and one each in consolidations and accounting systems.

Beginning in February I will take evening work in preparation for the May C.P.A. examination. Next September I plan to begin work on an evening Master of Business Administration program.

Experience

For the last six years I have worked at a variety of part-time and summer jobs in order to cover my educational expenses. During 19____ I worked for the firm of Jackson and Clark, Certified Public Accountants, where my duties included general ledger work, monthly financial statements, payroll taxes, and general accounting.

For the past two years I have been working, full-time during the summers and part-time after class, for the public accounting firm of Patterson & Co. During this time I have gained experience in the areas of general, tax, and insurance accounting which should prove very valuable to your company.

Box 221 BAM
December 3, 19____
Page Two

Among my varied duties at Patterson and Co., I have been the assistant to the Administrative Manager of the Tax Department. In this position I have come into contact with managerial accounting, a field which interests me very much. I also participated in two employee training programs, one in taxes and another in insurance accounting.

Personal

I am 22 years of age, 5'9", and weigh 150 pounds. I am in excellent health, unmarried, and live at home.

References

I have spoken to the persons listed below and they have assured me that they will be happy to offer an objective, written opinion of my capabilities and personality.

Mr. Peter T. Patterson, Partner
Patterson & Co.
111 South Monroe Street
Madison, Wisconsin

Mr. Mark W. Kelly, Chairman
Department of Business Law
University of Wisconsin
Madison, Wisconsin

Mr. Carl R. Jansen, Partner
Jackson and Clark
111 West Washington Avenue
Chicago, Illinois

Mr. Erwin R. Port, Commr.
County Dept. of Buildings
130 North Wells Street
Milwaukee, Wisconsin

I would very much appreciate an opportunity to meet with you, at your convenience, to discuss further my background, salary, and future potential with your company. I may be reached any afternoon at FInancial 6-7200, extension 344, or any evening at SUnnyside 3-2916.

Sincerely yours,

Robert T. Murtain

Robert T. Murtain

1411 North Clearview Street
St. Louis, Missouri
March 3, 19____

Box 233 FAX
St. Louis Daily News
St. Louis, Missouri

Gentlemen:

Your advertisement offered an unusual opportunity for a
marketing trainee—I would like to offer you one in return.
With an MBA degree from Northwestern University,
diversified work experience, and a desire to learn and grow
professionally in an expanding company, I am sure I can be
of value to your firm.

This June I shall receive my MBA degree from the Graduate
School of Business of Northwestern. While concentrating my
studies in marketing, I have also developed effective skills
in decision-making techniques, policy determination, and
marketing management and communications. I received my
undergraduate degree from Missouri State, where I majored
in economics.

I have worked every summer to help defray my college
expenses, indicative of my ability and ambition to accept a
wide range of responsibilities. These summer jobs include
assisting the accountant of a small company, proofreading
and writing technical manuals, and expediting fabrication of
electronic components for a satellite.

I have always been interested in what motivates America's
buyer—both wholesaler and consumer—and have completed
research in this area in both my undergraduate and
graduate studies. I have also learned a good deal from my
work assignments, and I am now eager to put my education,
experience, and ambition to work in a business environment.

On the basis of my education I feel a salary of $850 to $950
per month would be satisfactory, but I am sure an equitable
figure can be reached at the time of an interview. May I
come in, at your convenience, and discuss my background
and education in greater detail? I can be reached late
afternoons and evenings at 747-8322.

Sincerely,

Keith Thompson

Keith Thompson

Keith Thompson
1411 North Clearview Street
St. Louis, Missouri
747-8322

Photograph

Job Objective

Management position in marketing
with a growing company. Eventual
objective to become an officer in
a medium-sized firm.

Major Qualifications

University background in business administration
Experience in the field of accounting and office work

Education

Master of Business Administration Degree, Northwestern
University, June, 19____

Courses in Marketing

Marketing Communications
Marketing Logistics
Marketing Planning and
  Management
Pricing Strategy
Market and Sales Analysis
Retailing Management

Courses in Related Fields

Business Communications
Human Elements of
  Management
Logic of Problem Analysis
Statistical Methods
Private Enterprise and
  Public Policy
Management Processes and
  Organization Structure
Financial Planning and
  Management

Business Policy Formu-
  lation
Quantitative Analysis for
  Business Decisions
Accounting Fundamentals
Accounting Control and
  Financial Reporting I & II
Logic of Decision Making
Problems of Business
  Regulation

Bachelor of Arts Degree, Missouri State University,
June, 19____
Major area: Economics

Business Related Courses   2

Cost Accounting	Advertising
Industrial Psychology	Economics of Industry
Price Theory	Social Control of Industry
Money and Banking	

Work Experience

Gayle and Gompers Corp.
1414 South Jackson Road
St. Louis, Missouri

Summer 19____ and 19____
Duties: Accounts receivable, payroll supervision, and
           routine accounting assignments. Also the
           writing, editing, and proofreading of technical
           manuals.

Electronic Development Company
101 South Madison Avenue
St. Louis, Missouri

Summer, 19____
Duties: Expediter in purchasing department
           Correspondent to suppliers

Other part-time and summer jobs included routine office
work, road laborer, clerk in a law office, and salesman in a
men's clothing store.

Personal Data

Physical details: age, 23 years; height, 5'11"; weight, 180;
                   health, excellent

Hobbies and interests: Swimming, handball, folk music,
                       reading

References

Mr. Robert T. Gayle, President	Mr. Michael Coffee, Plant Mgr.
Gayle and Gompers Corp.	Electronic Development Co.
1414 South Jackson Road	101 South Madison Avenue
St. Louis, Missouri	St. Louis, Missouri
Dr. Henry Hale	Dr. J. T. Jackson, Dean
Professor of Marketing	Missouri State University
Northwestern University	Carver, Missouri
Evanston, Illinois	

1023 Roscomare Road
Los Angeles, California 90024
May 15, 19____

Space Age Corporation
Aircraft Division
1955 West Granville Avenue
Burbank, California 90756

Attention: Mr. H. A. Franklin, Director of Employment

Gentlemen:

I am answering your advertisement for a Senior Management Systems Analyst because I feel that the Space Age Corporation is looking for a bold, imaginative man.

I feel that my background, experience, and interests are uniquely suited to working in a creative environment in the field of purchasing systems and procedures as well as related areas. This, briefly, is why I think so:

1. Experience in writing, revising, and coordinating purchasing policy at the corporate level for the Saturn Aviation Company, Inc.

2. Exposure to a wide variety of purchasing systems, procedures, and related areas among the multiple divisions of Saturn.

3. A good working knowledge of government procurement regulations including: ASPR, NASAPR, AECPR, FPR, DPC, AFPI, and others.

4. I feel strongly challenged to tackle the ever-growing communication problems of defense industry management.

I have included a résumé of my experience, education, and personal data for your further information.

I would certainly appreciate the opportunity of an interview where we can discuss my background and other qualifications in greater detail, as well as my possible future with the Space Age Corporation. Please call my home (213-476-4222) so that a time can be arranged to suit your convenience.

Sincerely yours,

Edward T. Counter

Edward T. Counter

Enclosure

-2-

EDWARD T. COUNTER

1023 Roscomare Road   Los Angeles, California 90024

213 476-4222

EXPERIENCE

SATURN AVIATION COMPANY, INC.
Van Nuys, California   June 19____ TO Present

Staff Assistant, Corporate Material, General Office
36 months

Responsible for assisting Manager-Material staff in development of new and revision of existing Corporate Material Directives. Principal duties include: maintaining working knowledge of Government procurement regulations, Company directives, Company basic procurement agreements; reviewing and analyzing information emanating from corporate sources for policy development and implementation; coordinating Material policy and procedures with all levels of division and Corporate management.

Methods Analyst—Supersonic Division   24 months

Responsible for advising and assisting Material staff in various administrative functions. Duties included: the maintenance and administration of personnel records and the processing of personnel data received; development and maintenance of statistical data and graphic displays relating to work load and other activities for work measurement and other management requirements. Interviewing small

-3-

business suppliers and dealers and otherwise implementing the company's policy toward the small businessman.

THE FLOURNOY CORPORATION
Research Division
Whittier, California   May 19____ TO June 19____

Supervisor of Services   14 months

Staff assistant to manager of research with responsibility for operational analysis and control of research services for research branch of 55 people. Work assignment was highly diversified, requiring line and staff responsibility in areas of personnel, purchasing, budgeting, building and equipment maintenance, and related duties.

ECONOMY AIR FREIGHT AIRWAYS, INC.
San Francisco, California   June 19____ TO April 19____

Station Manager   20 months

Responsible for all traffic and maintenance functions including handling flight movements, servicing aircraft, receiving and processing cargo, billing and manifesting, load planning, and crew coordination. Accounting responsibilities covered payroll reporting, treasury reports, rating and invoicing, accounts payable and receivable, budget control and related areas.

District Sales Manager   14 months

Responsible for all sales activity on West Coast with a sales staff of seven men. Organized and directed

-4-

sales promotion activities and sales training. Created direct mail promotion and all necessary follow-up. Sales volume increased well over 100% in the period of my responsibility.

EDUCATION

Bachelor of Science Degree, June 19____
University of Illinois
School of Business Administration

Major area of concentration: Management

Master of Business Administration, June 19____
University of Southern California
Graduate School of Business Administration

Major area of concentration: Quantitative Analysis
Systems and Pro-
cedures

MILITARY

Served with the United States Air Force, May 19____ to May 19____
Honorably discharged with the rank of Major
Decorated

PERSONAL

Age   32
Health   Excellent
Married, 3 children

REFERENCES

Furnished on request

1521 Martel Street
Los Angeles, California
June 2, 19____

Personnel Director
North American Aviation, Inc.
1700 East Imperial Highway
El Segundo, California 90246

Dear Sir:

Through several acquaintances who are employed by North American, I have learned of the many commercial and defense projects in which your firm is engaged. Because of my undergraduate degree in engineering and my graduate work in business administration, I feel that I can be an asset to your firm.

I would like to work for North American in the area of project coordination. I have already been exposed to this area in the two summers I was employed by Southern California Edison Co. Careful administration of my assignments brought commendation from my supervisors who commented on my initiative and responsibility.

In February, 19____, I received my Bachelor of Science degree in Electrical Engineering from the University of Southern California. This same institution will award me a Master of Business Administration in just one week. While in school I was an officer in the student branch of the Institute of Electrical and Electronics Engineers, and president of our chapter of Eta Kappa Nu, the national electrical engineering honor society. In addition I took part in various other undergraduate and graduate activities.

In both my previous work experience and my extracurricular activities, I have had the opportunity to work successfully with and through many types of people. On the basis of my background, I know I can prove of benefit to North American.

I would appreciate an opportunity at your convenience to discuss my qualifications. At that time I can answer any questions you have. My phone number is 292-3333.

Sincerely yours,

James Kennedy

James Kennedy

James Kennedy
1521 Martel Street
Los Angeles, California

Phone 292-3333

Photograph

JOB OBJECTIVE

A position in project coordination. Eventual objective to be a project manager.

MAJOR QUALIFICATIONS

University background in electrical engineering and business
    administration
Experience in program coordination

EXPERIENCE

Southern California Edison Company
Fifth and Grand Avenues
Los Angeles, California

    Summer of 19____
    Duties: Programming and coordinating activities leading
            to the establishment of new generating facilities

    Summer of 19____
    Duties: Analysis and coordination of activities in
            research of new power sources

EDUCATION

Master of Business Administration degree, University of
Southern California, Los Angeles, California, June, 19____

    Courses in Business

Accounting Concepts	Business Economics
Communications	Financial Analysis
Legal and Social	Business Strategy
Environment	Plus many related courses
Quantitative Methods	in the specific area of
Financial Management	Administrative Management

Courses in Engineering and Mathematics   2

Calculus	Electric Circuits I, II, III
Probability and Statistics	Electronics I, II, III
Random Processes	Computer Design
Computer Programming	Control Systems

AWARDS AND ORGANIZATIONS

Eta Kappa Nu (national electrical engineering honorary
   society), President
California State Scholarship
Institute of Electrical and Electronics Engineers, Member
Institute of Electrical and Electronics Engineers—U.S.C.
   Student Chapter, Treasurer, Secretary

PERSONAL DATA

Physical details: age, 23 years: height, 6'1"; weight, 180
   pounds; health, excellent
Marital status: Single
Citizenship: United States of America
Draft status: II-S

REFERENCES

Dr. Robert M. Lamp
Professor of Engineering
University of Southern California
Los Angeles, California 90007

Dr. M. T. Regal
Associate Prof. of Electrical Engineering
University of Southern California
Los Angeles, California 90007

Mr. John M. Dorsey
Project Coordinator
Southern California Edison Co.
Fifth and Grand Avenues
Los Angeles, California

Dr. F. W. Workman, Assistant Dean
Graduate School of Business Administration
University of Southern California
Los Angeles, California 90007

2707 South Standard Avenue
Los Angeles, California
November 29, 19____

Personnel Office
Burke Technological Center
6401 Laughton Street
Los Angeles, California

Gentlemen:

This morning's *Los Angeles Times* carried your advertisement
for a "college graduate who is looking for a challenging and
interesting position in industrial accounting." With my
educational background, practical experience, and
willingness to work in an interesting position that offers a real
challenge, I am sure I can be of value to your company.

Next February I shall receive my Bachelor of Science degree
from University of California at Los Angeles, where I have
majored in accounting and minored in finance and
management. Beginning in January I plan to take work in
preparation for the May C.P.A. examination.

For the last six years I have worked at a variety of part-time
jobs: engineer trainee, electrical apprentice, customer service
assistant, and accounting clerk. During the past two years,
I have gained working experience which will be very valuable
to your organization. Details of these jobs, my education, and
other information may be found on the attached data sheet.

I know that I can fill the challenging position you have open,
and I would appreciate an opportunity to meet with you at
your convenience to discuss in detail my qualifications,
salary, and future potential with your company. I may be
reached every afternoon at FInancial 6-9200, extension 32;
or any evening at PAlisades 4-1282.

Sincerely yours,

Thomas T. Peterson

Thomas T. Peterson

enclosure

THOMAS T. PETERSON
2707 South Standard Avenue
Los Angeles, California

PAlisades 4-1282

Photograph

Job Objective

Professional position as an accountant
with an aggressive firm. Eventual objective to serve as comptroller of
a good-sized organization.

Major Qualifications

University training in accounting and
    business
Varied experience with a large public
    accounting firm

Education

Bachelor of Science Degree in Commerce, University of
California at Los Angeles, February 19_____

Courses in Accounting

Elements and Principles
    of Accounting
Interpretation
Intermediate Accounting
Advanced Theory and
    Practice

Cost Accounting
Consolidations
Auditing Theory
Auditing Practice
Taxes I and II

Courses in Related Fields

Corporate Finance
Money and Banking
Production Management

Problems in Marketing
Business Communications
Business Law I and II

Experience

Kelly and Kelly, Certified Public Accountants   2
111 West Monroe Street
Los Angeles 3, California
  Part-time (after class) February 19____ to present
  Full-time summers of 19____ and 19____
  Duties: Assistant to Administrative Manager of Tax
Department, Assistant to Office Manager, routine
   accounting work, physical inventories, and
   referencing tax returns

Campbell and Company, Certified Public Accountants
411 West Washington Street
Los Angeles, California
  Part-time (after class) September 19____ to February
   19____
  Duties: Routine accounting work, ledger posting, monthly
   statements for small businesses, and quarterly
   payroll taxes

Social Activities and Organizations

Vice-President of Young Democrats
Member of Accounting Society
Member of the Society for the Advancement of Management

Personal Data

Physical details: age, 22 years; height, 5'9"; weight, 145
  pounds; health, excellent
Special interests: philosophy and golf
Draft status: 1-A

References

Mr. Robert T. Kelly   Dr. Thomas L. Lewis, Chairman
Kelly and Kelly   Department of Accounting
111 West Monroe Street   University of California
Los Angeles 3, California   Los Angeles, California

Mr. Thomas Johnson   Professor M. T. Colinworth
Senior Partner   Department of Finance
Campbell and Company   University of California
Certified Public Accountants   Los Angeles, California
411 West Washington Street
Los Angeles, California

1313 West Scott Street
Des Plaines, Illinois
May 11, 19____

Mr. Robert T. Book
Western Electric Company
Hawthorne Station
Chicago, Illinois

Dear Mr. Book:

Your company can benefit greatly from my educational background, part-time experience, and willingness to work hard.

Next month, I shall receive my Bachelor of Science degree from De Paul University's College of Commerce. Maintaining an overall B+ average at this fine institution has enabled me to obtain an excellent, well-rounded education and, in particular, an above-average knowledge of accounting.

In order to meet college and personal expenses, I worked four years at Martin and Allen, Certified Public Accountants. After one year of proofreading, I was promoted to the accounting department. As a staff member, my duties included auditing, preparing individual and corporate tax returns, and compiling financial statements. This valuable experience not only helped me supplement my studies with practical application, but it also taught me how to associate with clients, understand assignments, and communicate ideas.

During high school, I worked at Kopper Kitchen Restaurant in Des Plaines, Illinois. I started as a cook, and after one year held the position of assistant manager. From both of my former employers I have received bonuses for ideas that improved company efficiency. This, I think, will indicate to you that I am a person willing to work hard and perform a job correctly.

In June I will start Northwestern's evening C.P.A. Review in preparation for the November examination. I also plan to take graduate courses in accounting systems and control to further broaden my education.

I would appreciate an opportunity to discuss with you in detail my education, experience, and other qualifications. My telephone number is MOnroe 6-1231.

Very truly yours,

Robert A. Connors

Robert A. Connors

Robert A. Connors
1313 West Scott Street
Des Plaines, Illinois

Home phone: MOnroe 6-1231
Work phone: FInancial 6-1200

Photograph

JOB OBJECTIVE:

Professional position as an auditor with a C.P.A. firm and
eventual managerial capacity in such a firm

EDUCATION:

Bachelor of Science degree, De Paul University's College of
Commerce—June 19_____

COURSES IN ACCOUNTING:

Elements	Cost Accounting
Principles	Auditing Theory
Interpretation	Auditing Practice
Intermediate Theory	Taxes I and II
Advanced Theory	Consolidations
Systems	Governmental Accounting

COURSES IN RELATED FIELDS:

Business Law I and II	Corporate Finance
Economics I and II	Money and Banking
Income Determination	Business Communications
The Stock Market	Business Report Writing
Marketing Problems	Ethics

MAJOR QUALIFICATIONS:

University education in accounting. Four years part-time
experience in accounting firm. Two years assistant manager
in drive-in restaurant.

EXPERIENCE:

Martin and Allen, Certified Public Accountants
315 West Wabash Avenue
Chicago 4, Illinois
Period from October, 19____, to June, 19____

EXPERIENCE: (continued)   2

Duties: First year—proofreading. Remaining three years
—member of accounting staff—auditing;
preparing individual and corporate tax returns,
both state and federal; compiling financial
statements, reports on examination and S.E.C.
10-K reports.

Kopper Kitchen Restaurant
64 East Lake Street
Chicago, Illinois
Period from September, 19____, to June, 19____
Duties: First year—short-order cook. Remaining two
years—assistant manager at night, supervising
four men

Other part-time jobs: Stock boy in pet shop; saxophone
player in musical combo

ACTIVITIES, HONORS, AND ORGANIZATIONS:

National Honor Society—High School
Des Plaines Library Art Club
Writer for De Paul University's Literary Magazine,
"Trajectories"
Winner of De Paul University's Art Contest

PERSONAL DATA:

Physical details: Age 23; height 6 feet, 1 inch; weight
175 pounds; health excellent
Marital status: Single
Hobbies and interests: Reading, art, music, sports, and
painting
Draft status: IIA

REFERENCES:

Mr. John Foreman, C.P.A.   Professor Edwin Sloan
Audit Manager   Professor of Accounting
Martin and Allen   De Paul University
315 West Wabash Avenue   Chicago, Illinois
Chicago 4, Illinois

Mr. Harold Jackson   Professor Martin Contrant
Kopper Kitchen Restaurant,   Department of Finance
Inc.   Northwestern University
1900 East Queen Court   Evanston, Illinois
Chicago, Illinois

IMPORTANT REMINDERS
FOR THE JOB SEEKER

There are several factors which are worth emphasizing for the writer of the application letter.

Appearance is vital. When the prospective employer reads your letter, he should be impressed with its excellent proportion, generous use of white space, obvious organization, and easy "readability." You want him to say as he reads, "My, this is a well-organized, logical person."

Check the letter's *correctness* and use of *English*. Personnel directors have told me that a college student's or graduate's letter must be completely error-free. All that is required to achieve this is editing and care. And as one employment supervisor stated:

> There is no more important letter he will ever write unless he proposes marriage by mail . . . and this job letter should be perfect. We can understand when a letter from a shop supervisor exhibits an error or two, but not when the message comes from a college-trained man. After all, if he is careless in his letter, what can we expect in his handling of our ledgers?

So check your letter carefully and make sure it is clear, concise, complete, and correct.

Does the letter have a *"you" attitude*? Have you attempted to point out how the *company* will benefit from your skill, service, and ambition? The personnel director is not particularly concerned with how his firm will give *you* experience; provide *you* with interesting and challenging situations; and offer *you* promotions and pay increases. He is interested in learning how your education, your experience, your travels can be successfully used in the advancement and progress of the firm.

> My degree in accounting and two years of part-time experience with Merril and Maxwell, CPA's, should prove of value to your company.

> If your company can use a professionally trained advertising man who has loads of energy and ambition, plus three years' experience, I'm the man for your firm.

Your letter should also be *specific* and *original*. The letter that is general as to what the applicant has done in the past and can do in the future usually makes little impact on the reader. We live in a world of specialization and, in professional areas especially, we like to know precisely what the job seeker can do for us.

It isn't enough to indicate that your degree is in business administration; what specific area? And there is too much left to the imagination with, "I held a management position for two years with Croxton and Croxton."

"I was the office manger of Croxton and Croxton's Southfield division," or "personnel assistant in charge of training." On the other hand, the applicant must be careful not to give the reader the impression (unless he sincerely means to) that he would only be happy doing "inventory control" or that he can "only accomplish payroll accounting." There is certainly a middle ground that should be indicated.

And of course the letter of application should be *original*. Never copy a paragraph, and certainly not a complete letter, from any source. Anyone can find examples of clever letters in texts, paperbacks, and a dozen other sources. But you can be sure that most personnel directors have read almost all the "model" letters many times.

THE JOB INTERVIEW

As we all know, the letter of application will rarely result in a job offer; we hope, however, that through the letter we can secure an interview and that is the way it should be written—with the objective of securing an interview, not a job.

A job is offered only after we have "sold" ourselves at the interview, and for this reason as much time and care should be spent on that phase of job seeking as on the preparation, planning, or even writing of the letter. The half hour spent talking to the prospective employer is vital. We must give the evidence of a pleasant personality, ability to communicate, knowledge of our area, our future objectives, the information we have about the company, our level of courtesy, and familiarity with topics of professional, political, and cultural interest. This requires preparation.

New York Life Insurance Company has issued an excellent booklet titled *Making the Most of Your Job Interview*. It begins with the statement:

> The employment interview is one of the most important events in the average person's experience, for the obvious reason that the 20 or 30 minutes he spends with the interviewer may determine the entire future course of his life. Yet college recruiters are continually amazed at the number of applicants who drift into job interviews without any apparent preparation and only the vaguest idea of what they are going to say. Their manner says, "Well, here I am." And that's the end of it. In more ways than one.

Many college graduates are interviewed on campus by corporate recruiters. Others are interviewed as a direct result of the letter of application which they have submitted. In both cases, the applicants' preparation for and conduct during the discussion should be similar.

The job applicant should consider several carefully worded questions he might ask. These may be concerned with future opportunities within the firm, compensation in addition to the base salary (hospitalization, annuity funds, tuition refund plans, stock option programs, profit sharing, etc.), plans for company expansion and diversification, job duties, travel requirements, advancement policies, and a host of others.

The answers to these questions are vital to you, and will surely determine which job you choose. Furthermore, this two-way discussion gives you an opportunity to relax as the interviewer speaks. And it opens up important new avenues for discussion.

In addition to preparing questions, you should secure some information about the company. What are its primary products? Where are its plants? What is its financial history and present situation? How many employees does it have? What kind of growth picture does it reflect?

Background data can be secured from a number of sources, among which are:

The company's annual report
Thomas' Register of American Manufacturers
Moody's Manuals
Standard and Poor's Corporation Records
Dun and Bradstreet Reference Book
Poor's Register of Directors and Executives
College Placement Directory
College Placement Annual
Government booklets (for federal departments, bureaus, and divisions)

To further prepare for your job interview, you might think of twenty or so questions the interviewer is likely to ask and how you will answer them. If you think that is a task which requires little thought, examine the following typical questions.[3] How would you answer them?

Tell me about yourself.
Why are you interested in our company?
What are your plans for the future?
Why did you choose your particular field?

---

3. The New York Life booklet contains a list of 94 questions most frequently asked during a job interview, as reported by 92 companies. Some of those questions are listed here.

What qualifications do you have that you think will make you successful in your field?
What kind of boss do you prefer?
What do you think determines a man's progress in a company?
What is the source of your spending money?
What job in our company would you choose if you were entirely free to do so?

Just a quick survey of the questions above shows us how important preparation is. To take an interview without a clear analysis of your own needs and desires, and the company's objectives, is foolhardy.

Of course, no comment is necessary concerning neat dress, erect posture, and the need to speak clearly, correctly, and completely during the interview. The importance of these factors is well known.

The interviewee should take care not to ramble or make political hay if asked about foreign policy, national affairs, or his profession. Freedom of expression is respected, but comments should be concise and delivered in good taste.

If questioned about courses, instructors, and former employers, the applicant should remember, "If you can't say anything good about him, say nothing." The interview is not the place for disparaging others. And the job seeker should be frank and honest in all his replies about himself. A statement which is not true will surely trip him up sooner or later.

Don't be coy with the interviewer. If he offers a job and you aren't prepared to accept it at that moment, don't stall, or accept it with the mental reservation that you will turn it down if you receive a better offer that afternoon. Tell him directly that you have other interviews scheduled, and that you want to defer a decision, for the benefit of the company as well as yourself. Because the interviewer is usually a reasonable person, he will accept an honest approach of this type.

Find an opportunity during the interview to state your major attributes factually, but not boastfully.

"My extracurricular activities were somewhat limited because I had to work while attending school. My job in the bookstore helped me to pay almost 80 per cent of my college expenses."

"My knowledge of Spanish is good enough for me to carry on correspondence and routine business activities with your Latin American accounts."

"I was fortunate to receive a General Bank and Trust Company scholarship as a freshman. I held it, on the basis of grades, for all four years."

THE FOLLOW-UP LETTER

You would not usually send a follow-up letter as a result of an initial, brief, exploratory interview. However, if you have been interviewed at length and you are very much interested in the position, you might very well consider a follow-up note. Very few persons take the time or make the effort to do this. When the interviewer receives such a letter, it is an unusual experience for him. You can be sure he will read and be impressed with it.

The written follow-up to the interview should be concise, sincere, and courteous. Basically, its purpose is to thank the interviewer for the time and effort he expended in talking to you and to review briefly your own qualifications. It should be mailed the same day, or the day following the interview.

May 27, 19____

Dear Mr. Cates:

Thank you very much for the time you spent with me this morning. I found your discussion of the Fairmont Company most interesting, and the openings you described very challenging.

You will recall that I received my commerce degree from California State last year, acquired a CPA certificate a few months ago, and have been employed for one year as a junior accountant with Continental Aerospace Company.

I would certainly like an opportunity to work more extensively in an electronic data processing position such as the one you described. I do hope you will call me at GR 6-4622 for further discussion.

Sincerely yours,

October 3, 19____

Dear Mr. Robinson:

Thank you very much for taking the time to show me Barton's office and manufacturing facilities yesterday. I was certainly impressed with the efficiency, friendliness and overall climate of the firm.

Now that I know something about your company's directions and objectives, I feel that my degree in industrial engineering, my two years of part-time work in motion and time study, and my desire to work hard should all be of value to your company.

If I can supply you with additional information on my education and experience, I shall be happy to come in at your convenience. In the meantime, I hope you will consider me favorably for the position we discussed.

Sincerely yours,

Perhaps the most important quality of the follow-up letter is sincerity. A letter that contains obviously insincere statements, or overly enthusiastic praise, will surely fail in its purpose. Keep it concise, direct, sincere, and mail it promptly after the interview.

The entire process of securing a position is a vital one; it deserves your full attention, your very careful preparation, and your maximum effort.

QUESTIONS FOR STUDY

I. Complete any of the following problems assigned. You may wish to review the chapter and note key points before attempting to solve the problem.

1. What attributes do sales and application letters have in common?

2. Under what circumstances would a two-part letter of application be superior to a one-part letter?

3. Design a series of six questions which a job applicant might ask of a company interviewer.

4. What specific attributes should a "follow-up to an interview" letter contain?

5. Select an advertisement from the classified section of your local newspaper. Reply to the ad using a two-part letter of application. You may make no assumptions which are not accurate except that you expect to receive your college degree in six weeks, and you have successfully completed all courses leading to that degree. Clip the advertisement to your letter.

6. Send an unsolicited one-part or two-part letter of application to a firm that you would like to work for after you receive your degree. Assume your graduation will take place within two months.

7. Split into groups of five and conduct a mock job interview. Establish the job, job requirements, qualifications of the interviewee, salary level, and education and experience backgrounds necessary to secure the job. One individual should play the role of interviewer, one the job applicant, and three should act as observers.

The interviewer and interviewee should make all necessary assumptions for the role-playing exercise. The observers should offer a carefully structured critique at the conclusion of the interview. Roles should be rotated so that each person has an opportunity to play two or three different roles in the various interviews held.

8. Assume that you were interviewed yesterday for a position which you would like to secure. Although you feel you made a favorable impression, you know that at least six well-qualified persons in addition to yourself were interviewed by the personnel director.

Write Mr. Cunningham, the personnel director, a brief follow-up letter.

9. Offer your constructive criticism of the one-part letters of application on pages 285-291. Remember to note factors that are competently done as well as those which need improvement.

10. Offer your constructive criticism of the two-part letters of application on pages 292-307. Remember to note factors which are competently done as well as those which need improvement.

PART THREE

Letters

CHAPTER ELEVEN

Writing Effective Letters

Every company, big or small, communicates to dozens of different publics. These are all *external* to the firm: suppliers, dealers, manufacturers, customers, vendors, prospective purchasers, regulatory bureaus, government agencies, community groups, educational institutions, and on and on. Of the many types of written or printed external communications, such as newspaper and magazine advertisements, direct mail pieces, telegrams, reports, and letters, it is certainly letters which are used most frequently. It is true that communication takes place during a salesman's presentation, a manager's phone call, or a casual discussion at lunch. However, when a record is required or facts need to be spelled out—prices quoted, offers made, or deliveries promised—then a letter is needed.

The number of business letters written and delivered each day is countless, and it is largely these letters which keep the wheels of industry turning, as one transaction after another is completed.

THE BUSINESS LETTER AND THE COMPANY IMAGE

In many firms the business letter is the primary means of external communication. There are several reasons for this: a letter establishes a tangible record which can be used for later reference; distances can be spanned quickly at relatively small costs; the time spent traveling to another person's office and carrying through a discussion can be eliminated; and routine business matters can be completed efficiently with the help of letter guides and forms.

For example, take a large insurance company with thousands of policyowners and hundreds of agents from coast to coast. Questions about premiums, cancellations, medical bills, changes in beneficiaries, overpayments, past due accounts, conversions, reinstatements, and a thousand and one other situations arise each day. Letters flow into the home (or central) office from a variety of different sources. And replies must go out, all on the company's stationery and written by hundreds of different employees, and all contributing to the company's image.

When policyowner Mrs. Baxter of Three Forks, South Dakota, reads the letter she receives at her farm home, she has a mental picture of the company; so too does Mr. Smythe as he sits in his apartment on the forty-fifth floor of a Chicago apartment building; and so does the corporate officer who is considering the purchase of major policies for his company. Each person, young or old, rich or poor, from the policyowner to the corporate officer, from the community member to the secretary of the state insurance commission—each one builds an image of the company on the basis of the letter he reads.

If the letter is curt, the company appears abrupt; if the letter is hackneyed, stereotyped, and dull, the company appears backward and stodgy; if the letter is discourteous or tactless, the company appears pompous and high-handed; if the letter is unattractive and sloppy, the company appears careless and negligent.

On the other hand, when the letter is clear and concise, the firm seems well organized and competent; when the letter is courteous and friendly, the company seems concerned and helpful; when the letter is attractive and neat, the company seems efficient and accurate. And so it goes: regardless of who wrote the letter, the message will reflect—to the reader—the image of the company.

The firm's manager may protest that a particular letter was carelessly written by an inexperienced, tactless new employee and is not an accurate reflection of company policy. But his protests will be to no avail. To the reader, the curt, overbearing, sarcastic letter does reflect the company. Say what you will, the image has been drawn, and good will and sales suffer.

The best solution, of course, is to have all the employees of a company write clearly, tactfully, and concisely. To accomplish this goal, management must be responsible for training its correspondents to write well. And the correspondents not only must be taught the mechanics of good letter writing, but they must understand how very important their job is to the company.

Because the managements of many companies in the United States do recognize the importance of effective letters, they have carried through various programs in this area. Some very large corporations have departments whose primary function is to evaluate company correspondence and train employees in letter writing. Perhaps one of the most ambitious programs is that of New York Life Insurance Company. This firm holds classes, reviews correspondence, issues bulletins, and, at frequent intervals, reminds its employees of the importance of effective correspondence.

Other companies follow different patterns. Some engage outside consultants for evaluation and training purposes, and many firms subscribe to letter improvement bulletins sent out periodically by companies specializing in this service. Most firms today are aware of the importance of good company correspondence—and are doing something about raising their standards or keeping them high.

MECHANICS

The training carried on for correspondents and management personnel in most organizations usually places little if any emphasis on the form and mechanics of the business letter, because these areas are considered the responsibility of the typist. However, the manager should have some familiarity with the topic. For that reason, Appendix C contains suggestions in this area.

The mechanics and form of the business letter vary considerably from one company to another. One firm requires that its employees use block form; another prefers modified block. One organization recommends identifying initials of dictator and typist, and another company omits them entirely. These minor variations in the form of the letter exist, and serve to express the ideas and individuality of companies. The "correct" form, therefore, is the one that a particular firm requires that its employees use. It is for this reason that many companies publish correspondence manuals and guides, written for the company, which indicate the firm's preference in letter layout, use of abbreviations, address style, signatures, and so on.

The mechanics of a business letter should be correct, but an error in typing or letter layout will not lose nearly as much good will as a tactless or sarcastic statement. Thus it is knowledge of the *principles* of business writing that is so important.

PRINCIPLES OF COMMUNICATION

TONE

Although we frequently refer to it, *tone* is an indefinable quality in business writing. Often an individual will say, after reading a letter, "The

319

tone of Acme's message was extremely friendly," or "tactful," or "impersonal," or "very positive." Our interpretation of the tone seems to depend on our reactions to the words used, the phrasing of the sentences, the order of the ideas. And this interpretation and evaluation of the tone as "friendly," "formal," "courteous," "high-pressured," then becomes the characteristic (friendly, formal, courteous, high-pressured) we tend to apply to the company as a whole.

Naturalness

There was a time when a good deal of attention was given to eliminating stiffness in business letters: hackneyed phrases, stereotyped expressions, obsolete and archaic references, and pompous statements. Although the number of letters we find today that contain such expressions is relatively few, there are times when we use fairly meaningless statements that should be revised.

If you find that you sometimes use hackneyed expressions, drop them for more natural statements. It is doubtful that you use the following, or other, stereotyped expressions in speaking; why use them in writing?

As in the above	Enclosed please find
According to our records	Esteemed order
Advise	Hand you
As indicated	Hand you herewith
As per	Hereby acknowledge
At hand	Hoping to hear
At early date	In accordance with
Attached hereto	Previous to
Attached please find	Prior to
At your earliest convenience	Permit me to say
Avail yourself of this opportunity	Pursuant to
Beg to state	Re or In re
Beg to remain	Recent date
Contents duly noted	Take this opportunity
Contents noted	Trust that
Due to	We wish to state

The use of one or two of these in a letter is certainly not bad; it is when a letter is filled with them that we receive an impression of a cold, severe, impersonal, and unfriendly company. Compare the two letters which follow. Notice that the messages are similar but the tone is not. What would your feelings be toward the companies that mailed them?

Dear Mr. Baxter:

Received yours of the 15th and beg to state that item 204 of merchandise requested in your basic communication is out of stock and same can therefore not be shipped but will be back-ordered as per our policy.

Enclosed please find duplicate shipping ticket listing items being forwarded as per your request.

Hoping this proves satisfactory, we beg to remain,

Dear Mr. Baxter:

Thank you very much for your order #2146. It is always a pleasure to hear from you.

All the merchandise you requested, with one exception, has been packaged and shipped via Midwest Fast Freight. It should arrive no later than January 20.

During the past month we have had an extremely heavy demand for the #204 Desk Lamps and they are temporarily out of stock. However, we are happy that they proved to be a popular and profitable item for our dealers.

We do expect a supplementary supply within 48 hours. The quantity you requested will then be sent via "special freight" and should arrive by January 26. Will this be satisfactory, Mr. Baxter? If not, please call us collect. We are always eager to serve you in every way we can.

It is true, of course, that the second letter required a little thought and probably cost the company a bit more in typing time than the first. But it is surely worth the investment. The longer letter reflects sincerity, warmth, and a natural tone that builds good will. The short one creates the impression of a company that is cold, unfriendly, and hardly concerned with going out of its way to satisfy a customer.

Such reasoning (evaluating an entire company on the basis of its letters) might very well be false, but the reader often has little on which to base his interpretation of the firm except the words in a letter addressed to him.

The Connecticut Life Insurance Company published a booklet for its employees titled *Speak When You Write*. Its eighteen pages are filled with suggestions on how to inject this natural, friendly tone into communications so that good will for the company will increase. The key perhaps is in the title—which of course should not be taken too literally. Connecticut Life does not literally mean "speak when you write." If we did write as we talked, our written communications would probably be quite wordy and repetitious. What is really meant is write as *you sound* when you talk. In this way your written communications will reflect the natural, friendly spontaneity of your spoken words.

Courtesy

In this modern, hurried world of ours, we sometimes overlook an opportunity to extend a little courtesy to those with whom we communicate. Letters often conclude with a phrase such as "Your merchandise was shipped on January 14." Why not add a "Thank you very much," or "Your business is always appreciated," or "We were happy we could ship this equipment immediately as you requested"? When *thank you, please, I appreciated*, or similar expressions are used in a letter—and used sincerely—they help create good will.

Optimism

There are specific words and phrases in our vocabulary which evoke an unfavorable mental reaction which we tend to associate with the product or service to which the words refer. We have already discussed words as symbols for situations, experiences, and reactions; we know how words often make pictures in our minds. Thus, a department store does not put up a sign saying, "Complaint Department," because it would stimulate an unpleasant association. The terms "Adjustment Bureau" or "Customer Service Department," on the other hand, make the customer look forward to a helpful, favorable, and positive situation.

What would be a customer's reaction to an order form with the printed statement, "To avoid errors and mistakes in shipping, complete the order form as directed"? His immediate "picture reaction" to this sentence is obvious. He can only see his order delayed or lost, and anticipate being billed for merchandise he never received—it would be far better to tear up the order form and do business elsewhere. Thus, the messages on most order forms do everything possible to stimulate a favorable reaction, a pleasant picture. Toward that end they may state, "Please complete the order form as requested for accurate and rapid shipment of merchandise."

What is it about these two statements which triggers different reactions? It is the words themselves. Certain words in our culture, used in a specific context, induce mental associations which are not favorable (negative).

Negative: We hope you won't be dissatisfied with the new All-American line.

Positive: We are sure you will be satisfied with the new All-American line.

Negative: We don't believe you will encounter trouble and difficulty in the installation of the new equipment.

Positive: For quick and efficient installation of the new equipment, please follow the directions contained in the instructional manual.

Under most conditions, it is wise to avoid the words which precipitate this negative or unfavorable response. Words such as *trouble, dissatisfaction, complaint, hope, if, neglect, errors, negligence* usually result in unfavorable mental associations with the product or service under discussion.

However, the negative tone is not always undesirable. It can be used to generate impact in a positive statement. This device is frequently used in advertising:

Negative problem: Have you provided for your advancing years?

Positive solution: Let us show you how enjoyable your retirement can be with Parker Protection.

Negative problem: Are you concerned that bad breath and teeth discoloration will offend those around you?

Positive solution: For sparkling teeth and mountain-fresh breath, use Glisten toothpaste every day.

The negative tone, when used in this way, certainly helps to sell many of America's products: insurance, health items, safety and personal hygiene products. But in every instance the negative tone must be handled with care, for negative symbols are much more likely to be remembered (and associated with a product) than the pleasant, positive picture. This may be the reason why more and more insurance today is *not* sold as "death benefits or protection from disaster"—all negative, but for "living comfort, peace of mind, and security"—all positive.

A brewery once announced that its beer was "bitter free." The message which followed went on to speak, in smaller type, of the product's "mellowness and mildness." However, it was the negative term which people remembered and associated with the product, probably because of the strong and emphatic quality of the word "bitter."

The same principle is found in automobile and cigarette advertising. Rarely does the manufacturer use negative themes (accidents, collision, death; cancer, heart attacks) for fear that negative connotations will be associated with the product by the prospective purchaser.

Tact

The quality of tact in communication is certainly abstract and, as such, somewhat difficult to define. If you were to ask the man in the street, he might say that "tact is saying the right thing at the right time in the right way." But when you are trying to write a tactful letter, what is the right thing to say? when is the right time? what is the right way? It is clear that the standard definition of tact is not an adequate guide.

Like so many factors in communication, tact is intimately involved with words, their use, and their interpretation. If we say, "You failed to include the order form," or "We were surprised you did not understand the directions," or "We received your letter in which you claimed we did not ship," we are certainly being tactless. Is it because of the *denotations* of the key words, "You failed," "We were surprised," or "You claimed," or is it their *connotations*? Here we see an excellent example of how important the personal interpretation of words can be. Words which have simple, basic meanings can assume special connotations in specific contexts and result in statements which are interpreted as tactless and discourteous.

What is the answer? It's simple. Avoid the words or phrases which might antagonize or embarrass. Comments on another's error can be made so that the other person will not "lose face" if you choose the right words.

Tactless: We received your letter in which you claim we did not send . . . .

Better: Thank you for your letter concerning our shipment of December 3.

Tactless: We were surprised you did not understand the specifications we sent . . . .

Better: We are sending a more complete set of specifications for the job which we feel will . . . .

Tactless: You failed to indicate the color you preferred . . . .

Better: Please indicate the color you prefer and we will ship immediately.

CONSIDERATION—THE "YOU" ATTITUDE

Perhaps there is no quality in business writing that has received more attention than the "you" attitude. We discuss it, write about it, and lecture on it. Yet, it seems an elusive and a difficult concept to understand and to use.

Because of our nature and the society in which we live, our interests, activities, and goals usually center in us. Most of us are impatient when our problems, our situations, our purchases are not examined from our point of view. We usually analyze the situations in which we are involved from our position and with our perceptions, and we often communicate our ideas and feelings from the same standpoint. The problem is often compounded because we are not even aware that the other person may have a position, feelings, and reactions which we have not been considering. Our decisions and actions always seem very logical to us. But how often do we ask ourselves how logical our actions are from the other person's viewpoint? (See Rogers and Roethlisberger, "Barriers and Gateways to Communication," Part IV).

Essentially this is what a "you" attitude is—viewing a situation from the other person's point of view. It requires a sensitivity to others, an appreciation of others, a respect for others. And this interest must be sincere, for, if it is not, the other individual will be aware that it is false and resent it.

The use of the "you" attitude is most important when a difference of opinion exists. It is at precisely such times—when we are stoutly justifying and substantiating our point of view—that it is vital to appreciate the other person's.

To become aware of another's point of view will often require two attributes: sensitivity to his needs, and the ability to communicate your appreciation of his situation to him.

It must be emphasized that the "you" attitude is not necessarily *agreement*. It is quite possible to communicate a strong "you" attitude while disagreeing with the principles of the other person. People do not necessarily want us to agree with them; but they do want us to understand and appreciate their point of view. The secretary who wants a new $400 electric typewriter will be more willing to accept a "no" if her employer first indicates that he understands *why* she wants a new machine. The merchant will be more likely to accept a refusal if he is assured that his interpretation is valid but franchise restrictions and government regulations will not permit a change in labeling.

The following letters illustrate the difference between a "you" attitude and a "we" or "I" attitude.

"We" Attitude

Dear Mr. Burling:

For several years we have shipped you and our other customers quantities of our Kentron Line from our St. Louis manufacturing plant and our Madewell Line from Chicago.

Although we have been happy to do this, you can appreciate that the cost to us for double shipping has often been excessive. This is especially true when orders are small, and our profit margin is consequently completely absorbed. Naturally no company is happy with such a situation. We certainly are not.

Beginning April 15, however, we will consolidate shipping procedures and we will forward both the Kentron and the Madewell Lines from Chicago. This will certainly save us money and will afford faster receipt of merchandise by our customers. In addition there will be less billing as well as other bookkeeping procedures for our firm to carry through.

We believe that you will agree that this new arrangement will prove wiser and more satisfactory for us as well as all concerned.

"You" Attitude

Dear Mr. Baxter:

We are happy to announce a change in our shipping procedure which will prove beneficial to you in many different ways.

For several years, as you know, we have been shipping you our Kentron and Madewell Lines from warehouses in St. Louis and Chicago respectively. Processing your order from two different cities sometimes resulted in service to you which was not always the most efficient or rapid.

Beginning April 15, however, our shipping will be consolidated. All products will be shipped directly to you from Chicago. This will result in several definite benefits to you.

Your orders will now be filled and shipped within 24 hours of our receipt of them.

Shipping costs will be reduced, and the savings achieved will be passed on to our customers in the form of lower prices.

We will maintain larger inventories so that you will enjoy complete selections at all times.

We are happy to add this new procedure to our list of services. This, plus our high-quality products, sold at very competitive prices, assures you of fast merchandise turnover and top profit margins.

In the letter to Mr. Baxter the writer obviously has some appreciation of Mr. Baxter's point of view. He is concerned with Baxter's profits and convenience. In the letter to Mr. Burling, however, the writer has given no evidence of such appreciation. He is concerned only with his own point of view.

This sensitivity to the needs, feelings, and desires of others will produce the "you" attitude in communications, but this attitude must reflect a sincere interest in people. If a writer attempts to introduce this "you" attitude into his letters purely as a device to secure additional profits, chances are good that he will not be successful. He may unknowingly go too far in his statements concerning the reader's interests. Thus, the insincerity becomes apparent, and the reader may very well say "Nonsense, I don't believe it!"

If a business letter has a sincere and effective "you" attitude, it needs little else, for the "you" attitude ensures that all other principles will be followed. If the writer is sincerely concerned with the reader's point of view and feelings he will be courteous in tone, his comments will be friendly and natural, he will organize his thoughts carefully, he will see to it that his letter is attractive, and his writing will be clear and correct.

EFFECTIVE COMPOSITION

Completeness

When facts or ideas are inadvertently omitted from business letters, we have a tendency to brush this off with "Oh, I forgot all about that." The result, however, is that another letter must be written to ask us about the items we omitted, and we in turn must reply again, to deal with the items we forgot about the first time. Perhaps no great harm is done in one isolated case, but if ten per cent of the letters a firm sends out are not complete, and the company mails approximately three thousand letters a week, the cost can be staggering. Not only is there the writing, typing, and mailing of unnecessary letters (at about three dollars each), but the recipient's irritation when he finds that one of his questions was not answered is costly. The result can only be a loss of good will and, quite possibly, a customer.

There are other factors involved which are more difficult to measure. If, for example, Company Z writes to firms A, B, and C for information concerning cost, shipping dates, and guarantees on plastic widgets, and the replies received are complete from firms A and B but not from C, will Z write to C and ask for the shipping dates which were omitted? Not unless C's prices were significantly lower. Z will probably make a decision between A and B. Company C will not be considered because its letter was not complete.

It is not unusual for an industrial consultant engaged to evaluate correspondence procedures in a company to examine first *incoming* files of letters. From such an analysis he may find that ten per cent of the incoming letters contain such statements as "Thank you very much, but will you elaborate on . . ."; "We appreciated receiving . . . , send us additional details"; "Thank you . . . please be more explicit." And so these go, indicating that in many cases the original letter which was sent out lacked important details and required this type of follow-up to make the original communication complete.

When we communicate with others, we cannot always be sure of precisely what they want, and from time to time our letters will not cover every point; however, we should avoid omitting important facts through carelessness. The key to writing letters that are as complete as we can make them with the facts at hand is simple: organize before we write.

Good Organization

Before the simplest letter is written, the writer should know precisely what topics he will cover. Some writers carefully read the letter to which they are replying and make notes in the margin or at the bottom of the page. Others find it more convenient to make notes on a piece of scratch paper, or draw up an outline of their reply. Still others prefer to outline mentally. The mechanics don't matter, so long as the writer has a guide to writing or dictating the reply letter. By checking the guide against the inquiry letter, the writer can ensure that his reply will be complete.

Here, for example, is a letter we have just taken out of its envelope. Let us read it, make an outline, and write a reply, making sure that *our* letter is as complete as we can make it.

Glen S. Robin
Robin Office Equipment Company
1414 North Jackson Avenue
Chicago, Ill. 60626

Dear Mr. Robin:

We received your recent announcement concerning the Bright-as-Day fluorescent desk lamps. They seem to be precisely what we have been looking for and we would like to have you send us two dozen charged to our account.

Your circular indicated that one free desk lamp would be included with each dozen purchased, provided the order was entered before June 1. Unfortunately it is now two weeks past that date, but we do hope that you will nevertheless send us two lamps without charge. Your announcement also indicated that the color of these desk lamps was gray; if possible we would like to get them in beige to match our office decor.

Our employees have discussed the new electric Shelley Pencil Sharpener. It apparently saves work and produces an extremely fine point. Do you carry this product and do you recommend it, or do you feel that it is just another office "toy"?

What about the No. 107 Easy File cabinet which we ordered some time ago and which you were out of stock on? Are you going to ship this to us or are they no longer available?

Our check for last month's merchandise will be a little late but you may expect to receive it prior to the 15th.

Here is a letter to which we must reply as quickly as possible. But we should not do so unless we first organize our presentation. Let us look at the outline which we have jotted down and which we will use as a guide in replying to the above letter.

1. Acknowledge the order for lamps.
2. Explain tactfully that offer of a free lamp with each dozen no longer is available—agreement with manufacturer.
3. Comment on and promote electric pencil sharpener—recommend Efficiency Brand, not Shelley.
4. Desk lamps come only in gray, not beige.
5. Easy File cabinet due out in 30 days.
6. Sorry check will be late—discount of course not possible.

The next step is to check the outline. Such an examination quickly shows us that point 4 should follow 2 (why break the discussion on lamps into two different segments?); that change can quickly be made. Our review also tells us that we have neglected to include a sales paragraph on the new Easy Roll typewriter tables. After those two changes have been made and the outline checked again, we are quite certain our letter will be complete and now we are ready to dictate. But under no circumstances should any communication be carried through without first making up a plan. If we do, we run the risk of writing a letter that is confused, unorganized, or incomplete. And of course, the result is costly and unnecessary correspondence.

Conciseness

There is probably nothing more disconcerting than reading a letter which seems to ramble on and on. We must read it all because it involves a business transaction with which we are vitally concerned. But it is nevertheless irritating to plow through unending paragraphs, meaningless phrases, and unnecessary words.

Overall length is no sure guide. A letter covering a third of a page may be short but overly wordy. On the other hand, a three-page letter may be properly concise. We should strive to write business letters which do not waste words, where every phrase, every clause, every statement says what needs to be said.

Wordy: It should be observed that not very many, in fact only 15, cases of absenteeism took place in the second month of this year, February; the very month, in fact, when the new system was begun.

Revised: Only 15 cases of absenteeism were recorded during February, the month the new system was begun.

Wordy: We found after careful investigation and research that several different organizations and companies were satisfactory, and offered programs which were designed to improve the ability of our engineers in the vital and important area of report writing.

Revised: We learned that six firms in the New York area were qualified to offer programs in report writing for engineering personnel.

Wordy: We have found that many customers of this firm have been quite concerned and upset by our new policy on deliveries. This new delivery policy requires a minimum order from each and every customer; these orders are to have a minimum dollar value of $50.00.

Revised: Many of our customers have become concerned about our new delivery policy which requires a $50.00 minimum order.

These are examples of how sentences can be edited, made more concise, and thus improved. Notice how the meaning becomes clearer, understanding easier, and impact greater when unnecessary words have been dropped and phrases made shorter.

Clarity

It is difficult to say how much confusion has been caused by lack of clarity in business communications. The sentence which can be interpreted by the reader in two different ways, or is not understood at all, is most disturbing. How should the reader interpret this statement: "If the safety bracket for the 333 Press has been completed, send it at once"? What should he ship? If he sends the press and the bracket is desired, he will have a staggering freight bill to pay. If he sends the bracket and it was the press that was wanted, time and a customer may be lost.

Whatever you write, whether it is a six-line memo or a three-page letter, it should be checked for clarity. If there is the slightest doubt in your mind about the clarity of what you have set down, you should immediately cross it out and rewrite it.

Clarity can often be achieved by breaking rambling sentences into two or three short ones, replacing vague words with exact ones, and making diligent use of a dictionary and thesaurus. The greatest writing of all times, the writing which has lived through the ages, and the writing to which we still turn with love and respect has always been simple and clear. So, too, should be the expression of our ideas—great or small.

Diction

Statements can be clear, unified, and coherent, but yet not as accurate and precise as they should be. If you mean "thoroughly examined," you should not say "looked over"; if you mean "A proportional stratified sample was taken," you should not write "A survey was made."

Because business communication is often the basis for making decisions, precision and accuracy in diction (word choice) are very important. One or two words, carelessly chosen, may convey a thought which is far from the one desired.

Vague: Sales of the Kenwood Lumber Company have gone up during the past two or three years.

Precise: Sales of the Kenwood Lumber Company increased by 4 per cent in 1968 and 8 per cent in 1969 over the gross sales figures of 1967.

Vague: Quality control is assured by running tests on the mixture periodically.

Precise: Quality control of the cookie mixture is maintained by testing samples taken at 9:00 A.M., 1:00 P.M., and 3:00 P.M. each day.

Our use of general, vague, or incorrect words in place of precise and accurate terms is often due to our habit of completing tasks the easiest way possible. It takes effort to use the dictionary and thesaurus to find the precise word; it is easier to use a word which is handy and on the tip of our tongue. It is often these easily available words that convey fuzzy ideas. On the other hand, a long or esoteric word is not necessarily better than a short, familiar one. Our objective is to impart information and ideas; if our readers will grasp those ideas better if we use familiar, everyday words, then we should use them.

Correctness

As careful as we are in our writing, we sometimes make mistakes. A word is misspelled, the apostrophe is not placed correctly, the wrong punctuation mark is used, or a plural instead of a singular noun is used. These errors are made—but they shouldn't be.

It is a strange quirk of human nature, but most people notice immediately if something is awry. An error in grammar or punctuation will be immediately apparent, more so than all the correct items. Because the reader focuses on the error, voluntarily or not, he will necessarily give less attention to the content, the message of the letter. Some of its impact is lost.

And because letters are often all the recipient knows of a company, errors in basic English must diminish, to some degree, his opinion of that company. Management must see to it, therefore, that its correspondents have mastered not only the intangibles like tact, courtesy, clarity, precision, but also the basic principles of good English.

Attractiveness

The final principle has little to do with effective statement of ideas, but everything to do with communication—for communication depends as much on how a message is received as on how it is sent out. Your ideas may be brilliant, your statements clear, tactful, concise, accurate, and in correct English—but if those beautiful statements are thrown together haphazardly on paper, with no form or balance, the recipient will probably not even read them; if he does, it will be with prejudice. The careless erasure, the negligent strikeover, the jagged margin, the poorly spaced and placed message on the page, certainly reflect little credit on the company sending the letter or the manager who signs it.

Although the handling of the mechanical aspects of the business letter, such as typing, style, and format, is the task of the secretary, the manager should have some familiarity with the topic (see Appendix C). And it is the manager's responsibility to see to it that letters going out over his name meet his standards of attractiveness.

QUESTIONS FOR STUDY

I. Revise the following sentences eliminating phrases that are hackneyed, tactless, negative, and wordy.

1. You will not be unhappy if you decide to purchase and stock Carlin's Valves.

2. Your firm will encounter no difficulties or troubles if you decide to install our Mark III Frigid Air Conditioning system.

3. If you always include complete shipping instructions and your code number, we will be able to process your order without error.

4. We received your letter in which you claimed we did not ship your complete order on January 4.

5. We hope that you will have no difficulty installing your automatic cutter; please follow directions enclosed to avoid problems.

6. I was surprised that you did not understand our objectives in this case.

7. We know that you will appreciate our situation in this case regarding our refusal of your request for the free case of Snappettes with your dozen-case order because of your request being received almost a month after the special offer ended.

8. You neglected to include the invoice for the merchandise which was shipped on August 3.

9. You don't seem to understand that all the information requested on the credit application form is needed if we are to open a charge account for you.

10. Under ordinary circumstances we would not feel that it is necessary to request your full compliance in following the routine steps necessary in a legal situation of this sort, but to maximize your benefits and because of the fact that your child is not of legal age, we urge that all documents be completed precisely and filed according to the instructions contained in Reg. 254AT.

11. As per your valued instructions of April 28 we herewith hand you, as per your request, all necessary data for account 239.

12. May we take the liberty to inform you that henceforth we will be available for order processing on Saturdays.

II. Revise the following sentences where necessary. Eliminate phrases that are hackneyed, tactless, negative, and wordy.

1. In reference to yours of the fifth, we hand you herewith our check for $128.50.

2. It is our unbiased and considered opinion that under circumstances such as these, it would be to your best interests to pay your past due bill within a time period of 10 days.

3. We beg to state that all merchandise herewith requested is to be delivered to our place of business no later than December 10.

4. Please be advised, in reference to yours of the second, that requirements of the State of New York in this regard have been noted and will be carried through.

5. We hope you will now find it possible to place an order with us and avail yourself of the 5 per cent discount being offered to special customers such as yourself.

6. Now that we have repaired your motor, we hope that you will not continue to encounter operational failures with it.

7. If you encounter problems with your Kelton unit, please call and we will do our best to alleviate the situation.

8. We were extremely sorry to learn from your letter of May 2 that the 1 h.p. motor we shipped arrived with the wrong plug attachment, a broken base, and a cracked safety shield. We are sending your replacement today.

9. It is difficult for me to understand how you arrived at your request for a $94 credit.

10. We feel very strongly, at least to some degree, that all merchandise purchased during the period previous to the opening day of the sale is not eligible nor should it receive the 2 per cent discount which is explained in our sales advertisements.

III. Answer the following questions as concisely as possible.

1. "Perceive the world from the decoder's point of view if you wish to communicate effectively." How does this statement relate to a "you" attitude?

2. Differentiate between a "you" attitude and an "I" or "we" attitude.

3. From a semantic point of view, what happens in the process of decoding as a result of negative statements being used by the encoder? (You may wish to comment on word connotations and words as symbols.)

IV. Each pair of the statements which follow convey essentially the same idea. Why do we feel that the one listed first in each pair is less tactful than the second, and what is the role which word connotations play in the interpretation of these statements?

1. "We received your letter in which you claim we did not ship."
"We received your letter in which you indicated we did not ship."

2. "You failed to list the colors desired for the file cabinets ordered, and we therefore find it difficult to complete your request."
"Your order will be shipped immediately after we hear from you as to the colors you prefer for the file cabinets listed on your Purchase Order 4-212."

3. "I was surprised that you did not understand our policies for customer return of merchandise."
"Our customers may return merchandise for full credit on the basis of the policy printed on the reverse of all invoices."

V. "To be a good writer, one must be a severe critic of his own efforts." Assume you have written the letters which follow. Edit them carefully and then submit a completed version.

1. Mr. Robert T. Compton, President
Apex Manufacturing Company
4112 North 14th Street
Chicago, Illinois 60615

Gentlemen:

Just three weeks ago we received six one-horsepower motors from you people on our purchase order F-121-A.

As you probably recall, we have been purchasing motors from you for many years to run our equipment and by and large we have had no quarrel with the quality of the merchandise, although your price is sometimes out of line, until three weeks ago when we received six one-horsepower motors as per P.O. F-121-A.

Three of the motors were immediately put into use and within two weeks, two have become inoperable. We have checked the lead, current supply, etc., and find everything in order except the motors. We believe that perhaps your manufacturing process in these two cases was faulty and you will therefore want to make proper changes.

Hoping to hear from you in the near future, we remain,

2. Caelson, Caelson, and Caelson
Caelson Towers
145 North Fourth Street
New Orleans, Louisiana

Gentlemen:

May we take this opportunity to thank you most graciously and sincerely for placing your order for office furniture with our firm.

All the merchandise which you requested, with one exception, has been shipped from our warehouse via Western Van Lines and should arrive within 10 days of today's date. The item in question —reception room lamp tables (2)—were temporarily out of stock, but will be shipped to you to complete the order.

You asked about a matching coffee table for the reception room and we would suggest that at the moment you might cancel the idea. Your reception area is relatively small and to place a coffee table in it might result in a very cluttered appearance. Perhaps a slant-type wall magazine rack would be wiser to utilize for the display of periodicals. As you can see, we are much more interested in your welfare than in securing just another sale.

And, oh yes; getting back to the lamp tables—they will be shipped in approximately two weeks of this date.

Miss Betty Cavanaugh will stop by this coming week to talk to you about art accessories for the offices and reception areas. I'm sure you'll find her suggestions valuable as to paintings, reproductions, statuary, etc.

VI. Secure three actual business letters and submit a brief criticism on each. Substantiate your critical comments by referring to specific portions of the message or by quotations from it. Remember to note those points which merit commendation as well as those areas which require improvement.

Structure your comments around the following points:

1. The principles of clarity, appearance, tact, "you" attitude, tone, etc.

2. The effectiveness of the letter in achieving its intended objective in light of the reader to whom it is directed.

CHAPTER TWELVE

Communications Requiring Answer or Action

Every letter written, whether personal or business, is written for a reason. A personal letter may be to congratulate, to encourage, to further a relationship, to ask a favor, to thank, to express friendship. A business letter may be used for all those ends, plus to ask for credit or an adjustment, to place an order, to collect a bill, to make a sale, to request information, or to reply to any of the others.

Although all business letters have certain attributes in common—neatness, courtesy, "you" attitude, coherence, etc.—the organization of a letter refusing credit is quite different from that of a letter welcoming a new customer. Obviously the content depends on the message you have to communicate; the organization must vary as well.

As our society has become more complex, so have the services and products which are available. Frequently today a relatively simple component may be manufactured from raw materials which are secured from a dozen different sources. Often too the item itself must conform to government specifications or be interchangeable with a similar product manufactured by another firm. Thus, a company must request information, as well as order supplies, from a variety of sources. To secure the data and the raw materials often requires a great deal of correspondence, much of which is concerned with asking and answering questions. A good example of a company operating at this level is the Lockheed Corporation. This firm manufactures aircraft, ships, electronic equipment, and missile components, and engages in undersea and space research, plus many other activities. Of course, Lockheed manufactures thousands of items but it also purchases from some 20,000 suppliers. To secure the necessary materials from all these companies requires a mountain of forms and letters, which move in and out of the company each year. The same problems are encountered by many other firms.

In this and the following chapters, therefore, we shall discuss the various *kinds* of business letters, and lay down some guidelines to help you write effective business letters efficiently.

The first major area includes inquiries, requests, orders, claims, collection letters, applications—in effect, letters which require an answer or some sort of action.

INQUIRIES AND REQUESTS

Essentially, an inquiry desires an answer and a request desires action, but they are both petitions for favor. An inquiry asks for information; a request asks for someone's services as a speaker, endorsement of a product, a free sample—in short, it requires action beyond a simple written reply.

Before you begin to write a letter of inquiry or request, you must know, of course, exactly what your purpose is—what information or action do you want? Keep in mind that you, and the recipient of your letter, are busy. Make an outline. Include every point you want an answer to and every point necessary to make your desires absolutely clear.

Your inquiry may be simple and brief: Who is the distributor in our area? How quickly can he ship a carload? Is a discount available? Or it may be complex and difficult: What would be involved in air conditioning our offices? What kind of market is there for our product on the West Coast? What does the Civil Rights Act mean to us? The principle is the same—be complete, be clear, be courteous. And, particularly when the problem is a complex one, get to the point immediately. Your first sentence or two should state the subject, so that from the very beginning the reader can think to the problem; he will not have to wade through extraneous greetings and references and bush-beatings. He will be more likely to answer well if you ask well.

We can see how much effort would be wasted if Office Manager Lyons sent us an inquiry in which he simply asked about air-conditioning equipment for his firm and omitted important details.

Dear Mr. Martin:

Because our firm is located in a Chicago loop area which gets very hot in the summer, we are considering air conditioning these quarters.

Your firm has been recommended to me by several people in the Office Managers' Association and I am therefore writing you for information.

We occupy an area of approximately 24,000 square feet and we would like to have this entire space air-conditioned. Will you, therefore, send me information concerning the cost and feasibility of this project?

If Mr. Lyons' letter were no more detailed than this, we would have to write back and ask him if he was interested in window units or central air conditioning, what was the capacity of his electrical supply lines, the layout of his space—several rooms, one large room, a large room with dividers? These questions might require several more letters, costing money, wasting time, and irritating people.

The following letter makes the same inquiry, but in such a way that the desired information can be provided promptly.

Dear Mr. Martin:

For some time we have been considering the feasibility of air conditioning our offices. It is our understanding that your firm has made many installations of the type we require.

We occupy 24,000 square feet of office space on the ninth floor of the Stewart Building at 140 East Lincoln Boulevard. Because we use only a portion of the Stewart Building, it would be necessary for us to have some type of individual unit or units rather than a central system which would utilize the building's duct work. It is my understanding that our present electrical outlets are wired to accommodate almost any electrical demands placed on them.

Specifically, I would like to have your answers to the following questions:

1. How many and what type of air conditioning units would you suggest?
2. Are units available which are quiet enough so as not to interfere with office efficiency?
3. Would it be possible to have such an installation completed before the end of June?
4. Do you handle the engineering problems, as well as equipment and installation, or would it be necessary for us to secure additional professional assistance?

I am enclosing a floor plan of our offices which indicates walls, window openings, and furniture placement. I believe you will require this before you can give us an estimate of the cost of the job.

Because we would like to make a decision on this project prior to April 28, when we have an executive meeting scheduled, I would appreciate a reply from you by April 23. You may be sure that any information of a confidential nature will be respected as such.

This letter of inquiry has several attributes which every letter of this type should possess:

1. Reason for inquiry, in the first or second sentence.
2. The inquiry itself, with specific questions listed.
3. Indication of the date by which a reply is needed.
4. Assurance that information will be considered confidential (if applicable).

The two letters that follow include these criteria. In both cases the reader would be able to reply intelligently because of the completeness of the material.

Dear Mr. Jameson:

As you may have heard, our firm is seriously considering the purchase of the Aero Air Craft Plant in your city. From the point of view of total space, location, physical facilities, and other attributes, this plant appears satisfactory. However, we are not quite sure whether we will find an adequate labor supply in Baseside, inasmuch as Aero has not used this plant for some eighteen months and the city itself is not very large.

We would be most grateful if you, because of your position, could inform us as to the availability of personnel in the following categories:

1. 800 unskilled production workers;
2. 35 engineers—mechanical and electrical;
3. 40 clerical personnel;
4. 35 office personnel—typists, stenographers, and miscellaneous.

In addition to this information, can you also send me data on the educational institutions in the area? Are there nearby high schools and colleges for our personnel who would be interested in night classes? What universities are available for those of our people who wish to pursue further education? Do you think it will be possible for us to fill our future needs of approximately 15-20 business and engineering graduates per year from the surrounding universities?

You may be sure that the information you give me in answer to these questions will be held in confidence, if you so desire. We request that this inquiry be kept confidential.

Inasmuch as our board of directors will meet on May 10 to make a decision concerning the possible purchase of this plant, I would appreciate a reply from you by April 28. Thank you for your assistance.

Dear Mr. Miller:

Thank you very much for the brochure you sent me recently concerning your new plastic line. Our preliminary tests indicate that your Futura Plastic will meet our particular needs, provided certain modifications can be carried through. At the moment, however, we are concerned with certain production problems and a particular delivery schedule.

Your answers to the following questions will assist us in making a specific decision on whether or not to move ahead:

1. Can you mold a container identical to the one described in the enclosed specification sheet?
2. Can you guarantee that such a product will retain its shape even when heated to 160° F?
3. Can you deliver 30,000 such units, beginning August 15, in quantities of 2000 per week for 15 weeks?
4. Is it possible to secure this item in code colors of red, green, and blue (10,000 of each)?

We would like to have the answers to these questions, plus the estimated cost per unit, by January 14. Shortly thereafter, we shall be able to give you a definite reply concerning our purchase of the material. Of course, we shall hold in confidence the information you give us.

As a result of both letters above, action can be taken and an intelligent reply sent to the inquirer. And this is the objective of every letter of inquiry: to elicit an intelligent and complete reply. If the inquiry is well organized and well written, the person who receives it will not have to ask the writer for important information and specific details which were omitted from the original communication before he can reply properly.

The inquirer should make it as easy as possible for the recipient to reply. He can do this by listing his questions in an orderly fashion and by limiting himself to essentials; obviously it is unrealistic to ask so many questions that replying to the letter would require an unreasonable expenditure of time or money. The writer may even wish to assist the recipient of his inquiry letter by including a self-addressed envelope. And, of course, the writer must recognize when not to ask for information by letter: If a problem is too complex, too abstract, or too detailed, it may be necessary to set up an interview or a conference for discussion of the problem.

Request letters follow the same pattern as inquiry letters. Because they are asking for action, however, rather than just an answer, they should be even clearer, if possible, and they should be written far in advance of the proposed date of action.

Dear Mr. Robertson:

We are holding a week-long workshop for our middle-management employees, beginning October 14. The workshop will consist of talks and discussions on various phases of business. The seminars are to be led by men prominent in each field.

We have scheduled discussion of "Corporate Investments" for Tuesday afternoon, October 15. We should be grateful if you could be with us to lead the discussion, preceded by a 20- to 30-minute talk.

The meeting will begin at 1:30 p.m. in the Eagle Room of the Mereside Hotel. The group consists of 25 men and women. And will you and your wife join us for dinner afterward?

I do hope you can help us. Will you let me know by September 5?

Because the writer of the above letter is requesting a favor, he makes the project interesting; he calls the reader a "prominent man"; he gives all necessary details; he subtly assumes the reader will accept; and finally, he invites him—and his wife—to dinner.

ORDERS

Because of the weight of sheer numbers, most firms today use a printed order blank rather than placing orders by letter; it is more efficient and less costly to use forms and blanks. Nevertheless, every order must include certain information if it is to be filled correctly; whether you use a form or a letter, you must be certain to include the following data:

1. Catalog number
2. Quantity
3. Description of merchandise (model number, size, color)
4. Unit price; total price
5. Precise identification of purchasing unit or purchaser
6. Where merchandise is to be shipped
7. How merchandise is to be shipped (rail, truck, mail)
8. Payment method (c.o.d., open account, check enclosed, etc.)
9. Delivery date desired
10. Miscellaneous information which may be included:
    a. order number
    b. date of order
    c. salesman's name
    d. information on substitutions
    e. instructions for "back order"

The businessman or consumer who writes a letter to place an order should be sure that it includes as much of the above data as possible. The criterion is whether the order can be filled to the complete satisfaction of the letter writer from the information he has included in his letter.

Dear Sir:

Please send me the following merchandise, all of which is listed in your winter catalog. Please send the order c.o.d. to the address below.

2146	3 Ashtrays	$1.25 each	$3.75
3104	2 Vases	4.25 each	8.50
2578	1 pr. Cufflinks	3.50 each	3.50
3777	1 Umbrella, red	5.50 each	5.50

Inasmuch as several of these items are to be used as Christmas presents, I would appreciate receiving them no later than December 18. If you are out of stock on any of these items, please make no substitutions.

CLAIMS

Business transactions do not always run smoothly. Regardless of how careful or efficient business organizations are, various steps in their operations will go wrong from time to time. Merchandise may be shipped to a wrong address or arrive in less than perfect condition; billing may be incorrect; details for an order may be confused; badly needed articles may be delayed; quality may not be at the level expected.

When these situations occur, a claim letter is usually sent. And because most people in industry recognize that errors do take place, the letter—if it is reasonably and properly written—will bring the desired adjustment. Claims must be handled efficiently, for in one year's time the amount of money involved can reach a very significant level.

One Los Angeles firm, as an illustration, recently found that many of its vital dollars were being drained away because of poor claim procedures. A management consulting firm found that the company had submitted some $60,000 in claims to suppliers, shippers, and dealers in one year. However, it had received only $8000 in adjustments. Investigation disclosed that the claims which were entered were incomplete and inaccurate and that follow-ups were almost nonexistent. The poor ratio of adjustments received to claims entered was the fault not of the firms to whom the requests were submitted, but of the company entering the claims.

In an attempt to improve the situation and secure a more favorable adjustment record, a brief training program was given to those persons concerned with claims. Once these individuals began writing complete, clear, and specific claim letters, the amount of adjustments rose dramatically. It was estimated that in the year following the initial survey of this company, adjustments received increased some $30,000 as a result of improved communication in this one area.

There are various levels of claim problems. If we are not satisfied with a situation we may simply enter a complaint. If a transaction does not go precisely as we have requested and it is a matter of correcting a very understandable situation, we become involved in a *routine* claim. If, however, the situation has several facets and there is a question as to who is responsible, we would enter a *nonroutine* claim.

ROUTINE CLAIM LETTERS

Routine claim letters are usually associated with relatively minor situations. When the wrong quantity, size, color, or model has been shipped, a routine claim will usually correct the situation. Or perhaps an error has been made in pricing, discount privileges, or other matters of a routine nature. In such cases, all that is necessary is a clear, specific, concise letter listing the facts of the situation.

> Dear Mr. Hollins:
>
> Our order #415 was delivered to our warehouse this morning via Michigan Transport Service.
>
> All the items we requested arrived in excellent condition with one exception. If you will refer to our original order, you will note that we requested your #606 fluorescent desk lamp. Apparently, an error was made in the processing of this order, because we received your #608 model instead of the one we requested.
>
> Will you kindly pick up those you sent out and substitute an equal quantity (30) of the model #606?
>
> Because we already have orders for several of the #606, we would appreciate your attention to this within the next few days.

Note that the writer says clearly that, with the one exception, the delivery was thoroughly satisfactory. He says not "you made an error," but "an error was made." He mentions the demand for the product, and he assumes his claim is completely valid and will be taken care of (positive tone).

NONROUTINE CLAIM LETTERS

In many business situations where an error occurs, the facts are not always clear-cut and obvious. The buyer may feel that he has $140 due him because the damage took place prior to his receipt of the merchandise. The seller, however, feels that it left his premises in perfect condition. Or perhaps the buyer maintains that he did not receive a case of merchandise though the seller insists that he did. These situations and a hundred others will result in nonroutine claim letters being written. They are nonroutine because there is a difference of opinion as to precisely who is at fault. But errors do occur and settlements must be made. Sometimes the adjustments are in favor of the seller; sometimes they favor the buyer. One thing is certain: The seller does not relish receiving a claim letter nor does the buyer like to write them. At the moment, however, we are concerned with the buyer and the claim he enters.

The letter he writes should be so well written that it will result in a specific answer. We hope that that answer will be a "yes, we will credit your account." If, however, the buyer cannot secure an affirmative reply, he should strive for one that suggests a compromise. And if he can secure neither, then he should look for an answer that says "no." Of course, the "no" is not very satisfactory, but at least he knows where he stands. He may now take his business elsewhere if he is unhappy, or accept the "no" he has received. Obviously a follow-up to a "no" would depend on the strength and size of the claim. However, the reply which the claimant should make every effort to avoid receiving is the one that conveys "no answer." Such a response is merely a brush-off or a delaying action which goes like this:

> We will look into it; may we suggest that you do the same. Please be assured that this will be settled to our mutual satisfaction. Now let me call your attention to a special we are running. . . .

This kind of letter is no better than none at all. Time has been wasted, and as the days and weeks go by without an adjustment, the strength and immediacy of the claim decline.

However, claim letters can be written so that they will result in a definite answer. The following outline should be generally followed in the composition of an effective claim letter:

1. An introductory statement referring precisely and specifically to the transaction.
2. A specific statement of the loss or damage incurred.
3. A specific statement of the adjustment desired.
4. A statement which will motivate favorable action.
5. A friendly close.

When the buyer is certain that his claim is correct from every point of view, and the adjustment that he is requesting is honest in every respect, then he should check his letter to be sure that the tone is positive (but not accusing), the statements specific, and the details precise. On the other hand, if he is not sure who is at fault or exactly how the damage or loss occurred, then he can only write honestly and request that both parties do what is necessary to reach an equitable solution.

If his letter reflects a tone of uncertainty, the recipient will very probably seize upon that tone to delay making an adjustment. The following statements, for example, have been changed to reflect a much more positive tone:

> We believe the damage took place . . . .
> The damage took place . . . .

> We think you did not include . . . .
> . . . was not included.
>
> It is our feeling that perhaps the loss . . . .
> The loss took place on January 10.

Just as the tone should be positive, so too should the statements of loss or damage be specific and precise. Note the contrast between the original and revised versions of the sentences below:

> We suffered a considerable loss.
> Our loss was $58.12.
>
> The damage was quite extensive and we believe that . . . .
> The damage was extensive and amounted to $114.52.
>
> It would be wise for you to look into this and make a fair adjustment.
> A fair adjustment in this situation would be $144.00.
>
> We imagine that it would be quite expensive for us to replace the damaged watch.
> Replacement of the damaged watch would come to $85.50; this is the amount of the adjustment requested.

Sometimes the writer, in an effort to be courteous, will not be as positive and as specific as he should, lest his statement be interpreted as "pushy." It is important to be courteous, to give the reader credit for good will and care; but an element of uncertainty or vagueness may give the adjustor an opportunity to send a response that will result in delay and unnecessary correspondence. When the claim letter is framed to include the five points listed above and its tone is positive and its statements specific, the reply will usually be favorable (if the claim is valid).

> Dear Mr. Fox:
>
> On March 15 we received our order #207 from you. You may recall that this included a large quantity of lawn furniture, barbecue accessories, and outdoor cookware.
>
> If you will check our original purchase order, you will find that we requested six dozen sets of your Patio Grill Sets. Three dozen were to be sent in the regular style at $2.50 each and the remainder in the deluxe at $3.50 per set.

We have just started to display this merchandise and we have found that you inadvertently sent us five dozen of the regular and only one dozen of the deluxe. However, we have been billed according to our original purchase order.

Although we are aware that claims are to be submitted within ten days of receipt of merchandise and almost five weeks have now gone by, we nevertheless feel that you will understand our position in this case and credit our account for the $24.00 which is due.

Inasmuch as this is the first claim of this nature that we have submitted in some three years of satisfactory business relations with you, we know you will handle it as we request. In the future we shall check the markings on each package to avoid such a situation.

Notice in the letter above that the writer is so specific and precise in his presentation of facts, and the tone of the letter is so positive, that it has apparently never occurred to him that the reader would question the claim. The letter below, however, presents a contrast and certainly permits the reader to send back an equivocal reply.

Dear Mr. Wolf:

On March 28 your truck delivered the Empire Conference Table which we ordered on February 2.

Because our executive office facilities were not completely decorated at the time of delivery (as we had hoped they would be), the table was stored in our warehouse. Two days ago the painting and decorating of the conference room was completed and the table was brought in. It was at that time that we noticed a deep scratch running across the top of the table.

You may be sure that we were very upset, for we feel that the damage probably occurred prior to our receiving this piece of furniture. We do hope that you will want to make the proper adjustment in this case and we will look forward to hearing from you at your convenience.

There are obviously many opportunities for the recipient of this letter to legitimately delay taking specific action. The word "probably" will surely result in a letter asking for further investigation. Then, too, the writer did not indicate whether the table had been left with its protective wrappings on while stored, and he certainly neglected to point out what adjustment he would consider equitable. Should the table be replaced or refinished? And finally, he made no reference to former business associations which might help motivate a favorable response. Thus when the claimant receives an adjustment letter which awards him nothing but does suggest further investigation, he will have no one to blame but himself.

The letter which follows, like the one above to Mr. Fox, permits the adjustor to answer only with a "yes" or a "no" or a compromise.

Dear Mr. Wilshire:

On June 27 we ordered 110 yards of your Superior Brand Leather at $2.10 per yard. This was requested on our purchase order #2131.

For some unexplained reason, we received our shipment from you one month after it had been entered, instead of within the usual ten days. When the merchandise arrived, we found that you had shipped us the correct quantity but in your Deluxe Espanol Brand. This was billed to us at $3.50 per yard.

Because we were under a deadline arrangement with one of our clients, we had no alternative except to cut this leather and fabricate it into the furniture items (chairs) he had ordered.

Of course, you can appreciate that our price quotations to him were based on the cost of the Superior Brand Leather. We, therefore, had no way of making up the $1.40 difference per yard and we could only bill him at the original price we quoted him. You can see that your error, though certainly unintentional, resulted in a loss to us of $154.

Because of our long and favorable business association, we believe that you will see the situation as we do and will want to credit our account for one half the amount in question: $77. May we hear from you regarding this adjustment at your earliest possible convenience.

Here again there are almost no questions the recipient can ask which would delay the adjustment. Why was the more expensive leather used without communicating with the manufacturer? Precisely what was the loss? Exactly what kind of adjustment is required? Each of these questions and others are answered and the only action the receiver of the letter can take is to send back an affirmative or negative reply.

CLAIMS AT THE CONSUMER LEVEL

All too often, discussions on claims situations are concerned only with those made between one company and another. But what about Joe Average who has purchased a faulty television set, automatic washer, wrist watch, automobile, or refrigerator? We frequently hear him complaining, but when asked what he has done about the situation, he responds with, "How can I fight a giant corporation like . . . ?"

The truth is that he *can* enter a successful claim against a major company. Unfortunately, he frequently suffers (and loses money) in silence. He should not. He should complain; if his letter is written as suggested above, he will probably receive the satisfaction to which he is entitled. But he must keep in mind that major corporations receive dozens of claim letters each day, of which perhaps 50 per cent are legitimate. If he will write his letter specifically, courteously, and accurately, and enclose necessary substantiating data, such as bills, chances are very good that he will receive the adjustment he deserves. Certainly it would be foolish for a major American corporation to pay a television star $100,000 a week and then not take care of a faulty $20 relay switch in an automatic washer. The companies want to build good will with the American consumer; quality products and friendly service will help achieve that goal. When the consumer has difficulty, it is just as important for him to write an excellent claim letter as it is for the wholesaler.

Mr. Robert T. Farmont, President
General American Appliance Corporation
25 East Edison Parkway
New York, New York

Dear Mr. Farmont:

On March 28 I purchased a model #505 General American Refrigerator. This was secured from Star Appliance Dealers located in our city at 1511 West Marble Avenue.

You may be sure that this was not a hasty purchase. My husband and I checked several different models and examined the various companies' products carefully. We finally decided that the best and most attractive refrigerator on the market was yours, and we were delighted when it was delivered to our home.

After we had it for approximately seven weeks, we found to our disappointment that your beautiful appliance did not function as efficiently as we had been led to believe. Although the model #505 is sold as a "self-defrost" unit, it certainly did not live up to this qualification. At the end of the first three weeks we had to turn it off and chip away at the large chunks of ice which had formed in the refrigerator and freezer sections. Star Appliance Dealers sent out a repair man, but three weeks later we were again chipping away.

A second complaint to Star resulted in our being told that their guarantee period had expired and that we should get in touch with a commercial repair service.

I think that you will agree with me that a $375 refrigerator should give much better service and satisfaction than what we have experienced from your product.

We feel that you will want to see to it that this appliance is properly repaired or that we receive a new one as quickly as possible. I have always felt the General American Appliances were of excellent quality and made by a reliable firm. I know that you will want me to continue to feel this way in the future.

This letter is, like other good claim letters, specific, precise, and positive. Under ordinary conditions, it should result in favorable action.

One of the key factors is to be restrained and tactful in describing the situation and requesting an adjustment. To bluntly accuse the recipient of your letter of intentionally causing you a loss can only result in hard feelings and unfriendly relations. Every claim letter should be based on the premise that the error was completely inadvertent. No one likes being accused, and when a claim letter is unreasonable in its comments and its requests become demands, the effect on the recipient is likely to be negative.

QUESTIONS FOR STUDY

I. Offer your constructive criticism of the following inquiry, request, and claim letters. Remember to indicate which sections of the letters deserve favorable comments, as well as where improvements can be made. Be as specific as possible in your evaluations.

1. Dear Mr. Berman:

   Your firm was recommended to me as a possible supplier for factory lighting fixtures.

   We are presently renovating our Fairfield Avenue plant and are desirous of installing more powerful and intensive illumination because of the meticulous nature of the production which our production personnel must carry through in the production area.

   We have looked through your latest catalog and we find nothing that seems to fit our basic lighting needs. We look forward to receiving your suggestions.

2. Dear Sir:

   We have recently purchased six desk pen sets, your catalog number A-204, for our senior management personnel.

   These have proved extremely satisfactory and it was suggested at a recent meeting that these might prove to be very effective Christmas gifts for some of our clients.

   Can you give us the answers to the following questions no later than November 1 so that we may plan accordingly:

   1. Is it possible to attach a small brass plate to the marble base of each set with the engraving:

   To Mr. _____

   with

   Best Wishes

   The Offenbach Corp.

   Christmas 1971

   2. Will you package and ship all units directly to our clients on the basis of the list we supply?
   3. Will you guarantee safe arrival (or replacement) of all units prior to December 20?
   4. What will the charge be for a quantity of 50? of 100?

   Thank you very much for your cooperation.

3. Dear Dr. Flowers:

We have recently been talking to Mr. Robert Faverman concerning an opening we have for corporate training director. Because of your close association with Mr. Faverman at the University of California, we felt that you might be able to give us some important background information on him.

We are especially interested, Dr. Flowers, in your opinions of Mr. Faverman in the following areas:

1. His ability to get along with top management and "sell" them on the need for training of their personnel in necessary areas.
2. His creative imagination in designing programs for all levels of management personnel.
3. His instructional ability.
4. His supervisory ability in organizing and delegating tasks to subordinate personnel in the Training Department.

Details that you can add to the above regarding Mr. Faverman—his ability to communicate, appearance, sense of humor—will all be appreciated.

Because of our desire to make a decision in the near future, I would appreciate your reply by June 15. Of course, all information you forward will be retained in confidence.

Thank you very much.

4. Dear Dr. Kempton:

The members of the Kansas City Engineering Association hold a monthly meeting which features a cocktail hour, dinner, and a speaker.

We wonder if you would be available to be our speaker for the March meeting scheduled for the 28th at the Engineers' Club at 318 South Jackson Boulevard. We begin our "Happy Hour" at 5:30, dinner is served an hour later, and the speaker goes on at 7:30 for about a 45-minute presentation.

Because of your research and publications in the area of cardiac conditions, it was felt that an address on "The Young Executive and Cardiac Stress" would be valuable and very timely if carefully prepared.

Unfortunately our budget does not permit us to offer you an honorarium, but we can promise an excellent dinner and a responsive and interested group.

May we count on your acceptance of our offer?

5. Dear Sir:

We received our order #215, shipped via your truck, on April 27.

If you will note our original purchase order, dated April 15, you will see that it calls for 12 white table lamps, catalog number 205, among other items. Unfortunately the lamps we received were blue. Please pick these up and deliver the white no later than May 5. Inasmuch as several of these have already been sold to our customers, and early May delivery promised, we would appreciate your immediate attention to this request.

6. Dear Mr. Petre:

Early this month we placed an order of 112 replacement chairs for our employee cafeteria.

As you may recall, these were your model 242 but modified to include a swivel seat. We now find that after only two or three weeks' use, a sizable number of these chairs do not "swivel" easily, or at all, and are extremely noisy when people get in or out of them.

Will you arrange to pick up the faulty chairs and correct the condition or supply us with new ones? Of course we will have to have replacement chairs in the cafeteria to substitute for those you remove. Remember to bring those along. Can you make arrangements to correct this situation by the end of this month?

We were under the impression you used high-grade ball bearings, but you apparently don't.

7. Dear Mr. Conway:

On March 30 you delivered our Order 271A23 via Fast Line Freight Company.

Included in that order were one dozen Contemporary Office Tables, your catalog number 412.

Shortly after they arrived we opened the individual cartons so the tables could be put on display. It was at that time that we noticed that the base of 4 of these units was water marked. Because these tables are oiled walnut, this imperfection is clearly visible. Closer inspection of the cartons revealed that apparently water had come into contact with the cartons to a depth of two or three inches, as indicated by the discoloration line.

Because of these facts, you will understand why no notation as to damage was made on the receipt we signed.

Nevertheless we need these tables and would appreciate your replacement of these items by April 15. We have retained the original cartons for your use and feel that you have a valid claim against the carrier. If we can help in that regard, we shall be happy to do so.

Because of our years of pleasant association, we hope you will handle this claim as requested.

8. Dear Sir:

On November 24 we received our order 379ACT delivered in your truck.

This shipment included six table model RCA AM-FM radios, model 209. We have just noted that three of these radios have deep scratch marks on the right side. Obviously they cannot be sold in this condition. Will you kindly pick these up on your next delivery and replace them with an equal number in excellent condition.

The damage probably took place in your shipping room rather than here, and for that reason, I know you will wish to rectify this situation.

9. Dear Mr. Carmody:

On June 15, we ordered an Excello Color TV set, model 209. This was delivered, as requested, on July 1.

Our plan was to have this unit installed in our new Employee Lounge on July 1. However, the painters and carpet men did not finish until late in July. Thus we requested and had one of your men complete the installation on August 2.

On August 25 the set "went out" and your repair man told us the picture tube was "shot" and other items needed repair. He indicated that our 30-day warranty had expired and repair costs would be $185 including labor.

Inasmuch as the set was stored from July 1 until August 2 and not removed from the carton, I think you'll agree that the set did "go out" within the 30-day warranty period. Of course it was technically in our possession for almost twice that period, but I'm sure you will appreciate our point of view and make the necessary repairs without charge. Your reputation for fair play is well known and we hope you will act favorably in this instance.

II. Complete any of the following problems assigned. You may wish to review the chapter and note key points before solving the problem.

1. It is your understanding that the Midwest Office Equipment Company has a trade-in service for typewriters. You presently have 18 manual machines in your office and would like to replace them with automatic electric models. Write to Midwest and attempt to determine if they are agreeable to a trade-in arrangement and what line or lines of automatic machines they carry. If they have brochures describing the various equipment, it would be helpful for you to review them before going further.

2. Although you have purchased cartons from National Paper Company for many years, you have never had occasion to secure any that were manufactured of fire-retardant material. You have recently received an order for merchandise to be delivered to Veterans' Administration Hospitals. One of the requirements is that your product must be packaged in safety cartons according to Department of Defense specification AD 108.

Although you have checked National's latest catalog, you find no mention of the availability of fire-resistant or fire-retardant cartons. Can they manufacture their models #209 and #210 to conform to the government specifications? If so, what will they cost?

3. A communications consultant recently engaged by your firm has made several suggestions to improve internal corporate com-

munications. One of these involved the use of plant bulletin boards. You understand that both Fullerton Manufacturing and the Freeman Corporation specialize in school and plant bulletin boards. Write a letter (a copy of which will go to both firms) inquiring about the cost of 12 units. You would like them framed in three-inch aluminum approximately 3 by 5 feet, ½ inch cork face on ½" or ¾" plywood. How much is added to the cost when they are equipped with glass sliding doors? Is there an additional charge for locks on the doors? Do these companies have standard models? Are they less expensive and immediately available? Assume any other facts which are necessary in your letter.

4. You were recently invited on a tour of the new National Oil Corporation building. In the course of the tour, your group was told by the Management Training Director that National has made four films for use in management development programs. The training director ran about ten minutes of one titled "Building National's Corporate Image." You were very much impressed by it, and saw many communication implications in it. Write to National Oil and inquire if it would be possible to use the film in your Management Communication classes. If the film is available, you would like to show it to your classes on March 10 and 11. If the film has a "discussion guide" booklet, you would like to borrow that also.

5. You have recently received a contract from the Southern California Aerospace Corporation to manufacture the cabinets for the new commercial 1012 jet passenger aircraft. Write to Sperling Manufacturing Company and inquire if they are interested in submitting a bid on the drawer pulls or handles and locks.

They are to be manufactured according to the specifications and design which you enclose. You will need a total of 4000 handles delivered in 1000-unit lots. The first lot must arrive in Burbank, California, no later than June 1 and the balance in 1000-unit lots every 30 days thereafter.

6. You recently purchased 24 four-drawer filing cabinets from Parker Office Equipment Company. You requested their model 405 ("All-Safe") which comes equipped with individual drawer locks, roller-bearing drawers, and two steel separators per drawer. Shortly after the cabinets arrived, your maintenance staff began to place them. However, they reported that although the cartons were stamped "Model 405," these cabinets did not have individual drawer locks. For security reasons, it is vital that 12 of the cabinets be so equipped. However, locks are not necessary on the other 12. You check Parker's

invoice and find you have been charged for Model 405. Write a claim letter to the company which is 600 miles away. Determine what you wish to ask of Parker. Perhaps they can have locks installed on 12 cabinets locally? or they can pick up 12 and deliver an equal number of Model 405, or give you a reduction in price, or . . . .

7. On November 5 you purchased 500 "Sunlight" bath towel-wash cloth sets in pink, blue, and yellow from Sanford Towel Corp. These moved out of your store very briskly during the Christmas season. Since about January 10 you have had at least 15 returns and almost every day brings another claim or two. The problem is in the color of the items after washing. The wash cloths in each of the three colors are appreciably lighter than the towels after a washing. You don't know why, but you do know that many of your steady customers are upset and the situation has caused much ill will. Of course, you have taken the 210 cartons (which you have left from the original 500) off the shelf. You not only want them picked up and a credit entered, but also credit for those sets which have been returned and those which will come back in the future. It is true that Sanford has a 30-day return policy, and that applies only to unused merchandise, but in this case you feel the rule should be overlooked.

8. On October 12 you ordered 12 dozen desk pen sets from the Mitchell Company in New York, to be used as Christmas gifts to your clients. These units have an excellent quality pen mounted on a white marble base. The cost per unit, including a 3-line message inscribed on the base, was $5.70. All 12 dozen were delivered on December 12, although Mitchell gave you a November 20 delivery date. It was at the time of the late delivery that you noted the error. On every one of the 144 sets the inscription read "Best Wishes from the Shield Company," instead of "Best Wishes from the Sheald Company."

Because you were 1200 miles from the Mitchell Company, and you wanted these delivered no later than December 20 to your clients in various parts of the country, you rushed them to a local engraver without calling Mitchell. Emory Engravers polished the word "Shield" off and engraved them correctly. This was all done within 24 hours but you had to pay a premium price because of overtime and the difficulty of the polishing job. In any event you have a bill for $216 from Emory Engravers which you feel Mitchell should pay. Write Mitchell and enter your claim.

9. On May 14 you received a shipment of furniture from Contemporary Wholesale Furniture Dealers on Order 195F. The mer-

chandise was delivered by Contemporary. You have just taken two end tables from stock (part of order 195F). As you were about to place them in a window display, you noted that the tops of both had a series of scratches. Your stock man tells you, "I sure don't remember banging them, but you never can tell what happens. I guess they looked O.K. when they came in although I don't remember checking them in. Maybe we got them damaged from Contemporary."

You don't know who is at fault, but the possibility is good that it may be the manufacturer. Write a claim letter to Contemporary. Decide on your position before you write the letter.

10. About three months ago, you received a request from the Washington Service Group. This organization asked your railroad to sponsor a Saturday rail trip for 60 boys (from 12 to 15 years of age). The director told you that all these youngsters were from disadvantaged homes and most had never been on a train in their life.

After a great deal of effort on your part and with the hesitant approval of your superiors as well as the Commerce Commission, you arranged it.

The 100-mile round trip (which included a complimentary lunch) took place last Saturday. Although the three adults who accompanied the boys did a good job, the conductor reports one cracked sink in the men's toilet, two ripped coach seats, and two broken window shades. You know these were all inadvertent and the result of healthy spirits. Nevertheless the damage does come to $160.00, plus $80.00 for labor repair costs.

You have no alternative, as the assistant passenger agent, but to write to the Director of the Washington Service Group.

CHAPTER THIRTEEN

Communicating
a Favorable Response

All the types of letters in the preceding chapter except perhaps the first, inquiries, require an answer of "yes" or "no." The order can or cannot be filled, the request can or cannot be granted, the adjustment will or will not be made.

Everyone wants to receive a favorable reply; everyone likes to be able to give one. Everybody is happy; it is an easy letter to write. An unfavorable reply, on the other hand, causes unhappiness. The writer must try to soften that reaction as much as possible, without lessening the purpose or definiteness of his denial. A "no" letter is difficult to write.

So let us take a look at favorable letters, then one at unfavorable letters.

ANSWERING INQUIRIES
AND REQUESTS: YES

ROUTINE

When a major corporation places a double-page spread in a national magazine, it is not unusual for the advertisement to bring in one or two thousand inquiry letters: Where can I buy your television set? Is the model pictured in the lower-left-hand corner available in walnut? What are the dimensions of the set pictured in the upper center of the page? What is the address of the dealer nearest my home?

All of these inquiries should be answered, because each one represents a potential sale. But it would not be practical to answer each individually, so these firms have replies prepared. These may be form letters, brochures, pamphlets, or even postcards. The form is relatively unimportant, provided the inquiry is answered as fully and as soon as possible. Further, and perhaps most important, the reply, in whatever form, should express thanks for the inquiry and interest in further dealings with the inquirer.

NONROUTINE

There are, however, many letters of inquiry or request which cannot be adequately answered with a printed form or pamphlet. These require an individual letter.

When you can answer an inquiry or grant a request, say so near the beginning of your letter. Don't leave the recipient in suspense. When he receives the good news, he will then give greater attention to the rest of the letter than if he were still waiting for a "yes" or a "no."

Dear Mr. Hayworth:

We received your letter of May 15 in which you inquired about the recent training program conducted for our office personnel. I am happy to give you the information you requested.

The training was carried through by Communication Services located here in New York. We selected middle-management people whose job responsibilities require that they write a good many business letters and reports. The class was limited to sixteen members and met for two hours each Tuesday afternoon, on company time. Twelve such sessions were held. Communication Services provided the instructor, text, and all hand-out material. Home assignments were given to the participants and these were evaluated by the instructor and returned to the students.

We found the program to be very valuable. Our employees enjoyed it and came away with many ideas which are clearly evident in their day-to-day writing assignments. We have scheduled a second class for this fall and we know that it will be as profitable as the one which was just concluded.

If there is any other information which you desire in this area, I should be very happy to cooperate with you.

Dear Mr. Kahill:

We have received your recent inquiry concerning our research and manufacture of the new aluminum circuit breakers, Model 101.

You will find all the technical information as well as the specifications in the enclosed technical manual. I believe you will be especially interested in pages 38 to 42 as well as the diagram in appendix III.

If you have not seen the article by R. T. McKenzie which appeared in *Science Monthly* this last May, be sure to read it. Mr. McKenzie has described the results of his research, which seems related to the work you are doing. I know you will find McKenzie's article of benefit.

In your letter you indicated that you were interested in the information we are sending you from a research point of view, with the possibility of utilizing our products in a subsequent manufacturing process. If we can, therefore, supply you with quantities of our fine electronic components, we will be happy to do so. You will find that our quality is high and our prices attractive.

If there is any other way in which we may assist you, Mr. Kahill, please do not hesitate to write.

Dear Mr. James:

I was delighted to receive your invitation to speak before your Principles of Business class. I shall be there on Monday, 28 November, in time for the 11:00 class, and then lunch with the department.

Can you find me a ride back into town after lunch?

I look forward to meeting you and your students.

In all of these letters, a general organizational pattern was followed:

1. An introductory statement acknowledging the inquiry.
2. The grant itself.
3. Listing of the necessary information or reference to the source where it may be found.

4. A constructive suggestion, if possible.
5. A sales appeal (if applicable).
6. A friendly close.

ACKNOWLEDGING ORDERS
THAT CAN BE SHIPPED

Most of the business transactions between buyer and seller are routine. Merchandise is ordered on Monday and delivered on Wednesday. These are often stock items and few if any problems ever arise. If a portion of the order is not delivered on Wednesday it will probably be sent out the following week.

However, when products are manufactured on the basis of special instructions, or are to be delivered within a limited period of time, it is usually wise for the seller to acknowledge that the order has been received. This permits a formal understanding to take place between buyer and seller so that possible problems at a future date may be eliminated. If the buyer requests a Black and Johnson Cutter, Model 304, to be delivered within 30 days, and he receives an acknowledgment of the facts of the purchase from the seller, he may then assume that understanding has taken place. However, if he receives an acknowledgment from the seller which indicates that a Model 403 cutter is being prepared for shipment, he can wire and correct the error immediately. Had the wrong cutter been shipped, both parties would have suffered. A simple acknowledgment has added to the efficiency of operations of the companies.

Basically, there are several reasons for acknowledging orders which have been submitted:

1. To inform the buyer that his order has been received and is being acted upon.
2. To tell the buyer that his order is appreciated—a simple act of courtesy.
3. To confirm the order as originally entered. This gives the buyer the opportunity to check the acknowledgment and determine if the seller is shipping precisely what the buyer wants. If the buyer learns from the acknowledgment form that his request has been misinterpreted and he is scheduled to receive merchandise or services he did not order, he can call and make the necessary corrections. Without the acknowledgment form, he would have had no way of knowing about the error until after it had been made. As a result, both parties would have been inconvenienced and money would have been wasted.

Many acknowledgments can be made by means of a form or guide letter; some cannot. This distinction lies largely in whether the buyer is a steady customer or a new one.

STEADY CUSTOMERS

Those firms that do acknowledge orders from steady customers usually use postal cards, form letters, or duplicate invoices. The postal card contains only a brief message indicating the order has been received, is being processed, and will be shipped shortly. There is usually no effort made to list the items so that the buyer may verify the order as entered.

The form letter usually performs the same function as the postal card. However, it may be said to be a gesture which is a little more courteous because it travels in a stamped envelope.

The most efficient and least expensive means of acknowledgment is the duplicate invoice which is sent to the buyer. This is typed at the same time as the invoice (along with other needed copies). This duplicate of the invoice fulfills all three points we listed above as reasons for acknowledging orders: It informs the buyer that the order is being processed; it is an expression of courtesy and consideration; and it permits the buyer to check the specific details of the order.

Every now and then a personal letter of acknowledgment should be sent to steady customers, as an expression of pleasure in the business relationship. A good customer likes to know that he is not just taken for granted.

Dear Mr. Ryan:

This is just a short note to tell you that your order of April 28 has been received and is being shipped according to your usual instructions.

We want you to know that your purchases, which have been made so regularly during the past year, are always appreciated. Of course, we haven't written you an individual letter for each of the orders, but we want you to know that we will always make very effort to supply you with quality merchandise at the lowest possible prices.

If you have any special needs that we can fill, please give us an opportunity to assist you. We appreciate your confidence in us and we shall try to earn it for many years to come.

365

A letter such as this tells the customer that he has not become simply another account number to the seller. It is this kind of "unnecessary" act which helps build good will.

NEW CUSTOMERS

Although it is obviously impossible to send a personal letter to a steady customer for every order, it is necessary to do so for a new customer. We want him to know that we truly appreciate adding his name to our customer list. This message also gives us an opportunity to tell him what some of our procedures are and to be sure that the terms of sale and payment are clearly understood.

This letter can effectively be made up as a guide letter and individually typed when the need arises. The reader should feel the red carpet has been rolled out for him, but the letter should not be so effusive as to sound insincere.

The new customer is primarily concerned with his order; this should therefore be mentioned first. Following this fact other details may be given on the company's services, policies, and practices.

Dear Mr. Dietrich:

Thank you very much for your initial order. All merchandise that you requested is in stock and will be shipped via Illinois Central Railroad on June 8. The terms of sale agreed upon will be followed through.

The merchandise which you order in the future will be shipped within three days. When bills are paid within ten days of receipt of merchandise, a profit-making 2 per cent discount may be taken. In a year's time this can add up to a very meaningful savings. When payment is not made within ten days, it is due, net, within thirty days.

As you probably know, Martins is extremely interested in promoting plant safety and housekeeping. Each month we publish a poster in each of these areas. We will be happy to send you a quantity for posting on your employee bulletin boards if you so desire. In addition to this, our industrial management department is at your service to answer relatively routine questions concerning storage of merchandise, movement of merchandise in the plant, and plant layout.

These are only a few of the services that we here at Martins are delighted to offer to our customers. As our relationship continues in the years ahead, you will become aware of many other services which are available to you and other Martins customers.

We look forward to a long and mutually satisfying relationship between you and Martins. If there is anything we can do to further that relationship, please let us know.

For further verification of the order, a duplicate of the invoice may accompany a letter such as the one above.

MAKING ADJUSTMENTS: CLAIM GRANTED

The number of items which most firms handle today is greater than a generation ago; billing procedures are more complex; inventory controls are more difficult; handling and shipping of merchandise require more attention; and as a matter of fact, the entire process of getting goods from source to consumer requires many more steps today than it did in the past. Because there are more factors involved, there are greater possibilities for error. And errors do occur. But most businessmen recognize that such situations are likely to arise, so their claims or adjustments, when things go wrong, are tempered with patience.

Furthermore, intelligent managers are aware that a claim or a complaint can often assist by bringing attention to an area which needs improvement or change in their own firms. And in addition, they accept most claims as being legitimate and fair. There is the further fact, of course, that the people who submit claims are customers and it is upon their business that the seller's firm stands. Thus, it is important to handle quickly and courteously the claims and complaints that come in. This must be done with care and discretion so that the seller is recognized as fair; but he must be sure he does not gain a reputation for being too soft and accepting any claim, nor too severe and refusing all.

Most claims which are entered are legitimate, and it is on this basis that firms usually establish a fairly generous adjustment policy. If there is a question as to the fault, companies will usually give the benefit to the buyer. Their future business is involved, and the profits that go with that business. Certainly there will be some claims submitted which have no merit and the seller may accept them and make an adjustment, but the individuals or firms that frequently make such requests are sooner or later recognized and properly dealt with.

An adjustment policy is often governed by that which is accepted in the trade. Furniture manufacturers from coast to coast have agreed on a standard return privilege; appliance manufacturers have set down an industry-wide repair policy; and other fields have established their ground rules. When this is done, obvious advantages are gained by the seller in an adjustment situation.

The way in which the adjustment is made is a vital factor in building or losing good will. An adjustment which is given grudgingly will usually do more harm than one which is refused, but carefully and courteously explained. We have probably all been in a situation where we have requested a refund. Although it was granted, we were interrogated and questioned and made to feel guilty about submitting the claim at all. We probably walked out of that place of business intending never to return. Had the seller, on the other hand, given us a reasonable, intelligent, and courteous explanation for a refusal, we would have accepted it and more than likely he would have retained our good will. The key to granting any adjustment is to do it graciously. The following letter, although it grants the adjustment, will probably lose the account.

Dear Mr. Hoefler:

We received your letter of December 3 in which you requested that we credit your account for $28.50 for discounts on orders which you received in July and August.

As you may or may not know, the standard policy throughout the furniture industry is that a 2 per cent discount is granted only when bills are paid within ten days of date of invoice. If we do not follow this policy, and give such discounts to every Tom, Dick, and Harry, we would surely lose money; this would be very bad for our company. The discounts which you claim you are entitled to are all for orders which you paid late, whether you know it or not.

However, we are granting your claim and we hope this satisfies you. We also hope you will be more careful in the future.

Any adjustment which is made in a carping, grudging, and tactless manner will be resented.

BUYER AT FAULT

Not infrequently in business the buyer will submit a claim which is not justified, but in most of these cases he honestly believes it is. He may run the machine over its rated capacity and he now requests a replacement; he may return the furniture forgetting that he has overlooked the ten-day return period privilege; he may order merchandise at a special price long after the last date announced for the sale. When these claims are granted, it is purely for the purpose of building good will.

When the buyer is at fault and the claim granted, it is usually wise to structure the letter so that an explanation precedes the favorable adjustment.

Dear Mr. Milton:

We received your letter of July 5 in which you requested that we pick up the American 1/3 h.p. motor and replace it with a 3/4 h.p. unit.

We were sorry to learn that the 1/3 h.p. motor which we sold you on June 15 did not prove satisfactory. In your letter, however, you indicated that it was used to power a Jackson-Smith Industrial Saw, model #208. We checked this with our chief engineer because we are always desirous of furnishing our customers with the best and most efficient materials available.

He found that the manufacturer of this saw recommends that a 3/4 to 1 h.p. unit be used with this particular model. Apparently this was overlooked by the people in your shop and our 1/3 h.p. unit was used. Of course, we realize that incidents such as this occur and we are sending out the larger motor as you requested. However, for your satisfaction and the most efficient operation of equipment in the future, we suggest that the manufacturer's recommendations be checked and followed.

The new motor should be delivered to your warehouse no later than August 10; at that time our driver can pick up the original unit. If we can assist you in any way in the future, Mr. Milton, please call on us.

We stated earlier that good news should be given immediately in a business letter. This is not true, however, when granting a claim in which the buyer is at fault. If he opens his adjustment letter and finds there is an immediate grant, he may not read further to learn that he was at fault. And even when he does read the entire letter, the psychological impact of the explanation may be lost. It is for this reason that it is recommended that a courteous, straightforward explanation be included which points out to the buyer how he was at fault, before the grant is made. In most cases the following organizational structure is recommended:

1. A statement referring to the specific transaction.
2. A statement explaining tactfully and discreetly how the buyer is at fault. Care should be taken to avoid putting him in a situation where he may lose face.
3. A statement granting the claim graciously.
4. A sales appeal, if appropriate.
5. A friendly close.

This pattern was used in the letter to Mr. Milton above. Compare the effectiveness of that letter with that of the following one, where the pattern has not been followed.

> Dear Mr. Fischer:
>
> We are happy to tell you, in reference to your letter of April 15, that we have credited your account for $72.50.
>
> We can understand how you felt when the merchandise you purchased was not up to the quality you expected.
>
> However, your technicians should not have attempted to correct whatever was wrong with the #207 switching unit. This is a highly complex piece of electronic equipment and it is for this reason that we carefully seal it and place the statement on every cover which says: "To be opened by manufacturer's personnel only; call manufacturer for service."
>
> For your best interests, we suggest that you follow our recommendations in the future.

This letter to Mr. Fischer can result in further complications. If he reads just the first paragraph, he may comment, "Boy, this was easy." And if he doesn't read any further, he may repeat the action which caused the claim in the first place. It is for this reason that the proper organization of such a letter is important.

Perhaps equal in importance with the organization is the tone. It should be direct, courteous, and open-handed.

> Poor: Although you made the mistake, we are giving you the money.
>
> Revised: We are pleased to make the adjustment under these circumstances.

> Poor: If you had read the instructions, this would never have happened. But we are going along with you anyway.

Revised: The adjustment has been made as you requested. May we suggest that in the future the installation instructions be followed carefully for complete satisfaction.

Poor: We can't imagine why you would feel your claim is justified; nevertheless, we have credited your account.

Revised: Oversights are certainly made from time to time and on this basis we have credited your account.

SELLER AT FAULT

When the buyer is at fault when he requests an adjustment, the seller may grant the claim, refuse the claim, or offer a compromise. When it is the seller who is at fault, however, there is no alternative: he must grant the claim.

Before Receiving a Claim

Generally the seller is not aware that he has made some mistake until the claimant tells him so. However, in those situations where the seller determines shortly after he has made a shipment that something is wrong, he should attempt to correct the error before the buyer asks for an adjustment. Maybe the seller will discover that a particular lot of merchandise has not been manufactured properly, but only after the merchandise is on its way to the customer. Or the seller may receive a justified complaint from only one of several buyers. In any of these situations, he should immediately get in touch with the other buyers who have been shipped similar faulty merchandise and offer to make proper adjustment. The seller who does make an adjustment prior to receiving claims and complaints will secure an amount of good will which no advertising can purchase. Adjustments made under these circumstances are the mark of a reliable house and the reputation gained by such action proves invaluable.

Answering Claims

The letter granting a claim when the seller is at fault is a difficult one to write. The seller must indicate that he has made an error, but in such a way that the buyer will not lose confidence in him and take his business elsewhere.

What makes this such a difficult assignment is the fact that people act like people. Although any of us will readily admit that we are likely to make an error—and do—we cannot understand how those from whom we purchase can make such "dumb and completely inexplicable mistakes." Thus when a seller does make an error in dealing with us, we often enter a claim, accept the adjustment, and then take our business elsewhere. This reaction holds true for many consumers; however, at the wholesale level the businessman does recognize that mistakes are likely to happen, and he will usually accept the adjustment in good faith.

What is the proper order of points in the letter where the seller is at fault and grants the claim? If the message opens with a grant, the reader may never read on to the explanation of how the situation occurred. He has already read the item—the grant—which is of major interest to him.

To reverse the order is also subject to criticism. After all, the buyer is primarily interested in whether he is going to receive a credit of $52.00, and he is not very much concerned with the fact that your computers suddenly began to punch holes incorrectly. Probably, the situation and prospective reader should determine the order of your letter.

There is indeed a question as to whether an explanation should be included at all. A detailed discussion of how and what went wrong in our company may only compound the situation and erase what little confidence the customer has in us. Perhaps the best thing to do is to open by saying that we made a mistake, that we are making an adjustment, and that we will do our best to see that a similar case does not arise in the future. Of course, there are instances where an explanation will clear up a situation and will be accepted as perfectly logical and plausible. But in many situations, trying to explain how an error happened only serves to emphasize our own shortcomings.

New York Life Insurance Company had this to say in one of its *Effective Letters Bulletins:*

> Mistakes are bound to happen. As company correspondents we have the alternative of compounding the mistake or minimizing it.
>
> Considering the millions of paper operations involved in the day-to-day workings of a large company, proportionately few errors are made. But letters do go out billing a policy owner for a premium that's already been paid, billing him for the wrong amount, notifying him that his policy is lapsed when it isn't, telling him he hasn't sent a necessary form when he has.
>
> Generally, of course, management decides how such errors are to be rectified but it's the job of the correspondent to convey these decisions in language and tone that are most likely to win back the confidence of the policy owner.
>
> Let's look at an example. Say a policy owner has been

billed for a previously paid premium. He writes back and says, "But I already paid it." We check, find out he's right and say:

> In your letter of January 6 you claimed that the premium payment of $68.03 due on December 1 was paid by you under date of November 28. A check of our records indicated that this was not so.
>
> However, a further check revealed that you were correct in your assumption for the reason that a member of our clerical staff neglected to enter your payment on our books.
>
> We hope that this error caused you no undue concern.

Not only is this grudging—"our records revealed that this was not so," "your assumption," "UNDUE concern,"—it is also a fine example of buckpassing—"a member of our clerical staff neglected . . . ." This is a flimsy excuse at best and, anyhow, as a member of the company, the clerk's errors reflect on the company. Wouldn't it be better to say:

> You are right, Mr. Jones. We checked and found out that you did pay your premium on November 28, just as you said.
>
> Please forgive us—you can be sure we'll try to see that this doesn't happen again.

Let's take another example. A policy owner whose policy is fully paid-up receives a lapse notice regarding his policy. He writes in asking "how come?" and this is the reply he receives:

> Upon receipt of your letter of January 14, 1961, a thorough check was made of our records which bears out your statement that a lapse notice was sent you for a December premium on your above-numbered policy.
>
> You are correct in assuming that your policy is paid-up and that no further premiums are due.
>
> It is a pleasure to be of service to you.

Again no apology, just a grudging assent that he was right—for once. Why not:

> The notice you received was intended for another of our policy owners, Mr. Brown. You are perfectly right in assuming that your policy is paid-up and that no further premiums are due.
>
> I'm awfully sorry this happened, and should you receive another of these notices (we'll try to see that you don't) just ignore it.

Here's one more example—a bit different from the others, since this is more of a mix-up than a mistake. Suppose a letter was sent to a policy owner, asking him to sign and return an enclosed form. He sends the form, but for some reason, we never receive it, and a couple of weeks later, he receives this letter from us.

> We are writing to you regarding the delay in furnishing the Company with the claim form previously requested in our letter of December 19. It has not been received nor have we heard from you as to when it will be received.
>
> Will you kindly let us know when we may expect to receive this form since if it is not in our possession within the next two weeks, we will be obliged to close our file.

A letter like this will undoubtedly inspire a reader with all the kindly instincts of a chicken hawk, but for the sake of argument, let's say that this particular reader just writes back a mild note saying he'd sent the form. A few days later, we tell him:

> In reply to your letter of January 23, we wish to advise that we have no record of having received the claim form forwarded to you for completion on December 19.
>
> If, as you state, you signed and returned this form, it is possible that you inadvertently forwarded it to our field office.
>
> We are, however, enclosing another form. Please complete it in ink and in duplicate and forward it directly to the undersigned. Thank you.

First of all we say that if he did send the form, which is doubtful, ("as you state,") he sent it to the wrong place. Then, with an implied sigh, we give him another chance and enclose a second form. No apology—dignified or otherwise—only a dogged insistence that the form was not received. And that's not important. What's important is that it is our job to be of service to this man. Maybe he sent the form, maybe he didn't. No matter. It's up to us to give him the benefit of the doubt. Even the law says a man is innocent until he's proven guilty. So why not say something like:

> Thank you for writing us about that elusive claim form. We always like to give prompt service on such things,

but unfortunately in your case, we couldn't because the form you sent just didn't get to us.

At any rate, here's another form. Would you fill it out in duplicate, sign and return it to us? As soon as we receive it, we'll be happy to take care of the matter for you.

It doesn't hurt to say "I'm sorry about this," or "I hope this didn't alarm you too much," or even a straightforward, simple, "Please forgive us."

It's much easier to lose face by not apologizing than by apologizing. A customer is flesh and blood with feelings and emotions like our own. An apology, properly made, is likely to appeal to his most reasonable self.[1]

The following indicates a good organizational pattern for an adjustment letter when the seller is at fault:

1. An opening which refers to the situation and makes a grant.
2. An explanation of how the incident occurred, if such an explanation sounds reasonable. If it will only magnify a careless error, it should be omitted.
3. An attempt to regain the customer's confidence.
4. A sales appeal, if it seems appropriate.
5. A friendly close.

In the letter to Mr. Canfield below, an explanation is offered which will probably help make the entire situation more understandable to the buyer. In the second letter below, however, there is no explanation of how the incident happened, for if it were offered it would only emphasize a very careless procedure within the seller's company.

Dear Mr. Canfield:

You had every reason in the world to be upset when your order #509 did not arrive on July 5, as we had promised. You were correct in selling the higher priced Maxwell units at the sale price you advertised for the Kolton. We will surely take care of the $36.50 loss which you sustained. A credit for that amount has been entered in your account.

As you may or may not be aware, we have two "Canfields" in our files. Your firm is listed as the Canfield Corporation and

1. *Effective Letters*, "We're Sorry," January-February, 1961. Copyright, 1961, New York Life Insurance Company.

is, of course, in Chicago. The other company we carry as Canfield's and Associates in St. Louis. Our regular shipping clerk is well aware of the difference and has never made a mistake between the two. However, he has the bad habit, like our other employees, of requesting a vacation each year, and his substitute mistakenly shipped your order to St. Louis.

We are extremely sorry about this, Mr. Canfield, and you can be sure that we will do everything in the future to avoid such a situation.

I have enclosed our summer catalog and I do hope you will give our substitute shipping clerk an opportunity to prove his efficiency; he and I will be very pleased to receive your order.

Dear Mr. Lapidus:

Our sincere apologies for the beautiful "goof" we pulled. A check for $28.00 is enclosed.

There was no excuse for our delivering your order #209 to the wrong warehouse. Your instructions were clear and explicit, but through our oversight, they were not followed. We are sincerely sorry.

Our salesman in your area has sent us a note indicating your interest in our new Empire Line. I am enclosing a bulletin describing all of the items in this line. This is the first release we have made on it, and I am sure that you will find this to be a quality product at a highly competitive price. If you will drop me a note, I can have a complete set of samples of the Empire Line to you within three days. I am sure you will find them attractive and an excellent addition to the stock you carry for the Junior Miss customers in your area.

THIRD PARTY AT FAULT

In most transactions between buyer and seller today, a third party is involved: a shipper, carrier, broker, or storage agent. It may be that the loss or damage involved in the claim took place while the merchandise was in the hands of a third party. In such a situation, the seller will normally reply with a courteous letter and extend to the buyer whatever assistance he can. If some of his accounts are small retail merchants, he may even offer to process the claim for them.

Dear Mr. Canterbury:

We were extremely sorry to hear that several of the lamps included in order #705, which we shipped via Rapid Freight Lines, did not arrive in satisfactory condition.

As you know, this carrier, like all others, inspects merchandise before accepting it. We have their receipt indicating that this order was turned over to them in excellent condition.

For this reason you will probably want to get in touch with Rapid Freight as quickly as possible and enter a claim for the four damaged lamps. I have enclosed two blank copies of Interstate Commerce Commission Form 202 which you can complete and forward to the carrier.

If I can assist you in any other way, Mr. Canterbury, please let me know and I will be happy to cooperate.

Dear Mr. Middleberry:

We were very sorry to hear that the display case (model #49), which we sold you on September 5, arrived with one of the rear glass panels broken.

When this item was accepted by Chicago and Eastern Railway, it was checked by them and found to be in excellent condition. Apparently the damage took place while the case was en route to you.

We have completed Interstate Commerce Commission Form 202 in duplicate and enclosed both copies with this letter. If you will sign them on the line indicated and return them to us, we will forward the claim to the railroad. If you would prefer to do this, however, just complete the forms and mail them to the railroad's Claim Office at 215 East Adams Avenue in Springfield, Illinois.

Please let us know if we can assist you in any other way.

Naturally, it is costly for the seller to get involved in a claim where he has no legal responsibility. However, the good will which may accrue to him in such circumstances will be well worth the effort expended.

MISCELLANEOUS ADJUSTMENT SITUATIONS

Other instances arise in addition to those listed above. At times both parties can be at fault, in other cases the fault is not known, and sometimes the problem is the result of a misunderstanding. Each of these situations, and others, must be handled on its own merits and in conformity with the adjustment policy of the seller. Regardless of what the circumstances are, all such adjustment letters should carry a strong sales and good-will message.

> Dear Mr. Dayton:
>
> You're correct. Your order #506 did call for six dozen ladies' Casual Line footwear. Why we sent you sixteen dozen (and billed you for this number) is beyond me.
>
> You may return them, of course, and as a matter of fact, we will be happy to pick them up when we deliver the merchandise which is scheduled to arrive in your store one week from today.
>
> May I suggest, however, that you seriously consider retaining the extra ten dozen. This line is moving far beyond our expectations and we think that you will find this merchandise a most satisfactory sales item. Our advertising on this item is now in full swing and a double-page spread will appear in the June issue of the *Women's Shopping Guide*. We know that this, plus the high quality of this footwear, will help increase your sales.
>
> Naturally, we will save shipping and bookkeeping costs if you elect to retain all of the original shipment. For your cooperation, we would like to have you deduct 5 per cent from the bill which covers this merchandise. Please call me collect, extension 205, and let me know if this proposal is satisfactory to you.

Sometimes a claim can be adjusted through the expedient of "educating" the customer. This may be done through courteous instructions or suggestions which tell him how to handle the product.

Dear Mr. Huchinson:

We are as concerned as you that your new Lawn King Mower does not give you the satisfaction you have every right to expect. From the description of the difficulty you are having, it seems to me that the solution and correction are relatively simple.

You say that you turned the little knob next to the starting control to #7 immediately before starting the motor. This is proper and correct, but if the gas mixture is left at seven, the motor will stall in exactly the fashion you have described. Once the motor is turning over, the gas mixture should be reduced to #2 or #3. Try it this way and I am quite sure your Lawn King Mower will give you the satisfaction it gives thousands of other home owners in the United States.

If however, this unit does not give you the service which you have every right to expect, we will make arrangements to see that an exchange is carried through for you.

The competent business manager recognizes that an equitable adjustment policy can contribute greatly to a company's image, business, and reputation.

QUESTIONS FOR STUDY

I. Please offer your constructive criticism of the following letters. Remember to indicate which sections of the letters deserve favorable comments, as well as where improvements can be made. Be as specific as possible in your evaluations.

1. Dear Miss Kellogg:

We are happy to comply with your request and send you the 25 foreign policy booklets you asked for. We hope you and the other members of your organization will find them instructive and valuable.

Because this is your initial use of our American Education Series booklets, we are happy to provide them on a complimentary basis. We have enclosed our catalog which lists all our publications and quantity prices and discounts. Your order for materials can be filled within three days of receipt of your request. Please use the blanks enclosed.

2. Dear Mr. Bragg:

Your request for information for use in your graduate studies is hereby acknowledged as received.

As you probably know, your area of electronic sensors is a delicate one. Our government has indicated that our efforts in this direction are classified; however, we have checked with the Security Officer in the area, and he has agreed to permit us to release the information you requested.

You will therefore find enclosed the drawings you wanted and we hope they serve your purpose; after you use them they should be returned to us, which we would appreciate.

3. Dear Mr. Blackstone:

Yes, we certainly would be happy to assist you in designing and writing your new employee orientation manual.

We were faced with the similar problem of a rapidly growing work force and vast differences in employee backgrounds; we know how difficult it is to put together a pamphlet that serves everyone.

I would strongly suggest that you use a spiral binder approach so that changes may be printed on new pages and easily inserted. And I would certainly use sketches to add humor and break the monotony of the printed page. Topic headings and an index are also helpful to the reader.

I've enclosed two copies of our latest edition. You may find them helpful for guide purposes. Please call or write, Mr. Blackstone, if I can help in any other way.

4. Thank you, Mr. Daily,

For your order #2121 which we received on February 23. It is being given our usual careful attention.

Although we don't have the opportunity to thank you often in the computerized business world of today, we do want you to know that we appreciate your confidence in permitting us to fill your lighting requirements.

If our salesman isn't immediately available or if you have some special needs, or even a question, please pick up the phone and call us collect. We want to assist you in every way possible, Mr. Daily.

5. Dear Miss Zebco:

I guess if I were about 30 years younger, I would be sending you a Valentine during this week. But because I am the perennial "39," I'll use a business letter.

I just wanted you to know that your latest order for supplies has been filled and is on its way to you. But I also wanted you to know how much we appreciate your business and that of the other 600 hair-styling shops we supply in the Midwest.

You're my Valentine, Miss Zebco, and I hope I'll be drawing hearts for you for many years to come.

6. Dear Mr. Gotz:

Welcome to Farmington's. The red carpet has been rolled out and our staff would like to sing you a chorus of "Glad to Have You Aboard."

Your first order (AT 303) has been processed and will leave here tomorrow in one of Farmington's bright blue trucks. You should receive your merchandise within 48 hours.

This will be true of all your future orders, Mr. Gotz; delivery to your warehouse within seven days after your order has been received. And as our salesman indicated, payment made within ten days of receipt of merchandise assures you of an important 2 per cent discount. Of course, you may take up to our maximum period of 30 days to pay your net bill.

Requests for adjustments must be made within 20 days of receipt of merchandise and returns can only be made to our driver when he has a completed yellow "Returns Authorization" form.

We will be happy to work with you, Mr. Gotz, in many different ways: market surveys, special deliveries, and economic analysis of your area. Let us know when we can be of help.

7. Dear Mr. Kentenber:

We received your letter of March 20 in which you requested that we pick up the 18 sheets of #202 plastic which we delivered on your Purchase Order 140FR.

We have made arrangements to have our truck stop at your Hawthorne plant on March 29 and secure these items. A credit memo for $425.00 will be sent to your accounting department.

I would like to call to your attention, Mr. Kentenber, that these sheets were manufactured according to your formula and are not regularly carried in our stock in this composition, weight, or size. You can see, therefore, that your request places us in a rather awkward position. Our sale of this merchandise to another source in the near future is only a possibility. Nevertheless, we understand how our customers' needs change.

Please let us know if we can assist in any other way.

8. Dear Mr. MacElroy:

We received your letter inquiring about the return of one of our #2412 Electronic Heat Treating units.

We were concerned because this is one of our most reliable and widely sold items. We turned the situation over to our Chief Engineer, Mr. Karbon, who visited with your R and D Director, Mr. Jones.

After several meetings both of these men agreed that you required a unit with a top heat capacity of 1800° F. Our #2412 unit was constructed to function best at a high level of 1200° F and is so advertised and represented. Your order, however, did request the #2412 unit which we shipped.

Situations of this type do occur and for that reason we are picking up the #2412 within 10 days and giving you full credit even though it has been used.

Of course we are happy to work with you in situations like this, Mr. MacElroy. And again, I want you to know that our engineering and research staff are always available to assist you in research, design, and consulting areas. Please call on us when we can help.

9. Dear Mr. Twining:

I can fully appreciate your feeling when your TRMX Field Unit order was cut way back by the government.

As you indicated, we did manufacture the 2124 Triple-Safe Locks to your specifications. On the other hand, we recognize that you now have 2000 on hand which will serve no purpose. We will therefore pick these up and issue you full credit.

I have talked to the Purchasing Department Manager of one of our large customers and he has assured me that he can use these units. All we need is a formal requisition from him which should be forthcoming in ten days. So "all's well that ends well."

It might be helpful, in the future, if we agreed on "step manufacture and delivery." Thus we could assemble and deliver according to your monthly needs. The slight additional cost for this is usually well worth it.

10. Dear Mr. Prosser:

Yes, we will be able to accept for full credit the 40 Marquette Switching sets (#706) you wish to return.

I did check your original purchase order, Mr. Prosser, and it clearly calls for the "Residential" Marquette units. However, it is common practice to classify any building with four or more apartments as "Commercial." Surely if you were going to use these sets in four eight-flat buildings, you should have requested the "commercials." Of course, the limits and use of all our units are all clearly marked on the cartons in which they are packaged.

As you can see, Mr. Prosser, we are always happy to cooperate with our customers.

11. You're right, Mr. Cutter.

We *did* ship the wrong merchandise and we're now working to correct our error.

We still haven't determined how we went into production on 250 large size (8″) #421 Double Lock Clamps when your Purchase Order clearly calls for the small 4″ size. But we did manufacture and deliver them, and we are certainly aware of the problem we created.

The #420 units are now in the final manufacturing stage, and should be shipped tomorrow. Please return the #421 (8″ Double Lock Clamps) to the driver. If you find you can use these, please retain them and we will be happy to deduct 8 per cent from that purchase order. This is roughly the sum we will save in accounting and handling costs.

You may be sure, Mr. Cutter, that we will check our orders more carefully in the future.

12. Dear Mr. Lamborn:

We have carefully audited your December and January billing, and determined that you did purchase $1,832.50 worth of merchandise during that period.

On January 8 we did pick up and return merchandise from Order 48FX which amounted to $207.50. Although the driver issued you a hand credit memo he did not report that nor complete an official credit form (as he is supposed to) for our credit department. Consequently an IBM credit card was not completed for our computer.

What it all amounts to, Mr. Lamborn, is that your account balance is really $1,625 and if you will forward your check for that amount, it will clear your account.

13. Dear Mrs. Robinson:

Now that our busy Christmas season is behind us, we have a few loose ends to gather up and apologies to make. One of these apologies is certainly due you for we did bill you for $74.00 worth of merchandise which was purchased by another Robinson family also living in Pasadena.

I'm sure there is an explanation for this which would involve our temporary holiday help, increased volume of sales, etc., but I'm sure you're primarily interested in the correction—

which has been made. And we're interested in retaining your good will—which we sincerely hope has been done.

We have enclosed two tickets to our Winter Fun-in-the-Sun Fashion Show and Tea which is scheduled for 3:00 p.m. February 8. We do hope you and a guest will attend and enjoy viewing the latest in cruise and holiday wear.

14. Dear Mr. Farmer:

Immediately after receiving your claim letter of September 5 we called Rapid Route Freight Service. We now understand clearly why you received your Order 49AT51 on August 27 instead of on our promised date of delivery of August 22.

Unfortunately the truck which carried your order was involved in an accident just west of Kansas City. Because the truck also carried some merchandise of a special type, it was placed under guard. By the time it was towed into Kansas City, inspected, and the merchandise transferred to a substitute vehicle, a good deal of time was lost.

I am well aware that we promised Order 49AT51 in time for your weekend August 25-28 sale. Certainly too we can understand that you were forced to purchase a quantity of #214 Star Lamps from a local supplier to meet your customers' requests.

Please let us know what your extra expenditures and costs were, Mr. Farmer, so that we can credit your account. And if you would like to return any or all of Order 49AT51 because of the late delivery, please let us know and arrangements will be made.

Thank you for your understanding and cooperation.

15. Dear Mr. Norrell:

We received your letter concerning the Model 2481 Electric Motor which you recently purchased from us.

Your explanation leads us to think that the load on the motor is heavier than it should be, and for that reason it frequently turns itself off and requires that you reset it.

If the two pieces of equipment are heavy duty and you run them simultaneously on this motor, the answer may be there. May I suggest that you restrict your operations to one piece. I think you will then secure plenty of power from the 2481 motor. Why not try it this way and let me know the results.

We're happy to cooperate in any way possible.

II. Complete any of the following problems assigned. You may wish to review the chapter and note key points before solving the problem.

1. Reply to Professor John House of the Finance Department of California State College. He has requested 60 copies of your annual report for use by his two classes in Money and Banking. Unfortunately you can only spare 35 copies; perhaps he can use these in one class, collect them and use them again in his second class.

2. The PTA of the Burnside Elementary School has requested 500 copies of your booklet "How to Keep Your Home Safe from Fire." You are not only happy to comply with the request but you can also send along one of your fire safety engineers to make a 20-minute color-slide presentation. Although your firm sells commercial and residential fire insurance, the booklets and the presentation are completely objective and contain no sales appeals.

3. Next month you will launch your annual Spring Sale which usually results in heavy sales from your steady customers. This would be a good time to send each of your retail accounts a letter acknowledging their purchases of your products (children's wear) during the previous months.

4. During the last two months your sales force has carried through an all-out campaign to secure new accounts. Your firm has been quite successful and you have secured approximately 10 to 15 new customers each week in your district.
    Prepare a letter which can be used to acknowledge a new account's initial order for golf and tennis equipment (assume brand names) and also tells them about your payment policies, your advertising assistance allowances, delivery schedules, return privileges, and special discounts for quantity purchases.

5. You have recently purchased the Bel Air Appliance Center. In most cases, the consumer makes a purchase which is delivered within 10 days to 2 weeks. You feel it would be a good idea to acknowledge the order and thank the customer for his purchase within 24

hours of the sale. Prepare such a letter keeping in mind that the expenditure of several hundred dollars for a freezer, color TV, or stereo set is usually made only after very careful consideration by the consumer.

6. Mr. and Mrs. Theodore Abbott have recently purchased a Maynard Color TV-Stereo combination from you (Bel Air Appliance Center) for $980.00. You cautioned the Abbotts about picture reception, telling them that color was critical and the picture might not be sharp and clear because their home was located in a canyon area. They assured you their aerial was mounted at the top of a nearby hill and the signal should be excellent. Two months have gone by since they purchased their set, and you have received at least 15 calls from the Abbotts. Your installer has visited them three times and assures you "they're getting the best picture possible in their location."

Because the set is now definitely "used," you are reluctant to take it back; however, offer to do so, and give them full credit if they are not completely satisfied.

7. The Hi-Speed Corporation, a fabricator of piece parts for major aerospace companies, has made purchases from you for several years.

They recently ordered 800 pieces of your #210B strip aluminum according to their design specifications. They were, of course, going to cut this to size and further fabricate it into a finished piece part.

You have just received a phone call from them in which they tell you that a mistake was made. Because of the aircraft into which the part will go, the strips should have been made of your #410B titanium line. Hi-Speed indicates that it has 600 uncut pieces of the #210B on hand and would like them picked up.

Although you decide to go along with the request, you are irritated because you will be required to stock the 600 pieces and you aren't sure how long it will take for you to dispose of them. Of course, there is a handling and shipping charge which you will have to charge against Hi-Speed.

8. Approximately eight months ago Bellview Furniture opened for business. Their initial order from you was very large, and subsequent purchases have been excellent.

Mr. Karlton recently mentioned to your salesman that almost 100 per cent of his sales are for contemporary and modern lamps and he really made an error when he secured so many of the traditional styles in that first order.

Write Karlton and tell him if he has a quantity of those lamps in unopened cartons which are in first-class condition, you will accept their return for full credit. These are to be lamps secured only in Order 41368, of August 12 of last year.

9. Your computer equipment did it again! Campbell Can Corporation requested and received their order 4851 on September 3. It was made up of your special hi-strength coiled aluminum (catalog #202). This aluminum is used by Campbell to manufacture a specific item for the Army. For some reason an identical order was delivered on September 13. How or why it happened (a machine or human error?) seems immaterial. Offer to pick up the duplicate order and issue full credit.

10. Mr. and Mrs. Costello recently purchased a Kleen Time Vacuum Cleaner from your Chicago outlet. Unfortunately, neither the Chicago store or warehouse had model 421 in Sunburst Yellow in stock. You called both Milwaukee and Gary where you have other outlets. Both managers agreed to check and call you back. The Gary manager did call back and said he had the 421 and you requested that he ship it to Mrs. Costello. The Milwaukee manager apparently did not understand that he was to return your call. He shipped a 421 to Mrs. Costello also. Unfortunately, the second vacuum sweeper arrived when Mrs. Costello was not home. The driver left it with a neighbor.

Mrs. Costello is confused; she complains that she has two bills for $105.00 each and two vacuum cleaners. A letter of explanation seems to be in order.

11. On August 15, Mrs. Cleveland of Kelly Accounting Company called you and said that she had received a $168.50 bill for the office desk (model 21) which had been returned on August 1. You assured her the credit was probably "in the works." On September 17, she called and was quite angry as she complained about getting a "past due" bill for the same desk. You told her to forget it and you immediately sent a memo to the Accounts Receivable department explaining the situation.

Today, October 20, you receive a very cold, formal note from Kelly telling you they have now received a delinquency notice from you for an item they've never received. Enclosed were photo copies of the credit receipt signed by the driver who picked up the desk, as well as copies of all your past due notices.

Kelly has been an excellent customer for 12 years. From the tone of the letter, you have apparently lost them because of a silly bookkeeping error. The problem is all straightened out now in your company; see what you can do with a letter to Kelly.

12. Spear Engineering Corporation purchased 18 of your Model 48F Double-Purpose Pumps about three weeks ago. However, they recently called and complained that the pumps were not delivering the quantity of water needed or desired.

This concerned you because you were sure these models would serve the necessary purpose described at the time of purchase. You immediately sent one of your engineers out to Spear and he reported back the trouble was in the size of water line—¾″—hooked into the pumps. The pumps function best when the quantity of water is greater than what can be delivered by a ¾″ line. A 1½″ or 2″ line should have been used.

Write to Spear and make the strong suggestion that the size of line should be changed. You're sure that when that is done, the pumps will function much more efficiently.

CHAPTER FOURTEEN

Communicating an Unfavorable Response

Although we do not like to do it, we must sometimes tell people "no." This may make them unhappy; it may cause them to take their business elsewhere; or it may, because it is honest and sincere, gain us respect and good will. It is important, when saying no, to say it courteously, promptly, and with the recipient's point of view well in mind.

ANSWERING INQUIRIES AND REQUESTS: NO

Everyone who asks us for information feels that his inquiry is legitimate and that he should receive a favorable reply. Our primary objective in the unfavorable reply to an inquiry is to keep the good will of the person to whom we write while still not giving him the answer he desired. Saying "no" while retaining a friendly relationship requires a good deal of skill and tact. The following organizational plan will help accomplish the aims of a letter containing an unfavorable reply:

1. An introductory statement acknowledging the inquiry.
2. An explanation of the situation which makes the refusal necessary.
3. The refusal, implied or expressly stated.
4. A constructive suggestion.
5. A sales appeal, if applicable.
6. A friendly close.

Here are three examples of letters which follow the plan suggested above. Note that in each case the refusal is not stated directly and emphatically, but is implied because of the explanation which precedes it. When reasons are given for the refusal, it is not then usually necessary to tell the recipient of a letter "it is therefore impossible," "we must refuse," or "we cannot carry through your request." As a matter of fact, after most individuals read through a reasonable explanation, they will usually refuse themselves by some such silent statement as "Well, now I understand why they can't do this."

Dear Mr. Cooper:

Thank you very much for your recent inquiry concerning our management training programs here at Black Stone Steel Corporation. Your tentative plans sound excellent and we are sure that your personnel will benefit from the training which you intend to establish.

The course which we have worked out for the engineers in our Research and Development Department is the result of several years' effort. Inasmuch as some of the areas which it pursues are of a classified nature, because of either our designation or the government's, you can appreciate why it is not possible for us to send you a detailed outline of the program.

Although you did not indicate that you were interested in a training program for office personnel, I am sending you an outline of the course which we have in this area. It may be that this will prove of some value to you.

You may also wish to write to the College of Engineering, State University Extension Division. They have developed an off-campus program for engineers which may be of interest to you. May I also recommend an article in the June issue of *Engineering Research* which described several corporate training programs for engineering development. If you have not seen it, you may wish to check it.

If there is any other way, Mr. Cooper, in which we can assist you, I do hope you will write.

Dear Mr. Conkling:

Thank you very much for your recent inquiry concerning the Century Filing Cabinets which we sold you three years ago. You will recall that these were especially designed to be used for storage of outdated files and the cabinets themselves were relatively inexpensive.

We manufactured 5000 of these units, offered them to all our accounts, and quickly sold them. For us to go into production for the six units you require would make the price quite prohibitive.

We do have a suggestion, however, which we feel would be in your best interest. The All Purpose Filing Cabinet, which we now carry in stock, is similar to the Century except for a sturdier construction. I am sure it will suit your needs admirably and will prove to be almost exactly what you had in mind. We would also be happy to extend to you the quantity price on the All Purpose to make this offer still more attractive. On this basis the cost will be only $3.40 per unit more than the Century Filing Cabinet.

If you will call me collect, I will have these units shipped to you immediately.

Dear Mr. Harrison:

Thank you for inviting me to speak to your economics class. Unfortunately, I shall be attending a conference in Washington that week.

Perhaps you might try Professor Charles O. Sething at City University. He has written two books on the subject you are studying and he knows the subject thoroughly.

Do ask me again. And good luck.

In all these letters the explanation is complete and accurate. After each implied refusal a positive offer or suggestion is made. Notice that there are no statements which might arouse negative or unpleasant associations in the mind of the reader. Once the refusal is made, even if only by implication, it is not referred to again, and there are no abject apologies.

The reason for the refusal is given, the refusal is tactfully implied, and a suggestion is made by the writer in such a way that apparently the reader would be ill advised not to accept it.

Whether you can reply favorably or unfavorably to an inquiry or request is important, but it is also vital that the inquiry be answered promptly. Too often in industry today individuals are made to wait an unreasonable time after they have made an inquiry. When questions come in concerning products or services, make every effort to reply within twenty-four hours. If you can tell the inquirer "yes," so much the better, but do not make him wait several days to receive a "no, we're sorry." If you let him know your decision immediately, he can then take further action to benefit himself. He may wish to accept your counter-offer or, if you cannot meet his wishes, he then has adequate time to turn elsewhere. But if he is made to wait several days, and he then receives the "no," it will make him more unhappy. Perhaps it will be too late for him to make other arrangements.

Of course, we have always said that an immediate answer should be sent to every letter we receive, but in the case of an inquiry it is especially vital that a reply go out at once.

ACKNOWLEDGING ORDERS
WHEN THERE IS A PROBLEM

Not every order which comes in can be filled completely and efficiently. There are times when all the merchandise requested is not in stock; when the order isn't clear; when the credit status of the customer is questionable; and a half dozen other situations.

INCOMPLETE ORDERS

At times an order will be received that is either incomplete, indefinite, or not clear. It is usually unwise to guess at what the customer means, for if the wrong merchandise is shipped, it will be returned and ill will and expense will result. It is better to use a form acknowledgment which will correct this situation.

Dear Mr. Conway:

Thank you very much for your order of March 17, #204, which arrived today. All the merchandise that you requested is in stock and will be shipped via California Freight Lines.

You may recall that you listed four dozen American Beauty two-quart cooking containers. However, you did not indicate whether you prefer these with the copper or stainless steel bottoms. If you will check your preference on the enclosed air mail card, your order will be processed precisely as you desire and shipped immediately.

I am also enclosing a flyer on our new outdoor grill line. If you wish to order a quantity of these fast-moving items, you can do so on the same card.

Notice in the letter above that the approach is tactful and positive. The writer did not say, "You neglected," or "You forgot to list." He simply indicated that the oversight was inadvertent and as soon as the correct information was received, the merchandise would be shipped immediately.

MERCHANDISE TEMPORARILY OUT OF STOCK

The letter informing a customer that the merchandise he ordered is temporarily out of stock must be well written; if it is not, he may well attempt to find another source of supply. And the danger is that he may remain as a customer with that other source.

Dear Mr. Rattner:

Thank you for your Order #207 of June 25. All the items with one exception have been shipped and should arrive at your place of business no later than July 7.

In the case of the light gray shark-skin, #505, we are temporarily out of stock because of an unusually heavy demand for this fine fabric. However, our New England mill is sending us a replacement order of this particular merchandise via air freight. As soon as it arrives here, the 50 yards that you requested will be immediately cut and shipped to you. I would estimate that it should arrive no later than July 13.

Please call me collect if these arrangements are not satisfactory. If I do not hear from you, I shall assume that the suggestions made above are acceptable. We do want to do everything possible to meet your needs.

In this letter a strong positive tone is used. The writer did not say "we will hold the merchandise until we hear from you." He did say that the merchandise would be immediately shipped. As a matter of fact the entire tone of the letter gives the impression that it has never occurred to the writer that the customer may not accept the suggestions. And perhaps this approach will motivate the customer as the writer intended.

MERCHANDISE NOT HANDLED

A customer may request merchandise which the seller has never handled. This may come in as a separate order, or it may be one item in a large order.

What to do about this request? If we suggest a source of supply, we will create good will with the customer. However, there are some practical dangers inherent in this procedure. The source of supply will probably make every effort to satisfy the customer and it may be that we will lose the customer to the very source we suggested. On the other hand, business ethics almost demand that we make such recommendations.

A letter handling such a situation might follow the general outline suggested below.

Dear Mr. Hart:

We received your Order #202, dated January 14, and are happy to tell you that all the merchandise, with one exception, will be on its way to you by this afternoon.

Although we handle all types of office supplies, we have never stocked the Arco Filing Cabinet. This is recognized as an excellent unit; however, our customers' needs at this level have always been fulfilled by the Apex Line, which we do stock.

However, your request specifically lists your preference for the Arco. These may be secured from the Dearborn Office Furniture Corporation, located in Chicago.

It has been a pleasure doing business with you, and we know that you will be satisfied for many years to come with the consistently high quality of merchandise we handle and the competitive prices we offer.

When the merchandise requested by a customer is only related to the usual items handled, and does not compete directly with an item in stock, it is a good deal easier to make a recommendation.

Dear Mr. Flynn:

Thank you for your recent note inquiring as to whether or not we handle automobile seat covers as well as our usual line of automotive accessories.

As you may know, we stock over 5000 parts for cars. We have considered putting in a line of seat covers, safety belts, and so on, but have not as yet.

Through our own experience, we have found that the Los Angeles Auto Seat Company is an excellent firm. The quality of their merchandise is high and their prices quite acceptable. I recommend that you get in touch with them. Ask specifically for Mr. Kameron, who has always given us excellent service.

Enclosed you will find our latest parts catalog. Check through it; we know you will find many items of interest.

In some instances, a firm will secure the item (which it does not handle) from a supplier and forward it to its customer. This is a matter of courtesy —usually no profit is made—but a third party (who might be a competitor) is not thereby introduced.

ORDERS WHICH MUST BE REFUSED

There are a variety of different reasons why orders must sometimes be refused, even when the merchandise is in stock and available for immediate shipment. A few such cases are:

1. The buyer is a poor credit risk.
2. The buyer has exceeded his credit limit.
3. Company regulations concerning a franchise or distributorship agreements would be violated.
4. Filling the order might be contrary to government regulations.
5. Filling the order would be unprofitable because of the limited quantity ordered, distances to be shipped, or modifications requested.
6. Extremely limited supply in stock which must be retained for steady accounts.

Dear Mr. Calloway:

Thank you for the completed order and credit application blank. Both were received today.

We have checked the credit sources which you have listed, and we find that your references speak highly of you. However, your ratio of assets to liabilities, plus the debts which you have incurred in your new location, would seem to indicate that it would be in your best interests to purchase on a cash basis.

The advantages which are received from this arrangement are important. A 2 per cent cash discount, low inventory, and no end-of-month bills, all add up to money-making features.

Please call me collect and I will see to it that the merchandise you ordered is on its way to you, on a c.o.d. basis, almost immediately.

Dear Mr. Franklin:

We were delighted to receive your request to stock the new Precision Watch line of the American Jewelry Corporation.

Some months ago we visited Indianapolis and at that time selected twelve jewelry outlets to handle the Precision Watch. Unfortunately, we did not get in touch with you. However, we did assure each of the twelve dealers that Indianapolis would have a maximum of one dozen franchises. In all fairness to these outlets, therefore, and in conformity with our agreement, we can open no others at this time.

If, however, one of these twelve does not wish to retain his franchise, we will immediately get in touch with you to determine your availability.

We certainly appreciate your interest in the Precision Line. We have enclosed the new American Watch catalog in the hope that you will find other non-franchise items of interest to you.

Dear Mr. O'Connor:

Thank you for your request of April 30 for 2 dozen #307 kitchen utensil sets. I have checked our files and found that this is the first order we have had the pleasure of receiving from you. You are, therefore, perhaps not completely familiar with some of our operations which have been designed for our customers' benefit.

In an effort to secure shipping and office savings, we have established $75 as the minimum amount for any order. The savings which are thereby secured are passed on to our customers. We are sending you a copy of our general catalog via air mail. When you check through it, I am sure you will find many cost-saving items which your customers will want to purchase. If you will be kind enough to supplement your original order so that the minimum figure is $75, we would be delighted to process it immediately and ship it c.o.d.

These are a few of the acknowledgment situations which arise. Notice that they are all handled tactfully, positively, and with a strong sales orientation.

HANDLING ADJUSTMENTS:
CLAIM NOT GRANTED

The only cases in which a claim would not be granted are when the buyer is definitely at fault (and, as we have seen, not always then) or when there is no real "fault" but, because of government or industry regulations, the claim cannot be granted.

As is the case with the letter granting an adjustment even when the buyer is at fault, the explanation of a refusal to grant a claim should precede the actual refusal. Although people would not enter claims if they did not wish them to be granted, they will understand and accept a refusal if it is presented courteously and reasonably. Such a letter should follow this plan:

1. A statement referring to the specific transaction.
2. A statement explaining tactfully and discreetly how the buyer is at fault. Care should be taken to avoid putting him in a situation where he may lose face.
3. The refusal, either implied or expressed.
4. A sales appeal, if appropriate.
5. A friendly close.

Dear Mrs. Hardy:

We received your letter of April 15 and the package containing our Beach Fun bathing suit which you recently purchased for your daughter.

We were, of course, concerned to learn that she did not find the suit satisfactory and wished to exchange it for a different model. Under ordinary circumstances we do everything possible to please our customers in the matter of adjustments, for we recognize how important you and thousands of other purchasers of our product are to the Beach Fun Company.

Immediately after your daughter's swim suit arrived, we sent it to our Customer Service Department. They have indicated to us that the garment has been worn several times. This presents a problem, for in keeping with the statutes of this state, garments of this type may not be restocked and sold after they have been used. I am sure that you were not aware of this regulation, but because of it you will understand why we are not sending out the model you requested in exchange.

The suit you sent to us is being returned along with the addresses of several dealers who handle the Beach Fun line in your city. We know that you will find all the latest styles and fashions in beach wear on display in our dealers' stores.

At times the sting of the refusal may be lessened by offering some concession, a free item, or a carefully structured sales appeal. This has been done in the two letters which follow.

Dear Mr. Shay:

We received your letter of November 5, in which you asked us to credit your account for $22.50 for one dozen large bottles of Sunshine Vitamin A tablets.

For the protection of you as well as our other accounts, we are very careful to follow the FDA ruling on returning items of this type. All of our literature states the industry-wide ruling that "pharmaceuticals must be returned unopened within ten days of purchase."

The Sunshine Vitamins which you sent back were purchased twelve months ago. The potency of this item has now been lessened; in addition, the return policy mentioned above also applies. The items which you sent us, therefore, will be returned with your order #2029, which is due to be shipped at the end of this week.

I am enclosing a special bulletin on Clear Sight sunglasses. These fine optical glasses are manufactured by one of America's leading lens companies. Check the price list enclosed and you will find that all listings are 30 per cent below those which are printed in our summer sales catalog. Please pick up the phone and call me collect; tell me precisely how many dozen of each model you can use and I will add them to your order, plus a free aluminum Clear Sight counter display stand.

Dear Mr. Stark:

We received your letter of December 3 concerning your request for credit to your account for $28.50.

As you are probably aware, the discount policy throughout the furniture field permits a 2 per cent reduction when bills are paid within ten days of date of invoice. The amount thereby secured is passed on to our customers and represents our saving in billing and handling.

In the case of your July and August orders, with which this $28.50 discount is concerned, we have checked and found that they were inadvertently paid 18 (#209), 16 (#402), and 22 (#991) days after the discount period. This oversight in handling bills payable sometimes occurs and has certainly happened to us. Nevertheless, you will understand that in all fairness to our other accounts, as well as to our own position in this case, we cannot agree to your request.

We think you will feel as we do that this action is equitable; however, if some special circumstances are involved in your case, we will be very happy to review the facts.

I have enclosed our new brochure on the Patio Aluminum line of outdoor funiture. Our preferred customers may take a 10 per cent discount from the prices listed from now through the end of the month. Why not indicate your needs on the enclosed order form and return it so that we can ship you a quantity of this high-quality, excellent mark-up line of furniture.

Although these letters are refusals, the positive approach in the last paragraph or two seems to say to the reader, "Business is business; we are sorry that we must say 'no,' but we believe you will understand. Now let's continue our transactions."

QUESTIONS FOR STUDY

I. Offer your constructive criticism of the following letters. Remember to indicate which sections of the letters deserve favorable comments, as well as where improvements can be made. Be as specific as possible in your evaluations.

1. Dear Mrs. Tedry:

I was happy to receive your letter and learn that you are doing so many interesting things in the health sciences in your sixth-grade class.

I agree with you that your students would benefit from a visit to our hospital to visit the labs, pharmacy, food preparation center, a vacant surgical room, the emergency center, and one of the patient floors. However, we do have a City Department of Health ruling to contend with: it strictly prohibits children fourteen years of age or less from visiting areas where patients are confined.

Although this ruling does not apply to other areas of the hospital, I wonder how much each child would really observe if he had to compete with thirty others. And of course there is the factor of the slight disruption of hospital routine created by such a large group.

May I suggest an alternate plan, Mrs. Tedry? We have an excellent film titled, "A Complex but Gentle Giant." This tells the story of what goes on in a large, busy hospital. Although it was made by the American Nursing Council and is largely used for recruiting nurses, your students would find it very valuable and interesting. The camera gives the viewer close-ups of all types of procedures and techniques and the commentary is excellent.

One of our staff could bring the film to your class, or you may, if you wish, use our hospital auditorium. In both cases, a competent person would be present to answer questions.

Just call me at ER2-4132, extension 259, and we can make arrangements for the showing of the film at a time that will suit your schedule.

2. Dear Mr. Easton:

I have just been informed by our Shipping and Receiving Department that you returned for credit cartons containing eight #208 room heaters and five table model AM-FM Zenith radios, #500, on October 12.

Because you have been in business for many years it would seem to me that you would be aware that once merchandise has been removed from the original carton (as these have been), and put on display (as these apparently have been), they can hardly be returned. Furthermore our return policy (merchandise must be returned within 10 days of receipt) has obviously been violated as we've shipped none of these items since June 1 of this year.

I would also like to point out that three of the radios are slightly damaged. So for all these reasons you can see why we must refuse your request although we are delighted to cooperate in any way possible with good customers such as you.

3. Dear Sir:

Thank you for your recent inquiry concerning our "Travel The Wide-Wide World" display which was exhibited during the recent World Trade Fair in London.

I would be the first to agree that it is a creative and imaginative display, and we are flattered that you would like to incorporate it into your County Fair Program. However, it would be almost impossible for us to remove all our company markings and insignia from the models. Of course we recognize that you could not very well permit a display to advertise one airline without requesting other firms to participate on an equal basis.

And in addition, we have already scheduled our exhibit for the Annual Aviation Week Conference to be held in New York during the same week as your County Fair.

In any event, we are very happy that you wrote us, and we hope you will give us another opportunity to cooperate with you in some other way.

4. Dear Mrs. Gray:

Thank you for your letter of March 4. Certainly the work in which you and the other members of the Midwest Women's Association are engaged is most commendable. Your efforts in behalf of physically handicapped children are extremely important contributions to our society, and we are all indebted to you.

As you can appreciate, we receive several requests each day for contributions of our appliances to be used in fund-raising efforts. However, the number involved is prohibitive and would result in additional costs which we would have to pass on to the consumer; at the same time we would be placed in a non-competitive position as compared to other firms.

However, we do have a plan which other organizations have found helpful. Two years ago we commissioned the famous chef, Henry Bils, to write *Favorite French Dishes*. This 300-page, hard-cover book is fully illustrated in color. We will be happy to send you twelve copies free of charge. They may be sold for a minimum of $5.00 each and the funds added to your treasury.

You should receive these within a few days; please accept them with our best wishes for the success of your Spring Fund Drive.

5. Dear Mrs. Corley:

Thank you very much for your kind invitation to speak to the Sponsors of the Children's Health Center on March 8. I am indeed flattered.

As you may have heard, a national meeting on Children's Respiratory Diseases is scheduled for the first two weeks in March at the New York Medical Center. I was designated as our medical school's representative, and accepted some time ago.

May I have a "rain check"? I shall be happy to cooperate for one of your future meetings.

6. Dear Mr. Campbell:

Thank you for your Order 421F of March 28. All the merchandise which you requested is in stock, and will be shipped on April 5.

In the case of the 12 dozen number 2522 waste baskets, we do have a small problem. Did you prefer them in walnut or mahogany finish? Or did you prefer six dozen of each? (See page 62 of our catalog for full description.)

Please call me collect so we may complete the processing of your order and have the merchandise on its way to you just as quickly as possible.

7. Dear Mr. Fairmont:

We appreciated your order 578FF and the completed credit application form.

In some thirty years in the furniture industry, we have found that a new retail business requires about one year to become established. It is after that period of time that an open account best serves the retailer's purpose.

We note that although you have been in your present location for only four months, you are doing very well. We would therefore be delighted to have you resubmit your application in November so that we may take action on it at that time.

In the meanwhile we want to call your attention to our 2 per cent discount on all cash or c.o.d. orders and our 72-hour service. We stand ready to serve you with quality merchandise at competitive prices. Please call Kelly's for outstanding values.

8. Dear Mr. Carmichael:

We were certainly concerned when we received your claim for replacement of the 12 Electro-Mark III switches you purchased on April 28.

Because we wanted to know precisely what happened to cause problems, we immediately requested one of our engineers, Mr. Costello, to visit your plant, pick up the switches, and determine how we could help.

Mr. Costello talked to your Mr. Klein and found that these switches were used in conjunction with your Double Mixer Units. These are powered by 3 h.p. motors, and it is because of this that problems arose.

All Mark III switches, as the instructions note, are rated for use with motors up to 2 h.p. only. For heavier requirements, our Mark IV and V switches should be utilized.

We are processing an order for 12 Mark V switches at a special price of $4.25 each. Please call me collect, and I will ship the switches immediately.

Our spring catalog is enclosed; I think you'll be especially interested in the automatic conveyors and the prices listed on page 21. Pick up the phone and we'll enter your request immediately.

9. Dear Mr. Kavely:

We received the carton containing the Armstrong Toaster which you returned to us. We can appreciate your feelings inasmuch as you purchased the unit just four weeks ago.

We have checked the mechanism and we found that the three ceramic plates are broken and the heating rods have been split away from the wiring. Apparently this unit was dropped or inadvertently struck by a heavy object. Perhaps you did not notice, but the exterior base is badly dented; this may have been the point of impact.

Had the malfunction been due to faulty mechanism or production, we would immediately comply with your request. However, you can appreciate our position in this case. Your toaster has been repackaged and is being returned via parcel post.

Enclosed is our new folder, "Hot Weather Recipes," which we know you will enjoy reading and using.

10. Dear Mr. Kingly:

We received the foot support brace which you returned to us.

We are sorry that it has given you no comfort during the last two months. However, we are at a loss to know what to do with the item. Surely this soiled unit cannot be returned to stock and sold again. In addition, local City Health Department rules make it impossible for us to resell an article of this type.

We are returning the brace and we know you will understand why we cannot take favorable action in this case.

II. Complete any of the following problems assigned. You may wish to review the chapter and note key points before solving the problem.

1. You have just received a request from the Bellview Children's Aid Society to use your company's parking lot area for a Fund Raising Pancake Breakfast affair. You check with your Safety Officer and he tells you that the firm's liability insurance policy does not permit the parking area to be used for "games, recreation, or social affairs." This is due to the severity of injuries which might result from accidents taking place on the hard surface. Although you would like to cooperate, you fear that such use in violation of the policy might result in its being cancelled. Write to the Bellview Children's Aid Society and tactfully refuse. Perhaps the local park could be used instead.

2. Mr. Connory of the physics department of Jefferson High School would like to bring his Physics Club (48 members) through the electronic components department of your company. Unfortunately some of your products are classified as "secret" by the Department of Defense and tours are not permitted without official Washington clearance. Perhaps Mr. Connory would like to have his group hear an address by your Research and Development manager; that can be arranged.

3. Franklin Junior College is arranging a major affair for Saturday, November 21. There will be a beauty parade prior to the big game, half-time festivities and other events. As a matter of fact the governor has accepted an invitation to attend. The chairman of the program has written and asked your Chevrolet agency to supply three white convertibles for "Official Use" for that day. Arrangements for these must be made through Detroit; you don't have the cars and even if you did, you would be reluctant to take a chance on new vehicles being damaged. Your own car is a light gray convertible which may be used if the committee wishes.

4. Your research department has perfected a new method for packaging very fragile glass equipment used in outdoor signs. Very general aspects of the method were described in a recent issue of *Packaging Methods*. Several companies have written asking for specific details, and samples of the packaging materials.
Actually the method and materials are so new and excellent, your firm plans to secure a patent and market the procedure commercially.

Prepare one letter which can be sent to all those who have and will inquire, and tactfully refuse the request for the present time.

5. Because you are a relatively large mail-order house, you receive several hundred orders from consumers each day. About 3 per cent of these orders neglect to include one or more important facts: color, size, or model of item; shipping instructions, etc. Prepare a form letter in which you acknowledge the order but request additional information necessary to process it.

6. In very few cases, in the same operation described in problem 5 above, the customer forgets to include his money although his letter or completed order form indicates that he believes that he has. Prepare another guide or form letter which acknowledges the order but refuses to fill it until the proper sum of money is received.

7. Consumers will sometimes write directly to you and request that you ship one of your appliances to them (TV set, stereo, or radio). They will even include a check at times or request c.o.d. delivery. You are a manufacturer and sell your products through some 25,000 outlets of various types in the United States. Write a letter which refuses the order but encloses a booklet which lists "your nearby Conroy Dealers."

8. Your weekly newspaper ads carry a brief statement inviting consumers to enjoy the convenience of a "Martin's Charge Account." As a result, you receive about 20 applications each week. One or two of these, after investigation, must be turned down. Complete a letter of refusal to the consumers involved.

9. Mr. Jarwith has purchased furniture from you for his two busy San Francisco stores for two years. During that entire period he has always paid for all merchandise on a c.o.d. basis Although you and he have discussed an open account, he has always said, "Oh no; I pay cash or I don't buy."

Today an order from him arrived for $1245 worth of merchandise. Attached was a note which said, "Please charge and ship immediately."

A credit check requires at least seven days. Write and refuse to send the merchandise out immediately on a credit basis. Perhaps Jarwith can wait a week, or perhaps he will accept this order on a c.o.d. basis and charge those in the future.

10. Talbott Drugs has written you and requested one of your free

"Diet for Health" signs. These are electric, automatic, and may be mounted in the diet food section of a store. Your customers that purchase upwards of $1500 worth of Slim Line Diet products per month are eligible for a free sign. This is noted in your sales literature. However, Mr. Talbott's operation is small; his purchases, although steady, never exceed $500 per month. Write and refuse Talbott's request. The signs are available to you at $79.00 each, and you secure them from White Sign Corporation.

11. Although your firm has a liberal adjustment policy, you sometimes have problems with accounts that do not abide by your policy. Claims for damaged appliances from your accounts must be entered within ten days of receipt of merchandise and if the claim is over $25.00, it is subject to inspection.

Barber's Appliance Outlet has had numerous claims, most of which you have accepted. However, today's letter from him tells you he received an RCA TV set from you last month (35 days ago) which he sold to a nearby bar. He said the cabinet was badly damaged and he sold it at $50 below cost. Because the set was to be mounted above the bar for customers' viewing, the appearance of the cabinet was not very important.

Write to Barber and note your policy. Refuse to grant the claim but remember that he has been a fairly good customer for some years.

12. Your department store handles a full line of small appliances. From time to time an individual will secure item(s) from discount outlets and attempt to return them to you for full retail price credit. To avoid this, all small appliances which you sell are identified on the base with your store insignia. This is a barely visible mark. Prepare a letter of refusal to be sent to those persons who mail an appliance in and request an adjustment even though the item was not secured from one of your stores. You should not assume that every one who requests an adjustment does so with intent to defraud. Perhaps some individuals received such appliances as gifts and were told the item was purchased from you.

CHAPTER FIFTEEN

Credit and
Credit Communications

Over the years, the American economy has become more and more credit-oriented. Consumer, commercial, industrial, investment, and government credit levels have risen remarkably. "Buy now, pay later" has become the watchword. Credit permits us to enjoy luxuries now—cars, boats, and vacation trips for family recreation; appliances of all types for the home; and orthodontia, music lessons, art training, and college education for our children's welfare.

At the industrial-commercial level, we see 50-story skyscrapers going up like mushrooms, factories expanding in all directions, and companies spawning plant additions daily. Businessmen can carry an inventory much larger than their cash level ordinarily would permit; they are therefore in a position to secure many more sales. All this is accomplished on the basis of credit.

In commenting on levels of credit, Beckman and Bartels said:

> The extent to which credit is used is an indication of its importance in business. There are no data to show the *total volume* of credit business, but careful estimates based on the United States census data indicate that over 25 per cent of all retail store sales are on credit and that about 85 per cent of all sales by wholesalers and manufacturers' sales branches are on credit. It is further estimated that between 90 and 95 per cent of all business transactions involve the use of some credit instrument, including checks.[1]

The figures cited above are staggering. As our society becomes more credit-oriented, there is perhaps need for re-evaluation of our credit

1. T. N. Beckman and R. Bartels, *Credits and Collections in Theory and Practice* (New York: McGraw-Hill Book Company, Inc., 1955), p. 8.

structure. Certainly an economic system that has such a wide credit foundation may at times be in a state that is less than firm. The thoughtful student and responsible businessman have an obligation to make their views known on the benefits and dangers of credit.

The fact that an extremely small percentage of the credit extended is written off as a loss certainly indicates the basic integrity of people and the efficiency of the credit system. But granting and accepting credit are not to be taken lightly. Even the most honest man, through negligence, a business situation, or the times, may not always be able to meet his obligations. The credit manager is the one who must watch every step of the credit process to ensure maximum benefits to his own company as well as to the credit user.

Credit is an estimate of the ability and the desire of the individual or company to pay debts at a later date. This ability and desire are usually weighted by the credit manager on a careful analysis of the classic C's: capital, character, conditions, and capacity.

The granting of credit is a very carefully organized procedure. At the commercial level, we have credit reporting firms such as Dun and Bradstreet issuing thousands of reports each year. At the consumer level, there are dozens of organizations which can supply credit data reports on most of the adults in the United States.

THE CREDIT MANAGER

The credit manager is surely one of the key individuals in an enterprise. The manner in which he administers his department has a profound effect on the progress of the firm. The credit manager who grants credit too liberally can overextend the resources of a company. On the other hand, if his viewpoint is very conservative, he will not extend the quantity of credit he should, and competitors will secure the accounts he was reluctant to underwrite. In such instances his firm's sales may not advance or may even decline appreciably.

Management today recognizes the need for a thorough, progressive, carefully administered and controlled credit system. In this system, the credit manager plays the dominant role—and he frequently does this through the letters and reports he writes.

Among the various situations he encounters which require correspondence are:

1. Acknowledging applicants' requests for credit.
2. Acknowledging receipt of credit data.
3. Requesting credit information from references furnished by applicants.

4. Sending credit information in response to requests from other credit managers.
5. Granting credit.
6. Refusing credit.

ACKNOWLEDGING A REQUEST FOR CREDIT

In both consumer and commercial situations, corporations often encourage customers to open charge accounts. The obvious reason for such action is the knowledge that the customer who enjoys a credit line with a firm will usually supply most of his needs from that company. Furthermore, the mechanics of a sale are often expedited when credit, rather than cash, is the basis for the transaction.

At times a regular cash customer will ask that a credit account be opened or a new customer will make such a request. In both cases, the acknowledgment should be swift and courteous.

Dear Mrs. Schnee:

Thank you very much for requesting that we add your name to the list of over 200,000 Chicagoans who have charge accounts with Conway's.

We are enclosing one of our standard forms which we would like to have you complete and return to us within 10 days.

The information secured will, of course, be kept confidential.

We will write to you approximately two weeks after you have completed and returned the enclosed form to us.

In the meantime, please visit your nearest Conway's and take advantage of our daily specials on quality merchandise.

Dear Mr. Ragan:

Thank you for your recent request for information on a credit account with our firm. You may be sure we will be proud to add your name to our growing list of satisfied customers.

I have enclosed one of our standard application forms. Please complete and return it to us with your financial statement (certified if possible). All data received will be handled in confidence, of course.

For over four generations, Bakers has brought quality furniture to dealers throughout the United States. We are proud to sell this prestige line, and we know you will be, too.

Under separate cover I have sent you our new wholesale catalog and price list. We know you will find many items listed which you will want to include in your next order.

Dear Mr. Scott:

Thank you very much for your order of January 14 for various items in our Atlantic Line and your request to open a credit account.

As you know, credit information is needed. Will you, therefore, complete the enclosed form or send us a copy of your most recent financial statement. Of course this will be handled in confidence.

Your order will be processed and shipped immediately after an evaluation is made. If you would like to have the merchandise immediately, we will be happy to ship it to you on a c.o.d. basis less our usual 2 per cent discount. Please use the enclosed airmail return postal card to let us know your preference.

Notice that in all the letters above the tone is optimistic and positive. In the one to Mr. Scott, for example, the statement "Your order will be processed and shipped immediately after . . ." is much better than "We will hold your order until . . . ."

ACKNOWLEDGING RECEIPT OF CREDIT DATA

In some industries or even consumer situations, fifteen to thirty days may be required to secure the information needed to make a decision. In such cases it is sometimes wise to let the applicant know that his request for credit is being processed. Such a letter is especially necessary if it is obvious that an unusual delay will be encountered in securing all data necessary.

Dear Mr. Kingston:

Thank you very much for sending us the completed credit application form and a copy of your financial statement.

An evaluation is now being carried through; you will hear from us just as quickly as possible.

We have already requested our salesman in your area to stop in, introduce himself to you, and leave you a copy of our latest catalog. I'm sure you will find Carl Downes to be most cooperative and eager to fill your needs for all types of Carlton Kitchen Ware.

We are certainly looking forward to a mutually satisfactory business relationship.

REQUESTING CREDIT INFORMATION

When you request information on an individual or a company that has applied to you for credit, you are basically sending out an inquiry letter. A vital attribute of such a letter is that it be easy to answer. To achieve this, the letter can be reduced to a few courteous statements with room provided for fill-ins, or a complete form can be attached to a brief cover letter.

For a Consumer Credit Applicant:

Gentlemen:

The above named individual has applied for a retail credit account with us.

Your comments on his financial responsibility, his credit reputation, and his payment record with you will prove very valuable to us.

The information you send will be kept confidential.

A stamped envelope is enclosed for your convenience. Thank you for your cooperation.

When did applicant have an account with you?
_____

What item(s) was purchased? _____
His high credit was $_____
His payments were _____   _____   _____
                      prompt   slow   delinquent
Does he have an open account with you now? ___   ___
                                        Yes   No

Other Comments: _____
_____
_____

For a Wholesale Credit Applicant:

Gentlemen:

The _____ Company has listed your firm as one with which they do business. We would greatly appreciate your giving us information on your business relations with this organization.

If you will complete the enclosed form and return it in the envelope provided, we will be most appreciative. You may be sure all information supplied will be kept confidential.

This form accompanied the letter above:

TO   Carlton Manufacturing Corp.
_____

CUSTOMER   Penway Industrial Service
_____

ACCOUNT HISTORY

Sold Since _____ Terms _____
Highest Recent Credit _____
Owing on O/A _____ On Notes _____
Past Due on O/A _____ On Notes _____

414

MANNER OF PAYMENT

_____	Discounts
_____	Prompt & Satisfactory
_____	Days slow, considered good
_____	Days slow, considered unsatisfactory
_____	Pays C.O.D., customer's request
_____	Pays C.O.D., our requirement
_____	Placed for collection
_____	Collected by attorney

COMMENTS _____

_____

_____

Authorized Signature _____

SUPPLYING CREDIT INFORMATION

Quite frequently the credit manager is asked to send information on his accounts to other places of business. Usually this requires little more than completing and signing a form. At other times the request is broad and the respondent is asked to send "background credit data." Usually a brief letter, such as the following, will prove satisfactory:

Gentlemen:

We are happy to send you confidential credit information on The Mary Lee Dress Shop.

Business Relationship: Since 1967
High Credit: $550.00
Payment Record: Prompt

If there are other specific data which you require, we will attempt to cooperate in every way possible.

When it is necessary to return a negative evaluation, care should be exercised in the choice of words. Statements should be qualified and opinions stated tactfully. There are also legal implications involved which suggest the use of discretion.

Gentlemen:

We received your request of January 4 for credit information on the Campton Company.

We have had some difficulty in collecting from this firm since they opened an account with us 18 months ago. At the present time all our transactions with them are handled on a C.O.D. basis.

Some companies, in sending out replies of this nature, feel it is wise to omit the name of the firm on which the evaluation is made. A reference, instead, is made to the date of the inquiry.

GRANTING CREDIT

As noted earlier, it is always quite easy to tell people, "Yes, you can have what you asked for." But in the credit letter, we should also attempt to build sales and good will.

This letter has still a further task, and that is to set down the terms of credit in a clear and specific manner. This is to ensure prompt and correct payment and to avoid misunderstandings (and ill will) at a later time concerning due dates, discount privileges, and related factors.

To the Consumer Applicant:

Dear Mrs. Rattner:

It is a pleasure to add your name to our list of charge account customers.

We have enclosed two charge plates: one for your use and one for another member of your family. All you need do next time you shop at Daro's Department Stores is to select your merchandise, request that it be charged, and hand the salesperson your Daro Charge Plate. It's that simple.

You will receive a bill between the first and the third of each month. Payments should be made prior to the fifteenth of that same month.

We know you will enjoy shopping at Daro's, for every effort

is made to keep our quality high and the variety of merchandise extensive.

Whenever you have a question concerning merchandise which you have purchased, please do not hesitate to visit our Customer Service Department. Our watchword is "Customer Satisfaction" and we will do everything possible to merit your complete confidence.

I do hope you will call on me if I can be of service at any time in the future.

To the Commercial Applicant:

Dear Mr. Kelly:

It's a pleasure to open a credit account for your firm with Kingsley Lumber Corporation.

All you need do after giving your Kingsley salesman an order in the future is to say "charge it." He will be happy to do so.

All bills are payable by the 12th of the month for merchandise purchased during the previous month. Bills handled in this manner enjoy a profit-making 2 per cent discount. Net payments are required by the 25th.

We are also pleased to offer you many other Kingsley services. Our Consumer Sales Advisory Department representative will visit you periodically or when you have some special problem. And the Kingsley Display Department will supply you with sales-building materials for your place of business and items for direct mail distribution.

We are here to serve you and we hope you'll give us many opportunities to do just that in the years to come.

Dear Mr. Jameson:

Welcome to Denton's Drug Distributors' list of satisfied credit accounts.

For almost 75 years we have served the retail drug merchants of the Chicago area to their complete satisfaction. We think you'll agree that "Denton's Always Satisfies" as you become better acquainted with our extensive line of quality merchandise offered at very competitive and profit-building prices.

In the enclosed brochure you will find our payment and credit policies. Read them carefully so that you may profit from our discounts and understand our credit payment practices. May we suggest that this booklet be filed for ready reference.

In addition to quality products, we offer you a complete window and display department, a direct mail and sales promotion advisory service, and participation in our yearly retail management seminar and workshop.

We are delighted to have you aboard, Mr. Jameson. We look forward to a long and pleasant cruise.

From the letters above, it is easy to see that a pattern is followed in letters granting credit:

1. A friendly opening.
2. The credit grant (this may very well be part of the opening).
3. A clear and specific statement concerning company credit policies and practices (or reference to a booklet describing these in detail).
4. A brief paragraph describing other company services and designed to build good will.
5. A friendly close.

If possible, these letters should be individually typed and signed. It isn't necessary to make each one different; they can be typed from a guide letter, but the use of the recipient's name and some personal reference is wise. This can be easily accommodated in a guide letter.[2]

REFUSING CREDIT

It is always difficult to say "No" to people, and especially so when an evaluation of the applicant's personal character is involved. The problems of ego involvement enter into the case.

The organizational pattern for this letter is similar to all refusal correspondence. The key is to explain the reason for the negative action before the request for credit is denied.

2. See Chapter Nineteen for a discussion of guide letters.

Refusing the Consumer Credit Applicant:

Dear Mrs. Larkin:

Thank you very much for your recent request for a charge account with Sanders' Shopping Center.

We have carefully checked the information you submitted and found that you now carry several open accounts with rather heavy balances.

Rather than burden you with an additional account which will require your end-of-month attention, we suggest that you continue on a cash basis with Sander's. In this way your transactions will be completed immediately. As you know, our various service departments will be delighted to assist you.

I am enclosing our January Brochure describing our Yearly White Sale. I'm sure you'll want to take advantage of Sander's fine quality linen and bath supplies at remarkable savings.

At times the credit manager will find that the information he secures on a consumer is so negative that to explain or mention it as a basis for the refusal would be unwise and might very well arouse antagonism. After all, how can you point out that you've checked and found Mrs. Smith to be a consistently delinquent account and an overall poor risk? In such instances it is wiser not to explain but simply to refuse tactfully. This will save face for the applicant and perhaps serve to retain his or her good will.

Dear Mrs. Halsted:

Thank you very much for your recent request for credit with Wilson Women's Wear Shoppes.

We have carefully checked the information you supplied. We do feel that at this time you would be wiser to continue making your purchases on a cash basis. In this way you will be able to take advantage of the many services cash buying affords. If, at some time in the future, you care to reapply for a charge account, we will be delighted to again evaluate your request.

We are enclosing two tickets for our January 20 Cruise Wear Show. Please bring a guest and join us at 3:00 P.M. for this exclusive gala showing of designer fashions under the direction of Madame Blanc of Paris. Refreshments will be served and we know you will find the afternoon most enjoyable.

In the refusal to the consumer, extra care must be taken in diction, for such a person may not be as understanding or as objective about a refusal as a company accountant or executive might be.

Refusing the Commercial Credit Applicant:

In this situation, the usual refusal pattern is almost invariably followed. However, it is important to project a sincere "you" attitude. Perhaps it would be to his advantage to use an open account for his purchases in the future, but at the moment, it is your sincere and considered opinion that buying on a C.O.D. or cash-with-order basis is in his best interests. You must explain your refusal and yet retain his good will. Just one or two incorrectly chosen words will turn your explanation into a lecture and antagonize him.

Examine the three letters which follow. The first one offers a brief explanation and the refusal. The second letter is a good deal more involved, and yet it carries a note of sincerity. Whether to use the first or the second type of letter will depend largely on your evaluation of the recipient and what approach he might accept or reject.

The third letter is unsatisfactory. It reflects a lecturing, pompous, "we" attitude approach that is sure to bring the irritated comment, "I asked for credit. Tell me 'yes' or 'no' but don't give me a lecture on how to run my business!"

Dear Mr. Larson:

Thank you very much for sending us the credit information which we requested.

We have carefully evaluated the data and we are happy to tell you that your references speak highly of you. However, your asset-liability ratio is such that we suggest you buy on a C.O.D. or cash-with-order basis.

This will result in an immediate savings of 2 per cent, the maintenance of current inventory levels, and rapid service.

Your order has been prepared and can be shipped immediately. Just call collect and we'll send the merchandise right out.

I've also enclosed a flyer describing our "special sale to special customers." Why not add a few of these items to your order when you call me?

Dear Mr. Klein:

Thank you very much for completing and returning to us the credit information we requested.

We have carefully evaluated all the data you sent and we feel that it would be to your best interests to remain on a cash basis at this time. Let me explain the reasons for this decision and I think you'll agree with my suggestion.

Your ratio of assets to liabilities is below the generally accepted level of 2 to 1. In addition, you are just getting settled in the community and you have incurred a good many expenses through the purchase of new fixtures, remodeling costs, advertising, and heavy initial purchases.

Cash buying for the next year or so will give you the advantage of an immediate 2 per cent discount, lowered inventory levels, and no end-of-month bookkeeping problems.

We sincerely believe that you will be able to build your credit rating and fill your merchandise needs through this method of buying.

Our salesman, Bob Campbell, is scheduled to call on you at the end of this week. I know you'll be interested in the specials he has on small appliances. With the wedding season fast approaching, I'm sure you will find many products that will move rapidly as gift items. Bob will explain our advertising allowances which are available and which help boost your profit margin. And of course, he will be happy to give you additional information concerning cash buying.

Please call me collect, Mr. Klein, if you have any comments or questions regarding our business arrangements. We want to work with you in every possible way.

Dear Mr. Mills:

We received your letter and completed credit information forms. We have examined these and have concluded that you would benefit from buying on a cash basis.

As you are probably aware, you are thoroughly over-extended at the present time. If you could secure $5000 on loan and pay off some of your bills, you would be moving in the right direction. Of course, you should not get involved with an unusually high rate of interest, for that will only increase your burden. Perhaps increasing your home mortgage might be a solution.

We also feel that the receivables which you have are probably higher than they should be. Why not tighten up on your debtors and secure cash in this manner?

We have the merchandise in stock about which you inquired. May we send it out on a C.O.D. basis?

Notice in each of the three letters above that we do have an explanation and a refusal. However, the tone conveyed differs appreciably in each letter, and will govern the reader's response—whether favorable or unfavorable.

This credit letter is a vital one. It must be well written, for the applicant we refuse today may be a most desirable credit account in five years. Thus it is essential to secure and maintain his good will.

QUESTIONS FOR STUDY

I. Offer your constructive criticism of the following letters. Remember to indicate which sections of the letters deserve favorable comments, as well as where improvements can be made. Be as specific as possible in your evaluations.

1. Dear Mr. Parker:

It was a pleasure to receive your request to be added to our selected list of credit accounts.

We have enclosed one of the standard credit forms used throughout the jewelry industry which we would like to have you complete and return to us. You will also note that the form requests a certified financial statement.

We look forward to working with you, Mr. Parker, as we do with our 4000 other retail accounts. We have, since 1920, instituted a variety of services designed to increase our retailers' sales: advertising campaigns, holiday tie-in store displays, contest sponsorship, counsel on direct mail, seminars on store and personnel management, and other efforts.

I have requested our salesman in your district, Joe Jemper, to stop by and introduce himself to you. Mr. Jemper will also leave you a copy of our new catalog and policy booklets.

May we ask that you return the completed forms in 10 days, Mr. Parker. You may be sure that all the data you supply will be retained in confidence.

2. Dear Mrs. Spear:

Thank you for your request to open an account with Kendry's Women's Wear.

We have enclosed one of our credit information forms; please complete and return it within 2 weeks. Of course all the data you list will be kept in confidence.

Until we have had an opportunity to evaluate the information, please continue to fill your clothing needs at Kendry's. Between January 5 and 25 we are featuring many outstanding values on cruise and vacation wear. Stop in today and shop . . . and, of course, complimentary tea and cakes are available each afternoon between 2 and 4 in our Sussex Room.

3. Dear Sir:

Your Order 2151 arrived today along with your request to charge the merchandise.

We have checked our records and find that you have not been approved for credit, nor, as a matter of fact, have you ever applied. It is true that you have been making cash purchases for almost 18 months, but not on a credit basis.

I have enclosed all necessary credit application forms. Please complete and return them along with a financial statement if you want to secure an open account. As for your order 2151, we can fill that and ship it C.O.D. almost immediately or hold it up until the credit check has been completed.

Please let us know what action you prefer.

4. Dear Mr. Altonway:

We have recently received an application for credit from:

Mr. Robert Falloway
1201 South Washington Street
Evanston, Illinois 60202

He claims that he has had a credit line with your firm for four years.

Will you send us information on what type of risk he is, plus other data such as payment record.

Thanks.

5. Dear Mr. Sulton:

It is a pleasure to say "Welcome to Leeds." We have opened an account for you, and we will be happy to cooperate with the managers of your three stores.

As we agreed, each store manager will have an $800-per-order limit which will be entered on a monthly basis. All bills will be submitted to your main office, and are, of course, eligible for a full 2 per cent discount when payment is made within 10 days. The usual net payment is due within 30 days.

I have enclosed our booklet, "What Leeds Can Do for You." It describes our promotional discount policy, cooperative display programs, and related activities. We certainly want to cooperate in every way possible to help boost your sales.

Please call me direct whenever you have a question or whenever I can assist in any way.

6. Dear Mr. Getz:

It was a pleasure meeting with you last week. Your various completed forms arrived and have been evaluated. We are certainly happy to add your firm's name to our list of "Preferred Accounts."

Mr. Vern Cable is the salesman in your area. He will be calling for an appointment to meet with your canned fruit buyer. I'm sure Mr. Cable will be happy to work with your buyer in every way possible: discount privileges, lot purchases, advertising tie-ins, etc.

The enclosed card, "Credit Control at Carpenter's," will be of interest to your controller. It lists payment and discount policies as well as other information.

Please call me, Mr. Getz, if there is anything we here at Carpenter's can do at any time.

7. Dear Mrs. Farley:

We received your recent request for credit with Kennelly's. Thank you very much for your completed application.

We are sorry to tell you, however, that we must turn you down. We have checked and found that you are now carrying three other open accounts in the city and that your payments to all are not up to standard.

Why not just continue to buy from us on a cash basis and take advantage of our quality merchandise and low prices?

8. Dear Mrs. Barley:

Thank you for your recent request for credit with Kennelly's.

We have evaluated your application carefully, and have found that you now have open accounts with several excellent local firms. These obligations appear to be rather heavy and we feel it would not be in your best interests to add another.

Kennelly's has been a leading supplier of home and personal

needs to Cincinnati area families since 1920. We do want you to continue shopping with us, Mrs. Barley. We will serve you in every way possible.

9. Dear Mr. Ralston:

We have carefully evaluated the completed credit form which you sent us, and though we would be happy to say, "O.K.," in this instance, we cannot.

We have found that you are over-extended with several whole-sale firms and that you would be wise to purchase from us on a cash basis. This will give you an immediate 2 per cent discount plus building a fine reputation.

Why not pick up the telephone and let me know what your paper and bag needs are. I can have an order on its way to you the same day.

10. Dear Mr. Carbone:

It was a pleasure for us to receive the reference letters which we have received concerning you. All the firms spoke very highly of you personally and your future potential in the furniture field.

However, it was also evident that you are now somewhat extended. Certainly this is not unusual for a business that is only 6 months old.

We do feel that because your present asset-liability ratio is somewhat out of balance, you would be wise to continue your purchases with us on a cash basis. This will result in several major advantages such as immediate discounts, no end-of-month bills, and overall reputation.

We have noted that one of your best items has been our Contempo Record Cabinet. As you may recall, these have sold for $88.00 per dozen. However, we are offering them to our preferred customers at only $67.00 per dozen, until March 8. This is a 25 per cent reduction over our usual sale price. Just return the enclosed order card, and your shipment will be on its way within 3 days.

II. Complete any of the following problems assigned. You may wish to review the chapter and note key points before solving the problem.

1. Your firm, Office Aids, sells business machines and office supplies to a large number of companies in the New York area. Prepare a letter which may be used as a guide to be sent to those firms that have applied for a credit account and have been approved. Make any reasonable assumptions concerning rules, services available, and miscellaneous factors.

2. In some instances, the company mentioned in Problem 1, Office Aids, must reject a credit applicant. Write the letter taking care of such a situation when the applicant has been found to be a poor credit risk due to very slow payments to other creditors, and a generally unsatisfactory financial position.

3. You are the owner of Parker Fashions in Broadway, New Jersey. Assume this is a suburb of a large urban center. The population of the suburb is made up of families in upper income levels, many of whom know each other. From time to time, one of the applicants for credit must be rejected. Write such a letter, keeping in mind the individual's possible close social relationship with many of your best customers.

4. Parker Fashions advertises in the weekly *Broadway News*. The advertisement usually carries a small message at the bottom inviting charge accounts. Quite often an individual will telephone to inquire about an account. Write the letter which accompanies the blank "request for information" forms which are mailed to the applicant.

5. Sometimes you receive an order for auto parts and supplies (products which you distribute) from either steady cash customers or new customers which are marked, "Please charge." Many of these requests come from outlets which will be good credit risks. However, you cannot send the merchandise out on a charge basis until you have run a credit evaluation. Write the letter which will accomplish the following: (1) acknowledge the order; (2) offer to send it on a cash basis, or hold it until the evaluation is completed; and (3) request completion and return of the "request for information" forms which are enclosed.

CHAPTER SIXTEEN

Collection Letters

In most companies the functions of credit and collection are assigned to one department; the extension of credit and the collection of unpaid bills are intimately associated. On the other hand, the frequent friction which exists between the credit and collection department and the sales department is unfortunate. It is not unusual for the credit and collection department to entertain a rather severe and conservative point of view on credit extension and delinquent accounts. The sales department representative, however, often asks, "How can we sell with such tight credit policies?"

The letter which establishes credit is really a letter "selling" future business. And surely the primary purpose of the collection letter is to sell the delinquent account on paying his past-due balance, continuing his business relationship on a cash basis, and promoting a friendly relationship. Thus, in a large measure, the collection letter carries heavy selling responsibilities.

Although we often speak of form collection letters—and use them extensively—the entire collection operation must frequently be tailored to individual cases.

Consumer accounts that become delinquent require different types of communications from those used for the wholesale or commercial account. And the collection letter sent to the "good risk" is certainly different in content from the one sent to the "poor risk." There are many other factors which vary, yet from the necessity of time and the burden of numbers, we formulate "standard" collection letters which contain variations so that they can be adapted to different situations. Perhaps this is why form collection letters are not particularly successful; they do lack the individual, personal approach. Yet the problem is one of numbers. How can we possibly send personal, individually typed letters to each of our 5700 delinquent retail or wholesale accounts, who owe us anywhere from $2 to $2000 each? And so we compromise. We begin our collection series with forms, which bring a substantial reply, and then we go into a more personal approach in an attempt to secure payment from the more difficult accounts.

As we have already noted, credit and collection procedures differ when we are dealing with consumer accounts as opposed to industrial, commercial, or manufacturing accounts. Surely our approach with Mrs. Johnson, whose husband earns $8500 per year, is different from our treatment of National Automotive Parts Company with annual sales of ten million dollars. And yet, they do have factors in common: they both may be classified as "good risks"; they are both delinquent in their payments; and they are both customers whose sales and good will we wish to retain.

You will recall that, before granting credit, a company examines the applicant's capital or financial position; his character or past business and personal history; the conditions which exist at the time in his type of business; and the capacity of his firm to do business and carry on successful operations.

After evaluation of these four areas, plus other contributing factors, the account is classified as a good, fair, or poor risk. And then, after further evaluation, the classification is extended to "good risk—good pay" or "good risk—poor pay," or "poor risk—fair pay," or whatever title is considered appropriate. An account may be a good risk, but for some reason he does not like to part with his money, so he is classified as a "good risk—poor pay." On the other hand, we have the new businessman who owes for his fixtures, his merchandise, his equipment, and his vehicles. Yet he makes every effort to pay his bills within the discount period so that his credit reputation will improve. Thus, at the moment, he is classified as a "fair risk—good pay."

STEPS IN THE COLLECTION SERIES

Most corporations, in dealing with delinquent accounts, divide their collection procedure into three steps: form reminders; personal letters; and finally, collection agencies or court action.

THE REMINDER

Shortly after a bill has become past due, most firms send out a reminder. The assumption is that the account has been overlooked and "this is just to remind you that this sum is due."

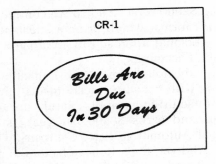

Stickers, in a variety of colors and messages, or rubber stamps with a brief request for payment, are often affixed to a duplicate invoice.

Other types of reminders are printed on cards, small sheets of stationery, and even on rolls of tape (in different colors to indicate different levels of urgency) which can be cut off and fixed to the invoice.

Various companies have found that the most effective type of reminder is a short, sincere, handwritten note on the face of an invoice. This should be signed by the treasurer, controller, or other company officer. Stickers, cards, and rubber-stamp messages are often ignored by the delinquent account, but the personal note will often be read and acted upon favorably.

THE PERSONAL LETTER

Most people are honest and pay their bills promptly. Because of a variety of circumstances, ready cash is not always easily available. However, the combination of the desire to pay and a reminder or two are usually enough to result in the payment of a delinquent account.

But there are many instances where the bill still remains unpaid and it is necessary to send more than a reminder to the debtor. A personal letter, or two, or three, will usually produce payment or explanation. People will generally act like people when they are treated like people, and not like computer cards.

THE COLLECTION AGENCY

If a series of personal letters to a debtor does not result in payment, it will finally be necessary to turn the account over to an agency for collection. This should be only a last resort, because it is good neither for the debtor nor for the creditor.

Once an account is turned over to an agency, that debtor will become a poor risk; he will have difficulty getting any kind of credit in the future. And the creditor admits his inability to collect and his bad judgment in extending credit in the first place.

VARIABLES IN COLLECTION LETTERS

Before we can send any collection letters, we should know whether the account has been classified as a good, fair, or poor risk. And what further evaluations have been made? Is he a "fair risk—good pay"? Or perhaps a "good risk—fair pay"? On the basis of our classification, several factors in our collection actions will vary:

1. The tone of the letter sent to the poor risk will surely be more insistent and less lenient than that of the letter sent to the good risk;

because he is a poor risk, we know that funds are not usually readily available to him. A more severe, insistent, and demanding tone is used in this instance.

> *Poor risk:* Your bill is now three months past due and we insist on immediate payment.

> *Poor risk:* We have now sent you two reminders and a letter. We have received no response concerning your delinquent account. Legal action will be started within 14 days of the date of this letter if payment of this past-due balance of $47.85 is not received.

> *Good risk:* Because you have been an excellent account of ours for over 15 years, we know there must be a good reason for non-payment of your past-due account of $390.00. Please call me collect so that we may discuss it.

> *Good risk:* For over ten years you have paid your accounts promptly and taken advantage of the discount privilege. That is why your present past-due balance of $480.00 disturbs us. We know there must be a reason. Mr. Campbell of our office will be in your area on March 5, and will stop by to see you. I'm sure arrangements can be worked out.

2. Among the various types of appeals (see discussion below), there are some which are more adaptable to the good risk than to the poor. An appeal to fear or self-interest might be wiser to use with the poor risk than an appeal to pride. Thus the *type of appeal* may vary.

3. Normally more letters are sent to the good risk than the poor risk before drastic action is instituted. Where the good risk may receive from four to seven letters, the poor risk may get two to four. The poor risk may well be delinquent to several firms and being subjected to many pressures. If we insist on sending him seven letters before taking action, it may be too late to recover anything. Perhaps three weeks earlier, while we were sending him letter number four, he paid what he could to creditors more insistent than we and now can make no further payments to anyone. The *number of letters sent* may vary according to the type of risk.

4. The man who has been in business for 20 years, has adequate capital, and whom we've classified as a good risk will certainly be given more time between collection letters than the poor risk. If we give the fellow who is a poor risk too much time, he may pay off other creditors while we are still sending out letters and watching the days pass. *Time varies between letters.*

5. The poor risk's account will be turned over to a collection agency or lawyer more quickly than the good risk's delinquent bill. Here again, if we are too lenient with the poor risk, we may find ourselves arranging a court date only to find that the delinquent has paid off as well as he could and has, perhaps, left town. And we are busy sending out collection letter four or five! *Time before action* may vary according to type of risk.

APPEALS USED TO MOTIVATE PAYMENT

When an individual or a firm owes money to a creditor, it is not because he wants to. He has troubles and probably owes several other creditors at the same time. He has a limited amount of money on hand and half a dozen creditors that are asking for the funds. He can use the money he does have available to pay other debts, buy more merchandise to carry on business, allocate it for advertising to increase sales, or turn it over to you.

Where shall he place the limited number of dollars for the maximum effectiveness? For you to simply say "Send it to me" may not be very effective when weighed against the insistent demands he is receiving from others. It is necessary for you to show him why he should pay you —for *his* benefit. Here is where the collection correspondent can use the "you" attitude very effectively.

The strengths of the appeals vary, but they are all designed to make the debtor want to pay his bill, or to send along an explanation of why he can't pay at present and what his plans are for the future. The appeal may be based on ethics and fair play; good credit reputation; self-interest; the saving of time and trouble; status; fear of court action; or a combination of two or more of the above.

Quite frequently a collection letter will use more than one of the appeals listed above. However, the effective letter (or series of letters) emphasizes the ways the debtor benefits by paying his bill. Never, or infrequently, do the letters point out how the creditor will gain. In the six examples below, note how the various appeals have been used.

Dear Mr. Corbett:

On March 17 we sent you order #217 as you requested it . . . we shipped it air express at our expense so that we could make the delivery date you asked for.

The order came to $574.50, due on April 15. Although we have sent you several reminders and have made two phone calls, we have not heard from you.

We know that you want to be fair about this. Therefore, will you put your check for $574.50 in the stamped envelope enclosed and return it to us immediately?

Dear Mr. Jason:

When you applied to us for a credit account, we carried through a standard credit check. We were very pleased when our inquiries brought responses which praised highly your credit reputation.

Perhaps you have merely overlooked this past-due bill of $294.50. If so, please remit the sum today. If there is some difficulty, and we can assist in any way, please let us know.

We know that it took years for you to build such a reputation and we are sure that you want to retain your outstanding rating. And so we are at a loss to explain why you have not paid or responded to the notices we have sent you.

We want to say, when someone calls us about your credit, "It's excellent!" Won't you help us maintain your fine credit reputation by sending us your check today?

Dear Mr. Lindemann:

We're not sailors, but at the moment we're at sea. We can't understand what happened to your check for $365—an amount which is now almost two months past due.

Surely it is in your best interests to pay this bill today. Time can be saved and trouble avoided if you will complete the check now and send it in.

If, on the other hand, there is some reason why you haven't paid this balance due, we want to know about it. We've always valued your business and friendship, and we want to retain both for many years to come.

Dear Mr. Shelley:

"Nothing seems to work," my accountant has just told me. And unfortunately he was talking about his efforts to collect your unpaid bill of $165.00.

It's a pity that he hasn't been successful, for I've had faith in you and I've wanted to continue our pleasant business relationship. However, there seems to be little left we can do except turn your account over to our legal department for action.

If we don't receive your check for $165.00 by April 28, we'll have to take that step. Won't you help us avoid this drastic move? Send in your check today.

Dear Mr. Delento:

Let's recapitulate your delinquent account situation up to this point.

On January 4 we sent you $870 worth of merchandise which when added to your balance of $450 brought your account to $1320.

Through February, March, and April we sent you reminders and called you regarding this past-due sum.

We have obviously done all we could to help you retain your credit reputation. However, on May 15 your account will be turned over to the Furniture Credit Association for collection.

They in turn forward the names of all delinquent accounts to furniture manufacturers and suppliers throughout the United States. All Association members are then required to stop shipments to such delinquent accounts.

You can see what this will do to your reputation and sources of supply. Why destroy what you've worked so many years to build? Please forward your check to us prior to May 15.

The letters above are typical of those sent out to collect from past-due accounts. The different appeals, or combination of appeals, are clearly evident. Notice that few, if any, collection letters bother with a "sales appeal" unless the letter is the first or second in a series. The primary purpose of the letter is to secure money due, and any discussion which clouds that central message is usually eliminated.

However, for large corporations it is almost impossible, from the point of view of cost, to send personal letters to all delinquent accounts. Furthermore, it is usually not necessary, for a short, courteous form letter will motivate most persons to forward part or all of the sum due, or an explanation for non-payment. Because this is true, most companies have form collection letters prepared.

Whether it is a form letter or individually typed, the collection message should always:

1. Be courteous and restrained. Insults, accusations, and sarcastic comments serve no useful purpose.
2. List specific dates when payment is due or when more drastic action will be taken—and stick to these dates.
3. List the precise amount due in every letter in a series from the first three-line reminder to the last carefully worded appeal.
4. Include a "you" attitude which clearly shows the debtor how *he* will gain from making the payment requested.

THE COLLECTION LETTER SERIES

It is extremely difficult to write one series which can be used for all types of risks. As noted earlier, the tone, number of letters, and other factors differ. For that reason it is usually wise to make up three different series, one for each group: good, fair, and poor risks.

The series may be preprinted and provided with blank spaces, which can be filled in with the proper dates and amounts due. Or guide letters can be written which are bound into a folder and used as models for individually typed messages. Obviously the latter method is more effective because of the personal tone and better appearance of the letters, but they are more expensive to process than prepared form letters.

TO A GOOD RISK

(Two reminders have been sent.)

Letter One:

Dear Mr. Felton:

This is just to call your attention to your past-due balance of $_____ . Perhaps you've overlooked it in the rush of daily activities; however, we would appreciate receiving your remittance by return mail.

Carson's prices and products were never more attractive than at present. Why not check your needs and get in touch with your Carson salesman today?

Letter Two:

Dear Mr. Felton:

It has now been _____ days since your account for
$_____ has been marked "Past Due." We are puzzled
and can only assume that you inadvertently overlooked this
bill.

We certainly did "what was right" in filling your requests
promptly for quality furniture at competitive prices. They
say "Turn about is fair play"; therefore won't you do what's
right and pay this bill today?

I've enclosed a stamped envelope for your convenience. Please
return it with your check for $_____ .

Letter Three:

Dear Mr. Felton:

The head of our accounting department has just been in to
see me about your delinquent account of $_____ .

I must say I was surprised; there must be a very good reason
for your non-payment. Why don't you pick up a pen and jot
a note on the reverse side of this letter telling me what the
problem is? We want to help in any way we can.

For some time you have been one of our valued customers
and you have enjoyed a fine credit reputation. Surely we both
want that credit rating of yours retained. Won't you help me
to help you by sending me a check today or an explanation
for the non-payment of your bill for $_____ ?

Letter Four:

Dear Mr. Felton:

We are at a loss to understand why you have taken no action
to pay or reduce your bill of $_____ which is now
_____ days past due.

We have written you several times and have received no response. You can appreciate our position, for we must now

think of turning your account over to the National Furniture Wholesalers Association for collection.

We do want to avoid this for it means that your name is published and distributed industry-wide as a "delinquent account." Obviously such an announcement does your credit rating almost irreparable damage.

We have no recourse except to forward your name to the Association within 15 days or by _____ , 19_____ . Won't you help us to avoid such action by mailing us your check for $_____ , or a substantial part of this sum, prior to the date indicated?

Letter Five:

Dear Mr. Felton:

After several reminders and letters concerning your past-due bill of _____ , we are now forced to consider taking drastic steps to collect. This means turning your account over to our attorneys for court action.

This will not be desirable for either party. For you it means the payment of not only the sum due but court costs of no inconsiderable amount, and in addition there are the time and trouble involved.

Why not save yourself all this difficulty by sending us your check for $_____? If we do not hear from you by _____ _____ , your account will be turned over to McAlister, Kelley, and McAlister for legal action.

TO A POOR RISK

(Two reminders have been sent.)

Letter One:

Dear Mr. Larkin:

This is to call your attention to your past-due bill for $_____ _____ .

It is quite possible that you simply overlooked this amount, but we know that you want your credit record to reflect prompt payments.

Therefore will you send us your check today?

Letter Two:

Dear Mr. Larkin:

Your bill for $_____ has not been paid. We are at a loss to understand this, for we know the merchandise and service you received from us were satisfactory.

We must, of course, insist on payment when due. When accounts are not cleared, we send a notice of delinquency to the Appliance Association. Our next step is legal action.

Please send us your check today.

Letter Three:

Dear Mr. Larkin:

Your account has now been delinquent for_____ days. You are doubtless aware of this for we have written you several times about this unpaid balance of $_____ .

Unfortunately you leave us no recourse unless we hear from you by _____ . If your check does not arrive by that date, we will submit your name to the Association of Wholesale Appliance Dealers. You will then be classified as a delinquent account and all member dealers will be so notified.

Why not avoid the stigma of such classification by sending us your check for $_____ today?

Letter Four:

Dear Mr. Larkin:

This is to inform you that we have not received any satisfactory settlement or explanation of your past-due account of $_____ .

On _____ , 19_____ , your account will be turned over
to Mr. Thomas Shane of the legal firm of Shane and Shane,
120 South La Salle Street, Chicago, Illinois. After the above
date all communications should be made to Mr. Shane, who
will be in charge of court action to be taken against you to
collect your outstanding debt with us.

UNUSUAL COLLECTION LETTERS

There is something to be said for the imaginative collection letter. At
best, collecting money is a difficult task. Sometimes the right proportions
of humor, fact, and appeals to common sense—all cast in relation to the
reader—work very well.

Dear Subscriber:

Not so long ago you hired several thousand eyes . . .

They were eyes trained to see clearly . . . discriminating eyes
to turn surely to things worth seeing . . . photographic eyes to
mirror all they saw.

And you said to these eyes, go out to all the scattered corners
of the earth, where I cannot go myself—see what is happening to the world and to the people who make up the world—
and send me once a week a true picture of what you see.

And the several thousand eyes went to work for you—as they
work for millions of others who want to see in order to understand.

These eyes are seeing for you now—in parliaments and planes,
in factories and laboratories, on farms and ships and city
streets.

And each week in the pages of LIFE they are bringing you
what they see, exactly as they see it. . . .

The "wages" you contracted to pay these several thousand
eyes were very low—the price of a subscription to LIFE.

I hope the service you receive under this contract is all you
expect—and more . . .

And that you will pay the "hire" listed on the enclosed bill
—*today*.

Dear Subscriber:

In Oklahoma City recently café owners opened a school to
teach their waitresses to smile pleasantly.

And before you laugh, you might admit that smiling waitresses have a lot to recommend them.

Here at TIME, we've always felt the same way about "collection" letters.

We just smile pleasantly and say: "Our bill for your current
subscription is enclosed."

Wonder if you wouldn't like to substantiate our faith in smiles
by sending us your check, please, today?

Dear Subscriber:

Not 1001 nights but 92 days ago you again commissioned us
to be your story teller. You bade us appear before you each
week of the year, to bring you all the curious and exciting and
significant news of all the world.

And lo, we have fulfilled your commission faithfully.

Now it is the third month since you asked us to play Sche-
herazade to your Sultan for another year—and still TIME
arrives regularly at the appointed hour, laden with tales to
inform and entertain you . . .
   Tales stranger than any fiction ever written . . .
   Tales of great heroism and man-made disaster . . .
   Tales of the magic wrought in laboratories . . .
   Wondrous tales of artists and bards and mimes.
But throughout all these 92 days and nights we have waited
in vain for your check—and this is enough to make even Sche-
herazade lose confidence.

Please won't you reassure us by settling this small account
today?

Notice in the letters above that the level of language, the style of humor, and the type of appeals would all be acceptable to the *Time-Life* readers.[1]

The four following letters have also proved very effective and have been used (with variations) by many companies.

Dear Mr. Barwig:

That rubber band stapled to the top of this letter is very significant, for it has much in common with credit.

Both rubber bands and credit perform valuable functions when used correctly. But when either one is stretched too far, it breaks, with results that can prove to be disastrous.

In your case, the rubber band of credit has been stretched very thin . . . in fact we think it's close to breaking.

Let's keep the usefulness of your credit intact. Send in your check for $_____ no later than _____ . Then both your credit and the rubber band will continue to function perfectly.

Dear Mr. Kranz:

That paper clip up at the top of this letter hasn't been left there by a careless stenographer.

That's Elmer our pet paper clip.

His purpose in life is to hold two pieces of paper together. But Elmer has enlarged his scope of usefulness and has accepted two very definite tasks which we've asked him to do.

ONE ... to hold your check for $_____ to this note and thus clear up your past-due account and . . .

TWO ... by so doing, to bind the friendly relationship which has always existed between us.

When returning your check, don't forget to send Elmer. You know, he's our Credit Manager.

1. Letters reproduced by permission of Time, Inc.

A Two-Sided Story

OUR SIDE	YOUR SIDE
On March 28, we sent you a notice about your past-due bill of $_____ .	
Since that date, we've sent you several other reminders and letters but we haven't had a reply.	
We are really puzzled. Surely there must be something wrong . . . the bill? our service? business conditions? a misfortune?	
We sincerely want to work with you but we can't if we don't know what is wrong.	
Won't you take a few minutes to tell us your side of the story in the attached space? Then use the stamped envelope to send us your reply.	
We want to work with you. Give us some help by replying today.	

Dear Mr. Farber:

You may well wonder what that piece of jig-saw puzzle is doing at the top of this letter.

Well, it's really quite simple. Our auditor has been checking our books. He finds that everything balances and is complete except for one missing item . . . your check to cover your past-due account of $_____ .

Obviously, he can't finish the audit to his satisfaction without your check and I can't finish my puzzle without the missing piece.

Won't you help us both by returning your check and the jig-saw puzzle piece today?

443

On the other hand, when letters become too "cute" and too funny, their effectiveness is diminished. In recent years there has been a trend not only toward cute and "off-beat" collection letters, but to cards, verses, and even telegrams. Here are a few—recommended for laughs, but not for use.

Dear Mr. Prettler:

Perhaps you've heard about the dentist who couldn't collect for the set of false teeth he made for one of his patients.

One day he went to see the recalcitrant debtor, but he returned to the office quickly. His nurse asked him what happened and the crestfallen dentist wailed, "He not only didn't pay me, but he bit me with my own teeth!"

Now, I don't think you're going to bite me, but for heaven's sake, how about paying up . . . today. It's only $_____ .

Dear Mr. Berger:

Have you read about the bachelor who submitted his income tax return and brazenly listed a dependent son?

One of the auditors in the Internal Revenue Service returned the form to the bachelor and attached a note, "This must be a stenographic error."

Shortly thereafter the form came back to the Income Tax Division—still listing the dependent son but the bachelor had added below the auditor's note, "You're telling me!"

One thing we're sure of here at Martin Manufacturing, and that is that your past-due bill for $_____ is not a stenographic error. We've gone over every detail and the only message we want you to write is your name at the bottom of your check.

Dear Mr. Baxter:

Can you send us the name of a competent attorney in your area? We may have to sue you for $_____ which you owe us.

Perhaps these examples only emphasize the likelihood of the story concerning the delinquent account who had already received five letters from the National Manufacturing Company but had not sent as much as a post card in return. Finally the sales manager of National, completely perplexed, boarded a plane and flew down to see the delinquent account.

When the sales manager entered the debtor's place of business, he found the store crowded with customers and prosperity in the air.

"For heaven's sake, Brown. You're obviously doing very well. Why in the world haven't you paid your 5-month old bill?"

"Oh, I can pay easily enough," answered Brown. "It's just that I enjoy your collection letters so much, I'm waiting to get the complete series before I pay."

It's conceivable that humorous collection letters might have a boomerang effect. The debtor may not take seriously the cute, clever, or funny collection letter, especially if several creditors are pressuring him at the same time. He may decide that if one of his creditors finds the situation humorous, perhaps that creditor is a logical choice for delayed payment.

QUESTIONS FOR STUDY

I. Offer your constructive criticism of the following letters. Remember to indicate which sections of the letters deserve favorable comments, as well as where improvements can be made. Be as specific as possible in your evaluations.

1. Dear Mr. Roth:

It's been well over three weeks since we sent you our last reminder concerning your past-due bill.

Because you have been an excellent customer for several years, we are at a loss to understand why you have permitted your account to become delinquent.

We know you are as eager as we are to see that your fine credit reputation is retained. Please send us your check for $740 which will clear your account and maintain your excellent credit reputation. If for some reason you can't do that conveniently, please send us part of it and your comments.

We want to work with you, Mr. Roth, in every way possible.

2. Dear Mr. Frederick:

Your complete lack of attention to our reminders and letter of two weeks ago is most difficult to understand.

We assume that you are a man of reason. However, we find your recent actions impossible to understand. Surely you know that we need the $560 you owe us, for we have bills to pay also. And certainly too you are aware that your firm's reputation will be badly damaged if we don't hear from you by May 10.

Remit today!

3. Dear Mr. Fairwhether:

There's an old song that goes, "We'll take the high road and you take the low road, and we'll all meet in . . . ."

That may be acceptable for songs but not for doing business as far as we're concerned.

We want to travel on the *same* road with you, and we want to keep abreast. Right now, however, we seem to be on different highways.

We've been waiting patiently on the corner of Jackson and Van Buren for the $295 you owe us but you're apparently on a different road.

How about getting back on the track and clearing your past-due bill—now 60 days delinquent. We sure don't want to send a posse down the road for you, but we do want that $295.

4. Dear Mr. Kaufman:

On March 14 we shipped you $480 worth of merchandise. On April 12 we added to that with a $560 order. Through May and early June we sent you several reminders of this past-due account of $1040.

We know you want to retain your fine credit rating, for on June 18 you told our salesman, Mr. Cameron, that a check would be mailed shortly.

It is now July 2 and your account still stands at $1040.

If we do not hear from you within 10 days, Mr. Kaufman, we will be required to take serious steps.

5. *A Collection Series*

Dear Mr. Hodgkiss:

Perhaps you have overlooked the two reminders we sent you recently concerning your past-due balance of $_____ .

May we remind you of this and ask that you remit this sum as quickly as possible.

I've enclosed our autumn sales brochure which I know you'll want to review.

Dear Mr. Hodgkiss:

We don't understand; perhaps you can explain.

On _____ , approximately _____ days ago, we shipped you the merchandise you requested. Since that time, we have sent you several reminders concerning your bill of $_____ .

However, we have had no response.

We shall expect a payment or an explanation within a reasonable time or we will have to take additional steps that will prove detrimental to your credit reputation.

Dear Mr. Hodgkiss:

Your bill for _____ , now _____ days past due, is still on our books.

We are aware that you value your credit reputation highly. It would seem to us that you would want to do everything possible to protect it. Yet our communications to you have proved unsuccessful.

If we do not hear from you by _____ , we will turn your account over to Henly and Henly, Attorneys, for collection.

II. Complete any of the following problems assigned. You may wish to review the chapter and note key points before solving the problem.

1. Mr. Robert T. Elkins opened an account with you two years ago. His purchases of lamps and decorative home items from you have averaged about $600 per month. He paid his bills promptly until five months ago. At that time his account stood at $940. You sent him several reminders and letters and he finally responded 21 days ago with a $250 check. However, he has made no further payment on the $690 past-due balance. Write the necessary collection letter.

2. You own a neighborhood women's dress and sportswear shop. Although you do not encourage credit accounts, some of your steady customers ask, from time to time, if they may charge a purchase. You usually agree, and payment is usually prompt. However, some accounts do not pay when they should. A further problem is that they shop elsewhere while their account with you remains delinquent.

   Write a letter which can be sent to such accounts; attempt to collect while retaining good will.

3. Assume you are the credit manager for a department store located in a middle-class suburb just outside of New York. Approximately twenty of your accounts each month do not pay when scheduled although most send their checks eventually. Prepare a collection series for this group.

4. You have six salesmen who sell brief cases, attaché bags, wallets, and related items to retail outlets on the west coast. You have relatively few delinquent accounts, but from time to time this does happen. Prepare a short reminder letter and two collection letters which can be used as models. One letter should be standard and the other quite severe.

5. Mr. Robert Campbell was an excellent customer of yours for nine years. About five months ago he told your salesmen that you had overcharged him, sent him damaged merchandise, and in general did not treat him correctly. You did everything possible to placate him and adjust the situation, but he remained angry and paid $540 of a $610 bill slowly and reluctantly. He has now had a balance of $70 for over two months. Write the letter that will attempt to collect this.

6. On June 10, Dr. Thomas Pine, a faculty member at the nearby state university, purchased two suits and miscellaneous merchandise from you. His total bill was $290 which he charged. After you sent him two reminders, he sent you a check for $90. You have called him three or four times without luck. On your last call, he said something about the suits not fitting and you suggested he bring them in for alteration. However, he has never appeared.

Write the letter which will bring some action. Remember that most of your accounts are also on the staff of the university.

CHAPTER SEVENTEEN

Sales Communications

The growth of the use of direct mail in the last twenty years has been phenomenal. All one must do to be aware of this growth is to observe the number of pieces of mail he receives at home today as compared with twenty years ago; to observe the volume of sales literature delivered to every office; and to note the number of major companies which are now offering their products by mail as well as over the counter.

ADVANTAGES OF DIRECT MAIL

Direct mail is not limited just to selling products or services. It can pave the way for salesmen; keep contact with customers between a salesman's calls; sign up new accounts; stimulate the inactive customer to return; develop interest among prospects not yet visited by salesmen; answer inquiries; build good will; distribute samples; and a score of other profit-building activities.

But how does direct mail compare with newspaper and magazine advertising? Will money spent on direct mail bring a greater return than the same sum expended on radio or TV time?

I doubt that there are reliable answers to these questions, for different products, directed to different prospects, may sell better if the advertisement appears in a trade magazine or on radio or TV rather than in a sales letter.

But on the whole, selling by direct mail has proved to be an effective, inexpensive, and profitable method of doing business.

When compared to radio, television, or newspaper advertising, direct mail has an impressive number of advantages to offer.

Here is what two authorities in the direct mail field have to say about this area of sales activities.[1]

Here are ten advantages which direct mail offers you when your advertising needs personalness, selectivity, flexibility:

1. You can be more exact in selection of and delivery to individuals or markets you wish your advertising to reach. From the list of the "Wisest Men at $1 for 7 Names" offered by one list house, to the massive National Occupant lists which carry the addresses of most American homes (98.5 per cent accuracy guaranteed), to that list right in your lap—present customers, past customers, and the people they would recommend—you can hit exactly at the market you wish.

2. You can be personal and confidential with direct mail . . . you can wrap a personal message in the secrecy of an envelope when the message is the "between-you-and-me" type.

3. You have less competition for the reader's attention with direct mail. Because of its physical make-up, direct mail doesn't have to compete with other advertising or editorial matter to the same degree or in the same way that display advertising does. When the reader has a mailing in his hand, the "distraction" from other elements is less.

4. You have few limits in format to restrict the creative expression of your advertising ideas. The selection of color, shape, size, and format has few restrictions except those of feasibility, practicality, and the U.S. Post Office. For this reason, creative ingenuity in expressing an advertising idea is almost unlimited.

5. You have great flexibility in the selection and use of creative materials and reproduction processes. All forms of the graphic arts, all those elements which can give direct mail a third or fourth dimension—die cuts, folds, sound, smell— can be adapted to give you a custom-built advertising impact.

6. You can interpret your advertising story . . . with a "reader-only" individualism, with novelty, with realism. You can get attention with such things as odd shapes, pop-ups, cutouts, folds, etc. And at the same time you can get the difference of novelty . . . the impact of realism in your advertising message.

7. You can produce direct mail as you need or want it.

1. From *Planning and Creating Better Direct Mail* by J. D. Yeck and J. T. Maguire. Copyright 1961 by McGraw-Hill. Used by permission of McGraw-Hill Book Company.

No publication date will make you wait for the impact of your advertising to be felt in your market. You can make a quick promotion when needed, make "emergency mailings" when circumstances call for them.

8. You can use the "control" inherent in direct mail for research, for testing—appeals, ideas, etc.—for reaching highly selective audiences. The individual, personal qualities of direct mail are ideal for research. And with well-selected portions of lists, you can test mailings before you throw your whole advertising effort in the hopper.

9. Your timing of mailings can be accurate, exact. To help you hit your market at the time you wish, mail departure and arrival schedules can be obtained from your post office. This means you can have mailed material hitting at its target, as planned.

10. You can offer a complete "reply" package so that the reader has ease of answering. With an enclosed, easily mailable, postpaid reply piece—business reply card, envelope, order blank, and the like—you can get easy, immediate action from readers.

These are some of the obvious advantages of direct mail. There are others: a sales letter will frequently penetrate (to the president's desk, for example) where other advertising media may not; it can be directed to widely separated geographic areas for much less money than sales personnel can be sent; it can introduce a product prior to the personal call; and it can accomplish a dozen other tasks for you quickly, selectively, and inexpensively.

PUBLIC RESPONSE TO DIRECT MAIL

Public acceptance of direct mail has increased tremendously. It is true that many persons, in firms and in homes, decry the quantity of mail they receive. But they would scream louder if the mail stopped. Businessmen, physicians, lawyers, accountants, engineers, educators, grocers, housewives, and almost everyone else is indebted to direct mail. The letters which arrive in homes, offices, factories, and plants inform readers about the products and services they use daily. The letters note changes in prices of products, improvements in design, different methods of application, new items, special sales offers, and a hundred other bits of information which help keep readers up-to-date and knowledgeable in their areas of activity and interest.

WRITING THE SALES LETTER

Writing the letter which sells a product or service can be an exciting adventure. To do a good job requires vivid imagination, skill in the basic concepts of written communication, and the sales ability to create desire through words.

The writer must possess imagination so he can project himself into the reader's position and recognize the latter's hopes, needs, and desires. This is not easy, for the world usually revolves around our needs, our hopes, our desires. But these must be put aside, for the sales letter writer must become the person he is attempting to sell; he must see, appreciate, understand, and feel that person's needs as though they were his own.

Imagination is also necessary to recognize new needs, new uses, new reasons why the prospect should have the product. And imagination is needed to select the words which will build a compelling picture of the product in the reader's mind.

Skill in composition is required in every communication, but in the sales letter especially. The organizational development of the letter must be logical and smooth. Persuasive point must be constructed unobtrusively on persuasive point from the introduction to the final statement which motivates the purchase of the product or service.

The sentences must be crystal clear so that they seem to flow from one idea to another. Never should the reader be required to stop and reread to understand a statement. His progress should be swift and sure and always assisted by the clarity of the statements which effortlessly move him along from one idea to another.

The word choice must be accurate and precise so that it evokes the exact response desired. There should never be a question about possible interpretations or reactions. The words should be so selected that only one response and/or interpretation may be received from the words.

And the total composition which conveys the message must be concise. Today's reader does not have the time, patience, or inclination to read through three pages if the message can be contained in one.

The sales correspondent must combine his imaginative ability with his communication skill to build desire. His words must motivate the reader to favorable action. It can't be just a "white or blue blouse." It must be a "highly styled, easy care blouse, fashioned in figure flattering silk and available in Wedgwood blue or snow white." It can't be "a modern office desk." A better picture is achieved if we say, "Contemporary styling in oiled walnut or glistening mahogany to enhance your present office decor and provide your secretaries with an efficient, convenient, and attractive work area."

INITIAL STEPS

There are several steps the sales writer must carry through before he writes his letter. He must:

1. Conduct a product analysis
2. Complete a market analysis
3. Review the needs of the prospect
4. Select the attribute(s) of the product which will fulfill the need
5. Plan the presentation

Product Analysis

The sales letter writer must know his product intimately and thoroughly if he hopes to sell it successfully. He must know how it is made, what its components are, where the raw materials came from, what research has gone into it, what it will do, how it will do it, and a dozen other factors. He must also know a good deal about competing products which are on the market.

And knowing all this—thoroughly—he will be assisted in doing a good job of selling. Such detailed information not only permits him to talk knowledgeably about the product or service, but it also adds two vital selling factors to his presentations:

1. Sincerity and belief in his product and
2. The ability to anticipate almost any question or objection which the prospect might raise.

There are many ways in which a product analysis may be conducted. The sales writer may visit the manufacturing and office areas of the company producing the product. Through observation and discussion with those directly involved with the product or service, he can secure information.

Data may be gathered and entered on chart forms concerning the quality level of the raw materials used and their sources; the production techniques employed; the quality control standards imposed; the method of operation of the product; the performance levels of the product; its design and appearance; the product's differentiating features as compared to competitive items; repair and service facilities offered; and prices and terms.

These are just some of the areas about which information can be secured. The areas examined can be used as headings on a chart, and the applicable data filled in under each head. When the sales writer is finished, he possesses an excellent resource chart from which to draw information for sales letters and sales promotion pieces of various types.

Market Analysis

Today most companies will bring a new product out only after very sophisticated market analysis.

Thousands—sometimes hundreds of thousands—of dollars are invested in producing a product. It would be silly to spend these huge sums of money without first determining whether or not a profitable market exists for the product. Such market analysis will determine:

The potential number of buyers
Present sales and acceptance of competitive products
Present buying habits and geographical concentrations of potential buyers
The likes, drives, and status symbols of the potential buyers (teenagers vs. college professors, for example)
What the potential buyer wants in this product
The buyer's buying power
Under what conditions and terms the buyer will act
The short- and long-range selling potential of the product
Possible tie-in with other products

Answers to these questions and others may be secured from secondary as well as primary sources.

Company records, earlier market studies for similar products, government statistics on buying habits, journal articles which discuss the future sales potential in various fields are only some of the secondary sources which are easily available. Primary sources of information are also extremely valuable. Interviews and questionnaire surveys of a sample of the potential buyers are frequently used. Also valuable is the personal and unobtrusive observation, at the very moment of selection, of just how or why a buyer decides to purchase one product instead of another.

Discussion with people who have had years of experience in the field—manufacturers, advertising executives, and salesmen—is also helpful.

Needs of the Buyer

Our market analysis should indicate whether or not our product or service will sell and which group or groups in the population we may expect to become our buyers.

Now we must place these specific groups under the magnifying glass, so to speak, and determine what their needs and drives are and what appeals we should use to motivate them to select our product.

Most of our daily activities revolve around our efforts to fulfill our needs. These needs are usually divided into physical, social, and egoistic.

In today's society our physical needs—food, shelter, warmth, etc.—are usually met, and thus we concentrate on our social and egoistic needs. Our social needs include our desire to give and receive affection, to affiliate with others and be affiliated with, and our need to take care of others and to be taken care of (nurturance). (See "Communication in Management" by Mason Haire, Part IV.)

Unlike the social needs, which concern our relationship with others, the egoistic need involves our relationship with ourselves. This need may be filled by the recognition we receive, our status symbols, position of authority we occupy, the achievements we secure, and similar situations of concern to ourselves.

Most of us desire or wish to secure:

Love	Saving of time
Security	Good health
Social distinction	Warmth
Comfort	Approval from others
Pleasure	Respect
Efficiency	Prestige
Position of authority	Delicious food

The specialists in consumer motivation have produced lists of human drives or motives which include from fifty to several hundred items. Of course many of these wants are offshoots of those listed above, and overlap each other.[2]

But they must be taken into account, for *consumers usually buy on the basis of the need which the product will fulfill rather than the product itself.*

The buyer of an expensive automobile is usually purchasing prestige and respect rather than transportation; a woman may want from her mink coat status and position instead of warmth; a young man may be looking for individuality, nonconformity, and distinctiveness in owning a foreign sports car rather than transportation; the teenager may be purchasing beauty and popularity rather than "just" cosmetics, soap, or clothes.

And so it goes, very well exemplified in the time-worn phrase: "Sell the sizzle—not the steak."

---

2. Vance Packard in several of his popular books *(The Hidden Persuaders, The Status Seekers, The Pyramid Builders, The Waste Makers)* discusses the buying drives of the American consumer.

Major Appeal

In selling, it is necessary to select one or two outstanding attributes of the product or service offered and emphasize these in the sales message. The characteristics chosen will help fulfill the needs—real or imagined—of the prospect.

This is necessary for two primary reasons. Everyone is so busy today, he doesn't have the time nor inclination to examine and weigh ten or fifteen wonderful attributes of the product. He asks, "Why is it better than the other cars, autos, typewriters, shavers, or television sets on the market? Give me a short, quick answer and I'll decide for myself whether to purchase your product or not."

Secondly, the seller is interested in showing the prospect how his product surpasses competing items. When the seller selects and emphasizes one or two attributes which his product has, and his competitors' products do not have, he draws attention to so-called superior features. But this major appeal is always based on the needs of the prospect.

Let's look at some examples of how this works in practice. We have just been requested to sell prospects on the idea of coming to our appliance store to purchase the new Arctic Refrigerator-Freezer for $325. We are to mail out 50,000 letters to prospects who live in the greater Chicago area, and try to induce them to come to our downtown location to make their purchase.

Our refrigerator-freezer has many outstanding attributes, but our prospects are not interested in all the Arctic's features. And furthermore, the needs of our prospects vary. Some live in $40,000 to $70,000 homes in upper-class suburbs; some live in densely populated neighborhoods; incomes among our prospects vary from $6000 per year to $60,000. The size of families fluctuates from two to ten. These people are all excellent prospects but their needs and what will motivate them to buy will be different.

We must therefore select different major appeals and match these with what we hope are our prospects' needs. Of course this means that we may mail several thousand copies of each of four, five, or six different letters.

In one letter (directed to upper-income areas), our major appeal may be an automatic ice cube maker, new contemporary styling, or a new temperature-controlled butter keeper or vegetable crisper; to another group (perhaps suburban or rural), a frost-free freezer. For the low-income group, we may focus on price, installment buying, time-payment plans, and trade-in deals. And in the letters sent to neighborhoods containing large family units, we might underscore Arctic's size, storage capacity, and efficiency. Of course, the refrigerator-freezer and its price never change, but the major appeal and need fulfillment do.

It is interesting to see how the advertisements for the same cars, the same soap, the same cigarettes, and a thousand other items change from magazine to magazine or newspaper to newspaper. The messages and appeals present various selling points of the product in an effort to match the different needs of the various buying groups. The same changes are made in the sales letters according to the prospect group which is being addressed.

The selection of the major appeal must be based on careful market analysis. If we are attempting to sell a product to a consumer, our choice of a central appeal point will probably differ from that used in the letters sent to wholesalers.

In the former case, special attention might be given to need fulfillment that is based to some degree on emotion—status, prestige, beauty, securing an attractive husband or beautiful wife, and other items of this nature. The businessman, however, is more practical. Central appeals directed to him are more successful when based on profits, business efficiency, and rapid turnover of products.

THE PARTS OF THE SALES LETTER

Today every individual, whether a housewife or corporate executive, receives a large quantity of sales literature. Because much of the material is of no interest to him or is poorly presented, he often discards messages without reading them. Our first problem in sales writing, therefore, is to secure the reader's attention and interest in such a way that he will read our messages.

Arousing Interest

Listed below are some of the devices, ideas, and plans which are used. How clever, "tricky," or unusual one should become clearly depends on who the reader is and what the nature of the product is.

But in all cases, the sales correspondent should be careful that his attention-catching idea isn't so arresting as to be classified as a tasteless gimmick which may reflect badly on the quality of the product. And it shouldn't be so unusual that the reader's interest focuses on the attention device and not on the item to be sold.

1. *Samples of the product.* Although this can be a rather costly way of attracting attention, it is one of the most effective. Who can discard a sample swatch of cloth, slice of plastic, piece of metal, or square of

rubber without first carefully examining it? Some companies have even had their letters printed on a sample (wood, plastic, cardboard) of their product.

When the prospective buyer can see, feel, bend, tear, taste, or smell the *actual* item, he is more likely to go back to the sales letter which accompanied the sample, and read it carefully.

2. *Photographs or sketches of the product.* Some items are too big, bulky, or in some way not adaptable to a sample. In such cases, a good photograph permits the prospect to see the product and integrate it into the word picture supplied in the letter.

3. *Gadgets and gimmicks.* Various plastic, paper, metal, cardboard, and wooden figures are used successfully. They may be reproductions of the product or some related item that will tie in with the product or service offered. These may be attached to the letter, be a part of the message, or be a separate item altogether. Sometimes they are clipped or pasted to the letter, sometimes they pop up or out or fold down.

Every large city has several agencies which specialize in the sale of advertising novelties and stickers of this type.

4. *Different openings to attract attention.* Unusual messages, type sizes, and word arrangements can be used to attract the reader's attention:

    a. Unusual offer:
        "An Executive Brief Case at no cost to you!"
        "Four DeLuxe Safety Tires for the Price of Two!"

    b. Surprising statement:
        "How would you like to make $50,000 per year?"
        "Here's a salesman who draws no salary."

    c. Inside address opening: .
        Here's How
        America's Teenager
        Can Always Score High:

    d. Vital facts about the product:
        "Eight hours a day, seven days a week, month in and month out, Canfield Chemical Co. has used Marton hoses to transfer liquid chemicals from ships to storage facilities."

    e. Story opening:
        "It was 3:00 a.m., January 14, when the phone next to Doc Garyl's bed rang shrilly. He reached out, instantly awake, to take in the seriousness of the message. . . . The Atlantic Flyer, bound for Florida, had just crashed into the Daily B & M Freight. . . ."

    f. Reference to prospect's problem:
        "Are You Too Being Robbed of Your Sleep on These Hot, Sticky, Uncomfortable Nights?"

Notice in several openings above that the reference is personal: you. This tack immediately involves the reader, and can be accomplished with most openings.

Openings of sales letters should also be positive, and so designed as to awaken in the prospect favorable associations with the product or service. And they should always be pertinent and concerned with the sales item. The reader is usually irritated if he finds that his interest has been awakened by some device that has nothing to do with the product.

Building the Picture

Now that we have aroused the prospect's interest and we have him reading, our next task is to describe the product carefully and show him how its purchase will benefit him.

We must not only describe the product so that he can almost see and feel it, but we must do this in such a way that he *desires* to purchase it. In our description we answer the questions of "what does it look like?" and "how is it made?"

> The Academic Brief Case is made of only number-one steer hides whose strength and durability guarantee years of wear. The heavy-duty National Zipper and triple heavy-duty nylon thread stitching add to the years of wear you will receive. The disappearing handles and Kentor Lock are valuable extras. And the four roomy interior sections provide individual compartments for your valuable papers, documents. . . .
>
> All this and impressive beauty too. The sheen, elegance, and appearance of the Academic Case have been responsible for the "Open Sesame" to many office doors. The rich golden tan or emphatic black are the two most popular executive colors. . . .

The words which are used to describe the product or service must evoke a real picture in the prospect's mind. Of course we can't inundate him with details but there should be enough so that he can really visualize the sales item. And the details should be presented in such a way as to add strength to the central appeal. If the letter is accompanied by an enclosure, brochure, or pamphlet, the details, sketches, and pictures can go in there. If not, they must be carefully selected and presented in the letter.

But even while he reads, the prospect asks, "What will it do for me?" "How will I benefit?" And these questions must be answered early in the letter, if we are to "hold" the prospect. He is told how some need of his will be fulfilled: how the product or service will provide him with profit, prestige, comfort, security, love, beauty, economy, health, or some other factor which he desires.

> Cool, pleasant, restful nights for you and your family can be yours in the warmest, most humid weather. This is what an Arctic Howe Air-Conditioning System guarantees you.

> A full 25 per cent profit margin is secured every time you sell a Tru-Lite Lamp. And they are selling like hot cakes throughout the country as a result of unexcelled quality, competitive price, and national radio-TV-newspaper-magazine advertising. The average furniture dealer can clear approximately $200 per week by just selling 20-25 Tru-Lite Lamps. Here is a prestige money-maker for you.

In handling the description of the product and the explanation of the prospect's benefits, it is again wise to be specific, positive, and detailed in reference to the primary selling appeal. It isn't necessary to first describe the product and then show the prospect how he will benefit. The order can be reversed or the two steps can be integrated.

Proving Your Point

But Americans are a skeptical lot and they often say, "Sounds great, but I don't believe it will do all that. Prove it!" And prove it we must if we expect the prospect to make the purchase.

A dozen different methods can be used to secure belief in what has been said. The type of proof selected will in large part depend on who the prospect is and the nature of the product. Where a testimonial from a movie star may impress this high school prospect, it might merely cause a scientist to respond with an irritated shrug.

Some of the common types of proof are:

1. *Samples.* Carefully examine the enclosed swatches of cloth—cloth that is used to tailor America's finest suits. Note the silk-like quality of the Italian sharkskin, the beauty of the English tweeds, the design of the American worsted-silks, and the attractiveness of the smartly styled gabardines. Each can be hand tailored to . . . .

2. *Guarantee.* And you will be happy to know that your National Stove is backed by a full 5-year guarantee on parts and service plus the National Home Makers Seal of Approval.

3. *Free trial.* Therefore, with no obligation or risk on your part, we

will be happy to send you the next six issues of *National Affairs*. After you have read a few copies of this vital national news magazine . . . .

4. *Names of previous purchasers.* After your firm has received its Executive Conference Table, you will find it as useful and as attractive as have International Harvester, General Motors, Western Electric, and many other American corporations.

5. *Testimonials.* "There can be no doubt," said Martel Plant Superintendent, Bill Peterson, in a recent letter to us, "that Kelley Safety Equipment is directly responsible for our safest year on record."

"The National Brief Case," wrote Prof. L. Ryan of DePaul University, "has carried a multitude of papers and books for me and looks as attractive and impressive today as the day I purchased it almost ten years ago."

6. *"Outside" agency records.* Conclusive tests conducted by the chemistry department of Central Illinois University during the winter of 1969 indicated that every one of the Teltax cans of paint examined contained . . . . These samples of Teltax were purchased at random throughout Illinois, Michigan, and Indiana. Surely . . . .

The United States Testing Company, Inc., carefully evaluated each of our new lines and found . . . .

7. *Money-back guarantee.* We are so sure you will find the new Arctic Frozen Fruit line so tasty, delicious, and satisfactory that we promise to refund *double* the price you have paid for any item which does not meet with your complete satisfaction. All you need do is . . . .

The proof in the sales letter should be restrained, specific, and well documented. It should overcome any doubts the prospect has, and it should convince him that the product or service will prove of value to him.

Although proof is normally placed after the description, it need not be. Sometimes the proof can be so startling and dramatic as to serve the twofold purpose of arousing interest and convincing the prospect to make the purchase.

> Dear Mr. Canfield:
>
> In its first year on the market, Cartell's Drafting Lamps were purchased by the engineering divisions of U.S. Steel, General Electric, Standard Oil, Caterpillar Tractor, Zenith Radio and Television, and 1875 other leading manufacturers! . . .

Making the Sale

We have aroused the interest of our prospect through a well-written opening; we have made him want to possess the product or service through our description of it; and we have proved to him that it will give him full value. Now he must take the most important step of all—he must buy it. But most people hesitate before they buy. They think before they buy. And this is to the good. Our only concern is that they may delay purchase to the point where the desire or the impulse to buy may disappear. Henry Hoke, editor of *The Reporter of Direct Mail Advertising*, says the two big barriers to action are (1) human inertia and (2) the competition for the reader's money.[3]

For this reason, the "buy" section of the sales letter should reflect an appeal sufficiently strong to move the prospect to action. And we hope immediate action. The longer he delays, the less likely he is to act favorably.

The action does not necessarily have to be the purchase of a product. It may simply involve "purchasing" the next step. It may be sending for a brochure, agreeing to see a salesman, or accepting a demonstration.

The type and tone of the approach to use in the action section will depend on the prospect. Sometimes incentives are offered to the potential buyer so that he will act quickly:

Premiums
Special Price
Special "deals" for limited time
Limited supply available

Other important factors in the action section are telling the prospect *what* to do and *how* to do it.

"Cut out the coupon"
"Sign and mail"
"Check box, sign, and mail"
"Include a quarter, add your signature, and mail"

And of course, the reader may be further motivated to reply quickly if you provide him with a stamped return card, a card with his name and address already typed or printed on, or a double-fold card that simply requires his tearing off one portion for return.

Dear College Student:

Attracting attention	An electric typewriter at less than you would expect to pay for a manual!

3. Henry Hoke, "How to Think About Direct Mail," *The Reporter of Direct Mail Advertising* (1951), p. 6.

But it's only for a limited time that we offer the International PT Electric Typewriter at a price of $119.95.

Description
of the
product

Here's a typewriter that's guaranteed to save you time as you score higher grades. You'll type faster, easier, and cleaner on this quality machine. Power Touch keys repeat automatically when held down; the Power Touch paragraph key indents 5 spaces and resets with each new margin. There are also a copy control which handles up to 10 carbons without extra pressure on keys; a plastic line finder which has a line drawing aperture for making tables; a full 88-character keyboard; quick set margins; a page gauge; and an automatic carriage centering device.

These are just a few attributes of the International PT Electric. We could go on and tell you about the sturdy steel frame, white plastic keyboard, baked-on blue enamel finish, all steel vinyl-clad carrying case and dozens of other outstanding details, but we won't because we want you to see and try this outstanding typewriter yourself.

The proof

It's available until October 30 at your College Bookstore or the local dealer listed on the enclosed flyer . . . and at the almost believable price of $119.95. And, of course, the PT comes with International's famous 5-year guarantee.

Don't let another week slip by without a PT International. And as a special bonus, when you order your Power Touch typewriter, you may have—completely free of charge—one set of Change-a-Type faces in either mathematics, engineering, pharmacy, Greek, or language symbols.

The action

See your International Dealer today, while the PT is still priced at only $119.95.

COVER LETTER AND ENCLOSURE

Most sales letters cover one page, although in some cases a sales letter of several pages has proved very successful. However, most experts, when faced with the need for a rather long, involved presentation, prefer to use a variation of the basic sales letter.

This usually consists of a letter accompanied by a brochure, a pamphlet, or a flyer. Prospects do not object to reading through an attractively laid out and well written enclosure if it is concerned with a product they are seriously considering buying. However, they do object to wading through six typed pages of a sales letter. It is because of this that most people in direct mail prefer the cover letter and enclosure to the extensive sales letter.

Authorities in the field of direct mail seem to feel that the cover letter can be designed in either of the following two methods:

1. Very general and designed to arouse sufficient interest in the reader so that he will be motivated to turn to the enclosure.
2. Containing the four parts of the sales letter—interest, description, proof, and action. However, each section is treated so briefly that the total letter would be inadequate were it not for the enclosure which expands on each of the parts.

Cover Letter Arousing Interest

Please accept -

Cool days and pleasant nights during the warmest, most uncomfortable weather Chicago has to offer.

Yes, that's what an Arctic Central Air Conditioning System can give you at an amazingly low price. Comfort . . . Cool comfort . . . Pleasant comfort . . . Inexpensive comfort . . . Delightful comfort.

Those fatiguing, tiring, blistery hot days and sleepless, perspiration-drenched nights will be gone forever once your Arctic System is installed.

Surely the comfort of you and your family is worth just pennies a day.

Examine the enclosed brochure and then return the postal card to us. One of our expert engineers will stop by to see you —no obligation, of course—to show you how easy and inexpensive it is to own an Arctic Air Conditioning System.

Cover Letter Covering The Four Points:

Please accept -

Cool days and pleasant nights during the warmest, most uncomfortable weather Chicago has to offer.

Yes, that's what an Arctic Central Air Conditioning System can give you at an amazingly low price.

The unit occupies very little space in your yard and may be placed behind shrubs or bushes. Its operation is whisper-quiet, thoroughly efficient, and almost completely maintenance-free.

Cool, refreshing air flows through the present ductwork in your home and provides comfortable days and restful nights.

Our expert engineers will make a scientific survey to determine the exact size unit your home requires. Then with no fuss, muss, or bother to you, the Arctic System will be installed in one afternoon.

You may be sure you will be as satisfied as the 9400 Chicago-land homeowners who purchased a unit last year. The Arctic System has also been approved by the American Home Builders' Association, and carries our five-year guarantee on parts and services.

Examine the enclosed brochure and then return the postal card to us. One of our expert engineers will stop by to see you —no obligation, of course—to show you how easy and inexpensive it is to own an Arctic Air Conditioning System.

The design, color, layout, and copy of the enclosure can be as imaginative as the writer wishes it to be. Naturally what he does will always be governed by his prospect group and his budget. Surely the enclosure directed to the businessman will be more conservative than that sent to teenagers. But with modern high-speed printing devices which reproduce photographs and color artwork with remarkable fidelity, the only limitations on the sales writer are money and his own imagination.

MAILING LISTS

The best sales letter will not sell if it does not get into the hands of a potential buyer. It is for this reason that special attention is always given to the mailing list.

The competent sales writer examines his list of names periodically to be sure that it reflects the characteristics of a good mailing list.

1. Is each name spelled correctly?
2. Is every person a good prospect for the product or service?
3. Do all persons listed have several basic attributes in common?
4. If the list is large, has it been divided into logical divisions such as geographical location, economic level, ethnic characteristics, etc.? When this is done, different appeals can be used in different sales letters selling the same product.
5. Have all persons' names been removed who have moved, died, or expressed no interest in the product?
6. Have new accounts', customers', and prospects' names been added?

Most firms develop their own mailing lists, which are usually made up of the names of customers. Certainly a list of this type has much to recommend it. These people have already established a friendly relationship with you, and they are sympathetic to the concept of buying through the mail.

But every firm desires to expand its sales and for this reason always adds to its list of customers' names. For those persons who have never done so, looking through the catalog of a mailing list firm is a surprising experience. Thousands of different lists are available, covering some of the most obscure vocations imaginable. College students are subdivided into a dozen categories—male, female, at denominational schools or public, majoring in various fields, or members of various ethnic groups, in universities or in junior colleges. But if you want a list of clock manufacturers, blacksmiths, sculptors, female World War II veterans, compact car dealers, or bell collectors, such a list may be purchased. And if the mailing list firm does not have a list for you in some particularly unusual field, they will compile one.

In almost every case, it is worthwhile to pay a little more to a reputable firm which keeps its lists up-to-date. There is no point in buying a list, saving a few dollars, and then learning that an appreciable percentage of the names belong to persons who have moved, died, or changed jobs.

But it isn't always necessary to buy a list. Company records are excellent sources; lists may be rented or borrowed from other merchants, and organizations—professional, social, or business—will sometimes provide a membership list.

Public rosters also provide good sources: tax rolls, vital statistics listings, auto registrations, and voters' lists are possibilities.

Then there are literally hundreds of different types of directories available in a business library. Not only telephone and city directories, but directories of lawyers, doctors, manufacturers of aircraft components or auto parts or rugs, shippers, clothing dealers, building contractors, and a hundred and one other categories of professions and businesses here and abroad. These listings provide names, addresses, and vital facts concerning the operation. All one needs to secure these lists is pencil and paper and the time to make a copy.

Davis, *Guide to American Business Directories*, lists directories in 77 different areas of activity. *Trade Directories of the World, A Guide to Foreign Business Directories*, and *Guide to American Directories for Compiling Mailing Lists* are other sources.

There are also available directories of corporations such as *Moody's Investor Service, Standard and Poor's Corporation Services*, and *Thomas' Register of American Manufacturers*.

The businessman can also compile a mailing list by offering a premium or a prize which requires that the prospect complete a card with his name and address.

So building a mailing list is frequently dependent on one's ingenuity and efforts, if not his ability to purchase a list from a commercial firm.

QUESTIONS FOR STUDY

I. Offer your constructive criticism of the following letters. Remember to indicate which sections of the letters deserve favorable comments, as well as where improvements can be made. Be as specific as possible in your evaluations.

1. "It works like magic!"

> That's what thousands of persons are now saying about the Wadsworth Water Control Unit. And you will feel the same way once you start to use yours.

> Just attach it to your outdoor water outlet, connect it to your sprinkler system, pool inlet valve or anywhere you would like a specific amount of water delivered. Just set the dial for 100 to 2000 gallons of water, and when that precise amount has run in, your Wadsworth Water Control Unit will automatically stop the flow of water. You need not be present or even at home; the Wadsworth Unit is completely automatic.

> The Unit is a precision instrument, manufactured of non-rusting

aluminum to exacting specifications. Thousands have been sold in the last few years to individuals as well as hundreds of park and recreation services supervised by local, county, state, and government agencies. Supervisor Watson of the Kenton County Park Service of Ohio wrote that:

> "The Wadsworth Unit has saved our agency thousands of dollars by cutting down on the number of men needed to supervise summer watering activities. And, in addition, we never over-water or under-water our fine flowers and grass areas."

Once you try it, we are sure you will agree with Mr. Watson and the thousands of other satisfied Wadsworth Water Control Unit users. Just return the enclosed order form with your check or money order for $9.95 and we will have your unit on its way immediately. Of course it comes to you with a money-back guarantee in the event you're not completely satisfied . . . but we're sure you will be. Order yours today.

2. Who says, "You can't take it with you"?

You certainly can when you have your Sportsmen's Outdoor Grill.

This compact unit, made of stainless steel, is a joy to have. It folds like magic and fits into its own 16″ by 16″ carton with carrying handle. It unfolds in a jiffy, stands on its sturdy steel legs, and gives the outdoor chef a full 200-square-inch grill surface.

And to top it all off, your unit comes with a spit, motor, and battery. You can roast your pheasant immediately on the slowly rotating spit and baste and season the bird to taste.

As to its acceptance, we need only cite the fact that over 100,000 have been sold since it appeared on the market last year. And it has become standard equipment for each of the 400 Colorado Mountain Rescue Patrols.

We know you will enjoy giving one of these to a friend or to yourself. They are available either with or without motor and spit. Just check your preference on the enclosed card and return it today.

3. A full 22 per cent margin when you sell a set of Palmer's Patio Lights at the nationally advertised price of $6.95 per unit!

Palmer's Patio Lights consist of a string of eight colored lights wired at 5-foot intervals and attached to a heavy-duty outdoor extension cord 40 feet long. There are three styles from which to choose, and you will find your customers buying one of each as they change the motif of their outdoor gatherings. The Party Line is especially popular, with the Oriental Occasion and the Hawaiian Luau running close behind.

All units are approved by the Underwriters Laboratories and sold with a money-back guarantee. You can order them in dozen lots, either in cartons of four sets of each of the three lines or packed twelve of a type to a carton.

The enclosed folder describes the Palmer Patio Lights in more detail, lists prices, and tells you how you can secure three free sets for yourself when you order before June 1. Order today; you'll be happy you did.

4. It's almost June and you're probably getting a little worried about gifts for the three bridal showers and two weddings scheduled during the coming weeks.

Worry no more; the solution is here in Hamilton's Hardwood Boards.

These beautiful and practical Cutting and Serving Boards have been the pride of New England housewives for three generations . . . and they're now going national.

Constructed of alternating strips of light and dark hardwoods, carefully laminated together, they go from work counter to serving table in a jiffy. The tiny rubber base mounted at each corner assures you of not marring the finest table and the Swedish stainless steel knife attached permits the artist to carve, cut, and slice before his admiring guests.

Hamilton Hardwood Boards are available in four sizes, with or without attached knife, and range from $3.95 to $12.95 each. Of course they are sold with a money-back guarantee.

Select one for each of the parties coming up . . . and be sure you don't forget yourself. The enclosed order blank, when completed and returned to us, assures delivery of Hamilton Boards within ten days.

5. "I should really start from scratch."

If you have recently said this to yourself as you looked at your towel supply, let us spur you on with a wonderful solution.

During May only, Hubfield's is offering its regular charge account customers a full 20 per cent reduction on all Hillcrest towels. These classic cotton terry towels are thick and luxurious, assuring you of years of wonderful wear.

You have four different groups to choose from: the Dundee available in four different solid colors; the Baxter in the new flower patterns; the Robinaire with its impressive crown pattern; and the Paxton for those who want the finest. They are all available in a full range of colors to match any decor. Every one of the four lines is especially priced and available either in the 12- or 18-towel sets or individually. The savings which are available in the 18-towel family sets are especially impressive. It's almost like getting several towels free of charge.

Go through the enclosed pamphlet soon—better yet, today. Check the pattern and color you prefer and order today. You are assured of Hubfield's quality and guarantees—but remember, time is limited.

II. Complete any of the following problems assigned. You may wish to review the chapter and note key points before solving the problem.

1. Your firm manufactures various wax products. Your leading item is dinner-table candles. These are available in various lengths and sizes and are thoroughly described in your brochure, "Caleb's Candles." Write a sales letter to be addressed to the fund-raising chairman of PTA's, church groups, private organizations, local charities, etc.

Explain that your product can be packaged with the organization's name and insignia on each candle wrapper and that the product can be sold at bazaars, fund-raising affairs, teas, church gift shops, etc. For the next sixty days, your firm is offering a 20 per cent discount over the wholesale prices listed in the brochure. The minimum order accepted under these terms is $150.00. All orders totaling $400 or more may take a 25 per cent instead of a 20 per cent discount. A copy of "Caleb's Candles" is to be enclosed with each letter.

2. Your firm manufactures various sport clothing. One of your lines includes bulky sweatshirts with the school name and crest imprinted. Send a sales letter to fraternity and sorority presidents offering these sweatshirts for sale. The buyer can have any sorority or fraternity name or initials imprinted (in place of the school name and crest) on the front, and any three words (maximum of 18 letters) on the back. Such statements as "Go Tigers," "We're Tops," "Follow the Leader," can be used on the back.

The card which you enclose with your letter lists the type styles of initials available and prices. Two free shirts are available for every dozen ordered. Minimum order: one dozen.

3. Your firm has recently designed and manufactured a sign-making kit for the retail merchant. It contains patterns, letter and number templates, paper, paint, brushes, correction units, spacers, and other items.

The entire unit will permit the independent dealer to quickly make window and store posters, sales cards, counter announcements, and miscellaneous signs. All work looks professional, can be completed quickly, and should save the average merchant hundreds of dollars each year if he is now buying his signs.

Other advantages include increased sales as a result of the signs, instant availability of a sign, and crisp, fresh-looking announcements available at all times. Replacement items such as paper, paint, and brushes may be ordered from your firm at wholesale prices.

You have three kits available ranging from $75 to $125 each.

Your sales letter should attempt to secure a request for your salesman to call to explain and demonstrate these units.

4. Secure an actual sales letter directed to a consumer (perhaps one that has come to your own home) and evaluate it.

Your evaluation should be very specific and should analyze the appeals used, the method of arousing interest, describing the product, proving its worth, and securing the sale. This should all be done in reference to the specific prospect to whom it was directed.

Submit both the sales letter and the criticism.

5. Complete the same assignment as in No. 4 above, except this time, choose a sales promotion piece directed to a business firm.

6. Assume that you have a mailing list of 50,000 college students. Attempt to sell each of them a new high-intensity study lamp called "The Winner."

This very attractive item folds into a four-by-four-by-four-inch cube, has an extension arm that places the light source from 6 inches to 16 inches from the desk top, is manufactured of unbreakable plastic, comes in ivory, white, or black, is fully guaranteed for one year, and sells for only $7.95 or two for $15.00.

Assume any other facts you feel are necessary.

7. You are the manager of the Vacation Isle Hotel in Florida. Send a sales letter and descriptive brochures to company sales managers recommending they consider the Vacation Isle as a perfect spot for high-ranking salesmen who have reached specific sales quotas.

This sales-incentive program is based on the firm sending a minimum of ten salesmen and their wives in any one month in March, April, or May. All golf, swimming, tennis, and related facilities are included plus three meals each day.

Assume all necessary information that you would need as the manager of the Vacation Isle Hotel.

8. Outline a sales letter campaign to sell the Diplomat attaché case. List four different prospect groups: college instructors, college students, businessmen, and the college and stationery store buyer. Note the different appeals, price, proof, and format of the messages.

Assume price, qualities, and attributes of the Diplomat and indicate which of these you would use with the different prospects.

9. Write two sales letters selling the Diplomat noted in No. 8. Direct one letter to college students, the other to business executives.

10. Complete a sales letter and sales brochure presenting the Diplomat attaché case (see problem 8) to the college bookstore buyer. Your sales enclosure should be a "dummy" with all copy written out and placed. The photos or sketches you want included should be described so that the artist or photographer knows precisely what you want. Indicate by squares or circles where in the dummy you want the art work placed.

CHAPTER EIGHTEEN

Good Will Letters

There is another letter which is somewhat similar to the sales letter, but instead of selling a product or a service, it sells friendliness, sincerity, and good relationships. This is the good will letter.

It is the letter that doesn't *have* to be sent but is. It is the business letter which has as its purpose the building of good will, not selling, not inquiring, not adjusting.

In today's hectic world of business, there is seldom the time (or the inclination) to carry through the extra and really somewhat unnecessary step of sending out a letter which says little more than "thank you; we're happy to know you and feel fortunate that we can do business with you."

Many businessmen will tell you that this kind of letter is nonsense, but they are wrong. They will tell you that the customer or supplier knows that all is well—why bother to tell him? But it is human nature to want to be thanked. There are few of us who don't experience a little bit of inner excitement and self-satisfaction when someone thanks us sincerely for what we have done.

Those persons who question the value of good will letters have probably misused them or have been the recipients of the insincere, hard-sell type. For a good will letter to be successful, it must be sincere. There is no place in this letter—absolutely no place—for sales pitches on products or services. On occasion one may wish to sell the idea of resuming business relations when an association has been broken off. But usually the recipient will feel irritated if the apparent good will letter turns out to have the ulterior purpose of trying to make a sale.

Few of us receive true good will letters today. The businessman often doubts their value and sends none, or mails out inexpensive form letters (which shout their insincerity). As for the individual, he rarely has time to write, so he buys his good will letter in the form of a greeting card. He then carries through the tremendous task of signing it. How much more all of us appreciate the short, sincere note, but all we receive (and usually send) are the pseudo-sophisticated, humorous greeting cards which are provided for every occasion from birthdays to promotions on the job to best wishes and love on Arbor Day.

The successful good will letter should be brief, sincere, and concerned only with a discussion (usually a thanks) of the relationship between the firms, or perhaps a comment on the occasion of the letter (Christmas, Thanksgiving, New Year's, etc.).

USE OF THE GOOD WILL LETTER

Once the businessman is convinced of the value of good will letters, he will find numerous situations in which to use them. The two major categories are:

1. Letters which extend good wishes or thanks. These are usually sent to steady customers and are sometimes mailed in conjunction with a national holiday.
2. Letters which attempt to build good will with an account that has terminated or cut down his business relations.

TO THE STEADY CUSTOMER

All too often, the steady customer is taken for granted; he becomes an account number. We give him special attention only when he interrupts his relationship with us. By that time, it is probably too late. The best time to thank him is when his orders are consistently coming in.

Dear Mr. Campbell:

Just a word to say "thanks" for giving us an opportunity to serve you.

Here at Shelley's we always try to bring our customers the best possible products at the lowest possible prices. We certainly hope we've succeeded in that goal in our business relationships with you.

It is the steady customer, such as you, that has made Shelley's the largest manufacturer of frames in the West. The savings we secure through efficient operations, we pass on to our customers . . . and we are delighted to do so, for it is your work, effort, and cooperation that makes Shelley's number one in the industry. For this distinction, we want to thank you most sincerely.

You may be sure we will continue to do everything possible to merit your continued support and patronage. Please call on us when we can be of special assistance to you.

Dear Mr. Stone:

With the Thanksgiving season approaching, it seems to be particularly fitting for us to say "thanks to you."

Too often most of us take our good fortunes for granted . . . but we shouldn't. Here at Kelley's we have much to be thankful for . . . the world's leading nation, good health, wonderful fellow workers, pleasant plant conditions, and cooperative customers such as yourself who keep us working month after month.

You and hundreds of other customers of Kelley's are responsible for our present position. For our part, we have done everything we could to bring you the best possible paper products at the most competitive prices. And you have given us your support through your steady purchases.

So we say, simply and sincerely: Thank you for your confidence in us. We shall continue to do the best we can, and we hope you won't hesitate to call and tell us how we can assist you in your daily operations.

Dear Mr. St. Clair:

With a new year beginning in just a few days, it seems particularly appropriate to look back over our shoulder at the months that have flown by.

They have been good months for Franklin Fixture Company largely because of customers like yourself. For your purchases, cooperation, understanding, and loyalty, we say, sincerely and gratefully, Thank you very much.

You may be sure that in the year ahead we will do everything possible to merit your continued patronage and good will.

The letters above all have one purpose and that is to promote good will. They are simple and straightforward. However, there is a variety of situations which arise where good will letters can be used to welcome a new account and comment on his order, attempt to increase the purchases of a customer, or re-activate one who has terminated his relationship with us.

TO THE NEW CUSTOMER

Perhaps your salesman has been working for some time to get this account. That first order has just been shipped. Let the new customer know that not only the salesman but the company president appreciates his order.

> Dear Mr. Melton:
>
> Welcome to Clayton's. We are delighted to have you as one of our customers, and you may be sure we will do everything possible to merit your business and good will.
>
> Our activities have always revolved around the wishes and demands of our customers. You come first. If you have some special desires or requests on shipments, merchandise, account payments, or product modifications, let us know. We will work with you.
>
> Each month our salesman will bring you window flyers and display materials. He also will be happy to make arrangements for you to secure our special counter and floor display cases. And then there are traveling demonstration units which he can schedule for your place of business.
>
> All in all, Mr. Melton, we are delighted to welcome you and we want you to know that we will work with you . . . from president to stock boy. Just tell us how, and we'll jump into action.

TO THE ABSENT CUSTOMER

The wide-awake businessman will survey his accounts periodically. When he does, he is likely to find an impressive number of customers who have become inactive. Some were excellent accounts; others mediocre. But they were accounts and as such added to the company's profit margin.

It is relatively unimportant why they no longer buy. It may have been a tactless comment, the personality of the salesman or truck driver, a price which proved rather high, or service rather slow. But the fact is, they are not customers now! The situation certainly deserves a letter, a good will letter which may bring them back.

Dear Mr. Palmer:

We miss you!

Yes, it's that simple. We all miss you: your salesman, stock boy, shipping clerk, truck driver, and accountant. These are some of the people at Rotel's who miss you; there are many others.

Perhaps it's our fault that you no longer make your purchases here. Won't you call me collect, please, and let me know why we haven't seen you, and I'll do my best to correct the situation.

We value your business and friendship and we want to keep them both. If your absence has been due to a Caribbean cruise which you took, don't bother to call. Just send your requests in. But if you haven't ordered because of a more serious reason, please phone me so that I can do everything possible so we may again enjoy your patronage.

In this letter, we are faced with a rather strong negative tone ("perhaps it's our fault"). However, this frank, sincere approach may be good, for certainly we know something is wrong. And an open discussion may well clear the air, so that the business relationship can start over.

Here is an approach that talks to the absent customer primarily about the future.

Dear Mr. Palmer:

Good news for you and other customers of Carlson's.

Beginning on May 1 we will hit the newspapers, magazines, and radio commercials in an all-out summer campaign designed to increase your sales of Carlson's products.

Although our advertising will emphasize our entire line, we will give special attention to our new Style-Bright sweaters.

Extremely heavy newspaper and magazine exposure will place the Style-Bright sweater in sharp focus. Window display materials, sample sweaters, store banners, and allowances for neighborhood advertising campaigns will be available for our accounts.

We want to work with you on this and all other business activities. Just check, on the enclosed card, the time and day convenient for you and our salesman will call on you.

TO THE "INCOMPLETE" CUSTOMER

A surprising number of accounts may purchase only part of their needs from you. This may be because they aren't aware of how extensive your line is, or they have never tried certain items which you handle because they are satisfied with another source of supply.

If you can secure all or almost all of their business, your sales will rise appreciably though the increase in the cost of selling is only minimal. Your desire is to make a better customer of him.

Naturally, if you can determine why he purchases only some of his products from you, you can more intelligently construct your letter. If not, a general approach, such as the following, may prove of value:

Dear Mr. Swibel:

For some time you have proved to be one of our valued customers, and we certainly appreciate your business. But we also find that many of our best customers are not completely familiar with the many products and services which we have available and which can increase their profit margins.

One of our most successful policies is our "double discount over five" arrangement. This means that our usual 2 per cent discount for payment within 10 days is doubled when the sum paid is over $5000. This is a tremendous addition to your margin.

We also pride ourselves on having not only a complete line of men's and women's dress shoes, but also specialized numbers of all types: golf, tennis, bowling, safety, orthopedic, and other hard-to-find models.

And if you haven't talked to our salesman about the New England men's sock line, discuss it with him on his next visit.

We will supply a complete stock of fine quality socks on consignment together with a beautiful walnut-finish floor display case. The case harmonizes with the decor of most stores, and the quality of the merchandise will please your customers and add to your sales.

These are only a few of the reasons why you should look to us for ways to increase your level of business. We want to serve you in every way we can.

EVALUATION

A good will letter program may not result in any immediate, tangible results. It is a practice that requires a long-range point of view. But it is valuable and worthwhile.

Check the good will letter before it goes out. Does it carry a personal pen and ink signature? If it is processed, does it look neat and attractive? Is the letter always sent by first class mail? Does the letter itself express a friendly tone and a "you" attitude? And above all, is it honest and sincere?

Customers should not be taken for granted. The seller should maintain contact and there is no better way than with good will letters.

QUESTIONS FOR STUDY

I. Offer your constructive criticism of the following letters. Remember to indicate which sections of the letters deserve favorable comments, as well as where improvements can be made. Be as specific as possible in your evaluations.

1. Dear Mr. Bodell:

In the rush and hurry of daily business activities, we sometimes overlook communicating a simple "thank you" now and then. And perhaps we at the Bolton Corporation have been guilty of doing just that. Nevertheless, we are sincerely appreciative of the confidence you have placed in us.

You, and the many other dealers who handle Bolton Products, are really our "bosses." We try to serve you well and bring you the finest children's wear available. And as "bosses" you have given us valuable help through your suggestions. Please keep them coming; we need your guidance to achieve our objectives: quality merchandise at competitive prices.

Again, our appreciation to you for your support. We shall work with you in the future in every way possible.

2. Dear Mrs. Golden:

One of our salespeople remarked this morning, at our regular Tuesday meeting, "Hey, today is the first day of spring." Now, perhaps that isn't very significant to many persons, but to us it is; you may recall that we opened for business on the first day of spring just two years ago . . . and you, Mrs. Golden, visited us during that "Opening Week" sale.

Our records show that you and many of our other good friends in the Bel Air community have been back many times since . . . and we want to say, "Thank you . . . Thank you very much."

We have attempted to serve you well by bringing you excellent merchandise at attractive prices plus outstanding service. We hope we have succeeded and will continue to merit your support.

But spring is for flowers . . . and we have one for you. We won't tell you more than that . . . just that we have a flower for you that we know you will enjoy for years to come. Please stop by to pick up yours and give us an opportunity to say, "Thank you for your patronage, Mrs. Golden."

3. Dear Mr. Gould:

We were delighted to hear from Al Alberts that you met with him recently and placed your first order for Miller Pipe Products. Thank you very much.

As Al undoubtedly told you, we pride ourselves on offering our customers quality and service along with competitive prices.

One of the services that we are proud of and we hope you will use is our free drop shipments in the greater Milwaukee area. When your customers in this area place an order for over $500 of Miller Pipe Products, we will drop it at their address if you so direct. And there is no shipping charge.

We also stand ready to make reasonable modifications in products for your special jobs; the only charge to you is our direct labor cost. And, in addition, we will be happy to supply you with sales promotion material at no charge.

So, Mr. Gould, we at Miller Pipe Products stand ready to serve you in every way possible. We're as close to you as your phone. . . GR 4-4200.

4. No, Mr. Campbell,

The tiny silver whistle attached is no gag. We want you to whistle whenever you need us. And we do hope you will use it soon, for we haven't heard from you in too long a time.

As you know, we value our customers highly, and nothing pleases us more than to be whistled at . . . either in admiration or for service. So, won't you whistle soon. We promise to respond immediately with quality, service, and a smile.

5. Dear Mr. Fagel:

Too often today in the world of business, people, companies, and institutions have become numbers, symbols, punched cards, or printed tapes.

And too often too, we forget that behind these impersonal identification methods are people—people who are our good friends.

So, if we may, we would like to stop the clattering machines and whispering computers to say, "Thank you, good friend Fagel, for letting us serve you during this past year. We have been delighted to fill your construction and building equipment needs."

Now with another year opening before us, we will return to the high-speed business needs of today. But we won't forget our good friends for whom we are working, and if you will tell us how— from time to time—we will work harder and better to bring you exactly what you want.

II. Complete any of the following problems assigned. You may wish to review the chapter and note key points before solving the problem.

1. You have owned a large neighborhood jewelry store for several years. For some time you have noted a trend among some of your cus-

tomers. A fairly large number have been shopping for gifts in the downtown centers and at discount houses. Prepare a good will letter to be sent to your entire mailing list that stresses your appreciation of their patronage as well as your service and return privileges.

2. Your corporation manufactures garden supplies which are sold through your sales staff to neighborhood hardware stores, garden shops, and miscellaneous outlets. Prepare a good will letter to be mailed at Thanksgiving time.

3. Prepare a good will letter to be sent to former customers of the men's department of Campbell's Department Store. These accounts have made no purchases from this men's department in eighteen months or more.

4. Send a good will letter to all your franchise dealers who represent you as a Tasty Treat Pie Shoppe. You have 1800 franchised dealers in the United States. The letter is to arrive on the first or second day of the new year.

5. As the General Sales Manager of the Bon Ton Food Company, send a good will letter to each of your salesmen. Bon Ton has 140 salesmen operating under six division sales managers. These men have been employed by Bon Ton for anywhere from two to twenty years.

6. Your term of office as President of the Accounting Club will be up in two weeks. Prepare one good will letter to be sent to each of your four officers.

7. You are in the highly competitive furniture field. Many of your dealers purchase from several different firms. Send a good will letter to a selected group of your accounts who purchase only a limited number of items from you. Thank them for their patronage and remind them of the advantages of securing a larger variety of items from your firm.

8. You manufacture and sell hospital equipment on a national scale. You have twenty salesmen representing you. Prepare a good will letter to be directed to either the hospital administration or the purchasing department head who has made an initial purchase from your company. Your Chicago office has a complete display of all your equipment. You also have facilities for modifying equipment to serve the special requirements of doctors or needs of patients.

CHAPTER NINETEEN
Guide and Form Letters

The intelligent and discriminating use of form and guide letters by management can improve a firm's sales and customer relations and save thousands of dollars. There is no point in dictating a letter which must be typed (at a cost of $2.75 to $3.50) if a form or guide letter will accomplish the same end at a fraction of the cost.

GUIDE LETTERS

Many companies have found it valuable to compose a series of guide letters for a variety of situations. Copies are made and complete sets are bound into a notebook or spiral binder. Each letter is numbered for easy reference.

A copy of the notebook is then given to each person who may be concerned with the area. This includes executives and correspondents as well as the secretaries or typists who are required to do the typing.

Let us say that Mr. Reiner has just received an initial order from a new customer, Mr. Calloway. All he need do is tell the typist to send Guide Letter #3 to Mr. Calloway, making sure to fill in the correct name, address, order number and other details. Of course letter #3 has been carefully written, edited, and revised and is probably better than one Mr. Reiner can dictate "off the cuff."

Or perhaps there is a claim situation which must be refused very tactfully and which arises rather frequently. The guide letter which has been prepared does an excellent job, but probably required several hours to write initially. It certainly makes sense to use it rather than take the hour or so to design the tactful, carefully worded reply needed in this case.

In some cases it is helpful to number the paragraphs in each guide letter. Thus the dictator can ask the typist to send Mr. Dalton Guide Letter #10 except "substitute this paragraph for paragraph #3."

Using guide letters takes getting used to. But if a good set of letters is written initially, and company personnel are encouraged to use them, they can prove valuable.

Guide letters, all in all, serve the following purposes for management:

1. They permit the use of carefully written and excellent letters for many situations.
2. They are economical. Because one letter can be used many times for the same situation occurring with different customers, time in letter composition is thereby saved.
3. A guide letter may be sent out quickly as a follow-up on a situation. To prepare and write a specific letter may require an extra day or two.

SITUATIONS FOR USE

Guide letters can be written and successfully used in the following situations:

Welcome letter to new customers.
Letters to customers who have been absent for some time.
Collection letters (those sent early in the collection series).
Refusals of claims, requests for contributions of merchandise and funds, credit, and other recurring situations requiring a denial.
Letters introducing new products; explaining credit procedures, delivery or payment methods; or other changes.

ENCOURAGING THE USE OF GUIDE LETTERS

Pride of authorship is a very important factor in the writing of business letters. Most persons enjoy writing them, take pride in their efforts, and usually feel their letters are far superior to anyone else's in the office. Because of this, many men are reluctant to use letters which they haven't written, but which they must sign.

A good solution to this problem is to first distribute a notebook of draft copies of guide letters to those who will use them, with a request for suggestions for revision and improvement. In this way, those who will sign the letters have also had something to do with their composition. Because of this, there is less reluctance to use them.

Another step required to maintain a high level of use is to constantly encourage the employment of guide letters. And still another factor is the frequent up-dating and revision of the letters so that they will be current and applicable to everyday situations.

FORM LETTERS

Form letters are those which are usually reproduced in large quantities. One hundred thousand form sales letters may be run off and sent to prospects or a hundred form acknowledgments of orders may be reproduced and used as needed.

Form letters are usually processed on high-speed printing equipment. The firm's letterhead stationery is used and the message is multigraphed or multilithed. Many times, specific typewriter type is used so that the letters may be personalized in the company office. Thus the letter can be produced in the print shop using characters which duplicate the style of type of the typewriters which the firm owns. The inside address and salutation can then be filled in and the entire letter appears to have been individually typed. It is even possible, through careful letter composition, to provide for "fill ins" of dates and names in the last few words of a paragraph.

The personal appearance of this type of letter, which apparently has been individually typed, may motivate the reader to take the action the writer requests. On the other hand, there are some people who resent the obvious attempt to hoodwink them into believing that a form letter has been individually typed.

My personal feeling is that form letters should be designed to appear like form letters and nothing more. Most persons recognize the need for them and accept the fact that individual letters cannot possibly be sent to a large number of prospects.

AUTOMATICALLY TYPED LETTERS

Still another type of form letter is the one produced on an automatic typewriter. Here a carefully written letter is composed and transferred to a punched tape or other memory device. When that particular letter is desired, the master is slipped into the typewriter, the inside address and salutation typed on the stationery manually, and the "on" button pressed. The automatic typewriter then types the letter automatically. Some large corporations or letter-reproducing companies maintain a battery of these typewriters. One typist can move from machine to machine manually typing in inside addresses, salutations, order numbers, prices, or names. She then turns the machine "on" and it types the letter effortlessly, quickly, economically, and perfectly. If a "fill-in" is required in the body of the letter, the machine will automatically stop. After the insertion has been made, the automatic control again takes over.

USE OF FORM LETTERS

Form letters can be used for many of the same purposes as guide letters:

> acknowledging orders
> letters to new customers
> basic letters in the collection series
> acknowledging payments
> simple claim situations
> simple adjustment situations
> routine inquiries
> answers to inquiries
> routine announcements

However, the chief use of form letters is for sales promotion and sales follow-up situations. Millions of such letters are sent out annually in the United States.

Both guide and form letters thus serve very useful purposes. They help build sales and good will and do so economically and efficiently.

QUESTIONS FOR STUDY

I. Complete any of the following problems assigned. You may wish to review the chapter and note key points before solving the problem.

1. Your firm manufactures electrical appliances which are distributed nationally. Prepare a guide letter to be mailed to individuals who request free appliances which may be sold to raise funds for schools, churches, and so on. In your letter you must regretfully refuse these individual requests even though you recognize the merits of the endeavor. However, you do receive between 25 and 50 such requests each month. Your firm does contribute large sums to national charities on a yearly basis.

2. Prepare a guide letter to be used for new customers. This letter is to be sent after the first order has been received by one of your company's salesmen.

3. Design a guide letter to be sent to all those persons who request a replica of our new jet passenger transport. It is true that we have these replicas but we supply them to travel agents for display purposes only and they remain our property and must be returned so that other travel agents may use them.

As a national airline we would like very much to send them out to individuals, school classes, and various organizations, but the cost to us would be prohibitive.

4. As a local rapid transit line, we receive 15 to 30 letters each day inquiring about lost articles. We check with our central lost and found and if the item hasn't turned up, we send a letter to the individual. Prepare such a letter to be used as a guide.

5. Try to sell a guide and form letter service to the local department stores. Include two or three of your guide letters as samples.

Point out the advantages to the store of having such a service and how economical it can prove to be.

PART FOUR

Readings

COMMUNICATION IN MANAGEMENT

Mason Haire

One of the major responsibilities of a leader is the establishment and utilization of a communication system. His communications with his subordinates are the medium through which he directs their efforts. By means of these communications the leader defines the goals of the organization and the subgroup; he tells the subordinate what is expected of him, what resources are available, how well he is doing, and the like. The communications from the superior are the things on the basis of which the subordinate is able to form a stable organization of his work world. They are the medium through which the superior can administer reward and punishment and, by a utilization of the Law of Effect, help the subordinate to learn what the boundaries of the situation are, and which behaviors are approved and which disapproved. Without a rich flow of communications from the superior, the subordinate cannot know what the situation is, which direction he should be going, how well he is doing, and the like; without good communication he is in an impossibly insecure position.

On the other hand, the communication from the subordinate to the superior is a real necessity to the successful leader. It is on the basis of these communications that the superior knows his subordinates. It is on the basis of these communications that the superior can diagnose misperceptions on the part of his subordinates of the goals of the group, of their own role and what is expected of them, of their degree of success, and the like. Upward communications provide the first symptoms of tension and difficulties in the group as they reflect aggressions and insecurities. Further and perhaps most important, it is on the basis of these messages that the superior can see the role which he himself plays, can tell the way in which he is seen by his subordinates, and consequently can fashion his behavior accordingly. A sensitivity to the movement of communications is one of the prime requisites of a successful leader, and the utilization of communications both to and from the leader can be one of his greatest assets.

"TWO-WAY" COMMUNICATION

So far, this description of the problem of communication sounds very much like the emphasis on so-called "two-way communications" which is one of the current fads of personnel philosophies. Indeed, to a certain extent it is just such an emphasis. However, the problem of communication is not nearly so simple. The problem of communication is not merely to provide an opportunity for person A to say something to B and for B to say something back to A. Each of them is concerned that the other not only hears what he says, but also accepts it, integrates it into his view of the world, and acts on it, rather than distorting it, rejecting it, or hiding it away. . . .

One of the easiest mistakes to make in the practice of communication is to feel that because we have heard ourselves say something, the other person necessarily has heard us say it too, and moreover, has heard much the same thing that we heard ourselves say. The steps in the normal communication process probably usually go something like this: Suddenly A thinks of something. He thinks, "I must tell B so-and-so." He goes over to B and says "So-and-so." At this point, A is quite apt to be through. He has put the idea in words. He has got it outside himself, and he has heard it out there, so he usually assumes that it has taken the next step—that is, that it has gone from being outside A to being inside B. Consequently A is quite apt to walk away confident in his communication. However, he may go further. He may ask B, "Do you get it?" or "Is that clear?" Now, by and large, these are questions to which B is only allowed to answer "Yes"; for B to say anything else suggests an inadequacy in him, so the answer is apt to be irrelevant to the communication. However, even if B is a strong character, and his "Yes" means actually "Yes, I do understand what you said," he still can only mean "I understand what I heard," not "I understand what you heard yourself say." If the communication is of any importance, A must have more information than this; he must know something of what B heard.

At first glance this seems to make the problem of communication almost impossible. On the one hand, we are apt to think that no serious misunderstanding will arise if A assumes that B heard A say the same thing that A heard himself say, and on the other hand, it seems very difficult for A ever to find out what B did hear, if he can't trust the answer when he asks B, "Did you understand that?" Indeed, it is difficult to communicate. We are probably saved mostly by the fact that there is a very great tolerance in the degree of understanding that we require of one another; very little precision is asked of most of our communications. However, it is still possible for A to find out a good deal more about what B heard. Even though he can't trust B's response when he asks him directly, there are other techniques. If A, after he has made his statement, simply does not walk away, and does not ask any questions, but only stands a moment in an expectant pause, he will create a situation in which B is much more likely to tell him what he heard. B, feeling that the matter is not closed, and that some sort of response is required of him, will probably either ask questions, revealing his conception of the communication, or repeat the gist of it, so that A now knows not only what he heard himself say, but, to some extent, what B heard.

COMMUNICATION AND THE ORGANIZATION OF THE ENVIRONMENT

. . . The other problem—the fact that B may have heard A say something different from what A heard himself say—is more serious. Each individual has the problem of organizing a sensible and coherent world for himself out of an external environment which does not make sense in itself. The same problem is present in communication. When A talks to B, he never tells B everything. He relies on B to fill in gaps, to relate the material to larger patterns, and to organize the whole thing into a sensible order. In doing this B will very often organize the material in such a way that the words no longer mean the same thing to him that they did to A. A little thought will probably call to mind instances in which each of us spoke confidently about something, only to find that our listener was interpreting a key word differently and had distorted the whole thing completely. However, an example may show the point even better.

Immediately above, you will see a square made up of nine dots. The problem is to draw four straight lines which join all nine dots. Try the problem yourself. Copy the dots on another piece of paper and see if you can do it. You are not allowed to lift your pencil from the paper, and every time you change the direction of a line (turning or retracing) it counts as another line. You are not allowed to fold the paper.

It usually seems very hard to do. Five lines would do it nicely, but four seems very difficult. However, it is not difficult at all. If you will look at the figure on p. 494, you will see how it can be done. It looks funny, but it is only four lines, and it does go through all the dots.

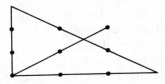

Almost everyone will try to solve the problem while staying inside the square of dots. Many people even say, "Oh, but you told me to stay in the square." Actually the instructions did not say that the lines must be in the square. In fact, there is no square there. The dots are an example of the situation in which the environment provides an amibiguous stimulus, which the perceiver organizes into a square. Rather than see nine unconnected dots, we typically see them joined together in a good square, and this organization, which we provide, leads us to interpret the instructions in a particular way. It does not matter that the instructor heard himself clearly and knows that he did not say to stay within the square. To make sense of the environment, the problem solver will add his own instructions, and to make sure of the communication, the instructor should get some response back from the subject to indicate how this particular piece of the world is interpreted. Very nearly the same kind of thing happens at work when a subordinate is given part of the information on the superior's belief that the rest is unnecessary. The subordinate, being faced with the necessity of making sense out of many parts of his environment, will organize it as best he can, and often not in the manner intended.

This is an example of a situation in which principles of organization arising from factors within the outside environment dictated the kind of sense the observer would make of the world. Other kinds of pressures act to determine particular organizations, too. Very often motivations and emotions tend to alter the way in which things are seen and heard, and these must be taken into account in assessing our communication. Industrial organizations are hierarchical, and what the boss says has meaning because the boss said it. His words are not just words; they are the boss's words. If he says "Things aren't going well," he may refer to his own feeling of inadequacy about managing; the insecure subordinate may hear him suggesting that he (the subordinate) is falling down on the job. If the boss says "Things are going to expand here soon," he may be referring to plans for new space and new machinery, and knowing the content of his own ideas, he clearly hears the reference. The ambitious subordinate, however, equally clearly hears a promise of possibilities of advancement, and if they are not forthcoming, he will be resentful since he has had an explicit promise. In all these cases, the motivations and emotions of the listener and the kind of need systems to which he refers the statement determine its meaning. In order to avoid gross mis-understanding, it is essential for A to know not only what he heard him-self say but what B heard.

Such misunderstandings are not at all uncommon outside industry. During World War II, an aerial-gunnery student was taking a training flight over the Gulf of Mexico. The pilot, enjoying the ride and the scen-ery, pointed over the side of the plane, in a friendly spirit, to call the student's attention to a speedboat below. The gesture was clear to him, but the student referred it to his own acute terror of being in the air, and interpreting it to mean that his worst fears were realized, he parachuted over the side. In many senses the two people were not acting in the same world, and the pilot's attempt to communicate without fitting his sym-bols to the world of the listener was typical of a very common error in communication patterns.

Often the meaning of a fact may become, for various reasons, very special to one person or a group of people, and a reference to it will elicit quite different responses in them than in others. It is essential, in such cases, to realize this fact, and to trim communication techniques to fit the organization of the listener. . . . Under the influence of a strong motive the facts may be distorted so that they actually look different to the per-son. When one gets up at night to investigate a strange sound and goes into the darkened living room, the coat thrown over a chair momentarily and temporarily actually is a terrifying figure, and it is responded to as such. It does not matter that another person may know that it is only a coat, or that the investigator himself may subsequently learn that it is only a coat. At the time of his misperception, under the influence of his motivation, the only thing that is real is his experience, and his experi-ence covers a threatening figure rather than a discarded coat. The psy-chological environment may not agree entirely with what we know to be physically present, but what is psychologically present—molded by our fears and hopes as well as by other mechanisms—is the thing that determines our behavior.

PSYCHOLOGICAL MECHANISMS PROTECTING ORGANIZATIONS

There is still another characteristic of human beings, arising out of the individual's problem in organizing his environment, which acts to im-pede and distort communications. Once we have achieved a satisfactory organization of a piece of the world we tend to retain it, even in the face of contradictory information. Facing an ambiguous situation generates an acute anxiety in us. When the situation is one which has considerable importance to us—as when we must decide which paths of action will lead to success, or what philosophy of life or political point of view is best—the pressure is increased. It then becomes extremely important to us to bring some order into the facts and to achieve a stable organization on the basis of which our behavior may be directed. Once such an organization is achieved, we tend to retain it and protect it, rather than to admit other facts and let it change, because the possibility of change involves leaving the security of an existing organization that works.

Several techniques are common for this kind of protection of existing organizations. In the first place, we tend to select those sources of information which will present facts in harmony with our present pattern, and to avoid sources of information which do not fit easily with our organizations. Beyond this, if we are confronted with discrepant information, it is a characteristic of human mental process to distort the information, to reject or overlook it, to reinterpret it or explain it away, and as a final resort, to eliminate it gradually through selective forgetting. All these processes act to preserve and protect existing organized attitudes and pictures of the world, and whenever one aims to change such an attitude they must be taken into account. They are of sufficient importance to communication to warrant a more detailed examination.

One of the greatest difficulties in effecting a communication which will change our minds lies in the fact that we all tend to select sources of information which purvey material with which we already agree. This is not at all a deliberate conscious choice to bolster our own prejudices or to avoid seeing the other side of the question. Rather it is because the information from these sources tends to make sense to us, is understood easily, and is couched in the kinds of phrases we understand. All these things at once select the source for us and protect us from having to change our minds. The phenomenon is quite common in industry. When a group assembles to discuss the kinds of problems raised in this book, we find that the personnel men go to personnel meetings, the vice-presidents to vice-presidents' meetings, and the foremen to foremen's meetings. Each finds himself in a group where the others have the same general kinds of organization of the world that he has. As the meeting goes on, the personnel men say personnel kinds of things to one another, they hear their own points of view presented in different words, and they go away reinforced in their original opinions. Similarly with the others. This example is not meant to belittle personnel men or vice-presidents or foremen in particular. Rather it is a characteristic of all of us, and the tendency to choose sources of information which present facts in agreement with already existing organizations is one of the large barriers to communication designed to change a person's mind.

During the war the Treasury Department produced a movie about buying war bonds. It was one of a series of techniques directed toward changing people's behavior in this particular dimension—toward increasing bond purchases. A test was conducted to determine its effectiveness in changing people's minds and actions. A particular community was chosen for study, and a sample of the audience interviewed in detail to find out who went and what kind of effect the movie had had. Tickets to the movie had been distributed free through service clubs, women's clubs, religious groups, newspaper offices, and the like, so that they were available to almost everyone who might want to go. However, when the interviews were conducted it was found that the people who attended were those who were already giving blood at the blood banks and were already buying bonds. The movie had attracted the people who were already convinced. Those for whom participation in activities closely related to the war effort seemed important were attracted by the idea of the movie, and they chose to go to see the film urging them to participate. Those who did not participate in such activities were not interested in the film, and by and large did not go. Unfortunately this is the fate of many of our attempts to change people's minds. The people who already agree are the only ones who listen.

In many cases, however, all of us find ourselves confronted with facts which are at variance with our already existing view of the situation—facts which threaten our organization of the world. A simple selection of the media which carry facts to our liking is not enough. We cannot successfully avoid being faced with discrepant information. At this point, in order to protect existing organizations and to avoid the insecurity of ambiguity, there is a group of psychological mechanisms that act to reject and distort information in the interest of preserving a stable organization.

One of the things that we very often do is simply to overlook such incongruent facts. Most of us probably do this particularly in the cases of complicated problems and problems which are close to our personal values. Certainly there is a good deal of such overlooking or rejecting of information in connection with our assessment of the personalities of our families and our friends, and probably even more in the case of our own personalities. We think of ourselves as having certain sorts of characteristics, and even though we may act quite differently on occasion, these items are conveniently omitted from our picture because they do not fit. Similarly, on complicated issues it is often possible to overlook the relevance of various items of information which are at variance with our view of the situation.

To take another example from wartime bond campaigns, a survey was conducted early in the war to determine why people bought war bonds. Most of them (65 per cent in April, 1943) said it was to finance the war; at this time 14 per cent said it was to help prevent inflation. A tremendous advertising campaign was conducted in the next few years, with the prevention of inflation an important theme. In June, 1945, 68 per cent of the people thought bonds should be bought to help finance the war and 14 per cent thought they should be bought to help prevent inflation. Certainly this is a very discouraging suggestion about the possibility of changing people's minds, even with a kind of publicity campaign that was virtually universal in its contact. After two years of this kind of publicity about the inflationary effect of a shortage of consumer goods and the increase in purchasing power, 54 per cent of the people either said that bond purchases had no effect on prices or said that they could not see any relation between the two. The disheartening suggestion is that the information about inflationary pressures was communicated to those who already realized them and the information about supporting the war reached those who already held this position. There is very little real evidence of any change in opinion.

In face-to-face communications, all of us have been in situations where people have been quite impervious to facts that were being presented. Indeed, in many arguments one often gets the impression that the "listener" is not, in fact, a listener at all. He is simply politely remaining silent until it is his turn to speak, meanwhile mustering his own arguments. His reply is apt to be almost totally irrelevant to the preceding speaker's statement. He often seems to have completely ignored the points. Such rejection obviously poses a real problem in communication and must be recognized if it is present.

More frequently, however, it is not possible to reject items completely. In these cases the tendency is to distort them so that they fit into the already existing organization. A fact is not complete by itself; it has meaning partly in terms of the context in which it is seen. Consequently, in many cases we find that a piece of information which has been intended by the speaker in a particular way is changed and remodeled by the hearer to fit another context. Indeed, when it is heard in the new context, there is no need to change it; the simple fact of its contextual relations will make the change. There is no question here of a deliberate and conscious attempt to distort, but only of a variation in meaning which comes from the interpretation given to a fact by including it in a particular context.

This kind of distortion is well illustrated in a series of experiments that have been done on the way in which people form impressions of a personality. If we were to ask people to describe the actions of someone who is "helpful, quick, and skillful" as opposed to another person who is "helpful, quick, and clumsy," the word "quick" which is in both descriptions means quite different things. In the first case it is the quickness of a person who is deft and sure and whose help is successful and welcome. In the second case the quickness is a blundering sort of rushing in where the helpfulness is more apt to be a liability than an asset. The meaning of the term depends, to a large extent, on the context in which it is seen. Similarly, if we are told that a person is "cool, industrious, capable, forceful, intelligent, effective," we have a very different picture from one who is "warm, industrious, capable, forceful, intelligent, and effective." The difference in the basic orientation of the organized view of the personality originates in the cool-warm difference, and it changes the meaning of all the items in the list.

In another experiment two groups of men were asked to describe the personality of a man on the basis of a picture and a brief description of what he does. One group consisted of union members of a central labor council; the other group consisted of industrial-relations and personnel men from industry. Both groups were shown the same picture and the same description, but management representatives were told it was a union officer, while the union representatives were told it was a member of management. In each case the description of the man given them was reinterpreted by them to fit their already existing view of what union men or management men were like, and the personalities described were quite different, each molded to harmonize with present organizations. Although each group had the same set of "facts" about the man to work on, they selected and altered them quite differently. It is entirely possible that members of the two groups, meeting in bargaining, could talk about such a man or about an issue in such a way that they used very nearly the same words but never really referred to the same thing.

As a last resort, we often provide the distortion in memory. A fact is retained in memory as part of an organized system there. If it does not fit well, it tends to be modified to fit into the essential character of the pattern of memory. The well-known changes that take place in a rumor as it is heard, remembered, and retold are an example of this kind of change. A graphic example can be seen in an experiment on memory for visual figures. Two groups of people were shown a series of figures and asked to reproduce them later. One of the figures looked like this: O-O . The group who were told it was a symbol for eyeglasses reproduced it later like this: OO . The group who were told it was a symbol for dumbbells reproduced it like this: O-O . The same "fact" was modified in memory to fit the essential character of the memory system. . . .

REJECTION OF THE MEDIA
OF COMMUNICATION

Still another psychological mechanism which acts to impede communication lies in the fact that people tend, in the interest of simplifying the problem of receiving information from the environment, to evaluate the whole medium of information through which information is received, and to accept or reject the medium and everything it carries, rather than to have to make specific judgments on separate items. Thus, for example, all of us have thrown advertising circulars out of the mail without giving them more than a casual glance. We have a general organization of the sources of communication, and we act on the implicit theory that there is a low probability of getting important information from this one. The medium is seen as one which carries certain sorts of material; since it isn't a kind of material which we particularly want, we reject the whole content without analysis. House organs probably often meet the same fate, and in many cases it seems impossible to make them into good communication media without changing their entire character in the minds of the potential recipients.

The extent to which this kind of rejection can go is shown in a survey conducted by the Treasury Department in connection with the war-bond drive which has been mentioned before. As part of the campaign, a pamphlet on bonds was mailed to every household in certain parts of the country. A check on the effectiveness of the pamphlet was conducted by interviewing a sample of the recipients in Baltimore. In spite of the fact that the pamphlet had been in every mailbox, two weeks later only 17 per cent of the people even recognized it when they were allowed to examine it, and 83 per cent of the people could not even remember having seen it two weeks before. Of the 17 per cent who recognized it, one-third only remembered having seen the cover, and consequently only about 10 per cent were even exposed to the material within. This gloomy result is probably characteristic of the fate of information carried in many media of communication where a generalized negative evaluation has been made of the kind of facts that are apt to be found within.

Wherever a form of communication has become routine and stereo-typed, it is liable to be judged in terms of the kind of information usually contained, and hence may become almost useless for conveying any other kind. Many of the techniques of communication that are in use in industry today no doubt are characterized in such a manner, and many of them suffer by it. In addition to the aura that the house organ has, which may make it inappropriate for carrying certain messages, such media as the annual report, weekly luncheons with supervisory groups, speeches on the occasion of awarding service pins, and the like, may tend to be stereotyped by the listener. "They usually talk about such-and-such, and so there's no need to listen." Formalized and routinized methods of communication are always in need of a constant reevaluation and analysis to determine how the communication channel itself is seen by the recipients, for the effect of its content is largely determined by the listeners' perception of the medium. . . .

In the face of a host of difficulties in communications, it seems strange that anything ever gets across. Indeed, it is difficult, and it is probably because of this difficulty that most human relationships are built in such a way that they do not demand great precision in communication except in simple specific denotations. By and large, people get along on the basis of an unexpressed realization that no two people see the world the same way, and that different people seldom mean the same thing when they speak the same words. However, in a closely interdependent organization there are many cases where the transmission of information and the changing of attitudes is essential. Some points to improve this necessary communication can be derived from an examination of the very difficulties themselves.

TECHNIQUES OF COMMUNICATION

The material to be communicated must be tailored on the basis of the listener's view of the situation rather than the content of the information itself; this point has already been stressed. Unfortunately, most of us are so used to building statements in terms of content, and so clear about what we are trying to say, that it is difficult to accomplish this reversal in approach. However, the greatest single aid to communication would probably be learning to *tailor information on the basis of the recipient's organization* of the situation.

A good example of the failure to tailor the information to the other person is often found in the booklets describing the company that are issued in many plants. In one specific case, the company published an expensive booklet on glossy paper in full color, for the purpose of providing indoctrination and orientation for new employees. An interview study of a group of employees who had been with the company for six months or less brought out the discouraging fact that not a single one of them had read the document. Why? The pamphlet, though beautifully done, was written for management to read. It told that there were many thousands of employees of the organization; that the investment per worker was so-and-so much; that the company paid an annual wage bill in astronomical figures. Information such as this is interesting and meaningful to the men who wrote the booklet, to their immediate superiors, and to the vice-presidential board which probably had to pass on it. However, the bulk of the new employees were girls in their teens for whom these figures, and particularly this way of stating them, had no meaning or interest at all. The money that was spent on the brochure was virtually a total loss.

Another method that would probably improve communications would be to *transmit information in small units.* A large organized mass of material tends to threaten existing patterns in the listener and so may be rejected. Small units transmitted little by little carry the same message over a period of time without the same likelihood of rejection. Cumulatively they may effect the change where they would be rejected out of hand if they were presented at once.

The importance of finding out what the listener has heard has come up repeatedly. As a check on what was, in fact, communicated, it is essential for the communicator to *provide an opportunity for "feedback"* from the recipient. Unless one has some way of finding out what was heard, either by observing subsequent behavior or by some kind of restatement, communication must remain pretty much a matter of shooting in the dark, with very uncertain results.

One of the most effective ways to provide for feedback, and at the same time an effective technique for communication, is to *provide an opportunity for participation* on the part of the recipient. If the material and situation are such that the recipient can be brought into a discussion and encouraged to state problems and solutions in his own words, many of the difficulties are overcome. For one thing, a constant index of his view of the matter is present. For another, he becomes involved in the material himself, so it is less apt to be a threat to his existing organizations, and consequently it is less apt to be rejected or distorted to protect private views of the world. Finally, such a practice frees the listener from the one-sidedness of much communication where he passively listens to what he is told. Now he participates in it and is part of it, and he no longer has to reject the material on the grounds that being told threatens his egoistic need-satisfactions and feeling of independence. Eliciting participation is often a relatively costly process in time and effort, and at first glance it seems unnecessary and prohibitively expensive. However, the returns are potentially very great, and with practice it becomes much easier to accomplish.

CHANGING ATTITUDES

One other point should be considered before we leave the problem of communication. We are usually interested in communication with the aim of changing other people's attitudes and with the eventual aim of changing their behavior. We want people to stop doing something they are doing or to start doing something they aren't doing, and we have the feeling that their behavior flows from their attitudes and that if their attitudes were different the behavior would change. Because of this we try to influence attitudes. Since this is so large a part of the field of communication, it is a good idea to look a little more closely at the problem of attitudes.

We often speak of someone "having" an attitude, as if the attitude were a tangible and separate thing, in much the same sense that he might have a Chevrolet rather than a Ford. This way of speaking about it has led us to try to change "his" attitude by persuasion, sweet reasonableness, or attack. Certainly all of us have been discouraged by the fact that we do not seem to change attitudes in this manner very often, and that, indeed, attack often seems to strengthen the person in the attitude he "has." If we look back over what we have said so far about the problem of an individual's making sense out of his complex environment, we see that we should not think of him as "having" an attitude but rather as having organized the world in a certain way. In this sense the word "attitude" should not be used as a noun, but rather as an adverb that modifies the verb "to see." An attitude is a way of seeing things. To attack it as "his" attitude is to miss the meaning of the organization of the other person's perception of the world. Instead, we must try to see the way in which he sees things and then help him to see other things there.

On a hot day the surf looks inviting and cool. We do not at all have the feeling that this is an attitude in us. Regardless of the past experience that leads it to look this way, within ourselves the invitingness is simply a part of the view of the surf. To try to attack this view by argument is likely to leave us quite unmoved. Indeed, if the argument continues, we may well come to a point where we defend it as a point of honor *because* it is attacked. If someone wanted to change our behavior (that is, to keep us from going swimming), it would be more appropriate for him to realize that it looks cool and inviting and to work from there. Perhaps he could point out other similarly cooling things that required less exertion, such as a long drink on a shaded porch. Perhaps he could lead us to see other things in the surf that would change our perception, such as the undertow or the danger of sunburn. His doing these things might change the way we see the surf and might consequently change our behavior. In this way he would have changed the adverbial character of the attitude, that is, he would have changed the way we saw. He would not have changed the attitude in the sense of having attacked and modified something that we had.

An attitude is not something that resides in the person. It is a characteristic of the way he sees things. This leads us to take quite different means to modify it. Usually it is better to work indirectly to do this rather than to attack it broadside. . . .

What we mean by morale is the effects of the way the plant force sees their working environment. It is the result of certain ways of seeing. To deal with it we need to understand as clearly as possible how they do see it, and then to consider what things within them or within the environment lead to this kind of perception. Then, perhaps, we are ready to try to alter the process of seeing, and in this way, the morale.

SUMMARY

1. Communication is important to the superior as part of his job of directing the work of his subordinates and of creating a situation in which they can help him to get the job done. At the same time the importance of communication to the subordinate is clear in terms of his problem of making a pattern for himself of the nature of the job and his role, and to help him keep a clear picture of the world in which he operates.

2. The chief difficulty seems to arise by virtue of the fact that people tend to organize information into meaningful wholes, and in the process they may receive different information from what the communicator intended to convey. More specifically, hopes and fears may serve to modify and distort information. There is a tendency to reject and distort items on the basis of already existing organizations of the subject, and to reject whole media of communication and to render them ineffective. Finally, it is important to keep practice in line with statements because of the role of the Law of Effect in the acceptance or rejection of communicated material.

3. In an attempt to find ways to improve communications, on the basis of these difficulties and the nature of people, we have seen the importance of tailoring material in terms of the recipient's organization of the subject. We have also seen the possibility of communicating in small units, the importance of a "feedback" which will allow the communicator to check what is actually getting across, and the value of participation as a technique for effecting communication. Both the problems and the solutions in the area of communication are part of every other phase of industrial problems. Wherever we turn in considering problems of human beings at work—in the area of leadership, of training, or wherever—we see evidences of these same barriers and the same techniques for overcoming them. In many senses, good communications seems to be the key to many of the problems in our industrial society.

4. In using communication to change attitudes, we must remember that an attitude is a way of seeing things. The word "attitude" is not a noun; it is an adverb modifying the verb "to see." Indirect approaches to changing the way people see things are much more apt to produce the change in behavior than are attempts to change an attitude by force of argument.

HOW WORDS
CHANGE OUR LIVES

S. I. Hayakawa

The end product of education, yours and mine and everybody's, is the total pattern of reactions and possible reactions we have inside ourselves. If you did not have within you at this moment the pattern of reactions which we call "the ability to read English," you would see here only meaningless black marks on paper. Because of the trained patterns of response, you are (or are not) stirred to patriotism by martial music, your feelings of reverence are aroused by the symbols of your religion, you listen more respectfully to the health advice of someone who has "M.D." after his name than to that of someone who hasn't. What I call here a "pattern of reactions," then, is the sum total of the ways we act in response to events, to words and to symbols.

Our reaction patterns—our semantic habits, as we may call them—are the internal and most important residue of whatever years of education or miseducation we may have received from our parents' conduct toward us in childhood as well as their teachings, from the formal education we may have had, from all the sermons and lectures we have listened to, from the radio programs and the movies and television shows we have experienced, from all the books and newspapers and comic strips we have read, from the conversations we have had with friends and associates, and from all our experiences. If, as the result of all these influences that make us what we are, our semantic habits are reasonably similar to those of most people around us, we are regarded as "well-adjusted," or "normal," and perhaps "dull." If our semantic habits are noticeably different from those of others, we are regarded as "individualistic" or "original," or, if the differences are disapproved of or viewed with alarm, as "screwball" or "crazy."

Semantics is sometimes defined in dictionaries as "the science of the meaning of words"—which would not be a bad definition if people didn't assume that the search for the meanings of words begins and ends with looking them up in a dictionary.

If one stops to think for a moment, it is clear that to define a word, as a dictionary does, is simply to explain the word with more words. To be thorough about defining, we should next have to define the words used in the definition, then define the words used in defining the words used in the definition . . . and so on. Defining words with more words, in short, gets us at once into what mathematicians call an "infinite regress." Alternatively, it can get us into the kind of run-around we sometimes encounter when we look up "impertinence" and find it defined as "impudence," so we look up "impudence" and find it defined as "impertinence." Yet—and here we come to another common reaction pattern —people often act as if words can be explained fully with more words. To a person who asked for a definition of jazz, Louis Armstrong is said to have replied, "Man, when you got to ask what it is, you'll never get to know," proving himself to be an intuitive semanticist as well as a great trumpet player.

WHAT SEMANTICS IS ABOUT

Semantics, then, does not deal with the "meaning of words" as that expression is commonly understood. P. W. Bridgman, the Nobel-prize winner and physicist, once wrote, "The true meaning of a term is to be found by observing what a man does with it, not by what he says about it." He made an enormous contribution to science by showing that the meaning of a scientific term lies in the operations, the things done, that establish its validity, rather than in verbal definitions.

Here is a simple, everyday kind of example of "operational" criticism. If you say, "This table measures six feet in length," you could prove it by taking a foot rule, performing the operation of laying it end to end while counting, "One . . . two . . . three . . . four . . ." But if you say—and revolutionists have started uprisings with just this statement—"Man is born free, but everywhere he is in chains!"—what operations could you perform to demonstrate its accuracy or inaccuracy?

But let us carry this suggestion of "operationalism" outside the physical sciences where Bridgman applied it, and observe what "operations" people perform as the result of both the language they use and the language other people use in communicating to them. Here is a personnel manager studying an application blank. He comes to the words "Education: Harvard University," and drops the application blank in the wastebasket (that's the "operation") because, as he would say if you asked him, "I don't like Harvard men." This is an instance of "meaning" at work— but it is not a meaning that can be found in dictionaries.

If I seem to be taking a long time to explain what semantics is about, it is because I am trying, in the course of explanation, to introduce the reader to a certain way of looking at human behavior. Semantics—especially the general semantics of Alfred Korzybski (1879-1950), Polish-

American scientist and educator—pays particular attention not to words in themselves, but to semantic reactions—that is, human responses to symbols, signs and symbol-systems, including language.

I say *human* responses because, so far as we know, human beings are the only creatures that have, over and above that biological equipment which we have in common with other creatures, the additional capacity for manufacturing symbols and systems of symbols. When we react to a flag, we are not reacting simply to a piece of cloth, but to the meaning with which it has been symbolically endowed. When we react to a word, we are not reacting to a set of sounds, but to the meaning with which that set of sounds has been symbolically endowed.

A basic idea in general semantics, therefore, is that the meaning of words (or other symbols) is not in the words, but in our own semantic reactions. If I were to tell a shockingly obscene story in Arabic or Hindustani or Swahili before an audience that understood only English, no one would blush or be angry; the story would be neither shocking nor obscene—indeed, it would not even be a story. Likewise, the value of a dollar bill is not in the bill, but in our social agreement to accept it as a symbol of value. If that agreement were to break down through the collapse of our Government, the dollar bill would become only a scrap of paper. We do not understand a dollar bill by staring at it long and hard. We understand it by observing how people act with respect to it. We understand it by understanding the social mechanisms and the loyalties that keep it meaningful. Semantics is therefore a social study, basic to all other social studies.

It is often remarked that words are tricky—and that we are all prone to be deceived by "fast talkers," such as high-pressure salesmen, skillful propagandists, politicians or lawyers. Since few of us are aware of the degree to which we use words to deceive ourselves, the sin of "using words in a tricky way" is one that is always attributed to the other fellow. When the Russians use the word "democracy" to mean something quite different from what we mean by it, we at once accuse them of "propaganda," of "corrupting the meanings of words." But when we use the word "democracy" in the United States to mean something quite different from what the Russians mean by it, they are equally quick to accuse us of "hypocrisy." We all tend to believe that the way we use words is the correct way, and that people who use the same words in other ways are either ignorant or dishonest.

WORDS EVOKE DIFFERENT RESPONSES

Leaving aside for a moment such abstract and difficult terms as "democracy," let us examine a common, everyday word like "frog." Surely there is no problem about what "frog" means! Here are some sample sentences:

"If we're going fishing, we'll have to catch some frogs first." (This is easy.)

"I have a frog in my throat." (You can hear it croaking.)

"She wore a loose, silk jacket fastened with braided frogs."

"The blacksmith pared down the frog and the hoof before shoeing the horse."

"In Hamilton, Ohio, there is a firm by the name of American Frog and Switch Company."

In addition to these "frogs," there is the frog in which a sword is carried, the frog at the bottom of a bowl or vase that is used in flower arrangement, and the frog which is part of a violin bow. The reader can no doubt think of other "frogs."

Or take another common word such as "order." There is the order that the salesman tries to get, which is quite different from the order which a captain gives to his crew. Some people enter holy orders. There is the order in the house when mother has finished tidying up; there is the batting order of the home team; there is an order of ham and eggs. It is surprising that with so many meanings to the word, people don't misunderstand one another oftener than they do.

The foregoing are only striking examples of a principle to which we are all so well accustomed that we rarely think of it; namely, that most words have more meanings than dictionaries can keep track of. And when we consider further that each of us has different experiences, different memories, different likes and dislikes, it is clear that all words evoke different responses in all of us. We may agree as to what the term "Mississippi River" stands for, but you and I recall different parts of the river; you and I have had different experiences with it; one of us has read more about it than the other; one of us may have happy memories of it, while the other may recall chiefly tragic events connected with it. Hence your "Mississippi River" can never be identical with my "Mississippi River." The fact that we can communicate with each other about the "Mississippi River" often conceals the fact that we are talking about two different sets of memories and experiences.

FIXED REACTIONS TO CERTAIN WORDS

Words being as varied in their meanings as they are, no one can tell us what the correct interpretation of a word should be in advance of our next encounter with that word. The reader may have been taught always to revere the word "mother." But what is he going to do the next time he encounters this word, when it occurs in the sentence "Mother began to form in the bottle"? If it is impossible to determine what a single word will mean on next encounter, is it possible to say in advance what is the correct evaluation of such events as these: (1) next summer, an individual who calls himself a socialist will announce his candidacy for the office of register of deeds in your city; (2) next autumn, there will be a strike at one of your local department stores; (3) next week, your wife will announce that she is going to change her style of hairdo; (4) tomorrow, your little boy will come home with a bleeding nose?

A reasonably sane individual will react to each of these events in his own way, according to time, place and the entire surrounding set of circumstances; and included among those circumstances will be his own stock of experiences, wishes, hopes and fears. But there are people whose pattern of reactions is such that some of them can be completely predicted in advance. Mr. A will never vote for anyone called "socialist," no matter how incompetent or crooked the alternative candidates may be. Mr. B-1 always disapproves of strikes and strikers, without bothering to inquire whether or not this strike has its justifications; Mr. B-2 always sympathizes with the strikers because he hates all bosses. Mr. C belongs to the "stay sweet as you are" school of thought, so that his wife hasn't been able to change her hairdo since she left high school. Mr. D always faints at the sight of blood.

Such fixed and unalterable patterns of reaction—in their more obvious forms we call them prejudices—are almost inevitably organized around words. Mr. E distrusts and fears all people to whom the term "Catholic" is applicable, while Mr. F, who is Catholic, distrusts and fears all non-Catholics. Mr. G is so rabid a Republican that he reacts with equal dislike to all Democrats, all Democratic proposals, all opposite proposals if they are also made by Democrats. Back in the days when Franklin D. Roosevelt was President, Mr G disliked not only the Democratic President but also his wife, children and dog. His office was on Roosevelt Road in Chicago (it had been named after Theodore Roosevelt), but he had his address changed to his back door on 11th Street, so that he would not have to print the hated name on his stationery. Mr. H, on the other hand, is an equally rabid Democrat, who hates himself for continuing to play golf, since golf is Mr. Eisenhower's favorite game. People suffering from such prejudices seem to have in their brains an uninsulated spot which, when touched by such words as "capitalist," "boss," "striker," "scab," "Democrat," "Republican," "socialized medicine," and other such loaded terms, results in an immediate short circuit, often with a blowing of fuses.

Alfred Korzybski, the founder of general semantics, called such short-circuited responses "identification reactions." He used the word "identification" in a special sense; he meant that persons given to such fixed patterns of response identify (that is, treat as identical) all occurrences of a given word or symbol; they identify all the different cases that fall under the same name. Thus, if one has hostile identification reactions to "women drivers," then all women who drive cars are "identical" in their incompetence.

Korzybski believed that the term "identification reaction" could be generally used to describe the majority of cases of semantic malfunctioning. Identification is something that goes on in the human nervous system. "Out there" there are no absolute identities. No two Harvard men, no two Ford cars, no two mothers-in-law, no two politicians, no two leaves from the same tree, are identical with each other in all respects. If, however, we treat all cases that fall under the same class label as one at times when the differences are important, then there is something wrong with our semantic habits.

ANOTHER DEFINITION
OF GENERAL SEMANTICS

We are now ready, then, for another definition of general semantics. It is a comparative study of the kinds of responses people make to the symbols and signs around them; we may compare the semantic habits common among the prejudiced, the foolish and the mentally ill with those found among people who are able to solve their problems successfully, so that, if we care to, we may revise our own semantic habits for the better. In other words, general semantics is, if we wish to make it so, the study of how not to be a damn fool.

Identification reactions run all the way through nature. The capacity for seeing similarities is necessary to the survival of all animals. The pickerel, I suppose, identifies all shiny, fluttery things going through the water as minnows, and goes after them all in pretty much the same way. Under natural conditions, life is made possible for the pickerel by this capacity. Once in a while, however, the shiny, fluttery thing in the water may happen to be not a minnow but an artificial lure on the end of a line. In such a case, one would say that the identification response, so useful for survival, under somewhat more complex conditions that require differentiation between two sorts of shiny and fluttery objects, proves to be fatal.

To go back to our discussion of human behavior, we see at once that the problem of adequate differentiation is immeasurably more complex for men than it is for pickerel. The signs we respond to, and the symbols we create and train ourselves to respond to, are infinitely greater in number and immeasurably more abstract than the signs in a pickerel's environment. Lower animals have to deal only with certain brute facts in their physical environment. But think, only for a moment, of what constitutes a human environment. Think of the items that call for adequate responses that no animal ever has to think about: our days are named and numbered, so that we have birthdays, anniversaries, holidays, centennials, and so on, all calling for specifically human responses; we have history, which no animal has to worry about; we have verbally codified patterns of behavior which we call law, religion and ethics. We have to respond not only to events in our immediate environment, but to reported events in Washington, Paris, Tokyo, Moscow, Beirut. We have literature, comic strips, confession magazines, market quotations, detective stories, journals of abnormal psychology, bookkeeping systems to interpret. We have money, credit, banking, stocks, bonds, checks, bills. We have the complex symbolisms of moving pictures, paintings, drama, music, architecture and dress. In short, we live in a vast human dimension of which the lower animals have no inkling, and we have to have a capacity for differentiation adequate to the complexity of our extra environment.

WHY DO PEOPLE REACT
AS THEY DO?

The next question, then, is why human beings do not always have an adequate capacity for differentiation. Why are we not constantly on the lookout for differences as well as similarities instead of feeling, as so many do, that the Chinese (or Mexicans, or ballplayers, or women drivers) are "all alike"? Why do some people react to words as if they were the things they stand for? Why do certain patterns of reaction, both in individuals and in larger groups such as nations, persist long after the usefulness has expired?

Part of our identification reactions are simply protective mechanisms inherited from the necessities of survival under earlier and more primitive conditions of life. I was once beaten up and robbed by two men on a dark street. Months later, I was again on a dark street with two men, good friends of mine, but involuntarily I found myself in a panic and insisted on our hurrying to a well-lighted drugstore to have a soda so that I would stop being jittery. In other words, my whole body reacted with an identification reaction of fear of these two men, in spite of the fact that "I knew" that I was in no danger. Fortunately, with the passage of time, this reaction has died away. But the hurtful experiences of early childhood do not fade so readily. There is no doubt that many identification reactions are traceable to childhood traumas, as psychiatrists have shown.

Further identification reactions are caused by communal patterns of behavior which were necessary or thought necessary at one stage or another in the development of a tribe or nation. General directives such as "Kill all snakes," "Never kill cows, which are sacred animals," "Shoot all strangers on sight," "Fall down flat on your face before all members of the aristocracy," or, to come to more modern instances, "Never vote for a Republican," "Oppose all government regulation of business," "Never associate with Negroes on terms of equality," are an enormous factor in the creation of identification reactions.

Some human beings—possibly in their private feelings a majority—can accept these directives in a *human* way: that is, it will not be impossible for them under a sufficiently changed set of circumstances to kill a cow, or not to bow down before an aristocrat, to vote for a Republican, or to accept a Negro as a classmate. Others, however, get these directives so deeply ground into their nervous systems that they become incapable of changing their responses no matter how greatly the circumstances may have changed. Still others, although capable of changing their responses, dare not do so for fear of public opinion. Social progress usually requires the breaking up of these absolute identifications, which often make necessary changes impossible. Society must obviously have patterns of behavior; human beings must obviously have habits. But when those patterns become inflexible, so that a tribe has only one way to meet a famine, namely, to throw more infants as sacrifices to the crocodiles, or a nation has only one way to meet a threat to its security, namely, to increase its armaments, then such a tribe or such a nation is headed for trouble. There is insufficient capacity for differentiated behavior.

Furthermore—and here one must touch upon the role of newspapers, radio and television—if agencies of mass communication hammer away incessantly at the production of, let us say, a hostile set of reactions at such words as "Communists," "bureaucrats," "Wall Street," "international bankers," "labor leaders," and so on, no matter how useful an immediate job they may perform in correcting a given abuse at a given time and place, they can in the long run produce in thousands of readers and listeners identification reactions to the words—reactions that will make intelligent public discussion impossible. Modern means of mass communication and propaganda certainly have an important part to play in the creation of identification reactions.

In addition to the foregoing, there is still another source of identification reactions; namely, the language we use in our daily thought and speech. Unlike the languages of the sciences, which are carefully constructed, tailor-made, special-purpose languages, the language of everyday life is one directly inherited and haphazardly developed from those of our prescientific ancestors: Anglo-Saxons, primitive Germanic tribes, primitive Indo-Europeans. With their scant knowledge of the world, they formulated descriptions of the world before them in statements such as "The sun rises." We do not today believe that the sun "rises." Nevertheless, we still continue to use the expression, without believing what we say.

ERRONEOUS IMPLICATIONS
IN EVERYDAY LANGUAGE

But there are other expressions, quite as primitive as the idea of "sunrise," which we use uncritically, fully believing in the implications of our terms. Having observed (or heard) that *some* Negroes are lazy, an individual may say, making a huge jump beyond the known facts, "Negroes are lazy." Without arguing for the moment the truth or falsity of this statement, let us examine the implications of the statement as it is ordinarily constructed: "Negroes are lazy." The statement implies, as common sense or any textbook on traditional logic will tell us, that "laziness" is a "quality" that is "inherent" in Negroes.

What are the facts? Under conditions of slavery, under which Negroes were not paid for working, there wasn't any point in being an industrious and responsible worker. The distinguished French abstract artist Jean Hélion once told the story of his life as a prisoner of war in a German camp, where, during the Second World War, he was compelled to do forced labor. He told how he loafed on the job, how he thought of device after device for avoiding work and producing as little as possible—and, since his prison camp was a farm, how he stole chickens at every opportunity. He also described how he put on an expression of good-natured imbecility whenever approached by his Nazi overseers. Without intending to do so, in describing his own actions, he gave an almost perfect picture of the literary type of the Southern Negro of slavery days. Jean Hélion, confronted with the fact of forced labor, reacted as intelligently as Southern Negro slaves, and the slaves reacted as intelligently as Jean Hélion. "Laziness," then, is not an "inherent quality" of Negroes or of any other group of people. It is a *response* to a work situation in which there are no rewards for working, and in which one hates his taskmasters.

Statements implying inherent qualities, such as "Negroes are lazy" or "There's something terribly wrong with young people today," are therefore the crudest kind of unscientific observation, based on an out-of-date way of saying things, like "The sun rises." The tragedy is not simply the fact that people make such statements; the graver fact is that they believe themselves.

Some individuals are admired for their "realism" because, as the saying goes, they "call a spade a spade." Suppose we were to raise the question "Why should anyone call it a spade?" The reply would obviously be, "Because that's what it is!" This reply appeals so strongly to the common sense of most people that they feel that at this point discussion can be closed. I should like to ask the reader, however, to consider a point which may appear at first to him a mere quibble.

Here, let us say, is an implement for digging made of steel, with a wooden handle. Here, on the other hand, is a succession of sounds made with the tongue, lips and vocal cords: "spade." If you want a digging implement of the kind we are talking about, you would ask for it by making the succession of sounds "spade" if you are addressing an English-speaking person. But suppose you were addressing a speaker of Dutch, French, Hungarian, Chinese, Tagalog? Would you not have to make completely different sounds? It is apparent, then, that the common-sense opinion of most people, "We call a spade a spade because that's what it is," is completely and utterly wrong. We call it a "spade" because we are English-speaking people, conforming, in this instance, to majority usage in naming this particular object. The steel-and-iron digging implement is simply an object standing there against the garage door; "spade" is what we *call* it—"spade" is a *name*.

And here we come to another source of identification reactions—an unconscious assumption about language epitomized in the expression "a spade is a spade," or even more elegantly in the famous remark "Pigs are called pigs because they are such dirty animals." The assumption is that everything has a "right name" and that the "right name" names the "essence" of that which is named.

If this assumption is at work in our reaction patterns, we are likely to be given to premature and often extremely inappropriate responses. We are likely to react to names as if they gave complete insight into the persons, things or situations named. If we are told that a given individual is a "Jew," some of us are likely to respond, "That's all I need to know." For, if names give the essence of that which is named, obviously, every "Jew" has the essential attribute of "Jewishness." Or, to put it the other way around, it is because he possesses "Jewishness" that we call him a "Jew"! A further example of the operation of this assumption is that, in spite of the fact that my entire education has been in Canada and the United States and I am unable to read and write Japanese, I am sometimes credited, or accused, of having an "Oriental mind." Now, since Buddha, Confucius, General Tojo, Mao Tse-tung, Syngman Rhee, Pandit Nehru and the proprietor of the Golden Pheasant Chop Suey House all have "Oriental minds," it is hard to imagine what is meant. The "Oriental mind," like the attribute of "Jewishness," is purely and simply a fiction. Nevertheless, I used to note with alarm that newspaper columnists got paid for articles that purported to account for Stalin's behavior by pointing out that since he came from Georgia, which is next to Turkey and Azerbaijan and therefore "more a part of Asia than of Europe," he too had an "Oriental mind."

IMPROVING YOUR SEMANTIC HABITS

Our everyday habits of speech and our unconscious assumptions about the relations between words and things lead, then, to an identification reaction in which it is felt that all things that have the same name are entitled to the same response. From this point of view, all "insurance men," or "college boys," or "politicians," or "lawyers," or "Texans" are alike. Once we recognize the absurdity of these identification reactions based on identities of name, we can begin to think more clearly and more adequately. No "Texan" is exactly like any other "Texan." No "college boy" is exactly like any other "college boy." Most of the time "Texans" or "college boys" may be what you think they are: but often they are not. To realize fully the difference between words and what they stand for is to be ready for differences as well as similarities in the world. This readiness is mandatory to scientific thinking, as well as to sane thinking.

Korzybski's simple but powerful suggestion to those wishing to improve their semantic habits is to add "index numbers" to all terms, according to the formula: A_1 is not A_2. Translated into everyday language we can state the formula in such terms as these: Cow$_1$ is not cow$_2$; cow$_2$ is not cow$_3$; Texan$_1$ is not Texan$_2$; politician$_1$ is not politician$_2$; ham and eggs (Plaza Hotel) are not ham and eggs (Smitty's Café); socialism (Russia) is not socialism (England); private enterprise (Joe's Shoe Repair Shop) is not private enterprise (A.T.&T.). The formula means that instead of simply thinking about "cows" or "politicians" or "private enterprise," we should think as factually as possible about the differences between one cow and another, one politician and another, one privately owned enterprise and another.

This device of "indexing" will not automatically make us wiser and better, but it's a start. When we talk or write, the habit of indexing our general terms will reduce our tendency to wild and woolly generalization. It will compel us to think before we speak—think in terms of concrete objects and events and situations, rather than in terms of verbal associations. When we read or listen, the habit of indexing will help us visualize more concretely, and therefore understand better, what is being said. And if nothing is being said except deceptive windbaggery, the habit of indexing may—at least part of the time—save us from snapping, like the pickerel, at phony minnows. Another way of summing up is to remember, as Wendell Johnson said, that "To a mouse, cheese is cheese —that's why mousetraps work."

BARRIERS AND GATEWAYS TO COMMUNICATION

Carl R. Rogers and F. J. Roethlisberger

Communication among human beings has always been a problem. But it is only fairly recently that management and management advisers have become so concerned about it and the way it works or does not work in industry. Now, as the result of endless discussion, speculation, and plans of action, a whole cloud of catchwords and catchthoughts has sprung up and surrounded it.

The following two descriptions of barriers and gateways to communication may help to bring the problem down to earth and show what it means in terms of simple fundamentals. First Carl R. Rogers analyzes it from the standpoint of human behavior generally (Part I); then F. J. Roethlisberger illustrates it in an industrial context (Part II).

PART I

It may seem curious that a person like myself, whose whole professional effort is devoted to psychotherapy, should be interested in problems of communication. What relationship is there between obstacles to communication and providing therapeutic help to individuals with emotional maladjustments?

Actually the relationship is very close indeed. The whole task of psychotherapy is the task of dealing with a failure in communication. The emotionally maladjusted person, the "neurotic," is in difficulty, first, because communication within himself has broken down and, secondly, because as a result of this his communication with others has been damaged. To put it another way, in the "neurotic" individual parts of himself which have been termed unconscious, or repressed, or denied to awareness, become blocked off so that they no longer communicate themselves to the conscious or managing part of himself; as long as this is true, there are distortions in the way he communicates himself to others, and so he suffers both within himself and in his interpersonal relations.

Condensed from *Harvard Business Review*, XXX, 4 (July-August 1952), 46ff. © 1952 by the President and Fellows of Harvard College; all rights reserved.

The task of psychotherapy is to help the person achieve, through a special relationship with a therapist, good communication within himself. Once this is achieved, he can communicate more freely and more effectively with others. We may say then that psychotherapy is good communication, within and between men. We may also turn that statement around and it will still be true. Good communication, free communication, within or between men, is always therapeutic.

It is, then, from a background of experience with communication in counseling and psychotherapy that I want to present two ideas: (1) I wish to state what I believe is one of the major factors in blocking or impeding communication, and then (2) I wish to present what in our experience has proved to be a very important way of improving or facilitating communication.

BARRIER: THE TENDENCY TO EVALUATE

I should like to propose, as a hypothesis for consideration, that the major barrier to mutual interpersonal communication is our very natural tendency to judge, to evaluate, to approve (or disapprove) the statement of the other person or the other group. Let me illustrate my meaning with some very simple examples. Suppose someone, commenting on this discussion, makes the statement, "I didn't like what that man said." What will you respond? Almost invariably your reply will be either approval or disapproval of the attitude expressed. Either you respond, "I didn't either; I thought it was terrible," or else you tend to reply, "Oh, I thought it was really good." In other words, your primary reaction is to evaluate it from your point of view, your own frame of reference.

. . . Although the tendency to make evaluations is common in almost all interchange of language, it is very much heightened in those situations where feelings and emotions are deeply involved. So the stronger our feelings, the more likely it is that there will be no mutual element in the communication. There will be just two ideas, two feelings, two judgments, missing each other in psychological space.

I am sure you recognize this from your own experience. When you have not been emotionally involved yourself and have listened to a heated discussion, you often go away thinking, "Well, they actually weren't talking about the same thing." And they were not. Each was making a judgment, an evaluation, from his own frame of reference. There was really nothing which could be called communication in any genuine sense. This tendency to react to any emotionally meaningful statement by forming an evaluation of it from our own point of view is, I repeat, the major barrier to interpersonal communication.

GATEWAY: LISTENING
WITH UNDERSTANDING

Is there any way of solving this problem, of avoiding this barrier? I feel that we are making exciting progress toward this goal, and I should like to present it as simply as I can. Real communication occurs, and this evaluative tendency is avoided, when we listen with understanding. What does that mean? It means to see the expressed idea and attitude from the other person's point of view, to sense how it feels to him, to achieve his frame of reference in regard to the thing he is talking about.

Stated so briefly, this may sound absurdly simple, but it is not. It is an approach which we have found extremely potent in the field of psychotherapy. It is the most effective agent we know for altering the basic personality structure of an individual and for improving his relationships and his communications with others. If I can listen to what he can tell me, if I can understand how it seems to him, if I can see its personal meaning for him, if I can sense the emotional flavor which it has for him, then I will be releasing potent forces of change in him.

Again, if I can really understand how he hates his father, or hates the company, or hates Communists—if I can catch the flavor of his fear of insanity, or his fear of atom bombs, or of Russia—it will be of the greatest help to him in altering those hatreds and fears and in establishing realistic and harmonious relationships with the very people and situations toward which he has felt hatred and fear. We know from our research that such empathic understanding—understanding *with* a person, not *about* him—is such an effective approach that it can bring about major changes in personality.

Some of you may be feeling that you listen well to people and yet you have never seen such results. The chances are great indeed that your listening has not been of the type I have described. Fortunately, I can suggest a little laboratory experiment which you can try to test the quality of your understanding. The next time you get into an argument with your wife, or your friend, or with a small group of friends, just stop the discussion for a moment and, for an experiment, institute this rule: "Each person can speak up for himself only *after* he has first restated the ideas and feelings of the previous speaker accurately and to that speaker's satisfaction." . . .

If, then, this way of approach is an effective avenue to good communication and good relationships, as I am quite sure you will agree if you try the experiment I have mentioned, why is it not more widely tried and used? I will try to list the difficulties which keep it from being utilized.

Need for Courage. In the first place it takes courage, a quality which is not too widespread. I am indebted to Dr. S. I. Hayakawa, the semanticist, for pointing out that to carry on psychotherapy in this fashion is to take a very real risk, and that courage is required. If you really understand another person in this way, if you are willing to enter his private world and see the way life appears to him, without any attempt to make evaluative judgments, you run the risk of being changed yourself. You might see it his way; you might find yourself influenced in your attitudes or your personality.

This risk of being changed is one of the most frightening prospects many of us can face. . . .

Heightened Emotions. But there is a second obstacle. It is just when emotions are strongest that it is most difficult to achieve the frame of reference of the other person or group. Yet it is then that the attitude is most needed if communication is to be established. We have not found this to be an insuperable obstacle in our experience in psychotherapy. A third party, who is able to lay aside his own feelings and evaluations, can assist greatly by listening with understanding to each person or group and clarifying the views and attitudes each holds. . . .

Size of Group. . . . Thus far all our experience has been with small face-to-face groups—groups exhibiting industrial tensions, religious tensions, racial tensions, and therapy groups in which many personal tensions are present. . . . What about trying to achieve understanding between larger groups that are geographically remote, or between face-to-face groups that are not speaking for themselves but simply as representatives of others? . . .

Yet with our present limited knowledge we can see some steps which might be taken even in large groups to increase the amount of listening *with* and decrease the amount of evaluation *about.* To be imaginative for a moment, let us suppose that a therapeutically oriented international group went to the Russian leaders and said, "We want to achieve a genuine understanding of your views and, even more important, of your attitudes and feelings toward the United States. We will summarize and resummarize these views and feelings if necessary, until you agree that our description represents the situation as it seems to you."

Then suppose they did the same thing with the leaders in our own country. If they then gave the widest possible distribution to these two views, with the feelings clearly described but not expressed in name-calling, might not the effect be very great? It would not guarantee the type of understanding I have been describing, but it would make it much more possible. We can understand the feelings of a person who hates us much more readily when his attitudes are accurately described to us by a neutral third party than we can when he is shaking his fist at us.

Faith in Social Sciences. But even to describe such a first step is to suggest another obstacle to this approach of understanding. Our civilization does not yet have enough faith in the social sciences to utilize their findings. The opposite is true of the physical sciences. During the war when a test-tube solution was found to the problem of synthetic rubber, millions of dollars and an army of talent were turned loose on the problem of using that finding. If synthetic rubber could be made in milligrams, it could and would be made in the thousands of tons. And it was. But in the social science realm, if a way is found of facilitating communication and mutual understanding in small groups, there is no guarantee that the finding will be utilized. It may be a generation or more before the money and the brains will be turned loose to exploit that finding.

SUMMARY

In closing, I should like to summarize this small-scale solution to the problem of barriers in communication, and to point out certain of its characteristics.

I have said that our research and experience to date would make it appear that breakdowns in communication, and the evaluative tendency which is the major barrier to communication, can be avoided. The solution is provided by creating a situation in which each of the different parties comes to understand the other from the *other's* point of view. This has been achieved, in practice, even when feelings run high, by the influence of a person who is willing to understand each point of view empathically, and who thus acts as a catalyst to precipitate further understanding.

This procedure has important characteristics. It can be initiated by one party, without waiting for the other to be ready. It can even be initiated by a neutral third person, provided he can gain a minimum of cooperation from one of the parties.

This procedure can deal with the insincerities, the defensive exaggerations, the lies, the "false fronts" which characterize almost every failure in communication. These defensive distortions drop away with astonishing speed as people find that the only intent is to understand, not to judge.

This approach leads steadily and rapidly toward the discovery of the truth, toward a realistic appraisal of the objective barriers to communication. The dropping of some defensiveness by one party leads to further dropping of defensiveness by the other party, and truth is thus approached.

This procedure gradually achieves mutual communication. Mutual communication tends to be pointed toward solving a problem rather than toward attacking a person or group. It leads to a situation in which I see how the problem appears to you as well as to me, and you see how it appears to me as well as to you. Thus accurately and realistically defined, the problem is almost certain to yield to intelligent attack; or if it is in part insoluble, it will be comfortably accepted as such.

This then appears to be a test-tube solution to the breakdown of communication as it occurs in small groups. Can we take this small-scale answer, investigate it further, refine it, develop it, and apply it to the tragic and well-nigh fatal failures of communication which threaten the very existence of our modern world? It seems to me that this is a possibility and a challenge which we should explore.

PART II

In thinking about the many barriers to personal communication, particularly those that are due to differences of background, experience, and motivation, it seems to me extraordinary that any two persons can ever understand each other. Such reflections provoke the question of how communication is possible when people do not see and assume the same things and share the same values.

On this question there are two schools of thought. One school assumes that communication between A and B, for example, has failed when B does not accept what A has to say as being fact, true, or valid; and that the goal of communication is to get B to agree with A's opinions, ideas, facts, or information.

The position of the other school of thought is quite different. It assumes that communication has failed when B does not feel free to express his feelings to A because B fears they will not be accepted by A. Communication is facilitated when on the part of A or B or both there is a willingness to express and accept differences.

As these are quite divergent conceptions, let us explore them further with an example. Bill, an employee, is talking with his boss in the boss's office. The boss says, "I think, Bill, that this is the best way to do your job." Bill says, "Oh yeah!" According to the first school of thought, this reply would be a sign of poor communication. Bill does not understand the best way of doing his work. To improve communication, therefore, it is up to the boss to explain to Bill why his way is the best.

From the point of view of the second school of thought, Bill's reply is a sign neither of good nor of bad communication. Bill's response is indeterminate. But the boss has an opportunity to find out what Bill means if he so desires. Let us assume that this is what he chooses to do, i.e., find out what Bill means. So this boss tries to get Bill to talk more about his job while he (the boss) listens.

For purposes of simplification, I shall call the boss representing the first school of thought "Smith" and the boss representing the second school of thought "*Jones.*" In the presence of the so-called same stimulus each behaves differently. Smith chooses to *explain*; Jones chooses to *listen.* In my experience Jones's response works better than Smith's. It works better because Jones is making a more proper evaluation of what is taking place between him and Bill than Smith is. Let us test this hypothesis by continuing with our example.

WHAT SMITH ASSUMES, SEES, AND FEELS

Smith assumes that he understands what Bill means when Bill says, "Oh yeah!" so there is no need to find out. Smith is sure that Bill does not understand why this is the best way to do his job, so Smith has to tell him. In this process let us assume Smith is logical, lucid, and clear. He presents his facts and evidence well. But, alas, Bill remains unconvinced. What does Smith do? Operating under the assumption that what is taking place between him and Bill is something essentially logical, Smith can draw only one of two conclusions: either (1) he has not been clear enough, or (2) Bill is too damned stupid to understand. So he either has to "spell out" his case in words of fewer and fewer syllables or give up. Smith is reluctant to do the latter, so he continues to explain. What happens?

If Bill still does not accept Smith's explanation of why this is the best way for him to do his job, a pattern of interacting feelings is produced of which Smith is often unaware. The more Smith cannot get Bill to understand him, the more frustrated Smith becomes and the more Bill becomes a threat to his logical capacity. Since Smith sees himself as a fairly reasonable and logical chap, this is a difficult feeling to accept. It is much easier for him to perceive Bill as uncooperative or stupid. This perception, however, will affect what Smith says and does. Under these pressures Bill comes to be evaluated more and more in terms of Smith's values. By this process Smith tends to treat Bill's values as unimportant. He tends to deny Bill's uniqueness and difference. He treats Bill as if he had little capacity for self-direction.

Let us be clear. Smith does not see that he is doing these things. When he is feverishly scratching hieroglyphics on the back of an envelope, trying to explain to Bill why this is the best way to do his job, Smith is trying to be helpful. He is a man of goodwill, and he wants to set Bill straight. This is the way Smith sees himself and his behavior. But it is for this very reason that Bill's "Oh yeah!" is getting under Smith's skin.

"How dumb can a guy be?" is Smith's attitude, and unfortunately Bill will hear that more than Smith's good intentions. Bill will feel misunderstood. He will not see Smith as a man of goodwill trying to be helpful. Rather he will perceive him as a threat to his self-esteem and personal integrity. Against this threat Bill will feel the need to defend himself at all cost. Not being so logically articulate as Smith, Bill expresses this need, again, by saying, "Oh yeah!"

WHAT JONES ASSUMES, SEES, AND FEELS

Let us leave this sad scene between Smith and Bill, which I fear is going to terminate by Bill's either leaving in a huff or being kicked out of Smith's office. Let us turn for a moment to Jones and see what he is assuming, seeing, hearing, feeling, doing, and saying when he interacts with Bill.

Jones, it will be remembered, does not assume that he knows what Bill means when he says, "Oh yeah!" so he has to find out. Moreover, he assumes that when Bill said this, he had not exhausted his vocabulary or his feelings. Bill may not necessarily mean one thing; he may mean several different things. So Jones decides to listen.

In this process Jones is not under any illusion that what will take place will be eventually logical. Rather he is assuming that what will take place will be primarily an interaction of feelings. Therefore, he cannot ignore the feelings of Bill, the effect of Bill's feelings on him, or the effect of his feelings on Bill. In other words, he cannot ignore his relationship to Bill; he cannot assume that it will make no difference to what Bill will hear or accept.

Therefore, Jones will be paying strict attention to all of the things Smith has ignored. He will be addressing himself to Bill's feelings, his own, and the interactions between them.

Jones will therefore realize that he has ruffled Bill's feelings with his comment, "I think, Bill, this is the best way to do your job." So instead of trying to get Bill to understand him, he decides to try to understand Bill. He does this by encouraging Bill to speak. Instead of telling Bill how he should feel or think, he asks Bill such questions as, "Is this what you feel?" "Is this what you see?" "Is this what you assume?" Instead of ignoring Bill's evaluations as irrelevant, not valid, inconsequential, or false, he tries to understand Bill's reality as he feels it, perceives it, and assumes it to be. As Bill begins to open up, Jones's curiosity is piqued by this process.

"Bill isn't so dumb; he's quite an interesting guy" becomes Jones's attitude. And that is what Bill hears. Therefore Bill feels understood and accepted as a person. He becomes less defensive. He is in a better frame of mind to explore and re-examine his own perceptions, feelings, and assumptions. In this process he perceives Jones as a source of help. Bill feels free to express his differences. He feels that Jones has some respect for his capacity for self-direction. These positive feelings toward Jones make Bill more inclined to say, "Well, Jones, I don't quite agree with you that this is the best way to do my job, but I'll tell you what I'll do. I'll try to do it that way for a few days, and then I'll tell you what I think."

If I have identified correctly these very common patterns of personal communication, then some interesting hypotheses can be stated:

(a) . . . Jones has a better map than Smith of the process of personal communication.

(b) The practice of Jones's method . . . depends on Jones's capacity and willingness to see and accept points of view different from his own, and to practice this orientation in a face-to-face relationship. This practice involves an emotional as well as an intellectual achievement. It depends in part on Jones's awareness of himself, in part on the practice of a skill.

(c) . . . Most educational institutions train their students to be logical, lucid, and clear. Very little is done to help them to listen more skillfully. As a result, our educated world contains too many Smiths and too few Joneses.

(d) The biggest block to personal communication is man's inability to listen intelligently, understandingly, and skillfully to another person. This deficiency in the modern world is widespread and appalling. In our universities as well as elsewhere, too little is being done about it.

STRENGTHENING MOTIVATION THROUGH COMMUNICATION

Edwin Timbers

One of the principal responsibilities of every supervisor is to put the "see" into his communications. The mere possession of communication media, however, will do little to accomplish this objective. Supervisors have all the communication tools they need to communicate information and ideas with great proficiency, but the fact remains, nevertheless, that they are not affecting attitudes and behavior as they should. Obviously, the answer to today's communication problems lies not in the media we possess, but in how we use these media. . . .

THE BASIC HUMAN WANTS OF THE EMPLOYEE AT WORK

What are the basic human wants that can be satisfied, at least in part, by a company communication program? Prominent in any list of job-related wants are recognition, communication, belonging, and emotional security.

RECOGNITION

Possibly the most important want of any employee is to have others recognize his dignity and worth as an individual. This want can in some measure be satisfied merely by each supervisor making an effort to get more than superficially acquainted with each of his employees. So important is this obvious step that it should be standard management practice at all levels in every company. This point is stressed for two reasons: First, the employee will be flattered by his supervisor's interest in him as an individual, and, from the inception of their relationship, rapport

From *Advanced Management Journal* (April 1966), pp. 64-67. Reprinted by permission.

between supervisor and employee will be considerably strengthened. Second, in getting acquainted, the supervisor must listen. In listening, he develops the employee as a communication source, for the supervisor by listening implies that what the employee says is worth hearing. This implication usually flatters the employee and motivates him to increase his contacts with his supervisor. As a result, the upward flow of communication, the so-called "neglected half of communication," is stimulated.

COMMUNICATION

The great majority of employees want their supervisors to keep them informed about what is going on and what is anticipated in the company. Conversely, they want to have the ear of their supervisors, want them to listen to their problems, complaints, and achievements with understanding. In satisfying this want of his employees, the first obligation of each supervisor is training them to do their jobs. With new or untrained employees, the four-step job instruction training approach is best, and every level of supervision should be carefully and thoroughly trained in the use of this instructional technique. Regardless of the employee's initial skills and preparation, his supervisor's training responsibility continues, for new and better ways of doing work, new equipment, and better materials are continually being developed. Furthermore, without training, workers tend to regress and become careless and sloppy. Training, consequently, is a continuing supervisory responsibility which should be based on the supervisor's first-hand knowledge of the skills, strengths, and weaknesses of his subordinates. Such knowledge can best be obtained by careful and frequent observation and listening.

After basic training, worker skills can be refined not only by formal coaching but also by frequent and apparently casual contacts between supervisor and worker. The virtues of such informal coaching are that it is natural and spontaneous; it enables the employee to keep abreast of the latest methods; and it motivates him to do his work better. Employees appreciate and welcome good coaching. In coaching employees some do's and don'ts should be mentioned:

Tell the employee why the job is done in a certain way and why it is done at all. Help him to see the importance of the job by understanding why it is necessary. Not only will he take greater pride and care if he sees its importance, but he will be able to work much more intelligently in a crisis if he is guided by the light of understanding.

Avoid overinstructing. This kills his initiative, dulls his creative edge, and denies him the pleasure of figuring it out for himself.

Get "feedback." Have the employee play back your ideas, information, or instruction in his own words. If he says what you meant to say, your communication effort was successful. But if he errs, there has been a flaw in sending, in receiving, or both. You then repeat this process until the employee sees what you see. This technique used in oral communication is a virtually foolproof method of putting the "see" into communication. It is standard operating procedure in the U.S. Army Infantry to get such feedback on all oral field orders, and there is no doubt that this procedure has saved many lives in battle. It can also save many dollars in industry.

Save the employee's face. When you criticize, do so privately. Make your criticism constructive by showing the employee a better way. Always direct your comments to the employee's work and not to him personally.

Recognize the employee's progress. Compliment him on his good work and, at the same time, encourage him to strive for even greater achievement.

A FEELING OF BELONGING

One of our strongest desires is to belong and to be accepted by a group or groups. Man is undeniably a social animal. Aristotle once said, "a man who lives outside society is either a god or beast." This feeling of belonging, however, is not acquired by mere nominal membership in a group. It is acquired by *participation*, by the individual's contributing something of value to the group's work, and by the group's recognizing the contribution as worthwhile.

Communication can do much to satisfy the desire to belong in two ways: First, each supervisor should consult with his subordinates before instituting changes in processes, personnel, or equipment, a practice known as *consultative management*. Supervisors should make it a habit to ask their employees what they think, then listen and get their ideas. Whenever you ask someone, "what do you think?" you flatter him. You say to him, in effect, "I value your judgment." Not only does this approach raise employee morale and strengthen supervisor-employee rapport, but it often opens the floodgates to a flow of valuable ideas which can increase efficiency and cut costs. Every supervisor should be mindful of the fact that no one is quite so conversant with the details of a job as the man who does it daily. Many employees get good ideas from time to time about improving their jobs. These ideas should be tapped.

Consultative management is particularly important when changes are contemplated. Most of us tend to resist change. We have adapted ourselves, sometimes painfully, to the status quo, and we dislike having the pattern of our lives upset, especially when changes come abruptly and unexpectedly. To induce your employees to accept change cooperatively and to introduce it as smoothly as possible, get them to participate whenever practicable in planning and implementing it. If you do this, they will probably produce a number of valuable ideas that never occurred to you, ideas that will make the change better for all concerned. But, best of all, they will support the change because they had a hand in it. It is *their* change, a product of their efforts. In addition to their participation, it is important that all employees affected by an impending change clearly see how they will individually and collectively benefit from it. Satisfy their desire to know what is in it for them.

Second, each level of management should *make more frequent use of group problem solving.* Group problem-solving meetings have one merit, perhaps their greatest, which is often overlooked or glossed over. This merit is the tremendous lift which this method can give a group's morale, for this is participation at its best. In addition to the morale factor, such meetings provide an ideal milieu for horizontal communication, for the rapid exchange of ideas between supervisors across departmental lines. Such exchanges promote mutual understanding, enhance cooperation and coordination of effort, and knit the players of the company team more closely together.

EMOTIONAL SECURITY

Few conditions contribute more to a sense of emotional security than being employed by a well-managed organization. All of us like order and predictability. We like to know what we can and cannot do. We like to know how we are doing. And we like to feel that we can predict fairly accurately where we are going. In companies having good communication between management and employees, the employees know these things, for, in such companies, employees are well trained and well informed; jurisdictional lines are carefully drawn; each employee knows what he is supposed to do, where, when, how, and why he is supposed to do it; penalties for poor performance are firm, fair, and clearly understood; and credit for good work is freely and promptly given.

In summary, communication is the conveyance of meaning designed to motivate people to take desired action. People act most readily to satisfy their wants. Communication is the principal means by which the supervisor can help his employees satisfy their job-related wants. Communication, therefore, is the supervisor's most important tool.

COMMUNICATION BEGINS AT THE TOP

Communication must be an integral and vital part of management's philosophy. As all management philosophies, it must originate with top management and be a continuing network for the exchange of information and ideas up, down, and across the company structure. It must be as much a part of management planning as production schedules, procurement of materials, and the maintenance of equipment. And it must function continuously, not just when a crisis occurs. Management, therefore, must be communication conscious at all times. This does not mean that supervisors should bare their souls to their employees or completely divulge every decision and plan, but it does mean that every supervisor should consider the advisability of complete disclosure with due regard to the limitations applicable to his situation. And, if something should be told, the supervisor must, of course, decide when, where, to whom, and how.

While any plant-wide or company-wide communication program must start at the top and radiate downward through every echelon of management, the first-line supervisor is the key in any continuing communication program. He is the king-pin who can unite or sunder the labor-management segments of the company team. To the worker, he personifies the company, and it is he who is the key link in most upward communication from worker to top management. Likewise, it is he who must interpret company policy to the worker, pass on information, and transmit orders and instructions.

Up to this point, we have considered only the vertical half of the communication function. It is equally important, however, that ideas and information be communicated across the company structure as it is that they be communicated up and down. This means that management personnel at each level must view themselves as links in a horizontal chain of communication. No matter how effective a company's vertical communication may be, if its supervisors are not communicating well with each other and if they do not know, understand, and accept each other's problems and needs, there can be only ineffectual teamwork and poor cooperation.

ELIMINATING COMMUNICATION ROADBLOCKS

How can interdepartmental barriers to communication and understanding be overcome? The best and quickest way is by frequent face-to-face discussions at each level of management, provided such discussions are approached with an open mind and a spirit of friendly helpfulness. Such interdepartmental discussions should be aimed primarily at exchanging knowledge, creating understanding, and gaining acceptance of each other's problems and needs. These meetings should take place as often as practicable until each supervisor is so thoroughly familiar with and appreciative of the needs and problems of his peers that he consistently and unhesitatingly coordinates his efforts with theirs.

A second, and equally formidable, communication roadblock is the barrier of status and position. It particularly inhibits the flow of upward communication. Some men "freeze up" in the presence of their superiors and experience mental blocks which prevent them from expressing themselves fully or clearly. Other men take the position that "what the boss doesn't know won't hurt him" and deliberately screen out all unpleasant information which might upset their superiors. Often these self-appointed censors screen out information that management urgently needs to function intelligently.

What can management do to "thaw out" its employees, to put them at ease, and get them to "open up"? The first and most important step is to establish by the daily example of top management a free and permissive climate favoring upward communication. Once this climate has been established at the top it will quickly permeate the entire organization.

There are two intangible but essential elements in a good communication climate: an attitude that is people-centered rather than production-centered and an open door in fact as well as in word.

This is not an atmosphere that can be established by words, but only by deeds, by management's daily example on the job. Besides practicing what it preaches, management must make it clear to all supervisors that they should make time for communication. The driving insistence that every moment of a supervisor's time be spent on production is too frequently the preoccupation of some top managers. Such thinking has no place in modern management, for experience had abundantly demonstrated that the supervisor's job is handling people and that devoting enough time to communicating with them is an integral and inescapable part of that job.

Is there one best way of communicating? Not for all situations and messages, but face-to-face communication is preferable whenever it is practicable. It is personal and warmer than other media. It can convey more meaning than written or telephonic communication, because the parties can also communicate via gestures and facial expressions. It is quick and inexpensive. It permits immediate feedback and clarification. When each level of management communicates with the next lower level by meetings, three distinct benefits accrue:

1. Management's leadership at each level will be strengthened by regularly scheduled, face-to-face meetings.
2. The information conveyed at such meetings will usually be much more complete and accurate than that transmitted on the grapevine.
3. The workers will look increasingly to their supervisors rather than the union or the grapevine for company information.

SUMMARY AND CONCLUSION

Management is *man management*. As Lawrence Appley has said, "management is personnel administration." The results managers get can be achieved only through people. Since the supervisor cannot slavedrive people for a prolonged period without having it backfire, he must motivate them affirmatively by the carrot rather than the stick. A good communication program is a powerful motivational influence, because it makes it possible for employees to satisfy many of their basic wants, such as recognition, communication, belonging, and emotional security. Communication activities contributing to the satisfaction of these needs are induction, training, coaching, counseling, listening, informational meetings, consultative management, and group problem solving.

The cardinal prerequisite for a successful communication program is a proper climate. This must first be established at the top-management level, from which it will radiate downward throughout the entire organization. To sustain this climate, management must be employee centered, keep an open door, listen, and allow time for communication. Finally, all persons in the organization with important communication responsibilities should be located and trained in the most effective use of communication skills.

Removing barriers to communication, establishing a favorable communication climate, and improving the supervisor's skills as a communicator are among the foremost challenges and opportunities facing modern management. One of the measures of an organization's success is the extent to which its management has recognized and met this challenge.

AN EXPERIMENTAL APPROACH TO ORGANIZATIONAL COMMUNICATION

Alex Bavelas and Dermot Barrett

Communication as a critical aspect of organization has been attracting more and more attention. If one may judge from articles and speeches, much of the current thinking on communication centers around categories of problems which arise in day-to-day operations—"getting management's point of view to the workers," "stimulating communication up the line as well as down," "obtaining better communication with the union," "establishing more effective communication within management, and especially with the foremen." Knowing how such questions usually arise, it is not surprising that their discussion invariably resolves itself into considerations of *content* and *technique*: on the one hand, analyses of what management ought to be saying to the worker, the union, the foreman; on the other hand, descriptions of devices which can best say it—bulletin boards, letters, films, public address systems, meetings, etc. In its extreme form this approach becomes one of searching for a specific remedy for a specific ill. Helpful and practical as this may be, it is doubtful that such activity can lead to the discovery and understanding of the basic principles of effective organizational communication. Breakdowns and other difficulties at some point of a communication system are often only superficially related to the local conditions which appear to have produced them. They may, rather, be cumulative effects of properties of the entire communication system taken as a whole. But what are these properties, if, indeed, they exist?

FORMAL AND INFORMAL SYSTEMS

An organizational system of communication is usually created by the setting up of formal systems of responsibility and by explicit delegations

From *Personnel*, XXVII, 5 (March 1951), 366-371. Reprinted by permission of the American Management Association, Inc.

of duties. These categories include statements, often implicitly, of the nature, content, and direction of the communication which is considered necessary for the performance of the group. Students of organization, however, have pointed out repeatedly that groups tend to depart from such formal statements and to create other channels of communication and dependence. In other words, informal organizational systems emerge. One may take the view that these changes are adaptations by the individuals involved in the direction of easier and more effective ways of working, or, perhaps, not working. It is no secret that informal groups are not always viewed by managers as favorable to the goals of the larger body. Also, it is by no means obvious that those informal groupings which evolve out of social and personality factors are likely to be more efficient (with respect to organizational tasks) than those set up formally by the managers. Altogether, if one considers how intimate the relations are between communication channels and control, it is not surprising that the managers of organizations would prefer explicit and orderly communication lines.

IS THERE "ONE BEST WAY"?

Unfortunately, there seems to be no organized body of knowledge out of which one can derive, for a given organization, an optimal communication system. Administrative thinking on this point commonly rests upon the assumption that the optimum system *can* be derived from a statement of the task to be performed. It is not difficult to show, however, that from a given set of specifications one may derive not a single communication pattern but a whole set of them, all logically adequate for the successful performance of the task in question. Which pattern from this set should be chosen? The choice, in practice, is usually made either in terms of a group of assumptions (often quite untenable) about human nature, or in terms of a personal bias on the part of the chooser. The seriousness of this situation is illustrated by the following example.

Let us assume that we have a group of five individuals who, in order to solve a problem, must share as quickly as possible the information each person possesses. Let us also assume that there are reasons which prevent them from meeting around a table, and that they must share this information by writing notes. To avoid the confusion and waste of time of each person writing a message to each of the others, a supervisor decides to set up channels in which the notes must go. He strikes upon the pattern shown in Fig. 1.

In this arrangement each individual can send to and receive messages from two others, one on his "left" and one on his "right." Experi-

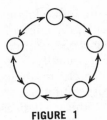

FIGURE 1

ments actually performed with this kind of situation show that the number of mistakes made by individuals working in such a "circle" pattern can be reduced by fully 60 per cent by the simple measure of removing one link, thus making the pattern a "chain" as shown in Fig. 2. The relevance of such a result to organization communication is obvious, simple though the example is. The sad truth, however, is that this phenomenon is not clearly derivable either from traditional "individual psychology" or from commonly held theories of group communication.

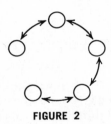

FIGURE 2

AN INTEGRAL PROCESS
OF ORGANIZATION

Perhaps some headway can be made by approaching the general problem from a somewhat different direction. In the affairs of organizations, as well as in the affairs of men, chance always plays a part. However good a plan may be, however carefully prepared its execution, there is a point beyond which the probability of its success cannot be increased. With the firmest of intentions, agreements and promises may be impossible to carry out because of unforeseen events. Nevertheless, an organization whose functioning is too often interrupted by unforeseen events is looked upon with suspicion. Bad luck is an unhappy plea, and it may well be that the "unlucky" organization is more to be avoided than the simply incompetent one. On the other hand, few things about an organization are more admired and respected than the ability to "deliver" despite widely varying conditions and in the face of unusual difficulties.

In a very broad sense, it may be argued that the principal effort of organizational activities is the making of favorable conditions for the achievement of certain goals. In other words, an effort is made to increase, as much as the economics of the situation will permit, the probabilities of succeeding. This is the essence of the manager's job. The development of training and selection programs, the improvement of methods and the specification of techniques, the organization of research and development activities, the designation of responsibility and the delegation of duties—all these processes have one organizationally legitimate purpose: to increase the chances of organizational success. Upon this point rest almost all of the notions by which we are accustomed to evaluate organizations—in part or as a whole.

An organization is, in short, a social invention—a kind of "machine" for increasing certain sets of probabilities. . . . Probabilities of success are increased, however, only by taking relevant and appropriate actions. For the manager, these actions reduce in most instances to the gathering and evaluating of information in the form of reports, schedules, estimates, etc. It is entirely possible to view an organization as an elaborate system for gathering, evaluating, recombining, and disseminating information. It is not surprising, in these terms, that the effectiveness of an organization with respect to the achievement of its goals should be so closely related to its effectiveness in handling information. In an enterprise whose success hinges upon the coordination of the efforts of all its members, the managers depend completely upon the quality, the amount, and the rate at which relevant information reaches them. The rest of the organization, in turn, depends upon the efficiency with which the managers can deal with this information and reach conclusions, decisions, etc. This line of reasoning leads us to the belief that communication is not a secondary or derived aspect of organization—a "helper" of the other and presumably more basic functions. Rather it is the essence of organized activity and is the basic process out of which all other functions derive. The goals an organization selects, the methods it applies, the effectiveness with which it improves its own procedures—all of these hinge upon the quality and availability of the information in the system.

PATTERNS OF COMMUNICATION

About two years ago a series of studies was begun whose purpose was to isolate and study certain general properties of information handling systems. The first phase of this research program[1] is directed at a basic

1 These studies are supported jointly by the Rand Corporation and the Research Laboratory of Electronics at M.I.T.

property of all communication systems, that of connection or "who can talk to whom."

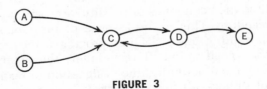

FIGURE 3

This property of connection can be conveniently expressed by diagrams. The meaning of the picture in Fig. 3 is obvious. Individuals A and B can send messages to C but they can receive messages from no one; C and D can exchange messages; E can receive messages from D, but he can send messages to no one. The pattern shown in Fig. 3, however, is only one of the many that are possible. A group of others is shown in Fig. 4. An examination of these patterns will show that they fall into two classes, separated by a very important difference. Any pair of individuals in each of the patterns, d, e, and f can exchange messages either directly or indirectly over some route. No pair of individuals in each of the patterns a, b, and c can exchange messages. Patterns like a, b, and c obviously make any coordination of thought or action virtually impossible; we will be concerned from this point on only with patterns like d, e, and f.

Since the individuals in any connected pattern like d, e, and f can share ideas completely, should we expect that the effectiveness of individuals in performing group tasks or solving group problems would be

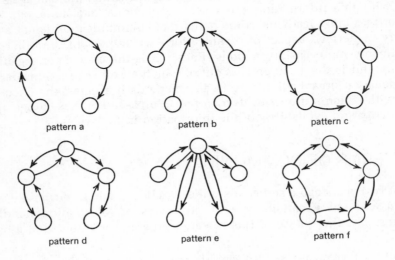

FIGURE 4

the same in patterns d, e, and f except for differences in ability, knowledge, and personality? Should we expect differences in quality and speed of performance? Is it likely that the individuals working in one pattern would show significantly better morale than the individuals working in a different pattern? Sidney Smith and Harold J. Leavitt conducted a series of experiments[2] which yielded very definite answers to these questions. An experimental design was used which made it possible to equate the difficulty of the tasks which the groups performed, and which permitted the cancelling of individual differences by randomizing the assignment of subjects to patterns. Also, the experiment was repeated with different groups enough times to establish the consistency of the results. A brief summary of the findings is given in Fig. 5. The use of qualitative terms in Fig. 5 in place of the quantitative measurements which were actually made blurs the comparison somewhat, but it gives a fair picture of the way these patterns performed. Since the original experiments were done by Smith and Leavitt, this experiment has been repeated with no change in the findings.

The question very properly arises here as to whether these findings can be "explained" in the sense of being related to the connection properties of the patterns themselves. The answer to this question is a qualified yes. Without developing the mathematical analysis, which can be found in Leavitt's paper, the following statements can be made:

For any connected pattern, an *index of dispersion* can be calculated. Relative to this index, there can be calculated *for each position in each*

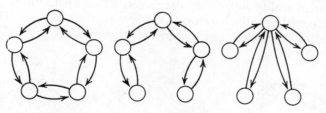

Speed	slow	fast	fast
Accuracy	poor	good	good
Organization	no stable form of organization	slowly emerging but stable organization	almost immediate and stable organization
Emergence of Leader	none	marked	very pronounced
Morale	very good	poor	very poor

FIGURE 5

2 Harold J. Leavitt reports these experiments in detail in the January, 1951, issue of the *Journal of Abnormal and Social Psychology*.

pattern an *index of centrality,* and an *index of peripherality.* The data suggest strongly that the rapidity with which organization emerges and the stability it displays are related to the gradient of the indices of centrality in the pattern. In Fig. 6 these indices are given for each position. It should be added at this point that in the patterns in which leadership emerged, the leader was invariably that person who occupied the position of highest centrality.

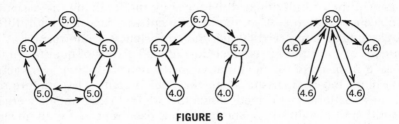

FIGURE 6

The index of peripherality appears to be related strongly to morale. In Fig. 7 the indices of peripherality are given by position. Those individuals who occupied positions of low or zero peripherality showed in their actions as well as in self-ratings (made at the end of the experiments) that they were satisfied, in high spirits, and generally pleased with the work they had done. Those individuals who occupied positions of high peripherality invariably displayed either apathetic or destructive and uncooperative behavior during the group effort, and rated themselves as dissatisfied and critical of the group's operation.

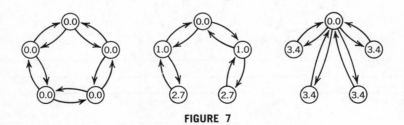

FIGURE 7

A word of caution should be given concerning the slow, inaccurate, but happy "circle" pattern. Subsequent experiments by Sidney Smith indicate that this pattern possesses unusual abilities for adaptation to sudden and confusing changes of task—a quality lacking in the other two patterns.

A PROMISING FIELD FOR RESEARCH

Clearly, these experiments are only the beginning of a long story. The findings, although they promise much, settle nothing; but they do suggest that an experimental approach to certain aspects of organizational communication is possible and that, in all probability, it would be practically rewarding. As the characteristics of communication nets and their effects upon human performance *as they occur in the laboratory* become better understood, the need will grow for systematic studies of actual operating organizations. The job of mapping an existing net of communications even in a relatively small company is a complicated and difficult one, but it is not impossible. Some work is beginning on the development of field methods of observation. The importance of bridging the gap between the simple, directly controlled experiment and the very complex, indirectly controlled social situation cannot be overestimated.

CONSIDERATION IN CHANNEL SELECTION[1]

Arlyn J. Melcher and Ronald Beller

INTRODUCTION

The existence of the formal and informal aspects of organizations is widely known. Even so, there has been little progress in integrating the two in a theory of administration. Others have recognized the problem and called for a solution.

> Where formal organization theory stresses the deliberate planning of structural arrangements and correlation of the work to be done, informal organization takes account of the ways employees actually behave insofar as they deviate from the formal plan. . . . Until it has been corrected by what informal organization theory has to offer, formal organization theory is likely to be inaccurate and incomplete. The obvious challenge to the present generation is to work out a single theory of organization where heretofore there have been two.[2]

In part, the difficulty of working out a single theory of organization is the complexity of the problem. There are a number of dimensions to formal organization. These include formal channels of communication, formal policies, procedures, and rules, formal authority and duties assigned to each office, and Gesellschaft norms that the officeholder is expected to observe.[3]

Condensed from *Academy of Management Journal,* X, 1 (March 1967). Reprinted by permission.

1. The suggestions of Prof. Rance Hill, Department of Sociology, Kent State University, and Dr. James Thompson, Graduate School of Business Administration, Indiana University, on a previous draft are gratefully acknowledged.
2. Marshall E. Dimock, Gladys O. Dimock, and Lewis W. Koenig, *Public Administration,* rev. ed. (New York: Holt, Rinehart, and Winston, 1961), p. 132.
3. The Gemeinschaft-Gesellschaft continuum summarized and refined by Loomis clarifies the norms with which an officeholder is expected to conform. See Charles P. Loomis, *Social Systems* (New York: D. Van Nostrand, 1960), pp. 57-128.

The concept of "informal organization" is used so broadly that it may cover any deviation from the formally prescribed patterns. Progress in developing an understanding of the relationships between formal and informal aspects of organization probably requires that the problem be broken into parts.

This paper focuses upon the communications aspect of organization —a limited but important part of this area. Specifically, the questions posed are where the use of formal or informal communication channels or some combination would contribute to the effectiveness of the administrator and when verbal, written, or some combination of these methods would facilitate an administrator's effectiveness when using the formal or informal networks.

Some suggestions are made in this article for the substantive aspects of a theory of channel selection. The primary purpose of this paper, however, is to present a more systematic approach to the development of theory than presently exists.

THE PROBLEM OF CHANNEL SELECTION

Where there is broad acceptance that unofficial channels are and must be used extensively, there is still the question of *when* it would be more effective to use the formal channels and when the informal channels. Little of the extensive literature on the subject of communication is relevant to the problem of channel selection. A good part of the published material deals with effective speaking and writing, leadership of conferences and committees, and similar personal skills.[4] Most of the other books and articles discuss the design of the formal communication systems. Some authors focus upon special networks such as suggestion plans[5] and grievance procedures;[6] others deal with general problems of

4. Illustrative examples are Charles E. Redfield, *Communication in Management* (Chicago: University of Chicago, 1958); Elizabeth Morting, Robert Finley, and Ann Ward (eds.), *Effective Communication on the Job* (New York: American Management Association, 1963); J. Harold Janis (ed.), *Business Communication Reader* (New York, 1958).

5. Stanley G. Seimer, *Suggestion Plans in American Industry* (New York: Syracuse University Press, 1959); Herman W. Seinwerth, *Getting Results from Suggested Plans* (New York: McGraw-Hill, 1948); *Suggestions from Employees* (New York: National Industrial Conference Board, 1936).

6. Neil W. Chamberlain, *Collective Bargaining* (New York: McGraw-Hill, 1951), pp. 96-119. Also Wilson Randle, *Collective Bargaining: Principles and Practices* (New York: Houghton Mifflin Co., 1951), pp. 466-492.

information flow associated with utilization of computers,[7] or the specification of hierarchical relationships that define the route for formal communication. The writers who deal with informal communication networks typically approach the topic on a descriptive level. Attention is primarily directed toward relating the ways in which deviations from the formal structure occur.[8]

A few investigators have offered clues to the functions alternative channels may serve.[9] Still, there is no framework that directs attention to the consequences of using official and unofficial channels. Since there is no systematic way of dealing with the problem, there is a nearly complete absence of theory.

ALTERNATIVE CHANNELS AND METHODS OF USING CHANNELS

The manager has a number of alternatives facing him in communicating. He can follow official channels,[10] proceed in the more nebulous area of using unofficial channels, or combine the two. While using these channels, the manager may contact others by written media, by voice (either face-to-face, or through other less direct means such as the telephone), or with some combination. There is a fairly complex set of alternatives to choose from in communicating.

7. Robert H. Gregory and Richard Van Horn, *Business Data Processing and Programming* (Belmont, California: Wadsworth Publishing Co., 1963); Joseph Becker and Robert M. Hayes, *Information Storage and Retrieval: Tools, Elements, Theories* (New York: John Wiley and Sons, 1963); John Peter McNerney, *Installing and Using an Automatic Data Processing System* (Boston: Graduate School of Business Administration, Harvard University).

8. For a summary of some of the literature see Delbert C. Miller and William H. Form, *Industrial Sociology* (New York: Harper and Brothers, 1951), pp. 272-307; Leonard Sayles, *Managerial Behavior* (New York: McGraw-Hill, 1964); Keith Davis, *Human Relations at Work* (New York: McGraw-Hill, 1962), pp. 235-260; Joseph A. Litterer (ed.), *Organizations: Structure and Behavior* (New York: Wiley and Sons, 1961), pp. 138-204; Peter M. Blau and W. Richard Scott, *Formal Organizations; A Comparative Approach* (San Francisco: Chandler Publishing Co., 1962), pp. 87-192 and 222-263; Henry Albers, *Organized Executive Action* (New York: John Wiley and Sons, 1961), pp. 339-342; Keith Davis, "The Organization That's Not on the Chart," *Supervisory Management* (July, 1961), pp. 2-7.

9. Lyndall Urwick, "The Manager's Span of Control," *Harvard Review*, XXXIV, No. 3 (May-June, 1956), pp. 39-47; also "Fitting in the Specialist Without Antagonizing the Line," *Advanced Management*, XVII (January, 1952), pp. 13-16; Chester Barnard, *Functions of the Executive* (Boston: Harvard University Press, 1938), pp. 122-123.

10. A number of terms will be used interchangeably in this paper. Official, organization, and formal are used synonymously. Unofficial, nonorganizational, and informal are also used interchangeably. The official channels are defined as those that coincide with

CHARACTERISTICS OF
THE CHANNEL MEMBERS

The characteristics of the message sender, receiver, intermediaries, and higher level supervisors are important variables in channel selection.[11] An outline of the relevant personality variables is given in Figure 1.

Characteristics of the Channel Members

1. The goal vs. means orientation of those who are directly or indirectly involved in communication.
2. The reliability of those involved to interpret and relay the communication.
3. The language capabilities of the recipient and intermediaries.

FIGURE 1

It is necessary to evaluate the communication potential of those who might be directly or indirectly involved in communicating. The term "potential" is used to represent their capabilities and restraints on the exercise of their abilities.

1. *Goal vs. Means Orientation.* The degree of commitment of the sending, receiving, and reviewing agents to follow the formal prescriptions of rules, procedure, and authority is a key consideration in selecting methods and channels. As others have observed, some individuals regard the formal prescription as ends. The policies, rules, and other restrictions are adhered to, even though it is impossible to carry out the assigned responsibilities by doing so.[12] Others are goal-oriented and observe the formal prescriptions when they support their efforts, but freely deviate

the formal chain of command. Messages follow the hierarchical pattern and cannot bypass any organization member on any level. For example, in the diagram below, a message from 31 to 34 would go to 21, then to 1, on to 22, and finally to 34.

Unofficial channels are all communication routes which do not coincide with the formal structure. A message from 31 to 34 might go directly to 34 or indirectly through any number of intermediaries, some of whom may form a segment of the formal channel—e.g., 31 to 22 to 34; the path is a segment of the formal channel.

11. The message sender, receiver, and intermediaries in the respective channels will be referred to as channel members.

12. Robert K. Merton, "Bureaucratic Structure and Personality," *Social Forces,* XVII (1940), pp. 560-568; Melville Dalton, *Men Who Manage* (New York: John Wiley and Sons, 1959), pp. 241-261.

from them when they impede achievement of goals. The latter attitude is well expressed by a Chinese general, 2000 years ago, who was questioned by his officers about a proposal that would violate government policy, but would counter a threatened annihilation of his unit:

> . . . His officers asked how he was to take this initiative without first obtaining permission from the Chinese civil commissioner who was accompanying the army; an objection which exasperated Pan Ch'ao.
>
> 'Our life and death is to be decided today; what do we care for the opinions of a common civil servant? If we inform him of our plan, he will surely take fright and our projects will be divulged.'[13]

Where those involved are committed to attaining ends rather than following procedures, greater reliance can be placed on nonorganization channels and verbal exchanges.

2. *Communication Reinforcement.* A second determinant of channel selection is the "potential" to contribute to the communication that is to be relayed to others. The recipient and intermediaries can frequently aid the overall effort by adding useful information, by arriving at subsolutions to problems faced by the next member, and by checking the reliability and accuracy of the information transmitted. On the other hand, if the message will be misinterpreted readily or confused by intermediaries, it may be necessary to eliminate some individuals from the channel and require combinations of written and verbal amplification.

Certain individuals may be particularly useful in the communication process. The person could be the "funnel," referred to by Dalton,[14] who is apt to "talk out of turn and carry secrets to the right people," assuring almost predictable communication. The individual might be the leader of one of the informal groups to which the potential receiver belongs. It would also be helpful to identify those who might deal in nonorganizational channels for some personal reward.

3. *Language Capabilities.* The language capabilities of those potentially involved in communication may restrict or eliminate some from the channel. Modification can be made in the way the communication is expressed and supplementary information provided if it is needed for understanding or to establish the pertinence of the communication to the immediate administrative problem.[15] In practice, some individuals

13. Rene Grousset, *The Rise and Splendor of the Chinese Empire* (Berkeley: University of California Press, 1964), p. 72.

14. Dalton, op. cit., pp. 232-234.

15. See Albers, pp. 329-332; Lester Tarnpol, "Attitudes Block Communication," *Personnel Journal*, XXXVII (February, 1959), pp. 325-328.

would be excluded and revision would be made in the content and method of communicating in order to adjust to the language capabilities of others.

CHANNEL CHARACTERISTICS

Each communication channel and method of using the network has specific characteristics which are relevant to communication. Six key elements are speed, feedback, selectivity, acceptance, monetary cost, and establishing accountability.

1. *Speed.* Where the written or verbal approach is given, unofficial channels generally are more direct and faster than official networks. Where the channel is given, verbal contacts usually are speedier than written. The combination of unofficial channels with verbal communication normally is the fastest. However, any combination of verbal followed up by written forms is as fast when the written message is used for recording rather than immediate communication purposes.

2. *Feedback.* The more complex the message, the greater the need for two-way interaction between the sender and receiver. This helps the sender to determine the understanding by the receiver and the effectiveness of the channel selected (i.e., whether the channel performed as the sender anticipated in terms of speed, accuracy). Feedback is automatic in face-to-face contact where both can get what Thayer[16] calls "instructions" in interpreting words, gestures, facial expressions, inflection, tone, emphasis, etc. Thus, verbal communication provides greater and quicker feedback compared to written messages since it provides a complete circuit while written media typically provide a one-way transmission.[17] Even when feedback is actively sought by the sender of written messages, the inherent delay in such a process can lead to erroneous actions.

3. *Selectivity.* Those sending messages frequently wish to exercise control over circulation of the message in the organization. The legitimacy of the communication is an important factor determining the need for control. In other cases, there may be a plan for gradual dissemination of information where only a small group is initially informed of developments. Unofficial channels may permit a greater degree of control than formal channels since the sender can be more selective in determining who will be initially included. Those suspected of leaking secrets to unauthorized personnel would be excluded.

16. Lee Thayer, *Administrative Communication* (Homewood, Illinois: Richard D. Irwin, 1961), p. 70.

17. Redfield, *op. cit.,* p. 74; Blau and Scott, *op. cit.,* p. 118.

4. *Acceptance.* One vital skill is the ability to persuade others to take desired actions. Persuasive efforts normally require a large amount of personal interaction between the participants. The channel selected for message transmission is crucial to the effort to enlarge the receiver's "area of acceptance."[18] Where persuasion or arriving at consensus is involved, it is essential to operate on the informal verbal level as positions can be changed without loss of official status. When agreement is achieved, the decision should then be formally processed and written. The latter is necessary since those that were not involved in making the decision are more likely to accept it when the decision is an official act of the authorized office. Barnard observed that the formal organization structure performs a valuable function in defining communication authoritativeness and authenticity.[19] This means that the hierarchical status differentiation is accepted as *prima facie* evidence of these qualities essential to message acceptance. Thus, requests for and giving of information upward in the hierarchy, and communicating decisions or information downward, are likely to receive greater acceptance when official channels are followed.

5. *Cost.* The monetary cost of using the various channels may be important in selecting a channel. For example, in a geographically dispersed organization, this factor could become important since it is expensive to travel from one location to another in order to meet face-to-face. Long-distance calls, closed circuit television, and other methods that enable verbal person-to-person exchanges may be substituted on economic grounds. Written communication may need to be used where many are competing for the recipient's time. It is considerably cheaper to queue written messages than it is verbal. A great deal of time can be wasted getting in to see the boss.

6. *Accountability.* Performance measurement and control depend on a clear establishment of accountability in carrying out assigned responsibilities. There must be accountability for (1) making past, present, and future decisions, (2) giving orders and requesting or giving information, (3) initiating communication contacts, and (4) utilizing organization resources in gathering information, or in carrying out orders. Written communications following formal channels are the most effective way of establishing accountability. The communication could initially take place on an informal level to speed up the process, but the communication would have to be officially recorded (written and sent along formal channels) if accountability is to be clearly established.

18. Barnard, *Functions of the Executive,* pp. 167-171.
19. Barnard, "Functions of Status Systems," *loc. cit.*

CONCLUSION

A practicing manager is faced with a choice of methods and channels when he is (1) establishing a program for a previously nonprogrammed activity, (2) reviewing an existing program for possible improvement, (3) working in an organizational context that is changing (new problems, personnel changes, increased cost and time pressures), or (4) orienting himself in a new job. At these times, a judgment must be made on the value of the alternative official or unofficial channels and written or verbal communication. The specification of channels and the methods of using the channels clarify the alternatives available to the manager. Administrative effectiveness probably is critically affected by how quickly a manager familiarizes himself with the orientation of his superiors, subordinates, and members in other departments, the extent to which he integrates himself into the social system, and his awareness of the functional aspects of the alternative channels. He is then in a position to use the channels and media that would best fit the nature of the communication. It is unlikely managers have complete information on all these variables to arrive at rational judgments. The important point, though, is that they must make intuitive or explicit judgments about each of these items. Their general effectiveness is likely to turn upon whether they consider all the dimensions of communications that are involved.

While the theory offered in this article is of a tentative nature, it provides some hypotheses that can be further explored. Further, the framework provides a basis for systematically observing in research studies the behavior of effective and ineffective administrators. As projects along these lines are pursued, we will be in a position to take a big step forward in developing a theory of organizational communication and to move toward a single theory of administration.

THE ORGANIZATION AND ITS COMMUNICATIONS PROBLEM

Jay M. Jackson

Business executives, I am told, are very similar to other people: they have communication problems, too. They are concerned, of course, about better understanding among all persons. They are interested in overcoming barriers to communication between members of the public and their own particular industry. They are especially concerned, or should be, about problems of communication within an organization, since business administration by its very nature is a collective enterprise, and people in this profession must spend their days in organized groups, or organizations.

First, I want to discuss some characteristics of all organizations that create communication problems. Second, I shall present some conclusions based on recent research findings regarding the forces which determine the flow of communication in an organization. Next I shall consider the consequences of communication in a number of conditions that often exist within an organization. Finally, I shall attempt to indicate that what we call problems of communication are often merely symptomatic of other difficulties between people.

CHARACTERISTICS OF ORGANIZATIONS

What is it about organizations that seems to make communication especially difficult? An organization may be considered a system of overlapping and interdependent groups. These groups can be departments located on the same floor of a building, or they can be divisions scattered over the face of the earth. Other things being equal, people will communicate most frequently to those geographically closest to them, even within a relatively small organization. Spatial distance itself can thus be a barrier to communication.

Each one of the subgroups within an organization demands allegiance from its members. It has its own immediate goals and means for achieving them. It distributes tangible or intangible rewards to mem-

From *Advanced Management Journal* (February 1959), pp. 17-20. Reprinted by permission.

bers of the group, based on their contribution to these objectives. When any particular communication is sent to a number of subgroups in an organization, each group may extract a different meaning from the message, depending upon its significance for the things the group values and is striving to accomplish.

The groups in an organization often represent different subcultures —as different, for example, as those inhabited by engineers, accountants, and salesmen. Each occupational or professional group has its own value system and idealized image, based on its traditions. These are guarded jealously, since to a considerable degree they give the members of that group their feelings of identity. Other groups in an organization, based on experience, age, sex, and marital status, have to varying degrees similar tendencies. Each develops along with its peculiar value system a somewhat specialized system of meanings. What is required to communicate effectively to members of different groups is a system of simultaneous translation, like that employed by the United Nations. This simultaneous translation must be taking place both within the sender and the receivers of a communication.

It is also characteristic of organizations that persons are structured into different systems of relationships. A work structure exists: certain persons are expected to perform certain tasks together with other persons. An authority structure exists: some people have responsibility for directing the activities of others. The status structure determines which persons have what rights and privileges. The prestige structure permits certain persons to expect deferential behavior from others. The friendship structure is based on feelings of interpersonal trust.

These systems of relationships overlap but are not identical. Each has an important effect upon communication in an organization, by influencing the expectations people have regarding who should communicate to whom about what in what manner. Now, how often do people openly and freely discuss these matters and come to agreement? Since these areas involve ranking of persons and invidious distinctions, they are commonly avoided. Yet disagreements and distorted perceptions about questions of relationship in an organization are the source of many communication difficulties.

What intensifies these communication problems is the fact that relationships among persons in an organization are in a continual state of flux. Personnel losses, transfers, promotions and replacements are occurring. Decisions about new policies and procedures are being made, and often modify people's relationships. Some people are informed about changed relationships before others; some are not informed at all. Although it is common practice to communicate decisions to all the persons who are affected by them, the problem is often to determine who are the relevant persons. Unless we are extremely sensitive to the social structure of our organization, it is likely that we shall restrict communication too narrowly. The restrictive communication of decisions about change, however, can be extremely disruptive to any consensus people have about their relationships to one another, and thus can create for them problems of communication.

THE FLOW OF COMMUNICATION

Any solution of a communication problem must be based on analysis of the particular situation in which the problem occurs, and an application of general principles about communication. It is possible, on the basis of findings from research, to formulate a number of principles about the forces in an organization which direct the flow of communication.

You may have heard at one time or another that communication flows downward all right in an organization; the problem is to get communication from below. This is only partially true. In fact, any generalization that communication flows down, up, or across, is equally false. Communication is like a piece of driftwood on a sea of conflicting currents. Sometimes the shore will be littered with debris, sometimes it will be bare. The amount and direction of movement is not aimless, nor unidirectional, but a response to all the forces—winds, tides and currents —which come into play.

What forces direct communication in an organization? They are, on the whole, motivational forces. People communicate or fail to communicate in order to achieve some goal, to satisfy some personal need, or to improve their immediate situation. Let us examine briefly some of the evidence from research which supports this statement.

A study was made of the communication patterns among the personnel of a medium-sized government agency.[1] Everyone was included in the research, from the director to the janitor. It was found that people communicated far more to members of their own subgroups than to any other persons. They also preferred to be communicating to someone of higher status than themselves, and tried to avoid having communication with those lower in status than themselves. The only exception to this tendency was when a person had supervisory responsibilities, which removed his restraints against communicating with particular lower status persons. When people did communicate with others of the same status level in the organization, there was a strong tendency for them to select highly valued persons, and to avoid those they thought were making little contribution.

Let us see if we can find a principle which explains these results.

---

1. Jay M. Jackson, *Analysis of Interpersonal Relations in a Formal Organization*, Ph.D. Thesis, University of Michigan, 1953.

The formal subgroupings in an organization are usually based upon joint work responsibilities. There are strong forces, therefore, to communicate with those whose work goals are the same as one's own. A supervisor can accomplish his work objectives only by having relatively frequent contact with his subordinates: and he probably would like to have more contact than he has. The people in an organization who are most valued for their ability to contribute are those who can give the best information and advice. People seek them out. These findings all seem to point to the same conclusion:

1. *In the pursuit of their work goals, people have forces acting upon them to communicate with those who will help them achieve their aims, and forces against communicating with those who will not assist, or may retard their accomplishment.*

In the midst of one study of a housing settlement,[2] a rumor swept through the community and threatened to disrupt the research. The investigators turned their attention to this rumor and were able to trace its path from person to person. They were trying to understand the forces which led people to communicate. Later on they tested their understanding by deliberately planting a rumor in an organization and again tracing its path by the use of informants.[3] They concluded that people will initiate and spread rumors in two types of situation: when they are confused and unclear about what is happening, and when they feel powerless to affect their own destinies. Passing on a rumor is a means of expressing and alleviating anxiety about the subject of the rumor.[4]

Let us consider one more fact before we draw a general conclusion from these findings. Studies in industry, in a hospital, and in a government agency all yield the same result: people want to speak to higher status rather than lower status persons.[5] Why are there these strong forces on people to direct their communication upwards? Higher status persons have the power to create for subordinates either gratifying or depriving experiences. These may take the form of tangible decisions and rewards, or perhaps merely expressions of approval and confidence.

2. Leon Festinger, Dorwin Cartwright, *et al.,* "A Study of a Rumor: Its Origin and Spread," *Human Relations,* 1948, 1, pp. 464-486.
3. Kurt Back, Leon Festinger, *et al.,* "The Methodology of Studying Rumor Transmission," *Human Relations,* 1950, 3, pp. 307-312.
4. For an illustration of this in a hospital setting, see: Jay Jackson, Gale Jensen, and Floyd Mann, "Building a Hospital Organization for Training Administrators," *Hospital Management,* September, 1956, p. 54.
5. See Elliott Mishler and Asher Tropp, "Status and Interaction in a Psychiatric Hospital," *Human Relations,* 1956, 9, pp. 187-206; Jay Jackson, *Analysis of Interpersonal Relations in a Formal Organization,* Ph.D. Thesis, University of Michigan, 1953; Tom Burns, "The Directions of Activity and Communication in a Departmental Executive Group," *Human Relations,* 1954, 7, pp. 73-79.

Lower status persons need reassurance about their superiors' attitudes, evaluations, and intentions towards them. We can conclude that:

2. *People have powerful forces acting upon them to direct their communication toward those who can make them feel more secure and gratify their needs, and away from those who threaten them, make them feel anxious, and generally provide unrewarding experiences.*

People's needs largely determine content of their communication to others of different status. There is evidence that subordinates will often be reluctant to ask supervisors for help when they need it, because this might be seen as a threatening admission of inadequacy.[6] And superiors tend to delete from their communications to subordinates any reference to their own mistakes or errors of judgment.[7] I am sure that these findings are in accord with the experiences that many of us have had in organizations.

A third principle which helps us understand the flow of communication is this:

3. *Persons in an organization are always communicating as if they were trying to improve their position.*

They may or may not be aware of their own behavior in this respect. But the evidence indicates that they want to increase their status, to belong to a more prestigeful group, to obtain more power to influence decisions, and to expand their authority. It has been said that talking upwards is a gratifying substitute for moving upwards. Persons in an organization who are attracted to membership in a particular department or group will feel inclined to direct much more communication in that direction than will those who do not want to belong to it. If they are excluded or barred from membership and their desire to belong persists, they will increase their communication even further, as if this represented a substitute for actually moving into the desirable group.[8]

In a study of the role relationships of three types of professionals who work together in the mental health field[9]—psychiatrists, clinical psychologists, and psychiatric social workers—it was found that the di-

---

6. Ian Ross, *Role Specialization in Supervision,* Ph.D. Thesis, Columbia University, 1957.

7. This finding is from an unpublished study of a public utility company by Alvin Zander.

8. Experimental evidence exists for this statement in: Jay Jackson and Herbert Saltzstein, *Group Membership and Conformity Processes* (Ann Arbor: Research Center for Group Dynamics, University of Michigan, 1956), p. 89; see also: Harold Kelley, "Communication in Experimentally Created Hierarchies," *Human Relations,* 1950, 4, pp. 39-56.

9. Zander, A., Cohen, A. R., and Stotland, E., *Role Relations in the Mental Health Professions* (Ann Arbor: Institute for Social Research, University of Michigan, 1957).

rection, amount, and content of their communication to one another could be predicted largely from two factors. These were: their perception of the other professions' power relative to their own; and how satisfied they were with their own power position compared to that of the other groups. The general principle that forces act on persons to communicate so as to improve their relative position in the organization seems to be supported by all these findings.

THE CONSEQUENCES OF COMMUNICATION

Recent research also has something to tell us about the consequences that communication will have when various conditions exist within an organization. Again we find that it is not possible to state that a particular type of communication will always have the same effect, without specifying the conditions in which the generalization will hold true. At the present time, however, the evidence from research appears to warrant four general conclusions.

1. *The effect of any particular communication will depend largely upon the prior feelings and attitudes that the parties concerned have towards one another.*

Findings from a number of different studies support this statement. During World War II, hostile attitudes and negative stereotypes existed between the inhabitants of a housing project for industrial workers and members of the surrounding community. An action research project was undertaken to increase contact between these two groups of people.[10] It was found, however, that after increased contact the attitudes and feelings of these people had become polarized: those that were initially positive became more positive, and those that began by being negative became even more negative. The effect of stimulating greater contact could have been predicted only from a knowledge of the pre-existing attitudes and feelings.

In another study of the communication patterns in a large organization, it was found that increased communication did make people more accurate about others' opinions, but only when they initially trusted one another and already were in considerable agreement.[11] When people are in disagreement or do not trust one another, an increase in communication will not necessarily lead to greater understanding.

10. Leon Festinger and Harold Kelley, *Changing Attitudes Through Social Contact* (Ann Arbor: Research Center for Group Dynamics, University of Michigan, 1951).
11. Glen Mellinger, "Interpersonal Trust as a Factor in Communication," *Journal of Abnormal and Social Psychology,* 1956, 52, pp. 304-309.

It was found in another study that frequent communication among personnel made working for the organization either more or less attractive for them. The mediating factor was whether or not the persons who were in constant communication valued each others' contribution to the work of the organization.[12]

2. *The effect of any particular communication will depend upon the pre-existing expectations and motives of the communicating persons.*

Executives of a large organization were asked to indicate on a checklist how much time they spent with each other, and the subject of their interaction.[13] In one-third of the answers they were in disagreement about the subject of their communication. For example, one reported that he had been discussing personnel matters with another; the latter thought they had been discussing questions of production. When these executives differed, each assumed that the problem with which he was personally most concerned was what they had really been talking about.

The subjects of this study were men with an engineering background. They consistently overestimated the amount of time executives spent on production matters and underestimated the amount of time spent on personnel problems. The impressions their communication made upon them had been shaped by their own goals and motives.

From this and other studies it seems clear that the consequences of communication are limited by people's interest in achieving certain effects, and lack of concern about achieving others. They will be inclined to remember and feel committed to those decisions which are consistent with their own expectations and motives.

3. *The effect of a superior's communication with a subordinate will depend upon the relationship between them, and how adequately this relationship satisfies the subordinate's needs.*

Communication between superior and subordinate often has consequences which neither of them anticipates nor welcomes. It is especially difficult to avoid problems of misinterpretation or ineffectiveness in this area.

In one organization it was found that some employees who received frequent communication from their supervisor became more accurately informed about their supervisor's real attitudes; but this was not true for other employees who also had constant contact with their supervisor.[14] The difference was traced to whether or not a supervisor said he trusted his subordinates. When he did not trust them, he was more

12. Jay Jackson, *op. cit.*
13. Tom Burns, *op. cit.*
14. Glen Mellinger, *op. cit.*

guarded in what he said to them, revealing less of his true feelings. A lack of trust between superior and subordinate can thus act as a barrier to the creation of mutual understanding.

We have discussed how people's need for security directs their communication toward higher status persons in an organization. A study was conducted in a public utility company,[15] where it was possible to vary experimentally the kind of communication supervisors gave their subordinates. People became anxious and threatened in response to two different conditions: when communication from their supervisor was unclear, and when the supervisor was inconsistent in what he said from one time to another.

We have also pointed out that the persons in an organization tend to communicate as if they were constantly attempting to improve their positions. This is consistent with the finding that the experienced employees in an organization resent close supervision,[16] since it implies that their power and prestige are less than they want them to be.

The study of the senior staff members in a British engineering plant, referred to earlier, led to the discovery of a process of "status protection." When these men received instructions from their superiors, they often treated them as merely information or advice. In this manner they in effect achieved a relative improvement in their own position in the authority structure, by acting as if no one had the right to direct their activity.

Thus the findings from laboratory and field research point unequivocally to the supervisor-subordinate relationship as one of the crucial factors determining the effect of a supervisor's communication to subordinates. Another major factor is whether or not the subordinate stands alone in his relationship to the supervisor, or belongs to a group of peers in the organization.

4. *The effect of a superior's communication with a subordinate will depend upon the amount of support the subordinate receives from membership in a group of peers.*

An experimental study has demonstrated the remarkable effect of belonging to a group of equals on a subordinate confronted by a powerful and directive superior.[17] Being a member of a group decreased a per-

15. Arthur Cohen, "Situational Structure, Self-Esteem, and Threat-Oriented Reactions to Power." A chapter in Dorwin Cartwright, *et al., Studies in Social Power* (Ann Arbor: Research Center for Group Dynamics, University of Michigan, 1959).

16. This finding is from an unpublished study by Jay Jackson, Jean Butman, and Philip Runkel of the communication patterns and attitudes of employees in two business offices.

17. Ezra Stotland, "Peer Groups and Reaction to Power Figures." A chapter in Dorwin Cartwright, *et al., Studies in Social Power* (Ann Arbor: Research Center for Group Dynamics, University of Michigan, 1959).

son's feelings of threat and freed him to disagree with his supervisor and make counterproposals. The person who had the moral support of membership in a group reacted to his supervisor's communication with less defensive and more problem-oriented behavior.

There is a considerable body of evidence, too, that a group acts as a source of "social reality" for its members, providing them an opportunity to validate their ideas and opinions.[18] When communication from a superior is directed to a group as a whole rather than to isolated individuals, it is likely that more accurate transmission of information will be achieved.

PROBLEMS OF COMMUNICATION ARE OFTEN SYMPTOMATIC

From our discussion thus far, I think it should be clear that what we call communication problems are often only symptomatic of other difficulties which exist among persons and groups in an organization. To summarize what has been said or implied, I should like to point to four problems which people in organizations must solve in order to overcome barriers to communication.

1. *The problem of trust or lack of trust.* Communication flows along friendship channels. When trust exists, content is more freely communicated, and the recipient is more accurate in perceiving the sender's opinion.

2. *The problem of creating interdependence among persons: common goals and agreement about means for achieving them.* When persons have different goals and value systems, then it is especially important to create mutual understanding about needs and motives.

3. *The problem of distributing rewards fairly,* so that people's needs are being met, and so that they are motivated to contribute to the over-all objectives of the organization. Nothing can be so restrictive of the free flow of ideas and information, for example, as the feeling that you may not obtain credit for your contribution.

4. *The exceedingly important problem of understanding and coming to common agreement about the social structure of the organization.* I can think of nothing which would facilitate more the free and accurate flow of communication in an organization than consensus about questions of work, authority, prestige, and status relationships.

18. See, for example, Jay M. Jackson and Herbert D. Saltzstein, "The Effect of Person-Group Relationships on Conformity Processes," *The Journal of Abnormal and Social Psychology* (in press).

COMMUNICATION—A KEY TO MANAGERIAL EFFECTIVENESS

Carlton J. Whitehead

Observation of managerial activity indicates that managers spend the greatest part of their day communicating either as encoders or decoders.[1] Dubin summarized the empirical studies related to managerial behavior,[2] and these studies indicate that managers at various levels spend from 50 to 80 percent of their workday talking.[3] When the time spent in other than oral communication is considered, the preponderance of time spent communicating becomes even more substantial. This finding is not surprising since an analysis of such managerial functions as leadership, motivation, planning, and control indicates that communication is a basic variable in each one. I recently interviewed several managers in both large and small manufacturing organizations, asking, "What do you consider to be your most serious problem?" The overwhelming response showed that the problem was communication.

Because communication is so important to the managerial process, one place to begin in the effort to improve managerial effectiveness is with a penetrating examination of the communication process designed to increase the manager's understanding. A review of the literature indicates the major focus has not been on understanding the communication process. For example, there are a plethora of "how to" articles which do not substantially contribute to one's understanding of the process of communication and, consequently, have minimum usefulness. In addition, the literature is replete with exhortations to improve communicative skills; but these exhortations which are not accompanied by attempts

Carlton J. Whitehead, "Communication—A Key to Managerial Effectiveness," *MSU Business Topics*, Spring, 1967, pp. 54-58. Reprinted by permission of the publisher, the Bureau of Business and Economic Research, Division of Research, Graduate School of Business Administration, Michigan State University.

1 For example, see Robert H. Guest, "Of Time and the Foreman," *Personnel*, XXXII (1956), 478-86.

2 Robert Dubin, "Business Behavior Behaviorally Viewed," in Chris Argyris *et al.*, *Social Science Approaches to Business Behavior* (Homewood, Ill.: Irwin-Dorsey, 1962), pp. 12-13.

3 *Ibid.*

to increase the manager's understanding have limited impact on his behavior. Consequently, the effort of this article is directed toward understanding the dynamics of the communication process; it is hoped that
understanding can lead to beneficial application.

In what follows, the discussion of the process nature of reality should
provide background for understanding the nature of words and the process nature of communication. After considering the nature and role of
word signs, the interpersonal communication process is examined with
a brief analysis of some ramifications of the interpersonal model; and
finally, the implications of the analysis for the manager are briefly reviewed.

PROCESS NATURE OF REALITY

To really grasp the dynamics of the communication process, one must
perceive the process nature of the world and events therein. Unfortunately, in our daily activities, we often ignore the available scientific
knowledge of the world.[4] Science 1967 indicates that the world is composed of multifarious interacting processes occurring in all directions
resulting in continuously changing reality. For example, an apparently
stable scientific event such as a pencil represents to science, 1967,

> a mad dash of "electrons," which is different every instant,
> which never repeats itself, which is known to consist of ex-
> tremely complex dynamic processes of very fine structure,
> acted upon by, and reacting upon, the rest of the universe,
> inextricably connected with everything else . . . we should
> ascribe to an event infinite numbers of characteristics, as it
> represents a process which never stops in one form or an-
> other. . . .[5]

The importance of the process point of view to the manager is that he
realize he is dealing with a continuously changing environment and dynamic events. To view many events like a pencil as static entities results in insignificant distortion; however, to view volatile events like
the organization and its membership as static entities results in a highly

---

4 The succeeding discussion reflects the point of view of general semantics presented
in Alfred Korzybski, *Science and Sanity: An Introduction to Non-Aristotelian Systems and
General Semantics* (Lakeville, Conn.: The International Non-Aristotelian Publishing Co.,
1959).

5 Korzybski, *ibid.,* p. 387.

distorted view of the elements in the management environment. For example, a subordinate, Joe Green 1960, is not Joe Green 1965; nor is the Clover Corporation 1960, the Clover Corporation 1965. Awareness of the concept of process enables the manager to realize he is a changing person managing dynamic events, and such an awareness should help to establish an attitude of change. Consequently, he should be better prepared to operate effectively in the very dynamic situation presented by a business organization.

NATURE OF WORDS

Words are the tools of communication, guides to events; and, furthermore, they are the end product of the process of abstracting. Therefore, to understand the nature of words, one must understand the process of abstracting. How does one get from the scientific event to words about that event?[6] First, there is the *scientific event*—for example, a person, a tree, or a car—which has infinite characteristics. Finite man can abstract only a finite number of characteristics to form an object. The *object* is the picture in one's head, the image he sees when the event, for example a tree, comes into the field of his sense organs. The object is not the event but only one's abstraction of the event. Thus, the object is unique to a particular person in a distinct space-time interval and contains a limited number of characteristics.

When a person begins to abstract characteristics related to the object and make statements about the object, he is on the word level. For example, from the event, tree, a number of characteristics could be abstracted to form the object. Then characteristics of the object could be abstracted in the form of descriptive statements to describe and define the assigned label "tree." Thus, the word level as a minimum is a second order abstraction.[7] The object is the first order abstraction from the event; and the word level is an abstraction from the object level, namely a second order abstraction. Therefore, words are not the object they represent, only a map or stimuli to direct one to the object level. The measure of words, then, is how effectively they direct the receiver to the desired object. To say that one set of words is right and another is wrong is often based on a false assumption about the nature of words. The real question is does either or do both sets achieve their purpose? Consequently, it

---

6 The succeeding discussion generally follows Korzybski, *ibid.,* pp. 386-411.

7 Statements and inferences about the descriptive statements are even higher order abstractions.

is useless to quibble over words because they are only guides or stimuli; and frequently many different sets of words will point to the same object.[8]

A consciousness of the process of abstracting makes the manager aware that his unique object is only one of many possible and that the descriptive words he utilizes are only those of many possible combinations. This understanding is very important to productive interrelationships with superiors, subordinates, and peers, and vital to the process of communication.

INTERPERSONAL COMMUNICATION MODEL

Models of the communication process have been developed by a number of writers,[9] and four elements are common to most of these models—an encoder, a message, a channel, and a decoder. A source and a receiver are also included to facilitate projecting the interpersonal model presented here to both the many-person and the intrapersonal levels. The source is the originator or instigator of the message. Encoding is the psychological process of selecting and structuring the signs to be included in the message. A message is a structured set of signs, and this discussion is primarily concerned with word signs. Channel is often used with a variety of meanings.[10] However, here it is used to designate the medium or carrier of messages.[11] A receiver is the intended recipient of the message and can be either a mechanical device, one person, or many people. Finally, decoding is the process of interpreting and assigning meaning to messages.

Examination of the interpersonal model begins with a snapshot view of the communication process in a particular space-time interval. Assume M and N are two persons in unique environments (physical and psychological). Further, assume M desires to communicate with N uti-

---

8 For related points of view on the subject discussed here, see C. K. Ogden and I. A. Richards, *The Meaning of Meaning* (New York: Harcourt, Brace and Co., 1947); Stuart Chase, *Power of Words* (New York: Harcourt, Brace and Co., 1953); S. I. Hayakawa, *Language in Thought and Action* (New York: Harcourt, Brace and Co., 1947).

9 For example, see F. Craig Johnson and George R. Klare, "General Models of Communication Research: A Survey of the Development of a Decade," *The Journal of Communication*, XI (March 1961), 13-26.

10 See Wilbur Schramm (ed.), *The Process and Effect of Mass Communication* (Urbana, Ill.: University of Illinois Press, 1955), pp. 87-90.

11 David K. Berlo, *The Process of Communication: An Introduction to Theory and Practice* (New York: Holt, Rinehart, and Winston, Inc., 1960), p. 31.

lizing word signs.[12] Since words are stimuli, M must choose and structure the words so that the message will stimulate N to reconstruct the meaning motivating the message. M is faced with a formidable task because he must attempt to evaluate the environmental and experiential state of N since these and other variables determine N's cognitive structure, a basic factor in interpreting the message stimulus.[13] As observed by one group of writers:

> The responses of the individual to persons and things are shaped by the way they look to him—his *cognitive world.* And the image, or "map," of the world of every person is an individual one. . . . Each person has an individualized image of the world because his image is the product of the following determinants: (1) *his* physical and social environments, (2) *his* physiological structure, (3) *his* wants and goals, (4) *his* past experiences.[14]

Assume that M has gone through the process of evaluating N and has encoded his message accordingly. Now, M must select a means of bringing the message into the environment of N in a manner conducive to reception by N's sense organs. That is, a channel must be selected and utilized.

Assume the message is transmitted and received by the exterocepters of N. The process now occurring may be visualized in the following diagram:

Stimulus → Interpretive Process → Meaning → Behavior

N decodes (interpretive process) the message within his existing cognitive frame of reference. Part of the interpretive process involves N trying to evaluate the source, M, because just as the perceived nature of the receiver is a basic cue for encoding the message, the perceived nature of the source is an important cue to interpreting it. The end product of N's interpretive process is a meaning assigned to the message. N's

---

12 There are many kinds of signs; for example, shaking one's head, facial expressions, etc.

13 As related to the previous discussion of abstracting, the cognitive structure influences the particular object abstracted by the perceiver.

14 David Kretch, Richard S. Crutchfield, and Egerton L. Ballachey, *Individual in Society* (New York: McGraw-Hill Book Co., 1962), pp. 17-18.

behavior related to the message is based upon the meaning assigned to it.[15] Communication is called a process because the sequence as described above is inextricably related to all past and future communication of both M and N.

The question might arise, "When has communication taken place?" Communication has been consummated when a meaning similar to the one motivating the message has been assigned to it by the decoder. Communication occurs in degrees, and perfect communication is rare. The extent to which the assigned meaning deviates from the motivating meaning is the amount of miscommunication.

SOME RAMIFICATIONS OF THE MODEL

Several important implications related to the preceding picture of the communication process should be noted. First, a common meaning is the objective of communicating. But what is the nature of meaning?[16] Is meaning found in the message or within people who assign meaning to the message? A message is a stimulus to which a person must assign a meaning. Although word signs may have an intended meaning and a dictionary definition, the individual actively assigns meaning on the basis of his past experiences, needs, purposes, etc.[17] In essence, meaning is the internal response to message stimuli.[18]

Second, the model points up that every person is both an encoder and a decoder. A manager's role as a decoder is just as vital to effectiveness in communicating as his encoding role. Unfortunately, most emphasis is placed upon originating the message, with disproportionate attention given to decoding. If a person is to communicate effectively, he must devote as much time and effort to receiving and decoding messages as he does to encoding them. Through successful decoding of incoming messages, the manager can derive and maintain a healthy, realistic view of events and people in the environment.

Third, this model can be projected to the many-person level—the type of systems characteristic of much organizational communication.

15 Actually this is an oversimplification because N's overt behavior may differ from his internal response because of intervening variables, as for example, the social environment at that time.

16 For a classic in the area of meaning, see C. K. Ogden and I. A. Richards, *The Meaning of Meaning: A Study of the Influence of Language Upon Thought and of the Science of Symbolism* (New York: Harcourt, Brace and Co., 1956).

17 Hadley Cantril, "Perception and Interpersonal Behavior," *American Journal of Psychiatry,* CXIV (1957), 123.

18 Berlo, *op. cit.,* p. 184.

In such a system, the originator and encoder might be different people, as might the receiver and decoder. The exact nature of this type of communication depends upon whether the system is a many-to-many, a one-to-many, or a many-to-one system and the intermediaries involved.

Fourth, the model indicates that communicating is a precarious process. Even though the encoder is constructing a message in word signs, other signs, both planned and unplanned, frequently accompany it.[19] For example, non-word signs include timing of the message, environmental factors, facial expressions, tone of voice, and bodily movements. While many of these cues may not be either purposeful or conscious, nevertheless, they are frequently part of the total message stimulus perceived by the decoder. Consequently, the encoder may be surprised, and at times shocked, by responses that, without a deeper analysis, would appear to be not in keeping with the message. Thus, an additional burden of dealing with silent signs confronts both the encoder and decoder. Both the tasks of constructing and interpreting messages are made significantly more difficult.

A related problem of connotative meaning complicates the process. Connotative meanings are specialized individualistic meanings assigned to words, and they develop from experiences with the referent of the words.[20] For example, the symbol fire may arouse a strong response from one who has had a very frightening experience with fire.[21] For various persons, many words contain unintended cues which evoke unanticipated responses. Although the extreme form of this problem whereby highly emotional responses are evoked is the exception rather than the rule, numerous shocked, frustrated, and confused communicators have experienced it to some degree.

Finally, the model implies that transmission of messages becomes very vital to the process when face-to-face communication is not being utilized. Transmission of messages through the channels in the organizational communication networks creates many types of problems.[22] Often distortion of message stimuli occurs as messages flow through the networks either horizontally or vertically, both upward and downward. Filtering and other noise factors either accidental or intentional result in a less than adequate message stimulus for decoders to evaluate. Thus, for effective communication the manager must provide adequate channels for message transmission. Otherwise, he, his superiors, his peers, and

19 Edward T. Hall, *The Silent Language* (Greenwich, Conn.: Fawcett Publications, Inc., 1961).

20 Berlo, *op. cit.*, pp. 209-15.

21 Carried to the extremes, this becomes sign pathology. See Charles W. Morris, *Signs, Language and Behavior* (New York: George Braziller, Inc., 1955), pp. 198-201.

22 Jay M. Jackson, "The Organization and Its Communication Problems," *Advanced Management*, XXIV (February 1959), 17-20.

his subordinates will have inadequate informational stimuli to guide their behavior.

IMPORTANCE TO MANAGERS

Has this discussion implied that a manager needs to be only a good communicator? Emphatically not! A person can be a good communicator and a poor manager; however, a manager with inadequate communicative understanding and skills will be severely limited. Good communication does not necessarily lead to good management, but poor communication does limit managerial effectiveness.

Understanding the communication process can help to minimize managerial frustration. How often has the manager experienced the frustration expressed in "How could he do that when I told him . . . ?" Understanding the communication process helps one to know that telling does not necessarily result in communication having occurred. This understanding also gives the manager a tool for explaining some previously puzzling behavior. Furthermore, he has a tool for preventing or solving many problems that confront him. Management can help provide the organizational environment for more effective communication. Restructuring the organization and creating an atmosphere where the members are receptive to messages from above and feel free to transmit unfavorable as well as favorable messages upward or horizontally might be some of the efforts needed.

Finally communicative ability can be developed. It involves a skill and techniques that can be acquired through the learning process and practice. A person can achieve as much professional competence as his ability level permits, and this is a reasonable objective that can be reached through a conscientious effort. Likewise, the communicative ability of the organization can be developed. Effective communication in the organization is dependent primarily upon an adequate structure and an intense desire for it by management.

CONCLUSION

The manager is involved in managing a complex set of dynamic interrelationships and processes and, consequently, in dealing with continuously changing sets of realities. The largest part of his workday is spent in communicating. Because communication is so vital to the manager, a deeper understanding of the communication process is suggested as a starting point in the effort to improve his effectiveness.

Communication is a process that requires a sensitive evaluative effort by the manager in his role as an encoder and a decoder of messages. Effectiveness at communication is highly important to the managerial role because receipt and transmission of information is basic to the managerial function. Understanding the process of communication should sensitize the manager's awareness of the variables and complexities of the communication process and result in improvement of his communicative ability. Furthermore, he should be better prepared to understand that part of previously puzzling organization behavior which is primarily communicative behavior. Consequently, the manager is likely to be better prepared and more willing to provide the organizational climate and structure for improving organizational communication.

A high level of communicative ability and understanding will not necessarily result in good management; however, inadequate communicative ability and understanding will significantly limit managerial effectiveness.

CLEAR COMMUNICATIONS FOR CHIEF EXECUTIVES

Robert N. McMurry

As one retiring chief executive said to his successor, "Yesterday was the last day you heard the truth from your subordinates." In many companies, often despite feverish efforts to improve internal communications, top executives are almost totally insulated from what is actually taking place in their enterprises. The intelligence they receive, including formal reports, is all too often incomplete or, at best, slanted.

Of equal concern, *not all chief executives are temperamentally capable of accepting and assimilating information which happens to conflict with their personal values and predilections.*

Consequently, undertakings of great magnitude and of critical significance to the integrity of the business are often entered into on the basis of incomplete, inadequate, or incorrect information. Without knowing it, the chief executive is in the perilous situation of the shipmaster who blindly sails uncharted shoals. He is unaware of the seriousness of his situation until confronted with catastrophe itself. It is probable that this is a not infrequent cause of the failure even of small, presumably well-integrated businesses. It certainly often contributes to the fact that, as a rule, the chief executive who is a professional manager and not a proprietor has the least job security of anyone in his organization.

In order to assist the chief executive in solving his predicament, I shall attack the communication problem point-blank by examining:

• The barriers which fault the chief executive's knowledge of "what's going on" in the middle and lower echelons of his organization.

• The sources of error which hinder his ability to communicate effectively with subordinates.

• The major remedies needed to improve his "intelligence," to help him to see himself, his staff, his employees, and his organization as a whole.

• The reorganization steps that should be taken to improve the over-all function of his organization.

Condensed from *Harvard Business Review* (March–April), pp. 131-145. © 1965 by the President and Fellows of Harvard College; all rights reserved.

- The personal conflicts which must be overcome if he is to establish clear, comprehensive, and valid channels of communication with his people at all levels.

UPWARD FAILURES

The top business manager is often lulled into a false sense of security regarding communication flows. His first and most egregious error is to assume that his supervisory hierarchy provides a clear channel of vertical communication, either upward or downward, and that lateral inter-departmental communication is equally reliable. Actually, most levels of supervision are less communication *centers* than communication *barriers*. In addition, many company functions, such as production and sales, are frequently less inclined to be cooperative *allies* than to be bitter *rivals* for power, recognition, and executive favor; hence, communication between them is often poor. Both are prolific *sources* of information, but this does not mean that the intelligence which they provide is complete, accurate, objective, or generally valid and useful.

MISLEADING INFORMATION

In fact, much information provided the chief executive by his subordinates is either unintentionally or willfully and maliciously inaccurate. There are a number of reasons for this:

- No subordinate wishes to have his superiors learn of anything which *he* interprets to be actually or potentially discreditable to him. Hence, he consciously and intentionally endeavors to screen everything that is transmitted upward, filtering out those items of information which are potentially threatening.
- He learns what his superiors desire to hear. Hence, he becomes adept not only at avoiding the unpleasant, but also at "stressing the positive." Though the individual subordinate may consciously be entirely sincere and accountable, his personal anxieties, hostilities, aspirations, and system of beliefs and values almost inevitably shape and color his interpretation and acceptance of what he has learned and is expected to transmit.[1]
- Each subordinate is often desirous of impressing the top manager with the superiority of *his* contributions to the enterprise—and, by the

1. See my article, "Conflicts in Human Values," *Harvard Business Review* (May–June 1963), p. 130.

same token, of the pitiful inadequacy of the contributions of his rivals in other divisions and departments of the company. *Special pleading* of this nature is often most seriously misleading. How can the chief executive know which protagonist is telling the truth? In most instances, he cannot be sure. If he depends solely upon his own judgment, he will probably be wrong at least as often as he is right.

- Another source of error arises from the fact that the position of chief executive is one for which there is often substantial competition and rivalry. Hence, the incumbent is not always surrounded and supported by allies and friends, despite his staff's frequent servility, obsequiousness, and dramatic protestations of loyalty. While most subordinates would hesitate to give their chief executive a final push into the abyss, many are not at all reluctant to sit by and let him stumble into it blindly.

- Finally, and from the viewpoint of upward communication of the greatest consequence, there is the inability of many chief executives to comprehend and accept valid information even when it is brought to their attention. No wonder top managers are seldom told "the whole truth and nothing but . . ." by their subordinates.

RESULTING ERRORS

In effect, the typical chief executive is the prisoner of his position communications-wise. He is largely insulated from the everyday realities of the enterprise he leads. It is not surprising that under these conditions the top manager makes a number of costly, sometimes even fatal, errors. These principally appear as:

- The acceptance of misinformation concerning what is actually happening within the business on a day-to-day basis.
- The institution and perpetuation of ill-advised policies and practices.
- Loss of contact with and misinterpretation of customer, public, and employee attitudes toward the firm.
- Failure to have a reality-centered control on executive wishful thinking concerning the present state of the enterprise and its future outlook.

DOWNWARD DEFICIENCIES

The foregoing failures are in no sense limited to upward communications. Many chief executives believe that their supervisory hierarchies

—supplemented by printed material, such as the house organ, bulletin boards, letters to the employees' homes, and occasional addresses by company executives—suffice as channels to convey messages to company personnel. It is assumed, moreover, that as long as the message, whatever its content, is clear, concise, well illustrated, and dramatically presented, its reception will be satisfactory. This, unfortunately, is not always true. There is much more to communication than merely the cogent presentation of a message. If the communication is not understood, believed, and regarded as having a positive value for its recipients, it will fail in its mission. The over-estimation of the effectiveness of the communication media employed is one of the greatest sources of managerial error in dealing with customers, personnel, and the public.

FEEDBACK MISSING

Chief executives repeatedly fail to recognize that for communication to be effective, it must be two-way: *there has to be feedback to ascertain the extent to which the message has actually been understood, believed, assimilated, and accepted.* This is a step few companies ever take (perhaps because they fear to learn how little of the message has actually been transmitted).

Thus, the chief executive frequently is in every sense isolated; he is not only denied access to valid information about what is transpiring below him in his enterprise, but his facilities for communication downward (with other than a few of his immediate associates) are severely circumscribed. As a result, he is often forced to make major decisions on the basis of unreliable intra-company intelligence. Furthermore, his orders to those in the lower echelons may be distorted or even blocked at any supervisory level in between.

It is not surprising, in consequence, that even an able, experienced, and well-qualified chief executive not infrequently finds himself unable to cope with the problems such conditions create. This is especially true where the executive has been brought in from the outside and lacks immediate, personal knowledge of conditions. Under such circumstances, he is almost totally at the mercy of his subordinates in the area of communications.

EXECUTIVE'S DILEMMA

Not only are many top executives unaware of what transpires within their organizations; they are even less well informed concerning the competence and potential of their key personnel. Ironically, many think they know their subordinates well, and may even have strong personal likes and dislikes for certain individuals. The difficulty here is that these attitudes are often simply the results of *impressions* which have little or no inherent validity.

Few, if any, businesses today have any genuinely reliable *measures* of the inherent competence and quality of performance of their top, middle, and first-line managements. (Particularly sensitive are research, development, and engineering groups.) Most merit rating programs are subject to some 16 sources of error (see Exhibit I).

Much of the operating inefficiency and internecine strife that plague many firms arises in part from the top manager's failure to be properly apprised of what is actually taking place in the organization. Often he knows neither how well suited each member of top, middle, and first-line management is to his job assignment nor the nature and extent of the consequences of his subordinate's maladaption to his job where this exists.

MISPLACEMENT TRAGEDY

No greater tragedy can befall anyone than to be misplaced in his job, particularly if this means he is "over his head" in it. Under these circumstances, the likelihood of prompt and outright failure is great. Worse still is the living hell of uncertainty, anxiety, and indecisiveness which develops when he is not quite bad enough to fail, but not good enough to master his job. He is desperately uncomfortable, but he dare not quit. The consequences of the protracted tensions under which such a person exists are always bad. Not only do they affect his daily performance, but they may injure his health (lead to an ulcer, heart attack, or breakdown) or cause him to become an alcoholic and perhaps wreck his home life.

At best, job misplacement can lead to disappointment, frustration, and failure of the victim to realize his ultimate potential. At worst, it may literally kill him.

Unfortunately, much job placement can be compared to Procrustes' bed. In this legend, you may recall, if the occupant was too tall to fit the bed, they cut off his head and feet; if too short, they put him on the rack to stretch him out. Nowadays, if the incumbent does not fit the job assigned to him, he is trained, counseled, and admonished to develop the desired skills, traits, and attributes. It is assumed, perhaps naively, that he can be reshaped to meet the requirements of his job.

While this process is sometimes successful, there are many occasions when it is not. The "rehabilitating" process may even do irreparable

Exhibit I. Sources of Error Common in Merit Rating Programs

Most merit rating programs produce few findings, if any, of more than minimal validity. This is because they must be predicated largely on the personal judgments of supervisors or others familiar with an employee's work. The raters' assessments are subject to a minimum of 16 distinct sources of error. These are:

1. A willingness to rate subordinates who may be virtually unknown.

2. An unwillingness to take the time or make the effort to analyze subordinates thoroughly.

3. Differences in rater temperament—some are overfriendly, others are overcritical.

4. The "halo effect"—if the man is liked, he is seen as excelling in every trait; if disliked, as deficient in every trait.

5. The overweighting of recent occurrences, either favorable or unfavorable.

6. The "sunflower" effect—the need to give superiors information which will not embarrass the rater ("None of my men is less than 100 per cent—I wouldn't keep him").

7. The need to second-guess superiors—to tell them what they want to hear.

8. The need to play politics—to use the ratings to curry subordinates' favor.

9. The reluctance to make adverse ratings for fear they might have to be discussed with the employee.

10. The use of ratings for an ulterior purpose—to justify giving or withholding raises or promotions.

11. The lack of uniform criteria or standards of performance from rater to rater.

12. Personal prejudice or bias on the part of the rater—"All Swedes are squareheads."

13. Extreme rater indecisiveness—the inability to make a categorical judgment.

14. Lack of analytical ability on the part of the rater—the inability to see causal relationships.

15. "Central tendency"—the reluctance of the rater to rate either high or low, the wish to stick to "good" or "average."

16. A proneness to wishful thinking—"Everyone is promotable, perhaps in five years."

emotional damage. The current fad for "sensitivity training" is a case in point. Some subjects of this training have had to have psychiatric treatment to repair its ravages. More frequently, the "counseling" or training has no effect at all. In consequence, the individual is placed in a position for which he has few or even the wrong qualifications. Many of the job failures, nervous breakdowns, and "battles with the bottle" almost certainly have their causes in vocational misplacement and subsequent mishandling by well-intentioned but often unqualified personnel people. With the information now made available through the appraisal program described in this article, remedial steps can be taken.

LOYALTY CODE

Every enterprise has its quota of misplaced, often "problem," personnel, many of whom are not only maladapted but maladjusted. The only reason that their presence is not more glaringly evident to the chief executive is that nearly everyone in this group, and to a lesser extent throughout the rest of the company, participates in a massive, informal conspiracy of silence to conceal conditions from the supervisor responsible for correcting them. Under these circumstances, an unwritten code of loyalty within the group prevails. The common need to preserve the status quo, with the security this implies, unites even otherwise dissident factions. According to the code:

- No one initiates trouble in his department or unit—makes complaints to top management, asks embarrassing questions, or otherwise "rocks the boat."
- No one reports the inadequacies or derelictions of anyone else in the unit, even though that person may be flagrantly incompetent, obviously an alcoholic, or openly dishonest.
- "Troublemakers" (i.e., those who will not join the group's conspiracy) are, when possible, transferred out of the unit, given unpleasant assignments, or made so uncomfortable socially that they leave voluntarily.
- The chief executive and those closest to him (the "they" encountered in most employee ideologies) are often regarded as common enemies to be deceived, misled, and bamboozled in every way possible short of threatening the job security of the participants in the conspiracy. This not only makes for group solidarity, but also gives the subordinates a goal toward which to strive: the embarrassment or frustration of their supervisors. Generally, the participants use the age-old technique of "passive resistance"—the order is accepted deferentially, but then nothing happens.

LABOR TROUBLE

Many of the effects of inadequate communication are self-evident. If the company's top manager is unaware of what is happening in the lower echelons or has been deliberately misled, is unable to communicate effectively with his subordinates, or must work through and with a staff of whose competence and true level of performance he knows little, it is to be assumed that he will be operating under a severe handicap. Such a situation can hardly be prevented from having an adverse effect on over-all morale, productivity, and, ultimately, profits.

Less clearly evident, however, is the fact that *failures of communication, in conjunction with weak and incompetent first-line supervision, are the prime cause of much chronic, intractable labor trouble.* This accounts for the phenomenon of the employer who has excellent working conditions, pays premium wages, and offers exceptional fringe benefits, yet has continual labor unrest.

Because of vertical communications failures, incredibly bad conditions are often permitted by the top manager to exist for long periods of time. Consider this glaring example:

A manufacturing plant employed women to assemble casters. The women worked on a moving assembly line, while the components they used were stored in metal containers which rested on the floor beside them. Their complaint of several years' standing was that rats nested in the containers and bit their fingers when they reached in to obtain the component parts. Yet top management was never told.

This kind of phenomenon becomes of even greater significance in the light of the contributions of first- and second-line supervision to workers' distrust of—and hostility toward—company leadership. To most hourly rated employees, *the foreman is management:* the attitude toward him reflects the attitude toward the company as a whole.

DIMINISHING COMPETENCE

Just because its workings are usually concealed by inadequate communications, and so its effects are not recognized, many businesses are, to a greater or lesser extent, victims of what I call McMurry's Law of Diminishing Competence. It postulates that in any supervisory hierarchy *weakness begets greater weakness.* By this I mean that if a supervisor is weak (overly passive, dependent, submissive, or indecisive), his subordinates will tend to be even weaker. In other words, such an anxious individual cannot tolerate as a subordinate anyone who is as strong or stronger than he. Furthermore, this phenomenon tends to repeat itself at each level down the supervisory hierarchy.

Ingrown Ineptitude. If the organization is a "tall" one (i.e., has many intermediate supervisory levels), and the chief executive is weak and uncertain, his inadequacies will be multiplied and elaborated at each supervisory echelon. The outcome may be, and often is, unbelievable incompetence and ineptitude in the lower levels of supervision. Since weak supervision is, on the one hand, the prime source of poor employee morale, because it is never supportive and is often both erratic and punitive, numerous organizations harbor built-in guarantees of continuing labor unrest. On the other hand, many of these passive and weak individuals are intelligent, knowledgeable, and consummate company politicians. Hence, they are highly skilled at concealing or rationalizing their shortcomings and preventing them from being revealed to their supervisors.

Concretized Cliques. When the supervisory hierarchy has a substantial infusion of weak incompetents, self-perpetuating cliques tend to be formed. Such persons habitually staff their departments in their own images. Strength of character and superior competence are regarded by such supervisors as contraindications for acceptance. In consequence, where promotions take place largely from within—as is the practice in many companies—little control is exercised over the influence of the Law of Diminishing Competence. Not only does management as a whole come to be ingrown and blindly conforming, but strong, decisive managerial candidates are actively excluded from acceptance and promotion.

Atrophied Attitudes. The result, over the years, is the formation of a rigid and sterile bureaucracy such as is typical of government agencies. Many of the more competent, decisive, and aggressive individuals, being denied advancement up the management ladder, leave or become union officers. Nevertheless, so completely is even strong top management often isolated from the reality of what is taking place in the organization that it is practically never aware of the steady deterioration of morale and efficiency.

ALLEGIANCE TO STRENGTH

The qualifications of first- and second-line supervision are important from another point of view in the determination of the character of labor relations. This is true because of the operation of a second phenomenon, which I call McMurry's Law of Allegiance to Strength. In effect, this postulates that where two agencies—for example, the company acting through the foreman and the union acting through the steward or business agent—are competing for employee allegiance and loyalty, the one with the strongest, most aggressive, and decisive representative will nearly always win out. This is due to a simple truism: the stronger and more aggressive of the two will, if all other factors are even, be able to accomplish more for his followers than his less dynamic counterpart. Solely on the ground of self-interest, most employees will give their allegiance to the leader who can demonstrably win the most for them.

Self-Reliant Supervision. Hence, the winning of employee allegiance by the chief executive is less a matter of providing benefits and recreational and feeding facilities than it is of instituting strong, competent supervision. In this connection, it must be warned that the supervisor chosen must be *innately* strong and self-reliant—*these qualities cannot be inculcated by admonition or training.* The supervisor either has them or he does not. If he has them, they can be enhanced by training him in the skills of dealing with people; if the person does not have them, he should not be in a supervisory position. Since few executives have any valid measures for assessing their supervisors' attributes, in practice few have any means of knowing to what extent their supervisors are actually qualified for the positions they hold. Oddly enough, weakness in management shows itself very clearly to those who recognize the overt signs.

MAJOR REMEDIES

But this dilemma of the chief executive is not insoluble. There are three essential things which the astute chief executive can, and *must*, do if he is to establish clear, comprehensive, and valid channels of communication with his people at all levels.

(1) *He should recognize the primary dangers to good communication, if he is to improve his "intelligence" in the military sense.*

(2) *He should systematically and comprehensively inventory every member of his management and supervisory staff.*

(3) *He should periodically conduct an employee poll or morale survey which will provide him with a comprehensive overview of the human realities of his organization.*

RECOGNIZING DANGERS

The establishment of clear channels of communication throughout all levels of the organization hinges on the chief executive's recognition of these primary dangers:

• The tendency on his own part to perceive only "what he wants to see."

- The faulty medium of his supervisory hierarchy for both upward and downward communication.
- The inadequacy of most current supervisor and executive appraisal programs.
- The fallacious standards used in selecting candidates for promotion.
- The limited facilities for employee grievance drainage because of fear of supervisors and distrust of the personnel department.
- The possibility of chronic and legitimate employee dissatisfaction caused by company conditions, policies, and practices.
- The weaknesses of many supervisors, including some who are highly rated by upper management, which deteriorate morale, efficiency, and productivity.
- The risk of employee misunderstanding, disbelief, or refusal to accept a factual statement of company policies and the reasons behind them.

WHY COMMUNICATION GOES HAYWIRE

Frank W. Braden and John T. Trutter

The first step in learning to communicate more effectively is to find out what obstacles stand in your way. Sending or receiving a message accurately may seem like a simple process, but in actuality it is complex and difficult. A supervisor should be aware of the barriers between the speaker and the listener that can block and distort the intended message.

What are the barriers? Studies of communication problems have pinpointed four major ones: distortion or omission of information, the turning of inferences into facts, a know-it-all attitude and confusion over word meanings. Let's examine these obstacles to effective communication.

FAULTY TRANSMISSION

To illustrate what can happen to a message during its transmission, the authors have often conducted a demonstration with six volunteers. Five volunteers leave the room. The remaining one is shown a picture of a street scene and is given two minutes to observe and memorize as many details as possible. The picture is then put away. The second volunteer is called into the room, and the first tries to describe the picture to him. He in turn passes the description along to the third volunteer, and the process goes on until the last volunteer is reached. This last man describes the picture as he envisions it. Then he is shown the actual picture—and usually doesn't recognize it.

This is not surprising when you consider what happens to the message as it is passed from person to person:

- Fewer details are included each time the picture is described. The details are changed.
- Details are added that don't exist.
- Inferences that one party makes become definite assertions when another person passes on the description.
- Each person emphasizes different things in his description.

From *Supervisory Management* (January 1967), pp. 9-12. Reprinted by permission of the American Management Association, Inc.

Can the supervisor do anything to prevent loss of meaning and distortion in conveying his messages? Definitely yes. Effective communication depends on skills that can be learned. That was brought out sharply by a recent study in which policemen trained in reporting their observations did better than Phi Beta Kappa college seniors who had no such training. Supervisors who have worked on their communicating skills have been surprised at the sharp increase in the accuracy of their messages.

They have, for example, learned to keep the number of links in the message-transmission chain to a minimum. A safe limit is three links—such as supervisor to secretary to file clerk. Another effective principle is to use more than one media for more important messages—those containing vital figures should be given in both oral and written form.

You can eliminate distortion and omission in transmitting messages by:

- Keeping the number of items in the message as small as possible.
- Using sketches—when practical—to reinforce the message.
- Itemizing the points and putting them in a logical sequence.
- Underscoring the important points.
- Using associations that will bring the message home to the listener.

If you are on the receiving end, you can do several things to make sure you get the complete message without distortion. Experiments have shown that by asking questions freely, you can increase the "carry-through" of the message by 20 per cent. If you take notes, your comprehension will increase an additional 15 per cent. When you play back or review the message, the gain can be doubled.

INFERENCE OR FACT?

The failure to distinguish between inferences and facts leads to inaccurate communication. Many supervisors consider a declaratory statement to be a statement of fact. Actually, the declaratory statement may or may not be a fact. In the English language we use a declarative form both to make a statement before we make an observation and after we have done so. *A factual statement is possible only after observation.* The factual is limited to what we have actually observed, while the inferential goes beyond what we have seen. After an observation is made, a limited number of statements is possible. Before an observation is made, an almost limitless number of inferential statements can be made.

The difference between an inference and a fact can be illustrated this way: If you see a doctor's car parked outside your neighbor's house and you say, "Somebody's sick over at the Smiths'," you're stating an inference as if it were a fact. You would be more accurate if you said,

"There's a doctor's car parked in front of the Smiths' (the fact). Maybe somebody is sick there (the inference)."

An amusing incident related by Dr. Charles W. Eliot, one-time president of Harvard, provides another example of where fact leaves off and inference begins. Dr. Eliot had been in a New York club and had deposited his hat without obtaining a check. When it was time for him to leave, he returned to the entrance and the doorman promptly handed him his hat. Dr. Eliot asked, "How did you know that it was my hat?" The attendant replied, "I did not know that was your hat, but I do know that is the hat you gave me!"

Inferences that get turned into facts during their transmission can have serious consequences. They often cause false rumors to be spread through a department. An inference represents only a degree of probability. It goes beyond what you are actually observing and draws conclusions that are not necessarily true.

There is nothing wrong with a supervisor's expressing an inference —if he makes it clear to his listener that it is an inference and not a proven fact. But if a supervisor tells his boss flatly that a certain drill-press operator was loafing on the job, he must actually have observed the operator loafing. He cannot assume that the operator was goofing off simply because he was away from his machine for half an hour. A worker's absence is the basis for inferring that he may have been loafing, but not for asserting it as a positive fact.

CLOSED MINDS

Someone who thinks he knows everything there is to know about a particular subject also puts obstacles in the way of effective communication. A person afflicted with know-it-allness becomes rigid and dogmatic in his attitudes. He shuts his mind so tightly that he probably doesn't even hear any new ideas that are told to him. Instead, he is simply waiting for a chance to interrupt with what he knows is the conclusive word on the subject.

He should learn to put a comma after his beliefs, rather than a final period. This doesn't mean that he shouldn't have strong beliefs. But they must always be tempered by the realization that he can learn from other people who try to give him new thoughts and ideas. He doesn't have to accept them, but he should be ready to consider them. Only then can he grow and develop instead of remaining in a narrow mental groove.

We all can call to mind a person who seemingly delights in telling other people how much he knows, or, to put it realistically, how much he thinks he knows. You seldom enter into a discussion with him—you usually merely listen and soon become frustrated over the inability to get a word in edgeways. Or if you actually do succeed in saying your piece, you get the impression that the fellow actually is not hearing it at all but is thinking up what he can say to interrupt you.

The disease of know-it-allness leads to arrogance, the attitude of already knowing, a freezing up, and a stopping of the observing process. Thus it is a serious impediment to communication. Those who move higher in the business hierarchy particularly must be on guard against succumbing to it.

WORD CONNOTATIONS

A listener often forgets that in order to understand a speaker's words he must usually know the speaker's purpose in using them. This is true of most nontechnical words, which can have a wide range of meaning. For example, the word "run" has over 800 different uses. In addition, there are regional and vocational variations in the meanings of many words. New words are being coined all the time, and at the same time, established words develop new meanings or lose old ones. (In the Middle Ages, for example, a "solemn" party was one at which everyone drank himself into a stupor.)

Thus the listener must try to interpret the speaker's words from the speaker's perspective, not his own. Behind any set of words are things, people, relationships, feelings. If the listener looks for the meaning only in the word itself, he can easily misunderstand it. The word is acting as a pointer, and the listener should ask himself, "I hear the word, but how is the speaker using it?"

Since effective communication requires an effort by the speaker and the listener, both are at fault when misunderstandings occur. An awareness of this fact alone can help promote better communication.

SERIAL COMMUNICATION OF INFORMATION IN ORGANIZATIONS

William V. Haney

An appreciable amount of the communication which occurs in business, industry, hospitals, military units, government agencies—in short, in chain-of-command organizations—consists of serial transmissions. A communicates a message to B; B then communicates A's message (or rather his *interpretation* of A's message) to C; C then communicates his interpretation of B's interpretation of A's message to D; and so on. The originator and the ultimate recipient of the message are separated by "middle men."

"The message" may often be passed down (but not necessarily all the way down) the organization chain, as when in business the chairman acting on behalf of the board of directors may express a desire to the president.[1] The message begins to fan out as the president, in turn, relays it to his vice presidents; they convey it to their respective subordinates; and so forth. Frequently a message goes up (but seldom all the way up) the chain. Sometimes it travels laterally. Sometimes, as with rumors, it disregards the formal organization and flows more closely along informal organizational lines.

Regardless of its direction, the number of "conveyors" involved, and the degree of its conformance with the formal structure, serial transmission is clearly an essential, inevitable form of communication in organizations. It is equally apparent that serial transmission is especially susceptible to distortion and disruption. Not only is it subject to the shortcomings and maladies of "simple" person-to-person communication but, since it consists of a series of such communications, the anomalies are often compounded.

This is not to say, however, that serial transmissions in organizations should be abolished or even decreased. I wish to show that such com-

---

From Sidney Mailick and Edward H. Van Ness, Editors, *Concepts and Issues in Administrative Behavior* © 1962. Reprinted by permission of Prentice-Hall, Inc., Englewood Cliffs, New Jersey.

1. I place quotation marks around "message" to indicate that what is conveyed is not static, unchanging, and fixed. Despite their absence with later uses of the word, the dynamic nature of the "message" should be kept in mind.

munications can be improved if communicators are able (1) to recognize some of the patterns of miscommunication which occur in serial transmissions; (2) to understand some of the factors contributing to these patterns; (3) to take measures and practice techniques for preventing the recurrence of these patterns and for ameliorating their consequences.

I shall begin by cataloguing some of the factors which may influence a serial transmission.[2]

MOTIVES OF THE COMMUNICATORS

When B interprets A's message to C he may be influenced by at least three motives of which he may be largely unaware.

1. *The Desire to Simplify the Message.* We evidently dislike conveying detailed messages. The responsibility of passing along complex information is burdensome and taxing. Often, therefore, we unconsciously simplify the message before passing it along to the next person.[3] It is very probable that among the details most susceptible to omission are those we already knew or in some way presume our recipients will know without our telling them.

2. *The Desire to Convey a "Sensible" Message.* Apparently we are reluctant to relay a message that is somehow incoherent, illogical, or incomplete. It may be embarrassing to admit that one does not fully understand the message he is conveying. When he receives a message that does

---

2. During the past three years I have conducted scores of informal experiments with groups of university undergraduate students, business and government executives, military officers, professionals, and so on. I would read the message (below) to the first "conveyor." He would then give his interpretation to the second conveyor who, in turn, would pass along his interpretation to the third, etc. The sixth (and final) member of the "team" would listen to the message and then write down his version of it. These final versions (examples later) were collected and compared with the following original:

"Every year at State University, the eagles in front of the Psi Gamma fraternity house were mysteriously sprayed during the night. Whenever this happened, it cost the Psi Gams from $75 to $100 to have the eagles cleaned. The Psi Gams complained to officials and were promised by the president that if ever any students were caught painting the eagles, they would be expelled from school."

3. On an arbitrary count basis the stimulus message used in the serial transmission demonstrations described in footnote 2 contained twenty-four "significant details." The final versions contained a mean count of approximately eight "significant details"—a "detail loss" of sixty-five percent.

not quite make sense to him he is prone to "make sense out of it" before passing it along to the next person.[4]

3. *The Desire to Make the Conveyance of the Message as Pleasant and/or Painless as Possible for the Conveyor.* We evidently do not like to have to tell the boss unpleasant things. Even when not directly responsible, one does not relish the reaction of his superior to a disagreeable message. This motive probably accounts for a considerable share of the tendency for a message to lose its harshness as it moves up the organizational ladder. The first line supervisor may tell his foreman, "I'm telling you, Mike, the men say that if this pay cut goes through they'll strike—and they mean it!" By the time this message has been relayed through six or eight or more echelons (if indeed it goes that far) the executive vice president might express it to the president as, "Well, sir, the men seem a little concerned over the projected wage reduction but I am confident that they will take it in stride."

One of the dangers plaguing some upper managements is that they are effectively shielded from incipient problems until they become serious and costly ones.

ASSUMPTIONS OF THE COMMUNICATORS

In addition to the serial transmitter's motives we must consider his assumptions—particularly those he makes about his communications. If some of these assumptions are fallacious and if one is unaware that he holds them, his communication can be adversely affected. The following are, in my judgment, two of the most pervasive and dangerous of the current myths about communication.

1. *The Assumption That Words Are Used in Only One Way.* A study indicates that for the five hundred most commonly used words in our

---

4. The great majority (approximately ninety-three percent) of the final versions (from the serial transmission demonstrations) made "sense." Even those which were the most bizarre and bore the least resemblance to the original stimulus were in and of themselves internally consistent and coherent. For example:

"At a State University there was an argument between two teams—the Eagles and the Fire Gems—in which their clothing was torn."

"The eagles in front of the university had parasites and were sprayed with insecticide."

"At State U. they have many birds which desecrate the buildings. To remedy the situation they expelled the students who fed the birds."

language there are 14,070 different dictionary definitions—over twenty-eight usages per word, on the average.[5] Take the word *run*, for example:

Babe Ruth scored a *run*.
Did you ever see Jesse Owens *run*?
I have a *run* in my stocking.
There is a fine *run* of salmon this year.
Are you going to *run* this company or am I?
You have the *run* of the place.
Don't give me the *run* around.
What headline do you want to *run*?
There was a *run* on the bank today.
Did he *run* the ship aground?
I have to *run* (drive the car) downtown.
Who will *run* for President this year?
Joe flies the New York-Chicago *run* twice a week.
You know the kind of people they *run* around with.
The apples *run* large this year.
Please *run* my bath water.

We could go on at some length—my small abridged dictionary gives eighty-seven distinct usages for *run*. I have chosen an extreme example, of course, but there must be relatively few words (excepting some technical terms) used in one and in only one sense.

Yet communicators often have a curious notion about words *when they are using them*, that is, when they are speaking, writing, listening, or reading. It is immensely easy for a "sender" of a communication to assume that words are used in only one way—the way he intends them. It is just as enticing for the "receiver" to assume that the sender intended his words as he, the receiver, happens to interpret them at the moment. When communicators are unconsciously burdened by the assumption of the mono-usage of words they are prone to become involved in the pattern of miscommunication known as *bypassing*.

A foreman told a machine operator he was passing: "Better clean up around here." It was ten minutes later when the foreman's assistant phoned: "Say, boss, isn't that bearing Sipert is working on due up in engineering pronto?"

"You bet your sweet life it is. Why?"

"He says you told him to drop it and sweep the place up. I thought I'd better make sure."

5. Lydia Strong, "Do You Know How to Listen?" *Effective Communication on the Job*, ed. Dooher and Marquis (New York, 1956), p. 28.

"Listen," the foreman flared into the phone, "get him right back on that job. It's got to be ready in twenty minutes."

. . . What the foreman had in mind was for Sipert to gather up the oily waste, which was a fire and accident hazard. This would not have taken more than a couple of minutes, and there would have been plenty of time to finish the bearing.[6]

Since we use words to express at least two kinds of meanings there can be two kinds of bypassings: denotative and connotative. Suppose you say to me, "Your neighbor's grass is certainly green and healthy looking, isn't it?" You could be intending your words merely to denote, that is, to point to or to call my attention, to the appearance of my neighbor's lawn. On the other hand, you could have intended your words to *connote*, that is, to imply something beyond or something other than what you were ostensibly denoting. You might have meant any number of things: that my own lawn needed more care; that my neighbor was inordinately meticulous about his lawn; that my neighbor's lawn is tended by a professional, a service you do not have and for which you envy or despise my neighbor; or even that his grass was not green at all but, on the contrary, parched and diseased; and so forth.

Taking these two kinds of meanings into account it is clear that bypassing occurs or can occur under any of four conditions:

1. *When the sender intends one denotation while the receiver interprets another.* (As in the case of Sipert and his foreman.)

2. *When the sender intends one connotation while the receiver interprets another.* A friend once told me of an experience she had years ago when as a teenager she was spending the week with a maiden aunt. Joan had gone to the movies with a young man who brought her home at a respectable hour. However, the couple lingered on the front porch somewhat longer than Aunt Mildred thought necessary. The little old lady was rather proud of her ability to deal with younger people so she slipped out of bed, raised her bedroom window, and called down sweetly, "If you two knew how pleasant it is in bed, you wouldn't be standing out there in the cold."

3. *When the sender intends only a denotation while the receiver interprets a connotation.* For a brief period the following memorandum appeared on the bulletin boards of a government agency in Washington:

Those department and sections heads who do not have secretaries assigned to them may take advantage of the stenographers in the secretarial pool.

6. *The Foreman's Letter,* publication of the National Foreman's Institute (New London, Connecticut).

4. *When the sender intends a connotation while the receiver interprets a denotation only.* Before making his final decision on a proposal to move to new offices, the head of a large company called his top executives for a last discussion of the idea. All were enthusiastic except the company treasurer who insisted that he had not had time to calculate all the costs with accuracy sufficient to satisfy himself that the move was advantageous. Annoyed by his persistence, the chief finally burst out:

"All right, Jim, all right! Figure it out to the last cent. A penny saved is a penny earned, right?"

The intention was ironic. He meant not what the words denoted but the opposite—forget this and stop being petty. For him this was what his words connoted.

For the treasurer "penny saved, penny earned" meant exactly what it said. He put several members on his staff to work on the problem and, to test the firmness of the price, had one of them interview the agent renting the proposed new quarters without explaining whom he represented. This indication of additional interest in the premises led the agent to raise the rent. Not until the lease was signed, did the company discover that one of its own employees had, in effect, bid up its price.[7]

2. *The Assumption That Inferences Are Always Distinguishable From Observations.* It is incredibly difficult, at times, for a communicator (or anyone) to discriminate between what he "knows" (that is, what he has actually observed—seen, heard, handled) and what he is only inferring or guessing. One of the key reasons for this lies in the character of the language used to express observations and inferences.

Suppose you look at a man and observe that he is wearing a white shirt and then say, "That man is wearing a white shirt." Assuming your vision and the illumination were "normal" you would have made a statement of *observation*—a statement which directly corresponded to and was corroborated by your observation. But suppose you now say, "That man bought the white shirt he is wearing." Assuming you were not present when and if the man bought the shirt that statement would be *for you* a statement of *inference*. Your statement went *beyond* what you observed. You inferred that the man bought the shirt; you did not observe it. Of course, your inference may be correct (but it could be false: perhaps he was given the shirt as a gift; perhaps he stole it or borrowed it, etc.).

Nothing in the nature of our language (the grammar, spelling, pronunciation, accentuation, syntax, inflection, etc.) prevents you from speaking or writing (or thinking) a statement of inference *as if* you were making a statement of observation. Our language permits you to say "Of course, he bought the shirt" with certainty and finaltiy, that is, with as

7. Robert Froman, "Make Words Fit the Job," *Nation's Business* (July 1959).

much confidence as you would make a statement of observation. The effect is that it becomes exceedingly easy to confuse the two kinds of statements and also to confuse inference and observation on nonverbal levels. The destructive consequences of acting upon inference as if acting upon observation can range from mild embarrassment to tragedy. One factual illustration may be sufficient to point up the dangers of such behavior.

THE CASE OF JIM BLAKE

Jim Blake, 41, had been with the Hasting Co. for ten years. For the last seven years he had served as an "inside salesman," receiving phone calls from customers and writing out orders. "Salesman," in this case, was somewhat of an euphemism as the customer ordinarily knew what he wanted and was prepared to place an order. The "outside salesmen," on the other hand, visited industrial accounts and enjoyed considerably more status and income. Blake had aspired to an outside position for several years but no openings had occurred. He had, however, been assured by Russ Jenkins, sales manager, that as senior inside man he would be given first chance at the next available outside job.

Finally, it seemed as if Jim's chance had come. Harry Strom, 63, one of the outside men, had decided in January to retire on the first of June. It did not occur to Jenkins to reassure Blake that the new opening was to be his. Moreover, Blake did not question Jenkins because he felt his superior should take the initiative.

As the months went by Blake became increasingly uneasy. Finally, on May 15 he was astonished to see Strom escorting a young man into Jenkins' office. Although the door was closed Blake could hear considerable laughing inside. After an hour the three emerged from the office and Jenkins shook hands with the new man saying, "Joe, I'm certainly glad you're going to be with us. With Harry showing you around his territory you're going to get a good start at the business." Strom and the new man left and Jenkins returned to his office.

Blake was infuriated. He was convinced that the new man was being groomed for Strom's position. Now he understood why Jenkins had said nothing to him. He angrily cleaned out his desk, wrote a bitter letter of resignation and left it on his desk, and stomped out of the office.

Suspecting the worst for several months, Blake was quite unable to distinguish what he had inferred from what he had actually observed. The new man, it turned out, was being hired to work as an inside salesman—an opening which was to be occasioned by Blake's moving into the outside position. Jenkins had wanted the new man to get the "feel" of the clientele and thus had requested Strom to take him along for a few days as Strom made his calls.[8]

TRENDS IN SERIAL TRANSMISSION

These assumptions,[9] the mono-usage of words, and the inference-observation confusion, as well as the aforementioned motives of the communicators, undoubtedly contribute a significant share of the difficulties and dangers which beset a serial transmission. Their effect tends to be manifested by three trends: omission, alteration, and addition.

Details Become Omitted. It requires less effort to convey a simpler, less complex message. With fewer details to transmit, the fear of forgetting or of garbling the message is decreased. In the serial transmissions even those final versions which most closely approximated the original had omitted an appreciable number of details.

> There are Eagles in front of the frat house at the State University.
> It cost $75 to $100 to remove the paint each year from the eagles.

The essential question is, perhaps, which details *will be retained?* Judging from interviewing the serial transmitters after the demonstrations these aspects will *not* be dropped out:

A. Those details the transmitter wanted or expected to hear.
B. Those details which "made sense" to the transmitter.
C. Those details which seemed important *to the transmitter.*
D. Those details which for various and inexplicable reasons seemed to stick with the transmitter—those aspects which seemed particularly unusual or bizarre; those which had special significance to him; etc.

Details Become Altered. When changes in detail occurred in the serial transmissions it was often possible to pinpoint the "changers." When asked to explain why they had changed the message most were unaware that they had done so. However, upon retrospection some admitted that they had changed the details in order to simplify the message, "clarify it," "straighten it out," "make it more sensible," and the like. It became evident, too, that among the details most susceptible to change were the qualifications, the indefinite. Inferential statements are prone to become definite and certain. What may start out as "The boss seemed angry this morning" may quickly progress to "The boss was angry." . . .

8. The names have been changed.
9. For a more detailed analysis of these assumptions and for additional methods for preventing and correcting their consequences, see William V. Haney *Communication: Patterns and Incidents* (Homewood, Ill.: 1960), Chs. III, IV, V.

It became obvious upon interviewing the serial transmitters that bypassing (denotative and connotative) had also played a role. For example, the "president" in the message about the "eagles" was occasionally bypassed as the "President of the U.S." and sometimes the rest of the message was constructed around this detail.

> The White House was in such a mess that they wanted to renovate it but found that the cost would be $100 to $75 to paint the eagle so they decided not to do it.

Details Become Added. Not infrequently details are added to the message to "fill in the gaps," "to make better sense," and "because I thought the fellow who told it to me left something out." . . .

PICTORIAL TRANSMISSION

An interesting facet about serial transmission is that the three trends—omission, alteration, and addition—are also present when the "message" is pictorial as opposed to verbal. My procedure was to permit the "transmitter" to view the stimulus picture (upper left corner of drawing below) for thirty seconds. He then proceeded to reproduce the picture as accurately as possible from memory. When he finished his drawing he showed it to Transmitter₂ for thirty seconds, who then attempted to reproduce the first transmitter's drawing from memory, etc. Drawings 1 through 5 represented the work of a fairly typical "team" of five transmitters.

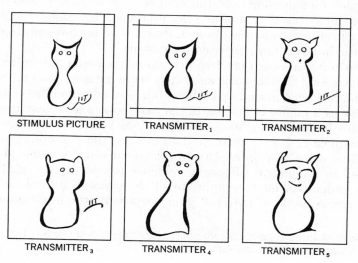

| STIMULUS PICTURE | TRANSMITTER₁ | TRANSMITTER₂ |
| TRANSMITTER₃ | TRANSMITTER₄ | TRANSMITTER₅ |

Details Become Omitted. Note the progressive simplification of the configuration in the lower right of the illustration and the eventual omission of it altogether. Note the omission of the border.

Details Become Altered. The border is an interesting example of alteration. The original border is quite irregular, difficult to remember. Transmitter$_1$ when interviewed afterward said, "I remembered that the frame was incomplete somehow but couldn't remember just how it was incomplete." Note how indefinitely irregular his border is. So subtle, in fact, that Transmitter$_2$ said he never recognized it as purposefully asymmetrical. "I thought he was just a little careless." Transmitter$_2$ drew a completely regular border—easy to remember but also easy to fail to notice. Transmitter$_3$ was surprised afterwards to discover that the drawing he had tried to memorize had had a border. It had apparently seemed so "natural," so much a part of the background, that he had failed to attend to it.

Details Become Added. Transmitter$_1$ perceived the stimulus picture as a cat and a cat it remained through the series. When shown that he had added a nose, Transmitter$_4$ admitted, "You know, I knew there was something missing from the cat—I knew it had a body, a head, ears, and eyes. I thought it was the mouth that was missing but not the nose." Providing everything *except* a mouth was far too enticing for Transmitter$_5$. "I thought the other fellow made a mistake so I corrected it!"

CORRECTIVES

Even serial transmissions, as intricate and as relatively uncontrolled communications as they are, can be improved. The suggestions below are not sensational panaceas. In fact, they are quite commonplace, common sense, but uncommonly used techniques.[10]

1. *Take notes.* Less than five percent of the serial transmitters took notes. Some said that they assumed they were not supposed to (no such restriction had been placed upon them) but most admitted that they rarely take notes as a matter of course. In the cases where all transmitters on a team were instructed to take notes the final versions were manifestly more complete and more accurate than those of the non-notetakers.

2. *Give details in order.* Organized information is easier to understand and to remember. Choose a sequence (chronological, spatial, deductive, inductive, etc.) appropriate to the content and be consistent with it. For example, it may suit your purpose best to begin with a pro-

10. Most of these suggestions are offered by Irving J. and Laura L. Lee, *Handling Barriers in Communication* (New York, 1956).

posal followed by supporting reasons or to start with the reasons and work toward the proposal. In either case take care to keep proposals and reasons clearly distinguished rather than mixing them together indiscriminately.

3. *Be wary of bypassing.* If you are the receiver, query (ask the sender what he meant) and paraphrase (put what you think he said or wrote into your own words and get the sender to check you). These simple techniques are effective yet infrequently practiced, perhaps because we are so positive we *know* what the other fellow means; perhaps because we hesitate to ask or rephrase for fear the other fellow (especially if he is the boss) will think less of us for not understanding the first time. The latter apprehension is usually unfounded, at least if we can accept the remarks of a hundred or more executives questioned on the matter during the last four years. "By all means," they said almost to a man, "I *want* my people to check with me. The person who wants to be sure he's got it straight has a sense of responsibility and that's the kind of man (or woman) I want on my payroll."

Although executives, generally, may take this point of view quite sincerely, obviously not all of them practice it. Querying and paraphrasing are *two-way* responsibilities and the sender must be truly approachable by his receivers if the techniques are to be successful.

This check-list may be helpful in avoiding bypassing:

Could he be denoting something other than what I am?
Could he be connoting something other than what I am?
Could he be connoting whereas I am merely denoting?
Could he be merely denoting whereas I am connoting?

4. *Distinguish between inference and observation.* Ask yourself sharply: Did I *really* see, hear, or read this—or am I guessing part of it? The essential characteristics of a statement of observation are these:

A. It can be made only by the observer. (What someone tells you as observational is still inferential for you if you did not observe it.)

B. It can be made only during or *after* observation.

C. It stays with what has been observed; does not go beyond it.

This is not to say that inferential statements are not to be made—we could hardly avoid doing so. But it is important or even vital at times to know *when* we are making them.

5. *Slow down your oral transmissions.* By doing so, you give your listener a better opportunity to assimilate complex and detailed information. However, it is possible to speak *too* slowly so as to lose his attention. Since either extreme defeats your purpose, it is generally wise to watch the listener for clues as to the most suitable rate of speech.

6. *Simplify the message.* This suggestion is for the *originator* of the message. The "middle-men" often simplify without half trying! Most salesmen realize the inadvisability of attempting to sell too many features at a time. The customer is only confused and is unable to distinguish

the key features from those less important. With particular respect to oral transmission, there is impressive evidence to indicate that beyond a point the addition of details leads to disproportionate omission. Evidently, you can add a straw to the camel's back without breaking it, but you run the decided risk of his dropping two straws.

7. *Use dual media when feasible.* A message often stands a better chance of getting through if it is reinforced by restatement in another communication medium. Detailed, complex, and unfamiliar information is often transmitted by such combinations as a memo follow-up on a telephone call; a sensory aid (slide, diagram, mock-up, picture, etc.) accompanying a written or oral message, etc.

8. *Highlight the important.* Presumably the originator of a message knows (or should know) which are its important aspects. But this does not automatically insure that his serial transmitters will similarly recognize them. There are numerous devices for making salient points stand out as such; for example, using underscoring, capitals, etc., in writing; using vocal emphasis, attention-drawing phrases ("This is the main point . . . ," "Here's the crux . . . ," "Be sure to note this . . ."), etc., in speaking.

9. *Reduce the number of links in the chain.* This suggestion has to be followed with discretion. Jumping the chain of command either upward or downward can sometimes have undesirable consequences. However, to the extent that it is possible to reduce or eliminate the "middlemen," the message becomes progressively less susceptible to aberrations. Of course, there are methods of skipping links which are commonly accepted and widely practiced. Communication downward can be reduced to person-to-person communication, in a sense, with general memos, letters, bulletins, group meetings, etc. Communication upward can accomplish the same purpose via suggestion boxes, opinion questionnaires, "talkbacks," etc.

10. *Preview and review.* A wise speech professor used to say: "Giving a speech is basically very simple if you do it in three steps: First, you tell them what you're going to tell them; then you tell them; then, finally, you tell them what you've told them." This three-step sequence is often applicable whether the message is transmitted by letter, memo, written or oral report, public address, telephone call, etc.

SUMMARY

After the last suggestion I feel obliged to review this article briefly. We have been concerned with serial transmission—a widespread, essential, and yet susceptible form of communication. Among the factors which vitiate a serial transmission are certain of the communicator's motives and fallacious assumptions. When these and other factors are in play the three processes—omission, alteration, and addition—tend to occur. The suggestions offered for strengthening serial transmission will be more or less applicable, of course, depending upon the specific communication situation.

An important question remains: What can be done to encourage communicators to practice the techniques? They will probably use them largely to the extent that they think the techniques are needed. But *do* they think them necessary? Apparently many do not. When asked to explain how the final version came to differ so markedly from the original, many of the serial transmitters in my studies were genuinely puzzled. A frequent comment was "I really can't understand it. All I know is that I passed the message along the same as it came to me." If messages were passed along "the same as they came," of course, serial transmission would no longer be a problem. And so long as the illusion of fidelity is with the communicator it is unlikely that he will be prompted to apply some of these simple, prosaic, yet effective techniques to his communicating. Perhaps a first step would be to induce him to question his unwarranted assurance about his communication. The controlled serial transmission experience appears to accomplish this.

THE SILENT LANGUAGE
IN OVERSEAS BUSINESS

Edward T. Hall

With few exceptions, Americans are relative newcomers on the international business scene. Today, as in Mark Twain's time, we are all too often "innocents abroad," in an era when naiveté and blundering in foreign business dealings may have serious political repercussions.

When the American executive travels abroad to do business, he is frequently shocked to discover to what extent the many variables of foreign behavior and custom complicate his efforts. Although the American has recognized, certainly, that even the man next door has many minor traits which make him somewhat peculiar, for some reason he has failed to appreciate how different foreign businessmen and their practices will seem to him.

He should understand that the various peoples around the world have worked out and integrated into their subconscious literally thousands of behavior patterns that they take for granted in each other.[1] Then, when the stranger enters, and behaves differently from the local norm, he often quite unintentionally insults, annoys or amuses the native with whom he is attempting to do business. For example:

In the United States, a corporation executive knows what is meant when a client lets a month go by before replying to a business proposal. On the other hand, he senses an eagerness to do business if he is immediately ushered into the client's office. In both instances, he is reacting to subtle cues in the timing of interaction, cues which he depends on to chart his course of action.

Abroad, however, all this changes. The American executive learns that the Latin Americans are casual about time and that if he waits an hour in the outer office before seeing the Deputy Minister of Finance, it does not necessarily mean he is not getting anywhere. There people are so important that nobody can bear to tear himself away; because of the resultant interruptions and conversational detours, everybody is constantly getting behind. What the American does not know is the point at which the waiting becomes significant.

From *Harvard Business Review*, XXXVIII (May-June 1960), 87-96. © 1960 by the President and Fellows of Harvard College; all rights reserved.

1. For details, see my book, *The Silent Language* (New York, Doubleday & Company, Inc., 1959).

In another instance, after traveling 7,000 miles an American walks into the office of a highly recommended Arab businessman on whom he will have to depend completely. What he sees does not breed confidence. The office is reached by walking through a suspicious-looking coffee-house in an old, dilapidated building situated in a crowded non-European section of town. The elevator, rising from dark, smelly corridors, is rickety and equally foul. When he gets to the office itself, he is shocked to find it small, crowded, and confused. Papers are stacked all over the desk and table tops—even scattered on the floor in irregular piles.

The Arab merchant he has come to see had met him at the airport the night before and sent his driver to the hotel this morning to pick him up. But now, after the American's rush, the Arab is tied up with something else. Even when they finally start talking business, there are constant interruptions. If the American is at all sensitive to his environment, everything around him signals, "What am I getting into?"

Before leaving home he was told that things would be different, but how different? The hotel is modern enough. The shops in the new part of town have many more American and European trade goods than he had anticipated. His first impression was that doing business in the Middle East would not present any new problems. Now he is beginning to have doubts. One minute everything looks familiar and he is on firm ground; the next, familiar landmarks are gone. His greatest problem is that so much assails his senses all at once that he does not know where to start looking for something that will tell him where he stands. He needs a frame of reference—a way of sorting out what is significant and relevant.

That is why it is so important for American businessmen to have a real understanding of the various social, cultural, and economic differences they will face when they attempt to do business in foreign countries. To help give some frame of reference, this article will map out a few areas of human activity that have largely been unstudied.

The topics I will discuss are certainly not presented as the last word on the subject, but they have proved to be highly reliable points at which to begin to gain an understanding of foreign cultures. While additional research will undoubtedly turn up other items just as relevant, at present I think the businessman can do well to begin by appreciating cultural differences in matters concerning the language of time, of space, of material possessions, of friendship patterns, and of agreements.

LANGUAGE OF TIME

Everywhere in the world people use time to communicate with each other. There are different languages of time just as there are different spoken languages. The unspoken languages are informal; yet the rules governing their interpretation are surprisingly *ironbound*.

In the United States, a delay in answering a communication can result from a large volume of business causing the request to be postponed until the backlog is cleared away, from poor organization, or possibly from technical complexity requiring deep analysis. But if the person awaiting the answer or decision rules out these reasons, then the delay means to him that the matter has low priority on the part of the other person— lack of interest. On the other hand, a similar delay in a foreign country may mean something altogether different. Thus:

In Ethiopia, the time required for a decision is directly proportional to its importance. This is so much the case that low-level bureaucrats there have a way of trying to elevate the prestige of their work by taking a long time to make up their minds. (Americans in that part of the world are innocently prone to downgrade their work in the local people's eyes by trying to speed things up.)

In the Arab East, time does not generally include schedules as Americans know and use them. The time required to get something accomplished depends on the relationship. More important people get fast service from less important people, and conversely. Close relatives take absolute priority; nonrelatives are kept waiting.

In the United States, giving a person a deadline is a way of indicating the degree of urgency or relative importance of the work. But in the Middle East, the American runs into a cultural trap the minute he opens his mouth. "Mr. Aziz will have to make up his mind in a hurry because my board meets next week and I have to have an answer by then," is taken as indicating the American is overly demanding and is exerting undue pressure. "I am going to Damascus tomorrow morning and will have to have my car tonight," is a sure way to get the mechanic to stop work, because to give another person a deadline in this part of the world is to be rude, pushy, and demanding.

An Arab's evasiveness as to when something is going to happen does not mean he does not want to do business; it only means he is avoiding unpleasantness and is side-stepping possible commitments which he takes more seriously than we do. For example:

The Arabs themselves at times find it impossible to communicate even to each other that some processes cannot be hurried, and are controlled by built-in schedules. This is obvious enough to the Westerner but not to the Arab. A highly placed public official in Baghdad precipitated a bitter family dispute because his nephew, a biochemist, could not speed up the complete analysis of the uncle's blood. He accused the nephew of putting other less important people before him and of not caring. Nothing could sway the uncle, who could not grasp the fact that there is such a thing as an *inherent* schedule.

With us the more important an event is, the further ahead we schedule it, which is why we find it insulting to be asked to a party at the last minute. In planning future events with Arabs, it pays to hold the lead time to a week or less because other factors may intervene or take precedence.

Again, time spent waiting in an American's outer office is a sure indicator of what one person thinks of another or how important he feels the other's business to be. This is so much the case that most Americans cannot help getting angry after waiting 30 minutes; one may even feel such a delay is an insult, and will walk out. In Latin America, on the other hand, one learns that it does not mean anything to wait in an outer office. An American businessman with years of experience in Mexico once told me, "You know, I have spent two hours cooling my heels in an executive's outer office. It took me a long time to learn to keep my blood pressure down. Even now, I find it hard to convince myself they are still interested when they keep me waiting."

The Japanese handle time in ways which are almost inexplicable to the Western European and particularly the American. A delay of years with them does not mean that they have lost interest. It only means that they are building up to something. They have learned that Americans are vulnerable to long waits. One of them expressed it, "You Americans have one terrible weakness. If we make you wait long enough, you will agree to anything."

Indians of South Asia have an elastic view of time as compared to our own. Delays do not, therefore, have the same meaning to them. Nor does indefiniteness in pinpointing appointments mean that they are evasive. Two Americans meeting will say, "We should get together sometime," thereby setting a low priority on the meeting. The Indian who says, "Come over and see me, see me anytime," means just that.

Americans make a place at the table which may or may not mean a place made in the heart. But when the Indian makes a place in his time, it is yours to fill in every sense of the word if you realize that by so doing you have crossed a boundary and are now friends with him. The point of all this is that time communicates just as surely as do words and that the vocabulary of time is different around the world. The principle to be remembered is that time has different meanings in each country.

LANGUAGE OF SPACE

Like time, the language of space is different wherever one goes. The American businessman, familiar with the pattern of American corporate life, has no difficulty in appraising the relative importance of someone else, simply by noting the size of his office in relation to other offices around him:

Our pattern calls for the president or the chairman of the board to have the biggest office. The executive vice president will have the next largest, and so on down the line until you end up in the "bull pen." More important offices are usually located at the corners of buildings and on the upper floors. Executive suites will be on the top floor. The relative rank of vice presidents will be reflected in where they are placed along "Executive Row."

The French, on the other hand, are much more likely to lay out space as a network of connecting points of influence, activity, or interest. The French supervisor will ordinarily be found in the middle of his subordinates where he can control them.

Americans who are crowded will often feel that their status in the organization is suffering. As one would expect in the Arab world, the location of an office and its size constitute a poor index of the importance of the man who occupies it. What we experience as crowded, the Arab will often regard as spacious. The same is true in Spanish cultures. A Latin American official illustrated the Spanish view of this point while showing me around a plant. Opening the door to an 18-by-20-foot office in which seventeen clerks and their desks were placed, he said, "See, we have nice spacious offices. Lots of space for everyone."

The American will look at a Japanese room and remark how bare it is. Similarly, the Japanese look at our rooms and comment, "How bare!" Furniture in the American home tends to be placed along the walls (around the edge). Japanese have their charcoal pit where the family gathers in the *middle* of the room. The top floor of Japanese department stores is not reserved for the chief executive—it is the bargain roof!

In the Middle East and Latin America, the businessman is likely to feel left out in time and overcrowded in space. People get too close to him, lay their hands on him, and generally crowd his physical being. In Scandinavia and Germany, he feels more at home, but at the same time the people are a little cold and distant. It is space itself that conveys this feeling.

In the United States, because of our tendency to zone activities, nearness carries rights of familiarity so that the neighbor can borrow material possessions and invade time. This is not true in England. Propinquity entitles you to nothing. American Air Force personnel stationed there complain because they have to make an appointment for their children to play with the neighbor's child next door.

Conversation distance between two people is learned early in life by copying elders. Its controlling patterns operate almost totally unconsciously. In the United States, in contrast to many foreign countries, men avoid excessive touching. Regular business is conducted at distances such as 5 feet to 8 feet; highly personal business, 18 inches to 3 feet—not 2 or 3 inches.

In the United States, it is perfectly possible for an experienced executive to schedule the steps of negotiation in time and space so that most people feel comfortable about what is happening. Business transactions progress in stages from across the desk to beside the desk, to the coffee table, then on to the conference table, the luncheon table, or the golf course, or even into the home—all according to a complex set of hidden rules which we obey instinctively.

Even in the United States, however, an executive may slip when he moves into new and unfamiliar realms, when dealing with a new group, doing business with a new company, or moving to a new place in the industrial hierarchy. In a new country the danger is magnified. For example, in India it is considered improper to discuss business in the home on social occasions. One never invites a business acquaintance to the home for the purpose of furthering business aims. That would be a violation of sacred hospitality rules.

LANGUAGE OF THINGS

Americans are often contrasted with the rest of the world in terms of material possessions. We are accused of being materialistic, gadget-crazy. And, as a matter of fact, we have developed material things for some very interesting reasons. Lacking a fixed class system and having an extremely mobile population, Americans have become highly sensitive to how others make use of material possessions. We use everything from clothes to houses as a highly evolved and complex means of ascertaining each other's status. Ours is a rapidly shifting system in which both styles and people move up or down. For example:

The Cadillac ad men feel that not only is it natural but quite insightful of them to show a picture of a Cadillac and a well-turned-out gentleman in his early fifties opening the door. The caption underneath reads, "You already know a great deal about this man."

Following this same pattern, the head of a big union spends an excess of $100,000 furnishing his office so that the president of United States Steel cannot look down on him. Good materials, large space, and the proper surroundings signify that the people who occupy the premises are solid citizens, that they are dependable and successful.

The French, the English, and the Germans have entirely different ways of using their material possessions. What stands for the height of dependability and respectability with the English would be old-fashioned and backward to us. The Japanese take pride in often inexpensive but tasteful arrangements that are used to produce the proper emotional setting.

Middle East businessmen look for something else—family, connections, friendship. They do not use the furnishings of their office as part of their status system; nor do they expect to impress a client by these means or to fool a banker into lending more money than he should. They like good things, too, but feel that they, as persons, should be known and not judged solely by what the public sees.

One of the most common criticisms of American relations abroad, both commercial and governmental, is that we usually think in terms of material things. "Money talks," says the American, who goes on talking the language of money abroad, in the belief that money talks the *same* language all over the world. A common practice in the United States is to try to buy loyalty with high salaries. In foreign countries, this maneuver almost never works, for money and material possessions stand for something different there than they do in America.

LANGUAGE OF FRIENDSHIP

The American finds his friends next door and among those with whom he works. It has been noted that we take people up quickly and drop them just as quickly. Occasionally a friendship formed during schooldays will persist, but this is rare. For us there are few well-defined rules governing the obligations of friendship. It is difficult to say at which point our friendship gives way to business opportunism or pressure from above. In this we differ from many other people in the world. As a general rule in foreign countries friendships are not formed as quickly as in the United States but go much deeper, last longer, and involve real obligations. For example:

It is important to stress that in the Middle East and Latin America your "friends" will not let you down. The fact that they personally are feeling the pinch is never an excuse for failing their friends. They are supposed to look out for your interests.

Friends and family around the world represent a sort of social insurance that would be difficult to find in the United States. We do not use our friends to help us out in disaster as much as we do as a means of getting ahead—or, at least, of getting the job done. The United States systems work by means of a series of closely tabulated favors and obligations carefully doled out where they will do the most good. And the least that we expect in exchange for a favor is gratitude.

The opposite is the case in India, where the friend's role is to "sense" a person's need and do something about it. The idea of reciprocity as we know it is unheard of. An American in India will have difficulty if he attempts to follow American friendship patterns. He gains nothing by extending himself in behalf of others, least of all gratitude, because the Indian assumes that what he does for others he does for the good of his own psyche. He will find it impossible to make friends quickly and is unlikely to allow sufficient time for friendships to ripen. He will also note that as he gets to know people better, they may become more critical of him, a fact that he finds hard to take. What he does not know is that one sign of friendship in India is speaking one's mind.

LANGUAGE OF AGREEMENTS

While it is important for American businessmen abroad to understand the symbolic meanings of friendship rules, time, space, and material possessions, it is just as important for executives to know the rules for negotiating agreements in various countries. Even if they cannot be expected to know the details of each nation's commercial legal practices, just the awareness of and the expectation of the existence of differences will eliminate much complication.

Actually, no society can exist on a high commercial level without a highly developed working base on which agreements can rest. This base may be one or a combination of three types:

1. Rules that are spelled out technically as law or regulation.
2. Moral practices mutually agreed on and taught to the young as a set of principles.
3. Informal customs to which everyone conforms without being able to state the exact rules.

Some societies favor one, some another. Ours, particularly in the business world, lays heavy emphasis on the first variety. Few Americans will conduct any business nowadays without some written agreement or contract.

Varying from culture to culture will be the circumstances under which such rules apply. Americans consider that negotiations have more or less ceased when the contract is signed. With the Greeks, on the other hand, the contract is seen as a sort of way station on the route to negotiation that will cease only when the work is completed. The contract is nothing more than a charter for serious negotiations. In the Arab world, once a man's word is given in a particular kind of way, it is just as binding, if not more so, than most of our written contracts. The written contract, therefore, violates the Moslem's sensitivities and reflects on his honor. Unfortunately, the situation is now so hopelessly confused that neither system can be counted on to prevail consistently.

Informal patterns and unstated agreements often lead to untold difficulty in the cross-cultural situation. Take the case of the before-and-after patterns where there is a wide discrepancy between the American's expectations and those of the Arab:

In the United States, when you engage a specialist such as a lawyer or a doctor, require any standard service, or even take a taxi, you make several assumptions: (a) the charge will be fair; (b) it will be in proportion to the services rendered; and (c) it will bear a close relationship to the "going rate."

You wait until after the services are performed before asking what the tab will be. If the charge is too high in the light of the above assumptions, you feel you have been cheated. You can complain, or can say nothing, pay up, and take your business elsewhere the next time.

As one would expect in the Middle East, basic differences emerge which lead to difficulty if not understood. For instance, when taking a cab in Beirut it is well to know the going rate as a point around which to bargain and for settling the charge, which must be fixed before engaging the cab.

If you have not fixed the rate in advance, there is a complete change and an entirely different set of rules will apply. According to these rules, the going rate plays no part whatsoever. The whole relationship is altered. The sky is the limit, and the customer has no kick coming. I have seen taxi drivers shouting at the top of their lungs, waving their arms, following a redfaced American with his head pulled down between his shoulders, demanding for a two-pound ride ten Lebanese pounds which the American eventually had to pay.

It is difficult for the American to accommodate his frame of reference to the fact that what constitutes one thing to him, namely, a taxi ride, is to the Arab two very different operations involving two different sets of relationships and two sets of rules. The crucial factor is whether the bargaining is done at the beginning or the end of the ride! As a matter of fact, you cannot bargain at the end. What the driver asks for he is entitled to!

One of the greatest difficulties Americans have abroad stems from the fact that we often think we have a commitment when we do not. The second complication on this same topic is the other side of the coin, i.e., when others think we have agreed to things that we have not. Our own failure to recognize binding obligations, plus our custom of setting organizational goals ahead of everything else, has put us in hot water far too often.

People sometimes do not keep agreements with us because we do not keep agreements with them. As a general rule, the American treats the agreement as something he may eventually have to break. Here are two examples:

Once while I was visiting an American post in Latin America, the Ambassador sent the Spanish version of a trade treaty down to his language officer with instructions to write in some "weasel words." To his dismay, he was told, "There are no weasel words in Spanish."

A personnel officer of a large corporation in Iran made an agreement with local employees that American employees would not receive preferential treatment. When the first American employee arrived, it was learned quickly that in the United States he had been covered by a variety of health plans that were not available to Iranians. And this led to immediate protests from the Iranians which were never satisfied. The personnel officer never really grasped the fact that he had violated an ironbound contract.

Certainly, this is the most important generalization to be drawn by American businessmen from this discussion of agreements: there are many times when we are vulnerable *even when judged by our own standards*. Many instances of actual sharp practices by American companies are well known abroad and are giving American business a bad name. The cure for such questionable behavior is simple. The companies concerned usually have it within their power to discharge offenders and to foster within their organization an atmosphere in which only honesty and fairness can thrive.

But the cure for ignorance of the social and legal rules which underlie business agreements is not so easy. This is because:

- The subject is complex.
- Little research has been conducted to determine the culturally different concepts of what is an agreement.
- The people of each country think that their own code is the only one, and that everything else is dishonest.
- Each code is different from our own; and the farther away one is traveling from Western Europe, the greater the difference is.

But the little that has already been learned about this subject indicates that as a problem it is not insoluble and will yield to research. Since it is probably one of the more relevant and immediately applicable areas of interest to modern business, it would certainly be advisable for companies with large foreign operations to sponsor some serious research in this vital field.

A CASE IN POINT

Thus far, I have been concerned with developing the five check points around which a real understanding of foreign cultures can begin. But the problems that arise from a faulty understanding of the silent language of foreign custom are human problems and perhaps can best be dramatized by an actual case.

A Latin American republic had decided to modernize one of its communication networks to the tune of several million dollars. Because of its reputation for quality and price, the inside track was quickly taken by American company "Y."

The company, having been sounded out informally, considered the size of the order and decided to bypass its regular Latin American representative and send instead its sales manager. The following describes what took place.

The sales manager arrived and checked in at the leading hotel. He immediately had some difficulty pinning down just who it was he had to see about his business. After several days without results, he called at the American Embassy where he found that the commercial attaché had the up-to-the-minute information he needed. The commercial attaché listened to his story. Realizing that the sales manager had already made a number of mistakes, but figuring that the Latins were used to American blundering, the attaché reasoned that all was not lost. He informed the sales manager that the Minister of Communications was the key man and that whoever got the nod from him would get the contract. He also briefed the sales manager on methods of conducting business in Latin America and offered some pointers about dealing with the minister.

The attaché's advice ran somewhat as follows:

1. "You don't do business here the way you do in the States; it is necessary to spend much more time. You have to get to know your man and vice versa.

2. "You must meet with him *several times* before you talk business. I will tell you at what point you can bring up the subject. Take your cues from me. [Our American sales manager at this point made a few observations to himself about "cookie pushers" and wondered how many payrolls had been met by the commercial attaché.]

3. "Take that price list and put it in your pocket. Don't get it out until I tell you to. Down here price is only one of the many things taken into account before closing a deal. In the United States, your past experience will prompt you to act according to a certain set of principles, but many of these principles will *not* work here. Every time you feel the urge to act or to say something, look at me. Suppress the urge and take your cues from me. This is very important.

4. "Down here people like to do business with men who *are* somebody. In order to be somebody, it is well to have written a book, to have lectured at a university, or to have developed your intellect in some way. The man you are going to see is a poet. He has published several volumes of poetry. Like many Latin Americans, he prizes poetry highly. You will find that he will spend a good deal of business time quoting his poetry to you, and he will take great pleasure in this.

5. "You will also note that the people here are very proud of their past and of their Spanish blood, but they are also exceedingly proud of their liberation from Spain and their independence. The fact that they are a democracy, that they are free, and also that they are no longer a colony is very, very important to them. They are warm and friendly and enthusiastic if they like you. If they don't, they are cold and withdrawn.

6. "And another thing, time down here means something different. It works in a different way. You know how it is back in the States when a certain type blurts out whatever is on his mind without waiting to see if the situation is right. He is considered an impatient bore and somewhat egocentric. Well, down here, you have to wait much, much longer, and I really mean *much, much* longer, before you can begin to talk about the reason for your visit.

7. "There is another point I want to caution you about. At home, the man who sells takes the initiative. Here, *they* tell you when they are ready to do business. But, most of all, don't discuss price until you are asked and don't rush things."

THE PITCH

The next day the commercial attaché introduced the sales manager to the Minister of Communications. First, there was a long wait in the outer office while people kept coming in and out. The sales manager looked at his watch, fidgeted, and finally asked whether the minister was really expecting him. The reply he received was scarcely reassuring, "Oh, yes, he is expecting you but several things have come up that require his attention. Besides, one gets used to waiting down here." The sales manager irritably replied, "But doesn't he know I flew all the way down here from the United States to see him, and I have spent over a week already of my valuable time trying to find him?" "Yes, I know," was the answer, "but things just move much more slowly here."

At the end of about 30 minutes, the minister emerged from the office, greeted the commercial attaché with a *doble abrazo*, throwing his arms around him and patting him on the back as though they were long-lost brothers. Now, turning and smiling, the minister extended his hand to the sales manager, who, by this time, was feeling rather miffed because he had been kept in the outer office so long.

After what seemed to be an all too short chat, the minister rose, suggesting a well-known café where they might meet for dinner the next evening. The sales manager expected, of course, that, considering the nature of their business and the size of the order, he might be taken to the minister's home, not realizing that the Latin home is reserved for family and very close friends.

Until now, nothing at all had been said about the reason for the sales manager's visit, a fact which bothered him somewhat. The whole set-up seemed wrong; neither did he like the idea of wasting another day in town. He told the home office before he left that he would be gone for a week or ten days at most, and made a mental note that he would clean this order up in three days and enjoy a few days in Acapulco or Mexico City. Now the week had already gone and he would be lucky if he made it home in ten days.

Voicing his misgivings to the commercial attaché, he wanted to know if the minister really meant business, and, if he did, why could they not get together and talk about it? The commercial attaché by now was beginning to show the strain of constantly having to reassure the sales manager. Nevertheless, he tried again:

"What you don't realize is that part of the time we were waiting, the minister was rearranging a very tight schedule so that he could spend tomorrow night with you. You see, down here they don't delegate responsibility the way we do in the States. They exercise much tighter control than we do. As a consequence, this man spends up to 15 hours a day at his desk. It may not look like it to you, but I assure you he really means business. He wants to give your company the order; if you play your cards right, you will get it."

The next evening provided more of the same. Much conversation about food and music, about many people the sales manager had never heard of. They went to a night club, where the sales manager brightened up and began to think that perhaps he and the minister might have something in common after all. It bothered him, however, that the principal reason for his visit was not even alluded to tangentially. But every time he started to talk about electronics, the commercial attaché would nudge him and proceed to change the subject.

The next meeting was for morning coffee at a café. By now the sales manager was having difficulty hiding his impatience. To make matters worse, the minister had a mannerism which he did not like. When they talked, he was likely to put his hand on him; he would take hold of his arm and get so close that he almost "spat" in his face. As a consequence, the sales manager was kept busy trying to dodge and back up.

Following the coffee, there was a walk in a nearby park. The minister expounded on the shrubs, the birds, and the beauties of nature, and at one spot he stopped to point at a statue and said: "There is a statue of the world's greatest hero, the liberator of mankind!" At this point, the worst happened, for the sales manager asked who the statue was of and, being given the name of a famous Latin American patriot, said, "I never heard of him," and walked on.

THE FAILURE

It is quite clear from this that the sales manager did not get the order, which went to a Swedish concern. The American, moreover, was never able to see the minister again. Why did the minister feel the way he did? His reasoning went somewhat as follows:

"I like the American's equipment and it makes sense to deal with North Americans who are near us and whose price is right. But I could never be friends with this man. He is not my kind of human being and we have nothing in common. He is not *simpatico*. If I can't be friends and he is not *simpatico*, I can't depend on him to treat me right. I tried everything, every conceivable situation, and only once did we seem to understand each other. If we could be friends, he would feel obligated to me and this obligation would give me some control. Without control, how do I know he will deliver what he says he will at the price he quotes?"

Of course, what the minister did not know was that the price was quite firm, and that quality control was a matter of company policy. He did not realize that the sales manager was a member of an organization, and that the man is always subordinate to the organization in the United States. Next year maybe the sales manager would not even be representing the company, but would be replaced. Further, if he wanted someone to depend on, his best bet would be to hire a good American lawyer to represent him and write a binding contract.

In this instance, both sides suffered. The American felt he was being slighted and put off, and did not see how there could possibly be any connection between poetry and doing business or why it should all take so long. He interpreted the delay as a form of polite brush-off. Even if things had gone differently and there had been a contract, it is doubtful that the minister would have trusted the contract as much as he would a man whom he considered his friend. Throughout Latin America, the law is made livable and contracts workable by having friends and relatives operating from the inside. Lacking a friend, someone who would look out for his interests, the minister did not want to take a chance. He stated this simply and directly.

CONCLUSION

The case just described has of necessity been oversimplified. The danger is that the reader will say, "Oh, I see. All you really have to do is be friends." At which point the expert will step in and reply:

"Yes, of course, but what you don't realize is that in Latin America being a friend involves much more than it does in the United States and is an entirely different proposition. A friendship implies obligations. You go about it differently. It involves much more than being nice, visiting, and playing golf. You would not want to enter into friendship lightly."

The point is simply this. It takes years and years to develop a sound foundation for doing business in a given country. Much that is done seems silly or strange to the home office. Indeed, the most common error made by home offices, once they have found representatives who can get results, is failure to take their advice and allow sufficient time for representatives to develop the proper contacts.

The second most common error, if that is what it can be called, is ignorance of the secret and hidden language of foreign cultures. In this article I have tried to show how five key topics—time, space, material possessions, friendship patterns, and business agreements—offer a starting point from which companies can begin to acquire the understanding necessary to do business in foreign countries.

Our present knowledge is meager, and much more research is needed before the businessman of the future can go abroad fully equipped for his work. Not only will he need to be well versed in the economics, law, and politics of the area, but he will have to understand, if not speak, the silent languages of other cultures.

LISTENING IS A TEN-PART SKILL

Ralph G. Nichols

White collar workers, on the average, devote at least 40 per cent of their work day to listening. Apparently 40 per cent of their salary is paid to them for listening. Yet tests of listening comprehension have shown that, without training, these employes listen at only 25 per cent efficiency.

This low level of performance becomes increasingly intolerable as evidence accumulates that it can be significantly raised. The component skills of listening are known. They boil down to this:

Learning through listening is primarily an inside job—inside action on the part of the listener. What he needs to do is to replace some common present attitudes with others.

Recognizing the dollar values in effective listening, many companies have added courses in this skill to their regular training programs. Some of the pioneers in this effort have been American Telephone & Telegraph Co., General Motors Corporation, Ford Motor Company, The Dow Chemical Company, Western Electric Co., Inc., Methods Engineering Council of Pittsburgh, Minnesota Mining & Manufacturing Co., Thompson Products, Inc., of Cleveland, and Rogers Corp. of Connecticut.

Warren Ganong of the Methods Engineering Council has compared trainees given a preliminary discussion of efficient listening with those not provided such discussion. On tests at the end of the courses the former achieved marks 12 to 15 per cent higher than did the latter.

A. A. Tribbey, general personnel supervisor of the Wisconsin Telephone Company, in commenting on the results of a short conference course in which effective listening was stressed, declared: "It never fails to amaze us when we see the skill that is acquired in only three days."

The conviction seems to be growing that upper-level managers also need listening skill. As Dr. Earl Planty, executive counselor for the pharmaceutical firm of Johnson & Johnson puts it: "By far the most effective method by which executives can tap ideas of subordinates is sympathetic listening in the many day-to-day informal contacts within and outside the work place. There is no system that will do the job in an easier manner. . . . Nothing can equal an executive's willingness to hear."

A study of the 100 best listeners and the 100 worst listeners in the freshman class on the University of Minnesota campus has disclosed 10 guides to improved listening. Business people interested in improving their own performance can use them to analyze their personal strengths and weaknesses. The 10 guides to good listening are:

1. FIND AREA OF INTEREST

All studies point to the advantage in being interested in the topic under discussion. Bad listeners usually declare the subject dry after the first few sentences. Once this decision is made, it serves to rationalize any and all inattention.

Good listeners follow different tactics. True, their first thought may be that the subject sounds dry. But a second one immediately follows, based on the realization that to get up and leave might prove a bit awkward.

The final reflection is that, being trapped anyhow, perhaps it might be well to learn if anything is being said that can be put to use.

The key to the whole matter of interest in a topic is the word use. Whenever we wish to listen efficiently, we ought to say to ourselves: "What's he saying that I can use? What worth-while ideas has he? Is he reporting any workable procedures? Anything that I can cash in, or with which I can make myself happier?" Such questions lead us to screen what we are hearing in a continual effort to sort out the elements of personal value. G. K. Chesterton spoke wisely indeed when he said, "There is no such thing as an uninteresting subject; there are only uninterested people."

2. JUDGE CONTENT, NOT DELIVERY

Many listeners alibi inattention to a speaker by thinking to themselves: "Who could listen to such a character? What an awful voice! Will he ever stop reading from his notes?"

The good listener reacts differently. He may well look at the speaker and think, "This man is inept. Seems like almost anyone ought to be able to talk better than that." But from this initial similarity he moves on to a different conclusion, thinking "But wait a minute. . . . I'm not interested in his personality or delivery. I want to find out what he knows. Does this man know some things that I need to know?"

Essentially we "listen with our own experience." Is the conveyer to be held responsible because we are poorly equipped to decode his message? We cannot understand everything we hear, but one sure way to raise the level of our understanding is to assume the responsibility which is inherently ours.

3. HOLD YOUR FIRE

Overstimulation is almost as bad as understimulation, and the two together constitute the twin evils of inefficient listening. The overstimulated listener gets too excited, or excited too soon, by the speaker. Some of us are greatly addicted to this weakness. For us, a speaker can seldom talk for more than a few minutes without touching upon a pet bias or conviction. Occasionally we are roused in support of the speaker's point; usually it is the reverse. In either case overstimulation reflects the desire of the listener to enter, somehow, immediately into the argument.

The aroused person usually becomes preoccupied by trying to do three things simultaneously: calculate what hurt is being done to his own pet ideas; plot an embarrassing question to ask the speaker; enjoy mentally all the discomfiture visualized for the speaker once the devastating reply to him is launched. With these things going on subsequent passages go unheard.

We must learn not to get too excited about a speaker's point until we are certain we thoroughly understand it. The secret is contained in the principle that we must always withhold evaluation until our comprehension is complete.

4. LISTEN FOR IDEAS

Good listeners focus on central ideas; they tend to recognize the characteristic language in which central ideas are usually stated, and they are able to discriminate between fact and principle, idea and example, evidence and argument. Poor listeners are inclined to listen for the facts in every presentation.

To understand the fault, let us assume that a man is giving us instructions made up of facts A to Z. The man begins to talk. We hear fact A and think: "We've got to remember it!" So we begin a memory exercise by repeating "Fact A, fact A, fact A. . . ."

Meanwhile, the fellow is telling us fact B. Now we have two facts to memorize. We're so busy doing it that we miss fact C completely. And so it goes up to fact Z. We catch a few facts, garble several others and completely miss the rest.

It is a significant fact that only about 25 per cent of persons listening to a formal talk are able to grasp the speaker's central idea. To develop this skill requires an ability to recognize conventional organizational patterns, transitional language, and the speaker's use of recapitulation. Fortunately, all of these items can be readily mastered with a bit of effort.

5. BE FLEXIBLE

Our research has shown that our 100 worst listeners thought that note-taking and outlining were synonyms. They believed there was but one way to take notes—by making an outline.

Actually, no damage would be done if all talks followed some definite plan of organization. Unfortunately, less than half of even formal speeches are carefully organized. There are few things more frustrating than to try to outline an unoutlineable speech.

Note-taking may help or may become a distraction. Some persons try to take down everything in shorthand; the vast majority of us are far too voluminous even in longhand. While studies are not too clear on the point, there is some evidence to indicate that the volume of notes taken and their value to the taker are inversely related. In any case, the real issue is one of interpretation. Few of us have memories good enough to remember even the salient points we hear. If we can obtain brief, meaningful records of them for later review, we definitely improve our ability to learn and to remember.

The 100 best listeners had apparently learned early in life that if they wanted to be efficient note-takers they had to have more than one system of taking notes. They equipped themselves with four or five systems, and learned to adjust their system to the organizational pattern, or the absence of one, in each talk they heard. If we want to be good listeners, we must be flexible and adaptable note-takers.

6. WORK AT LISTENING

One of the most striking characteristics of poor listeners is their disinclination to spend any energy in a listening situation. College students, by their own testimony, frequently enter classes all worn out physically;

assume postures which only seem to give attention to the speaker; and then proceed to catch up on needed rest or to reflect upon purely personal matters. This faking of attention is one of the worst habits afflicting us as a people.

Listening is hard work. It is characterized by faster heart action, quicker circulation of the blood, a small rise in bodily temperature. The overrelaxed listener is merely appearing to tune in, and then feeling conscience-free to pursue any of a thousand mental tangents.

For selfish reasons alone one of the best investments we can make is to give each speaker our conscious attention. We ought to establish eye contact and maintain it; to indicate by posture and facial expression that the occasion and the speaker's efforts are a matter of real concern to us. When we do these things we help the speaker to express himself more clearly, and we in turn profit by better understanding of the improved communication we have helped him to achieve. None of this necessarily implies acceptance of his point of view or favorable action upon his appeals. It is, rather, an expression of interest.

7.   RESIST DISTRACTIONS

The good listeners tend to adjust quickly to any kind of abnormal situation; poor listeners tend to tolerate bad conditions and, in some instances, even to create distractions themselves.

We live in a noisy age. We are distracted not only by what we hear, but by what we see. Poor listeners tend to be readily influenced by all manner of distractions, even in an intimate face-to-face situation.

A good listener instinctively fights distraction. Sometimes the fight is easily won—by closing a door, shutting off the radio, moving closer to the person talking, or asking him to speak louder. If the distractions cannot be met that easily, then it becomes a matter of concentration.

8.   EXERCISE YOUR MIND

Poor listeners are inexperienced in hearing difficult, expository material. Good listeners apparently develop an appetite for hearing a variety of presentations difficult enough to challenge their mental capacities.

Perhaps the one word that best describes the bad listener is "inexperienced." Although he spends 40 per cent of his communication day listening to something, he is inexperienced in hearing anything tough, technical, or expository. He has for years painstakingly sought light, recreational material. The problem he creates is deeply significant, because such a person is a poor producer in factory, office, or classroom.

Inexperience is not easily or quickly overcome. However, knowledge of our own weakness may lead us to repair it. We need never become too old to meet new challenges.

9. KEEP YOUR MIND OPEN

Parallel to the blind spots which afflict human beings are certain psychological deaf spots which impair our ability to perceive and understand. These deaf spots are the dwelling place of our most cherished notions, convictions, and complexes. Often, when a speaker invades one of these areas with a word or phrase, we turn our mind to retraveling familiar mental pathways crisscrossing our invaded area of sensitivity.

It is hard to believe in moments of cold detachment that just a word or phrase can cause such emotional eruption. Yet with poor listeners it is frequently the case; and even with very good listeners it is occasionally the case. When such emotional deafness transpires, communicative efficiency drops rapidly to zero.

Among the words known thus to serve as red flags to some listeners are: mother-in-law, landlord, redneck, sharecropper, sissy, pervert, automation, clerk, income tax, communist, Red, dumb farmer, pink, "Greetings," antivivisectionist, evolution, square, punk, welsher.

Effective listeners try to identify and to rationalize the words or phrases most upsetting emotionally. Often the emotional impact of such words can be decreased through a free and open discussion of them with friends or associates.

10. CAPITALIZE ON THOUGHT SPEED

Most persons talk at a speed of about 125 words a minute. There is good evidence that if thought were measured in words per minute, most of us could think easily at about four times that rate. It is difficult—almost painful—to try to slow down our thinking speed. Thus we normally have about 400 words of thinking time to spare during every minute a person talks to us.

What do we do with our excess thinking time while someone is speaking? If we are poor listeners, we soon become impatient with the slow progress the speaker seems to be making. So our thoughts turn to something else for a moment, then dart back to the speaker. These brief side excursions of thought continue until our mind tarries too long on some enticing but irrelevant subject. Then, when our thoughts return to the person talking, we find he's far ahead of us. Now it's harder to follow him and increasingly easy to take off on side excursions. Finally we give up; the person is still talking, but our mind is in another world.

The good listener uses his thought speed to advantage; he constantly applies his spare thinking time to what is being said. It is not difficult once one has a definite pattern of thought to follow. To develop such a pattern we should:

▶ *Try to anticipate what a person is going to talk about. On the basis of what he's already said, ask yourself: "What's he trying to get at? What point is he going to make?"*

▶ *Mentally summarize what the person has been saying. What point has he made already, if any?*

▶ *Weigh the speaker's evidence by mentally questioning it. As he presents facts, illustrative stories and statistics, continually ask yourself: "Are they accurate? Do they come from an unprejudiced source? Am I getting the full picture, or is he telling me only what will prove his point?"*

▶ *Listen between the lines. The speaker doesn't always put everything that's important into words. The changing tones and volume of his voice may have a meaning. So may his facial expressions, the gestures he makes with his hands, the movement of his body.*

Not capitalizing on thought speed is our greatest single handicap. The differential between thought speed and speech speed breeds false feelings of security and mental tangents. Yet, through listening training, this same differential can be readily converted into our greatest asset.

MANAGEMENT COMMUNICATION AND THE GRAPEVINE

Keith Davis

Communication is involved in all human relations. It is the "nervous system" of any organized group, providing the information and understanding necessary for high productivity and morale. For the individual company it is a continuous process, a way of life, rather than a one-shot campaign. Top management, therefore, recognizes the importance of communication and wants to do something about it. But what? Often, in its frustration, management has used standard communication "packages" instead of dealing situationally with its individual problems. Or it has emphasized the means (communication techniques) rather than the ends (objectives of communication).

One big factor which management has tended to overlook is communication *within its own group*. Communication to the worker and from the worker is dependent on effective management communication; and clearly this in turn requires informal as well as formal channels.

THE GRAPEVINE

A particularly neglected aspect of management communication concerns that informal channel, the grapevine. There is no dodging the fact that, as a carrier of news and gossip among executives and supervisors, the grapevine often affects the affairs of management. The proof of this is the strong feelings that different executives have about it. Some regard the grapevine as an evil—a thorn in the side which regularly spreads rumor, destroys morale and reputations, leads to irresponsible actions, and challenges authority. Some regard it as a good thing because it acts as a safety valve and carries news fast. Others regard it as a very mixed blessing.

Whether the grapevine is considered an asset or a liability, it is important for executives to try to understand it. For one thing is sure: al-

Condensed from *Harvard Business Review*, XXXI, 5 (September-October 1953), 43-49. © 1953 by The President and Fellows of Harvard College; all rights reserved.

though no executive can absolutely control the grapevine, he can *influence* it. And since it is here to stay, he should learn to live with it.

PERSPECTIVE

Of course, the grapevine is only part of the picture of communication in management. There is also formal communication—via conferences, reports, memoranda, and so on; this provides the basic core of information, and many administrators rely on it almost exclusively because they think it makes their job simpler to have everything reduced to explicit terms—as if that were possible! Another important part of the picture is the expression of attitudes, as contrasted with the transmission of information (which is what we will be dealing with in this article). Needless to say, all these factors influence the way the grapevine works in a given company, just as the grapevine in turn influences them.

In this article I want to examine (a) the significance, character, and operation of management communication patterns, with particular emphasis on the grapevine; and (b) the influence that various factors, such as organization and the chain of procedure, have upon such patterns. From this analysis, then, it will be possible to point up (c) the practical implications for management.

As for the research basis of the analysis, the major points are these:

1. *Company studied*—The company upon which the research is based is a real one. I shall refer to it as the "Jason Company." A manufacturer of leather goods, it has 67 people in the management group. . . .

2. *Methodology*—The methods used to study management communication in the Jason Company are new ones. Briefly, the basic approach was to learn from each communication recipient how he first received a given piece of information and then to trace it back to its source. Suppose D and E said they received it from G; G said he received it from B; and B from A. All the chains or sequences were plotted in this way—A to B to G to D and E—and when the data from all recipients were assembled, the pattern of the flow of communication emerged. . . .

SIGNIFICANT CHARACTERISTICS

In the Jason Company many of the usual grapevine characteristics were found along with others less well known. For purposes of this discussion, the four most significant characteristics are these:

1. *Speed of transmission*—Traditionally the grapevine is fast, and this showed up in the Jason Company.

For example, a certain manager had an addition to his family at the local hospital at 11 o'clock at night, and by 2:00 p.m. the next day 46% of the whole management group knew about the event. The news was transmitted only by grapevine and mostly by face-to-face conversation, with an occasional interoffice telephone call. Most communications occurred immediately before work began, during "coffee hour," and during lunch hour. The five staff executives who knew of the event learned of it during "coffee hour," indicating that the morning rest period performed an important social function for the staff as well as providing relaxation.

2. *Degree of selectivity*—The grapevine here showed that it could be highly selective and discriminating.

For example, the local representative of the company which carried the employee group insurance contract planned a picnic for company executives. The Jason Company president decided to invite 36 executives, mostly from higher executive levels. The grapevine immediately went to work spreading this information, but it was carried to *only two of the 31 executives not invited*. The grapevine communicators thought the news was confidential, so they had told only those who they thought would be invited (they had to guess, since they did not have access to the invitation list). The two uninvited executives who knew the information were foremen who were told by their invited superintendent; he had a very close working relationship with them and generally kept them well informed.

Many illustrations like the above could be gathered to show that the grapevine can be discriminating. Whether it may be *counted on* in that respect, however, is another question. . . .

3. *Locale of operation*—The grapevine of company news operates mostly at the place of work. . . .

The significance of at-the-company grapevines is this: since management has some control over the work environment, it has an opportunity to influence the grapevine. By exerting such influence the manager can more closely integrate grapevine interests with those of the formal communication system, and he can use it for effectively spreading more significant items of information than those commonly carried.

4. *Relation to formal communication*—Formal and informal communication systems tend to be jointly active, or jointly inactive. Where formal communication was inactive at the Jason Company, the grapevine did not rush in to fill the void (as has often been suggested[1]); instead, there simply was lack of communication. Similarly, where there was effective formal communication, there was an active grapevine.

Informal and formal communication may supplement each other. Often formal communication is simply used to confirm or to expand what has already been communicated by grapevine. . . .

1. For example, see National Industrial Conference Board, *Communicating with Employees*, Studies in Personnel Policy, No. 129 (New York, 1952), p. 34.

SPREADING INFORMATION

Now let us turn to the actual operation of the grapevine. How is information passed along? What is the relationship among the various people who are involved?

Human communication requires at least two persons, but each person acts independently. Person A may talk or write, but he has not *communicated* until person B receives. The individual is, therefore, a basic communication unit. That is, he is one "link" in the communication "chain" for any bit of information.

The formal communication chain is largely determined by the chain of command or by formal procedures, but the grapevine chain is more flexible. There are four different ways of visualizing it, as Exhibit I indicates:

1. *The single-strand chain*—A tells B, who tells C, who tells D, and so on; this makes for a tenuous chain to a distant receiver. Such a chain is usually in mind when one speaks of how the grapevine distorts and filters information until the original item is not recognizable.

2. *The gossip chain*—A seeks and tells everyone else.

3. *The probability chain*—A communicates randomly, say, to F and D, in accordance with the laws of probability; then F and D tell others in the same manner.

4. *The cluster chain*—A tells three selected others; perhaps one of them tells two others; and then one of these two tells one other. This was virtually the only kind of chain found in the Jason Company, and may well be the normal one in industry generally.

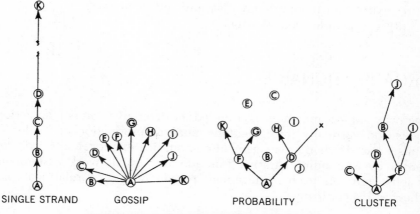

SINGLE STRAND   GOSSIP   PROBABILITY   CLUSTER

EXHIBIT I. TYPES OF COMMUNICATION CHAINS

ACTIVE MINORITY

The predominance of the cluster chain at the Jason Company means that only a few of the persons who knew a unit of information ever transmitted it—what Jacobson and Seashore call the "liaison" individuals.[2] All others who received the information did not transmit it; they acted merely as passive receivers.

For example, when a quality-control problem occurred, 68% of the executives received the information, but only 20% transmitted it. Again, when an executive planned to resign to enter the insurance business, 81% of the executives knew about it, but only 11% passed the news on to others. Those liaison individuals who told the news to more than one other person amounted to less than 10% of the 67 executives in each case. . . .

The above findings indicate that if management wants more communication, it should increase the number and/or effectiveness of its liaison individuals. This appears to be a large order, but it is entirely possible. Liaison individuals tend to act in a predictable way. If an individual's unit of information concerns a job function in which he is interested, he is likely to tell others. If his information is about a person with whom he is associated socially, he also is likely to tell others. Furthermore, the sooner he knows of an event after it happened, the more likely he is to tell others. If he gets the information late, he does not want to advertise his late receipt of it by telling it to others.

In other words, three well-known communication principles which are so often mentioned in relation to attitudes also have a major influence on the spread of information by liaison individuals:

(1) Tell people about what will affect them (job interest).
(2) Tell people what they want to know, rather than simply what you want them to know (job and social interest).
(3) Tell people soon (timing).

ORGANIZATIONAL EFFECTS

The way an organization is divided horizontally into organizational levels and vertically into functions, such as production and sales, obviously has effects on management communication, for it cuts each company's over-all administrative function into small work assignments, or jobs, and sets each management person in certain relationships to others in his company.

2. Eugene Jacobson and Stanley E. Seashore, "Communication Practices in Complex Organizations," *The Journal of Social Issues*, VII, 3 (1951), p. 37.

HORIZONTAL LEVELS

Organizational levels are perhaps the more dramatic in effect because they usually carry authority, pay increases, and status. From the communication point of view, they are especially important because of their number. In a typical firm there are usually several management levels, but only one or two worker levels; furthermore, as the firm grows, the management levels increase in number, while the worker levels remain stationary.

Communication problems are aggravated by these additional levels because the chain of communication is lengthened and complicated. Indeed, just because of this, some companies have been led to try to reduce the number of intermediate management levels. Our concern here is with the patterns of communication among individuals at the different levels.

At the Jason Company, executives at *higher* levels communicated more often and with more people than did executives at *lower* levels. In other words, the predominant communication flow was downward or horizontal. When an event happened at the bottom level, usually the news did reach a high level; but a single line of communication sufficed to carry it there, and from that point it went downward and outward in the same volume and manner (cluster chain) as if it had originated at the top.

Accordingly, the higher an executive was in the organizational hierarchy (with the exception of nonresident executives), the greater was his knowledge of company events. This was true of events which happened both above his level and below his level. Thus, if the president was out of town, a greater proportion at the fourth level knew of it than at the sixth level. Or—and this is less to be expected—if a foreman at the sixth level had an accident, a larger proportion of executives at the third level knew of it than at the fourth level, or even than at the sixth level where the accident happened. The more noteworthy the event, of course, the more likely it was to be known at upper levels—but, in a company of this size, it had to be quite trivial indeed before it failed to reach the ears of top executives.

The converse follows that in terms of communications transmitted and received the sixth and lowest level of supervision, the foreman level, was largely isolated from all other management. The average foreman was very hesitant to communicate with other members of management; and on the rare occasions when he did, he usually chose someone at his own level and preferably in his own department. Members of this group tended to be the last links in management communication, regardless of whether the chains were formal or informal.

A further significant fact concerns the eight departmental superintendents at the fourth level. Six of them supervised foremen directly;

two others, with larger departments, each had a single line assistant between him and his foremen. The two who had line assistants were much
more active in the communication chains than were the six others; indeed, all but one of the six appeared to have little to do with their foremen except in a formal way.

Perhaps the clue is that, with increased organizational levels, those
at the higher (and hence further removed) levels both recognize a greater
need for communication and have more time to practice it!

FUNCTIONAL GROUPS

Functionalization, the second important way in which an organization
is "cut up," also has a significant impact on communication in management. The functions which are delegated to a manager help to determine the people he contacts, his relationships with them, his status, and,
as a result, the degree to which he receives and transmits information.
More specifically, his role in communication is affected (a) by his position in the chain of command and (b) by his position in the chain of
procedure, which involves the sequence of work performance and cuts
across chains of command, as when a report goes from the superintendent
in one chain of command to the chief engineer in another chain of command and to the controller in still another.

In the Jason Company the effects of functionalization showed up
in three major ways:

1. *Staff men "in the know"*—More staff executives than line men
usually knew about any company event. This was true at each level of
management as well as for the management group as a whole. For example, when the president of the company made a trip to seek increased
governmental allotments of hides to keep the line tannery operating at
capacity, only 4% of the line executives knew the purpose of the trip,
but 25% of the staff men did. In another case, when a popular line superintendent was awarded a hat as a prize in a training program for line
superintendents, within six days a larger proportion of the staff executives than of the line executives knew about this event.

The explanation is not just that, with one staff executive to every
three line executives, there were more line executives to be informed.
More important is the fact that the *chain of procedure* usually involved
more staff executives than line executives. Thus, when the superintendent
was awarded his hat, a line executive had approved the award, but a
staff personnel executive had processed it and a staff accounting executive had arranged for the special check.

Also the staff was more *mobile* than the line. Staff executives in
such areas as personnel and control found that their duties both required
and allowed them to get out of their offices, made it easy for them to walk
through other departments without someone wondering whether they

were "not working," to get away for coffee, and so on—all of which meant they heard more news from the other executives they talked with. (In a larger company staff members might be more fixed to their chairs, but the situation in the Jason Company doubtless applies to a great many other businesses.)

Because of its mobility and its role in the chain of procedure, the staff not only received but also transmitted communications more actively than did the line. Most of these communications were oral; at least in this respect, the staff was not the "paper mill" it is often said to be. It seems obvious that management would do well to make conscious use of staff men as communicators.

2. *Cross-communication*—A second significant effect of functionalization in the Jason Company was that the predominant flow of information for events of general interest was between the four large areas of production, sales, finance and office, and industrial relations, rather than within them. That is, if a production executive had a bit of news of general interest, he was more likely to tell a sales, finance, or personnel executive than another production executive.

Social relationships played a part in this, with executives in the various groups being lodge brothers, members of the same church, neighbors, parents of children in the same schools, and so on. In these relationships the desire to make an impression was a strong motivation for cross-communication, since imparting information to executives outside his own area served to make a man feel that the others would consider him "in the know." Procedural relationships, discussed earlier, also encouraged the executives to communicate across functional lines.

Since communications tended not to stay within an area, such as production, they tended even less to follow chains of command from boss to sub-boss to sub-sub-boss. Indeed, the chain of command was seldom used in this company except for very formal communications. Thus Exhibit II reproduces a communication chain concerning a quality control problem in production, first brought to the attention of a group sales manager in a letter from a customer. Although it was the type of problem that could have been communicated along the chain of command, the exhibit shows that, of 14 communications, only 3 were within the chain of command and only 6 remained within one fuctional area—sales—where the information was first received.

The fact that the chain of command may affect management communication patterns less than procedural and social influences—which has shown up in other companies too[3]—means that management needs to devote considerably more attention to the problems and opportunities of cross-communication.

3. See Carroll L. Shartle, "Leadership and Executive Performance," *Personnel* (March 1949), pp. 377-378.

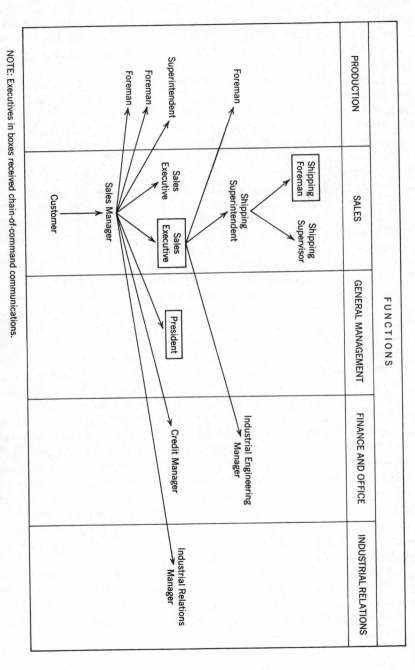

NOTE: Executives in boxes received chain-of-command communications.

EXHIBIT II. COMMUNICATION CHAIN FOR A QUALITY CONTROL PROBLEM

3. *Group isolation*—The research in the Jason Company revealed that some functional groups were consistently isolated from communication chains. Also, there were other groups which received information but did not transmit it, and thus contributed to the same problem—the uneven spread of information through the company. Here are three examples at the foreman level illustrating different degrees of failure to participate in the communication process and different reasons for this failure:

(a) The foremen in one group were generally left out of communication chains. These men were of a different nationality from that of the rest of the employees, performed dirty work, and worked in a separate building. Also, their work fitted into the manufacturing process in such a way that it was seldom necessary for other executives to visit their work location.

(b) Another group often was in a communication chain but on the tail end of it. They were in a separate building some distance from the main manufacturing area, their function was not in the main manufacturing procedure, and they usually received information late. They had little chance or incentive to communicate to other executives.

(c) A third group both received and transmitted information, but transmitted only within a narrow radius. Although they were in the midst of the main work area, they failed to communicate with other functional groups because their jobs required constant attention and they felt socially isolated.

In sum, the reasons for group isolation at the Jason Company were: geographical separation; work association (being outside the main procedures or at the end of them); social isolation; and organizational level (the lower the level of a group, the greater its tendency to be isolated).

Obviously, it is not often feasible for management to undertake to remove such causes of group isolation as geographical or social separation. On the other hand, it may well be possible to compensate for them. For example, perhaps the volume of formal communication to men who happen to be in a separate building can be increased, or arrangements can be made for a coffee break that will bring men who are isolated because of the nature of their work or their nationality into greater contact with other supervisors. In each situation management should be able to work out measures that would be appropriate to the individual circumstances.

CONCLUSION

The findings at the Jason Company have yet to be generalized by research in other industries, but they provide these starting points for action:

(1) If management wants more communication among executives and supervisors, one way is to increase the number and effectiveness of the liaison individuals.

(2) It should count on staff executives to be more active than line executives in spreading information.

(3) It should devote more attention to cross-communication—that is, communication between men in different departments. It is erroneous to consider the chain of command as the communication system because it is only one of many influences. Indeed, procedural and social factors are even more important.

(4) It should take steps to compensate for the fact that some groups are "isolated" from communication chains.

(5) It should encourage further research about management grapevines in order to provide managers with a deeper understanding of them and to find new ways of integrating grapevine activities with the objectives of the firm.

(6) "Ecco analysis," the recently developed research approach used at the Jason Company, should be useful for future studies.

If management wants to do a first-class communication job, at this stage it needs fewer medicines and more diagnoses. Communication analysis has now passed beyond "pure research" to a point where it is immediately useful to top management in the individual firm. The patterns of communication that show up should serve to indicate both the areas where communication is most deficient and the channels through which information can be made to flow most effectively.

In particular, no administrator in his right mind would try to abolish the management grapevine. It is as permanent as humanity is. Nevertheless, many administrators have abolished the grapevine from their own minds. They think and act without giving adequate weight to it or, worse, try to ignore it. This is a mistake. The grapevine is a factor to be reckoned with in the affairs of management. The administrator should analyze it and should consciously try to influence it.

EXPLAINING CHANGES: IF YOU DON'T, THE GRAPEVINE WILL

A. S. Hatch

What happens when a subordinate notices a change that he thinks will affect him or the group? He wants to find out as much as possible about the change—particularly if he senses in it a threat, or the possibility of a threat, to his well-being, comfort or security.

The change may be as small as an unusual number of closed-door conferences between the boss and another subordinate, a new employee in the work group or a change in the kind of activity being carried on in part of the work area. Or it may be as large as the installation of automatic equipment in another department.

REPORTS FROM THE GRAPEVINE

Explanations from the grapevine—and these explanations are inevitable —tend to attach sinister, threatening implications to the fragments of information that filter out. Yet all too often these explanations are the first to reach employees who have begun to wonder.

Arriving first, this kind of explanation tends to satisfy the subordinate's sometimes acute need to know and makes him less likely to hear and accept an official explanation that arrives later on. As a general rule, then, any plan for change ought to carry with it plans for communicating it to all who are directly and indirectly concerned as early as possible.

A common reason for withholding any information about a change until the last detail is completed and confirmed is to avoid reporting changes of plan. In some cases handled this way, the change takes place before people are informed about it at all.

Condensed in *Supervisory Management* (April 1967), pp. 38-40, from *IEEE Transactions on Engineering Writing and Speech* (Vol. EWS-9). © 1966 by The Institute of Electrical and Electronics Engineers, Inc., and reprinted with their permission.

But the longer the delay in communicating, the greater the number of people who become involved as the plan for change progresses; and the more people involved, the greater the chance that rumors will spread. Numerous cases involving change indicate that early release of information on the broad purpose of a planned change, with a general comment on its direction, is better than withholding information until details are settled.

Details may follow as they become available; if it becomes necessary to report changes in plan, experience suggests there is often motivational value to be gained in discussing the reasons for the change. In general, there is less to be lost in early communication of available information than there is in holding all communication for want of details.

GETTING THE MESSAGE ACROSS

How should a supervisor go about informing subordinates of a change? He is at a different communication distance from each subordinate—a distance measured by the ease or difficulty of communicating with that subordinate. A further complication is that it's easier for the boss to transmit over these communication lines than for his subordinates to do so—which means that he doesn't always get all the feedback he'd like on how information is received.

How he has handled the factors that affect his communicating relationship with subordinates will help determine how effective he is in telling them about a change, selling them on it if necessary and finding out how they feel about it. Generally, the more uniformity he has established in communicating with his subordinates, the more he will be trusted.

GROUP VS. INDIVIDUAL COMMUNICATION

In most cases, it is better to talk about a change to subordinates in a group, rather than individually. And it helps if this method of communication has been standard procedure. In the usual work group, each employee is quite sensitive to the length of the communication line between him and his boss, and how it compares with the relative length of the lines of each of his co-workers. Such a sensitivity is compounded during periods of change.

The supervisor who has emphasized individual lines of communication to the exclusion of group communication will face more—and wilder

—rumors during such times. Secretiveness, jealousy, politicking and a penchant for gossiping already flourish—encouraged by him. Subordinates are unlikely to cooperate wholeheartedly to help make the change.

On the other hand, the supervisor who has kept his subordinates equally and simultaneously informed on matters of common interest will find the announcement of change a simpler task, acceptance of it more immediate and the group more cooperative in carrying it out.

Emphasis on individual communication, then, tends to emphasize individuality and differences; emphasis on group communication emphasizes common interest and spontaneous cooperation.

This does not mean that the effective supervisor spends all his time in meetings and conferences called for the purpose of sharing information on changes with subordinates. It does mean that he recognizes the motivational value of shared information about a change, and the damage that can result from unequal distribution of information when the reason for the difference is not obvious in the working relationship, or when it is not made clear. He knows what effect being in the dark can have on a subordinate when others are obviously in the know. He is aware that consistent, implied confidential treatment of some group members can create tensions in the group as a whole.

HOW TO MAKE EMPLOYEE PUBLICATIONS PAY OFF

William Scholz

With a few notable exceptions, the answer to the problem of making employee publications pay off might well be both simple and blunt: "Do away with them!"

Coming from a practitioner of employee communication, this may be branded as heresy. But the inescapable fact is that, in the majority of cases, the time, money, and effort presently being expended on employee communication are sizable debit items without a single balancing entry on the black side of the ledger. To paraphrase Sir Winston Churchill, it can truly be said that never have so many words been addressed to so large an audience with so little result.

In *Communication in Management*, Charles Redfield put it more urbanely but no less forcefully: "It is regrettably true that, at a time when the means of communication have reached their greatest development, there is less intelligibility in communication between individuals and groups than at any stage in our history."

One needs only to glance at a typical company publication with its columns of personals and studious avoidance of facts about the business, let alone controversial issues, to have grave misgivings as to the value of the medium as it is presently being used.

Yet, ineffectual as they often are, employee newspapers or magazines are published by practically all large companies and most middle-sized and smaller organizations. As a matter of fact, the enormous sum spent annually by American industry on these publications—well over $100 million—constitutes probably the largest *single* expense item in the whole range of employee relations activity. Further, according to Opinion Research Corp., most of the companies that have employee publications consider them their major channel for getting information to employees. The least expensive form of mass communication to employees, company publications are the only medium of employee communication that

From *Personnel,* XXXII (March 1956), 449-457. Condensed and reprinted by permission of the American Management Association, Inc.

regularly reaches wives and families as well as the employees themselves. It has been estimated that they make their way into 75 million American homes.

Obviously, these publications are so closely interwoven with the entire fabric of employee communication that we cannot seriously consider abandoning them. Quite apart from their already deeply entrenched position as the backbone of employee communication and their as yet unrealized, but enormous, potential as molders of opinion, the fact of the matter is that there is no adequate alternative to them.

Employees are in the process of forming opinions every day—about management, about their company, about the major national issues under debate. If we don't want their attitudes to be based on hearsay, on biased propaganda, or the grapevine, it is up to us to give them the facts from which informed opinions can be drawn.

WHAT EMPLOYEES WANT TO KNOW

After evaluating the communication experience of hundreds of companies and looking at the findings of countless employee opinion polls, the National Association of Manufacturers found that employees want and are interested in getting specific information about:

1. Their company—its background, organization, and general operation; its products and how they are made and used.
2. Company policies—especially new policies affecting themselves and their fellow-workers.
3. Company plans—changes in location, methods or machinery, and how their jobs will be affected by them.
4. Their jobs—how they will be affected by strikes, material shortages, defense needs, etc.
5. How their jobs fit into the scheme of things and their chances for advancement.
6. The outlook for business and the prospects for steady work.
7. The company's income, its profits and losses, and its plans for the future—such as expansion or new products.
8. Should circumstances make layoffs necessary, the reasons why, and how they, as individuals, are affected.

Like most Americans, employees tend to take the material and spiritual benefits of our way of life for granted. They look upon the right to enjoy the fruits of their labor as their due. They are confused by widespread economic and ideological fallacies and are unaware of the forces that threaten us. This places a further obligation on management to provide employees with the information they need to know and understand:

1. The facts about profits.
2. What competition is and how it functions.
3. The basic economic facts of life in terms of their own company's operations—and in terms of their own daily experience.
4. What causes inflation and what can be done to prevent it.
5. How vital it is for them to fulfill their civic responsibilities.
6. The issues in the struggle of freedom and private enterprise vs. government planning and socialism.

To carry out this urgently important job of providing information to employees, their families, and their neighbors, calls for not just a single medium like an employee newspaper but a broad-scale, continuous employee communication *program* using a variety of media.

SOME QUESTIONS FOR MANAGEMENT

As a first step toward making employee publications pay off we must obtain frank answers to such questions as these posed by Hugh Forster, Public Relations Manager of Armstrong Cork Company:

What are we trying to accomplish through our employee communications? What is their basic purpose—their justification for the expense they involve? Are we trying to get employees to vote Republican, to build morale—make employees happy and satisfied with their jobs? Are we trying to justify our business system, explain the role of profits, arouse sympathetic understanding of the business or management point of view? Do we want to combat the propaganda of organized labor, eliminate employee grievances, slowdowns, strikes?

Though many of these objectives may be parts of our overall goal, the basic purposes of employee communication are to facilitate the profitable operation of the business and to promote the understanding, approval, and support of the employees of its objectives and the free market system in which it operates. If communications don't achieve this, they're not paying their way.

If it is to pay off, a communication program necessitates an appraisal of employees' knowledge and attitudes, ascertaining what gaps to fill in and what to correct, and fixing priorities and sequences.

How do we regard employee communications? Do we look upon them as a gadget or an accessory—something we do because everyone seems to be doing it? Is it a function delegated to one particular department, something that can be turned on and off like a faucet?

Employee communications should be regarded as an integral part of purposeful management toward a specific objective—profit. They should be woven into the fabric of day-to-day operations at all levels and cannot be divorced from operations any more than they can be delegated to one department.

Is the environment of our company in harmony with our communications? Do our operating policies and practices conflict with the statements we make to employees? Do we claim that performance is rewarded, yet promote on straight seniority, or politics, or something other than skill or ability?

Environment determines the effectiveness of our communications. Our words will be effective only to the degree that our actions are in agreement with them.

Do we mistake the media of communication for the ideas to be communicated? Do we feel that the mere fact of having a company magazine is the answer to our communication problem, rather than the quality of the publication itself? Are we deluding ourselves by being smug about having employee meetings, yet paying too little attention to who conducts them or what subjects are discussed? Do we think that letters to employees' homes will be good, no matter how they are written or what subjects they treat?

The ideas to be communicated and the manner in which they are expressed are far more important than the actual media used to carry them. We shouldn't assume that simply because we have a magazine, plant newspaper, or management news letter, illustrated annual reports, employee meetings, information racks, and the rest of it, that we are doing a good communications job. We *could* be doing a terrible, even a harmful one.

Are we prone to imitate rather than innovate? Do we start a communication project merely because we heard that another company used it successfully, or do we analyze our own particular problems and then determine what we should do and how we should do it?

Are our people accustomed to getting their information orally, or reading it? Do we have now, or are we willing to hire, top-flight writers capable of putting together an effective employee publication? Is management willing to discuss openly in it the vital facts about our business which would make it worth reading or must its contents be limited to the innocuous platitudes so frequently found in company magazines? Are our publications designed to be a vital, useful tool to achieve the objectives of management—or are they simply another employee perquisite whose sole aim is to entertain?

Do we try to measure objectively the effectiveness of our communication efforts? Do we check up on ourselves or are we so proud of our handiwork that we assume it's good just because we are doing it? Is our overall communication program helping our business to run smoothly and earn a satisfactory profit?

WHAT BETTER COMMUNICATION CAN ACHIEVE

The mere spending of time, talent, and money does not automatically assure an effective communication effort. We must have specific objectives, we must employ the appropriate media effectively, and, finally, we should be able to show a profit in terms of the results that have been obtained in relation to the effort expended.

Among the *results* we might reasonably expect from improved communication with employees are:

1. Better coordination of the organization: a clarification of the responsibility of organizational components and individual workers; avoidance of confusion, duplication, and conflict; improved functioning of interrelated work operations through common knowledge of relationships.

2. Improved individual performance through the development of intelligent participation gained from a knowledge of objectives and workings of the whole enterprise in relationship to individual responsibility.

3. Improved morale: a greater sense of identification on the part of individual employees with the interests of the company, which carries over into community and public relations; improved personal outlook and orientation in general through a better understanding of the social, economic, and political conditions of the environment and through better citizenship.

4. Improved consumer relations: uniform, prompt, and correct service resulting from knowledge of company policies, practices, and standards; wholesome, constructive, and promotional relationships with consumers arising from a sense of identification with and self-interest in the company.

5. Improved industrial relations—employees fully informed as to management's problems are better able to give balanced consideration to issues in labor negotiations.

It is admittedly difficult, perhaps even impossible, to determine and prove conclusively just how important a part effective communication plays in improving employee relations and contributing to a company's profit. It would be the height of naivete to try to prove that a full-blown employee communication program, let alone one particular medium, was a panacea for all of management's troubles. Yet impressive evidence exists that employee communication *does* pay off.

As *The Wall Street Journal* recently pointed out:

Efforts to keep the communications line open in both directions seem to be paying off for many corporate enterprises, large and small. Management spokesmen testify they have improved rates of production, headed off labor disputes, and cut down on worker turnover by adopting a two-way policy of talking and listening.

A number of company managements, including those of General Electric Company and Standard Oil of New Jersey, claim the development of good internal communications has been largely responsible for their recent peaceful relations with unions and better performance by workers.

PROFIT-MAKING OPPORTUNITIES FOR EMPLOYEE PUBLICATIONS

At General Electric we have isolated nine specific areas where effective communication, primarily through the use of employee newspapers and letters to employees' homes, can be made to pay off:

1. *During union negotiations, to gain solid support for the company's efforts to reach agreement without a strike. . . .*
2. *When strikes do occur, to get employees back to work. . . .*
3. *In union representation elections, to give all employees full information on which to base a sound decision. . . .*
4. *To maintain high participation in all employee benefit plans and to gain the good will inherent in the company's contribution to these plans. . . .*
5. *To promote health and safety and to improve the safety record. . . .*
6. *To increase productivity and reduce losses. . . .*
7. *To develop teamwork, by speeding the flow of information at all levels. . . .*
8. *To gain the confidence and support of plant community neighbors. . . .*
9. *To help protect management's right to manage the business. . . .*

SOME NEEDED IMPROVEMENTS

Certainly, it must be said that part of the secret of making employee publications pay off lies in improving both their appearance and their literary quality. Much more attention needs to be given to these basic principles:

1. Provide reader reward. Communicate useful information, important news, facts with a "pocketbook appeal."

2. Minimize mental work. State the central idea clearly and directly, graphically if possible.
3. Offer validation. Prove assertions with photographs, statistics, testimonials, quotations from experts, etc.

The real touchstone of success in employee communication, however, is in having the wisdom to set challenging objectives and the courage to pursue them relentlessly. Like the farmer who refused to subscribe to an agricultural magazine because "he wasn't farming half as well as he already knew how to," management's primary communication problem is not one of mechanics, but one of dynamics.

Communication, in the experience of many companies, is not a way to *spend*, but rather a way to *make* money. They have learned that a good communication program, coupled with sound operating and human relations practices, can integrate and motivate the entire management team, help develop supervisors as real leaders, inculcate favorable employee attitudes, and build employee confidence in top management. It can pay dividends in increased output, reduction of waste and spoilage, and avoidance of costly resistance to changing technology. And it can drastically reduce the most unnecessary losses of all—the tragic lost earnings and profits from slowdowns, walkouts, and strikes.

Improved attitudes, productivity, quality, and profits are the ultimate pay-off of a good communication program.

IN CONFERENCE
Robert F. Bales

There is a widespread interest in the process of decision making among executives in business, the military, government, research, civic affairs —indeed, in every sort of organization set up to produce anything by cooperation. Technical experts are called in to give advice; management committees must decide on basic policies; labor teams must plan and regulate their work; staff meetings take place daily at every level. Decision making is the pinpoint focus of the vast social machinery that makes up our democratic society and its economy.

Most decisions are made "in conference." Then they normally require a long series of further conferences for their implementation. Probably no serious estimate has ever been made of the total number of hours American businessmen spend per year "in conference." But the number must be astronomical.

COMMITTEE OPERATION

Yet think how little we know about the actual operation of a committee, and how little we are able to predict or control its success or failure. Many a "good idea" has emerged at the other end of the committee operation as a kind of "bad dream," mangled and amputated in its essentials, patched together with fantasies into a monster that finally dies at the hands of some committee further on down the line. It is no matter for wonder that committee meetings are often viewed with mixed feelings of apprehension and cynical humor. . . .

DIRECT EXPERIMENTS

One aspect of this broad front of scientific development is the direct experimental study of committee meetings where decisions are made.

Not many years ago nobody seriously supposed that the subtle as-

Condensed from *Harvard Business Review* (March-April 1954), pp. 44-50. © 1954 by The President and Fellows of Harvard College; all rights reserved.

pects of face-to-face human relations could be studied experimentally in the laboratory. All sorts of skeptical objections appeared, even among social scientists, when a few of their more hopeful colleagues began to set up small groups of subjects under laboratory conditions and study social behavior by direct observation. Now a number of such laboratories are in operation, and findings of possible practical importance are beginning to appear.

One of the early installations was set up by the Laboratory of Social Relations at Harvard University in 1947. This laboratory and some of its findings will serve as an illustration of the type of research now going on in a number of centers:

On the third floor of Harvard's Emerson Hall there is a specially designed room for the purpose of observing the operation of committees and similar types of small groups. Containing chairs and a table which can be varied in size, it is well lighted and surfaced in acoustic tile. On one wall is a chalkboard and on another a large mirror. Behind the mirror is an observation room, for in reality the mirror is a one-way glass through which a team of observers on the other side may watch without disturbing the subjects. While the subject group is aware that it is being watched, the illusion is such that any self-consciousness is only brief and the "mirror" is ignored and soon forgotten.

The groups vary in size from two to seven members, depending on the particular problem under discussion. The problem for discussion may be industrial, governmental, military, or educational in character, but in any case it has to do with administration and requires a decision or recommendation of some kind.

During the discussion the observers behind the "mirror" note the action within the group: who speaks, to whom he speaks, and how he speaks. The actual subject matter is not the primary concern, except as it indicates the speaker's feelings.

An ingenious machine, built by the laboratory, makes it easy for the observer to classify each statement as it is made. Observers are trained until they are able to classify within a second or so any remark that is made into one of 12 descriptive categories. (Originally there were 87 categories of response, but gradually the list has been reduced to 12.) In addition, the conversation is sound-recorded for later checking.

Each experimental group takes part in 4 sessions of 40 minutes each. By the end of this time, an accurate appraisal of the way in which it operates *as a group* is possible, and the relationships between members can be predicted with some confidence should it ever meet again.

KINDS OF BEHAVIOR

All the behavior that goes on in a committee (or, indeed, in any verbal interchange) can be viewed as a sequence of questions, answers, and positive and negative reactions to the questions and answers. Three types of questions are distinguished: *asking for information, opinion, and suggestion.* Corresponding to these three types of questions are three types of answers: *giving information, opinion,* and *suggestion.* These answers are problem-solving attempts, and they call for reactions. Negative reactions include: *showing disagreement, tension,* or *antagonism.* On the positive side the corresponding reactions include: *showing agreement, tension release,* and *friendly solidarity.* These are the 12 categories of remarks used as a basis of analysis in the Harvard experiments.

SUCCESSFUL DECISIONS

It is interesting to note that, on the average, about 50% of all remarks made in meetings are answers while the remaining 50% consist of questions and reactions. Such a 50-50 balance (or something close to it) may be one characteristic of successful communication. Problem-solving attempts are needed to reach a decision, but that is not all. It may very well be that if enough time is not regularly allowed also for questioning and reaction to occur in the meeting, the members will carry away tensions that will eventually operate to vitiate an apparently successful but actually superficial decision.

PARTICIPATION OF MEMBERS

A decision is not a successful decision unless each member who is supposed to have been involved in its making is actually bound by it in such a way that his later behavior conforms to it.

By and large, members do not seem to feel strongly bound by a decision unless they have participated in making it. However, participation does not necessarily mean that each member has to talk an equal amount. As a matter of fact, even approximate equality of actual talking time among members is very rare; and, when it does appear, it is usually associated with a free-for-all conflict. A moderate gradient among members in talking time is the more usual thing.

More significantly, participation means that the meeting operates under the presumption that each member has an equal right to ask questions or voice negative or positive reactions to any proposal made, if he wishes, and a right to expect that, if he makes a proposal, it will receive an appropriate reaction from some other member. Because of time exigencies, most members, most frequently, allow a voiced proposal to represent what they themselves would say, and a voiced reaction to represent what they themselves might respond.

On the other hand, it is difficult to know when a member's feelings and interests are being adequately represented and when they are not. The difference is so subtle that he himself is not always able to tell. He may go away dissatisfied without knowing quite why. Hence there is probably no adequate substitute for some actual verbal participation of each member. A few words on his part will serve to express and solidify his involvement, and to avoid his subsequent dissatisfaction.

OPTIMUM BALANCE

There are about twice as many positive reactions in most meetings as there are negative reactions. One might suppose that the more successful the meeting, the fewer negative reactions and the more positive reactions one would find. But the evidence does not support this view. Rather, there appears to be a kind of optimum balance. Departures too far to either side are indicators of trouble.

Disagreement. Rates of disagreement and antagonism that are too high are sure indicators of trouble. Apparently, when ill feeling rises above some critical point, a "chain reaction" or "vicious circle" tends to set in. Logic and the practical demands of the task cease to be governing factors. Such an occurrence is an impressive experience when seen from the perspective of the observer behind the one-way glass in the laboratory:

The observer is unseen by the subjects, cannot communicate with them, and so in a basic sense is "not involved." He knows that no action will be taken on the decision of the committee. He may have heard the same case discussed hundreds of times before. Nevertheless, he is "caught in the illusion of reality" as the temperature of the group begins to rise.

Suddenly the credulity of the observer is strained beyond some critical point. The illusion that the group is dealing with some external problem breaks. It becomes perfectly transparent—to the observer—that emotions have taken over, and that what one member is saying does not refer at all to some external situation but to himself and the other members present.

"Facts" are unwittingly invented or are falsified. Other facts drop out of sight entirely. When one member insists that "people in this office should be treated like human beings," it is clear that he refers to himself and how he feels he should be treated in this group. When his opponent insists that "troublemakers should be fired," it is equally clear that he refers to the man who just spoke to him.

The decision, if any, reached by a group in this state has all the characteristics of a "bad dream," indeed.

Agreement. There can also be too many agreements and too few disagreements. This condition may be an indication either of lack of involvement in the practical demands of the task or of an atmosphere so in-hibited and constrained that nobody dares risk disagreement. In the ordinary mill run of opinions and suggestions, there is always a certain percentage so unrealistic, exaggerated, or unsuitable that not to disagree means not to solve the problem.

Closely related to the rate of agreement is the rate of suggestion. Groups in a smoothly operating condition tend to show relatively high rates of suggestion, as well as of agreement. But there is a joker in this finding. This condition is an *outcome* of smooth sailing, *not* a way to attain it.

As most people would suppose, giving facts is fairly safe. The prob-ability of arousing disagreement by reviewing the facts of the case is relatively low. But giving opinions is more risky, for in so doing a man gives his inferences and expresses his feelings and values, including his prejudices. Others are more likely to disagree, and the means of re-solving disagreements are much more vague and indirect than in the case of disputed facts.

Indeed, a suggestion can cause a real bottleneck. If a man agrees to the suggestion, he must embrace all it implies, assumes, or involves. He has bound himself to future action. Most people are quite sensitive to this kind of constriction, even though they know that a decision is necessary. That is why, as the rate of giving suggestions goes up, the rate of negative reactions also tends to increase.

REDUCING THE RISK

Of course suggestions are necessary before a decision is reached. The decision point is inevitably a crisis point. But this is the risk that all decision-making groups have to take. The wise strategist should seek to reduce his risks to a calculated minimum, which is something quite different from trying to escape them entirely.

But how? The laboratory observations suggest a reasonable solution. Most successful groups go through an ordered series of three phases or stages in the solution of a problem:

(1) They attempt to assemble the largest possible pool of common information about the facts of the case.

(2) They make inferences and evaluations, and try to form common opinions in a general way.

(3) Only in the final phase do they get around to more specific sug-gestions, after an extensive groundwork has been laid.

Not all groups do this, by any means. Some start the other end to, and some start with an outburst of opinions before they ever look at a fact. Indeed, many of the members are hardly conscious of any difference between a fact and an opinion.

It is probably not any excess of wisdom or extraordinary sensitivity that produces the typical order of stages. It is rather, we may suppose, the "brute logic of natural selection." A suggestion given at a premature stage simply dies for lack of support, or is trampled to death in the general melee. Gradually the discussion is forced back to facts, where agreement can be reached.

In an environment barren of consensus, only a fact can survive; and, where there is hostility, even facts find a slim foothold. But a rich background of common facts lays the groundwork for the development of common inferences and sentiments, and out of these common decisions can grow. No decision rests on "facts" alone, but there is no better starting point. To start the decision-making process at any other point is to multiply the risk of a vicious circle of disagreement—and at no saving of time in the long run.

DUAL LEADERSHIP

One of the most startling implications of the laboratory research so far is that the concept of "leader," if it is taken too literally, can cause the man who thinks he is one to disregard a most important fact—namely, that there is usually *another* leader in the group whom he can overlook only at his peril.

SEPARATE ROLES

The laboratory findings, while still tentative, indicate that the man who is judged by the group members to have the "best ideas" contributing to the decision is *not* generally the "best-liked." There are two separate roles—that of task leader and that of social leader. If a man comes into a task-leadership position because he is popular or best liked, he is ordinarily confronted with a choice: (1) If he chooses to try to keep the task leadership of the group, he tends to lose some of his popularity and to collect some dislikes. (2) If he chooses to try to keep his popularity, he tends to lose the task leadership. People differ in the way they solve this dilemma, although most tend to prefer to keep the popularity rather than the task leadership.

The difficulty becomes more acute with time. At the end of the group's first meeting there is 1 chance in 2 that the task leader will be the most liked. At the end of the second meeting the chances are reduced to 1 in 4. At the end of the third they are 1 in 6, and at the end of the fourth they are only 1 in 7.

There are apparently few men who can hold both roles; instead, the tendency is for these positions to be held by two different men. Each is in reality a leader, and each is important to the stability of the group. The task leader helps to keep the group engaged in the work, but the pressure of decision and work tends to provoke irritation and injure the unity of the group. The best-liked man helps to restore this unity and to keep the members of the group aware of their importance as particular individuals, whose special needs and values are respected. These men complement each other, and they are both necessary for smooth operation of a committee.

It is especially important for these two men to recognize each other's roles and in effect to form a coalition. The most stable groups observed have been those in which this coalition has taken place. There are indications that such durable groups as the family and simple small communities are constructed this way, and apparently the coalition also takes place in many administrative staffs, sometimes consciously but more often accidentally.

These findings challenge some very basic concepts of leadership. Millions are spent each year by business, government, and the armed forces in developing means for recognizing leaders, and much has been written about the "characteristics" of leadership. Yet it appears that whatever superior qualities the individual may possess as a single individual, he may be unable, just because of the way groups work, to maintain a stable leadership position without a co-leader of complementary qualities.

COMMUNICATION NETWORKS

Significantly, among the half-dozen instances where the observation room and equipment at the Harvard laboratory have been duplicated are several installations by the military:

The Air Force has built a room at Maxwell Field, Alabama, for testing and predicting leadership ability. Other divisions of the armed forces are also engaged in the same kind of experimentation, for one of the most pressing problems they face is the development of leaders and the selection of personnel who have to work in small groups—bomber and submarine crews, intelligence teams, and communications centers—particularly in situations where immediate processing of information and rapid but wise decisions are a tactical necessity.

One of the persistent problems in rapid communications networks such as those found in military defense is how to keep the actual control over critical decisions in the hands of the person or persons who will later bear the formal responsibility for the decision. Practically, the decision-making function on the tactical level tends to gravitate to the person who is at the center of the communication network, where information about the tactical situation is immediately available. But this tactical information center tends not to coincide with the top spot in the chain of command, where formal authority and responsibility are centered.

Here again is an instance where it is unrealistic to operate with a simple notion of a single "leader" in whom all essential leadership functions can be vested. Although this problem appears most clearly in larger organizations, it is essentially a large-scale version of the same tendency toward division of labor in leadership that can be seen in a committee.

COMMITTEE MEMBERSHIP

If all this is true, the emphasis should shift from seeking the ideal leader to trying to compose the ideal total group. Accordingly, at Harvard the next few years will be devoted to observing groups for the specific purpose of assessing the personnel, and then attempting actually to compose new committees from them which will function in a predicted way. With the right kind of assessment of each person's action within a group, it may be possible to pick, say, two people who would appear to be complementary leaders, put them with three more "neutral" people, and thus form a committee which would theoretically function at a certain predicted level of effectiveness. This at least is a start in the direction of rational composition of total groups.

OPTIMUM SIZE

Just to take one of the elementary problems, the question of optimum size of a committee has received many interesting answers, but so far they seem to come mostly from numerology rather than from scientific research. For the particular task and time limits given to subjects in the Harvard laboratory, five seems to be the preferred number. Below that size subjects begin to complain that the group is too small, and above it that the group is too large. The fact that there is a distinct "saddle point" at five suggests that the notion of an optimum size is meaningful, if the task, time, and other circumstances are well enough specified. But the optimum size must surely vary according to conditions.

There seems to be a crucial point at seven. Below seven, for the most part, each person in the group says at least something to each other person. In groups over seven the low participators tend to stop talking to each other and center their communications on the few top men. The tendencies toward centralization of communication seem to increase rather powerfully as size increases.

At the same time, there are certain difficulties inherent in groups of as low as two and three members. In a two-man group no majority short of unanimity can form. Each person can exercise a complete veto over the other. One person can exercise power quite as effectively by simply refusing to react as he can by making suggestions, and this tendency toward withdrawal of one member appears with some frequency.

In a three-man group the tendency of two to form a combination against the third seems fairly strong. If this happens, the would-be task leader may be overcautious because he knows that, if his lieutenant disagrees with him, he may be left in the minority. The lieutenant knows he has this power but that, if he exercises it, the third man may step in to take his place. The third man on the outside of the coalition is left powerless whether he agrees or disagrees, so long as the other two agree, and tends either to withdraw or set up a damaging but unsuccessful protest. It is hard for a three-man group to have a "healthy" amount of disagreement. The structure is too sensitive to disagreement, and therefore it tends to an all-or-none extreme.

RECOMMENDATIONS

It is important to realize that basic research is a long, slow process which really cannot be short-cut by concentration on the need for practical results. Some of the generalizations ventured above actually go somewhat beyond the base of firmly established facts, and all of them should be taken with a generous grain of salt in any attempted application, since circumstances alter cases. With proper precautions, however, a summary of "rules of thumb" may be helpful in pinpointing some possible applications based on the experience of observing many laboratory groups:

(1) Avoid appointing committees larger than seven members unless necessary to obtain representation of all relevant points of view. Try to set up conditions of size, seating, and time allowed so that each member has an adequate opportunity to communicate directly with each other member.

(2) Avoid appointing committees as small as two or three members if the power problem between members is likely to be critical.

(3) Choose members who will tend to fall naturally into a moderate gradient of participation. Groups made up of all high participators will tend to suffer from competition. Groups made up of all lows may find themselves short on ideas.

(4) Avoid the assumption that a good committee is made up of one good "leader" and several "followers." Try to provide the group with both a task leader and a social leader, who will support each other. It is probably not a bad idea to include a "humorist" if the social leader does not have a light touch. A few strong but more silent men add judicious balance to the group.

A group of otherwise balanced composition can probably absorb one "difficult" member—one of the type, for example, who talks too much, is short on problem-solving ability, tends to arouse dislikes, and cannot be changed by ordinary social pressures. If such a member must be included, probably the best strategy is to "surround" him.

(5) In actual procedure, start with facts if possible. Even where the facts are thought to be well known to all the members, a short review is seldom a waste of time. A good general procedure is probably to plan to deal with three questions on each major agenda item:

"What are the facts pertaining to the problem?"

"How do we feel about them?"

"What shall we do about the problem?"

This is probably the preferred order. Take time to lay the groundwork before getting to specific suggestions, the third stage. It may be noted, by the way, that the order recommended is the exact opposite of that which is characteristic of formal parliamentary procedure.

(6) Solicit the opinions and experiences of others, especially when disagreements begin to crop up. People often think they disagree when actually they simply are not talking about the same experiences. In such cases they do not draw each other out far enough to realize that, although they are using the same *words*, they are thinking about different experiences. Try to get past the words and general statements the other man uses to the experiences he is trying to represent. Members of the group may agree with his experiences.

(7) When somebody else is talking, listen, and keep indicating your reactions actively. Most people are not much good at reading your mind. Besides that, they need the recognition you can give them by your honest reaction, whether positive or negative.

(8) Keep your eyes on the group. When you are talking, talk to the group as a whole rather than to one of your cronies or to one of your special opponents. Search around constantly for reactions to what you are saying. A good deal of communication goes on at a subverbal level. Nothing tones up the general harmony of a group like a good strong undercurrent of direct eye contact.

(9) When you scent trouble coming up, break off the argument and backtrack to further work on the facts and direct experience. In some instances the best way to get started on a cooperative track again after a period of difficulty is to agree to go out and gather some facts together by direct experience.

(10) Keep your ear to the ground. No recipe or set of rules can substitute for constant, sensitive, and sympathetic attention to what is going on in the relations between members. Do not get so engrossed in getting the job done that you lose track of what is the first prerequisite of success —keeping the committee in good operating condition.

STOP MISUSING YOUR MANAGEMENT MEETINGS

Your meetings are not an activity in themselves. They are a tool—a communications tool for getting action results in the plant. Plenty has been written about meetings. Much of it critical of the meeting as a time waster, a social event, a private soap-box, or an opportunity to dilute individual responsibility. But the meeting is potentially one of your most effective and productive management devices, if you understand its dynamics and expolit its possibilities.

Following are 10 rules to help you focus on the meeting process. If you understand and practice them, your meetings will be smoother. And you should notice an improvement in your action results in the plant:

1. PLAN TO SOLVE A PROBLEM – NOT TO HOLD A MEETING

The cost of a meeting—in wages and salaries alone—can be terrific. So don't waste time drifting. Plan. Know why you want to call a meeting. Ask yourself:
- What's the problem?
- What are the related facts?
- How can we solve the problem?

Too often we think we're planning when we're finding a good meeting place, checking on time and availability of members, and setting the date. But this is scheduling, not planning. The time you spend asking yourself hard questions—not about the meeting but about the problem—can be a real money saver.

2. USE THE MEETING AS A TOOL

There are good and bad reasons for calling a meeting—and you should know the difference. The basis for your use of meetings (or your neglect of them) may be worth questioning. A meeting is only one of several communications tools. Other tools are often just as good or better. Telephones, for instance. Or memos. Or private conversations.

A meeting may also be used as an escape or excuse. Ask yourself these questions from time to time:

- Is a meeting really necessary to accomplish this task?
- Could I get this job done at some other meeting, later?
- Am I calling this meeting to get some listeners and increase my own sense of importance? To get other people to do my homework for me? To pass the buck on responsibility?

Here are some good occasions for calling a meeting:

- When you must be sure your message will be understood. Most managers have experimented rather widely with written communications and are aware of the limitations of this one-way method.
- When you want to get subordinates' reactions and stimulate two-way communications. By himself, a subordinate is bound to tell you what he thinks you want to hear. In a meeting, he'll gang up with others and tell you the facts.
- When you need more facts or expert opinions.
- When you need creative new ideas, approaches, and solutions. The clash of ideas in a group can often produce superior solutions.
- When you must depend on others to carry out decisions. It's well known that people support what they help create.
- When you want to build better teamwork. Don't restrict meetings to crises. Members need to feel they have a part in the creation and growth of their organization.

3. PICK EACH MEMBER AS A RESOURCE

Think twice before you flip the switch to call your "kitchen cabinet" into a meeting. When you've got a problem, "Smith," "Jones," and "Green" may first come to your mind. The reason you call them may be that they are the smartest, quickest, and best informed members of your organization. Or is it because they can do you the most good in your future? Or because they usually agree with you? You should make sure you have good reasons for calling in these men.

But, depending on the problem, there are compelling reasons why you should call in various other kinds of people, without regard for their rank, age, position, or even whether you like them or not:

- The idea man. Maybe not all his ideas are good, but they may stimulate thinking.
- The company's informal "communicator." He seems always to know everything that's going on throughout the shop.

- The compromiser, who can help smooth things over.
- The technical expert.
- The man who should give his "blessing" to the project. He has informal power.
- The guy who has all the facts.
- A key member of the department that might block this project.

Representatives from interested groups (foremen or unions) who could help sell the project.

But it's important to be clear about what happens to a meeting each time you add a new member. According to communications experts, you're not merely ADDING to the complexity of the group—you are MULTIPLYING its complexity. A good rule of thumb is this: Use all the people you need as resources. But make it the minimum number.

4. SEE YOUR MEETING AS OTHERS SEE IT

When your members are with you—really going along with what you're trying to do in a meeting—the job is easy. But you can't assume this will happen automatically. Too often the members have other purposes in attending your meeting. They have other goals in mind. And they may work at cross-purposes to your meeting goals unless you do something about them—both before and during the meeting.

Before the meeting you might take these steps:
- Send the members the problem in advance. Ask them to do some thinking about it. Ask for plans, approaches, and possible holes in your plan.
- Distribute a tentative agenda. Ask for comments or additions to it. Be sure you acknowledge contributions when you meet.
- Brief members on the meeting and ask them to take action beforehand, such as preparing statistics or getting a few reactions to an idea.

Don't assume that announcing the agenda beforehand will eliminate conflicting interests at the meeting. Deal with them again at the start of the meeting. One way of handling this, especially in regular staff meetings, is through the use of "agenda budgeting." Here's a good procedure for budgeting an agenda:
- Use chart pad or blackboard to list agenda items you've selected for the meeting.
- Ask members for additional items they'd like to have covered.
- Help the group decide what priorities to give each item, labeling them, for example, as: urgent; important, today; important, this week; individual attention.
- Work with the group to budget time to be spent on each item.
- Review and revise time budgets during the meeting.

You may find that this joint agenda setting may take six or seven minutes. But this time spent in getting squared away for even an hour-long meeting is a worthwhile expenditure in "getting your people with you."

5. DON'T TOLERATE LATE ATTENDANCE, INTERRUPTIONS, ETC.

To set up ground rules, do these things before the meeting:
- Give at least 48 hours' notice of time and place. Impossible? You'd be surprised how often it can be done. And the number of "emergencies" somehow decreases.
- Tell how long the meeting will last. How can you tell? Once you start predicting, you'll become more and more accurate. Many men can tell within minutes.
- Tell exactly why the meeting is called. A good reason can make a lot of difference in the attitudes of those attending.
- Tell what the meeting is expected to accomplish. Don't say, "To discuss a new product." That's too vague. Say: "To set up production schedules for Model 7A."
- Tell each man why he's invited and what he's expected to do. Don't hamstring people with rigid assignments, but suggest beforehand: "Jones, would you be ready to look at this in terms of possible production snags?" "Rogers, would you just listen in? You'll be facing this problem next year."

And here's what you can do at the meeting:
- Insist on prompt attendance. And always be on time yourself for your own and others' meetings.
- Don't allow phone interruptions. Have calls held for answering at breaks or right after meetings.
- Have the meeting room checked beforehand for ventilation, quiet, paper, and pencils.
- Arrange the seating to fit the meeting.

6. SHARE THE RESPONSIBILITY FOR STARTING OUT RIGHT

The more important the meeting, the more concerned you may become about starting it off well. But the more concerned you get, the more likely you are to start off wrong. Why? First, because you're worried. And probably taking all the responsibility on yourself. You're not thinking about letting the other members share this responsibility. So they're not thinking about how they can help.

A second trap is related to the first. Maybe you're over-prepared. In your concern for the job, you forget to consider the feelings of these other members.

Much depends on your faith in the group's ability to solve problems, and your willingness to let them take the bull by the horns. There are a number of specific things you can do to avoid these two traps:
- Be sure everyone clearly understands the long-range objectives—where this meeting fits into the larger picture.
- Restate just what the meeting is for.
- Tell each person (again) just why he is there.
- Inform everybody of the meeting plan before you work on the agenda.

But don't be a mother hen. It's easy to over-plan what each member should do. After a general briefing, let members be flexible about how they participate.

7. CHANGE YOUR LEADER STYLE TO FIT THE TYPE OF MEETING

Meetings fall generally into five major categories. For each category you'll find one style of chairmanship is usually best:

Meetings for information giving—Addressing civic groups and explaining directives call for autocratic leadership because it's from you to them with no need for reactions.
- Meetings for information collecting—Interviewing employees, hearing union committee opinions, and getting reports call for shared leadership because lots of participation is important to get the facts. Members stimulate each other.
- Meetings for decision making—Planning a cost reduction program or setting up a work schedule calls for shared leadership because each member can perform useful functions, and follow-up is needed.
- Decision-selling—Getting acceptance of new organization set-up passed down by the front office calls for autocratic and shared leadership. Autocratic with regard to the decision, shared with regard to carrying it out. Again, commitments to action are needed.
- Meetings for problem-solving—Helping each other find the best ways to handle subordinates calls for shared leadership because it requires flexibility and the use of all resources available.

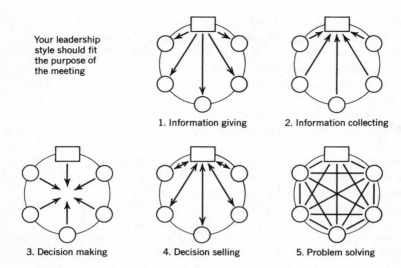

Your leadership
style should fit
the purpose of
the meeting

1. Information giving   2. Information collecting

3. Decision making   4. Decision selling   5. Problem solving

A meeting is a group of individuals interacting with each other in some pretty complex ways to try to get a job done. So it is vital that they stick together as a group and develop teamwork en route to the goal. What's more, most meetings don't reach the ultimate goal *at the meeting*, but later on, in actions back on the job. If a member is not really on the team during the meeting, he's less likely to do his share in carrying out the decision afterwards. So hold the group together.

Some aids to this objective:
• Help quiet members participate.
• Compliment the group on the progress it is making.
• Relieve the tension with a joke or story.
• Mediate arguments.

8. HARNESS MANY SKILLS
TO GET GOOD DECISIONS

Studies of the way decisions are made in meetings reveal that many groups, often at high levels, do a distressingly poor job of decision-making. To test your performance, keep tabs on the movements of decision-making meetings through these five phases:
• Pinning down the problem.
• Collecting information.
• Finding alternative solutions.
• Testing alternatives.
• Determining action.

Of course no meeting group is likely to proceed logically and systematically from the first to the last phase. But if your group jumps almost immediately to the last phase without further defining and redefining the problem, or concerning itself about facts, it will be behaving immaturely—the way many groups do in meetings.

Here are some factors that often tend to block good decisions—ask yourself if they affect your meetings:

• Grabbing at the first few alternatives suggested on the assumption they're the only ones.

• Jumping to a decision without testing it.

• Asking people to make a decision without data.

• Failing to *build in* an action commitment.

• Placing decision responsibility too high.

• Having the leader state his position too soon.

• Failing to take an experimental attitude. This is from a fear of failure —"Let's not take chances."

Below are six functions, all necessary parts of the decision-making process at your meetings. Ask yourself questions like these:

1. *Defining the problem*—How well was the information assembled? Was the importance of the problem really understood?

2. *Clarifying*—Was questioning encouraged? Were members asked to help clarify the problem?

3. *Keeping discussion on the beam*—Were members concerned about staying on the subject? Were temporary digressions permitted?

4. *Summarizing*—Who did the summarizing? Did he come in at the right time?

5. *Testing consequences of the emerging decision*—How did we know when we were ready for a decision? What checks were made on the decision's realities?

6. *Decision-making*—How was the decision made: Majority vote? Consensus? Silent consent?

9. DIAGNOSE AND TREAT THE HIDDEN AGENDAS

Long experience confirms the fact that even the best of people—when you get them together—do not always work logically or react intelligently. Below are some useful clues to this mystery. Dr. Leland P. Bradford, director of the National Training Laboratories, claims it results from a meeting's "Hidden Agendas."

"Groups work simultaneously and continuously on two levels," says Dr. Bradford. "One level is formally labeled. . . . This is the obvious, advertised purpose for which the group meets.

"Unlabeled, private, covered, but deeply felt and very much the concern of the group, is the other level. Here are the conflicting motives, desires, aspirations, and emotional reactions of the group members . . . problems which, for a variety of reasons, cannot be laid on top of the table—the Hidden Agendas."

Groups work hard on either or both of these agendas. A group may have been working hard on its surface agenda and getting nowhere. Suddenly it starts to move efficiently on its appointed job and quickly reaches a conclusion. Explanation: The group had to work on its hidden agenda and get it out of the way before it could go to work on its real job.

Some typical hidden agendas:
• The plant manager has a hip-pocket solution to the production-line problem being discussed. He wants the production planning committee to buy his solution. He waits his chance to slip it into the discussion. But meanwhile his mind is closed to everything else.
• The sales manager is in a meeting to discuss quality problems. Some of the problems are caused by errors in specifications made in the engineering department, which is managed by his best friend. Although he's not present, the engineering manager is an "invisible member" of the meeting.
• When a new committee is formed, even among people who know each other, each individual is concerned with his place in the group. Each wants to know what's expected of him and how far he should move. And depending on how important the group is to him, this need for respect or position or power will be more or less intense. Hidden agendas are almost always at work in these opening moments of a new committee's first meeting.

You need to be equally aware of the effect hidden agendas of various kinds may have on you in the leading role.

Hidden agendas often relate to you and your leadership. A man may compete with you (often without realizing it) for influence over the others. He may feel hostile to all leaders. He unconsciously may be dependent on you, need to lean on you. Another may support you because you have power to aid a special interest of his.

The group itself may have a hidden agenda in relation to you, the leader. (Ask yourself: Are you *really* its leader?)

Finally, of course, you may have your own hidden agendas. One of these may be your (carefully hidden) desire to box the ears of a subordinate. Another may be a hip-pocket solution to the problem at hand. Still another may be your need to maintain leadership at any cost.

Here are several ways of approaching hidden agendas:
• Be alert to their presence.
• Keep in mind that the meeting operates at two levels. Don't always

expect top-speed action on the surface task assigned. Other problems of personalities may be gnawing at each other underneath.
• Make people comfortable enough to bring out their hidden agendas. Encourage them to talk it over.
• Don't force discussion of a sub-surface problem that can't really be faced at the moment.
• Don't get angry or discipline the members for their hidden agendas. They can't help them—don't even know they have them.
• Help members develop ways of handling hidden agendas just as they handle surface agendas—by resolving the problem.

Hidden agendas are neither good nor bad. They're simply part of the game. But we need to be conscious of them and deal with them the way we deal with the surface problems. They're every bit as *real*.

10. BUILD A BRIDGE FROM THE MEETING TO THE GOAL

You want results, not meetings. You want results in terms of decisions carried out, actions taken, things done. Unless a meeting produces results afterwards—no matter how successful it seemed to be at the time—the meeting failed.

Too often what you're going to do afterward isn't planned until the meeting is over—then it's too late. Follow-up should be:
• Planned before meeting.
• Planned during meeting.
• Re-planned before the end of the meeting in terms of action.

Planning *follow-up* at the start of planning *the meeting* happens automatically if you are really viewing the meeting as a means, not an end. In this case you'll be looking at the ultimate goal and considering how the meeting will help move toward that goal.

A common method for planning follow-up is through minutes of the meeting. These minutes are often a colossal bore and practically useless because either too little or too much is recorded. Don't boil them down until the content is boiled away, and don't keep volumes of word-for-word notes. The key to the problem lies in making a distinction between meeting content and meeting procedures. Get on-the-spot highlights of what the meeting produces, not what goes on.

Follow-up action taken only at the close of the meeting may be too little and too late. Often a group makes a decision, sighs, "Thank Heaven that's done!" and files out of the conference room under the impression that the meeting goal has been reached. Far from it. You've merely made a decision.

The second phase of the problem is "How to get the action carried out successfully?" You're safer if you can create for yourself a mental picture of two meetings in one. The first meeting makes the decision, the second plans to carry it out. Possible approaches:

A. *Test its consequences* . . .
• What does it mean?
• How does it relate to other projects and policies?
• Is the decision possible? Is it realistic?
• How about cost, time, people to carry it out?
• What are the possible effects on other departments, customers, suppliers, the community?

B. *Test understanding and member commitment* . . .
• Is everyone clear about what this means?
• Is each one willing to go along?
• Are there any other concerns or misgivings?
• Does anyone see major pitfalls?

C. *Plan next steps* . . .
• Who does what?
• Who will coordinate?
• How about follow-up reports or meetings?
• What schedule of time, place, and people?

Follow-up that commits members to action and builds a bridge from the meeting to the goal is the final focal point for getting payoff from your meetings. But this payoff will also depend upon everything else we've been talking about.

One point in closing . . .

While all these rules can be useful to you, don't expect them to produce results in your meetings without a good deal of practice. They require, also, the development of skills—not only your own, but also those of the other members who participate.

THE INTERVIEW —
A MULTI-PURPOSE LEADERSHIP TOOL
Waldo E. Fisher

One common denominator characterizes the work of members of management: they all spend a lot of time solving problems. These problems will vary with the functions that are performed, but basically most of them deal with one or more production essentials: people, products, methods, markets, finances, equipment, and machines.

To solve these problems many management tools must be used. High on the list of these tools is the interview. It is surprising how often talking things over with others will suggest the solution to a problem or help to determine a course of action.

THE BUSINESS VALUE OF THE INTERVIEW

Because the interview is an effective instrument for getting and giving information and for winning acceptance of ideas, it is an indispensable communication device. It is invaluable in changing and developing attitudes and behavior and in creating the will to work together. It is also of primary importance in handling the following functions:

- Selecting new employees and inducting them into the organization in a manner which will make them effective members as quickly as possible.
- Presenting a point of view and tapping the experience of other persons.
- Explaining company policies, rules, regulations, complex orders, and innovations.
- Coaching and training employees.
- Reviewing employee performance on the job and helping ambitious and able employees to prepare themselves for greater responsibility.

- Handling complaints and grievances.
- Dealing with disciplinary situations.
- Counseling individuals confronted with personal problems affecting their work.

When it is realized (1) that in the final analysis an organization is a group of people who perform functions and activities essential to its successful operation and (2) that the interview is an invaluable instrument in selecting, training, appraising, developing, promoting, and counseling people, the importance of this instrument to management stands out clearly. For these reasons, management personnel should be fully aware of the nature and values of the interview and become proficient in its use.

WHAT INTERVIEWING INVOLVES

Ideally, an interview is a friendly and informal conversation between two people on a subject that they both want or need to explore. To be effective the interview should be planned, and the conversation conducted, as a two-way process. How much planning will be required and how much talking each person should do will depend on (1) the purpose of the interview and (2) the personalities of the participants.

Planning may be used to advantage in all types of interviews but is especially important when counseling and solving problems. Similarly, the distribution of the interviewing time between the participants will vary with the purpose depending, for example, on whether the interviewer is explaining company policies or standards or helping the interviewee to improve his performance or to change his attitudes or behavior.

Personality will also affect the distribution of time. An outgoing and well-informed interviewee who has considerable self-confidence and has no reason to be suspicious will usually talk freely with little or no encouragement, while one who is by nature taciturn or who is uninformed or unsure of himself will need to be drawn out and will be likely to place the burden of carrying the conversation on the interviewer.

In many interviews two sets of goals may be involved—those of the interviewer and those of the interviewee. These goals may be complementary, unrelated, or diametrically opposed. Irrespective of the goals, the function of the interview is to find a common ground for discussion which will facilitate a meeting of the minds of the participants.

Because the goals sought in the interviewing process vary in difficulty of attainment and because people differ greatly in capacities, interests, and temperament, no simple formula can be prescribed for conducting successful interviews. The competent interviewer will formulate clearly the things he wants to accomplish, plan his approach carefully, strive to be sensitive to human responses, and develop interviewing skills by applying accepted interviewing principles and utilizing correct methods.

TYPES OF INTERVIEWS

It may be helpful to attempt a classification of the kinds of interviews used in business situations. It should be recognized that the suggested categories cannot have hard and fast outlines since much overlapping will occur in actual practice. With this limitation in mind, the following classification is submitted:

Informative interview: The purpose of this type is to supply facts, opinions, policies, methods, and similar information to the interviewee.

Fact-finding interview: Here the interviewer is seeking information and advice which the interviewee, because of his training and experience, is in a position to offer.

Exploratory interview: The purpose in this instance is to obtain the opinions and judgment of the interviewee with respect to problems to be studied, programs to be introduced, methods to be utilized, or courses of action to be followed. This type of interview is sometimes used in resolving conflicting interests.

Appraisal interview: This type of interview is used in evaluating a person's suitability for employment with a company or his performance and behavior on the job in order to determine whether he should be considered for transfer, discharge, additional training, a merit increase, or promotion.

Counseling interview: The primary purpose of this type of interview is to deal with organizational problems involving people or personal problems affecting performance and working relationships: grievances, disciplinary cases, training and development, performance reviews, and personal problems of the interviewee that affect efficiency and teamwork.

The above classification is functional in nature, having been based on the primary purposes for which interviews are held. It is recognized that many interviews, especially in counseling, may require two or more of these functions in achieving the desired objectives. It will be observed that no separate category has been designated for problem solving. Actually problems, while occurring most frequently in counseling interviews, may arise during all kinds of interviews. Stating a topic in the form of a question tends to place it in the category of a problem.

PREPARING FOR THE INTERVIEW

The interview will be far more effective if time is taken to think through beforehand the objective sought and the methods by which the desired results can best be attained. The plan, however, should be general—not a detailed blueprint—and should be only a guide to be modified as circumstances require. Some of the principles and steps to keep in mind are:

1. KEEP YOUR GOAL IN MIND

Defining the purpose of the interview will give it direction, maximize results, and minimize irritations and wasted time and effort. The interviewer should contemplate the approach to use, the areas to cover, the information needed, the key and lead questions to ask, and possible solutions if a problem is involved.

What the interviewer will want to achieve will depend on the type of interview to be held: whether the principal goal is fact-finding, giving information, exploring possible courses of action, or appraising or counseling employees. Regardless of the type, it will be helpful to speculate beforehand about the specific things that are to be accomplished.

2. ADAPT THE INTERVIEW TO THE INDIVIDUAL'S PERSONALITY AND NEEDS

Because each person is a distinctive combination of traits, capacities, needs, attitudes, and aspirations, the interviewer should strive to utilize the approach and methods best suited to the personality and needs of the interviewee. The approach and method to be used will vary depending on the degree to which the individual is, let us say, mentally keen or slow, friendly or antagonistic, responsive or indifferent, emotionally disturbed or well-adjusted.

3. BRING TOGETHER NEEDED INFORMATION

The interviewer frequently will require pertinent information for his own use or to present to the interviewee. How does one decide what kind of information is to be compiled? Most interviews that are held in a business situation will be related to the factors often described as "The Six M's of Management": men, methods, machines, markets, materials, money. If the interviewer will speculate about the facts, policies, and programs related to each of these factors and which have a bearing on his problem, he will be likely to recognize the information that he will need. Most of this material is available in company records.

4. DEVELOP KEY AND LEAD QUESTIONS

In most interviews the principal task of the interviewer will be to get the individual to explore the subject under examination or tell why he responds, feels, or believes as he does, or prod him to make a decision or encourage him to solve a problem. These objectives can best be achieved by means of key and lead questions.

The key or primary questions set the pattern or structure of the interview and introduce and invite discussion of the broad areas covered by the interview. The lead or secondary questions draw out the interviewee by stimulating him to think and encouraging him to talk about the area opened up by the key question.

5. EXPLORE POSSIBLE SOLUTIONS IF A PROBLEM IS INVOLVED

When the topic under examination is a personal or organizational problem, the interviewer will find it helpful to speculate about possible solutions or courses of action that might be taken. The results of his speculation should not, as a general rule, be submitted by him during the interview. As we shall see later, such action often defeats the purpose of the interview. Its real value, as is also that of the key and lead questions, is to help the interviewer to think his way through the problem and enable him to guide the conversation into constructive channels.

The interviewer who has prepared for an interview will know what he hopes to accomplish, what he wants to talk about, how he will open the conversation, what questions to use to move toward his goal and get the interviewee to talking, and what courses of action to explore.

THE IMPROMPTU INTERVIEW

It will not always be possible to prepare for an interview. There will be matters that cannot wait such as when an employee comes with a grievance or personal problem that needs immediate attention. In that event, the interviewer will have to take the preparatory steps as he carries on the interview. He will want to obtain an understanding of the problem and so will help the interviewee to state it clearly. He will also get what facts he can from the interviewee but will recognize that additional facts may be needed especially if another employee is involved. Under these circumstances, the final decision will have to await further investigation.

The interviewer who plans for important interviews from day to day will adjust himself quickly to the needs of the impromptu interview and will pull out of his experience the key and lead questions and the possible solutions required to meet the situation.

CONDUCTING THE INTERVIEW

At the outset, it should be recognized that, because the personalities of those who participate in it vary greatly and the uses to which it is put are many, the interviewing process must be flexible. The interviewer, therefore, will want to utilize those principles and methods that he finds are best suited to his personality and to the situations with which he must deal. In particular, he will want to use the basic interviewing tools: interrogation, listening, observation, and evaluation. The following analysis presents the interviewing steps, to the extent that it is possible, in the order in which they are normally taken.

1. CREATE THE RIGHT SETTING AND PUT THE INTERVIEWEE AT EASE

The atmosphere must be conducive to a friendly and free exchange of ideas and experiences. What is needed is a relationship between the participants that will bring about mutual understanding, confidence, and participation.

Attitudes play an important part in bringing about this relationship. Experience has shown that most people respond positively to friendliness, courtesy, and to being accepted as equals. They want others to recognize their worth as persons and to respect their desire to be worthwhile. There still is no better way to achieve this relationship than to treat the interviewee as one would like to be dealt with under similar circumstances.

Because the interview is usually prearranged, it tends to become a formalized process. The skillful interviewer tries to overcome this tendency by putting the interviewee at ease. He makes it a point to be cordial and informal. He quickly finds a common ground for exchanging pleasantries and experiences having to do with mutual friends, events of current interest, or activities related to the purpose of the interview. But setting the tone and getting started should not become a time-consuming process which infringes on the business of the interview or even makes the interviewee less at ease.

2. SUPPLY PERTINENT INFORMATION

Early in the process, the interviewee should be given a clear understanding of why he is being interviewed. It is often helpful to review the events leading to the interview. Moreover, information that is needed by the participant to facilitate exploration of the subject under consideration should be presented early so as to avoid backtracking or interruptions to the smooth flow of ideas. The nature of the information to be presented will be determined in planning the interview.

3. SECURE INTERVIEWEE PARTICIPATION AND COOPERATION

The normal tendency of the non-professional interviewer is to dominate the interview. Except in the informative interview, the objectives sought are best attained if the interviewee is encouraged to do most of the talking by a friendly, observing, and responsive person who seldom interrupts.

a. Interrogation

This interviewing tool is especially helpful in getting the interviewee to participate. The role of key and lead questions in accomplishing this goal was discussed in the section on preparing for the interview. It may be helpful to point out that the "Why" questions are of especial significance since they often reveal the motives behind people's attitudes and behavior or the factors that have led to the selection of particular policies, programs, or courses of action.

b. Listening

Once the interviewee begins to talk, a second interviewing tool, listening, becomes important. There is a temptation to listen with only half one's mind, the other half speculating about other aspects of the interviewing process or even about unrelated things. The successful interviewer listens with an open mind, tries to comprehend the full meaning of what is being said, separates facts from opinions, evaluates the pertinent remarks, and tries to fit them into an overall pattern.

Some of the things said by the interviewee may run contrary to the interviewer's experience and convictions. He will be tempted to enter into an argument or to set the interviewee "straight in his thinking." Such action often satisfies his ego, but it uses up valuable time and energy and delays or may even preclude a successful interview. Interruptions on the part of the interviewer should be held to a minimum; they should be used primarily to encourage the interviewee to continue telling his story or to guide the conversation into more meaningful channels.

4. OBSERVATION

Observation is used throughout the entire interview but is of particular importance when the interviewee is relating his experiences and impressions.

Much can be learned about a person from the way in which he tells his story or reacts to a given situation. Facial expressions, postures, and gestures throw light on what is said. The tone of voice, a glint in the eye, flushed cheeks, clenched hands, a smile, a nod of the head, and other behavioral responses help to reveal personality traits and serve as red or green lights that indicate how the interview is progressing. But important as mannerism, responses, and the spoken word are, they are no substitutes for an understanding of the anxieties, needs, goals, and loyalties that motivate the individual.

5. EVALUATION

The next step is to relate to each other the facts, responses, and traits revealed by the interviewee's words and behavior, and to determine their importance and place in the overall.picture. Evaluation will go on throughout the interview, but the final appraisal must wait until interrogating, listening, and observing have had a chance to take place. Evaluation is necessary in order to form a reliable opinion as to the value of advice or counsel; to decide if an applicant should be hired, an employee retained, or how a person can be utilized more effectively; and to determine the best approach for helping an individual to develop himself or solve a perplexing problem.

6. WORK OUT A PROGRAM OF ACTION WHEN THE SITUATION DEMANDS IT

In certain types of interviews, notably performance reviews and counseling interviews generally, the participants often will find it desirable to work out a program of action. Experience has established the fact that any program or solution developed by the interviewee under the skillful guidance of the interviewer has a much better chance of being accepted and carried out than one that is made for him. When the interviewee helps to evolve the program, he will be more likely to have a greater sense of responsibility for it and more of a will to make it work.

7. TERMINATE THE INTERVIEW

In closing the interview, the salient points covered and particularly any agreements reached should be summarized. If a program of action has been formulated, the interviewer will want to review the specific things the interviewee agreed to do and the actions he himself offered to take. Should a follow-up interview be needed, a date should be set or the responsibility for arranging it assigned. The interview should be closed on a friendly note and a feeling of accomplishment when that is possible.

THE PROBLEM EMPLOYEE

From time to time, those who must work with or direct people will have to interview individuals with problems which prevent them from carrying out their duties and responsibilities as they should. How much help the interviewer can give such individuals will depend on the mental condition of the interviewee and the understanding and interviewing skill of the supervisor. The non-professional interviewer is not qualified to deal with deep-seated personal and emotional maladjustments. These conditions require psychotherapy and should be referred to the medical department.

But there are many problems of a less severe nature with which a supervisor will have to deal. In this class will fall difficulties involving grievances, discipline, motivation, status, and adjustments to changes in output standards, methods of productions, materials, machines, working conditions, and especially people. In dealing with these problems (particularly when emotions are involved), it is of little help to admonish, exhort, issue ultimatums, or hand down programs of action. A different approach and more refined interviewing methods are needed.

Professional counselors have developed some basic principles and techniques that should be of material help in dealing with these situations.[1] The problem employee frequently must be dealt with in perfor-

---

1. An excellent presentation of the role of the interview in counseling will be found in Carl R. Rogers, *Counseling and Psychotherapy* (Boston: Houghton Mifflin Company, 1942), especially pp. 11 to 47 and pp. 115 to 131.

mance reviews. A brief discussion of this type of interview, therefore, may be useful.

PERFORMANCE REVIEWS

Performance reviews are usually conducted as part of an employee appraisal program. Their immediate purpose is to let the employees know their supervisor's evaluation of how they are doing their work, how they can do it better, what their strengths and weaknesses are, and, if they are able and willing, how they can develop themselves and move up in the organization. Unless it is done well, this type of interview may boomerang and hurt instead of help personal relations.

The interviewer should keep in mind that in the final analysis he is trying to help the employee (1) become a more effective member of his team and (2) prepare himself for greater responsibility in the organization. Since most employees have a strong desire to be worthwhile and dislike criticism, it is well to begin with a positive emphasis by calling attention to traits in which the employee stands high or has shown recent improvement or to attitudes and incidents which reflect desired performance. Credit should also be given for aspects of his work that merit praise.

The interviewer will then want to shift to the employee's weaknesses and show how they affect his work and that of his fellow employees. Because no one likes to have his shortcomings enumerated, criticism should be resorted to only when it will be helpful and then used gently, tactfully, and constructively with emphasis on what the employee has or has not done rather than what he is or is not. Moreover, such criticism should be supported with observed examples and factual information.

The interviewer should not be disturbed if the interviewee disagrees with his appraisal. There may be a good explanation for unsatisfactory performance; circumstances inside or outside the organization may account for it. Differences of opinion have the advantage of disclosing misunderstandings or situations that need attention; so instead of trying to prove that the interviewee is wrong, it is far better strategy for the interviewer to ask him why he feels as he does and how he would remedy the situation. Such an approach will get him to think positively, help him to clarify his thinking, and often lead him to a solution of his problem or a program of self-improvement.

Generally speaking, in dealing with problem employees, the interviewer should seek to establish a personal relationship which will encourage and enable the interviewee to look carefully at his problem, analyze the reasons that lead him to feel and act as he does, and work out his own solution to it with the minimum of help. The interview should be a listening post and the interviewer a friend. Ask leading questions. Try to understand the meaning of what has been said. Respond sympathetically when appropriate. Restate and summarize from time to time the things that have been said to encourage the interviewee to continue his narrative. Refrain from making judgments by word or actions. These techniques help the interviewee (1) to feel as well as think his way through his difficulty and (2) to try his hand at developing a workable solution.

Check List for Appraising an Interview

1. *Opening of Interview*
   a. Was the setting of the interview conducive to obtaining the best results?
   b. Was the interviewer, himself, at ease?
   c. Did the interviewer appear as well prepared as possible?
   d. Did the interviewer put the interviewee at ease?

2. *Main Part of Interview*
   a. Did the interviewer demonstrate an awareness of the interviewee and let him participate to the fullest?
   b. Did the interviewer and the interviewee seem to jointly think their way through the problem under consideration?
   c. Did there seem to be a logical development as the interview progressed?

3. *Termination of Interview*
   a. Was there a mutual understanding of the decision and of who would do what and when, etc.?
   b. Was the interview terminated on a friendly, constructive note?

4. *Overall Rating*
   a. Did the interviewer seem to be skilled in interviewing?
   b. Any additional comments?

CONCLUDING REMARKS

What has been said about the interview—its nature, purposes, principles, and procedures—should have made it clear that interviewing is an art and not a formalized process. A knowledge of principles and techniques is a basic requirement for successful interviewing, but an understanding of people and skill in the use of these techniques are far more important. As we all know, skill—whether it is in interviewing, writing, painting, or athletics—is not only a matter of understanding but of practice.

The procedures outlined here to promote successful interviewing may have seemed involved and time consuming. But we must remember that people are exceedingly complicated beings. It would be a disservice to infer that they can be dealt with by a simple set of rules and procedures. Effective human relationships will always require a flexible approach supplemented by as much understanding, skill, experience, and wisdom as can be acquired.

The many pressures which characterize the work environment may make it seem hard to adhere to the approach recommended. But the results achieved by following these recommendations will make for more satisfying human relationships, better morale, and better employee performance which in turn should help increase output, improve service, and lower operating costs.

"WHAT DO YOU MEAN I CAN'T WRITE?"

John Fielden

What do businessmen answer when they are asked, "What's the most troublesome problem you have to live with?" Frequently they reply, "People just can't write! What do they learn in college now? When I was a boy . . . !"

There is no need to belabor this point; readers know well how true it is. *HBR* subscribers, for example, recently rated the "ability to communicate" as the prime requisite of a promotable executive.[1] And, of all the aspects of communication, the written form is the most troublesome, if only because of its formal nature. It is received cold, without the communicator's tone of voice or gesture to help. It is rigid; it cannot be adjusted to the recipients' reactions as it is being delivered. It stays "on the record," and cannot be undone. Further, the reason it is in fact committed to paper is usually that its subject is considered too crucial or significant to be entrusted to casual, short-lived verbal form.

Businessmen know that the ability to write well is a highly valued asset in a top executive. Consequently, they become ever more conscious of their writing ability as they consider what qualities they need in order to rise in their company.

They know that in big business today ideas are not exchanged exclusively by word of mouth (as they might be in smaller businesses). And they know that even if they get oral approval for something they wish to do, there will be the inevitable "give me a memo on it" concluding remark that will send them back to their office to oversee the writing of a carefully documented report.

They know, too, that as they rise in their company, they will have to be able to supervise the writing of subordinates—for so many of the memos, reports, and letters written by subordinates will go out over their signature, or be passed on to others in the company and thus reflect on the caliber of work done under their supervision.

From *Harvard Business Review* (May-June 1964), pp. 144-152. © 1964 by The President and Fellows of Harvard College; all rights reserved.

1. See also C. Wilson Randle, "How to Identify Promotable Executives," *HBR* (May-June 1956), p. 122.

Even the new data-processing machines will not make business any less dependent on words. For while the new machines are fine for handling tabular or computative work, someone must write up an eventual analysis of the findings in the common parlance of the everyday executive.

TIME FOR ACTION

Complaints about the inability of managers to write are a very common and justifiable refrain. But the problem this article poses—and seeks to solve—is that it is of very little use to complain about something and stop right there. I think it is about time for managers to begin to do something about it. And the first step is *to define what "it"—what good business writing—really is.*

Suppose you are a young managerial aspirant who has recently been told: "You simply can't write!" What would this mean to you? Naturally, you would be hurt, disappointed, perhaps even alarmed to have your *own* nagging doubts about your writing ability put uncomfortably on the line. "Of course," you say, "I know I'm no stylist. I don't even pretend to be a literarily inclined person. But how can I improve my writing on the job? Where do I begin? Exactly what *is* wrong with my writing?" But nobody tells you in specific, meaningful terms.

Does this mean that you can't spell or punctuate or that your grammar is disastrous? Does it mean that you can't think or organize your thoughts? Or does it mean that even though you are scrupulously correct in grammar and tightly organized in your thinking, a report or letter from you is always completely unreadable; that reading it, in effect, is like trying to butt one's head through a brick wall? Or does it mean that you are so tactless and boorish in the human relations aspect of communication that your messages actually build resentment and resistance? Do you talk "down" too much or do you talk "over your reader's head"? Just what do you do wrong?

Merely being told that you can't write is so basically meaningless and so damaging to your morale that you may end up writing more ineffectually than ever before. What you need to know is: "What are the elements of good business writing? And in which of these elements am I proficient? In which do I fall down?" If only the boss could break his complaint down into a more meaningful set of components, you could begin to do something about them.

Now let's shift and assume that you are a high-ranking manager whose job it is to supervise a staff of assistants. What can you do about upgrading the writing efforts of your men? You think of the time lost by having to do reports and letters over and over before they go out, the feasibility reports which did not look so feasible after having been befogged by an ineffectual writer, the letters presented for your signature that would have infuriated the receiver had you let them be mailed. But where are you to start?

Here is where the interests of superior and subordinate meet. Unless both arrive at a common understanding, a shared vocabulary that enables them to communicate with one another about the writing jobs that need to be done, nobody is going to get very far. No oversimplified, gimmicky slogans (such as, "Every letter is a sales letter"; "Accentuate the positive, eliminate the negative"; or "Write as you speak") are going to serve this purpose. No partial view is either—whether that of the English teacher, the logician, or the social scientist—since good business writing is not just grammar, or clear thinking, or winning friends and influencing people. It is some of each, the proportion depending on the purpose.

TOTAL INVENTORY

To know what effective business writing is, we need a total inventory of all its aspects, so that:

- Top managers can say to their training people, "Are you sure our training efforts in written communications are not tackling just part of the problem? Are we covering all aspects of business writing?"
- A superior can say to an assistant, "Here, look; this is where you are weak. See? It is one thing when you write letters that you sign, another when you write letters that I sign. The position and power of the person we are writing to make a lot of difference in *what* we say and *how* we say it."
- The young manager can use the inventory as a guide to self-improvement (perhaps even ask his superior to go over his writing with him, using the writing inventory as a means of assuring a common critical vocabulary).
- The superior may himself get a few hints about how he might improve his own performance.

Such an inventory appears in Exhibit I. Notice that it contains four basic categories—*readability, correctness, appropriateness,* and *thought.* Considerable effort has gone into making these categories (and the subtopics under them) as mutually exclusive as possible, although some overlap is inevitable. But even if they are not completely exclusive, they are still far less general than an angry, critical remark, such as, "You cannot write."

EXHIBIT I. WRITTEN PERFORMANCE INVENTORY

1. READABILITY

Reader's Level
- ☐ Too specialized in approach
- ☐ Assumes too great a knowledge of subject
- ☐ So underestimates the reader that it belabors the obvious

Sentence Construction
- ☐ Unnecessarily long in difficult material
- ☐ Subject-verb-object word order too rarely used
- ☐ Choppy, overly simple style (in simple material)

Paragraph Construction
- ☐ Lack of topic sentences
- ☐ Too many ideas in single paragraph
- ☐ Too long

Familiarity of Words
- ☐ Inappropriate jargon
- ☐ Pretentious language
- ☐ Unnecessarily abstract

Reader Direction
- ☐ Lack of "framing" (i.e., failure to tell the reader about purpose and direction of forthcoming discussion)
- ☐ Inadequate transitions between paragraphs
- ☐ Absence of subconclusions to summarize reader's progress at end of divisions in the discussion

Focus
- ☐ Unclear as to subject of communication
- ☐ Unclear as to purpose of message

2. CORRECTNESS

Mechanics
- ☐ Shaky grammar
- ☐ Faulty punctuation

Format
- ☐ Careless appearance of documents
- ☐ Failure to use accepted company form

Coherence
- ☐ Sentences seem awkward owing to illogical and ungrammatical yoking of unrelated ideas
- ☐ Failure to develop a logical progression of ideas through coherent, logically juxtaposed paragraphs

3. APPROPRIATENESS

A. Upward Communications

Tact
- ☐ Failure to recognize differences in position between writer and receiver
- ☐ Impolitic tone—too brusk, argumentative, or insulting

Supporting Detail
- ☐ Inadequate support for statements
- ☐ Too much undigested detail for busy superior

Opinion
- ☐ Adequate research but too great an intrusion of opinions
- ☐ Too few facts (and too little research) to entitle drawing of conclusions
- ☐ Presence of unasked for but clearly implied recommendations

Attitude
- ☐ Too obvious a desire to please superior
- ☐ Too defensive in face of authority
- ☐ Too fearful of superior to be able to do best work

B. Downward Communications

Diplomacy
- ☐ Overbearing attitude toward subordinates
- ☐ Insulting and/or personal references
- ☐ Unmindfulness that messages are representative of management group or even of company

Clarification of Desires
- ☐ Confused, vague instructions
- ☐ Superior is not sure of what is wanted
- ☐ Withholding of information necessary to job at hand

Motivational Aspects
- ☐ Orders of superior seem arbitrary
- ☐ Superior's communications are manipulative and seemingly insincere

4. THOUGHT

Preparation
- ☐ Inadequate thought given to purpose of communication prior to its final completion
- ☐ Inadequate preparation or use of data known to be available

Competence
- ☐ Subject beyond intellectual capabilities of writer
- ☐ Subject beyond experience of writer

Fidelity to Assignment
- ☐ Failure to stick to job as signed
- ☐ Too much made of routine assignment
- ☐ Too little made of assignment

Analysis
- ☐ Superficial examination of data leading to unconscious overlooking of important pieces of evidence
- ☐ Failure to draw obvious conclusions from data presented
- ☐ Presentation of conclusions unjustified by evidence
- ☐ Failure to qualify tenuous assertions
- ☐ Failure to identify and justify assumptions used
- ☐ Bias, conscious or unconscious, which leads to distorted interpretation of data

Persuasiveness
- ☐ Seems more convincing than facts warrant
- ☐ Seems less convincing than facts warrant
- ☐ Too obvious an attempt to sell ideas
- ☐ Lacks action-orientation and managerial viewpoint
- ☐ Too blunt an approach where subtlety and finesse called for

Furthermore, you should understand that these four categories are not listed in order of importance, since their importance varies according to the abilities and the duties of each individual. The same thing is true of the subtopics; I shall make no attempt to treat each of them equally, but will simply try to do some practical, commonsense highlighting. I will begin with readability, and discuss it most fully, because this is an area where half-truths abound and need to be scotched before introducing the other topics.

READABILITY

What is *readability*? Nothing more than a clear style of writing. It does not result absolutely (as some readability experts would have you believe) from mathematical counts of syllables, of sentence length, or of abstract words. These inflexible approaches to readability assume that all writing is being addressed to a general audience. Consequently, their greatest use is in forming judgments about the readability of such things as mass magazine editorial copy, newspaper communications, and elementary textbooks.

. . . It does not make much difference whether the sentences are long or short; if the reader does not have the background to understand the material, he just doesn't. And writing specialized articles according to the mathematical readability formulas is not going to make them clearer.

Nevertheless, it is true that unnecessarily long, rambling sentences are wearing to read. Hence you will find these stylistic shortcomings mentioned in Exhibit I. The trick a writer has to learn is to judge the complexity and the abstractness of the material he is dealing with, and to cut his sentences down in those areas where the going is especially difficult. It also helps to stick to a direct subject-verb-object construction in sentences wherever it is important to communicate precisely. Flights of unusually dashing style should be reserved for those sections which are quite general in nature and concrete in subject matter.

What about paragraphs? The importance of "paragraph construction" is often overlooked in business communication, but few things are more certain to make the heart sink than the sight of page after page of unbroken type. One old grammar book rule would be especially wise to hark back to, and that is the topic sentence. Not only does placing a topic sentence at the beginning of each paragraph make it easier for the reader to grasp the content of the communication quickly; it also serves to discipline the writer into including only one main idea in each paragraph. Naturally, when a discussion of one idea means the expenditure of hundreds (or thousands) of words, paragraphs should be divided according to subdivisions of the main idea. In fact, an almost arbitrary division of paragraphs into units of four or five sentences is usually welcomed by the reader.

As for jargon, the only people who complain about it seriously are those who do not understand it. Moreover, it is fashionable for experts in a particular field to complain about their colleagues' use of jargon, but then to turn right around and use it themselves. The reason is that jargon is no more than shop talk. And when the person being addressed fully understands this private language, it is much more economical to use it than to go through laborious explanations of every idea that could be communicated in the shorthand of jargon. Naturally, when a writer knows that his message is going to be read by persons who are not familiar with the private language of his trade, he should be sure to translate as much of the jargon as he can into common terms.

The same thing holds true for simplicity of language. Simplicity is, I would think, always a "good." True, there is something lost from our language when interesting but unfamiliar words are no longer used. But isn't it true that the shrines in which these antiquities should be preserved lie in the domain of poetry or the novel, and not in business communications—which, after all, are not baroque cathedrals but functional edifices by which a job can be done?

The simplest way to say it, then, is invariably the best in business writing. But this fact the young executive does not always understand. Often he is eager to parade his vocabulary before his superiors, for fear his boss (who has never let him know that he admires simplicity, and may indeed adopt a pretentious and ponderous style himself) may think less of him.

LEADING THE READER

But perhaps the most important aspect of readability is the one listed under the subtopic "reader direction." The failure of writers to seize their reader by the nose and lead him carefully through the intricacies of his communication is like an epidemic. The job that the writer must do is to develop the "skeleton" of the document that he is preparing. And, at the very beginning of his communication, he should identify the skeletal structure of his paper; he should, in effect, frame the discussion which is to follow.

You will see many of these frames at the beginning of articles published in HBR, where the editors take great pains to tell the reader quickly what the article is about and what specific areas will come under discussion during its progress. In every business document this initial frame, this statement of purpose and direction, should appear. Furthermore, in lengthy reports there should be many such frames; indeed, most major sections of business reports should begin with a new frame.

There should also be clear transitions between paragraphs. The goal should be that of having each element in a written message bear a close relationship to those elements which have preceded and those which follow it. Frequently a section should end with a brief summary, plus a sentence or two telling the reader the new direction of the article. These rather mechanical signposts, while frequently the bane of literary stylists, are always of valuable assistance to readers.

The final aspect of readability is the category that I call "focus." This term refers to the fact that many communications seem diffuse and out of focus, much like a picture on a television screen when the antennas are not properly directed. Sometimes in a report it seems as if one report has been superimposed on another, and that there are no clear and particular points the writer is trying to make. Thus the burden is put on the reader to ferret out the truly important points from the chaos.

If a writer wants to improve the readability of his writing, he must make sure that he has thought things through sufficiently, so that he can focus his readers' attention on the salient points.

CORRECTNESS

The one thing that flies to a writer's mind when he is told he cannot write is *correctness*. He immediately starts looking for grammar and punctuation mistakes in things that he has written.

But mistakes like these are hardly the most important aspects of business writing. The majority of executives are reasonably well educated and can, with a minimum of effort, make themselves adequately proficient in the "mechanics" of writing. Furthermore, as a man rises in his company, his typing (at least) will be done by a secretary, who can (and should) take the blame if a report is poorly punctuated and incorrect in grammar, not to mention being presented in an improper "format."

Then what is the most important point? Frequently, the insecure writer allows small mistakes in grammar and punctuation to become greatly magnified, and regards them as reflections on his education and, indeed, his social acceptability. A careless use of "he don't" may seem to be as large a disgrace in his mind as if he attended the company banquet in his shorts. And in some cases this is true. But he should also realize (as Exhibit I shows) that the ability to write *correctly* is not synonymous with the ability to write *well*. Hence, everyone should make sure that he does not become satisfied with the rather trivial act of mastering punctuation and grammar.

It is true, of course, that, in some instances, the inability to write correctly will cause a lack of clarity. We can all think of examples where a misplaced comma has caused serious confusion—although such instances, except in contracts and other legal documents, are fortunately rather rare.

A far more important aspect of correctness is "coherence." Coherence means the proper positioning of elements within a piece of writing so that it can be read clearly and sensibly. Take one example:

Incoherent: "I think it will rain. However, no clouds are showing yet. Therefore, I will take my umbrella."

Coherent: "Although no clouds are showing, I think it will rain. Therefore, I will take my umbrella."

Once a person has mastered the art of placing related words and sentences as close as possible to each other, he will be amazed at how smooth his formerly awkward writing becomes. But that is just the beginning. He will still have to make sure that he has placed paragraphs which are related in thought next to one another, so that the ideas presented do not have to leapfrog over any intervening digressions.

APPROPRIATENESS

I have divided the category *appropriateness* into two sections reflecting the two main types of internal business communications—those going upward in the organization and those going downward. This distinction is one that cannot be found in textbooks on writing, although the ideas included here are common-place in the human relations area.

There is an obvious difference between the type of communication that a boss writes to his subordinate and the type that the subordinate can get away with when he writes to his boss (or even the type that he drafts for his boss's signature). I suspect that many managers who have had their writing criticized had this unpleasant experience simply because of their failure to recognize the fact that messages are affected by the relative positions of the writer and the recipient in the organizational hierarchy.

UPWARD COMMUNICATIONS

Let us roughly follow the order of the subtopics included under upward communications in Exhibit I. "Tact" is important. If a subordinate fails to recognize his role and writes in an argumentative or insulting tone, he is almost certain to reap trouble for himself (or for his boss if the document goes up under the boss's actual or implied signature). One of the perennially difficult problems facing any subordinate is how to tell a superior he is wrong. If the subordinate were the boss, most likely he *could* call a spade a spade; but since he is not, he has problems. And, in today's business world, bosses themselves spend much time figuring out how to handle problem communications with discretion. Often tender topics are best handled orally rather than in writing.

Two other subtopics—"supporting detail" and "opinion"—also require a distinction according to the writer's role. Since the communication is going upward, the writer will probably find it advisable to support his statements with considerable detail. On the other hand, he may run afoul of superiors who will be impatient if he gives too much detail and not enough generalization. Here is a classic instance where a word from above as to the amount of detail required in a particular assignment would be of inestimable value to the subordinate.

The same holds true for "opinion." In some cases, the subordinate may be criticized for introducing too many of his personal opinions—in fact, often for giving any recommendation at all. If the superior wishes the subordinate to make recommendations and to offer his own opinions, the burden is on the superior to tell him. If the superior fails to do so, the writer can at least try to make it clear where facts cease and opinions begin; then the superior can draw his own conclusions.

The writer's "attitude" is another important factor in upward communications. When a subordinate writes to his boss, it is almost impossible for him to communicate with the blandness that he might use if he were writing a letter to a friend. There may be many little things that he is doing throughout his writing that indicate either too great a desire to impress the boss or an insecurity which imparts a feeling of fearfulness, defensiveness, or truculence in the face of authority.

DOWNWARD COMMUNICATIONS

While the subordinate who writes upward in the organization must use "tact," the boss who writes down to his subordinates must use "diplomacy." If he is overbearing or insulting (even without meaning to be), he will find his effectiveness as a manager severely limited. Furthermore, it is the foolish manager who forgets that, when he communicates downward, he speaks as a representative of management or even of the entire company. Careless messages have often played an important part in strikes and other corporate human relations problems.

It is also important for the superior to make sure that he has clarified in his own mind just what it is he wishes to accomplish. If he does not, he may give confused or vague instructions. (In this event, it is unfair for him to blame a subordinate for presenting a poorly focused document in return.) Another requirement is that the superior must make sure that he has supplied any information which the subordinate needs but could not be expected to know, and that he has sufficiently explained any points which may be misleading.

Motivation is important, too. When a superior gives orders, he will find that over the long run he will not be able to rely on mere power to force compliance with his requests. It seems typically American for a subordinate to resent and resist what he considers to be arbitrary decisions made for unknown reasons. If at all possible, the superior not only should explain the reasons why he gives an order but should point out (if he can) why his decision can be interpreted as being in the best interests of those whom it affects.

I am not, however, suggesting farfetched explanations of future benefits. In the long run, those can have a boomerang effect. Straight talk, carefully and tactfully couched, is the only sensible policy. If, for example, a subordinate's request for a new assignment has been denied because he needs further experience in his present assignment, he should be told the facts. Then, if it is also true that getting more experience may prepare him for a better position in the future, there is no reason why this information should not be included to "buffer" the impact of the refusal of a new assignment.

THOUGHT

Here—a most important area—the superior has a tremendous vested interest in the reporting done by his subordinates. There is no substitute for the thought content of a communication. What good is accomplished if a message is excellent in all the other respects we have discussed—if it is readable, correct, and appropriate—yet the content is faulty? It can even do harm if the other aspects succeed in disguising the fact that it is superficial, stupid, or biased. The superior receiving it may send it up through the organization with his signature, or, equally serious, he may make an important (and disastrous) decision based on it.

Here is the real guts of business writing—intelligent content, something most purveyors of business writing gimmicks conveniently forget. It is also something that most training programs shortchange. The discipline of translating thoughts into words and organizing these thoughts logically has no equal as intellectual training. For there is one slogan that is true: "Disorganized, illogical writing reflects a disorganized, illogical (and untrained) mind."

That is why the first topic in this section is "preparation." Much disorganized writing results from insufficient preparation, from a failure to think through and isolate the purpose and the aim of the writing job. Most writers tend to think as they write; in fact, most of us do not even know what it is we think until we have actually written it down. The inescapability of making a well-thought-out outline before dictating seems obvious.

A primary aspect of *thought*, consequently, is the intellectual "competence" of the writer. If a report is bad merely because the subject is far beyond the experience of the writer, it is not his fault. Thus his superior should be able to reject the analysis and at the same time accept the blame for having given his assistant a job that he simply could not do. But what about the many cases where the limiting factor *is* basically the intellectual capacity of the writer? It is foolish to tell a man that he cannot *write* if in effect he simply does not have the intellectual ability to do the job that has been assigned to him.

Another aspect of thought is "fidelity to the assignment." Obviously the finest performance in the world on a topic other than the one assigned is fruitless, but such violent distortions of the assignment fortunately are rare. Not so rare, unfortunately, are reports which subtly miss the point, or wander away from it. Any consistent tendency on the part of the writer to drag in his pet remedies or favorite villains should be pointed out quickly, as should persistent efforts to grind personal axes.

Another lapse of "fidelity" is far more forgivable. This occurs when an eager subordinate tends to make too much of a routine assignment and consistently turns memos into 50-page reports. On the other hand, some subordinates may consistently make too little of an assignment and tend to do superficial and poorly researched pieces of work.

Perhaps the most important aspect of thought is the component "analysis." Here is where the highly intelligent are separated from those less gifted, and those who will dig from those who content themselves with superficial work. Often subordinates who have not had the benefit of experience under a strict taskmaster (either in school or on the job) are at a loss to understand why their reports are considered less than highly effective. Such writers, for example, may fail to draw obvious conclusions from the data that they have presented. On the other hand, they may offer conclusions which are seemingly unjustified by the evidence contained in their reports.

Another difficulty is that many young managers (and old ones, too) are unsophisticated in their appreciation of just what constitutes evidence. For example, if they base an entire report on the fact that sales are going to go up the next year simply because one assistant sales manager thinks so, they should expect to have their conclusions thrown out of court. They may also find themselves in difficulty if they fail to identify and justify assumptions which have been forced on them by the absence of factual data. Assumptions, of course, are absolutely necessary in this world of imperfect knowledge—especially when we deal with future developments—but it is the writer's responsibility to point out that certain assumptions have been made and that the validity of his analysis depends on whether or not these assumptions prove to be justified.

Another serious error in "analysis" is that of bias. Few superiors will respect a communication which is consciously or unconsciously biased. A writer who is incapable of making an objective analysis of all sides of a question, or of all alternatives to action, will certainly find his path to the top to be a dead end. On the other hand, especially in many younger writers, bias enters unconsciously, and it is only by a patient identification of the bias that the superior will be able to help the subordinate develop a truly objective analytical ability.

PERSUASIVENESS

This discussion of bias in reporting raises the question of "persuasiveness." "Every letter is a sales letter of some sort," goes the refrain. And it is true that persuasiveness in writing can range from the "con man" type of presentation to that which results from a happy blending of the four elements of business writing I have described. While it would be naive to suggest that it is not often necessary for executives to write things in manipulative ways to achieve their ends *in the short run*, it would be foolish to imply that this type of writing will be very effective with the same people (if they are reasonably intelligent) *over the long run*. Understandably, therefore, the "con man" approach will not be particularly effective in the large business organization.

On the other hand, persuasiveness is a necessary aspect of organizational writing. Yet it is difficult to describe the qualities which serve to make a communication persuasive. It could be a certain ring of conviction about the way recommendations are advanced; it could be enthusiasm, or an understanding of the reader's desires, and a playing up to them. One can persuade by hitting with the blunt edge of the axe or by cutting finely with the sharp edge to prepare the way. Persuasion could result from a fine sense of discretion, of hinting but not stating overtly things which are impolitic to mention; or it could result from an action-orientation that conveys top management's desire for results rather than a more philosophical approach to a subject. In fact, it could be many things.

In an organization, the best test to apply for the propriety of persuasiveness is to ask yourself whether you would care to take action on the basis of what your own communication presents. In the long run, it is dangerous to assume that everyone else is stupid and malleable; so, if you would be offended or damaged in the event that you were persuaded to take the action suggested, you should restate the communication. This test eliminates needless worry about slightly dishonest but well-meaning letters of congratulation, or routine progress reports written merely for

a filing record, and the like. But it does bring into sharp focus those messages that cross the line from persuasiveness to bias; these are the ones
that will injure others and so eventually injure you.

CONCLUSION

No one can honestly estimate the billions of dollars that are spent in U.S.
industry on written communications, but the amount must be staggering.
By contrast, the amount of thinking and effort that goes into improving
the effectiveness of business writing is tiny—a mouse invading a continent. A written performance inventory (like Exhibit I) in itself is not the
answer. But a checklist of writing elements should enable executives to
speak about writing in a common tongue and hence be a vehicle by which
individual and group improvement in writing can take place.

By executives' own vote, no aspect of a manager's performance is
of greater importance to his success than communication, particularly
written communication. By the facts, however, no part of business practice receives less formal and intelligent attention. What this article as-
serts is that when an individual asks, "What do you mean I can't write?"
—and has every desire to improve—his company owes him a sensible
and concrete answer.

REPORTS
THAT COMMUNICATE
Michael J. Reiter

Modern accounting reports range far beyond the textbook classifications of balance sheet, income statement, and annual report. Much emphasis is being placed on preparation of reports that are highly analytical and interpretive. Today's accountant must be more than a gatherer of figures, more than an allocator of costs. Today's accountant must be a "management accountant." That is, he must have not only highly developed accounting skills and knowledge of accounting principles but also a far greater insight into the overall functioning of the business than ever before.

To meet the needs of modern business, management is challenging the accountant to produce more reports, bigger reports, and better reports. The greatest challenge lies not in gathering the varied data, not in analyzing for hidden trends, but rather in being able to transmit this data with all its pertinent meanings to management. Liken the accountant to the football spotter. From his vantage point the spotter watches the game. He sees a weakness in the opposing backfield. This information in the hands of his quarterback may mean the difference between victory and defeat. He picks up his telephone and relays the information to the bench. But on the bench the coach hears only static. There has been no communication. The key play is lost.

In this same way a business play can also end in a loss. For the accountant to have the information and be aware of a trend is not enough. To be able to communicate rather than just present is becoming a good accountant's prime skill. If he has this ability, he can increase the effectiveness of a management group by giving it the best tools possible with which to do its work.

SCOPE OF ACCOUNTING REPORTS

Accounting reports can be divided into three major groups or types: statistical reports, financial reports, and narrative reports. Under the heading of statistical reports we find reports on such facts as units pro-

From *Management Services* (January-February 1967), pp. 27-30. Reprinted by permission.

duced, number of complaints versus sales, and waste. The financial report group includes reports of receivables, budget reports, and, that statesman of the accounting world, the annual report. The final group includes the research report and variance explanations.[1]

Accounting reports for management could instead be divided on a frequency basis—into periodic reports of performance and special reports for planning and policy making. The periodic reports, such as budget reports, monthly statements, and sales reports, have become fairly fixed in form and content through accounting convention and company policy. Most organizations have standardized these reports to the point of presenting them on printed forms. Although this practice may sacrifice some communication effectiveness, the volume of periodic reports necessitates some degree of standardization.

PYRAMID STRUCTURE

The essential feature of periodic reports is that each is a supporting part of the report at the next higher level. Such an integrated system permits management by exception. A division manager can see which area of his organization—production, sales, or advertising—is causing a deviation. The production manager can pinpoint an off-budget department, and the general foreman can locate the specific part of the plant where the deviation occurs. In each instance the individual can direct his attention to the persons or operations at fault and initiate corrective action promptly.

Special reports are designed to give detailed information on specific operations or problems about which management decisions must be made. The special report should expand or supplement data that may be found only in part in various periodic reports. Special reports may be required to give comparisons of performance data other than those comparisons generally used. These reports deal as much in "how" and "why" as they do in "how much."

Many long-range planning decisions, for expansion or for changes in product mix, for example, cannot be made on the basis of the information given in the periodic reports. The special studies required to obtain the needed data must be thorough, and their presentation must be highly communicative. In selecting the format and reporting style the accountant must take into consideration the end use of the report, the complexity of the problem being studied, and the needs and temperament of the person who will receive it.[2]

1. C. E. Redfield, *Communication in Management* (Chicago: University of Chicago Press, 1958), p. 164.
2. W. C. Himstreet and W. M. Baty, *Business Communications* (Belmont, California: Wadsworth Publishing Co., 1964), p. 319.

PROBLEMS OF RECEPTION

All of us, whether accountants, engineers, or managers, tend to assume that when we report data we have gathered or state even a simple opinion it will be understood exactly as we meant it. Modern-day research in the field of communication clearly disproves this normal assumption.

Claude E. Shannon in 1948 presented a paper entitled "A Mathematical Theory of Communication" that laid the groundwork for the modern-day study of information theory or communication theory. This new field of study has shown us how much, or perhaps how little, we actually do communicate with our fellow man. Its theories, although enlightening, do not solve our communication problems for us. They do, however, point out the areas of difficulty and strongly emphasize the need for skill in the art of communicating with others.

Communication theory provides, in the "bit," a universal measure of the amount of information we can pass on to someone else. It tells us how many of these "bits" can be sent per second over different channels, be the channel oral or visual. Communication theory shows us how to state, or "encode," messages efficiently and how to avoid errors in transmission. This last is of great value to us; how to say what we mean.[3]

Communication theory tells us that the amount of information conveyed by a message is directly related to the receiver's uncertainty about what the source of the message will say. Here is an example: If you see what is obviously a one-dollar bill and a man tells you it is a one-dollar bill, the amount of information conveyed is negligible. If you see what looks like some kind of engine and are told its type, use, and other particulars, the amount of information conveyed is greater. The amount of information transmitted, then, depends in part on how uncertain the receiver is of what he will receive.

Of what value are these abstract theories and generalizations to the accountant who must write a report? How can an accountant apply such concepts as "transmitter," "receiver," and "noise" to his work? How can he better communicate?

KNOW THE "NOISES"

The first step to better communication through reports is to know what "noises" cause poor reports. These "noises" may be personal traits, lack of communication skills, or outside distortions. Accountants of one major company were accused by a top executive of "using a pattern of rubber-

3. J. R. Pierce, *Signals, Symbols and Noise* (New York: Harper & Row, 1961), pp. 1-9.

stamp expressions. They write badly and their reports are complicated, obscure, and tiresome."[4] Such a comment is not one that an accountant should be proud of. Yet it does point up a common "noise" in the form of shopworn expression and poor writing style.

"Noise" can take various forms. For example, you are a sales manager whose orders are not being filled because of production processing problems. You receive a report that reads like a technical dictionary. Buried somewhere in the "noisy" verbiage may be the length of time required for solution of the problem and the anticipated level of production until then, the facts you need to know. Yet you may tire long before you reach the page on which they are hidden. You are a victim of "noise." Another common example of "noise" is the qualified sentence: "Production is good, all things considered" or "Costs were fairly low, despite minor scrap problems."

Such distortions often result from accountants' lack of training in basic report writing. Many times such training on the high school and college level is relegated to the few courses in English that everyone is obliged to take. Courses in the field of accounting tend to deal with method and cover reporting only in terms of standardized forms. With more special reports to be done, the managerial accountant finds that not only are the figures important but so are the narrative comments on those figures.

Fear of authority and the "cover-up" attitude also produce distortions. Just how detailed should an accountant's analysis be? Information may well be lost because of fear of uncovering a skeleton in someone's business closet.

Distortion can also occur on the receiving end. The mere quantity of reports received may have become more important to the receiver than what the reports say; he rates a job by the poundage of paper produced. Or a manager may look upon a periodic report not as information on performance but as a prescription for conduct. This is especially likely to occur with budgets and variance reports. The tendency is to change performance so as to have a better report without trying to get at the real cause of a variance.

The managerial accountant, as "transmitter," must tune himself to perform his reporting function well. Of prime importance is his ability to put himself in the place of the manager or executive who will use the report. The accountant must be able to envisage what the report is supposed to do. He must be aware of the problem involved, be it expansion or new products or whatever. He must detail the narration of his report to answer as many as possible of the foreseeable questions. The

4. P. Douglass, *Communication Through Reports* (Englewood Cliffs, New Jersey: Prentice-Hall, Inc., 1957), p. 379.

scope of his study must be such that all factors involved in and affected by the decision management will make are completely covered.

To achieve this high degree of problem orientation, the accountant must have a close working relationship with both the receiver of the report and those from whom background information and primary data are obtained. He must think in the frame of reference of the receiver. Semantic issues must be settled before the narrative section of the report is written. When the narrative discusses overhead, asset, or discount, will the executive reading the report include the same items under these headings as the accountant who writes the report? To avoid confusion the accountant must become an extension of the person requesting the report.

Assuming that you have the requisites of a good "transmitter" and that you are alert to possible distortion factors, you have only to pick the proper "signals." Your "signals" will consist of the format used for data tables and charts, the key segments of the analysis narrative, and, most important, the words and style used.

Data tables may be large or may be in small segments, each dealing with one cost segment or area of the report. The prime requisite here is to keep tables in meaningful order and readable. Charts may run the gamut from line charts through bar graphs to pie segment charts, depending on which will best convey the significance of the data presented. Clutter should be avoided. Charts and graphs should be easy to interpret and clearly labeled.

Words and style are of great importance, particularly in the special reports. A foundation of good grammar is essential for good reports. Another handy tool is an unabridged dictionary. Reports such as accountants prepare cannot be polished by the average secretary.

The standard writing techniques for tone setting, proper flow, emphasis, and phrasing are as basic to accounting reports as to any other writing. Reader attention will be held if the basic principles are followed. Brevity and conciseness are also essential. Many an important fact is lost in a mass of verbiage. The use of new and different words and phrases will give life to reports. The same old worn-out statements can be an anesthetic rather than a stimulant to action.

GUIDEPOSTS TO GOOD REPORTS

A good report is not a matter of chance but almost a work of art. All of the rules in the many books written about reporting can be summed up in six key words. Good reports should possess *clarity*. They are clear and concise, are written in good style, and are easy to read. Good reports have *consistency.* They stay in the problem area and do not deviate. Meanings and terms do not change in midreport. Good reports display *adequacy.* They are complete in all respects. Coverage is not slipshod. Good reports possess *timeliness.* Their data and interpretation are in the light of present circumstances and practices. Good reports have *adaptability.* They show recognition of the possible different viewpoints on the problem at hand by presenting data to analyze these views. And, lastly, a good report has *interest.* Gone are the rubber-stamp phrases and mire of useless words. The report takes and holds the reader's attention. It not only shows but it also tells.

The managerial accountant, in properly fulfilling his reporting function, displays skills in composition, human relations, general business knowledge, and communication as well as accounting. He *must* communicate the necessary information in the proper manner so as to achieve the best end result. He must be a dynamic part of the decision making team.

WRITING SKILLS
CUT MANAGEMENT WASTE

J. Harold Janis

The management of written communications needs rethinking in the light of today's requirements.

Too much is being written that ought to be communicated in another way or ought not to be communicated at all.

Too much individual effort is going into kinds of writing that could be systematized with improved results; and too little thought is given to writing proficiency as a job requirement.

Unlike other job skills, writing is the only one in which almost everybody, including top management, claims amateur status. To put written communication in proper perspective—to make it work for instead of against the organization—management needs to find some new ideas to take the place of old myths. These myths are three:

It's best to put it in writing.

Nothing beats the personal touch.

Anybody can write.

Applied too literally, these ideas consume a lot of time and money that could serve business far more profitably. What is worse, they actually reduce communication effectiveness.

One well known bank, for example, sends out more than 2.5 million letters a year, exclusive of printed forms. This does not take into account a sizable number of interoffice memos and reports. With nearly 3,000 employes, the count comes to probably 1,000 written messages per employe per year. If the cost is put at $1.25 per message (a conservative figure), its written communications are costing the bank $1,250 for every employe from page girl to president.

This money might be considered well spent if all the messages reflected the time and personal attention that go into them. The fact is, however, that the company is being shortchanged. Actually it could get better results with much less effort.

What interferes is a kind of semantic illness that affects many organizations: adherence to verbal formulas long after the conditions that created them have disappeared.

Let's take a skeptic's look at some of these formulas.

"PUT IT IN WRITING"

The written word in business had its origin in the dual need to record documentary material and to communicate at distances.

The need to keep records is still present—though questions legitimately arise as to how, how many, and how long.

The need to communicate is also present—but in an age characterized by close-knit business communities, advanced methods of picture reproduction, and a wide variety of sound-communicating systems, writing is often unnecessary and inefficient.

Further, written messages of all kinds are so easily duplicated and distributed that they tend to pile up on desks and to clutter drawers and files. Some inform, some irritate, some are never read, and all take time and money.

FAULT: WORD THERAPY

Businessmen tend to put too much faith in the power of the written word. Often they write as if the very act of writing will cure what is a wrong policy, an overcomplex procedure, or a bad decision.

It is true, of course, that writing stimulates thinking and that half-formed ideas may reach fruition on paper. On the other hand, writing out an idea should also show up its weaknesses and inconsistencies. The fault is not in writing down anything that comes to mind, but in offering it up to an audience as business communication.

Remedy: Write all you want—but be sure you *communicate* only the results of sound management.

FAULT: HYPER-COMMUNICATION

Most businessmen are familiar with the "thank you" letter in answer to the "thank you" letter and the send-a-copy-to-everybody technique of thoughtless communicators. In other instances the public relations and advertising offices send out a heavier stream of written communications than the recipients can cope with—this on the theory that if you send a message often enough, some of it is bound to sink in.

Perhaps a more valid theory is that business should do a job, not do it again and again. Helpful as many good will and reminder communications are, there is a point beyond which the reader becomes bored and the sender's costs are disproportionate to the results.

Remedy: Think of the reader as having to pay for every message you send (he does—in valuable time and mental energy). If you are still inclined to write, make the message so effective that it has to be said only once. When a direct response is desired, make liberal use of return cards, stamped envelopes, and short-answer reply forms to keep follow-ups at a minimum.

FAULT: PROLIXITY

That's just plain too many words. Some of the most concise business messages were written in the days when businessmen turned them out by their own hands. They could not afford to make them wordy: Dictation, and especially machine dictation, changed all that. Nowadays it's as easy to dictate 200 words as to dictate 100—sometimes easier. But, while the dictator is cuddling the microphone, he is piling up a huge transcription bill, wasting his reader's time, and dissipating the strength of the message.

Remedy: Get rid of school-bound composition formulas. A letter or memo does not need a beginning, a middle, and an end. All it needs is a message. Why take three paragraphs to say "Go ahead" when "Go ahead" says it all. Also, stop thinking you have to fill the page. Stock a supply of half-size (or smaller) letterheads, and trim your dictation accordingly. Get in the habit of using small slips for brief handwritten messages that do not have to be put through the stenographic mill at all.

FAULT: WRONG MEDIUM

The notion that any message in writing is superior to a telephone call or a visit next door dies hard. In practice, writing can be the most expensive of all communication media. It consumes time in composition and in the lapse of days or weeks while the answer is in process. Writing is also a one-sided medium, with response uncertain in the extreme and often disagreeably final when it comes.

Remedy: Give proper weight to the advantages of telephone and in-person communication when time and flexibility are important. The give-and-take of a conversation or conference leads to better understanding and sounder decisions than the one-sided letter or memorandum.

FAULT: OVEREXTENSION
OF COMMUNICATION LINES

"It's our policy," said the executive, "to let everybody know everything." Although he was not to be taken literally, his company is suffering from too much information in the wrong places. Costly technical literature is

690

finding its way into the hands of uncomprehending schoolboys. Customers are treated, via house organ, to newsy notes about pregnant secretaries. Top-echelon officers are buried under memos from overcommunicative underlings.

Nobody is quarreling with the concept of a sound information or communication program, but let's keep it in hand. Written communication should be purposeful and relevant. It should also hit the target, not maim him.

Remedy: Design written and printed communications to fill specific needs, and limit distribution to carefully selected audiences. Provide machinery for screening incoming communications—summarizing, underlining, or discarding, where necessary—to save management's time.

"NOTHING BEATS THE PERSONAL TOUCH"

Whether this is so depends on what you mean by the personal touch. Efficient management needs to distinguish between two types of business writing.

The first is original or creative writing. It requires all the personal attention one can give it. It is time-consuming, and it is terribly unscientific. There is often more chance involved in a single memo than in an entire manufacturing process. This is the kind of writing every executive must do at one time or another. There are few short cuts.

The other kind of writing is repetitive writing. This kind of characterizes most of the company's correspondence and a fair share of its memos and reports. The situations that give rise to repetitive writing are those that have been dealt with many times before. Proper names or figures may be different each time, but the structure of the message is the same. The trouble here is that the writer gives his personal attention to a message that does not require personal attention. As a result two opposite faults occur.

FAULT: COMMONPLACE WRITING

With individual handling, each letter should represent the company at its attentive best. The reverse is true. Office pressures initially encourage imitation of past correspondence. Having to dictate the same kind of letter again and again, the writer quickly freezes both content and language. Hackneyed, unimaginative writing results.

Remedy: Systematize routine correspondence by supplying prefabricated letters, paragraphs, phrases. Well conceived, these can sound more natural than dictated material. They will be more concise, more correct, and more courteous, too. An index facilitates use and saves time. For volume production, investigate automatic typing systems.

FAULT: CUSTOM WRITING

The custom touch in communication is often taken to be synonymous with thoughtfulness. As a result, information that could go on printed sheets or forms is incorporated in personal letters. Letters that could be mass-produced are individually typed. Messages that could be printed on post cards are laboriously dictated.

Personally tailored communications can be flattering. But they have their disadvantages. They tend to be wordier and harder to read than canned messages; they take longer to prepare; and they cost more. Besides, the very letters and reports that management insists be custom written are often handled at the other end in the most routine fashion by subordinates on whom evidences of personal interest are wasted.

Another factor to consider is that mass business operations are creating public acceptance of impersonal service (as witness the success of supermarkets), and that personal service is often so bad that the customer is willing to accept any kind of service that fills his needs.

The same philosophy can be extended to business communications. Custom writing is becoming an anachronism in an automated world.

Remedy: Regardless of company tradition, discover the most serviceable (not necessarily the most personal) carrier for every type of written message. Plan letters, memos, and report forms which require a minimum of writing. Give proper weight to cost, speed, convenience, and flow of information. Personalization of printed or facsimile material can be achieved simply by attaching a calling card or brief note of transmittal.

"ANYBODY CAN WRITE"

Writing is a complex mental and physical activity that has received far less sympathetic attention in business than it deserves. Most executives spend 25 to 50 percent of their time writing. Many spend nearly all their time at it. How much do they really know about writing? How effectively are they doing the job? How much time would be saved if they could do it better? The management approach to written communication has several deficiencies.

FAULT: UNREALISTIC STANDARDS OF EMPLOYMENT

With all the writing business people must do, few are ever hired on the basis of writing ability. They are interviewed, tested, and judged for knowledge of subject matter, mechanical skills, and personal qualifications. But, unless a job calls for professional writing, as in advertising and public relations, a writing test is rarely given. As a result, many men and women know their specialties, but cannot write the letters and reports their jobs demand.

Remedy: Ask all prospective employes slated for writing tasks to submit to a test in composition. An autobiography to be written in an hour under ordinary office conditions is as good a test as any. It will reveal much not only about the applicant's writing ability, but about his background and attitudes as well. The composition test should be backed up by one of the standard objective English examinations.

FAULT: DEFICIENCIES IN TRAINING

Many training programs include no instruction in writing. Although instruction cannot make bad writers into good writers, it can help to eliminate the most obvious faults in English and improve style and tone.

Where training programs exist, they often display these weaknesses:

1. They concentrate instruction at the bottom (the repetitive level) and tend to ignore the top (the creative level).
2. They are too short, the demands on the students are too few, and the follow-up is too haphazard to accomplish any lasting results.
3. They do not provide a sufficiently systematic approach to repetitive writing—one that will materially reduce the need for dictation and individual verbal invention.

Remedy: Give training in writing on all levels, on a permanent company-wide basis, and with continuous supervision and ample aids for repetitive writing. A regularly issued training bulletin can help to maintain interest in the program. *Caution:* Every writer, however bad, has his pride. Tact and good will are required in any attempt to improve employes' writing skill.

FAULT: UNPROFESSIONAL APPROACH

Irrespective of the training program, employes should not be expected to do writing jobs that call for professional ability. Every department has such jobs. These tasks can consume a vast amount of time taken from regular duties, and the results are often less than satisfying.

Remedy: Use professional writers for professional writing jobs. Draft talent in the advertising and public relations department, hire an editor, or establish a communications staff. The professionals will do the work faster and better, and probably cheaper in the long run.

IMAGINATION HELPS COMMUNICATION

The Royal Bank of Canada

The Basic Skill in every profession and in most businesses is the ability to organize and express ideas in writing and in speaking.

No matter how clever an engineer may be technically, or an executive managerially, or a research man creatively, he does not show his worth unless he communicates his ideas to others in an influential way.

Language is the most momentous product of the human mind. Between the clearest animal call of love or warning or anger, and man's most trivial word, there lies a whole day of creation—or, as we would say it today, a whole chapter of evolution.

A business man is not called upon to present the elegance of a wit, a novelist or a poet. He must express himself accurately, clearly and briefly, but he need not denude his language of beauty and appeal.

The purpose of the writer is to communicate effectively. He needs a feeling for writing the right thing in the right way at the right time: not a barebones recital of facts, unless in a specification or legal document, but a composition of words which will convey his meaning and his sentiment.

This requires use of imagination, which is the cornerstone of human endeavour. John Masefield, the Poet Laureate, wrote: "Man's body is faulty, his mind untrustworthy, but his imagination has made him remarkable."

Writing imaginatively cannot be taught. It can be studied in examples —the writings of Defoe, Shakespeare, La Fontaine and Jules Verne show what can be done, but not how to do it. In this, writing is on a par with art and the product of an artisan's hands. The painter can no more convey the secret of his imaginative handling of colour than the plumber can teach that little extra touch he gives a wiped joint. All three, writer, artist, artisan, have secrets springing from within. After learning the principles, they go on to produce their works inspired by the dignity of accomplishment due to their gifts.

From The Royal Bank of Canada Monthly Letter, XLI, 7 (September 1960). Reprinted with permission of The Royal Bank of Canada.

Look at the drama built into small events by choice of words and use of imagination: Defoe gave us Crusoe recoiling from the footprint in the sand; Homer gave us Achilles shouting over against the Trojans and Ulysses bending the great bow; and Bunyan gave us Christian running from the tempter with his fingers in his ears. None of these was an epic event, but by their mastery of putting imagination into their communication these writers painted scenes which stirred us in the reading and linger in our memories.

A good piece of writing, whether it be a novel or a business letter does three things: it communicates a thought, it conveys a feeling, and it gives the reader some benefit.

THE WRITER'S TOOLS

What are the writer's tools? A wide range of language, for variety and to avoid the commonplace; active verbs, to keep the action moving; similes, which make words paint a thousand pictures; metaphor and parable, to make meanings clear; and rhythm, which contributes to smooth, easy reading.

To these tools, the writer adds imagination, always being careful to bring it within the scope of facts. Art in writing must not be used as an escape from reality.

This sort of writing is not so simple a thing as fluency, which soapbox orators have in abundance. It is not so simple a thing as grammatical exactitude, which can be hammered into boys and girls by a teacher.

But when it is properly done, imaginative writing is very powerful. Look at Cyrano de Bergerac in the drama by Edmond Rostand. The hero was valiant and romantic, but very sensitive regarding the size of his nose. This sensitivity prevented his making his court to the beautiful Roxane, but he wrote ardent letters to her for a handsome and stupid friend. The power of the written word won Roxane's love for his friend by proxy.

Good writing needs to be appropriate to the occasion, the purpose, the reader and the writer. It must not be too pompous for its load, or hesitant about what it seeks to do, or beneath the intelligence of the reader, or too arrogant for the writer's position.

Writing is only serviceable and good with reference to the object for which it is written. You say: "That is a beautiful dress"; but let the dress slide from the model's shoulders and lie in a heap on the floor, and what is it? A heap of material. Its virtue resides in its fittingness to its purpose.

What is written imaginatively in the daily work of office and industry will get desired results. If the writer looks further, what is written with imagination will live on when this Atomic Age is ancient history. Why? Because imagination is the one common link between human minds in all ages.

Imagination in writing finds expression through the use of accurate and illuminating equivalents for thoughts. You may show your imagination by dealing with something unfamiliar; by calling to attention a commonplace fact that is generally overlooked; by bringing into view familiar things in new relationship; or by drawing together relevant thoughts in a nosegay tied with your own ribbon.

An imaginative writer can look out upon the sprawling incoherence of a factory or a city or a nation or a problem and give it intelligible statement.

SOMETHING ABOUT STYLE

The style in which you write is the living embodiment of your thought, and not merely its dress.

When you put words together you convey not only your purpose in writing but your character and mood, both of which are important to your reader's understanding.

Let the occasion dictate the manner of your writing. Sometimes a manly rough line, with a great deal of meaning in it, may be needed, while a different set of circumstances demands the lubrication of sweet words. A blinding light is not always the best illumination: the delicate colours in moss-covered rock are enhanced by overcast, misty air.

Knowledge of techniques does not give the writer this discrimination. Technique is always a means and not an end. If we allow rules to govern our writing we become tongue-tied by authority. As Rembrandt remarked to someone who was looking closely into one of his paintings, seeking the technique, "pictures are intended to be looked at, not smelled."

We do not find ourselves tripping over technique in the inspired paragraphs of great literary works. Think of the forcefulness, the meaning, the simplicity of expression, in Lincoln's Gettysburg address, in Churchill's "fall of France" radio broadcast. Then contrast the great golden phrases of political campaigners, rising from nothing and leading to nothing: words on words, dexterously arranged, bearing the semblance of argument, but leaving nothing memorable, no image, no exaltation.

At the other end of the scale are those who write speeches and letters stodgily. Too many people who are nice people at heart become another sort when they pick up a pen or a dictaphone. They tighten up.

They become unnatural. They curdle into impersonality and choose starchy sentences. Their product is like a page printed with very old and worn-out type. In the vivid prose which marked some seventeenth century writers, James Howell wrote: "Their letters may be said to be like bodies without sinews, they have neither art nor arteries in them."

A letter in which something significant is attempted—a sale, a correction, a changing of opinion, the making of a friend—cannot be written in a neutral and bloodless state of mind.

In letter writing, imagination must supply personal contact. When you call in your stenographer to write a letter you are entering into a personal relationship with the reader. He is no longer a statistic in a mass market. He and you are human beings talking things over.

Most business communications have lucidity rather than emotion as their aim, but none except those which are frankly and openly mere catalogues can afford to exclude humanity. There should be some in-between space in your letters, some small-talk between the important ideas, some irrelevancies which temper the austerity of business.

THE READER'S INTEREST

No matter what your letter is about, the reader will want to know: "How does this effect me?"

It is a literary vice not to seek out the reader's interest. You may tell him what you want in impeccable language and forceful manner, but you fall short of success unless you pay attention to what he wants or can be made to desire. Your ideas must enter, influence and stick in the mind of the recipient.

As a writer, you may protest that some of the failure in communication may be blamed on the receiver, but it is your responsibility as sender to determine in advance, to the best of your ability, all potential causes of failure and to tune your transmission for the best reception.

Granted, something must be expected of the reader. Every writer is entitled to demand a certain amount of knowledge in those for whom he writes, and a certain degree of dexterity in using the implements of thought. Readers who demand immediate intelligibility in all they read cannot hope to go far beyond the limitations of comic strip language.

However, the writer is bound to eliminate every possible obstacle. He must not grow away from people. He must anticipate their questions. Let the salesman stand at a bargain counter and listen to what goes on in the minds of prospective customers. He will see women who spend ten minutes examining socks advertised at 35 cents a pair—do they stretch? are they washable? will they stay soft? are they tough enough to wear long? Those women are not up on the plateau of bulk sales, but down where a nickel counts.

That is the imagination of preparation. Then comes the imagination of expression. The most important demand of customers is for friendliness in those who seek to do business with them. A man may pride himself upon being an efficient, logical person, unswayed by sentiment in business matters, but at some stage in his every business deal there is a spark of emotional appeal and response.

You need to study your audience and then write what you want them to understand in the form that is most likely to appeal to them. Any other course is like the childish custom of writing a letter to Santa Claus and burning it up the chimney.

GIVE IMAGINATION WINGS

If you do not wish your letters to be read yawningly, write them wide awake. When a good idea strikes you for a letter, ride that idea on the dead run: don't wait to ponder, criticize and correct. You can be critical after your imaginative spell subsides.

The search for the exact word should never so usurp the writer's attention that the larger movements of thought on which the letter's argument depends are made to falter and so lose their fire. The first draft of a piece of writing should be done at white heat. The smoothing and polishing may follow later.

Some degree of novelty must be one of the materials in every instrument which works upon the mind.

By "novelty" it is not meant that the letter should be artificial. Great art consists in writing in an interested and straightforward way.

A good writer is not always original. You cannot hope to reproduce in your own words how Keats felt as he listened to the nightingale singing. It is far better to copy his ode. Mr. Churchill could not help it, even if he did not desire it, when his "blood, toil, tears and sweat" echoed Garibaldi, or when his first speech as Prime Minister, declaring it to be his policy "to make war," echoed Clemenceau's "Je fais la guerre." Shakespeare took his plots wherever he could find them, from older plays, English chronicles and Plutarch's *Lives*. His originality consisted in the skill with which he made a story over and covered the skeleton with the living flesh of his language.

If a man has vision and sympathy—ingredients of imagination—and adds sincerity, he will be able to beautify the familiar and illumine the dingy and sordid. Montaigne, one of the world's great essayists, said: "I gather the flowers by the wayside, by the brooks and in the meadows, and only the string with which I bind them together is my own."

Variety in expression is as necessary to a piece of written matter as it is to an attractive bouquet. Monotony in a letter is like a paralyzing frost.

The Greeks knew this: they set off the loveliness of roses and violets by planting them side by side with leeks and onions. Some fastidious or critical people may complain of unevenness in your writing because it is not sustained at a peak. But there is no one more tiresome than the man who is writing always at the top of his voice.

USE WORDS HONESTLY

The effort to bring up the highlights must not blind us to our obligation to be moderate. To be dynamic and forceful we don't need to give the impression of breathlessness. Strong words lose their force if used often. Don't say "the roof is falling in" when you mean that a crack in the ceiling needs patching. If you habitually term a dull party "a disaster" what have you left that is vivid enough to cover your feelings about an earthquake?

From the moment that a writer loses his reverence for words as accurate expressions of his thoughts he becomes second-rate. Even experienced writers testify to their constant search for the right word.

Follow the spirit of what you are saying in the way you write it. Sometimes you will use little, jolting, one-syllable words; in another composition your meaning and feeling may be conveyed better in cascading syllables like Milton's, or in earthy words that fit the urgency of the occasion.

There is no better way to learn the feeling of words than through reading poetry. The use of synonyms so necessary in poetry gives us a grasp of language and readiness in its use. Exercise your imagination by looking up the wide choices of words meaning the same thing, in varying shades of strength and attractiveness. A handy book to have on your desk is *A Dictionary of English Synonyms* by Richard Soule (Little, Brown, and Company, Boston).

Be careful to use qualifying words only where they contribute something to the sense you wish to convey. An excessive use of qualifiers vitiates the force of what you write.

Correct modification is an essential of perceptive accuracy, but every modification means a deflection in the reader's flow of understanding.

To test this, take some magazine which professes to popularize news events, and strike out every adjective and adverb which seems dispensable: note how much more authoritative and less tinted by opinion the items appear.

The business man should test business reports and letters by asking "What omission of fact or skimping of research or expression of prejudice does this adjective cover up?"

PICTURES IN WORDS

Our writing creates pictures in the reader's mind. We use metaphors to sharpen and extend the reader's understanding of our ideas by presenting him with images drawn from the world of sensory experience: "She has roses in her cheeks; he has the heart of a lion." If we say that a brook is laughing in the sunlight, an idea of laughter intervenes to symbolize the spontaneous, vivid activity of the brook.

In 240 words of a single soliloquy of *Hamlet*, Shakespeare gives us these imaginative phrases, now part of our everyday language: to be or not to be, the law's delay, the insolence of office, the undiscover'd country from whose bourne no traveller returns, the slings and arrows of outrageous fortune, 'tis a consummation devoutly to be wish'd, there's the rub, shuffled off this mortal coil, conscience doth make cowards of us all.

Metaphors are not confined to poetic writing: they occur in science and business writing, too: the flow of electricity, the stream of consciousness, the thinking machine, getting at the root of the problem, falling into error, indulging in mental gymnastics.

Local colour is an element in imaginative writing. Your highlights and your expressive phrases do not have to come from the classics. A good writer, even on the most prosaic of topics, will mix his own mind with his subject. True imagination, no matter how strange may be the regions into which it lifts its head, has its roots in human experience. What arises in your writing from what you have been through will be more vivid than what you glean from the writings and experience of others.

BACKGROUND FOR IMAGINATION

If the imagination is to yield any product useful to the writer, it must have received material from the external world. Images do not spring out of a desert.

The writer will train his mind to roam, to seek food, to experience events. He will read widely, observing words at work in a multitude of combinations.

A library has evocative power. Merely to sit within view of good books draws out the goodness in one. A library has driving power, too: it challenges us to convey meanings and feelings as these writers did.

The books in an executive's office should not consist solely of directories, almanacs, *Canada Year Book*, and the like. In literature are recorded all the thoughts, feelings, passions, and dreams that have passed through the human mind, and these can play their part in the efficiency of the letter writer today. Even on the battlefield, Napoleon had in his tent more than three hundred volumes ranging through science, art, history, poetry, travels, romance and philosophy.

To do all that has been suggested takes time. It requires preparation, practice and participation: preparation through reading and study, practice through revising and rewriting, and participation through putting something of yourself into every letter.

We must get out of the vicious system whereby we spend a forenoon verifying the price to be quoted to a customer, while refusing to spend two minutes in reconstructing a clumsy sentence in the letter we write him. To be slovenly and feeble is not only discourteous to the persons we address but bad business, because it leaves the door open for misunderstanding.

If you are going to describe an event or a product, do not be content with black marks on white paper: at least stipple in the background and use some colour in the foreground.

It is necessary, too, to be in earnest. Many people dream away their lives, talking of the writing they mean to do, and in the end they fall asleep, still babbling of the green fields of literature.

If you make only average grades in your letters when you could with a little effort top the class, you are bound to be disappointed with yourself. The writing of letters, business or personal or professional, is no mean ministry. It deserves the best that can be given it, and when it is rightly done it absorbs the mind wholly.

Why not be one of the knowledgeable elite instead of one of the conforming average?

They are probably best who, having a subject on which they wish to express themselves, sit down to write about it in a loving way. As Cyrano de Bergerac described his genius: "I have but to lay my soul beside my paper, and copy!"

Brief Guide to Usage

In the presentation of a speech, the writing of a report, or the composition of a letter, all of us, from time to time, have to stop and check on such questions as whether we want, in a sentence, "who" or "whom"; "continual" or "continuous"; or the question mark inside the quotation marks or outside.

The sections which follow may be used as a quick reference guide to answer these and other common questions. However, there are many excellent texts and handbooks available which offer a more comprehensive discussion of these areas of diction and grammar.

PUNCTUATION

USE A COMMA:

1. To set off an introductory phrase or subordinate clause from the independent statement.

   When I entered the crowded assembly hall, I immediately noted the presence of armed guards seated in the gallery overlooking the stage.

2. Before the coordinating conjunction (*and, or, but, for, yet,* or *nor*) linking two independent clauses. If the independent clauses are very short, the comma may be omitted.

   Key management personnel in the large organization should be carefully selected, and all managers should be informed of their specific responsibilities.

   Barry shouted and Betsy turned.

3. To set off nonrestrictive (or nonessential) phrases or clauses.

> Dr. John Kelly, who taught philosophy for 25 years, received frequent commendation from students and faculty.

> The present Chairman of the Board, as you may or may not know, began as a stockboy with this firm 41 years ago.

4. To set off phrases or words in apposition.

> Mrs. Spear, fashion director for Century Clothes, was elected president of the Designers' Association.

5. To set off a name directly addressed.

> If you will write me at your earliest convenience, Mr. Barclay, I'll arrange a tour for your group.

6. To set off a mild interjection.

> Oh, I didn't want you to purchase a new one.

7. To separate adjectives in a series when they modify the same noun.

> The very contemporary design had lines and patterns of red, green, blue, yellow, violet, and white.

8. To separate words or short phrases in a series.

> The sofa was clean and uncluttered, inexpensive but not cheap, and colorful but not garish.

9. To set off a quotation from the reference source in a sentence.

> "I shall arrive in Los Angeles before midnight," said Mrs. Kelley.

10. To indicate the omission of a word or words (usually verbal).

> Buckingham Way has been renamed Washington Street; Devonshire Place, Adams Avenue; and Kavenaugh Way, Jefferson Street.

11. To avoid confusion in interpretation or to assist in reading a sentence correctly.

> That that is, is; that that is not, is not.

USE A SEMICOLON:

1. Between coordinate, independent clauses not joined by a conjunction.

> Mrs. Spear submitted her monthly report to the Board; it was accepted without comment.

2. Before a conjunctive adverb (*hence, however, therefore, consequently, inasmuch as*) joining two coordinate clauses.

> The girls enjoyed their vacation; however, their funds were badly depleted by the end of the second week and they had to return.

3. Before a coordinating conjunction joining two independent clauses if the clauses are very long or have commas in them.

> When the race, which has been held every year since 1925, was scheduled, we had 22 contestants; but 5 additional entrants paid their fees to the official registrar, who immediately issued a verified certificate.

USE A COLON:

1. To introduce a list, a statement, a question, a series of statements, a quotation, and in some cases, a word.

> Each man should bring the following equipment: one sleeping bag, hiking boots, rainwear, a small shovel, and heavy outdoor clothes.

2. Before or after a specific illustration of a general statement.

> In the first week he broke a turning rod, dropped a glass test kit, and tore a rubber protection sheet: he was an extremely negligent worker.

> Winter arrived with a sudden fury: the temperature dropped to 15° below zero, six inches of snow fell, and the wind howled violently.

3. Following the salutation in a business letter.

> Dear Mr. Anderson:
> Gentlemen:

USE A DASH:

1. To set off—and emphasize—parenthetical material.

> Rolsted—you know he worked for us in the 1950's—retired in June this year.

2. To indicate when the idea in a sentence has been broken off abruptly.

> Do you believe that—

3. To indicate a sudden change in thought within a sentence.

> Do you believe that—no, I'm sure you would never accept it.

4. To precede a summarizing statement at the end of a sentence.

> Magazines were everywhere, the record player was on, clothes were tossed helter-skelter, food disappeared like magic, laughter filled the air—the girls were home for the weekend.

USE PARENTHESES:

1. To enclose ideas not directly related to the main thought of the sentence.

> Compton's periodic reports (following the format recommended by the National Trade Council) were submitted by all department managers to the general superintendent.

2. To enclose a numerical designation of a verbal statement. This is sometimes found in legal documentation.

> The escrow deposit of five hundred dollars ($500.00) will not be refunded except through court order.

USE BRACKETS:

1. To enclose an explanatory comment within a quotation or to insert a correction into quoted material.

> In her article on political upsets, Sarah stated, "Martin was defeated in the election of 1956 [he was defeated in 1952] and this marked the end of 36 years of Democratic treasurers in Wade County."

USE QUOTATION MARKS:

1. To enclose direct quotations.

> Sally said, "People don't change; their basic characteristics remain the same throughout their lives."
>
> "I don't agree," said Marty.

2. To enclose slang words or expressions.

> My teen-ager said it was the "grooviest" party she had ever attended.

3. At the beginning of each paragraph and at the end of the last paragraph in a quoted passage.

4. To enclose a quotation within a quotation. The initial quotation is enclosed in double quotation marks; the quotation within that in single; and a quote within that one in double.

Stevenson said, "If we are to live in peace, we must, as the Israeli representative has indicated, 'Appreciate the dignity of all people at all times.'"

The professor said, "All groups have the same pleasure values, although Carter disagrees with this when he says, 'Entertainment values are not the same for all age groups; a "trip" to some is attractive; to others, repulsive.'"

5. To enclose titles of articles, chapters in a book, or any part of a whole unit such as an opera, play, book, or magazine.

Thomas Carton wrote the article, "The Problems of International Finance," which recently appeared in *The Financial Quarterly.*

6. To enclose a question mark or exclamation point if it refers to the quotation. Place the question mark or exclamation point outside the last quotation mark if it applies to the statement as a whole.

Dr. Martin asked, "Isn't that their usual performance?"

Did Dr. Jameson say, "The students completed work at a very high level"?

Did you say, "Will all of them receive their degree in June?"

Dr. Meloan asked, "Did you write the article, 'Communication and Decision Making'?"

Kelly replied, "No, I did not, but I did submit one to *The Journal of Communication* titled, 'Is There a Relationship Between War and Words?'"

Special Note

In using marks of punctuation with quotations or quoted words or statements, remember

1. That commas and periods are almost invariably placed *within* quotation marks.

2. That semicolons and colons are almost invariably placed outside quotation marks.

3. That question marks, exclamation points, and dashes are placed within the quotation marks when they apply to the quoted material, outside when they refer to the whole statement.

USE A HYPHEN:

1. To divide a word at the end of a line.

2. To form compound nouns, verbs, and adjectives.

Mrs. Lyons was my mother-in-law.

He got angry when he saw that I had double-spaced the letter.

He is not a very well-known artist.

USE AN ELLIPSIS:

1. To indicate the omission of a part of a sentence use three periods. If the omission is at the end of sentence use four periods.

   The transaction was completed . . . and provided for Garson to receive the car plus miscellaneous items. . . .

USE AN EXCLAMATION POINT:

1. After interjections of very strong or sudden emotion.

   "I will not!" he almost shouted.

   Stop that noise!

2. See also the section on quotation marks.

USE A QUESTION MARK:

1. After a direct, but not an indirect, question.

   Have you completed your analysis of the Compton Company case?

   He asked if we were coming.

2. A question mark is not followed by a comma, period, or semicolon when used in a quotation.

   Glenn said, "Will you drive or shall I?"

3. See also the section on quotation marks.

USE A PERIOD:

1. After a complete declarative or imperative sentence.

   Effective communication is a vital management tool.

2. To indicate an abbreviation.

   He worked for Kingston, Inc., for over ten years.

USE AN APOSTROPHE:

1. To indicate the omission of one or more letters in a contraction or one or more digits in a numeral.

    He hasn't been home since he graduated in '70.

2. To indicate the plural of letters, figures, or words.

    Betsy received three A's and two B's on her report card.

    His essay contained one sentence with three and's in it.

    Her I's always looked like t's.

    She belongs to the Gay '90's.

3. To form the possessive case of nouns.

    The three boys' jackets were red.

    He purchased a dollar's worth of candy.

    That was my aunt's coat.

    The men's tools were left behind.

Note:

If the word in question already ends in s, add only an apostrophe; if it does not, add 's.

    The girl's coat was green.

    The girls' coats were green.

Note:

On the whole it is best to avoid the use of possessives with inanimate objects; e.g., sink's top, lamp's cord, or chair's leg. Sink top, lamp cord, and chair leg are standard.

Additional Uses of the Apostrophe to Indicate Possession

1. If two or more persons or objects own one item, possession is indicated on the last named only. If the writer wishes to indicate individual possession, an apostrophe is used with each name or object.

    Robin and Shelley's car. (Robin and Shelley own one car in partnership.)

    Robin and Shelley's cars. (Robin and Shelley own more than one car in partnership.)

Robin's and Shelley's cars. (Robin and Shelley each own one or more cars individually.)

2. In compound words, an apostrophe is added to the secondary or last word to indicate possession.

My brother-in-law's car was damaged in the accident (singular possessive).

My brothers-in-law's cars were all parked in front of the house (plural possessive).

3. Certain phrases involving time that seem to express possession use the apostrophe.

A month's pay was granted.

Three hours' time is not adequate for the job.

His dream was to take a four weeks' vacation in Hawaii.

4. The apostrophe is used to indicate possession with indefinite pronouns.

One's thoughts are sometimes private.

Anybody's ideas are acceptable in this brainstorming session.

5. Where an appositive is used, possession is indicated on it, rather than the basic word.

Bob Thomas the singer's coat was lost. (Because this sounds awkward, it is wiser to say *The coat of the singer, Bob Thomas, was lost.*)

6. Possession is indicated on the "junior" or "senior."

Martin Kelly, Jr.'s coat was a plaid.

Thomas Kale, Sr.'s store was sold.

7. When one-syllable words, especially names, end in s, and possession is to be indicated, an 's should be added. If the basic word has more than one syllable and ends in s, simply add an apostrophe after the s. To add an 's after the last s in the basic word (Williams's) results in an awkward sound (note the difficulty of pronouncing Mr. *Williams's coat*).

Mr. Jones's car
Charles' car

Here again it would be somewhat difficult to say *Charles's car; Charles' car* is preferred.

8. Pronouns in the possessive case do *not* use the apostrophe to indicate ownership; such words are already possessive.

The radio is hers.

The chair is yours, but the table is ours.

Its surface was scratched, but it's (this is a contraction of *it is*, not the possessive pronoun) really of no great importance.

PRONOUNS

Pronouns take the place of nouns and permit us to avoid constant repetition.

1. A basic rule for the use of pronouns is that they agree in person, number, and gender with the word to which they refer (antecedent).

   Joan gave her coat to the waiter and he took it to the check stand.

   The boys ran down the road to the oak tree and then they cut across the field.

   Shelley got her car from the parking lot attendant right away; the other girls had to wait for theirs.

2. Use a singular pronoun for antecedents connected by "or" or "nor." Note that the pronoun refers to one or the other antecedent singly, not to both collectively.

   Shelly or Betsy will give you her key if you arrive before noon.

   A rake or a hoe will serve no purpose if its handle is broken.

   Neither Mr. Carleton nor Mr. Frank will give you his advice without an assurance of confidence.

3. The pronoun should be plural if the antecedents are connected by "and."

   The car and the train blew their horns simultaneously.

   Barnes and Blackwell gave their brief cases to the messenger.

4. When two antecedents are simply different names for the same person, the pronoun is singular.

   The professor and conference leader received a scroll for his efforts.

5. When two antecedents refer to different persons, the pronoun is plural. Usually the second name is preceded by "the."

   The professor and the conference leader received scrolls for their excellent contributions.

6. When two or more antecedents are closely associated by usage or practice, a singular pronoun is used.

> Tea and toast has its place in a convalescent's diet.

7. Collective nouns take either a singular or plural pronoun, according to the sense of the sentence or the idea to be conveyed.

> The jury reached its verdict (one verdict coming from one jury).

> The jury put on their hats and coats and left for home.

8. Antecedents involving both genders usually take a masculine pronoun. For precision, however, a separate pronoun for each gender may be used.

> Each graduate will receive his degree at commencement.

> Each graduate will receive his or her degree at commencement.

9. The words which follow, when used as antecedents, should take singular pronouns. More and more frequently, however, many of them are being interpreted as plural.

anybody	everybody	somebody
neither	someone	nobody
either	none	any
each	everyone	one
		another

> Neither of the men paid *his* bill.

> Everybody in the room has *his* own opinion.

> None of the boys had *his* paper completed.

> Note that the sentences above really say, *Neither one of the men; Every single body in the room; No one of the boys.*

PERSONAL PRONOUNS

The choice between *I* and *me, she* and *her, they* and *them* sometimes causes confusion. Each explanation which follows includes the standard grammar rule as well as a short-cut method. To begin, let us review the pronouns in the objective and subjective cases.

	Singular	Plural
Subjective or nominative case	*I, you, he, she, it*	*we, you, they*
Objective case	*me, you, him her, it*	*us, you, them*

Nominative Case

1. A pronoun in the nominative or subjective case is selected when it serves as the subject of a sentence or a clause.

   Betty, Dorothy, and I (not *me*) have made arrangements for the party.

   Short-cut method: Would you say, "*I* have made arrangements," or "*me* have made arrangements"? Certainly you would choose the former. Therefore the sentence must be "Betty, Dorothy, and I have made arrangements for the party."

   Mr. Kelly and I (not *me*) were selected.

   Short-cut method: Would you say, "*I* was selected," or "*me* was selected"? Certainly you would choose "*I* was selected." Therefore the sentence must be "Mr. Kelly and I were selected."

2. A pronoun completing the meaning of a connective verb or predicate complement (*am, is, are, was, were, be, been,* or *will be*) should be in the nominative case.

   It was *he* who was selected.

   I believe it is *she* who should receive the award.

3. When the pronoun is the subject of an implied verb, the nominative or subjective case should be used.

   He is quicker than I (not *me*).

   Short-cut method: Would you say, "He is quicker than *me* am quick," or "He is quicker than *I* am quick"?

   He did more for the Church than they (not *them*).

   Short-cut method: Would you say "He did more for the Church than *they* did for the Church" or "He did more for the Church than *them* did for the Church"?

Objective Case

A pronoun in the objective case is chosen when it is the object of a verb or a preposition or when it serves as an indirect object.

   He mailed the books to Bob, John, and me (not *I*).

   Short-cut method: Would you say, "He mailed the books to *I*" or "He mailed the books to *me*"? Certainly it is the second; therefore the sentence must be "He mailed the books to Bob, John, and *me.*"

   He called Miss Johnson, Miss Short, and me (not *I*).

Short-cut method: Would you say, "He called I" or "He called *me*"? Obviously the second sounds better; therefore, the sentence must be "He called Miss Johnson, Miss Short, and *me*."

RELATIVE PRONOUNS

Some of the more frequently used relative pronouns are *who, whom, which, what,* and *that.* The two that are often confused are *who* and *whom.* However, informal usage seems to be accepting *who* for *whom* more and more.

Subjective case—Who
Who, like the personal pronouns in the subjective case, is used as the subject of a sentence or a clause.

Miss Costello is a girl who (not *whom*) I am sure will do well.

Short-cut method: Would you say, "I am sure *she* will do well" or "I am sure *her* will do well"? Certainly "*she* will do well" sounds better than "*her* will do well." Inasmuch as *she* and *who* are both in the same case, the sentence must be "Miss Costello is a girl *who* I am sure will do well."

Objective case—Whom
Whom, like the personal pronouns in the objective case, is used as the object of the verb or preposition or an indirect object.

The soldier whom (not *who*) she loved has been sent overseas.

Short-cut method: Would you say, "She loved *he*" or "she loved *him*"? Obviously "she loved *him*" sounds better than "she loved *he*." Because *whom* and *him* are both in the same case, the sentence must be "The soldier *whom* she loved has been sent overseas."

Miss Colgate is the girl to whom (not *who*) we gave the award.

Short-cut method: Would you say, "We gave the award to *she*" or "we gave the award to *her*"? The second choice is preferable and because *her* and *whom* are both in the objective case, the sentence must be "Miss Colgate is the girl to *whom* we gave the award."

Whoever and *Whomever*
Whoever is in the subjective case and *whomever* is the objective case. Their use follows the same principles as for *who* and *whom.*

The company will award contracts to whomever (not *whoever*) they find acceptable.

Short-cut method: Would you prefer "They find *they* acceptable" or "they find *them* acceptable"? The second choice is better and because *them* and *whomever* are in the same case, the sentence must be "The company will award contracts to *whomever* they find acceptable."

Mrs. Taylor, Miss Jones, and whoever (not *whomever*) else is selected will vacation in England.

Short-cut method: Would you say, "*She* is selected" or "*her* is selected"? Certainly it would be "*she* is selected" and because *she* and *whoever* are in the same case, the sentence must be "Mrs. Taylor, Miss Jones, and *whoever* else is selected will vacation in England."

CAPITALIZATION

1. Capitalize the first letter in the opening word in a sentence, a direct quotation, or each line of a verse.

    He was an outstanding student.

    Mr. Boynton said, "Effective communication is the executive's primary management tool."

    My heart leaps up when I behold
        A rainbow in the sky:
    So was it when my life began;
    So is it now I am a man:
    So be it when I shall grow old,
        Or let me die!
    The Child is father of the Man;
    And I could wish my days to be
    Bound each to each by natural piety.

2. Titles associated with names are capitalized.

    Senator Birmingham
    President Adams
    Aunt Anna
    Commissioner Baxter

3. Names of national groups, races, languages, or similar designations are capitalized.

    French
    Israelis
    Canadians
    English

4. Names of holidays, days of the week, holy days, and months of the year begin with a capital letter.

> Veterans' Day
> Wednesday
> Good Friday
> Rosh Hashanah
> June

5. Capitalize the first letter in words which designate names of historical periods, treaties, laws, government departments, conferences, commissions, and so on.

> Renaissance
> Clayton Act
> United States Supreme Court
> Bill of Rights
> Columbian Exposition
> United States Department of Transportation
> Harbor Commission
> Webster-Ashburton Treaty

6. Capitalize the first letter in words which refer to names, national or international organizations, or documents.

> House of Representatives
> Drug Council of the International Medical Association
> World Council of Churches

7. Capitalize the first letter of a word referring to a deity, a Bible, or other religious reference sources.

> The Bible, the Koran, and the Torah . . .
> Allah
> God, Lord, and Almighty
> the Congregation of the Missions
> To those persons who know He will . . . .

8. The first letter of each important word is capitalized in titles of magazines, books, essays, plays, and so on. Short prepositions, articles, and adverbs in such titles are not, except as first word.

> *Journal of Business Communication*
> *An Analysis of Government Taxation*
> *The Taming of the Shrew*
> *The Decline and Fall of the Roman Empire*
> *My Fair Lady*

9. Capitalize a general term that is part of a name: Santa Fe Railroad

Southern College of Arts and Sciences
Baptist Church
New Horizons Psychedelic Temple

10. Although words which refer to directions are not capitalized, words which are derived from directional terms are. Names of specific geographical areas or directional terms which have reference to parts of a nation or the world are also capitalized.

A path directly northwest of the tower.
Far East
Wild West
Orient
a Southerner

WORDS FREQUENTLY CONFUSED

Accent: to stress or emphasize; a regional manner of speaking.

Ascent: a rising or going up.

Assent: to agree; agreement.

Accept: to receive, to give an affirmative answer to.

Except: to exclude; to leave out; to omit.

Access: admittance or admission.

Excess: surplus or more than necessary.

Accidentally:

Incidentally: in both these cases, the "ly" ending is added to the adjective forms, *accidental* and *incidental*, and not the noun forms, *accident* and *incident*.

Ad: abbreviation for *advertisement*.

Add: to join; to unite; to sum.

Adapt: to accustom oneself to a situation.

Adept: proficient or competent in performing a task.

Adopt: to take by choice; to put into practice.

Advice: counsel; a recommendation (noun).

Advise: to suggest; to recommend (verb).

Affect: to influence (verb).

Effect: result or consequence (noun).

Effect: to bring about (verb).

Aggravate: to increase; to intensify; to make more severe.

Irritate: to exasperate or bother.

All ready: prepared.

Already: previously.

All right: completely right.

Alright: an incorrect usage of *all right*.

Allusion: a reference to something familiar.

Illusion: an *image* of an object; a false impression.
Delusion: a false belief.

Almost: nearly; only a little less than.
Most: an informal use for *almost*; correctly, it means greatest in quantity or the majority of.

Altar: a place to worship or pray.
Alter: to change.

Altogether: completely or thoroughly.
All together: in a group; in unison.

Alumnus (sing.): male graduate.
Alumni (pl.)
Alumna (sing.): female graduate.
Alumnae (pl.)

Among: refers to three or more.
Between: refers to two only.

Amount: quantity without reference to individual units.
Number: a total of counted units.

Anxious: upset; concerned about a serious occurrence.
Eager: very desirous; anticipating a favorable event.

Anyone: any person in general.
Any one: a specific person or item.

Assay: to evaluate.
Essay: to try or attempt.
Essay: a literary composition.

Balance: as an accounting term, an amount owed or a difference between debit and credit sums.
Remainder: that which is left over; a surplus.

Bank on: informal expression for "rely on."

Bazaar: an establishment that sells merchandise.
Bizarre: eccentric in style or mode.

Being as, being that: should not be used for *since* or *because*.

Beside: by the side of.
Besides: in addition to.

Biannually: two times a year.
Biennially: every two years.

Calculate: to determine by mathematical process. Dialect for "think" or "expect."

Can: refers to ability or capability.
May: refers to permission.

Callous: not sympathetic; hardened.
Callus: hardened area of skin.

Canvas: a coarse type of cloth.
Canvass: to solicit; survey.

Cannon: large gun.
Canon: a law; church official.

Capital: a seat of government; money invested; a form of a letter.
Capitol: a government building.

Carat: unit of weight generally applied to gem stones.
Caret: mark showing omission.
Carrot: vegetable.
Karat: unit for measuring the purity of gold.

Cease: to halt or stop.
Seize: to grasp or take possession.

Censer: an incense pot.
Censor: a critic.

Sensor: an electronic device.

Censure: to find fault with or to blame.

Criticize: to evaluate; to examine.

Cereal: any grain.

Serial: arranged in successive order.

Choir: organized group of singers.

Quire: measure of paper.

Cite: to quote from a source.

Sight: act of seeing; object or scene observed.

Site: a place, such as "building site."

Coarse: composed of large particles; unrefined.

Course: a direction of progress or a series of studies.

Collision: a clashing of objects.

Collusion: a conspiracy or fraud.

Command: to direct or order; an order.

Commend: to praise or laud.

Complacent: satisfied, smug.

Complaisant: obliging.

Complement: that which completes or supplements.

Compliment: flattery or praise.

Complexioned: refers to skin coloring or appearance.

Complected: dialect for "complexioned."

Confidant: one who may be confided in.

Confident: positive or sure.

Consensus of opinion: redundant; *consensus* means "general opinion."

Contact: meeting of surfaces. Frequently misused as a verb to mean "to ask," "to call," "to consult," or "to inform."

Continual: taking place in close succession; frequently repeated.

Continuous: no break or letup.

Council: an assembly of persons.

Counsel: to advise; advice; an attorney.

Consul: a resident representative of a foreign state.

Councillor: a member of a council.

Counselor: a lawyer or adviser.

Core: a center.

Corps: a body of troops; a group of persons in association.

Corpse: a dead body.

Credible: believable or acceptable.

Creditable: praiseworthy or meritorious.

Credulous: gullible.

Critic: one who evaluates.

Critique: an analytical examination of.

Criticism: an evaluation.

Currant: fruit.

Current: timely; motion of air or water.

Data:

Criteria:

Phenomena: The plural forms of *datum, criterion,* and *phenomenon.* Sometimes used as singular, collective nouns.

Deal: informal use for a business transaction; use instead "sale," "agreement," "plan."

Deceased: dead.
Diseased: infected.

Decent: correct; proper.
Descent: going from high to low.
Dissent: disagreement.

Decree: a proclamation of law.
Degree: difference in grade; an academic award.

Defer: to delay or put off.
Differ: to disagree.

Deference: respect.
Difference: unlikeness.

Depot: a storehouse for merchandise or goods.
Station: a place for passengers, a regular stopping place.

Deprecate: to express disapproval of.
Depreciate: to lessen in value because of use and/or time; to belittle.

Desert: a reward or punishment.
Desert: to abandon.
Desert: a barren geographical area.
Dessert: a course at the end of a meal.

Different from:
Different than: either may be used, although American usage prefers "different from."

Differ from: to stand apart because of unlikeness.
Differ with: to disagree.

Disapprove: not to accept.
Disprove: to prove wrong.

Disburse: to make payments; to allot.
Disperse: to scatter.

Discomfit: to frustrate; to disconcert (verb).
Discomfort: distress; not comfortable (noun).

Discreet: careful; prudent.
Discrete: separate (adjective).

Disinterested: neutral; not biased.
Uninterested: not concerned with; lacking interest.

Disorganized: disordered.
Unorganized: not organized or planned.

Dual: double or two.
Duel: a contest between two antagonists.

Dying: in the process of losing life or function.
Dyeing: changing the color of.

Each other: refers to two.
One another: refers to more than two.

Either:
Neither: refers to one or the other of two. With "either" use "or"; with "neither" use "nor."

Elicit: to draw forth, usually a comment.
Illicit: unlawful; illegal.

Eligible: acceptable; approved.
Illegible: impossible to read or decipher.

Elusive: difficult to catch.
Illusive: deceptive.

Emerge: to come out.
Immerge: to plunge into, immerse.

Emigrate: to travel out of one country to live in another.

719

Immigrate: to come into a country.
Migrate: to travel from place to place periodically.

Eminent: outstanding; prominent.
Imminent: impending, very near, or threatening.
Immanent: inherent.

Enthuse: a colloquialism meaning "to show enthusiasm."

Envelope: container for a communication.
Envelop: to surround; cover over or enfold.

Erotic: sexually arousing.
Erratic: unpredictable, irregular.
Exotic: foreign.
Esoteric: of interest only to a select few.

Exceptional: much better than average; superior.
Exceptionable: likely to cause objection; objectionable.

Expansive: capable of extension or expansion.
Expensive: costly.

Expect: informal use of "suppose" or "think."

Extant: living or in existence.
Extent: an area or a measure.

Extinct: no longer living or existing.
Distinct: clear, sharply defined.

Facet: a small surface of a cut gem stone; aspect of an object or situation.
Faucet: a spigot.

Facilitate: to make easier.
Felicitate: to greet or congratulate.

Faint: to lose consciousness (verb); feeble, weak (adjective).
Feint: to pretend or simulate; a deceptive movement.

Farther: refers to geographical or linear distance.
Further: more; in addition to.

Fate: destiny.
Fête: to honor or celebrate (verb); a party (noun).
Feat: an act of unusual skill.

Faze: to disturb, discomfit, daunt.

Fiancé:
Fiancés (pl.): the man to whom a woman is engaged to be married.

Fiancée:
Fiancées (pl.): the woman to whom a man is engaged to be married.

Flair: natural ability.
Flare: a signal rocket; a blazing up of a fire.

Formally: according to convention.
Formerly: previously.

Freeze: to turn solid because of low temperatures.
Frieze: ornamentation along the top edge of a wall, sometimes on hung fabric.

Genius: unusual and outstanding mental ability.
Genus: a grouping or classification, usually on a biological basis.

Grisly: ghastly; horrible; very bad.
Grizzly: a subspecies of bear.

Healthful: giving or contributing to health.
Healthy: having health.

Hoard: to collect and keep; a hidden supply.
Horde: a huge crowd.

Holey: having perforations or holes.
Holy: sacred, saintly.
Wholly: entirely; completely.

Human: pertaining to man.
Humane: kindly, considerate.

Immunity: safety from infection; exemption from regulation.
Impunity: freedom or exemption from punishment.

Imply: to hint at or to allude to in speaking or writing.
Infer: to draw a conclusion from what has been said or written.

In: indicates location within.
Into: indicates movement to a location within.

Incite: to stir up.
Insight: keen understanding; intuition.

Incredible: extraordinary; unbelievable.
Incredulous: skeptical; not believing.

Indignant: angry.
Indigenous: native to an area or country.
Indigent: needy; poor.

Individual: refers to a single item.
Party: a festive occasion; legal reference to a group or single person.

Ingenious: clever, resourceful.
Ingenuous: frank, honest, free from guile.

In regards to: incorrect; use "in regard to" or "as regards."

Inside of: informal use for "within" as "inside of five minutes."
Outside of: informal use for "except" or "besides" as "outside of those three members . . . ."

Irregardless: nonstandard for "regardless."

Its: a possessive singular pronoun.
It's: a contraction for "it is."

Later: refers to time; the comparative form of *late*.
Latter: refers to the second named of two.

Learn: to acquire knowledge.
Teach: to impart knowledge.

Less: smaller quantity than, without reference to units.
Fewer: a smaller total of units.

Let: to permit.
Leave: to go away from; to abandon.

Lie, lay, lain: to recline.
Lay, laid, laid: to place.

Likely: probable.
Liable: legally responsible.
Apt: quick to learn; inclined; relevant.

Load: a burden; a pack.
Lode: a vein of ore.

Loath: reluctant; unwilling.
Loathe: to hate; to despise; to detest.

721

Locate: informal for "settle"; "to make one's residence."

Lose: to cease having.
Loose: not fastened or attached; to set free.

Magnate: a tycoon; important official.
Magnet: a device that attracts metal.

Marital: used in reference to marriage.
Marshal: an official; to arrange.
Martial: pertaining to military affairs.

Maybe: perhaps (adverb).
May be: indicates possibility (verb).

Medal: a badge of honor.
Mettle: spirit or temperament.
Metal: a mineral substance.
Meddle: to interfere.

Miner: an underground laborer or worker.
Minor: one who has not attained legal age; of little importance.

Moral: a principle, maxim, or lesson (noun); ethical (adjective).
Morale: a state of mind or psychological outlook (noun).

Nice: pleasant, agreeable; finely drawn, subtle, as in "nice distinction."

Notable: distinguished.
Notorious: unfavorably known.

Observance: following or respecting a custom or regulation.
Observation: act of seeing; casual remark.

Off of: informal use for "off."

Ordinance: a local law.
Ordnance: military weapons; munitions.

Peak: top of a hill or mountain; topmost point.
Peek: a quick look through a small opening.

Peal: sound of a bell.
Peel: to strip off.

Per cent: should be used after a numeral (20 per cent).
Percentage: for quantity or where numerals are not used (a larger percentage).

Persecute: to subject to harsh or unjust treatment.
Prosecute: to bring legal action against.

Personal: private; not public or general.
Personnel: the staff of an organization.

Plaintiff: the complaining party in a lawsuit.
Plaintive: sorrowful; mournful.

Practical: not theoretical; useful, pragmatic.
Practicable: can be put into practice (not used in reference to people).

Precedence: priority.
Precedents: cases that have already occurred.

Proceed: to begin; to move; to advance.
Precede: to go before.

Principal: of primary importance (adjective); head of a school; original sum; chief or official.

Principle: a fundamental truth.

Provided: on condition; supplied.
Providing: supplying.

Quite: almost; entirely; positively.
Quiet: without noise.

Real: actual, tangible; also slang for "very" or "extremely."

Recent: newly created or developed; near past in time.
Resent: to feel indignant.

Respectfully: with respect or deference.
Respectively: in order named.

Resume: to begin again.
Résumé: a summing up.

Right along: informal for "without interruption" or "continuously."

Rise: to move upward; to ascend (rise, rose, risen).
Raise: to elevate; pick up (raise, raised, raised).

Salvage: to save (verb); material saved from a fire, shipwreck, etc. (noun).
Selvage: edge of cloth.

Sit: to be seated.
Set: to put in position (set, set, set).

Sometime: at one time or another.
Sometimes: occasionally.

Spoonfuls, carfuls, shovelfuls: the plural forms of spoonful, carful, shovelful.

Stationary: not moving; fixed.
Stationery: writing paper or writing materials.

Statue: a carved or molded three-dimensional reproduction.

Stature: height of a person; reputation.
Statute: a law.

Straight: direct; uninterrupted; not crooked.
Strait: narrow strip connecting two bodies of water; a distressing situation.

Than: used in comparison (conjunction): "Joe is taller than Tom."
Then: relating to time (adverb): "First he ran; then he jumped."

Their: belonging to them (possessive of *they*).
There: in that place (adverb).
They're: a contraction of the two words *they are*.

To: preposition: "to the store."
Too: adverb: "too cold."
Two: number: "two apples."

Toward:
Towards: identical in meaning and used interchangeably; *toward* is preferred.

Veracity: truthfulness.
Voracity: ravenousness; greed.

Vice: wickedness.
Vise: a clamp.

Waive: to give up; relinquish.
Wave: swell of water; a gesture.

Ways: procedures; also slang for distance.

Who's: a contraction of the two words *who is*.
Whose: possessive of *who*.

Your: a pronoun.
You're: a contraction of the two words *you are*.

723

EXPRESSING NUMBERS

Should numbers be expressed in figures or words in written communication? To help solve this question, a number of general rules have been established.

1. When several numbers are used in one sentence and they are all above ten, use figures. If they are below ten, write them out. If a sentence begins with a number, write it out. However, it is usually wiser to revise the sentence.

   We shipped 75 chairs, 90 tables, 32 lamps, and 32 pictures.

   You have requested two rugs, three TV sets, and eight area rugs.

   Seventy-five chairs, 90 tables, 32 lamps, and 32 pictures were shipped on December 3.

   On December 3 we shipped 75 chairs, 90 tables, 32 lamps, and 32 pictures.

2. When numbers are below ten, write them out; when they are above, use numerals. When some above and some below are used in one sentence, follow one pattern for consistency. Round numbers over ten are usually written out.

   He owned three shares of A.T.&T., seven shares of Sears, and fifty-five shares of Zenith.

   The scouts consumed 8 pies, 7 chickens, 8 quarts of milk, and 32 bottles of soda.

   He made two great throws, one of sixty feet and the other of fifty-five.

3. When two numbers are used in different contexts in the same sentence, one should be written out and the other indicated in numerals.

   The thirty-man team canvassed more than 50,000 homes.

4. When one number immediately follows another, express the smaller in words, the larger in numerals.

   He purchased five 59-cent notebooks for use in his spring quarter classes.

5. Place a comma between two unrelated numbers when they immediately follow each other.

   In 1975, 95 supersonic aircraft should be available for commercial use.

Dates:

1. Write out the month when expressing a date.

> June 27, 1974
> 27 June 1974

It is strongly recommended that numerals for both month and day not be used. Although North American custom is to place the month first and then the day, the reverse is true in many countries of the world. Confusion in interpretation can thus easily result.

> 1-4-74   Preferred: January 4, 1974
> 3/7/65   Preferred: March 7, 1965, or 7 March 1965

2. Only use *nd*, *rd*, *st*, or *th* with the day of the month when that day precedes the month or stands by itself.

> She became engaged on the 4th of January.

> In your order of the 2nd, you did not list the colors desired.

> Your shipment of the 1st was lost in transit.

> Please mail your check by March 28.

Addresses:

1. Street numbers should always be expressed as numerals except one, which should be written out.

> One East Wilshire
> 10 North Roscomare Road
> 215 South Kansas Street
> 2157 South Topeka Avenue

2. Use words for streets from one to ten inclusive; use numerals for streets after eleven. The letters *nd*, *rd*, *st*, or *th* may be used with numerals.

> 2115 West Fifth Avenue
> 1115 West Tenth Street
> 210 North 19th Street
> 400 East 121st Avenue

3. When a number is used as a street name, use a dash to separate it from the street number only if a street direction is not included.

> 210 - 10th Street
> 2100 - 7th Avenue
> 2111 West 45th Street
> 205 North 41st Street

Amounts of Money:

1. All sums of money, domestic or foreign, should be presented in figures.

    Johnson paid $155.60 for the merchandise.

    It is difficult for me to convert £275 into dollars.

2. For sums of less than a dollar, follow the figure with the word *cents* or with the cent sign (¢); the preferred alternative is to use the dollar sign with a decimal point.

    It cost 25 cents.
    It wasn't worth 65¢.
    Tom paid $.75 for the ball.

3. When expressing even or round sums of money, do not use the decimal and zeros.

    His payment was $275 dollars.

4. In legal statements the numerals should be enclosed by parentheses and the sum written out.

    A firm offer for the car of seven hundred forty dollars ($740) is hereby made.

Decimals and Fractions:

1. When a decimal fraction begins with a zero, do not place a zero before the decimal. If the decimal fraction begins with a whole number, precede the decimal with a zero.

    .04683
    0.1746

2. Simple fractions are written out. When whole numbers and fractions make up one unit, a decimal may or may not be used.

    It took him one half hour.
    It was 25.5 feet long.
    It was 25 1/2 feet long.

Miscellaneous quantities, units, and measurements:

1. Distance: Use numbers unless the amount is less than a mile.

    We were one third of a mile from the house.

    It is 9 miles to Kingston and 350 miles from there to Prampton.

2. Financial quotations: Use numerals.

   American Telephone and Telegraph hit 56 7/8 this afternoon.

3. Arithmetical expressions: Use numerals.

   Multiply 70 by 44 and you will have the area of the house in square feet.

4. Measurement: Use numerals.

   The land produced approximately 95 bushels per acre.

   He quickly found that 15 kilometers did not equal 16 yards.

5. Specific numbers: Use numerals.

   The engine number was 4638147.

   Write for Training Manual 255.

6. Time: Use numerals except when the word *o'clock* is used.

   The plane leaves at 7:17 P.M.

   He is due to arrive at ten o'clock.

7. Dimensions: Use numerals with either x or *by*.

   The room measured 10x15 ft.

   The trim size of the annual report was 8½ by 11 in.

8. Age: Use numerals except where approximations are used.

   She became 21 and got engaged on the same day.

   I would say that he's about seventy years old.

   For your information, Bob is exactly 3 years and 6 months old today.

9. Government units: Write out such expressions as Congressional units or districts.

   He served in the Eighty-seventh Congress and represented the Tenth Congressional District of the state.

10. Book or magazine references: Major units or divisions are indicated by Roman numerals; minor units by Arabic numbers.

    He found the reference in Volume XX, number 4, of the *Journal of Communications*.

    You will find Figure 4 next to Table 7 on page 83 of Section 4.

APPENDIX B

Secondary Research Sources

GUIDES TO BOOKS

Book Review Digest. New York: H. W. Wilson Co., 1905 to date.
This very valuable reference work lists books reviewed in more than 75 periodicals. For each book, quotations from a few reviews and citations to others are given. This digest appears every month (except July) and is cumulated annually. The arrangement is by book author, with subjects and titles listed in the index.

Books in Print. New York: R. R. Bowker Co., 1948 to date.
This guide lists books currently in print in the United States, with the exception of those on poetry, drama, and fiction, juvenile fiction, and Bibles. Each book entry lists the author, title, price, and publisher. Author and title volumes. Title volume includes a list of publishers and addresses.

Cumulative Book Index: A World List of Books in the English Language. New York: H. W. Wilson Co., 1928 to date.
This index supplements the *U.S. Catalog*. It lists books published in the English language throughout the world, but does not include government documents. The *CBI* is arranged by author, title, and subject. It is issued monthly (except August) with frequent cumulations.

National Union Catalog. Washington D.C.: Library of Congress, Card Division, 1963 to date.
Coverage has varied through the years. At present includes works catalogued by the Library of Congress and by approximately 750 other North American libraries. Indexed by author. Printed monthly, with quarterly, annual, and quinquennial cumulations.

Publishers' Weekly. New York: R. R. Bowker Co.
This is a weekly trade journal directed primarily to book dealers. The "Weekly Record" lists new books published. Includes price and subject of each item. Does not include government documents, subscription books, periodicals, or dissertations.

U.S. Catalog: Books in Print, 4th ed. New York: H. W. Wilson Co., 1933.
This work, with its supplements, provides a complete list of American publications from 1900 to 1933. Because of the tremendous number of books that have appeared in recent years, it is doubtful that a similar work will be issued again, but it is useful for background research.

GUIDES TO PERIODICALS

Accountants' Index and Supplements. New York: American Institute of Certified Public Accountants.
The original *Index* was published in 1920. Supplements have been published periodically from that date, generally every two years.
The supplements are indexed by author, subject, and title. They list published articles, books, and government pamphlets in accounting and related fields, together with source, author, date, and title.

Agricultural Index. New York: H. W. Wilson Co., 1916 to date.

Applied Science and Technology Index. New York: H. W. Wilson Co., 1958 to date.
This index, like the *Business Periodicals Index,* was begun in January 1958 to replace the *Industrial Arts Index.* The *Applied Science and Technology Index* indexes 226 periodicals in the fields of engineering, chemistry, physics, geology, metallurgy, aeronautics, automation, electronics, etc. It is published monthly and cumulated annually.

Art Index. New York: H. W. Wilson Co., 1929 to date.

Business Periodicals Index. New York: H. W. Wilson Co., 1958 to date.
This work indexes 174 periodicals in the fields of business, finance, labor relations, insurance, advertising, office management, etc. It is published monthly except July and cumulated annually. It is the basic index for the business field.

Catholic Periodical Index. Haverford, Pa.: The Catholic Library Association, 1930 to date.

This serves as an index to 124 outstanding domestic and foreign periodicals, newspapers, and bulletins. In addition, it notes many articles written from a Catholic viewpoint appearing elsewhere. It is published quarterly with cumulations.

Cumulative Index of the National Industrial Conference Board Publications. New York: National Industrial Conference Board, 1962 to date.

This valuable index, published annually, lists hundreds of classifications of NICB publications of interest to commerce and industrial managers and others. Topics range from "Absence" to "Workman's Compensation." A few phrases of description, date of publication, number of pages, and prices are given.

Dramatic Index. Boston: F. W. Faxon Co., Inc., 1909 to date.

Education Index. New York: H. W. Wilson Co., 1929 to date.

Engineering Index. New York: Engineering Index Service.

This index has been published in some form since 1884. Information concerning articles in engineering, chemistry, and physics journals is now printed on 3″ by 5″ cards and sent to subscribers. In addition, data from technical magazines, government bureaus, and research laboratories are recorded as well as abstracts of reports and reviews of books and articles. Once each year the data are cumulated in a large volume. The service is divided into 295 subject areas which may be subscribed to individually or completely.

Engineering Index Annual. New York: American Society of Mechanical Engineers, 1906 to date.

Funk and Scott Index of Corporations and Industries. Detroit: Funk and Scott Publishing Co., 1960 to date.

These volumes are published weekly, cumulated monthly, and bound annually. They index, describe, and date, by company and industry name, articles and speeches from investment services, financial magazines, brokerage house reports, document services, bank letters, financial newspapers, books and pamphlets having to do with finance, stocks and bonds, and Canadian publications in the same areas.

Index of Economic Journals. Homewood, Ill.: Richard D. Irwin, Inc., 1965.

Volume I	1886-1924	Volume IV	1950-1954
Volume II	1925-1939	Volume V	1955-1959
Volume III	1940-1949	Volume VI	1960-1963

About 115 American and foreign economic journals are indexed for English-language articles in each volume for the years given. This valuable index is divided into two sections: (1) the Author Index, where all the articles by an individual for the period covered

are brought together, and (2) a Classified Index with 23 subject areas, ranging from Economic Theory to Regional Planning and Development. The 23 subject areas are further divided into numerous sub-areas for easy reference. All entries list author, title of article, journal where found, and page number.

Index to Labor Union Periodicals. Ann Arbor: University of Michigan, School of Business Administration, Bureau of Industrial Relations, 1960 to date.

Published monthly and cumulated annually, this work indexes articles from fifty major union periodicals; the entries usually include two or three brief descriptive sentences.

Index to Legal Periodicals. New York: H. W. Wilson Co., 1908 to date.

Industrial Arts Index. New York: H. W. Wilson Co., 1913 to 1958.

This is a cumulative index of articles which appeared in more than 200 periodicals on business, finance, applied science, and technology. It was published monthly until January 1958, when it was replaced by the *Business Periodicals Index* and the *Applied Science and Technology Index.*

International Index—A Guide to Periodical Literature in the Social Sciences and Humanities. New York: H. W. Wilson Co., 1907 to 1965.

This index was issued quarterly and cumulated every three years from 1916 to 1958, every two years from 1960 to 1964, and again in 1965, when it was replaced by the *Social Sciences and Humanities Index.*

Management Index. Ottawa: Keith Business Library, 1963 to date.

Formerly *Business Methods Index, Management Index* is published monthly except July and is cumulated annually. It is a guide to new American, Canadian, and British books, pamphlets, magazine articles, training films, maps, etc., of interest to management. It is indexed by subject, with description and price. In addition, reprints of articles are available from the publisher.

Poole's Index to Periodical Literature, 5 vols. and supplements. Boston: Houghton Mifflin Co., 1888-1908.

This index lists, under subject only, important magazine articles which appeared between 1802 and 1908. *Poole's Index* is no longer printed, but its work has been carried on by the *Readers' Guide.*

Readers' Guide to Periodical Literature. New York: H. W. Wilson Co., 1900 to date.

In this invaluable reference guide, researchers working in many fields can find the names of periodicals carrying articles on their topics. If the library does not carry the set of magazines the *Readers'*

Guide cites, the name of a nearby library which does may be found in the *Union List of Serials* (see below). *Readers' Guide* appears twice a month (except for one issue each in July and August) and is cumulated frequently. It indexes about 130 well-known and popular current periodicals. It lists articles under author, subject, and title.

Social Sciences and Humanities Index. New York: H. W. Wilson Co., 1965 to date.

In April 1965, this index replaced the *International Index.* It is an author, subject, and title index of a selected group of 175 periodicals published in the United States and England. It also lists the periodicals indexed, the publisher of each, and the subscription price.

Ulrich's International Periodicals Directory. New York: R. R. Bowker Co. Volume I and Volume II published in alternating years, with an annual supplement to both.

A guide to some 7500 domestic and foreign periodicals. Emphasis is on periodicals published in North and South America and England. Volume I covers the fields of science, technology, and medicine; Volume II covers arts, humanities, business, and social science. Arranged by subject with author and title index. Entry includes title, publisher, address, editor, circulation; indicates whether it includes an index and book reviews, and in which major index, if any, the title appears.

Union List of Serials in Libraries of the United States and Canada, 3rd ed., 5 vols. New York: H. W. Wilson Co., 1965.

This comprehensive guide lists magazines and the libraries where they may be found.

GUIDES TO NEWSPAPERS

American Newspapers, 1821-1936; a Union List. New York: H. W. Wilson Co., 1937.

This excellent work indicates where existing files of newspapers published in the United States from 1821 to 1936 may be found.

Directory of Newspapers and Periodicals. Philadelphia: N. W. Ayer, 1880 to date.

This directory is published annually. It contains information on circulation statistics, rates, name of publisher, size of page, politics, and other facts of some 22,000 newspapers and periodicals published in the United States, Canada, Cuba, Bermuda, and islands belonging to the United States.

Index of the Christian Science Monitor. Corvallis, Oregon: H. M. Cropsey, 1960 to date.
> Published monthly, with frequent cumulations.

New York Times Index. New York: New York Times Co., 1913 to date.
> This index has been issued twice a month since 1948 and is cumulated annually. News is summarized and classified alphabetically and chronologically by subject, by person, and by organization name. Each article is indexed by heading, subhead entry, date, page, and column reference. An earlier index covering 1851-1912 is now available.

Standard Rate and Data Service.
> This service is issued in fourteen parts and cites a wealth of information in the fields of publishing, consumer markets, and advertising. Information includes advertising costs, audience, and circulation figures of newspapers, U.S. business magazines, U.S. consumer magazines, Canadian newspapers, radio, and magazines, radio and television network data, films, and public transportation vehicle advertising.

The Wall Street Journal Index. New York: Dow Jones and Co., 1958 to date.
> This index is published monthly and combined into an annual. It indexes and gives synopses of *Wall Street Journal* articles for the period indicated. Only the New York edition of the *Journal* is indexed, however.

GUIDES TO REPORTS, BULLETINS, AND BROCHURES

Alexander, Raphael. *Business Pamphlets and Information Sources.* New York: Exceptional Books, 1967.
> Subject listing of pamphlets, reprints, and paperbacks in various areas of business. Includes prices, publishers, and addresses.

Vertical File Index. New York: H. W. Wilson Co., 1932 to date.
> This is a monthly descriptive list of free and inexpensive pamphlets, with the prices and name and address of the publisher. These are grouped under subjects in the main part of the catalog with an alphabetical list of titles in the index. Includes reprints, government documents, and mimeographed material.

GUIDES TO GOVERNMENT PUBLICATIONS

Ames, John Griffith. *Comprehensive Index to the Publications of the U.S. Government, 1881–1893,* 2 vols. Washington, D.C.: Government

Printing Office, 1905. Reprinted Ann Arbor, Mich.: Edwards, 1953.
A valuable index to publications for the period noted.

Andriot, John L. *Guide to U.S. Government Serials and Periodicals.*
McLean, Va.: Documents Index, 1962 to date.
This publication lists items, prices, availability, and order numbers
of government serials and periodicals. In addition, it gives a brief
description, reason for preparation, and audience to which the item
is directed. Arrangement is by branch of government, department,
agency, and subagency. Includes releases, field agency publications,
and miscellaneous publications. Starting with 1967 edition, to be
published biannually with supplements.

Andriot, John L. *Guide to U.S. Government Statistics,* 3rd ed. McLean,
Va.: Documents Index, 1961.
All government publications which include statistical data are
listed by department and issuing bureau. Description of the publication, type of statistics, and frequency of publication are included.
Independent agencies, judiciary, executive, and legislative branches
are also included and indexed. Detailed subject index.

Childs, James Bennett. *Government Document Bibliography in the U.S.
and Elsewhere.* Washington, D.C.: Government Printing Office, 1942.
Reprinted New York: Johnson Reprint Corp., 1964.
This work lists catalogs, guides, and indexes to the documents of
the countries and states listed.

Leidy, W. Philip. *A Popular Guide to Government Publications,* 3rd ed.
New York: Columbia University Press, 1968.
Contains over 3000 titles of recent government publications most
likely to be of interest to the public. The title, publisher, price, and
publication date are given for each item listed. A short descriptive
comment accompanies most entries.

Poore, Benjamin P. *A Descriptive Catalog of the Government Publications
of the United States, Sept. 1774–March 1881.* Washington, D.C.: Government Printing Office, 1885. Reprinted Ann Arbor, Mich.: Edwards, 1953.
Material is arranged chronologically, giving for each document the
full title, author, date, and a brief abstract of the contents.

Schmeckebier, Laurence. *Government Publications and Their Use,* rev.
ed. Washington, D.C.: Brookings, 1961.
Intended as a basic guide to government publications and their
use. Describes the types of publications, availability, classification.

U.S. Library of Congress, Processing Department. *Monthly Checklist of
State Publications.* Washington, D.C.: Government Printing Office, 1910
to date.

A current bibliography of the publications of the states, territories, and insular possessions of the United States. Annual index may be used as subject index.

U.S. Superintendent of Documents. *Catalog of the Public Documents of Congress and of All Departments of the U.S. for the Period March 4, 1893-December 31, 1940*, 25 vols. Washington, D.C.: Government Printing Office, 1896-1945.

This detailed work indexes all government publications, both Congressional and departmental. Listings are made under author, subject, and title. This is a very worthwhile guide.

U.S. Superintendent of Documents. *Checklist of U.S. Public Documents, 1789-1909*. Washington, D.C.: Government Printing Office, 1911.

A bibliography of publication issued by all branches of the government. Full titles, prices, and instructions for ordering are listed. An invaluable monthly reference guide.

U.S. Superintendent of Documents. *Selected United States Government Publications*. Washington, D.C.: Government Printing Office.

This free publication, issued biweekly, lists current items of general interest, a brief description of their contents, and the price.

U.S. Superintendent of Documents. *United States Government Publications, Monthly Catalog*. Washington, D.C.: Government Printing Office, 1895 to date.

Air University Library Index to Military Periodicals. Maxwell Air Force Base, Ala.: Air University Library, 1949 to date.

This is a quarterly subject index to significant articles appearing in 68 English-language military and aeronautical periodicals.

Annual Department of Defense Bibliography of Logistics, Studies and Related Documents. Fort Lee, Va.: U.S. Army Logistics Management Center, c. 1960 to date.

Consists of citations of completed, in-process, and planned logistics studies and related material. Most citations contain an abstract of the content of the study and each publication is variously indexed. With quarterly supplements. Controlled distribution.

International Aerospace Abstracts. New York: American Institute of Aeronautics and Astronautics, Inc., Technical Information Service, 1961 to date.

This semimonthly publication is issued in coordination with *STAR (Scientific and Technical Aerospace Reports)*. It provides worldwide coverage of scientific periodicals, trade journals, books, and technical papers presented at meetings, in the field of aerospace science and technology. As such, it complements *STAR'S* worldwide coverage of report literature in the field.

735

Scientific and Technical Aerospace Reports. Washington, D.C.: Aeronautics and Space Administration, 1963 to date.

STAR is a semimonthly publication containing a comprehensive listing of abstracts and indexes of NASA reports and technical literature on the science or technology of space and aeronautics. Its abstracts give the essence of the reports they cover, not merely an indication of the content.

United Nations Documents Index. New York: United Nations, Dag Hammarskjöld Library, Documents Index Unit, 1950 to date.

Published monthly, with annual cumulations, this is the basic guide to current U.N. publications and documents.

United Nations Publications, 1945–1966. New York: United Nations Sales Section, 1967.

Lists all sales publications of the U.N. issued from 1945 to 1966, including sales number and price, by broad subject categories.

U.S. Government Research and Development Reports. Springfield, Va.: National Bureau of Standards, Clearinghouse for Federal Scientific and Technical Information, 1965 to date.

This is a semimonthly abstracting publication which lists reports of U.S. Government agencies such as Department of Defense, AEC, NASA, and others. These are not classified (as secret) and are listed under 22 categories from Aeronautics to Space Technology. Published under various titles since 1946. Basic guide to government report literature.

GUIDES TO BUSINESS AND CORPORATION DIRECTORIES

Davis, Marjorie V. *Guide to American Business Directories.* Washington, D.C.: Public Affairs Press, 1948.

This volume lists, under subject headings, a brief description of American business directories in some 77 different areas such as advertising, banking, chemicals, construction, food, insurance, and transportation. This book contains much of the information originally presented in a Department of Commerce pamphlet published in 1947.

Directory of Business and Financial Services. New York: Special Libraries Association, 1963.

A selective list of 1050 services, including newsletters, bulletins, reports, and other published services covering business, economics, and finance.

Directory of National Associations of Businessmen. Washington, D.C.: Government Printing Office.

This directory, published annually, lists more than 2000 national organizations, trade associations, business groups, etc., including the name, address, and chief executive officer of each group. This directory is issued through the Office of Technical Services of the U.S. Department of Commerce.

Directory of National Trade and Professional Associations of the United States. Washington, D.C.: Potomac Books, 1966 to date.

This annual publication includes name, address, executive officer, size of staff and membership of approximately 3500 associations.

Dun and Bradstreet Reference Book. Published by Dun and Bradstreet six times a year.

This guide lists nearly three million business firms in the United States and Canada, indicating type of business and financial rating. Also available in separate editions by states. Not available to libraries.

Encyclopedia of Associations, 5th ed. Detroit: Gale Company, 1968 to date.

This volume is loose-leaf under the subtitle *New Associations.* Loose-leaf additions are published three or four times a year. Lists more than 16,000 organizations with keyword subject index. Each entry notes association publications, if any.

Guide to American Directories, ed. B. Klein. Englewood Cliffs, N.J.: Prentice-Hall, Inc.

This cross-referenced volume, published annually, covers 300 major fields and describes and categorizes 3350 industrial, mercantile, and professional directories.

Moody's Investor Service. New York: Moody's.

Moody's Service publishes information on various firms for the use of persons wishing to make investments. Information on officers, dividends, loans, debts, and a balance sheet are all listed. Moody's Service is divided into five areas: Transportation, Industrials, Public Utilities, Banks and Finance, and Municipal and Government. Annual bound volumes supplemented by loose-leaf service. Moody's also offers other services:

> *Moody's Advisory Reports*
> *Moody's Bond Record*
> *Moody's Dividend Record*
> *Moody's Handbook of Common Stock*
> *Moody's Investors Advisory Service*
> *Moody's Stock Survey*

Poor's Register of Directors and Executives of the United States and Canada. New York: Standard and Poor's Corp.

This annual directory lists the names of executives and directors of major manufacturing and investment firms. It comprises six sections:

1. The Classified Index lists corporations under S.I.C. industry classifications.
2. The Corporation Directory lists for each company: names of officers and directors, number of employees, and principal products.
3. The Register of Directors lists key leaders in business and professional organizations, with offices, birth dates, and home addresses.
4. The Obituary section lists the deaths of executives occurring the preceding year.
5. The New Companies section lists organizations appearing for the first time in the current Directory.
6. The New Individuals section lists persons whose names appear for the first time in the current Register.

Standard and Poor's Corporation Services.

This is a loose-leaf service designed primarily for the investor. It offers current information of the structure and financial background of corporations. Additional services offered are:

The Bond Outlook	*Stock Reports Over-the-Counter*
Industry Surveys	*and Regional Exchanges*
Railroad Securities	*Listed Stock Reports*
Daily Dividend Record	*Facts and Forecasts Service*
Called Bond Record	*Listed Bond Reports*

Thomas' Register of American Manufacturers.

This is an excellent list of sources of supply. The names and addresses of manufacturers, producers, importers, and other suppliers are listed. *Thomas' Register* comprises five volumes. The first three list product classifications from A to Z; Volume IV lists manufacturers, trade names, trade papers, boards of trade and other commercial organizations; and Volume V assists the individual who is looking for specific products.

Trade Directories of the World. Queens Village, N.Y.: Croner Publications, 1960 to date.

This is a loose-leaf handbook listing business and trade directories in the United States and Canada. This directory is kept current through additions.

U.S. Department of Commerce. *A Guide to Foreign Business Directories.* Washington, D.C.: Government Printing Office, 1955.

First published in 1931 and revised in 1939, 1948, and 1951, this guide is a good initial source for further research.

MISCELLANEOUS SOURCES

Annual Survey of Manufacturers. Washington, D.C.: Government Printing Office.
> This work, issued annually by the Bureau of the Census, is based on a sample of manufacturing establishments and provides statistics on employment, payrolls, man-hours, inventories, new capital expenditures, and value of products shipped. It is a very valuable and easy-to-use source.

The Economic Almanac. New York: National Industrial Conference Board, 1940 to date.
> This biennial volume contains accurate and significant statistical data useful to persons concerned with current economic problems, often of the type not usually found in the *Statistical Abstract of the United States.* Topics include: prices, savings, consumption, labor force, foreign trade, standard of living, construction, public debt, and wages.

Facts on File. New York: Facts on File, Inc., 1940 to date.
> A weekly news digest of information on world and national affairs, Latin America, finance, economics, arts, science, education, religion, sports, obituaries, and miscellaneous. Cumulated.

Fortune Directory. Chicago: Time, Inc., 1956 to date.
> An annual publication which lists major U.S. industrial firms by sales, assets, and net profits. The geographical section lists products manufactured and the companies that manufactured them.

Historical Statistics of the United States, Colonial Times to 1957. Washington, D.C.: Government Printing Office, 1960.
> This volume, issued by the U.S. Department of Commerce, contains innumerable facts going back to 1789 and relating to consumer activities, business, manufacturing, and national affairs.

Continuation to 1962 and Revisions. Washington, D.C.: Government Printing Office, 1965.

Information Please Almanac, Atlas, and Yearbook. New York: Simon and Schuster, 1947 to date.
> This almanac deals with U.S. and world events and statistics of the year issued. It contains maps, reviews of the arts, analysis of the state of the economy, and many miscellaneous statistics. It is fully indexed.

Public Affairs Information Service. New York: Public Affairs Information Service, 1915 to date.

This is a weekly subject index for current literature, primarily in political science, government, economics, and legislation. Indexes books, documents, pamphlets, and selected articles in more than 1000 periodicals.

Statesman's Year-Book. London: Macmillan, 1864 to date.

Statistical Abstract of the United States. Washington, D.C.: Government Printing Office, 1879 to date.

A digest of facts on population, vital statistics, commerce, finance, immigration, and many other topics. Includes both governmental and private sources. This book is a treasure house of statistical facts in a great many areas. Published yearly by the U.S. Bureau of Foreign and Domestic Commerce.

The *County and City Data Book*, a supplement to the *Statistical Abstract*, lists selected data for all counties and for cities over 25,000 population.

Whitaker's Almanack. London: Whitaker, 1869 to date.

Especially valuable for information relative to the British Empire.

The World Almanac and Book of Facts. New York: World-Telegram, 1868 to date.

A very thorough annual containing much valuable information concerned with the economic, social, educational, and political activities of the world.

Ginsburg, Norton, ed. *Atlas of Economic Development.* Chicago: University of Chicago Press, 1961.

This atlas contains a comparative quantitative measurement of the economic growth of the nations of the world. Its various sections, complete with detailed maps, deal with demographic data, resources, industrialization, and foreign trade.

Columbia Lippincott Gazetteer of the World. New York: Columbia, 1962.

This geographical dictionary lists in alphabetical order the names of mountains, lakes, rivers, islands, towns, cities, and countries. For each, the location, altitude, and pronunciation are given. For cities, towns, and nations, the population, brief history, and information on industry are given.

Rand McNally Commercial Atlas and Marketing Guide. New York: Rand McNally.

This excellent atlas is revised annually and its maps are kept up to date. The individual interested in commerce finds this especially valuable. It contains agricultural maps of the United States, population statistics, retail sales data, transportation information, and much other information in the field of marketing.

GUIDES TO THE GUIDES

Besterman, Theodore. *A World Bibliography of Bibliographies*, 4th rev. ed., 5 vols. Lausanne: Sociétas Bibliographica, 1966.
> Bibliographies are arranged alphabetically by subject. Over 117,000 volumes are recorded. This edition is updated to 1963.

Coman, E. T., Jr. *Sources of Business Information*, rev. ed. Berkeley and Los Angeles: University of California Press, 1964.
> A valuable text in which the first four chapters are devoted to the methodology of locating business information sources. The remaining chapters deal with sources in specific fields, such as statistics, finance, accounting, management, and personnel. Each of these subject headings is broken down in detail by type of information needed, and each periodical or text source is completely described. At the end of each chapter there is a useful summary of sources cited, and a detailed index covers the entire volume.

Executive's Guide to Information Sources. Detroit: Business Guides Co., 1965.
> This work contains a detailed listing for management reference of 2300 business and business-related subjects, with a record of periodicals, organizations, bureaus, directories, bibliographies, and other sources concerned with each topic. The subjects are arranged alphabetically.

Georgi, Charlotte. *Literature of Executive Management: Selected Books and Reference Sources for the International Businessman*. SLA Bibliography No. 5. New York: Special Libraries Association, 1963.
> An index of books and other information sources under such headings as the philosophy of management, management of science and technology, management education and development, etc. Each entry is completely documented, with number of pages and price.

Johnson, H. W., ed. *How to Use the Business Library—with Sources of Business Information*, 3rd ed. Cincinnati: South-Western Publishing Co., 1964.
> A very handy and useful guide which, along with the usual subjects covered, comments on the value and availability of audio-visual aids, data processing, and materials from research foundations. The volume is recent, easy to use, and is completely indexed.

Kruzas, Anthony T., ed. *Directory of Special Libraries and Information Centers,* 2nd ed. Detroit: Gale Research Co., 1968.
> Lists more than 13,000 special libraries in the United States and Canada alphabetically by name and address, along with a note on the special collections.

Manley, Marian C. *Business Information—How to Find and Use It.* New York: Harper & Row, 1955.
> In this thoroughly indexed book, initial chapters describe uses and applications of business information as well as ways of satisfying special informational needs. The remainder of the text provides a bibliography of various information sources concerning business and economic conditions, banking and finance, marketing and market research, plant management, communications, etc.

Murphey, Robert W. *How and Where to Look It Up—A Guide to Standard Sources of Information.* New York: McGraw-Hill Book Co., 1958.
> This is an extensive and intensive work, a true laymen's guide to reference materials. Subject headings make this volume very fast and easy to use. Included are sections on annuals and almanacs, periodicals, books, directories, government publications, graphic information, and sources of bibliographic and geographic materials and information. Each chapter and subchapter includes a few pages on the uses and limitations of the materials, as well as indexed entries with very detailed descriptions. Certainly one of the most valuable of all guides to reference works. The volume is cross indexed by subject and title.

Shores, Louis. *Basic Reference Sources.* Chicago: American Library Association, 1954.
> Actually written as a textbook for research workers, this volume is valuable for its elaborate descriptions and explanations for the best use of more than 500 basic reference works, including dictionaries, encyclopedias, yearbooks, handbooks, directories, serials, indexes, and bibliographies.

Wasserman, Paul. *Information for Administrators—A Guide to Publications and Services for Management in Business and Government.* Ithaca: Cornell University Press, 1956.
> A volume which describes the available information and services from such sources as government agencies, business services, periodicals, newspapers, chambers of commerce, research organizations, as well as sources of information in local areas. The appendixes list depository libraries, bureaus of business and government research in American universities, information sources in foreign countries, etc.

White, Carl M., and associates. *Sources of Information in the Social Sciences.* Totowa, N.J.: Bedminster Press, 1964.

> Sections on sociology, anthropology, psychology, economics and business, education, and political science. Bibliographic essays and annotated bibliographies on each subject.

Winchell, Constance M. *Guide to Reference Books,* 8th ed. Chicago: American Library Association, 1967.

> Lists approximately 7500 reference works. It serves as a guide to bibliographies, indexes and abstracts, handbooks, annuals, directories, biographies, atlases, and serial publications. These are organized under general reference works, the humanities, social sciences, history and area studies, and pure and applied sciences. An extremely detailed author, subject, and title index locates specific items or categories. Covers material through 1964.
>
> First supplement, published 1968, covers 1965 and 1966. To be supplemented biannually.

Business Letter Style and Format

THE SECTIONS OF THE BUSINESS LETTER

The business letter is usually divided into six major parts: the heading, which includes the letterhead and the date; the inside address; the salutation; the body; the complimentary close; and the signature.

Heading

Inside address

Salutation

Body

Complimentary close

Signature

THE HEADING

The heading of the business letter contains the letterhead and the date. The former is given a good deal of attention by most firms because it contributes to the company image.

The letterhead that "shouts" at us with oversize pictures of the product, unattractive sketches of the plant, or "call us day or night" statements, does not usually convey the best image of the company. However, the firm which utilizes a relatively simple, dignified letterhead, designed carefully and with good taste, somehow conveys an image of competence and efficiency.

There are many specialists and advertising agencies to assist the businessman in designing a new letterhead or revising the one he has used for years. And this revision is necessary, for styles in letterheads change as does the company image. Certainly outmoded type styles or a picture of a 25-year-old car or office machine in the letterhead design will not contribute to a very favorable impression of the company. *Printer's Ink* magazine had this to say about the letterhead design and the message it conveys:

> In addition to identifying the sender, letterheads convey, both liminally and subliminally, an image of the company. The great mass of mail sent out by the average company gives its letterhead a significant role to perform in its sales-promotion and public-relations programs.[1]

Many of the large paper corporations will also assist in letterhead revision. Their staff artists will draw up a new letterhead or send out letterhead kits which contain sample designs of letterheads and different grades and colors of stationery, graph paper, and directions for a "do-it-yourself" approach.

The trend in letterhead designs today is toward simplicity and clean-cut type faces that reflect dignity and good taste. Reproductions of products or office buildings or factories, if included, are usually small and very well executed, so they will not detract from the overall letterhead "message" or from the letter itself.

Many firms are also using the empty space along the bottom of the page. A listing of the cities in which the company has outlets or plants, small pictures of the firm's products, or even the company address can be included. The type should be small and distinct, and the layout in balance with the information at the top of the stationery.

In addition to being attractive, meaningful, and in good taste, the letterhead should answer the questions of *who, where,* and *what.* The

---

1. *Printer's Ink,* August 15, 1958, p. 60.

"who," of course, is the name of the company presented exactly as the firm wishes to be identified. This includes the precise abbreviations ("Corp." or "Inc.") and designations ("Furniture manufacturers" or "Manufacturers of furniture").

The "where" includes street address, city, state, zip code number, telephone number, cable address, and other items of this nature.

The "what" tells the reader the nature of the company's operations. It is disconcerting to receive a letter from the R. T. Cronin Corporation at 102 East Adams Street in Los Angeles and not be able to determine whether the firm manufactures kitchen appliances or conducts national surveys.

The date should be written out using either of the following methods:

January 4, 1966

4 January 1966

It is recommended that the date not be typed as 1/4/69 or 1-4-69 even in intracompany memos. Many persons feel that this exhibits a distinct lack of courtesy. But a more important reason for avoiding this method is to eliminate the possibility of confusion or misinterpretation. Although most North Americans would read 4/7/69 as April 7, 1969, this would not be true in Europe and among most Latin Americans who would interpret this as July 4, 1969. Because of the different meanings which can be given to the same set of numbers, it is recommended that the month be written out.

THE INSIDE ADDRESS

The inside address should be sufficiently complete to ensure accurate and rapid delivery of the letter. The information in the inside address should duplicate the address on the envelope.

The date for the inside address are usually drawn from the letterhead of the piece of correspondence being answered. Exact company designations and titles (as they appear in the letterhead) should be followed for the inside address.

The recipient's name in the inside address should be preceded by his title—Mr., Mrs., Dr., General, Reverend, etc. If the individual occupies a supervisory office, both his title and area of responsibility can be indicated.

Dr. Lester Jameson, Director
Medical Research Department
Cicero Clinics
3148 North Cicero Avenue
Chicago, Illinois 60606

If the initials which designate degrees mean the same as the person's title, both title and initials should not be used.

Incorrect:
Dr. Robert Clock, M.D.
Dr. Richard Mann, Ph.D.

Correct:
Dr. Robert Clock
Robert Clock, M.D.

Dr. Richard Mann
Richard Mann, Ph.D.

Words in the inside address, such as *street, north,* and *avenue* should not be abbreviated unless the company specifically requires such action. On the whole, the use of abbreviations should not be encouraged for the inside address.

Street numbers should always be written in numerals with the exception of *one.* Street names should be written out from First to Tenth streets. After that, numerals should be used. The zip code should follow the state. The examples below illustrate these recommendations.

Dr. Albert Fine, Director
Conrad Research Center
Conrad General Hospital
1007 West 63rd Street
Los Angeles, California 90024

Miss Joan Star, Manager
Personnel Department
Foods, Inc.
One East 95th Street
Cincinnati, Ohio 45216

Reverend Peter Jackson
Lutheran Central Church
7 South Ninth Avenue
New York, New York 10010

John T. Kasper, Ph.D.
Department of Management
Illinois State University
Springfield, Illinois 62704

Rabbi Herman Schaalman
Temple Emanuel
5959 North Sheridan Road
Chicago, Illinois 60626

Thomas L. Lamp, M.D.
Allerton Medical Center
17 North Bolton Avenue
Columbus, Ohio 43227

THE SALUTATION

Every effort should be made to use the recipient's name in the greeting or salutation. Almost everyone responds much more actively and sincerely to his name than to *Dear Occupant, Dear Friend, Dear Sir,* or *Dear Purchasing Agent.*

Many firms have expended large sums of money to have a personally typed inside address and/or salutation added to thousands of form letters before mailing. It is felt (usually with reason) that the form letter receives a much better reaction from the reader because of the added personal touch.

When individual letters are typed and the name of the recipient is not known, it is customary to use *Dear Sir* or *Dear Madame* in the singular, and *Gentlemen* or *Ladies* in the plural. *My Dear Sirs, Dear Sirs,* and *Mesdames* are all considered obsolete.

Many individuals, in an effort to add a more friendly and informal tone to their letters, and to give some significance to the opening, use a "salutation phrase" instead of a salutation. These might be *Thank you, Mrs. Klay; We were happy, Mr. Conway; Enclosed, Mrs. Finer, you will find; Your order, Mr. Fay, was sent.* These phrases appear, in the letter, in place of the salutation.

These are certainly different and do attract attention. Some authorities argue that they may be too different and therefore resented by the recipient. However, I believe they can be used, with certain readers, very effectively. And in sales writing they may well serve a very useful purpose.

THE BODY

Any discussion of the "body" of the letter must, perforce, be concerned with the type of letter (sales, credit, collection, etc.) under consideration. From the point of view of appearance and format, however, the body should be attractively centered, broken into relatively short paragraphs, and surrounded by plenty of white space.

THE COMPLIMENTARY CLOSE

The standard forms used in most letters are *Yours truly, Truly yours, Sincerely, Sincerely yours, Yours sincerely,* and to a lesser extent, *Cordially* or *Cordially yours.* As in the case of the salutation, attempts have been made to make the complimentary close more meaningful and personal. Some companies close their letters with phrases such as *Buy Arctic Freezers Today, See Your Arctic Dealer, Arctic for Quality, Arctic is Yours Truly, Soft Glo for the Best in Lighting,* or *Truly a Fine Product.*

When such phrases are chosen with care and discretion, they often produce excellent results. However, the letter writer should not "reach" too far for an interesting close. What may be clever to him might be interpreted by the reader as "much too cute." Some firms will compose a close, use it on all letters for two weeks, and then switch to a new one. In effect most persons will not see the same one repeated under this system.

THE SIGNATURE

This section of the letter is handled in a variety of ways by America's companies today. In most firms the signature has three or four parts, with the trend toward the latter number. The four-part signature includes the name of the company, the signature of the writer, his typed name, and his title. If the signature has only three parts, the name of the company (which appears in the letterhead) is omitted.

The use of the words *per* or *by* in front of the signed name is obsolete and should be discouraged.

Sometimes one will find initials placed immediately below the signature. This is done when the secretary signs the writer's name and adds her own initials. However, this practice is often interpreted by the reader in a rather poor light. He may be irritated that the writer apparently could

Yours truly,

CAIN PRODUCTS CO.
John Kingly
Sales Manager

JK/js

Sincerely yours,

Robert Blake
Superintendent

RB:ks

Truly yours,

LOOP LAMP COMPANY
William Key, Manager

WK/vt

Sincerely,

BAINE, INC.
Partner

Robert Baine/mt

not find fifteen seconds to sign his own name, but had a secretary do it for him. This is understandable and therefore every effort should be made by the writer to sign every letter he sends out.

Of course it is possible that the writer could have dictated the letter in the morning and then have left on a business trip. In such case, he obviously would not be available to sign the letter when it is ready for his signature. However, the fact is that most individuals resent what the initials below a signature seem to imply.

OTHER FACTORS IN THE MECHANICS OF THE BUSINESS LETTER

THE ATTENTION LINE

Frequently we find that one person in a company with which we are doing business gives us excellent service. Mr. Kelly, for example, is aware that we prefer to have our merchandise shipped via Star Freight Lines; that our terms are always C.O.D.; that we like to have our items individually wrapped and packaged, etc. Thus, in order to have Kelly handle our requests, we send our communications to his *attention*. If we sent the letter directly to him, and he had left the company, it is very possible that the envelope would be *returned* to us or *forwarded* to him. However, if the letter is sent to his *attention* and he has left the company, the communication will normally be opened and processed by his successor.

The position of the attention line varies, although it usually appears in one of the following places:

Belmont Steel Company
1122 West Ninth Street
Belmont, Indiana

Gentlemen: Attention of Mr. Keelton, Treasurer

Belmont Steel Company
1122 West Ninth Street
Belmont, Indiana

Attention of Mr. Keelton, Treasurer

Gentlemen:

Belmont Steel Company
1122 West Ninth Street
Belmont, Indiana

       Attention of Mr. Keelton, Treasurer

Gentlemen:

Many firms use an abbreviation for *attention: Attn:* or *Att.,* and the pattern followed in the inside address is repeated on the envelope.

THE SUBJECT LINE

The subject line is another device used to speed handling or retrieval of correspondence from files. In addition, it can eliminate much of the first paragraph if it is worded carefully. Its position, like the attention line, varies according to company preference.

Kelvyn Clock Company
1515 West Granby Street
Springfield, California

Gentlemen: Subject: Your order #2136

Betsy B. Ice Cream
1000 West Nevada Avenue
Boulder, Colorado

       Subject: Your invoice #201,
            January 7, 1965
Gentlemen:

This *subject* line, like a *file number,* or in *reply refer to file number*_____ , can save time and increase office efficiency.

IDENTIFYING INITIALS

For many years it was customary to place the dictator's and typist's initials in the lower-left-hand section of the business letter. However, in recent years the trend seems to be toward omitting them. With the name of the writer in the signature section, it is obvious who dictated the letter, and if the letter was completed in a typing pool or even by a secretary, the value of having her initials on the letter seems questionable.

  On the other hand, many firms follow the practice carefully, especially when all letters from a department are signed by one man even though any one of six people may have done the dictating. In this instance, the dictator's initials are used and, of course, do not match the signature of the department head. The initials serve to identify the person who actually wrote the letter.

Some of the accepted variations in handling identifying initials are shown below. Note that both a slash mark and a colon are acceptable separators.

JS/rt   MRL:AO
LT/MR   TTA:bm

ENCLOSURE LINE

The enclosure notation is usually placed immediately below the identifying initials and serves as a reminder that some item such as a check, invoice, or reprint has been included in the envelope along with the letter.

Either the word *Enclosure* is typed or the abbreviation *Encl.* If only one enclosure is included, no numeral is used; if more than one item goes with the letter, the number of different items is indicated. Some firms and most federal government agencies identify each enclosure so that when one is withdrawn, it can be easily identified.

BM:rt   LMS/rd
Encl.   Enclosures 3

GM/tl   LM:ML
Encl. 3   Enclosure
  1. Birth certificate
  2. Visa
  3. Letter of reference

CARBON COPIES

Obviously if a letter is sent to Mr. Robert Blackstone, a copy of that letter should ordinarily not be forwarded to anyone else; the contents of a business letter are a private matter between the writer and addressee. It is easy to understand how offended Mr. Blackstone might become if another person indicated, through a comment or a note, that he was aware of information which had been contained in a letter sent by Acme Products to Blackstone.

To avoid such a situation, and because it is also a matter of ethics, we tell Mr. Blackstone that a copy of this letter addressed to him was sent to Mr. Clayton. The device of *cc:* (carbon copy) is used.

DM/ts
cc: Mr. Clayton

LT/sa
cc: Mr. Clayton
    Credit Department

Some firms will sometimes employ the initials *bc* or *bcc* which stands for *blind copy* or *blind carbon copy*. This is typed only on the copy and not on the original letter and tells the reader of the carbon copy that Mr. Blackstone is *not* aware that a copy has been sent to a second party. The ethics and propriety of using this device should be questioned seriously.

PUNCTUATION

The terms *open* or *closed* punctuation refer to end-of-line punctuation in the inside address, complimentary close, and signature. Almost all correspondence today uses open punctuation for it saves typing time and therefore money. One frequent variation found in open punctuation is the comma after the complimentary close.

Closed punctuation:

> Mr. Robert T. Scott,
> Morrell and Company,
> 1515 West Ohio Street,
> St. Louis, Missouri 63125.
>
> Dear Mr. Scott:
>
> _____
> _____
> _____
>
> Yours very truly,

Open punctuation:

> Mr. Robert T. Scott
> Morrell and Company
> 1515 West Ohio Street
> St. Louis, Missouri 63125
>
> Dear Mr. Scott:
>
> _____
> _____
> _____
>
> Yours very truly,

FORMAT

Almost every firm types its letters according to a consistent form. It may feel that one form complements the letterhead design better than another form; or that this method requires less time, or is more efficient. Whatever the reason, every company has a variety of forms from which to choose. Perhaps the most popular today are the block and full block forms. Also used quite extensively is the modified block form. The indented form is rarely used because it requires more time to set up and type.

BLOCK

FULL BLOCK

MODIFIED BLOCK

INDENTED FORM

Some years ago the National Office Management Association recommended a Simplified Letter form. This style omits the salutation and complimentary close as being meaningless, insincere, and wasteful of space and time. However, many persons did not care for this break with tradition, and frowned on the use of this form in the mail they received. Consequently, it has never been generally accepted by American business.

SIMPLIFIED LETTER FORM

The executive form is very attractive, and is rapidly coming into greater use. It is neat, well proportioned, and dignified in appearance. The hanging indention style is primarily limited to sales writing or firms who desire their correspondence to be "eye catching." As can be seen, it is difficult to type. And if an error is made in line placement, it will usually require that the entire letter be retyped.

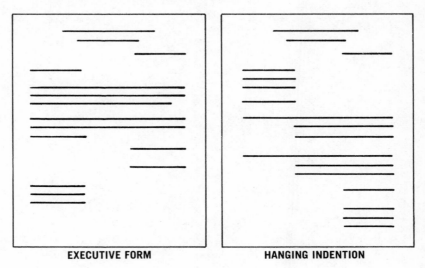

EXECUTIVE FORM   **HANGING INDENTION**

Index

3 4 5 6 7 8 9 10 11 12 13 14 15 16 17 18 19 20 21 22 23 24 25   74 73 72 71 70